GERMAN EXPRESSIONIST PAINTING

PETER SELZ lived in Germany until 1936, when he came to the United States. After the war he returned to Europe for extended periods to carry on the research embodied in this volume, together with other work relating to twentieth-century painting in France and Belgium. He taught at the Institute of Design in Chicago from 1949 to 1955, directing the programs in art history and art education for that institution when it became part of the Illinois Institute of Technology. Author of the article "Painting" in the current *Encyclopaedia Britannica,* and of many articles in art journals, Mr. Selz is now Chairman of the Department of Art, Pomona College, Claremont, California.

GERMAN EXPRESSIONIST PAINTING

BY PETER SELZ

UNIVERSITY OF CALIFORNIA PRESS

Berkeley and Los Angeles

University of California Press
Berkeley and Los Angeles

Cambridge University Press
London, England

© 1957
By the Regents of the University of California
Reprinted without change, 1968
Library of Congress Catalog Card Number: 57–10501
Printed in the United States of America
Designed by Rita Carroll

To My Wife
THALIA
and to the Memory of My Grandfather
JULIUS DREY

Introduction

In a recent eulogy of Edvard Munch, Kokoschka described expressionism as "form-giving to the experience, thus mediator and message from self to fellow human. As in love, two individuals are necessary. Expressionism does not live in an ivory tower, it calls upon a fellow being whom it awakens." (Oskar Kokoschka, "Edvard Munch's Expressionism," *College Art Journal,* XII [1953], 320.)

This statement might, in the loosest terms, justly describe most movements in the history of art, but Kokoschka seems to have meant it to differentiate expressionism from all other directions. The expressionist artist is not satisfied with formal construction or *belle peinture*. He seeks rather the I-Thou relationship of a Martin Buber, and hopes to establish a similar dialogue between himself and the observer.

The deep personal involvement on the part of both artist and viewer led naturally to a fervent conviction that expressionism was the ultimate fulfillment of art. Artists and critics believed that they were on the threshold of a creation vastly superior to previous endeavor. The term "expressionism," did not originally have this significance, although recently it has again been used with such extravagant claims.

The term is of recent origin. Although it may date back to the beginning of the century, it seems to have occurred in critical discussion for the first time in Berlin reviews of 1911 referring to former Fauves exhibiting in the Secession of that year. "Expressionism" was coined to distinguish strikingly between the new tendencies and impressionism. Critics quickly seized upon it to describe the modern movement in general, including cubism and futurism. During the second decade of the century, however, "expressionism" slowly came to mean a specifically German manifestation in painting and sculpture, and shortly in literature and the film.

The expressionist artist—in this more specific meaning of the term as it will be used in this book—rejects tradition, especially that of the most immediate past. He turns away from both conventionally realistic representations of nature and accepted concepts of beauty. When he finds an affinity with the art of the past—whether in the painting of Grünewald, El Greco, van Gogh, the late medieval woodcut, or South Sea sculpture—he is likely to consider it as a prototype of his own endeavors and to let it shine in his reflected glory.

The expressionist artist is concerned with the visual projection of his emotional experience. Generally he is driven by "inner necessity" to express his unresolved conflicts with society and his own personal anxieties. This often results in feverish accusations of society and urgent affirmation of self, expressed by the use of agitated form. The dramatic quality of urgency is rarely absent in expressionist painting, and the artist is more likely to attack the canvas than to caress it.

The expressionist movement may be seen in part as a reaction against the prevailing values of the deceptively stable society in which the artists grew up. In their reaction against materialism and rationalism they were attempting to affirm the values of the spiritual. Frequently they turned to religious subjects, or used art as a spiritual substitute for religion. Some expressionists dreamed of a new brotherhood of man or, beyond that, of a fusion of man and animal in cosmic universalism. Expressionism can be more fully understood if it is seen in relation to the relativistic and subjective trends in modern psychology, the sciences, and philosophy—trends of which many of the expressionist painters were acutely aware. The strong desire of the expressionist artist for self-knowledge and for comprehension of the meaning of human existence in its loneliness and threat of death can be compared with parallel trends in existentialism.

Ten years ago, when I began this study, the work of the German expressionists was little known inside or outside Germany. In Germany it had long been banned by the Nazi government. Here in the United States even artists and critics were relatively unfamiliar with the work of most of the expressionists. Because Paris had supplied the standards of modern art for several generations, creative emphasis was likely to fall on the constructive elements of harmonious relationships.

In the postwar years, however, a rapid change has taken place. The creative process itself has assumed chief importance, and the younger artists here and abroad often ask questions and seek solutions similar to those of the German expressionists of an earlier generation. At a time when a large body of painting is carried out in the abstract and expressionist vein, a reappraisal of the work of the expressionists, who felt the need to distort or to abandon the objective world, seems relevant and necessary.

Perhaps we now have sufficient historical perspective to make a first attempt at a comprehensive history of German expressionist painting. Until now there has been little definitive material available. Except for the *œuvre* catalogs of Kokoschka by Edith Hoffmann and Hans Maria Wingler, Will Grohmann's catalogs of paintings by Paul Klee and Schmidt-

Rottluff, and for Gustav Vriesen's book on August Macke, there are only incomplete listings of the works—particularly graphics—of the other artists.

Although there is a dearth of scholarly publications, there is an abundance of general descriptive and critical material. I found it necessary to sift through multitudes of documents such as reviews which were either too enthusiastic or too antagonistic to be of much critical or scholarly value. Further, a great deal of expressionist criticism is written so effusively as to be almost incomprehensible and certainly useless from the scholarly point of view. Not much scientific precision can be expected in essays heralding the arrival of an art that will improve the lot of mankind.

On the other hand, I have been fortunate in being able to discuss the movement with many of the artists themselves, as well as with the critics and historians who were intimately involved with the origins of the movement. It is questionable, of course, whether statements made by individuals about their activities forty years earlier can be considered as fully reliable or as primary source materials. Here I had to weigh carefully conflicting statements and contradictory evidence against genuine primary sources whenever extant. Exhibition catalogs and brief factual reviews in periodicals proved to be of particular help when questions arose as to validity or to the dating of the usually undated paintings. When no reliable confirmation of dates could be found, an analysis of the internal stylistic evidence sometimes furnished the key. This proved particularly feasible with the work of Kandinsky, Kirchner, Kokoschka, and Marc, whose styles underwent fairly perceptible changes in the period under examination. It proved more difficult with painters such as Otto Mueller, whose form experienced very little change. At times only approximate datings could be deduced.

The expressionist painters were generally eager to write about themselves and their ideas, and their writings have furnished this book with much source material. Their statements are also discussed from the point of view of esthetic thought. Unless these were previously published in translation, I have translated them (as well as the rest of the documentation) as literally as possible to permit the reader the most authentic insight into the period.

The writing of the history of a movement presents insurmountable problems, especially as to structure. Originally I had hoped to discuss each group of painters by itself and to analyze the development of each artist separately. This procedure, however, although doing justice to the individual artist, was not conducive to the principal aim of this book—the fullest possible understanding of the movement and its crosscurrents. After discarding an early draft along the lines of this "vertical" method, I attempted to proceed strictly chronologically, analyzing works by various artists executed simultaneously. This second method, highly useful for the later period, seemed artificial for the early years, when little or no contact existed among the painters in Dresden, Vienna, and Munich.

The present structure is admittedly a compromise between the "vertical" and "horizontal" methods. This compromise, in spite of some unavoidable repetitions, seemed most successful for the stated purpose of this book. It was not premeditated, but dictated by the nature of the material—the movement and the particular turns of its development in the period under investigation. This method, I hope, will establish for the reader the relationship between the creative personalities and the resultant style.

The scope of the discussion includes a good many painters—Kandinsky and Jawlensky, Schiele and Kokoschka, Klee and Feininger—who may not properly be called German painters but whose work forms an essential part of the total web. The book, however, limits itself to the early period of German expressionism, when the greatest vitality of statement occurred. After the First World War expressionism became an accepted manner in Germany, and the early dramatic quality too often lapsed into a theatrical gesture. By then the leading creative talents were already engaged in new and different discoveries.

Acknowledgments are due above all to Ulrich Middeldorf, formerly chairman of the Department of Art of the University of Chicago, who first suggested this subject when, in its initial phase, it was a doctoral dissertation. Joshua C. Taylor offered penetrating criticism during this early stage. I am also particularly indebted to my wife, Thalia Selz, not only for her great aid in the preparation and editing of the many drafts of the manuscript, but also for her numerous and original ideas and suggestions, especially concerning the analysis of certain paintings.

Special gratitude is also due those artists whose letters and often lengthy and fruitful interviews provided me with valuable documentation and new insight into their activities: Max Beckmann, David Burliuk, Lyonel Feininger, Erich Heckel, Johannes Molzahn, Gabriele Münter, Max Pechstein, Karl Schmidt-Rottluff. Of the same nature was the indispensable assistance rendered me by Sonia Delaunay, Nina Kandinsky, Maria Marc, Helene Rohlfs, and Nell Walden.

I recall with deepest appreciation the many stimulating discussions I had with Hans Bolliger, Klaus Brisch, Will Grohmann, Werner Haftmann, Kenneth Lindsay, J. B. Neumann, and Ernst Scheyer. Their views on various aspects of problems in German expressionism have been of the greatest value.

I wish to thank the Institute of International Education and the Belgian-American Educational Foundation for a Fulbright Award and a C.R.B. Fellowship, respectively, which enabled me to accomplish important travel and research in Europe.

Without the most painstaking and generous help of countless scholars, museum officials, collectors, and art dealers in the United States and Europe, I would never have been able to proceed beyond the barest beginnings of this work. Among those who have been of outstanding aid are Hildegard Bachert, Alfred H. Barr, Jr., Mr. and Mrs. John C. Best, Ralph Colin, Thomas Corinth, David W. Davies, Hugo Feigl, Günther Franke, Allan

Frumkin, W. Joseph Fulton, W. Greischel, Ludwig Grote, Mr. and Mrs. Fred Grunwald, P. Halm, George H. Hamilton, Egon Hanfstaengl, Dalzell Hatfield, Carl Georg Heise, Alfred Hentzen, Hans Huth, Sidney Janis, Otto Kallir, Mr. and Mrs. Paul Kantor, Bernard Karpell, Roman Norbert Ketterer, John Kirsch, Rex de C. Nan Kivell, Felix Klee, Charles Kleemann, Henry W. Knepler, Charles Kuhn, Frank Laurens, Mr. and Mrs. S. J. Levin, Wolfgang Macke, Mr. and Mrs. Yoland Markson, Mr. and Mrs. Morton D. May, John McAndrew, Henry Cord Meyer, Sibyl Moholy-Nagy, Ernest Mundt, Betty Peterson, Heinrich Petzet, Paul O. Rave, Hans Reichel, F. C. Schang, Alois Schardt, Werner Schmalenbach, Jason Seley, Peter R. Senn, Mr. and Mrs. Joseph R. Shapiro, Otto Stangl, Kate T. Steinitz, Justin Thannhauser, Curt Valentin, W. R. Valentiner, Jane Wade, Paul Westheim, Leonie von Wilckens, Frederick S. Wight, George Wittenborn, Bock von Wülfingen, Mr. and Mrs. Max Zurier.

This book was written while I was on the faculties of the Institute of Design of the Illinois Institute of Technology and of Pomona College. I am indebted to colleagues and students for their encouragement and consideration. I am especially grateful to Harry J. Carroll, Jr., for making many useful suggestions and for his tireless help in the preparation of the index. Finally, I want to express my appreciation to the staff of the University of California Press for their assistance in making this book a reality.

P. S.

Pomona College
Claremont, California

CONTENTS

Part Five
THE DEVELOPMENT OF EXPRESSIONISM
IN MUNICH

Part Six
THE PREWAR YEARS

ILLUSTRATIONS

Die Malerei stellt auf, was der Mensch sehen möchte
und sollte, nicht, was er gewöhnlich sieht.

GOETHE

PART ONE

Development in German Esthetics
Relevant to the Expressionist Movement

I

Art Criticism and Esthetic Thought

Twentieth-century art and esthetics are characterized by a growing disbelief in an objective reality. Emphasis has shifted from the outer world of empirical experience to the inner world that a man can test only against himself. As the subjective personality of the artist has assumed control, it has demanded, in place of the old passive contemplation, an active participation from the observer. This is perhaps the most important single factor in the development of the expressionist movement.

A similar trend in esthetic thought has occurred at the same time. About the middle of the nineteenth century, art historians began adopting the systematic methods of archaeologists and philologists. Men like Rumohr, Kugler, and Springer were concerned primarily with the classification of monuments, and they studied the techniques of artistic production with increasing attention. Scientific thought had a strong impact on art and the historiography of art, as it did on many other disciplines. Chevreul's "Law of Simultaneous Contrasts of Colors" (1838) undoubtedly affected the impressionists. Helmholtz's studies on the physiology and psychology of color vision, published in the 1880's, acted upon much of German artistic production. In 1876, Gustav Fechner came forth with an experimental method for the determination of esthetically satisfying forms. Both art historians and the estheticians hoped that the scientific method would help solve many of their problems.

Gottfried Semper (1804–1879) established a scientific and materialistic functional basis for art. According to this theory, symmetry, proportion, and orientation were universals in both art and nature. Art, however, was founded on the underlying physical need for clothes to hide and protect and, later, to adorn the body. In his scholarly treatise on the genetic development of style,[1] Semper maintained that the elementary craftsmanship of weaving was basic to the other crafts of pottery, wood carving, and metalwork. Architecture was derived from these crafts, and was in turn the foundation of the arts of painting and sculpture. Functional utility, the nature of the artifact, and the processes of operation were the fundamental causes of artistic creation. Semper said, in the introduction to his work, that the basis for the technical arts should be understood from a twofold point of view: as the attempted fulfillment of a material or symbolic need; and as a result of the materials, tools, and processes used in the production.[2]

Semper's great emphasis on function is understandable in view of the nonfunctional, overdecorated, mid-Victorian items he saw at the Crystal Palace exhibition of 1851. It is, however, also interesting that Semper considered the Gothic style, "which exhibits its bone structure like a panoplied sea crab," [3] nothing but an unfortunate delay between the Romanesque and a return to classical principles of the Renaissance. Further, Semper left little room in his scheme of values for the personal creativeness of the artist; utility is the decisive criterion: "Art knows only one master, Need! It [art] degenerates when it obeys the whims of the artist. With these bold words Semper began his career in a youthful blaze." [4]

Conrad Fiedler (1841–1895), agreeing with Semper on the possibility of an objective science of art, reinstated the individual contribution of the creative artist and criticized Semper for his omission:

. . . it seems to me that Semper buried all individual invention and boldness under his historic-artistic education, which he certainly possesses in the greatest degree and in the best sense. I have now gone over his writings again and I am constantly astonished at the insight which he gives me. But when he develops the origin of architectural forms, the individual contribution of the artist plays absolutely no part; it is never direct invention, never a free artistic act, but always a derivation, an offshoot, etc.[5]

To Fiedler the artistic personality was no longer a product of its time, but rather the creator of new forms and visions: "Each artist creates his own style by impressing upon his conceptual world the stamp of his own most personal spirit." [6] Fiedler separated art from esthetics, which deals with the concept of beauty in nature as well as in art. His most important contribution to the history of art criticism was the theory of pure visibility. Artistic creation is peculiar in that it deals only with visual perception: "Artistic activity can be explained thus: that in art the activity of the hand depends exclusively on the eye, on the interest in seeing." [7]

As the postimpressionist painters of Fiedler's era dominated the subject matter, as they annexed the elements of nature that were considered suitable for their personal expression instead of representing nature, Fiedler took strong issue with the theory of art as the imitation of nature. Imitative pictures, technical drawings, photography, and death masks only fix and explain objects. Imitation always takes us back to the original, and reproduces something already present in our consciousness. Art, on the other hand, gives form to something that cannot be expressed otherwise. It opens up to man the part of reality that neither thought nor emotion could ever penetrate; it is the "development of the intuitive consciousness." [8] Using nature to produce values of true visibility, art enables man to gain understanding and clarity from the confused profusion of images he sees in nature, "for art is nothing else but a means by which man conquers reality." [9]

On the same premise Fiedler also opposed the idealist philosophy, which found in art the expression or illustration of lofty ideas. If the purpose of art were the illustration of feelings and ideas, if it were merely to create visual symbols for spiritual thoughts, the contents of art would be of a nonsensual nature, and a sensual appearance would be only secondary. Truth in art would then depend upon the truth of an idea. Fiedler maintained, however, that in artistic creation idea and form are identical: "The content of the work of art is nothing but the formation [*Gestaltung*] itself." [10] Neither would Fiedler agree with the romantics, who stressed emotion as the causal agent for artistic creativity: "Works of art are not created with emotion; emotion, therefore, does not suffice for their understanding." [11]

Although Fiedler believed in the possibility of an objective, scientific explanation of art, he was also one of the first to introduce the concept of "inner necessity" into art criticism: "Artistic activity begins when man, driven by an inner necessity, grasps with the power of his mind the entangled multiplicity of appearances and develops it into configured visual existence." [12]

The term "inner necessity" was, however, not given the emotional emphasis with which, at a later period, Kandinsky was to endow it, or Arnold Schönberg, when he speaks of "inner compulsion." Although Fiedler evidently introduced the term to esthetic vocabulary, he was primarily concerned with the artist's visual clarification of forms. His esthetic theory was intimately related to the work of two artists who were close friends of his: the painter Hans von Marées and the sculptor Adolf von Hildebrand. Hildebrand (1847–1921) elaborated on Fiedler's theory of visual perception by asserting: "What the artist has to grapple with is a problem of visual manifestation solely. The subject he selects for representation need have neither ethical nor poetic significance." [13] The tasks of the artist are to bring order and rest into perception, to have a monumental, integrated vision of form, and to put man in a more secure relationship with nature. "The method by which he accomplishes this I should call the Architectonic Method." [14]

Although Hildebrand lived in the age of impressionism, he took strong issue with the impressionists' attempt to dissolve form and paint light reflections. [15] He felt that Rodin's concern with movement and effects of light and shade was leading away from the tectonic idea of true sculpture. The contrast between Hildebrand and his impressionist contemporaries is pointed out by Wölfflin:

He is linear and tectonic and has the greatest clarity of line, because from the beginning his form was cast in a "classical" mold. It is not true that Impressionism was the exhaustive expression of a period, else a phenomenon like Hildebrand would not have been possible. [16]

Hildebrand's idea of an architectonic art had orientation in space as its first requirement. But the task of the sculptor or the painter was not to reproduce the three-dimensional or cubic impression of nature, but rather to give a clear and restful idea of movement in repose. The classic relief preëminently fulfilled this idea.

Whereas Fiedler, by rejecting all rules of art, had in many ways come much closer to expressionist theory than had Hildebrand, the latter reëstablished an esthetics of absolute artistic laws. He found the realization of his concept of form only in classical Greek sculpture and in Michelangelo, and felt its lack in the *Farnese Bull,* in Cellini, in baroque sculpture, and even in Canova's neoclassic sculpture.

Fiedler's theory of vision and Hildebrand's book had important influences on later artists and art critics. "Hildebrand's *Problem of Form in Painting and Sculpture* was epoch-making in its effect on art criticism, which entered a new era with its publication. The first result of these new fermentations was Wölfflin's *Classical Art.*" [17]

This new theory of art as a matter of visual perception liberated the artist as well as the art critic from the various nineteenth-century standards of art as the expression of an idea, from the materialist theories, and from art as the representation of nature. Instead, the standard of value was established in the visual perception of the work of art itself.

Wölfflin (1864–1945), owing as much to Fiedler as to Jacob Burckhardt's sensitive esthetic analysis, expressed his admiration for Marées, Fiedler, and Hildebrand. He emphasized Fiedler's significant contribution —the stress on artistic conception:

So Fiedler had opposed the Aristotelian concept of "mimesis" as an erroneous concept of art and source of much wrong. Modern art pedagogy proceeds similarly, giving free rein to the artist's concept and not permitting a one-sided training of eye and hand toward perception and imitation. [18]

Wölfflin applied the theory of visual perception to an analysis of the development of style. He isolated a number of artistic forms, and arrived at polar principles for the definition of historical transformations. Although Wölfflin discussed and compared many individual artists, his striving toward a "history of art without artists" again shifted the emphasis away from the artist's individual contribution, which had been given such an important place in Fiedler's unsystematic writings.

Concurrent with the theories of Fiedler, Hildebrand, and Wölfflin was another theory of perception, which proposed the psychology of empathy as the basis of esthetic enjoyment.

The concept of empathy goes back to the late eighteenth century, when Herder imagined a youth sensing himself to be part of the upward-soaring tree, and when Novalis envisaged a merging of man's soul with the outward dwelling place. The word *Einfühlung* itself appeared first in the writings of Robert Vischer,[19] and the theory of empathy was developed into a comprehensive system by Theodor Lipps (1851–1914), who applied it to all aspects of art and esthetic cognition. Johannes Volkelt and Karl Groos were other important exponents of the theory in Germany.

Empathy may be defined as a hypothetical, psychic mechanism enabling man to experience esthetic enjoyment. It presupposes that the world is alien to man and that only an emotional identification can fuse the subject with the object. In a state of empathy the boundaries between personal identity and the artistic object disappear, so that separateness is replaced by oneness. The theory of empathy is based on the metaphysical concept of the subject existing in the object:

The first principle of empathy is this, that when I observe a form I am within it. And, if empathy is complete, I am *completely* in the form I observe. In empathy then, I am not the real self, but am inwardly separated from it, i.e., I am separated from everything that is tangential to my observation of the form. . . .

As far as this empathy exists, forms are beautiful. The beauty of spacial form is this "idealized," free, and complete existence within it. On the other hand, a form is ugly if I am not able to do this, if in the form or in observing it I feel myself inwardly unfree, frustrated, or constrained.[20]

The proponents of the theory of empathy did not believe that esthetic experience resulted from a long process of analysis and contemplation; they affirmed, rather, that the esthetic experience was an almost instantaneous projection of sensations and emotions. The object became animated in the emotion of the "empathetic" observer, and he could speak of a "weeping willow," a "rising mountain," "an active line taking a walk," or "gay" or "mourning colors." This theory became extremely important in expressionist criticism and esthetic theory. Vernon Lee, the leading exponent of empathy in British esthetics, explained: "We attribute to lines not only balance, direction, velocity, but also thrust, resistance, strain, feeling, intention, and character." [21] This same concept—that a line itself could carry the communicative meaning—appeared earlier in Signac's *D'Eugène Delacroix au néo-impressionnisme* [22] and in the writings of Henry van de Velde, who affirmed that "the line is a force which stems from the energy of him who drew it." [23] The concept appears in most esthetic theories of the twentieth century: for example, in Walter Crane's *Ideals in Art*,[24] in Sérusier's *ABC de la peinture*,[25] in Gleizes' and Metzinger's *Du Cubisme*,[26] and with particular emphasis in the Bauhaus publications of Kandinsky [27] and Klee.[28] The empathetic meaning of color, space, and shape can be similarly traced.

Interesting parallels could be drawn between the esthetic theories of the symbolists and the more systematic theory established in the writing and teaching of Theodor Lipps. These theories actually became fused in the last decade of the nineteenth century in the writings and in the work of August Endell, who had been a pupil of Lipps in the Faculty of Philosophy at the University of Munich and who later became one of Germany's outstanding supporters of Jugendstil.

The theory of empathy had transferred the emphasis from the esthetic object to the subjective response of the observer. Almost simultaneously

Alois Riegl (1838–1905) evolved a subjective esthetic theory stressing the creative act of the producer of that object.

Riegl, like Semper before him, was greatly concerned with the origin of art, but he took issue with Semper's largely materialistic and mechanical ideas: "Semper explained style . . . through technical conditions. For him the work of art was a mechanical product conditioned by utilitarian purpose, raw material and technique. And so it remained in German history of art until Riegl came onto the scene." [29]

Riegl interpreted the history of art as a history of artistic purpose [30] rather than of artistic ability. He postulated the idea that "the artist always could do what he wanted to do." [31] Art was not a matter of skill; rather, skill was a result of the artist's purpose. When imitation of nature was the standard of art, the artistic product could be judged by its relative adherence to this ideal. But when an increasing number of nonimitative works of art came to be known in the West, this concept could no longer be considered an absolute standard. And could the more realistic Egyptian servant statue really be considered a better work of art than the stiff, hieratic statues of the kings? These questions were discussed in Riegl's first important book, *Stilfragen*, published in 1893. Eight years later, in the introduction to his *Spätrömische Kunstindustrie*, Riegl wrote:

In contrast to this mechanistic concept of the character of a work of art I have advocated . . . a teleological concept, by recognizing in a work of art the result of a definite and deliberate artistic purpose, which wins out in the battle with usefulness, raw material and technique. These three latter factors, therefore, do not have the positive creative role which was assigned to them in Semper's theory, but they have rather an inhibiting, negative role: they form, as it were, the friction coefficient of the total product.[32]

In this same book Riegl also rose against the prevailing academic prejudice that measured all art by the standards of the classical Greek and that considered late Roman art decadent. He called attention to the peculiar excellence of the latter, which aimed at a different mode of expression and therefore necessitated a new form. Introducing the concept of artistic purpose as the entelechy producing art, Riegl transferred the standard from the external aspect of the finished product to the inner creative process, the subjective motivation of the artist.

Wilhelm Worringer (born 1881) combined Riegl's theory of "artistic purpose" with Lipps' theory of empathy, and elaborated further in *Abstraktion und Einfühlung*.[33] This book soon became almost the official guide to expressionist esthetics.

Worringer acknowledged his indebtedness to Riegl: "Modern art research must . . . accept as an axiom that the past could do all that it *willed*, and that it could not do only that which did not lie in the direction of its will." [34]

Worringer said that the artistic purposes of man have not always been the same, that at times man felt sympathetic to his natural surroundings, but that evidently in some epochs and cultures he felt antagonistic toward nature or threatened by it. Empathy, he insisted, was the driving force only when society tended toward the organic, toward naturalism, when it desired to melt into nature.

Empathy was undoubtedly the motivation of the classical artistic purpose, but cannot explain many other forms in art. For example, the lifeless form of a pyramid or the suppression of life manifested in Byzantine mosaics clearly shows that the need for empathy, which for obvious reasons always tends toward the organic, cannot possibly have motivated the creation of these works of art. Rather, the impulse seems to have suppressed the very need for which empathy offers satisfaction.[35]

Here, as in many other forms, the urge toward abstraction was decisive. Whereas empathy can be explained as a sympathetic relationship between man and the external world, the drive toward abstraction—geometric or otherwise—is the effect of the inner restlessness of man when confronted with nature. Worringer compared this restlessness with agrophobia in certain individuals. Abstraction is the drive to tear the object from its natural context in the world, to sever its relationships in order to clarify and stabilize it and give it a new and absolute form. Empathy produces "naturalism"; abstraction is the basis for "style." Franz Marc referred to Worringer's *Abstraction and Empathy* as one of the two attempts to create a basis for a new criticism,[36] and called it a book that "deserves general esteem and in which a severely historic intellect put down a train of thought, which might readily cause discomfort to the frightened opponents of the modern movement."[37]

Worringer became highly sympathetic to a new "style" in art: expressionism. His meeting with Kandinsky in Munich in 1908 was important for the further development of both men. Worringer became one of the spokesmen of expressionism, in which he saw a revolt of the spirit against sensualism and realism. In expressionism, he felt, the emphasis was again where it should be: on vision rather than on knowledge, on revelation rather than on observation. In an important article, published in 1919 in *Genius,* one of the leading organs of the movement, Worringer said: "The exciting element of expressionism, seen within the history of artistic development, was that—within the narrow, post-medieval European framework —it made the first completely consistent attempt to carry through the experiment of a complete spiritualization of expression."[38]

Worringer's first essay, *Abstraction and Empathy,* was so important for the development of the movement itself that Hans Tietze referred to expressionism as "having characteristics which became familiar to us through Worringer's book."[39]

The expressionist movement gave rise to a large body of critical documentation. Several of the artists, especially Kandinsky, made perhaps the most important contributions to this literature.[40] During and immediately after World War I a number of critical essays and monographs on the expressionist movement were written by historians, critics, and other writers.[41]

Typical of this literature, as well as being the first and most comprehensive discussion of expressionism from the point of view of esthetic theory, was *Expressionismus*, by Hermann Bahr (1863–1934).

Like Worringer, Bahr recognized a basic dichotomy in man's artistic expression, but saw something other than an abstraction-empathy polarity. He based his argument on Fiedler's theory of pure visibility, and agreed that the history of art is the history of vision and that a new way of seeing produces new forms. But Bahr distinguished between a passive, sensual, optical vision on the one hand and an active, mental vision on the other. Classical Greek vision expressed unity between man and nature. Seeing was more important than thinking in the classical-Renaissance tradition that reached its culmination in impressionism. Impressionism, according to Bahr, required feeling and sense reception without making any demands on the intellect. It was the vision of a materialistic age that valued only the senses but not the conflict between man and nature.

Bahr also stressed the importance of Riegl's contribution to art criticism [42] —the theory that man's artistic purpose makes him the activator rather than the echo of the world. In contrast to the "sense vision" of the classical tradition in Western art, primitive, Oriental, medieval, and expressionist art are parts of a sphere of art in which man determines nature. Mental vision, including tactile feeling and intellectual knowledge, is more comprehensive. The vision of the mind is abstract; therefore the art expression based upon it must deviate from nature. Just as sound for the composer begins in his brain and not in his ear, the vision of the painter may start in his mind rather than in his eye: "The aim of the painters of this newest trend is, as it were, eye-music. Their purpose is not the imitation of nature; therefore one does them injustice when one takes nature as a standard for their paintings." [43]

Bahr was conscious of the challenge to art of the new machine technology. His reaction, like that of the expressionists in general, was retreat. In modern times man is more insignificant than ever—he has become the tool of the machine; so the modern artist must search his own soul. Although the bourgeois generation of the late nineteenth century could find full expression in the materialistic art of impressionism, the new generation strives toward the spirit. [44] The painters of the new school represent man's longings, hopes, and fantasies rather than realistic images. " 'Painting,' says Goethe, 'predicates what man wants to see, and what man ought to see, not what he ordinarily sees.' If one really needs a program of Expressionism, this is it." [45]

The expressionist—the mental, the active—aspect is, however, only half of truly great art. The other half is the impressionist aspect—the purely visual, receptive art of sense enjoyment. Both aspects together yield the totality of inner and outer life. No period in art history has ever achieved the totality; only the baroque came close to this completeness. The new expressionist vision, Bahr argued dialectically, may offer the antithesis to the impressionism of the recent past and may lead to a synthesis of mental and sensual vision.

A similar optimism pervaded most of the critical writings. Hausenstein and Hartlaub predicted the subjugation of materialism and a new affirmation of the religious spirit. A strong religious revival was in fact one of the most significant factors in the movement. Typical is Edschmidt's exclamation: "Art is only a step on the road to God." [46]

The attempt to break with tradition and rationalism and the fervent search for new religious experience were related to the rediscovery of the Christian art of the Middle Ages. Unlike the Nazarenes or the pre-Raphaelites, the expressionists were not satisfied with the representation of God's creatures—they wished to reëxperience the Creation itself. "Art is a symbol of creation; it is an example, much as art exemplifies the cosmos." [47]

II

New Responses to Past Styles

Museums and reproductions of paintings and prints have made works of art from a large number of cultures and eras accessible to the twentieth-century observer. The German expressionist painter could thus experience the impact of primitive and tribal art, popular folk art, Near and Far Eastern art, Gothic art, the baroque, romanticism, and later also mannerism as well as postimpressionism. The academic determination, prevailing until the end of the nineteenth century, to measure all art by the standard of the classical Greek and the Renaissance, was broken. The new generation of artists, art historians, and critics found inspiration in the art of the nonclassical tradition:

Gothic, Baroque, primitive and Asiatic art, these suddenly revealed themselves—this, I think, is certain—as they never revealed themselves to any previous generation. These things had for long been looked at: now all at once we really saw them. Even although behind the walls of a distance which could never be bridged, they became to us unexpectedly transparent, and we saw into the most secret places of their mind and soul.[1]

Yet the artist is always limited in his choice of "influences" by the taste and tenor of his own time. The expressionist generation largely felt the greatest affinity to two periods in the German past: the style of the late Middle Ages and the esthetics of the romantic movement.

"THE SPIRIT OF THE GOTHIC"

Two years after the publication of *Abstraction and Empathy,* Worringer published his *Formprobleme der Gotik,* which also became highly important to the new generation of artists. Again he established a polarity: between Mediterranean and "Northern" vision—the former tending toward empathy, the latter toward abstraction. In his rejection of the "functionalist" theory, Worringer was much more extreme than any of his predecessors. He even negated the importance of the structural aspects of Gothic architecture, and placed his emphasis entirely on the expressive factor. He distinguished between mere building, which is concerned with material factors and practical purposes, and architecture, which is a creative art, "extracting from the dead materials an expression corresponding to a definite a priori will." [2]

After establishing this premise, Worringer fully reversed the old standards of value and placed Gothic art on a higher plane than Greek art. The Gothic achieved great form *in spite of* the material, whereas the Greek found its expression *by means of* the material. Greek art, he felt, merely appealed to the senses. Gothic art was on a higher, spiritual plane—it dematerialized to reach the transcendental. Using the contrast of Greek and Gothic architecture, Worringer expressed the feeling of transcendence he found in Gothic art: "The antonym of matter is spirit. To dematerialize stone means to spiritualize it. And with that statement we have clearly contrasted the tendency of Gothic architecture to spiritualize with the tendency of Greek to sensualize." [3]

Worringer finally linked expressionism with the German Gothic tradition. He traced the spirit of the Gothic—or Northern—art back to the Hallstadt and La Tène periods, through the linear fantasy of the intertwining band-and-braid ornament of the Vikings. He spoke of the "infinite melody of the Northern line," [4] which is of an essentially spiritual nature and which found its highest manifestation in the thirteenth-century Gothic cathedral. Like many other German writers of the time, he denied that France could be called the mother country of the Gothic. In France the Gothic was always colored with classical motifs, whereas the true Gothic was a style "peculiar as the common property of the Aryan people" [5]—whoever they might be. He saw the continuance of this Northern artistic purpose in Dürer's "Gothic roots" and the "pictorial pathos of Grünewald." The baroque was an art of the spirit, although expressed through a foreign, sensual language. The Gothic form-will had always existed as a sort of mystic undercurrent in German art. It appeared again in the great, fragmentary, enigmatic art of Hans von Marées, and Worringer prophesied that this racial phenomenon might come to a new climax in expressionism.

According to Worringer, the Gothic itself had its dualism of mind and spirit: the former expressed in scholasticism and the structural elements of the cathedral, the latter most perfectly revealed in the stained glass. Similarly, in modern art the rational element was expressed in Cézanne and the cubists, and the spiritual phenomenon appeared in van Gogh and might come to its culmination in expressionism.

The new concern with the medieval—this "revelation of the Gothic," as Worringer called it—engrossed not only extremists like Worringer, but also sober and conservative critics like Karl Scheffler. Scheffler, to be sure, was no friend of expressionism, which he called "self-destructive and eclectic"; [6] his periodical *Kunst und Künstler* was devoted primarily to the French and German impressionists. However, in his important *Der Geist der Gotik* ⁷ he assented to the new dictum that the decisive factor in art was the outward expression of inner emotion. He took issue with all "derived" styles and pointed to the great originality and spontaneity of the Gothic, which, he said, had been fully understood only in the immediate past.

In the nineteenth century the Gothic was still considered inferior to classical and Renaissance art by such art historians as Franz Kugler, Jacob Burckhardt, Gottfried Semper, Conrad Fiedler, and Adolf von Hildebrand. The fact that a conservative critic like Scheffler was able to place the Gothic on an equal if not higher level shows the change in evaluation that had occurred.

Not unlike Worringer, Scheffler set up a permanent dichotomy between the regular, orderly, knowing, static art form of the classical Greek and the irregular, imaginative, creative, dynamic form of the Gothic; the Gothic created forms of unrest and suffering on all levels, and was in opposition to the Greek spirit, which gave rise to forms of rest and happiness.⁸ This distinction seems to be an approximate application of Nietzsche's dichotomy of the "Apollonian" and the "Dionysiac." Like Nietzsche (and Bahr), Scheffler believed that the greatest art was a synthesis of the two polar factors.

Scheffler postulated a cyclical theory according to which young, growing, dynamic, masculine cultures created Gothic form. In their period of saturation and maturity, these cultures turned to the harmonious and formal classical; in their old age, new restlessness and desire again necessitated Gothic expression.

Thus to Scheffler, Gothic was an even wider concept than it had been to Worringer. Scheffler saw it in the totemic, highly expressive palaeolithic cave drawing, in the symbolism of Egyptian painting and sculpture, as well as in the architectural form of pyramid and pylon. It recurred in the Babylonian ziggurat, in the flamboyance of the Indian arabesque, and in the ornamental *décor* of Chinese bronzes. In European art, Gothic showed itself in the consciousness of death and the emotional quality in Etruscan sculpture as well as in the functional monumentality of Roman architecture, where it was the manifestation of violent desire rather than of classical balance. The mysticism of early Christian mosaics and manuscript illumination was most profoundly Gothic; the same spirit found its most complete manifestation in Gothic architecture. In the North, Gothic vision was retained even in the period of the Renaissance, and Grünewald bridged the gap to the new Gothic outburst of the baroque. In the nineteenth century, the Gothic spirit of romanticism quickly overcame neoclassicism and found new expression in impressionism, which was the product of an excited world feeling whereby the restless will gained form through struggle and carried its manifestation of man's unrest into the artistic transcription of a passionate state.⁹ The final manifestation of the Gothic spirit, in Scheffler's sense, was in the functionalism of the modern skyscraper, where the frank emphasis on the vertical was reminiscent of the Gothic cathedral itself.

Although Scheffler often severely criticized the expressionists, his journal gave increasing space to their work, and he frankly expressed the hope that the new generation of painters would follow the spiritual lead of the Gothic. The young painters "seek the archetype of the great primitivism; Giotto takes the place of Raphael and Michelangelo; Grünewald the place of Holbein. It is as if art were begun anew." [10]

Even the Renaissance and classical scholar Wölfflin turned to medieval art in this period of reëvaluation. In 1920 he published the *Bamberg Apocalypse* [11] with the announced objective of making this illuminated manuscript from Reichenau available to the large segment of the population that was showing an increasing interest in medieval art. In the introduction Wölfflin commented on the change in standards of criticism. The nineteenth century had classical and naturalistic standards, and judged works of art by their "correctness" and three-dimensional illusion. This value judgment, Wölfflin pointed out, was incorrect, because many art periods had different ends in mind. In eleventh-century miniatures, for example, it was neither modeling nor anatomically correct proportion, but rather the vivid and imaginative line that was most effective and forceful. "It is superfluous critically to note errors in proportion when there is a purposeful negation of correctness in order to give a stronger assertion to form by arbitrary distortion . . ." [12] Wölfflin explained that the artistic end was that of abstract values. To that end, representation might shift toward the fantastic; form might be dispersed without adherence to nature. Babylon's destruction, for example, might be represented in art simply by turning the city upside down; the importance of a gesture might be emphasized by exaggerating the proportions of a hand. [13] Wölfflin's descriptions of the eleventh-century miniatures resemble the contemporary analysis of expressionist painting, and a review of his publication [14] offers a series of interesting parallels between the Reichenau illuminations and modern painting.

In a later work [15] Wölfflin attempted to show the peculiar qualities of German art. He avoided the pitfalls and facile generalizations of Worringer and Scheffler, and showed that he was well aware of the complexity of an analysis of national style. Whereas the Italian artist concerned himself with regular, tectonic composition, the Northern artist stressed irregular, free-rhythmic movement. Italian art strove for grand simplicity, but the art of the North was held in a violent, dynamic tension. The Italian emphasis on the typical and on objective harmony was contrasted to the stress on the individual and on the subjective intuition of the German artist. The Italian painter saw in art the imitation of nature; the Northern artist concerned himself with the fantastic fruits of his imagination.

This new interest in medieval art, which the Germans considered their national heritage, occurred simultaneously in art history and criticism and in the creative arts. The result was a mutual stimulation among artists, critics, estheticians, and historians. The rediscovery of various medieval sources by the art historians influenced the trend of expressionist painting; the use of these elements by the painters affected critics and historians.

The artists found an immediate affinity to German medieval art through their enthusiasm for the early woodcut. Vallotton, Gauguin, and Munch had pointed the way in the technique of the modern woodcut.[16] Although the modern woodcut differed greatly in appearance and style from the medieval woodcut, there were basic resemblances in the directness of method as well as in the immediate symbolic effect.

The whole history of the woodcut, from its beginnings in the *Ars Memorandi* to work by the expressionists, was traced by Paul Westheim. "The early period and the most recent development of the woodcut are contiguous not in external gesture, and not only in the directness of technique, but in the direction of artistic purpose." [17] Max Friedländer saw a similar relationship.[18] Wolfradt felt that, in its clear statement of technique, its lapidary, and its direct language of form, the modern woodcut could be considered a regeneration of the primitive woodcut of the fifteenth century.[19]

Expressionist painting also sought its roots in the "spirit of the Gothic." Ernst Ludwig Kirchner said that the Brücke was in no way influenced by contemporary movements such as cubism and futurism, but "found its art-historical corroboration in Cranach, Beham, and other medieval German masters." [20] Kirchner emphasized the fact that Otto Mueller was drawn into the Brücke partly because "in his studio they saw Cranach's 'Venus,' which they themselves had always esteemed very highly." [21] Elsewhere Kirchner claimed to find the archetype of the new art in Dürer.[22] Max Sauerlandt, curator of the Hamburg Museum and a lifelong defender of the modern and progressive tendencies in German art, also saw an archetype to the art of the expressionists in that of their German predecessors: "In those years arose the new, hard, heroic beauty, a beauty of truly tragic bearing, which had grown strange to European painting since the heroic end of the Middle Ages in Grünewald and in Dürer's 'Apocalypse.' " [23]

THE ADMIRATION FOR GRÜNEWALD

Grünewald belongs to the expressionist painters as Fra Filippo Lippi belonged to the pre-Raphaelites. After centuries of oblivion, Grünewald had been rediscovered in the second half of the nineteenth century. The first scholarly treatise on him did not appear until 1911.[24] Arnold Böcklin had been one of the first painters to make repeated pilgrimages to Colmar to find new inspiration for his work.[25] But Böcklin was still willing to submit to the criticism of his friend Jacob Burckhardt, who rejected the Isenheim altarpiece as having been painted during an era "when everything was permitted." Later in the nineteenth century the symbolist novelist Huysmans wrote a eulogy on the Isenheim altarpiece.[26] As late as the 1880's, however, both the Kaiser Friedrich Museum in Berlin and the Germanic Museum in Nürnberg rejected the newly discovered *Karlsruhe Crucifixion* when it was offered them for purchase. In 1905 Max Liebermann, in a letter to Wilhelm von Bode, criticized Grünewald severely as "painted poetry." [27] Von Bode was still not interested in installing the Isenheim altarpiece at the Kaiser Friedrich Museum as late as the outbreak of World War I, and the work was sent to Munich instead. It is interesting in this connection that Max Beckmann wrote to Bode at the time and urged him to bring the altarpiece to Berlin.[28]

Grünewald, however, became the ideal of the new generation, which saw in his Isenheim altarpiece a freedom of creation following the intrinsic logic of content and composition rather than of nature. Grünewald, it was felt, penetrated to the core of human emotion and created a truth that went far beyond the doubtful truth of reality. Young artists recognized in Grünewald the fervent religious faith for which many of them had been searching. Here was the utmost expression of "artistic purpose." His figures revealed extremely intense emotions of suffering, mother love, piety. His form was the vessel of his emotion, and the mastery of light, color, and line was used only for the expression of inner feeling. Grünewald, like the expressionists, used color to create a rhythmic harmony that was an integral part of his total composition. The choice of color was determined by the emotional effect desired. The expressionists understood line to be more than the outline of form—they treated it as an independent vehicle of emotion; this use of line they found also in Grünewald's drawings. The expressionists did not consider perspective an essential element of space composition; here again they found a prototype in Grünewald. The varied physical sizes of the figures in Grünewald's *Crucifixion*—determined by significance in the event rather than by anatomical considerations—also appealed to the expressionists, who went much further in their distortions of the human figure.

Some artists, like the Rhenish expressionist Heinrich Nauen, showed ample evidence of Grünewald's influence in their own work, as can be seen by comparing a detail from Nauen's *Pietà* (cf. pls. 1a, 1b) with a detail of Grünewald's Isenheim *Crucifixion*. Others, like Ludwig Meidner, gave full rein to their verbal expressions of admiration for Grünewald:

Oh, a glowing, masculine, and unerring truth, like Master Multscher, Grünewald, Bosch, and Breughel. . . . We have to create the great visions. . . . Our visions must be clear and strong like those of Multscher and Grünewald.—Let us always think of these two! [29]

Similarly, art historians, like Max Deri, paid their respects to Grünewald as a pattern for the expressionists:

The strongest, the greatest and most agitated of the Expressionists in the European past was Matthias Grünewald. Next to him, everything that all other artists have done in this direction becomes tame. He puts the highest demands on the readiness of the spectator to experience the transposition from natural form to the most distorted configurations with the greatest seizure of innermost feeling.[30]

When the German critic Paul F. Schmidt first saw a large exhibit of Oskar Kokoschka's work, he compared the Austrian expressionist with Grünewald: "Kokoschka, a most original young man, is the first Viennese painter in whom one can say there is genius . . . Probably Germany has seen nothing so wild and fantastic since the death of Grünewald." [31]

Fechter recognized in the work of Kokoschka a special debt not only to van Gogh but also to the Gothic—above all to Grünewald. He considered the Isenheim altarpiece, with its ecstasy of emotion and intoxicating color, as one of the important sources of the new artistic search. [32]

The expressionists, who felt their isolation from modern society so acutely, hoped to find an affirmation of their search for the transcendental, absolute, and infinite in the art of the Middle Ages. It is certainly significant that from the wealth of available sources in medieval art it was Grünewald, and not the sculptors of Naumburg, who was acclaimed as the archetype of the new movement. Grünewald himself had lived during a period of great religious and social turmoil, encompassing the Chiliastic ecstasy, Anabaptist revolution, peasant wars, and the Reformation, at a time when the medieval order was bursting at the seams.

Grünewald may have distorted his bodies, but they never lose their physical beings. In spite of the apparent unorthodoxy of the altarpiece, there was no question of its immediate communicability to a large religious audience. But the expressionist distortions were to remain isolated; untouched by devotional character, they could never achieve the desired mass appeal. Yet the expressionists felt an affinity to the medieval artist, because he too was not primarily interested in representationalism. Where distance from nature was not a deliberate undertaking for the medieval artist, the modern artist removed himself purposely from nature—was antinaturalistic rather than anaturalistic.

As early as 1917 this conflict was seen by Gustav Hartlaub, one of the outstanding critics of the movement, [33] and soon others became aware of the dichotomy. Hausenstein, in his provocative essay on expressionist painting, pointed out the attempt to approach religion, but finally expressed his doubt that expressionism could succeed without faith in a dogma of revelation. [34] Worringer similarly began to doubt that expressionism would fulfill its spiritual mission. [35]

As expressionism became an accepted style after 1918—as its former ecstasy became a gesture and its passion a sensation—its promise of a religious renewal of society was obviously to remain unfulfilled. Therefore critics seriously doubted any affinity whatever with medieval art, since there was no longer the one ennobling and pervasive religious belief that gave force and coherence to the symbolism of the Middle Ages. Lacking a universal symbology, the modern artist must now find his own laws in his attempt to extricate himself from individual isolation. [36]

Richard Hamann commented on the vast difference between expressionist and Gothic man, stemming from basically different concepts of reality. Both the word and the idea were sacred realities for Gothic man, but now even reality was only an idea. In the Middle Ages divine power appeared in the merest leaf; modern man had made even of God an object—at best material for a still life. Hamann concluded that any relationship between expressionism and medieval art was nothing but a hoax.[37] Hamann obviously had no sympathy for the movement, but he also lacked the understanding for the very real utopian ideal that the Gothic and Grünewald had been for the expressionist generation. When this generation found little satisfaction in existing reality, it sought an intimate relationship with a desirable though unattainable myth of the past.

THE RELATIONSHIP TO THE ROMANTIC MOVEMENT

Although the romanticists had no knowledge of Grünewald, they did establish the first vital contact with early German art. Wackenroder placed Dürer on the same artistic level as Raphael, and emphasized divine inspiration, spontaneity of creation, and art's nonrational character in opposition to the standards of the eighteenth century. Friedrich Schlegel valued the poetic and imaginative aspects of art and "discovered" the school of Cologne and Altdorfer. Wackenroder and Schlegel were undoubtedly influenced by Herder, who had taught that there were no universal laws in art but that each artistic expression was an outgrowth of the special conditions of time, country, and the artist's own language.

The esthetics of romanticism in the late eighteenth century broke with the old-established "rules of art." The poets and painters were set free to create their own values, which became increasingly subjective and personal. Dynamic growth was considered superior to permanent standards. The sublime rose to the same level as the beautiful.

The work of the German romantic painters received comparatively little attention during the second half of the nineteenth century. Of far-reaching importance, therefore, was the 1906 Century Exhibition of German painting (1775–1875) in Berlin, including the major work of two important exponents of German romanticism: Runge and Friedrich.

This exhibition, coinciding with the beginning of the new movement in German art, was organized by Hugo von Tschudi. Tschudi was later dismissed as director of the German National Gallery in 1908, and was appointed director of the Bavarian State Galleries in Munich in 1909. In keeping with his enthusiasm for romanticism, Tschudi purchased works by Cézanne, van Gogh, Gauguin, Toulouse-Lautrec, Signac, Matisse, Denis, Vuillard, and Bonnard, and also became an important sponsor of the *Neue Künstlervereinigung*. When Marc and Kandinsky published their book *Der Blaue Reiter* in 1912, they dedicated it to Hugo von Tschudi. The resemblance of the name of the book to the *Blaue Blume* of German romanticism, which first appeared in Novalis' unfinished allegorical novel, *Heinrich von Ofterdingen* (1799), is too evident to be overlooked.

Novalis believed that art (poetry) was the spirit that yielded life to all things, in either nature or human activity. The dream became of prime importance to Novalis, because it revealed the most profound stratum of existence. "Our life is not a dream, but it should become one and it is likely to attain this end." [38]

The emphasis on the dream image and the paradoxical mixture of free thought and religious mysticism appear in both the romantic and the expressionist movements. In both, conscious and unconscious reality merge into a single realm.

Although it is true that there is comparatively little resemblance between German expressionist painting and German romantic painting, there is a close affinity in their affirmation of the intuitive aspects of art. Generally the expressionist painters, like the romanticists, considered the visible world only as a simile and recognized as their goal the perception of inner forces in the outer world.

In this connection it is interesting to compare fragments of letters by the German romantic painter Caspar David Friedrich with similar statements—emphasizing the introspective and subjective aspects of art—by Kandinsky and Marc. It is also significant that these fragments were published in the *avant-garde Genius*.

The painter shall not paint what he sees in front of him, but what he sees inside himself. But if he sees nothing dwelling within him, he had better also abstain from painting what he sees in front of him.

The artist's emotion is his law. Pure emotion can never be inimical to nature, but is always in conformity with it. The emotion of others must never be imposed upon the artist as law. Spiritual relationship engenders similar works, but this relationship is far different from apery.

Close your physical eye, so that you may see your vision at first with the spiritual eye. Then bring to light what you have seen in the darkness that it may evoke in the beholder a similar experience proceeding inwardly.[39]

A like emphasis on the spiritual is to be found in the following statements by Marc and Kandinsky, respectively:

Nature glows in our pictures as in every form of art. Nature is everywhere, in us and outside us; there is only one thing that is not altogether nature, but rather the overcoming and interpreting of nature: art. Art always has been and is in its very essence the boldest departure from nature and "naturalness." It is the bridge into the spirit world . . . the necromancy of the human race.[40]

Ever more strongly I realized that the center of gravity in art did not lie in its "formal expression," but in the inner impulse. . . .[41]

Herder's "spirit," which manifested itself in man in the form of culture and language, was still derived from the divinity. However, Herder's theory was very close to that of Kandinsky, who believed that in art "the abstract spirit takes possession of the individual human spirit and later rules an ever increasing number of men. In that moment individual artists succumb to *Zeitgeist*. . . ."[42]

The relationship between romanticism and expressionism was seen at an early date by a number of critics, including Ludwig Coellen, who published one of the first books on the new movement in connection with the international *Sonderbund* exhibition in Cologne in 1912. "The new painting is the romanticist opposition to the recent naturalism; it is the romanticism of modern art, and this is the accomplishment as well as the limitation of the new style." [43] Soon even Grünewald came to be considered a romanticist.[44] In 1920 Paul Ferdinand Schmidt noticed the connection between the revival of Grünewald and romanticism and the new art form. "The enthusiasm for Grünewald, the newly kindled love for Romanticism and the striking interest in so-called Expressionism . . . may all have their origin in the pure longing for a deep understanding of our essence." [45] The spirit of romanticism was finding its fulfillment in the new art as exemplified by Campendonk, Kandinsky, and Chagall.

What Romanticism a hundred years ago did not dare to do and was not able to do —what through fear it repressed in itself—today has broken out freely in the full force of creation. A Russian, with the freedom of a great barbarian from the East, liberated us from the convention of mimesis and realized in his way, Runge's dream of absolute musical color: Kandinsky. Another Russian, Marc Chagall, has endowed us with the courage necessary for the unlimited gigantic imagination of the irrational, fairy-tale logic or oriental dreams.[46]

The important parallels between the early-nineteenth- and early-twentieth-century ideas in German art must, however, not be overemphasized. The times had changed, and with them the artist's concept of the world. The passive contemplation of the romanticists had changed to the active participation of the early twentieth century; the Blue Flower of Novalis had become the Blue Rider of Kandinsky. The name—Blue Rider—implies both difference and similarity. The stress on the expression of emotion appeared in both romanticism and expressionism, but the form this expression was to take had changed considerably within a century.

PART TWO

Panorama of German Art
around 1900

III

The Sentiment of the Classic

Romanticism of a peculiar kind was kept alive by German painters during the second half of the nineteenth century—a romanticism of subject matter based largely on the classical tradition of the academy and rapidly becoming fused with the realism that made its inroads into Germany with Menzel and Leibl at mid-century. This type of fusion was by no means unique in German painting. Similar combinations of classical drawing and romantic subject matter can be found in France in the work of Chassériau, Delaroche, and Couture.

In Germany the painters of this particular style—Anselm Feuerbach, Arnold Böcklin, and Hans von Marées—enjoyed little popularity at the time of their greatest productivity. As much because of this lack of recognition as by choice, the *Deutschrömer* spent most of their creative periods in Italy. Not until the end of the century did they and their noted followers Franz Stuck and Max Klinger find great popular acclaim. Hans Thoma (1839–1924), originally a romantic landscapist, followed the taste for religious and mythological subject matter and peopled his realistically conceived Black Forest landscapes with classical nymphs and Wagnerian heroes. At the turn of the century these particular men were indeed hailed as the leaders of the new movement in German art. In a typical contemporary evaluation Max Schmid[1] wrote that Klinger, Böcklin, and Thoma represented probably the most significant manifestation of the newest German painting. These three men had become the spiritual leaders of the new period of fantastic art (*Phantasiekunst*). Free of imitation and conformity with foreign styles, they represented a pure German direction.[2] Klinger became the idol of members of the new generation, including even Paula Modersohn-Becker. Kubin too held Klinger in great respect, probably for the very thing in his work that repelled artists like Heckel— its overwhelmingly literary quality. Stuck, another member of this group, became teacher to Kandinsky and Klee.

Anselm Feuerbach (1829–1880) began his training in Düsseldorf under the guidance of the former Nazarene, Wilhelm von Schadow. He continued his studies in Munich and Antwerp, and worked in Paris under Couture from 1852 to 1854. In Paris he became familiar with Courbet's most recent work, which he rejected: "The so-called Realism is the easiest kind of art and denotes decay. If art copies life, then we have no need for it." [3] Descendant of a prominent family of philosophers and archaeologists, and a great admirer of Greek sculpture, German classic literature, and Venetian painting, Feuerbach hoped to become Germany's monumental history painter and the protagonist of a new idealism.

Spending most of his life in Venice and Rome and submitting consciously to the influence of Veronese and Palma Vecchio, Feuerbach searched for classical models, which he painted with excellent draftsmanship, adding color as additional decoration. Some of his figure compositions have a classical grandeur comparable to Corot, but only too frequently he was subject to overstatement when painting Roman women, to whom he added attributes and stereotyped expressions to transform them into Iphigenias or Medeas. His paintings were carefully premeditated: he felt it necessary to engage in considerable research in Greek mythology before doing his large *Medea,* and finally painted a vast canvas that lacks all spontaneity but still has the decorative effect of a spectacular stage set.

Feuerbach taught at the Vienna Academy from 1873 to 1875, but he had received only meager recognition by the time he died in Venice in 1880; his popularity came a generation later, during the formative years of the expressionist painters. The acclaim for Feuerbach at the turn of the century, however, was partly a reflection of the tremendous enthusiasm for Böcklin's work.

Arnold Böcklin (1827–1901), who fused classicist, romanticist, and realist trends in his work, may be considered a connecting link between the romanticists and expressionists. He expressed the greatest admiration for Caspar David Friedrich, to whose work his earliest landscapes show a clear affinity. Böcklin was in turn admired by men like the young Emil Nolde, who wrote: "How beautiful it would be if during one's life one could have so great an artist as Böcklin for a friend." [4]

Böcklin's early career was similar to Feuerbach's. Born in Basel, he began his studies at the Düsseldorf Academy and continued in Paris and Rome. He spent the latter half of the century in Italy, except for teaching at the Weimar Academy from 1860–1862 and for several longer periods of residence in Basel and Munich.

From his early landscapes Böcklin turned to mythological scenes and poetic illustration. Fascinated by Italian mountain landscape, he expressed his emotion by means of allegory. The mountain ravine was personified as a shepherd frightened by Pan; the experience of a tempest and rough sea became the birth of Venus, whereas a smoother sea developed into *Triton and Nereid.* Böcklin showed an extraordinarily rich invention in his creatures from myth, fable, and fairy tale, all rendered with meticulous care. His strange birds, dragons, and centaurs are disconcertingly realistic—one reason for the brief revival Böcklin experienced, first with de Chirico and later among the surrealists of the 1930's. The feeling of reality is evoked largely by his carefully representative draftsmanship. His symbols of fear, desire, joy, or longing are rendered by a theatrical gesture or literary allusion, and remain unconvincing as works of art. Typical is the supersentimentality of his *Amaryllis* or *Shepherd's Lament* of 1866 (pl. 2). Although his earlier sketches still have a freshness of concept, the final version of his paintings is generally overstated and highly sentimentalized. The long series from the early *Villa by the Sea* of 1864 to the final version of the *Isle of the Dead* of 1883 show this development perhaps most clearly.

Böcklin, like Feuerbach, was interested mainly in large mural decoration, but as no fresco commissions were forthcoming and since he lacked artistic sensitivity, he satisfied himself by using bright planes of pigment—after having carefully studied the techniques of the fifteenth-century Flemish painters—and applied them in clear lacquers on his canvases. He believed that the "painter even when painting small pictures, should always think in terms of the wall of the house." [5] The result is frequently a jarring, crowded effect of loud colors with little relationship between the hues. He then most carefully elaborated his surfaces, creating a highly finished enamel gloss, which also detracts from any power the original concept might have had.

This gloss was partly responsible for the great popular appeal of his paintings. More important, however, were the easily readable allegoric content and imagery, which was of a type that was most popular throughout Europe at the end of the nineteenth century. Such art offered an effortless escape from the unseemly ugliness of industrialization. The enthusiastic celebrations, in Germany and Switzerland, of Böcklin's seventieth birthday in 1897, as well as the flood of eulogistic monographs and articles that appeared at that time, attest to the popularity of Böcklin's Nordic versions of the classical world.

Critical opinion, however, was soon reversed. "The Böcklin worship threatened to become almost an obstacle to the further artistic development of the German nation." [6] In 1905 Meier-Graefe said, in his lengthy, provocative critical essay, *Der Fall Böcklin,* that Böcklin's powers of idea and invention, which had caused him to be eulogized, lacked spiritual depth and formal meaning and were therefore a dangerous enemy of art and of the spiritual life of the people. Especially in Böcklin's later works, Meier-Graefe noticed a heightened expression of antagonism to culture—an influence that the artist must resist for his own preservation. [7]

Deploring Böcklin's influence, Meier-Graefe introduced Germany to van Gogh, Gauguin, Cézanne, Toulouse-Lautrec, Vallotton, Munch, as well as Germany's own Hans von Marées.

Marées (1837–1887) was "the youngest of the three great German painters who in the second half of the nineteenth century went to Rome in order to realize in their work a monumentality and nobility which the growing trend towards bourgeois naturalism in the arts threatened to extinguish." [8]

Marées' first teacher, in the early 'fifties, was the Berlin animal painter Karl Steffeck. As Marées became acquainted with the techniques of the realists, he lightened his color and roughened his surfaces. Not concerned with realistic detail, he worked with large color masses. In the early 'sixties Marées arrived briefly at a technique somewhat related to early impressionism, but at the same time he was concerned with more static forms and careful structure. "While they [the French impressionists] endeavored to catch a purely painterly vision from a fleeting, momentary impression, he seeks to arrive at order, form and style by concentration of various results from direct observation, taking equal account of plastic form and painterly appearance." [9]

Marées arrived in Italy in 1864 with a commission, like Feuerbach, Böcklin, and Lenbach, to copy famous Italian Renaissance paintings for Count Schack of Munich. For almost ten years his artistic activity was almost stifled by the impact of Pompeian, early Christian, and Renaissance painting. He carried out the commissioned copies, but was able to paint only fragments of his own creation.

In Italy he met Conrad Fiedler. The two men became intimate friends, and shared a basic agreement about the meaning of art. Fiedler took Marées on an extended trip to Spain and France, and became his disciple as well as his life-long patron. After his return to Italy, Marées received a commission to paint frescoes for the library of the Naples Aquarium (1873). Unlike the other *Deutschrömer* he did not feel it necessary to resort to mythological history painting, but chose as his theme scenes from the life of the Neapolitan fishermen. He constructed his painting with plastic elements, and achieved a striking unity of color and form.

Throughout his life Marées struggled with problems of form, which he solved most successfully in his triptychs: *The Judgment of Paris* (1880–1881), *The Hesperides* (1884–1887), *Courtship* (1885–1887), and *The Three Horsemen* (1885–1887). *St. Hubert,* the central panel of *The Three Horsemen* (pl. 3), represents his late style, and shows his ability to discard all nonessentials and subordinate each detail to the totality of the composition. Here, as in his other works, he has arrived at a clear structure of his primarily vertical and horizontal forms. Marées placed little importance on the individual figure. Rather, he painted man in simple postures of standing, sitting, or lying. Marées' men are not men of action; rather, they are timeless creations of nature. Often they are seen in frontal poses with expressions that, like those of medieval ikons, are turned inward. Their significance is never that of the incidental, but of some universal law. They reflect a permanent order in which the reality of appearance has been rejected for the reality of artistic conception. Unfortunately, however, Marées' paintings do not always measure up to his formal ideas. Marées overpainted his canvases with layers of lacquer consisting of a mixture of tempera and oil. These layers produce an interesting quality of iridescence on careful observation, but give his paintings an unfortunately pale and muddy appearance when viewed from some distance.

Marées, who became of greatest importance to the German painters of the twentieth century, was hardly known during his lifetime. His Naples frescoes—similar in their classic form to the work that Puvis de Chavannes did at the same time in Paris—were hardly accessible to the general public, and his triptychs were hidden away in the Castle of Schleissheim. Only after his death was the public able to see Marées' work, in the Munich Glaspalast exhibit of 1891. Not until the twentieth century—when the Vienna Secession showed his work together with Hodler's and Munch's in 1903–1904, and when two large retrospective Marées exhibits were held by the Munich and Berlin Secession in 1908—was Marées received with real understanding. The publication of Meier-Graefe's three-volume work in 1910 [10] and the foundation of the *Marées Gesellschaft* after the war further assured Marées' permanent reputation.

Franz Marc considered Marées one of the few significant German painters of the nineteenth century.[11] Paul Fechter, in one of the first published discussions of the expressionist movement, spoke of the "spirit of Hans von Marées, hovering over the entire modern development [as the] recognition that art begins only beyond the representation of naturalism in all its variations." [12] Similarly, Joachim Kirchner, stressing the conceptual or ideational aspects of art, acknowledged Marées' importance for the expressionist generation: "With this transcendental note, which in the monumental formulation of these paintings found its fitting sacred expression, Marées became an unexcelled, shining example for the young generation, which was able to find in this artist the best leader into the realm of the spiritual." [13]

Max Klinger (1847–1920), who carried the sentiment of the classic into the twentieth century, is much more closely related to Böcklin than to Marées. His paintings, etchings, and sculpture were based on a most conscientious observation of naturalistic detail. This was considered to be the sound and necessary basis for modern fantastic art by his biographer Max Schmid [14] as well as by the vast number of people who considered him as one of the great German artists of the late nineteenth century.

Klinger studied with Gussow at the Berlin Academy, and spent an important year in Brussels close to Félician Rops and Antoine Wiertz before going to Rome in 1889. His rapid rise to popularity was responsible for his return, in 1893, to his native Leipzig, where he became celebrated as a master of grandiose dimensions. At a time when Gauguin and Redon found valid visual forms for their symbolic content, Klinger's world of fantasy and imagination resolved itself on canvas, paper, or marble in little more than theatrical attitudes or a disordered profusion of naturalistic forms.

Typical is Klinger's Beethoven monument of the 1890's (pl. 4), where the composer, dressed in a tablecloth and enthroned like Olympian Zeus, sits bent forward with folded hands, engaged in thought. Having learned that ancient sculpture was largely polychrome, Klinger used a great variety of materials: Pentelic marble for the flesh of the figure, Alpine onyx for the drape, gilded bronze for the throne, with ebony and a variety of patina on the moldings. The whole configuration is placed on a cloud of dark marble and confronted by a large ebony eagle.

Klinger's most ambitious painting is the *Christ on Mount Olympus* (1897). Strongly influenced by Wagner's idea of the *Gesamtkunstwerk*, this portable mural stands on a carved stone base. Two wings are separated from the central section by mahogany palms. The painting includes many of the major Greek divinities as well as Christ and the Christian virtues, each labeled with its proper attribute; the artist himself preserves admirable impartiality between Christianity and paganism. The figures are painted with astonishing realism: "He does not affect brilliant colors *à la* Rubens— red garments and blue cloaks—at the expense of truth. Rather he presents everything convincingly in the clear light of reality." [15] Another critic refers to this painting as a "dissertation . . . with figures which are supposed to express a great many ideas about Greece, but which all too clearly betray their origin in the Athens on the Pleisse." [16]

Comparing Klinger with Marées, Wilhelm Hausenstein criticizes Klinger's lack of artistic integrity and his vain attempt to achieve a grand style by means of technical facility and grandiose ideas whereas Marées possessed a true harmony of form and content. [17]

Klinger, although surely an artist of minor rank, is mentioned in this context because of his immense popularity at the turn of the century, in spite of his singular lack of both taste and judgment. Klinger did exert considerable influence on Alfred Kubin as well as on other twentieth-century artists. Georgio de Chirico, for example, expressed his admiration for both Klinger and Böcklin while he was studying in Munich, from 1909 to 1910.

Franz von Stuck (1863–1928) painted decorative allegories that were phenomenally successful. The son of a Bavarian miller, he studied at the Munich Academy and received a prize, when he first exhibited in the Munich International Exposition of 1889, with his *Guardian of Paradise*— an art-school model wrapped in a sheet and provided with realistically drawn bird's wings, flaming sword, and halo. By 1892 he was one of the leaders of young Munich painters who severed themselves from their older colleagues and, as the first group to adopt the name "Secession," set an example for similar movements throughout Germany and Austria.

Stuck became a professor at the Munich Academy, and was eventually knighted as well as appointed director of the academy. Both Klee and Kandinsky were among his students; Kandinsky frequently expressed his admiration for Stuck's fine draftsmanship. [18]

Stuck's chief motif was the female nude, which he consciously modeled after nudes in classical sculpture and Italian Renaissance painting. His figures were rendered with highly academic and "accurate" draftsmanship, and were always endowed with a quality that is both erotic and decorative. *The Sin* of 1895 (pl. 5) is a good example of his preoccupation with the combination of the nude female and snake that occurs in so many of his paintings (*The Sin, Vice, Sensuousness, Medusa*). In this painting Stuck was undoubtedly interested in the decorative possibilities of the snake coiled around the woman, the contrast in textures among flesh, hair, and snakeskin, as well as the symbolic quality of the snake, which not only has an obvious phallic significance, but is also associated with the idea of Woman, especially in German literature. It is not surprising that such paintings, as well as his centaurs, fauns, and nymphs, achieved immediate popularity. Further, their sinuous, linear quality is closely related to, and must be considered a part of, Jugendstil, the leading decorative style of the period.

Although Stuck was the teacher of some of the most important painters of the expressionist generation, his allegories must be considered the end rather than the beginning of a period. Writing in 1927, when Stuck's period of high acclaim had long passed, Hausenstein refers to him as the painter "who finishes with the pathos of catastrophe the Classicist Munich history painting, which derived from Cornelius and Kaulbach." [19]

Although Stuck and Klinger and Böcklin, revivers of ideational painting, were greeted for a brief time as the greatest of their period, their laurels were soon to pass on to Corinth and Slevogt. [20]

IV

Realism and Impressionism

Feuerbach painted his *Medea* in 1870; Marées' Naples frescoes were done in 1873; Böcklin's *Triton and Nereid* dates from 1875. But in this same decade there was important activity among the realist painters in Germany. Menzel's *Iron Foundry,* for example, was painted in 1875. In many ways Menzel was the leader of the realist movement in Germany, and his *Iron Foundry* is an excellent example of realism in both style and subject matter.[1] The other important German realist, Leibl, did his meticulously detailed *Women in the Church* between 1878 and 1880.

At first Wilhelm Leibl (1844–1900) developed his approach independent of Courbet's influence, though he paid considerable homage to the French painter when Courbet visited Munich in 1869. Opposed to the ideational art of his time, Leibl attempted to paint precisely what he saw—the rendering of the hem of a woman's skirt was as important to him as her facial expression. He lacked Courbet's boldness and, besides, was far more interested in accurate representation than in pictorial composition.

Leibl's paintings—although acclaimed by some critics as masterpieces—were not really popular in Munich. In the 'seventies he withdrew to the Bavarian countryside, where he settled down to painting the peasants with painstaking veracity.

His realism was carried into the new century by such painters as Charles Schuch, Wilhelm Trübner, Heinrich Zügel, and Albert von Keller, who combined an incisive realist perception with the impressionism filtering in from Paris and Berlin.

Impressionism was imported to Germany from France in the 'eighties and 'nineties. In France the impressionists were concerned primarily with rendering light and color, but the new technique in Germany was soon associated with the realist tradition established by Menzel and Leibl. Many German impressionists were closely concerned with the new social problems of the period of industrialization.

Max Liebermann (1847–1935), like Marées, emerged from the studio of Karl Steffeck in Berlin. However, the great multiformity of German painting during the second Empire can be clearly demonstrated by the contrast between these two painters. Marées worked in solitude in Italy without ever achieving any real degree of recognition in his lifetime, but Liebermann became the acknowledged leader of German painting.

Liebermann, more than any other painter, led German painting away from the literary subject matter of the ideational artists and brought it toward realism. When he went to Paris in 1873, he did not as yet become aware of the impressionists but instead became familiar with the work of Millet and the Barbizon painters, affirming his conviction that the artist should work directly from nature. Then he went on to Holland to stand in admiration before the paintings of Hals, whom he later referred to as "the most imaginative painter who ever lived." He explained that the artist's imagination was: "A concept of nature most adequate to the media of the painter." [2] Liebermann found this direct approach in Hals as well as in Josef Israels, the contemporary Dutch landscapist whom he considered his real teacher.

Liebermann's *plein-air* landscapes of the late 'seventies are very different from those of Monet or Pissarro; they are like seventeenth-century Dutch landscapes brought into the atmosphere of daylight. Real light enters his interiors, as in the *Dutch Sewing School* (1876) (pl. 6a) painted brightly in whites and blues. His own conquest of the bright world of color occurred long before his discovery of French impressionism.

Liebermann remained in Munich close to Leibl for a few years in an attempt to learn more about line and form. In the 'eighties he painted his almost monumental compositions, *The Net Menders* and *The Woman with Goats*. During this period his color was quite dark, with gray-green dominant.

Liebermann's realism was in strong opposition to the official Wilhelmian court painting. He chose the orphanage and the old-age home instead of the imperial ball for his motifs. This spreading opposition to an antiquated social system became, in Liebermann's paintings, a protest against worn-out esthetic ideas. He soon brightened his palette, this time in direct agreement with the Paris painters, particularly Manet and Degas. "There is really only a single German painter who can justly be counted among the Impressionists, who creates from an Impressionist *Weltanschauung*—Max Liebermann." [3]

Around the turn of the century Liebermann quickened the tempo of his line. Turning away from the social motif, he set out to catch momentary impressions of life by painting horseback riders, polo and tennis players, or bathers at the beach—such as his *Bathing Boys* of 1912 (pl. 6b). As leader of the Berlin Secession, he won recognition for impressionism in Germany and, making that style almost mandatory for the group, thereby opposed the new expressionist trends in the first decades of the twentieth century. But even in his most impressionist period, Liebermann remained within the Berlin tradition of Schadow, Blechen, Krüger, and Menzel. His contours were never submerged in light vibrations to the extent of those of

the French impressionists. His colors never achieved the richness or brightness of the French, but remained cooler and more sober; his line was always
his chief instrument.

Lovis Corinth (1858–1925) is often classified as a German impressionist, but the violent force and sensual quality of his work show a far greater
affinity to Rubens than to the more serene Monet.

Corinth was born in Königsberg and studied at the Munich Academy
before going to Paris, where he became a pupil of Bouguereau and Robert-
Fleury at the Académie Julian. He returned to Germany in 1887 and lived
in Munich in close association with the Secessionists and the Jugendstil
artists Eckmann, Obrist, and Behrens until 1900. However, his abrupt
break with "idealism," his apparent lack of concern for moral values, found
little favor in the Bavarian capital, and on the invitation of his close friend
Walter Leistikow he was glad to join the Berlin Secessionists. There he
became a leader and later president of the impressionist Berlin Secession, and
was most violently opposed to the expressionists when they were struggling
to gain recognition in Berlin. In his autobiography he spoke out violently
against the "Franco-Slavic international art," which he felt "threatened
German art and copied the art of the savages in order to draw attention to
itself." [4]

Throughout his life Corinth's painting bore the easily readable stamp
of a powerful vitality. Whether he painted scenes from classical mythology
or from the Bible, portraits, or nudes, his real content was always a sensual
flamboyance. His academic training stood in his way, because often a
literary characteristic seemed to interfere with his talent, which was one
of direct, vigorous visual expression; on the other hand, his portraiture, like
Graf Keyserling (1901) (pl. 7), belongs among the best achievements
of German impressionism.

In spite of his earlier antagonism to the expressionist movement, Corinth's last work—after a stroke in 1911, which resulted in partial paralysis
directly affecting his manner of painting—approached the style of expressionism. In his last portraits, religious paintings, and the magnificent Walchensee landscapes, he freed himself from all convention and turned toward
a highly expressive use of formal elements. His palette brightened, and in
his old age he began painting with the vivid, broken colors that make Julius
Held refer to him as the "most powerful colorist of German art since Grünewald." [5] In *Spring at the Walchensee* of 1922 (pl. 143) everything became
part of a vigorous over-all movement. He achieved a vibration of color that
goes beyond French impressionism to approach the expressionist landscapes
of Kokoschka or Nolde. Corinth came to be greatly admired by the younger
generation that he had opposed so stubbornly. Shortly before Corinth's
death, Kirchner wrote to his brother:

The old artist, even when sick and weak, creates better and deeper things than a
young and healthy artist. It is as if a curtain is lifted, and the aged artist sees more
truly and honestly. This has been true with all artists . . . it was also true with
Corinth. It was a miracle. At first he was mediocrity. At the end truly great.[6]

There is, however, a fundamental difference between Corinth's last work and later expressionist painting; although it seems close to expressionism, it is based on his visual perception and not on a preoccupation with his own emotions, as with the younger generation. Corinth's last landscapes seem rather like a fulfillment of his earlier search to manifest his immediate response to strong color sensations. They are a final manifestation of impressionism as a "bit of creation seen through the medium of a powerful temperament," [7] and are at the same time an intermediate step between the two artificial classifications.

Corinth had achieved an extraordinary effect by his vigorous handling of paint and his mastery of color. Max Slevogt's (1868–1932) imaginative and spontaneous creativity manifested itself in drawings and prints as much as in easel painting. His painting began with the dark tone composition he had learned as a student of Wilhelm Diez in Munich. But when in 1889, a few years later than Corinth, he went to Paris to study at the Académie Julian, his color lightened considerably; his line—under the impact of Rembrandt's work, which he studied in Holland—became nervously alive.

Slevogt returned to Munich in 1890, but accepted Liebermann's invitation to Berlin a decade later. He felt that the oppressive air of the academic Munich art world was no place for his highly imaginative work. In Berlin he found himself in a free, more cosmopolitan environment. His talent unfolded further in the direction of impressionism. He began to paint landscapes, still life, and portraits that often have a light, almost transparent quality and that show his love for light, color, and movement.

Slevogt had spent his adolescence and youth in the rococo city of Würzburg, where he had often seen and admired Tiepolo's frescoes in the Residenz. Now this background found pictorial expression, fused with the impressionism of his own time. "As the Paris Rococo is revived in the Frenchmen, especially in Renoir, but also in Monet and Sisley, so Slevogt's painting and his rich graphic work have the closest affinity to Würzburg Rococo." [8]

Rococo rhythm was combined with impressionist color and brush stroke in *Uniforms* (pl. 8)—a painting that is also a fine example of Slevogt's sarcastic sense of humor. The ornate uniforms go through all the motions of the parade, and the spectator never once misses the man behind the regalia. Slevogt's narrative imagination led him almost naturally toward illustration. In his illustrations for *The Magic Flute, Faust, The Iliad, Ali Baba,* and Cooper's *The Last of the Mohicans,* he used the technique he had learned from impressionism and developed away from the exactingly realistic illustration of Menzel toward poetic fantasies rendered by quick improvisations.

Slevogt was the only German impressionist who was given commissions to paint large mural decorations.[9] These are not monumental frescoes, but are light wall decorations of flowers, garlands, and fairy-tale images. If, unlike Corinth, Slevogt never went beyond the limits of impressionism, he did go to its limits and did solve many of its formal problems.

Liebermann, Corinth, and Slevogt, although influenced by their French contemporaries, each made creative contributions to the movement on their own. Their followers, however—like their counterparts among the French: Bastien-Lepage or Raffaelli—were adherents to a "style" that did much to crystallize, harden, and compromise the innovations of the earlier generation. Form can be dissolved properly only by those who have a full understanding of it, but the derivative impressionists lacked real feeling for form and rhythm. Thus, although the French technique was—often badly—imitated, little new was added to it by most of the German painters. Free inventiveness of the artist from his own emotional values was disdained by the new school, which emphasized only objectivity and realism. Even technique suffered badly, for color became increasingly gray and the original vitality a petrified formula: "Actually they vulgarized and coarsened their French models, whose subtle technical freedom was hardly understood by the decent and sober northerners . . ." But, this writer continues: "These correct art officials, attempting the joy of color out of a Prussian feeling for duty, could not suffice for too long a time." [10]

Fritz von Uhde (1848–1911), who at one time shared fame with Liebermann as Germany's outstanding impressionist, was actually one of the first *plein-air* painters in Germany. He quickly watered down the new style with sentimental social and religious overtones. In his ambition to bring the masses back to religion, he showed Christ in the house of the peasant or the factory worker's flat. Yet his religious paintings were neither conventional enough to gain the support of the churches nor of any consequence as artistic statements.

Leopold von Kalckreuth (1855–1928) exercised enormous influence in Weimar, Karlsruhe, Stuttgart, and Hamburg, and was elected head of the important *Deutsche Künstlerbund* at its inception in 1903. He, like Uhde, painted in a combination of sentimentalized romantic subject matter and impressionist technique.[11]

Other painters and teachers were Zügel in Munich, Trübner in Frankfurt, Bantzer in Cassel, Kühl in Dresden, and the much more original painter of Berlin street life, Lesser Ury. These men were the influential heads of the official schools of painting when the new generation, interested in very different problems, grew up. The impressionist group also directed the highly influential Berlin Secession.

THE BERLIN SECESSION

The Berlin Secession dates its history from the controversy that arose in 1892 when Munch was invited to exhibit as "guest of honor" at the *Verein Berliner Künstler*. Munch had discarded his experiments in pointillism and was painting highly evocative pictures of human suffering, love, and death —*The Sick Child, The Kiss,* and *The Death Chamber.* The immediate result of the exhibition was a wild protest from the academy under the leadership of its president, the painter Anton von Werner, and the chief conservative art critic Ludwig Pietsch. Impressionism was not yet accepted in Germany, and the new, provocative, and highly individualistic art of Munch was considered far beyond the bounds of propriety. The controversy grew to such an extent that the exhibition closed a week after it had opened, but the direct result was the temporary victory of impressionism —whose leaders had vigorously defended the Norwegian's right to exhibit —and a great deal of advantageous publicity for Munch. He was invited to exhibit his work in Dresden, Vienna, Cologne, and his art began to be diffused throughout Germany. In fact, except for brief visits to Norway and Paris, Munch stayed in Germany until 1908. He painted his most important works there—intended to be part of the great *Frieze of Life*—and he may certainly be considered the most important single influence on expressionist painting and print making.

The Dance of Life (1899–1900) (pl. 144), a part of the never completed frieze, shows clearly the extent to which Munch differed from the impressionists who had fought his battle. The objects of the world are not seen for the sake of their visual appearance, but have become emotional symbols. His intensity and provocativeness of mood had comparatively little to do with external representation. His highly personal style is much more closely related to symbolism and Jugendstil than to the realist-impressionist group that first sponsored his appearance in Germany.[12]

Many of the more advanced German painters supported Munch's right to exhibit, but only a few understood the meaning of his work. One of the few was his friend, the Polish writer Stanislaw Przybyszewski, who lived in Berlin.

The old kind of art and psychology was an art and a psychology of the conscious personality, whereas the new art is the art of the individual. Men dream and their dreams open up vistas of a new world to them, it is as though they perceived things with their mind's ears and eyes, without having heard or seen them physically. What the personality is unable to perceive is revealed to them by the individuality— something that lives a life of its own, apart from the life of which they are conscious.[13]

Such intelligent criticism remained isolated, and Munch's chief influence was not felt until the twentieth century. The censorship of his exhibition in Berlin had its more immediate effect. A group of painters, under Liebermann's leadership, left the *Verein* under protest. They first called themselves the "Eleven," and then adopted the name of their young colleagues in Munich: "Sezession."

The secessionists were by no means unknown painters, but had already gained wide reputation. Their exhibitions were meant to be rather small and highly selective. The Berlin Secession held its first exhibition in its own building in 1899. The show was an immediate success, and netted them the considerable sum of thirty-three thousand marks.[14] "The success of our first exhibition, which surpassed our boldest expectations, has proved that the foundation of the Berlin Secession did not derive from a temporary whim but conformed to a public need." [15] Under the capable direction of

Liebermann, Leistikow, and the art dealers Bruno and Paul Cassirer, the Secession exhibited the works of its members: well-established artists like Menzel, Leibl, and Böcklin, and also comparatively little-known painters like Corinth, Slevogt, Marées, and Hodler. Although the exhibitions of the Secession were limited to German art at the beginning, French painting also was soon shown, even including van Gogh, Cézanne, and Toulouse-Lautrec. "The Secession exercised in its exhibitions more and more the prerogatives of an exclusive artists' club, and this was for some time its very strength, because it counted among its members the most important creative artists." [16]

For some time the Secession, although strongly favoring impressionist trends, remained fairly liberal. After having moved into a new, large building on the Kurfürstendamm in 1905, it opened its doors to new men, including not only the rather conservative Max Beckmann, but also Nolde, Nauen, Kandinsky, and Jawlensky. Then in the winter of 1908, together with a retrospective show of graphic work by the nineteenth-century Berlin painter Franz Krüger, the Secession also had a small showing of graphic work by artists of the Dresden Brücke. Corinth exclaimed: "The Secession was ruined in 1908." [17] The leadership of this most powerful artists' group in Germany remained, however, in the hands of the impressionist group, which jealously guarded its prerogatives. When in the winter of 1909–1910 the Secession celebrated its tenth anniversary, it showed a few canvases by Cézanne and Hodler, but the featured artists were Liebermann, Corinth, Slevogt, Trübner, von Kalkreuth, and Anders Zorn. Liebermann, in the opening address, declared that impressionism was far from merely a direction; it was a *Weltanschauung* in which everyone could grow according to his ability. [18] When he said that "each art form which reached the helm, will and must be superseded by the succeeding form," [19] he referred to the triumph of impressionism. It is ironic that he undoubtedly did not realize that he was prophesying the end of the very style he had embraced with such conviction.

V

Regionalism, Worpswede, and Paula Modersohn-Becker

Near the end of the nineteenth century, painters from a number of German cities moved out into the countryside to live and paint, as the painters of Barbizon and Argenteuil had done before them. Mixed with this wish to be close to nature was frequently a nationalistic desire for a typically German art, which found its best expression in a fairly narrow regionalism. This move to set up rural communities continued into the period of expressionism, when the Brücke painters worked in the Moritzburg Lake region near Dresden and the Blaue Reiter moved to Sindelsdorf and Murnau in Upper Bavaria.

In the 'eighties and 'nineties many villages near large cities were settled, generally by rather insignificant painters. The most important of these settlements were Grötzingen near Karlsruhe, Cronberg near Frankfurt, Dittersbach near Dresden, Dachau near Munich, and Worpswede near Bremen.

DIE SCHOLLE AND NEU-DACHAU

Munich itself became the seat of one of the regionalist groups, which called itself *Die Scholle*.[1] The many painters of this group—Leo Putz, Fritz Erler, Erich Erler-Samaden, F. W. Voigt, Walter Georgi, Walter Püttner, Adolf Münzer, R. M. Eichler, Angelo Jank, G. Bechler, and Robert Wiese —were strongly indebted to Leibl and the Leibl school. They were, however, unsatisfied with the sincere modesty of Leibl's small paintings and with his objectivity of observation. Their ambition went beyond pictorial statements: "They wanted to sing a Hymn of Praise to Mother Earth, to their native soil, in their pictures. These are redolent of the pungent and healthy smell of earth. The striving after what is great is shared by the whole group alike, even down to size and technique in their paintings." [2]

Under the influence of impressionism and neoimpressionism, their palettes brightened considerably while their brush strokes broadened. By the time of their first joint exhibition in the Munich Glaspalast in 1899, the paintings of the Scholle had become stylized in shape, color, and line probably owing to the influence of the painters of Pont-Aven, quite well known in Munich by this time.

Fritz Erler, whose *Nordland* (1907) is somewhat reminiscent of Gauguin, was probably the most interesting member of the group. He combined the strong and bright color of impressionism with the linear-decorative tendencies of Art Nouveau, and built up his paintings from broad dabs of color into flowing, yet precisely defined contours to give them a posterlike appearance.

The painters of this group were eminently suited for poster design, book ornamentation, and magazine illustration. Most of them worked for the periodical *Jugend,* and must be counted among the important exponents of Jugendstil. As has happened frequently in the history of painting, many of these self-conscious painters of "messages" ended up as capable magazine illustrators working in a popular vein.

At approximately the same time three painters—Ludwig Dill, Arthur Langhammer, and Adolf Hoelzel—also under Leibl's spell in their early work, formed the Neu-Dachau group (1888). In contrast to the aims of naturalistic representation or of genre and narrative painting, the Neu-Dachau group, according to Hans Hildebrandt,[3] was concerned with the picture as a self-contained creation. The group affirmed that the total self of the artist, the entire visible environment, and the totality of the means of effective expression on the picture plane were at the painter's disposal.

Ludwig Dill, the oldest member of the group, had been a pupil of Piloty's in Munich. He had traveled widely in Holland, France, and Italy; he was one of the founders of the Munich Secession in 1892 and its president from 1894 to 1899. His work shows a growing awareness of the picture plane as a two-dimensional unity.

ADOLF HOELZEL

Adolf Hoelzel (1853–1934) became the theorist of the Dachau school and, going far beyond regionalism, one of the most significant teachers in twentieth-century German art. He was a pupil of Diez, and his early genre paintings are characterized by the meticulous execution and attention to minute detail of the Leibl school. On a trip to Paris he saw for the first time the work of Manet and Monet. As a result he decided to work out of doors and to loosen his technique. The Dachau moor landscape, with its hazy atmosphere, ancient trees, quiet waters, and high skies, became a perfect motif for Hoelzel and his friends, who wanted to paint in *plein-air* but who strove at the same time for harmoniously structured pictures. While Hoelzel was working in Dachau, his focus changed from the painted object to the means used. "The essence of art is the spirited use of the media." [4]

Hoelzel, emphasizing the importance of a constructive law, saw painting primarily in terms of rhythm, color, and formal relationships. As a teacher, first in Dachau and later in Stuttgart, he devoted a great deal of attention to a stylistic analysis of the masters of the past and present, especially Giotto, Van Eyck, Dürer, Rembrandt, Poussin, Puvis, Hodler, Marées, Cézanne, and Gauguin. He was one of the first German artists to realize the great importance of the postimpressionists.[5]

His paintings of the Dachau period are simplified and rather flat landscapes of the moors, in which a few trees are the sole motif. The void, empty spaces of light and air are stressed as much as the solid objects of tree trunks or foliage. These empty spaces form a clear, skeletal framework for the pattern of gray-silver tones: high in value for the areas of free space, and lower for the solid shapes surrounding them.

Hoelzel continued to experiment with the possibilities of form and the emancipation of pictorial elements from naturalistic representation. He was occupied with the problems of color and its distribution, harmony and balance, the interaction of colors in terms of quantity and quality to build up a pictorial structure. Without making it a principle of his creative endeavors —as Kandinsky was later to do—Hoelzel made experiments in nonobjective painting as early as 1910.[6]

Among the important painters of the next generation, Emil Nolde was the first to be drawn to Hoelzel. Nolde became Hoelzel's student in Dachau in 1899, and consequently changed his own style. Nolde was to bring Hoelzel's message to the Brücke painters when he later became affiliated with them.[7] Hoelzel himself later went to Stuttgart, where he taught at the Academy until 1919. His style there became one of abstract color patterns and line-plane relationships. His teaching of formal harmonies was of the greatest significance to twentieth-century German art. Among his pupils were painters as different as Otto Meyer-Amden, Josef Eberz, and Hans Brühlmann, as well as men like Johannes Itten, Oskar Schlemmer, and Willy Baumeister. Itten and Schlemmer at the Bauhaus and Baumeister, who became one of the leading German painters after the second World War, continued Hoelzel's experiment in "absolute art." The Hoelzel school was a highly important contemporary counterpart of expressionism in Germany until the two trends fused in the style of German painting after 1945.

From his early Dachau regionalism, Hoelzel developed toward a theory of universal art beyond the need for the object: "The object in the work of art does not form harmonies. The object is not necessary to the picture for the picture's musical meaning. This meaning results solely from the realization and completion of autonomous basic elements and possesses supreme value in its own right." [8] Even during the Dachau period, Hoelzel and his friends were interested in transforming the landscapes into structural statements, whereas their colleagues at Worpswede were primarily concerned with giving expression to the mood evoked by the north German moor and heath.

WORPSWEDE

Unlike the other artists' colonies, Worpswede became the permanent residence of a group of artists. These men carefully devoted themselves to painting the moors and peat bogs, black canals and streams, the old foot bridges, the windmills and the overcast skies, the meadows flowering with heather, the pine and birch forests, and the peasants who were themselves almost a part of the land—in short, the traditional subject matter of Dutch landscapists.

Fritz Mackensen, who had his early training at the Düsseldorf Academy, came upon the village of Worpswede almost by chance in 1884. He felt an immediate and strong attraction to it, but it was not until after his succeeding period of study in Munich that he decided to return to live in Worpswede. In Munich he studied under Kaulbach and Diez, but his own inclinations made him feel a stranger there. The painter Otto Modersohn, who had been Mackensen's friend from their student days in Düsseldorf, was similarly inclined. In 1889 the two men settled in Worpswede and, a year or two later, were joined by Hans am Ende, who had also been a Diez student in Munich.

Later other painters were attracted to the group, as was Rainer Maria Rilke, who in 1903 published a monograph on Worpswede: "A true poet's book, written in characteristic and beautiful prose, but actually rather a dreamy fantasy about the Worpswede landscape and the characters of the artists than an appreciation of their work." [9] Rilke's book does give an insight into the activities of the Worpswede painters; he himself was actually a member of the group during that period. He writes about their outdoor work as well as of their gatherings in the evening, when they spoke of

Böcklin, who had been able to see in nature its deepest and most significant traits, and who knew how to express it so beautifully. Memories of Rembrandt, his landscapes and etchings, arose and were connected with the thought of Böcklin. And when the painters were exhausted from discussion and no longer able to continue, they began to read. They read books from the North. Björnson, especially. . . .[10]

Otto Modersohn painted the moor landscape at dusk and during storms. His *Bad Weather* (pl. 9) is a highly romantic landscape, typical of Worpswede, in which a sweeping storm furrows the stream and makes the birch trees yield. The rather drab, gray-green color scheme adds to the general mood of melancholy evoked by this painting.

Fritz Mackensen was interested primarily in the peasants of Worpswede, whom he painted with a realism derived from Courbet but so sentimentalized as to lose much of its force. He spent three years on the large canvas, *Sermon in the Moors*, that was awarded the gold medal of the Munich Glaspalast exhibition of 1895. Suddenly the Worpswede painter, completely unknown heretofore, was in the public eye.[11]

Hans am Ende was perhaps most strongly influenced in his landscapes by Böcklin. His rarer portraits of the peasants and their children are done with a draftsmanlike precision that sets him apart from others of the group.

Several other painters joined the conclave at Worpswede. Fritz Overbeck came from Düsseldorf in 1891. His etchings and paintings are most closely related to Modersohn's; he avoided painting the human figure, and his work shows an interest even greater than Modersohn's in the untamed forces of nature.

Carl Vinnen, "the colorist among the Worpsweders," [12] was trained in the genre style of the Düsseldorf Academy. His claim to fame was his authorship of the *Protest deutscher Künstler* (1911), a chauvinist attack on the "international aspects of modern art whose baleful influence was to be seen in the corrupt painting of Expressionism." [13]

Heinrich Vogeler interpreted more lyrical moods. His paintings of springtime moors, peopled with fairy-tale figures, stem in mood as well as careful execution from the pre-Raphaelites. Vogeler, the most versatile of the Worpswede artists, was active not only as a painter and an etcher; he became one of the most popular book illustrators of his time, and was also responsible for Rilke's coming to Worpswede.[14] After 1900 he turned to designing book jackets, carpets, embroideries, furniture with peasant ornament, as well as silver and glass in the linear-floral manner of the international Jugendstil movement. Less provincial than his friends,[15] Vogeler was the chief link between the Worpswede group and the symbolist-Jugendstil style, which was also to affect—indirectly but strongly—the work of the most significant Worpswede artist: Paula Modersohn-Becker.

The great popularity that the regional Worpswede painters enjoyed in the late 'nineties could not last. None of them was of first rank. Further, they were ingrown and unaware of the latest discoveries of the French impressionists, as well as of Gauguin, van Gogh, and Cézanne. Their realism was sentimentalized in the popular manner of Bastien-Lepage; many of their paintings fail to register any individuality beyond that of examples of their style, the period, and the country. Exceptions were the two women in the group—the painter Paula Becker and the sculptress Clara Westhoff —both of whom struck out with far greater power and originality than their male associates.[16] Clara Westhoff, who did some sensitive sculpture in Worpswede and Paris, became Rilke's wife. Paula Becker, who married Otto Modersohn, became a significant painter.

PAULA MODERSOHN-BECKER

Paula Modersohn-Becker (1876–1907) first came to Worpswede in 1897 after taking drawing lessons in Bremen and London and serious academic training with various teachers in Berlin. She had studied portraiture, landscapes, nudes in water color, oil, pastel, and charcoal, in the prevalent academic manner. More important, perhaps, were her frequent visits to the museum of Berlin. Her letters told of her great admiration for Rembrandt's painting and Botticelli's drawing and the strong feeling she had for old German masters, such as Dürer, Cranach, and Holbein.

In 1897 she visited Worpswede and was immediately attracted to the land and its people. Her letters and diaries show her admiration for Worpswede's painters, especially Mackensen, Vogeler, and Modersohn.

She decided to study with Mackensen, who, unlike the others, had chosen the human figure as his chief motif. Although her diaries and letters spoke of her love for the breadth and stillness of the wide plains, the open spaces and great distances, the soft blue of the sky, the moor and the heath, she emphasized again and again that man was to be her principal motif. Her early paintings in Worpswede were very similar to Mackensen's work (for example, his *Infant*), but she soon gained a much more immediate understanding of the peasant than her teacher had. In her principal subject matter—mother and child—there was a minimum of portraiture. She saw first a simplicity and largeness of form and color in the motif of mother suckling child; the object became increasingly depersonalized in her work, so that it began to go beyond the representative toward the ideal or symbolic.

When Paula Modersohn-Becker held her first exhibit in Bremen in 1899, the public was very conscious of her difference from the other Worpswede artists, who had been accepted barely four years earlier. Her work was severely criticized. In all her painting there was a tendency toward simplification and basic forms, which was accomplished by increasing emphasis on line, removing her further and further from Worpswede tone painting. Recognizing the importance of the contour, she sought her own structural form and monumentality.

Finally, feeling that Worpswede could not offer enough stimulation, she went to Paris in 1900 for the first time. The entire city and its life excited her. This was especially true of the Louvre, where she made new discoveries to write about in every letter. There were other interests: Clara Westhoff, her friend and companion, studied with Rodin, whom Paula considered the greatest living artist.[17] In addition to the German "romantic classicists" Max Klinger and Arnold Böcklin, whom she greatly admired, she devoted much attention to Millet and, among the Breton symbolists, Charles Cottet and Lucien Simon. It is surprising that in all her Paris sojourns, she wrote about Cottet with more appreciation than for all other living painters; she may have found in his work the same intimacy and directness of expression for which she was striving.

The most important influences seem to have occurred without her conscious knowledge. She did not write about them, but worked them out visually. Cézanne was mentioned only much later (1907) in a letter to Clara Rilke, in which she recalled discovering Cézanne for herself at Vollard in 1900: "I think and thought . . . much about Cézanne, and how he was one of the three or four painters who has acted upon me like a thunderstorm and a great adventure. Do you remember in 1900 at Vollard?"[18] And in the last letter to her mother: "I wanted very much to go to Paris for a week. There are fifty-six Cézannes exhibited there."[19] In Cézanne she doubtless admired the tight structural composition and the penetration beyond surface appearance—both of which were part of her own aim.

When she returned to Worpswede and married Otto Modersohn in 1901, her style had changed. Much in the manner of Bonnard and Vuillard, she filled her canvas completely, leaving no part of the picture plane empty and giving everything an equal value. This highly decorative style changed again after her second trip to Paris in 1903. Perhaps it was van Gogh's influence, perhaps a development of her own style that bent toward a vibrating, curled and crimped line, especially obvious in the drawings of this period.

The drawing *Infant Nursing* (1904) (pl. 10) illustrates her preoccupation with the mother and child motif. Instead of the sentimental attitude with which Mackensen had treated the subject, Paula Modersohn-Becker's drawing indicates a clear and sober observation of nature. At the same time the line has become the immediate carrier of expression. With only a fragment of the mother's head, and with relatively few lines, she has, largely by implication, expressed her feeling of tenderness.

Her painting of the same period was not yet as advanced as her drawing. The *Old Peasant Woman* (pl. 11), also of 1904, was still painted in the dark potato color of the late nineteenth century. Yet she endowed the woman with great dignity by the simplicity and clarity of the painting: a clearly structured, flat pattern of light and dark areas. It is understandable why Cézanne acted upon her "like a thunderstorm and a great adventure," and it is also clear in which direction his influence had pointed.

In 1904 she painted her friend Rainer Maria Rilke (pl. 12), who always referred to her as the "blonde painter." For a long time she had felt that the imitation of nature was not the painter's task. As early as 1902 she wrote in her diary:

I believe one should not think about nature when painting, at least not during the conception of the picture. One should do one's color sketch exactly as one has perceived something in nature. But personal sensation is the main thing. When I have brought that into the picture, lucid in form and color, then I must bring enough of nature into it to make my picture look natural, so that the layman will only think that I had painted it from nature.[20]

The portrait of Rilke was actually one of the first paintings in which she simplified form severely. The use of light and dark, the large, black eyes, the simplified outline—all add to her incisive interpretation of the poet who later wrote about her: "She was the artist who exposed herself to the Paris of van Gogh, Gauguin, and Cézanne, to the presence of Maillol, and probably even Matisse and Henri Rousseau, and who at times went beyond the German successors of these artists."[21] Indeed, the Rilke portrait, in its intuitive interpretation, is remarkably similar to paintings that Nolde did about a decade later. When she met Nolde (whose name was still Hansen) in Paris in 1900, she noted in a letter to her family merely that he had done postcards of the Swiss mountains and was just turning with great earnestness to serious painting.[22]

Increasingly she felt the confinement of Worpswede, and twice more she returned to Paris, which she called the "world," in 1905 and in 1906–1907. Mackensen, whom she had admired so much before, now seemed petty, and his peasant paintings too much like genre pictures. She felt restricted even by the art of her husband, and knew that she must go her own way—so different from the Worpswede style.

The *Self-Portrait* of 1906 (pl. 145) has become highly symbolic. She painted herself, nude with a flower between her breasts, standing in front of a leafy screen budding with flowers. Depth is screened off, as in pre-Renaissance painting. Intense color has been applied in strong, planar brush strokes. Color, as well as line, forms the rather geometric shapes; this feeling for the structural is especially strong in the almost lapidary planes of the face.

Often, like Gauguin, Paula Modersohn-Becker has been called a primitive painter, but—also like Gauguin—she was not a true primitive. She adapted or developed a strong elementary quality, and deliberately worked toward simplification of form for the sake of more immediate expression.

Her final paintings, done during the last year of her life, were indeed under the influence of Gauguin, whose memorial exhibition she saw in Paris in 1906, yet at the same time show the most consistent development of her own style. Her symbolic tendencies were carried further in her *Self-Portrait* of 1907 (pl. 13). The flower has become a full-grown plant, perhaps because she was then approaching her long-desired motherhood. The background is no longer screened off—there is no more need for an excuse for two-dimensionality. She has emphasized her own figure by the long, narrow frame. The shape of the picture, the plant, the necklace—all lead the observer's eye to the point of focus of the picture: the large, wide-open eyes of the figure. Shadows are no longer used for realistic modeling but, like the whole treatment of light and dark elements and of color, are decorative elements in the static, frontal composition.

In these last paintings Paula Modersohn-Becker was considerably in advance, chronologically speaking, of the incipient expressionism in her native city of Dresden. She was unaware of developments there, and the Brücke painters knew nothing about her for a very long time. Her own development seems to have been in the direction of a highly personal symbolism. Her steady simplification of form and search for the essence of matter created a style close to that of expressionism. Often she is considered one of the significant precursors of the expressionist movement. The Brücke painters owe much of their form to van Gogh and Munch; Paula Modersohn-Becker, who began with preimpressionist Worpswede, was the first German painter to evolve a new, vital style under the inspiration of Cézanne and Gauguin.

She died late in the fall of 1907, three weeks after having given birth to a daughter. Her friend Rilke commemorated her in his poem *Requiem für eine Freundin*.

> For that you understood: the heavy fruit.
> You placed it there in front of you on platters
> And balanced then its heaviness with color.
> And much like fruit you also saw the woman,
> And you saw children thus: intrinsically—
> Driven into the forms of their existence.

VI

Jugendstil: A Major Source of Expressionist Painting

Jugendstil was one of the most direct sources of expressionism. Jugendstil —or Art Nouveau—was itself an integral part of a larger movement—symbolism—beginning in the late nineteenth century and having wide ramifications in both the plastic arts and literature. Symbolism in painting gained much of its impetus from the literary movement—it was even largely a literary kind of painting, at least in the work of men such as Puvis de Chavannes, Gustave Moreau, and Odilon Redon. The term itself—"symbolist"—was first used to denote those "decadent" (so they were called) literary gentlemen, like Stéphane Mallarmé and Paul Verlaine, who at their decadent literary soirées quietly discussed the nature of those concepts they considered relative to their esthetics: the Idea, the Soul, Beauty, Truth, Reality.[1]

THE SYMBOLIST MOVEMENT IN LITERATURE

Gérard de Norval and Charles Baudelaire were both writing verse replete with symbols of a special quality much earlier in the century—any word, for that matter, is a symbol. But the symbolist poets (Mallarmé, Verlaine, Arthur Rimbaud, Jules LaForgue) were the first group consciously to attempt to use symbolism as a poetical system, however loose.

The symbolists were preoccupied above all with the power of suggestion. To symbolize something is to evoke it, not to say what it is, not to narrate it, not to describe it.[2] *"To name* an object," says Mallarmé, "that is to suppress three-quarters of the enjoyment of the poem which comes from the delight of divining little by little; *to suggest* it, that's the dream." [3]

Opinions about *what* to suggest, however, were expressed quite differently. Mallarmé once said that the expression of beauty was the single aim of the poem. At another time he said that the poet, "inferring from SYMBOL

TO SYMBOL," seeks the reasons for nature and life.[4] Others agreed that only beauty was the object of the poem, or that poetry was "an explanation of a delicate and beautiful World," [5] or of a new world, a more "expressive landscape," whose construction was based on an exploration of real nature and the soul.[6] Still others felt that the purpose of the new poetry was "to suggest" everything about mankind, especially about the inner life that all men shared in common but that was different in each; or they maintained, as did Henri de Régnier, that the symbol was the expression of the idea, something grand and glorious and a little remote, at which men might aim.

Although the symbolist poets and estheticians capitalized their terms liberally, they seldom defined them, so that it is difficult to know exactly what Mallarmé meant by "Beauty," or Royère by the "Soul," or de Régnier by "Idea." Stuart Merrill describes Beauty as being an equivalent of Virtue and Truth, but the meaning of such abstract words for men like Merrill and, say, Arthur Rimbaud, might be as different as the two men themselves. The symbolists were chiefly concerned with suggesting the qualities of an enormous variety of intense emotions, of vague mystical feelings, of the whole inner life, whose power and significance were then beginning to be discovered. These poets were interested in giving expression to emotion, to feeling, and were extremely suspicious of reason. "Aux armes, citoyens!" cried Jules LaForgue, paraphrasing the *Marseillaise*. "Il n'y a plus de raison." [7]

To symbolize, then, was to suggest the beautiful, mysterious aspects of existence—the aspects that the poet considered to be at the same time the most valid and the most elusive. But how was the poet to suggest them? If by means of the symbol, what exactly was the symbol?

Most of the symbolists agreed on differentiating between the symbol and the allegory. The allegory was didactic: it sought to teach rather than to inspire; it addressed itself to the intellect rather than to the emotions; it was unspontaneous and therefore often inimical to art. The point of an allegory was something else, beyond itself; in a sense, like the metaphor, it described something rather than *was* the thing itself.

The symbol, on the other hand, seems to have been concurrently understood both as the key to the meaning and as the meaning itself. The symbol did not stand for something else; the symbol actually was what it stood for. It was close to the myth, and often identified with the myth—in opposition to the allegory—in that both symbol and myth were totally self-sufficient. They contained their meanings in themselves and did not refer the reader to something outside themselves, like the allegory.[8]

Actually the symbolists seemed to believe that the use of the symbol enabled the reader to reëxperience completely, and validly, the activity or thought or emotion about which they were writing. This was possible, they believed, because there were close "correspondences" or "affinities" between the sounds and rhythms of certain words and experience.[9] This is similar to the theories of the symbolist painters of the time, who "believed that for all emotion, all human thought there existed a plastic, decorative equivalent, a corresponding beauty." [10]

THE SYMBOLIST MOVEMENT IN PAINTING

Among the painters, Gauguin was concerned with finding such equivalents, colors that could be equated with emotions and that could reach to the center of thought. He found this "mysterious center of thought" lacking in impressionism; to him, as to the symbolist poets, the function of art was to reach that center. [11]

The meaning of symbolist painting is perhaps most concisely expressed by its leading theorist, Maurice Denis. Speaking of "true religious art," he stressed the value of symbolic form for its own sake, but he also saw it as a correspondence to truth itself:

. . . in place of evoking our old emotions before the subject represented, the work itself must move us. The perfection of the decoration corresponds to the invincible spiritual beauty; admirable configurations demonstrate the higher truth: proportions express concepts; there is an equivalence between the harmony of form and the logic of Dogma. [12]

It is without doubt in this sense that a painting like Gauguin's *Yellow Christ* (pl. 14) of 1889 is to be understood: the severe formal arrangement might here be taken as the equivalent of the structure of religious logic.

To the symbolist painters such as Gauguin, as well as to the poets, "Art is a universal language which expresses itself through symbols." [13] And "A symbol is necessarily a thing which represents another thing without explanation. It is the evocation of an idea without expressing it." [14]

Symbolist painting, like symbolist poetry, strives toward the condition of music in affecting the senses directly and without explanation. The theory that music is to be considered as the highest of the arts was postulated as early as 1818 by Schopenhauer, because music is "by no means like the other arts, the copy of the Ideas, but the copy of the will itself, whose objectivity the Ideas are." [15]

Schopenhauer's philosophy as well as Wagner's music were of considerable importance to the symbolist movement. It is not by accident that one of the mouthpieces of the movement was *La Revue wagnérienne.*

They venerate a renovation of verbal music, comparable to the renovation effected in instrumental music by Wagner, which does not at all abolish the airs, cadences, and repetitions, but gives them a particular sense and employs them only in order to produce certain very special emotions. [16]

Similarly, Gauguin's use of form, his flat surfaces of intense broad color areas, his precise dark outline, his simplified shape—all aim at a direct effect similar to that of music.

As early as 1882 the critic and novelist J. K. Huysmans [17] compared Redon's painting not only with the poetry of Baudelaire and Poe but also with music. [18] (The parallel of expressionists concerned with synesthesia, such as Kandinsky, comes immediately to mind.) Although Redon never joined the symbolist movement, the evocative quality of symbolist art is characteristic of his painting. Even his more literal drawings, such as *Face of a Man in the Sky* (pl. 15), have symbolist traits.

In the *Face of a Man in the Sky* a large head floats through the sky toward the sea, on which a tiny sailboat rides. The head is in heavy shadow except for a bright area around the large, heavy-lidded right eye, which gazes enigmatically down toward the sailboat. What does it mean? This cannot be answered without an explanation of Redon's own personal symbolism. The head comes out of space like a meteor; it has a little wing attached to it. Perhaps it is a self-portrait; at all events its meaning remains puzzling. The drawing is based on a series of contrasts. The round form of the head, emphasized by a faint ring traced around it, is in startling contrast to the completely straight line of the horizon and to the tiny, pointed sailboat. The plastically modeled head contrasts with the absolute flatness of the sky; the large dark areas contrast with the large light areas. But Redon also uses a repetition of form very effectively. This repetition is not dispersed over the entire drawing, but is concentrated heavily in one spot— around the head—to achieve an effect of turning through space. The round eyeball is set inside the round eye socket, inside the round area of cheekbone, inside the roundness of the head, inside the sort of Saturnian ring. This impression of spiral movement is not mitigated in force by its obviousness. Finally, the precision of the drawing is itself an amazing contrast to the ambiguity of meaning. It is as though the artist wished to state an enigma in terms of tangible forms but to leave any answer up to the spectator. In his autobiography, *A soi-même,* Redon said that the artist's purpose was "to use the logic of the visible world in the service of the invisible." [19] Years later Max Beckman expressed the same idea: "My aim is always to get hold of the magic of reality and to transfer this reality into painting—to make the invisible visible through reality." [20]

Parallels to this desire "to make the invisible visible" are apparent in most postimpressionist painting: in the swirling rhythms of van Gogh, in the measured cadences of Hodler's parallelism, in Munch's powerful expression of man's inner anxieties. Although these painters of the last decade of the nineteenth century had few stylistic characteristics in common, they all employed the suggestive use of form to evoke an emotional response. Redon himself spoke of "the effect of the abstract line acting directly on the spirit." [21] This concept was vastly different, not only from the sensitive descriptiveness of impressionism, but also from the rather banal, allegorical statements of the "neoromanticists"—men like Böcklin, Klinger, and Stuck, who were then enjoying the height of popularity in Germany. It is closely related, however, to the esthetic principles of Kandinsky and Klee.

Many of the painters who came to prominence in the 'nineties suggested the mystery of life by an ambiguous combination of elaborate literary metaphor and evocative form. The Dutch painter Jan Toorop (1858–1928), who had been under the influence of the pre-Raphaelites and was later a close friend of both Maeterlinck and Verhaeren, painted canvases like *The Young Generation* (1892) (pl. 17).[22]

The Young Generation is crowded with allegory and symbol. The young generation—the little child—sits in its brightly colored high chair in a lush garden and reaches out with its small arms toward the future. The child is in the center of light in the picture: youth is bright and hopeful. The older generation is already almost obliterated: the mother appears dimly in an exceedingly narrow doorway. There are hopeful promises: a bright bush glows at the brink of the water, two swans glide in the distance, and a Buddha is seated on the opposite bank of the pond. But evil threatens the child: a long snake, almost concealed among the vines, writhes down a tree. It seems to be lying in wait beside the railroad track that stretches along the lower margin of the picture and that is one of the most obvious symbols of passing time and the future. On the left is the straight vertical of a telephone pole whose insulators resemble buds. Symbols of an industrial age are placed in the same context with wild, organic forms—a fusion that is typical of much Art Nouveau work.

Less literary in its symbolism than *The Young Generation* is Thorn-Prikker's *The Bride* (pl. 18), which was painted in the same year (1892). *The Bride* relies on the suggestive use of form: clustered shapes in the background are not actually candles, but suggest them; there is no bridal wreath, but twining lines suggest it; the "bride" herself is implied by a long shape in a veillike garment patterned with decorative forms derived from flowers. A spiral line connects her on the one hand with the larger, harder-looking form of her "groom," and on the other with the flanking group of huge bud shapes. The picture is painted in subdued gray and greens; the eroticism is evoked entirely by means of suggestive line and shape.

Perhaps Edvard Munch came closest to a pictorial realization of the symbolist's endeavor to evoke an immediate response through the use of the plastic form itself without the intermediary factor of didactic allegory. His *The Cry* of 1893 (pl. 16) uses a minimum of descriptive or narrative elements. A writhing figure emerges from the picture plane, and its convoluted form is repeated throughout the landscape in the sinuous line of the shore and the equivalent rhythm of the clouds. This curved line is strongly emphasized by its contrast to the straight, rapid diagonal cutting through the imaginary space of the painting. The cry that the central figure seems to be uttering pervades the landscape like a stone creating centrifugal ripples in water. Munch has painted what might be called sound waves, and these lines make the human figure merge with the landscape to express a total anxiety that evokes an immediate response from the observer.

Gustav Schiefler, one of the first to recognize Munch and Emil Nolde and to prepare definitive catalogs of their prints, wrote:

Munch dared to paint incidents of the inner life: to formulate and make lucid concepts, emotions, experiences and memories in a manner that we knew from the psychoanalysis of modern literature and thought could be communicated by the word alone. Now we saw that brush and stroke were able to divulge even deeper things.[23]

Schiefler here realized the essential factor of the artistic purpose of symbolism as well as of the expressionism that followed it: the communication of emotion through the visual elements themselves.

JUGENDSTIL AND SYMBOLISM

Paintings like Toorop's *The Young Generation,* Thorn-Prikker's *The Bride,* and Munch's *The Cry* share not only a symbolist content and form but, more specifically, the sinuous line that is the most characteristic element of Jugendstil.

Jugendstil, a movement focused on the applied arts, opposed historical forms of ornament and substituted forms that were suggestive rather than definitive. Its emphasis was on the two-dimensional plane and, like symbolism, on the evocative possibilities of the visual elements themselves, especially line, plane, and shape. Because of similar creative impulses and a unity of *Zeitgeist,* much of this form is directly related to that developed by the symbolist painters. This intimate connection between Jugendstil (or Art Nouveau) and symbolism has been largely overlooked heretofore.[24]

Genuine artistic creations of Jugendstil are rare compared with the abundance of mediocre work. In an industrial age in which manufacturers were eager to use any kind of ornament—baroque, Byzantine, or bizarre—for quick and cheap imitation, the visual designs of men such as Emile Gallé, Otto Eckmann, August Endell, Henry van de Velde, or Joseph Maria Olbrich became quickly commercialized with much of the original excellence lost in vulgar imitation.

The symbolist ideas that pervaded both poetry and art inspired new forms, like the shapes of Gallé's vases. Perhaps the most creative exponent of Art Nouveau in France, Gallé made wavelike glassware covered with fantastic organic forms. He rejected traditional styles and created suggestive shapes that resemble those found in symbolist painting. Aphoristic phrases by Baudelaire or Maeterlink were sometimes burned into these vases, which —significantly—were called "études" (pl. 20a). Gallé, though he lived in Nancy and was evidently not in communication with other Art Nouveau artists and designers, arrived at similar forms because of similar conditions: familiarity with the thought of symbolism, a preoccupation with the free, organic growths in nature, an admiration for Japanese art, and a thorough understanding of material.

Although the symbolist movement in Germany produced no painter or sculptor of major significance in the 1890's, it was to a considerable extent responsible for the important revival of the decorative arts in Jugendstil. Symbolism was an all-inclusive movement in literature and the arts; Jugendstil was its subdivision dealing with the applied arts.[25]

The Jugendstil designers worked with a variety of personal formal means, foremost among which are the long, swinging curve, the broad color plane, the simplified shape, the interest in positive and negative space, the freedom in dealing with natural forms, and—perhaps most important—the two-dimensional, planar aspect of the picture. As early as 1903 [26] a distinction could be seen between a floral, naturalistic Jugendstil under the leadership of Otto Eckmann in Germany and a more abstract, linear, and constructive style as practiced by van de Velde. Eckmann, Riemerschmid, and to a large extent Obrist took their highly original deco-

Figure 1.   OTTO ECKMANN   Border design from "Pan"
1895–1896

ration from nature, much in the way that Toorop did. They stylized gracefully twining stalks, orchids, chrysanthemums, crocus, waves, swans' necks, women's hair, and floating clouds for their two-dimensional linear ornamentation (fig. 1).[27]

Van de Velde, Endell, and the Viennese group, on the other hand, worked with totally abstract forms almost from the beginning. Although van de Velde himself felt that the difference between his abstract style and the floral style was extremely important, this sharp distinction was hardly justified in the face of the great similarity of the two. Both varieties were manifestations of a desire to evolve a decoration that discarded the illusion of three-dimensional space and relied primarily on the emotional effect of the dynamic line.

As symbolist poetry based itself on the severely formal expression of the so-called undefinable and rejected description—indeed, even the naming of the object—so linear Jugendstil ornament, like symbolist painting, was an attempt to evoke an emotional or sensual awareness principally by means of the form itself. The art dealer Cornelius Gurlitt referred to Jugendstil as the "art of the symbolic line" as early as 1899, but it must be added that in Jugendstil the symbolism of the line frequently lies in its dynamism. It is not a line at rest; it suggests action.

Also in 1899 Henry van de Velde expressed a theory of the line as a force, which is thoroughly symbolist and goes even beyond Gauguin:

The line is a force which is active like all elemental forces; several lines brought in an opposing relation to one another have the same effect as several opposing elemental forces. This truth is decisive, it is the basis of the new ornament, but not its sole principle. Several times I have given expression to my hypothesis that complementary lines will soon be discovered.[28]

Exactly like colors, lines have their complementary values. A line demands a definite direction in another line, as purple demands orange and red calls for green.[29]

Van de Velde goes on to say that the line derives its force from its creator and communicates this energy to the spectator, who will be directed by it. This realization of the directive power of the line then leads van de Velde to his opposition to naturalistic form and his own theory of nonobjective ornament:

The difference between the new and the naturalistic ornament is just as great as that between the conscious and the unconscious, between right and wrong and between the healthy which gives life because it is the way it should be, and the other which is arbitrary, which takes its motifs at random from nature . . . which is disorderly and chaotic.[30]

As early as 1893 van de Velde made abstract woodcuts for the Flemish publication *Van Nu en Straks*.[31] These woodcuts are small black insets, characteristically Jugendstil in the use of the sinuous, active line and in the strong contrasts of black and white. A large, drooping, budlike form is clearly connected to forms in nature in the earlier vignette[32] (fig. 2) but the other no longer seems to represent any natural form or shape (fig. 3).[33]

Eighteen years later Kandinsky, presumably without knowledge of van de Velde's work, did designs for *Klänge* and for the cover of the first *Blaue Reiter* exhibition catalog. These designs are amazingly similar, except that in Kandinsky the line has been tautened, drawn into more angular curves or straight projections.

Similarly to van de Velde, August Endell, the architect of the Elvira Studio in Munich and German leader of the abstract Jugendstil, closely approached the theory of symbolist poetry as well as of abstract expressionist painting (for example, Kandinsky) when he wrote in 1898: "We stand at the threshold of an altogether new art, an art with forms which mean or represent nothing, recall nothing, yet which can stimulate our souls as deeply as only the tones of music have been able to do." [34]

The periodicals [35] that became the mouthpieces of Jugendstil are replete with literary as well as with pictorial allegory and symbol. A poem by Verlaine is likely to be found next to an abstract design by Endell, and the recurrent content seems to be an expression of the *fin de siècle* protest against the materialism and empiricism that had been rampant in all areas of life in the previous era. These magazines became almost the core of the

Figures 2 and 3.   HENRY VAN DE VELDE   Woodcuts from "Van Nu en Straks"   1893

movement. Jugendstil itself took its name from the Munich periodical *Jugend,* which in turn borrowed heavily from the English *Studio. Jugend* was an interesting mixture of a humorous popular tabloid and an art journal with cultural pretensions. The Berlin magazine *Pan,* published by Otto Julius Bierbaum and Julius Meier-Graefe, was much more erudite and therefore perhaps the least popular and short-lived of the Jugendstil publications. Its first issue offers interesting further evidence of the close relationship of the literary and artistic movements of the time.[36]

The third issue of *Pan,* also published in 1895, introduced Toulouse-Lautrec to the German audience with an article on the artist by the symbolist critic Arsène Alexandre and an original colored lithograph, *Mlle Marcele Lender au bust,* made by Lautrec for the magazine (pl. 19). Toulouse-Lautrec's decorative quality, his bold, twisting line, and his interest in flat pattern are typical of Art Nouveau; however, his intense involvement with his subject presents an interesting and important exception to the suggestive qualities of Jugendstil and symbolism. Like the expressionists of the following generation, he was intensely conscious of the place of man in society, although this consciousness took an altogether different form in his art from what came after it.

In its first year of publication (1895–1896), *Pan* became the principal rallying point of Jugendstil illustration and book decoration. It accepted work from Julius Diez, Otto Eckmann, Th. Th. Heine, Ludwig von Hofmann, Hermann Obrist, Walter Leistikow, and C. Strathmann. The Munich painters Fritz Erler and Pankok and the erstwhile sculptor August Endell were added to the second volume.

JUGENDSTIL: A MOVEMENT IN THE APPLIED ARTS

Unlike other manifestations of symbolism, Jugendstil was greatly concerned with the practical application of art. Later editions of *Pan,* as well as the other periodicals, became more specifically Jugendstil in their selection, and devoted increasing space to the applied and ornamental arts and less to painting and sculpture. Among the sources of Jugendstil were William Morris, the Arts and Crafts Movement with its emphasis on the honest use of materials, and Walter Crane's aim "to turn our artists into craftsmen and our craftsmen into artists." [37]

Many of the leading exponents of Jugendstil, as of the Arts and Crafts Society, began their careers as painters. Van de Velde painted impressionist and then neoimpressionist pictures and exhibited with *Les Vingt* [38] in Brussels before he turned from painting to architecture and all fields of applied design in the 'nineties. The Swiss sculptor Hermann Obrist turned to embroideries in 1894, and became the founder of the Vereinigten Werkstätten. 1894 was also the year of Otto Eckmann's last painting (*Lebensalter*). From then until his death in 1902 Eckmann was the most popular of the German Jugendstil designers in woodcut, book decoration, book jackets, stamps, typography, wallpaper, and carpets. Richard Riemerschmid abandoned painting for furniture design. Peter Behrens, who had begun his career as an impressionist, painted in a decorative, symbolist manner in the early 'nineties and then discarded painting entirely and became Germany's leading architect and an important typographer. Thorn-Prikker (1868–1932) went from Holland to Germany and turned from semiabstract symbolic paintings, such as *The Bride* of 1892, to stained-glass design in a similar vein and achieved considerable success in the revival of this medium. [39]

A few years after this widespread conversion of "fine" artists to the "applied" arts, there was a similar incipient movement in literature. Otto Julius Bierbaum concerned himself with what he called "applied lyricism." After his magazine *Pan* ended its brief career, he began in 1900 to publish anthologies of poetry designed for performance in vaudeville. He explained his purpose in one of the prefaces:

Art for the variety theater! But isn't that a shameful profanation? Are we not playing an unseemly joke on the muse of lyric poetry when we send her children out on the vaudeville stage? . . . We place our art in the service of vaudeville, for we have the notion that life in its entirety must be imbued with art. Today painters make chairs and are proud of the fact that these chairs are not mere museum pieces . . . so we too want to write poems which are not intended merely to be read in a quiet room, but which may be sung before a crowd anxious to be amused.[40]

The artist's desire to overcome his isolation from society was an important reason for this movement from the "fine" to the "applied" arts. In the two-dimensional visual arts the new esthetic that saw in the painting primarily a planar surface made this application to design possible.

THE AMBIGUITIES OF JUGENDSTIL

Another conditioning factor of Jugendstil, as of symbolism, was its conscious break with traditional means of expression. Jugendstil, especially, revolted against the series of revivals that characterized the nineteenth century, and postulated its intent to create a truly contemporary art. Joseph Maria Olbrich indeed inscribed this slogan in large letters on the Jugendstil building he designed and built for the Vienna Secession in 1898: *Der Zeit ihre Kunst.*[41]

This conviction was expressed by many of the artists and critics of the movement, perhaps most lucidly by S. Bing in an article—in which, incidentally, he described the derivation of the term "Art Nouveau" from the name of his own establishment at 22 rue de Provence in Paris:

Amidst this universal upheaval of scientific discoveries the decoration of the day continued to be copied from what was in vogue in previous centuries, when different habits and different masters were current. What an astonishing anachronism.[42]

Not only dealers, but also art historians and museum directors, were very active, helping to create this new style for a new time. In Germany and Austria men like Bode, Lichtwark, Brinckmann, von Seidlitz, and von Scala must be mentioned. Foremost among the critics was Meier-Graefe, whose influence on German taste was of greatest consequence.

During the last decade of the century, a feeling prevailed among the *avant-garde* that finally a new and contemporary style was being evolved, a style in which the flouting of convention—the attitude of "épater le bourgeois"—was thought to be "advanced," whether in the scathing social accusations of Ibsen's plays or in the apparent impudence of the unconventional Jugendstil whiplash ornament that appeared on the theater programs. To a very large extent, however, Jugendstil was merely an "anti" movement that often substituted a new kind of superficial ornament for traditional ornament.

Some Jugendstil ornamentation was indeed an original creative expression closely related to symbolism in its emotional content as well as in its suggestive form. Much of Jugendstil's production, on the other hand, was so repetitive as to become quickly frozen within a very brief time. This is one of the ambiguities characteristic of the style. Another is the fact that its avowed break with tradition was never complete. Many of its champions were so imbued with historicism that they mistook all manifestations of the style for truly original expressions. In many ways Jugendstil actually belonged to nineteenth-century historical styles. The century had run the gamut from the Egyptian revival of the first Empire to the baroque revival of the second. Now followed Art Nouveau, coming very close to being a rococo revival. As early as 1899 Karl Scheffler remarked on van de Velde's revival of the rococo tradition; this statement was quoted with pride a few years later by van de Velde himself.[43] It is important to realize, however, that the graceful and often playful line of the rococo has a very different effect from the elongated, dynamic, whiplash line of Art Nouveau.

Japanese art was another important historical influence on Art Nouveau. Two of the movement's innovators, S. Bing and A. L. Liberty, started as dealers in Oriental art; van de Velde freely admits his debt to the Japanese print.[44] This relationship is clearly pointed out in Clay Lancaster's article [45] and in an important earlier essay by Michalski.[46]

Most significant is the fact that the two-dimensional aspect of the Japanese color print—with its refutation of space illusion in favor of broad homogeneous planes, the evocative quality of the line, and the division of the picture space into large unified areas—was adapted by the Jugendstil artists. They, like the expressionists who followed them, generally did not work in the print media that are normally used for a three-dimensional illusion, such as engravings and etchings. Instead their interest was focused on the two-dimensional possibilities of the woodcut, where Jugendstil work leads most directly toward expressionism.[47]

Jugendstil designers also became interested in the flat batik technique that Toorop introduced from Indonesia to European crafts in The Hague.[48] This technique soon became widely used, recurring in the Dresden studio of the Brücke artists. One reason for the great interest of the Jugendstil artists in the Japanese print and in the batik was that the flat two-dimensional quality of these techniques made them eminently suitable for decorative purposes. These painters turned to all aspects of applied design in the hope of arriving at a union of the arts, an integration of design. Their great aspiration—certainly stemming from the same source as Wagner's—was the *Gesamtkunstwerk*. Some of them, like Endell, Eckmann, or Obrist, actually designed buildings and all the objects in them, including furniture, textiles, dishes, silverware, even the books on the bookshelves.

The first example of this integration of architecture and total interior design after William Morris' and Philip Webb's Red House at Bexeley Heath was Henry van de Velde's villa in Uccle, Belgium, which he built in 1894–1895. It is interesting to note that one of the reasons for this revolutionary design came close to the purpose of Morris: "I told myself—this was in 1892—that I would never allow my wife and family to find themselves in 'immoral' surroundings." [49]

Van de Velde, probably the most important representative of the whole Gesamtkunstwerk movement, was very conscious of its relationship to the British arts and crafts movement: "England's architecture, furniture, ornament had an effect on us as if a window had been opened, permitting a view on newly discovered landscapes. It was for us the discovery of a new land and a new light. Our reason was awakened to the logic of the appearance of objects." [50]

Morris and his circle felt that the immorality of design was largely caused by the machine, but van de Velde in the 1890's took an entirely different attitude toward mechanization. Engineering, in fact, was one of the major impulses of Art Nouveau.[51] In his lectures in the 'nineties van de Velde made these remarks:

The creators of the new architecture are the engineers.[52]

What we need is a logical structure of products, uncompromising logic in the use of materials, proud and frank exhibition of working processes.[53]

Why should artists who build palaces in stone rank higher than artists who build them in metal? [54]

August Endell made similar pronouncements, and stressed the importance of revealing structure in architecture: "Let the construction be seen; bring it to expression and all your misery will be over." [55] Yet Endell himself was responsible for the most fantastic and imaginative Jugendstil ornamentation.

The whole Jugendstil period was characterized by a series of ambiguities: a conscious attempt to break with tradition, but the inability to do so completely, as evidenced in the borrowing from the rococo and the Japanese print, as well as by an adherence to the William Morris tradition. There was, furthermore, the dichotomy between a desire for simple functional structure and evocative two-dimensional ornament. These unresolved ambivalences were largely responsible for the brief life span of the style after its initial success.

THE SUCCESS OF JUGENDSTIL

The year 1897 marked the high-water point, qualitatively, of Jugendstil in Germany. Early in that year the Seventh International Art Exhibition was held in the Munich Crystal Palace. "For the first time the arts and crafts were presented on an equal footing with the free arts after the model of the Paris Salons—symbol for a new equality of the applied arts." [56]

Soon after the Munich exhibition, a similar international "Raumkunstausstellung" opened in Dresden. Here van de Velde made his debut in Germany. The previous year the Belgian artist had been called to Paris at Meier-Graefe's suggestion to design the interior of Samuel Bing's large shop, called "Art Nouveau," the "meeting ground for all ardent young spirits anxious to manifest the modernness of their tendencies, and open also to all lovers of art who desired to see the working of the hitherto un-revealed forces of our day." [57]

In 1897 August Endell started the Elvira Studio (pl. 20b) [58] in Munich, certainly one of the most extreme Jugendstil creations and comparable to Gaudi's contemporary buildings in Barcelona. The year, moreover, marks the formation of the Vienna Secession and the advocacy of radically new principles of design by Adolf Loos in the new periodical *Ver Sacrum.*

The year 1897 was also the one in which Victor Horta built the Maison du Peuple in Brussels, the city that has often been considered the center of the style. This building of glass and iron is probably the most inventive structure of the entire decade. Across the Channel, Charles Rennie Mackintosh began building the Glasgow School of Art in that year. The new Glasgow style was introduced to England as well as to the Continent by Gleason White in the *Studio,* also in 1897. Britain never went to the excesses of an Endell or a Gaudi in its architecture of the 'nineties, but it must be remembered that, more than any other single country, she was responsible for the decorative style of Art Nouveau, which spread to the Continent in the famous English publications: the *Studio,* the *Dial,* the *Yellow Book,* and the *Savoy.*

This international style of the 'nineties went by different names in various countries. Somehow no one wanted to be responsible for it. The English frequently referred to it as "Art Nouveau," and the French as "Modern Style." In Germany it was variously called "Studio-Stil" after the English publication, or "Belgische" as well as "Veldesche" after van de Velde, until the term "Jugendstil"—after the Munich magazine—was generally adopted. The Austrians referred to it as the "Secessionstil." In France it went by a large number of names: in addition to "Modern Style," it was called "Style Nouveau," "Style de nouille," "Style de bouche de Métro," and "Décoration Style"; de Goncourt called it "Yachting Style." In Italy it went by the name of "Stile floreale" and "Stile Liberty" (after Liberty's Store in London and the printed textiles originating there). In Belgium it was called "La Libre Esthetique," the name of a leading group of artists in that country. [59]

The style also appeared in important contributions from America: the posters and book decoration by Will Bradley [60] and Louis C. Tiffany's Rockwood Pottery, which Bing brought from Cincinnati to Paris. Jugendstil elements were manifest in the Scandinavian countries, where these elements become fused with a revival of the direct, simple, and genuine quality of folk art and a relatively uninterrupted tradition in craftsmanship.

A revival of folk elements occurred also in Russia in the work of painters such as Vrubel, Bilibin, Roerich, Helen Polyenov, and Golovin. Much of their work, however, used folk-art motifs for an excessively refined and ornamental style, even in the fairy-tale illustrations of Bilibin and Polyenov, who shows her dependence on the Western Art Nouveau style. [61] Many of these artists, including Benois, Bakst, [62] Somoff, Sjeroff, and Diaghilev, who appeared first before the public in their publication *Mir Iskusstva,*[63] also became active in ballet design and stage *décor,* where they showed a most extraordinary feeling for decorative color and great ornamental resourcefulness: "For the time being . . . the vogue of the ballet obscured the more substantial and not less significant triumphs of the Russian brush and palette as seen in studio and exhibition wall. . . ." [64] A large exhibition of the Russian group was arranged by Diaghilev at the Paris Salon d'Automne of 1906. On its return to Russia the show stopped in Berlin, where Somioff's work seems to have left the greatest impression. Even before this exhibit was seen in the West, many of the same elements were to appear in the work of the Russian painters in Munich, including Kandinsky, Jawlensky, the Burliuks, Bechtejeff, and Werefkin.

Before the end of the century an attempt was made by Ernst Ludwig, Grand Duke of Hesse, to give greater stature to the international character of Jugendstil when he called seven of the leading personalities to Darmstadt in 1899. Hans Christiansen and Rudolf Bosselt came from Paris, Joseph Maria Olbrich from Vienna, Peter Behrens and several others from Munich. The following years the Darmstadt colony under Olbrich's leadership figured importantly in the Paris World's Fair. This exposition clearly showed the widespread character of the new style. Bing's "L'Art Nouveau" was in many respects the center of the exposition.

By the time of the World's Fair in Turin in 1902 Art Nouveau had achieved complete, though short-lived, popularity. The central pavilion of the Turin exhibition, extremely elaborate, combining Italian baroque with the new ornament, was designed by Italy's leading exponent of the "Liberty Style," Raimondo d'Avonco. The international popularity of Art Nouveau was assured: the very ornamental quality had an enormous public appeal—it always has.

THE END OF JUGENDSTIL

This international triumph was, however, also the end of the Jugendstil interlude. A general reaction set in. The concepts of van de Velde and even of Bing had become thoroughly distorted. Van de Velde exclaimed: "Away from the so-called Jugendstil, which has absolutely nothing in common with the spirit of the new direction." [65] Bing said: "Each article should be strictly adapted to its proper purpose." [66] Otto Wagner, once so closely allied to Vienna Secessionstil, rejected ornamentation in the Post Office Savings Bank in Vienna (1905) and preferred clearly to reveal construction. Adolf Loos, in many ways Wagner's follower, took strong issue with ornamentation in general and its application by Eckmann, Obrist, and even van de Velde.[67] He said: "The evolution of culture is equivalent with the elimination of ornament from objects of use," [68] in his very provocative essay significantly titled "Ornament and Crime." The term "Sachlichkeit" [69] was now heard throughout Germany for the first time, and a clear trend toward functionalism in architecture became apparent. The straight line, the right angle, and the simple plane took the place of curvilinear ornament; precision was the new byword in architecture.[70]

The brief experiment in the creation of a new unified style of all the visual arts—closely related to the movement in poetry—had come to an end. It was to be taken up again with very different results in Weimar in 1919, when Walter Gropius succeeded van de Velde as head of the School of Applied Arts and combined it with the art academy, which had been under the directorship of Mackensen, the Worpswede regionalist. Several of the painters whom Gropius invited to join the staff of this new undertaking had been closely connected with the expressionist movement in the intervening years and had started out under the dominant influence of Jugendstil.

JUGENDSTIL TO EXPRESSIONISM: THE WOODCUT

The connection of Jugendstil with expressionism is perhaps most apparent in the woodcut, which engrossed the artists of both movements. Although the expressionists preferred to maintain that their immediate inspiration for the direct woodcut technique came from the early German prints, it is clearly evident that their source is in the Jugendstil woodcut of the 'nineties.

The chronological precedence of the modern woodcut can be established as follows: Charles Rickets, Shannon, and Lucien Pissarro began in the late 'eighties by working directly on the block, to reverse the trend of having a woodcut merely reproduce a drawing. Their woodcuts, however, following the Morris tradition, were subordinate to the book of which they were a part, and aimed at harmony with the page.[71] Conscious of the work done in England, Felix Vallotton, however, was the first print maker whose concept of design was closely related to the direct cutting technique. Being very close to the symbolist movement, Vallotton was convinced that the shape itself must carry the communicative aspect of the work, and he began working in much larger and bolder contrasts of black and white. Vallotton's work was published in Germany as the first of Meier-Graefe's long series of monographs on artists. The critic pointed out as early as 1898 that Vallotton "can be considered the first artist who attempted the modern utilization of the wood." [72] Vallotton's first significant woodcut—interestingly enough, a portrait of the symbolist poet Verlaine—is dated 1891.

Vallotton's work was followed, in the history of the modern woodcut, by van de Velde's abstract woodcuts for *Van Nu en Straks* in 1893. Next came Gauguin's first woodcuts, done, not in Tahiti, but during his French sojourn in 1894.[73] Gauguin's woodcuts, unlike Vallotton's and van de Velde's, were published in small editions and remained relatively unknown for a considerable period. In 1894 also Otto Eckmann introduced the new manner of working in the woodcut in Germany; he was followed almost immediately by Behrens, Obrist, and Endell.

Munch's first woodcuts date from 1896. There is evidence that Munch was familiar with the work of Felix Vallotton,[74] and there is a correspondence between their work in the use of powerful, flat black areas and the often rigid, rough-hewn lines. Munch drew much from Gauguin [75] too: an interest in the texture of his wood block, the way of cutting the block, and the use of color. One of his finest woodcuts, *The Kiss* (1897–1902) (pl. 21), displays well what he learned from Vallotton and Gauguin. It also shows how differently he used these elements by his employment of the wood texture for its pattern effect. The striking off balance of the black mass of two clinging figures is pulled to a delicate equilibrium by the light, clustered areas of hands and face.

The woodcuts that appeared in the German Jugendstil periodicals, although never comparable in quality to Munch's, are most interesting for their interaction between mass and space, emphasized by an almost arbitrary pattern of light and dark, and for their active movement—dynamic lines crawling through space, and passive lines being bent by others—as well as for the design, which was directly related to the material and the tools.

The Jugendstil print makers were the pioneers of the graphic style of the expressionists, and it is frequently impossible to say where one movement stops and the other begins. Michel's article on the graphic arts, published in 1905 in Munich,[76] said that the woodcut must do justice to the material and express not truth to nature but to the artist's subjective emotion. Michel saw the model and inspiration for the new woodcut in the Japanese print and emphatically not in the "old German woodcut." He acknowledged the debt of the Munich print makers to Vallotton and Nicholson. The article was illustrated with work of Jugendstil graphics, including two early woodcuts by Kandinsky.

Ernst Barlach's early work belongs without question to Jugendstil. After his Russian trip in 1906 Barlach became the most significant exponent of expressionism in sculpture, but when he was a very young man he was a contributor to *Jugend* from 1897–1902. His cover for *Jugend* in 1899, for example, clearly shows the Jugendstil root of expressionism. Similarly, Feininger's somewhat later drawings for the *Chicago Tribune* are linear Jugendstil designs. The Brücke artists, as well as the Blaue Reiter, came from this Jugendstil background; the development of Viennese painting from Klimt to Schiele and Kokoschka is the development from Secessionstil to expressionism.

Symbolism, Jugendstil, and expressionism share above all their emphasis on form and its evocative potentialities, both in the expression of the artist and in the response of the spectator. Frequently, where symbolism merely suggests and understates, expressionism exaggerates and overstates.

PART THREE

Die Brücke

VII

The Formation of the Brücke

The formation of the Brücke in 1905 was one of the most revolutionary events in the history of modern painting. It must constantly be remembered that impressionism made its inroads into Germany a generation late, simultaneously with the postimpressionism of Cézanne, Seurat, and Gauguin. Jugendstil was just then achieving its highest stage of popularity. The young German painters were only slightly aware of the work of Munch and van Gogh. Fauvism had by no means traveled across the Rhine. Paula Modersohn-Becker, primitivist pioneer of expressionism in Germany, was not known beyond the limits of the artists' colony at Worpswede. Emil Nolde, who had been working his way toward a new pictorial expression for more than a decade, was not even a name, either to artists or to public.

Dresden, where the group began and passed through five significant years of development, was one of Germany's most beautiful cities. The capital of Saxony was relatively untouched by the Industrial Revolution, which had converted Leipzig, the other great city of Saxony, into a vortex of industry and commerce. Dresden, a jewel of early-eighteenth-century baroque architecture, had undergone relatively few changes after that time, and there were only a few modern buildings, though a number of them were important. One of these was Semper's *Hoftheater,* which, in spite of the architect's radical theories of functional design, was built to fit well into the total picture of the city. Dresden and its court remained a magnet for artists and intellectuals. Its opera, theater, and picture gallery were celebrated far beyond its own borders, as was the porcelain factory at nearby Meissen, where Japanese and Jugendstil forms were adapted to rococo tradition. Kirchner and Heckel spoke of the inspiration that the old culture of the city offered the young artists. Heckel, in a recent interview, mentioned his great love for the baroque city, with its sensuous, erotic charm and soft, river atmosphere. In this stable, mature, but rather saturated bourgeois setting, the Brücke had its inception.[1]

Dresden had also been the center of German poster design since the important poster exhibition in the Cabinet of Engravings in 1896. In the general trend toward the applied arts in Germany in the 'nineties, Dresden artists like Richard Müller,[2] Hans Unger, and Otto Fischer, all of whom were on the staff of *Pan,* turned to the design of posters. This concern with the applied arts was also allied to the entry of Jugendstil, in its international ramifications, into Dresden in the Art Exposition of 1897. Van de Velde, on Samuel Bing's invitation, made his all-important German debut here with an abundance of furnishings and complete room designs and installations. In 1899 the Dresdner Werkstätte für Kunsthandwerk was founded to execute designs, not only by Germany's leading Jugendstil artists, but also by van de Velde and Mackintosh. By 1906, the year of the Deutsche Kunstgewerbeausstellung, interior design objects had been stripped of much of their ornament, and the young painters who had rejected the elaboration of so-called Jugendstil decoration were beginning to admire the new, simplified designs by Riemerschmid and Behrens.[3]

Klinger was still the most celebrated and popular painter. The purchase of his *Pietà* in 1896 for the Gemäldegalerie was the most important event of that decade in the art life of the city.[4] His cerebral art, with its clear distinction between mythological content and eclectic but highly finished form, was to be seen in all the periodicals and exhibitions, and was highly praised in the press. At the same time, Klinger's pathos was greeted with lively derision by the young artists who were soon to unite their efforts in the Brücke.

KIRCHNER'S BEGINNING

Ernst Ludwig Kirchner (1880–1938) has come to be recognized, if not as the leader, as the initiator, of the Brücke. He was also its spokesman, either under his own name or as L. de Marsale, his *nom de critique.* Kirchner was born in 1880 in Aschaffenburg in Franconia; in 1889 his family moved to Chemnitz in Saxony, where his father taught at the Gewerbe-Akademie and where Kirchner became a student at the Chemnitz Realgymnasium.

He had already made up his mind that he wanted to be an artist. In his autobiographical notes, which he began at an early age, he said: "I have been drawing and painting since my third year—everything which was new and enigmatic to me—I drew for myself." [5] He followed his drawing classes in high school with great enthusiasm, praising his teacher and happily copying from plaster casts, Dürer, and nature. In 1898 he went to Nürnberg:

On my first study trip I came to the Dürer house in Nürnberg. I had known his work so well. It was quite confined there. Only the drawing of his mother hung above his work table. Quite self-conscious, I left again and visited the Germanic Museum and saw there for the first time the many very early woodcuts and incunabula with their blocks. This interested me very much and with new stimulation I went to my own wood blocks. This technique I had learned much earlier through my father.[6]

Kirchner's first known woodcuts date from 1900 or even earlier. It has long been taken for granted that they were done under the influence of Munch's woodcuts, a problem that will be discussed below. Although Kirchner emphasized his debt to the early German woodcut, he claimed that he himself found the technique of the direct woodcut, printed by the artist instead of an artisan. Under his *nom de critique,* he said:

While Kirchner was still in high school, his father once gave him several old wood blocks—they were trade-marks of old paper factories—so that he would make a few prints from them. Kirchner was greatly fascinated by the old blocks with their large-scale primitive drawings, and—inspired by them—he tried to cut drawings, etc., of his own into the wood of cigar boxes and tried to print them. In this way he learned the technique of the woodcut.[7]

Kirchner's earliest woodcuts, which he later refused to acknowledge, consist of flat color areas and cursive lines. They certainly belong to the general turn-of-the-century style of the new woodcut as seen in the work of Munch or Vallotton, with which he may or may not have been directly familiar at the time. His first paintings, however, were landscapes showing the influence of the provincial kind of impressionism then prevalent in many parts of Germany. It was to take considerable time for Kirchner's work to mature and for a certain unity of style to develop among his drawings, prints, and paintings.

In 1901 he began his architectural studies at the Technische Hochschule in Dresden. His father, who had once hoped to become a painter himself, was fully conscious of the struggles of an artist's life and, after considerable discouragement, insisted that Kirchner combine his studies in painting with architecture. Kirchner later wrote that he much preferred the more inclusive curriculum at the Technische Hochschule, which included solid geometry, higher mathematics, and architectural design in addition to the usual art academy program: freehand drawing, modeling, copying from plaster casts, life painting, and graphic reproduction.[8]

Kirchner's drawings of this period were energetic sketches in which he had begun to take down immediate visual impressions. He no longer made a distinction between actuality and fantasy; he treated imaginary scenes with much realism, and fused invention into drawings from nature. His thrusting line was still constrained, and at times awkward, often resulting in a chaotic network of pen strokes of varying thickness. These drawings, although lacking light and shade as well as any sense of atmosphere or structural form, manifested a quickness of observation and emotional energy.

In 1903–1904 Kirchner interrupted his architectural studies to study painting in Munich. These two semesters were of extreme importance in his own development and for his contribution to the Brücke. In Munich he worked for some time under W. Debschitz and Hermann Obrist, a leader of Jugendstil who had come to Munich from Switzerland. Obrist had turned from painting to embroidery in order to approach even closer to two-dimensional decoration without any space illusion.[9] These embroideries show a consistent development from naturalistic plant motifs to thoroughly imaginary ornament in which the original organic basis is hardly recognizable. Obrist's sculpture, like the *Model for a Monument* [10] of 1900, in its abstract but dynamic concept, points ahead to futurism and Boccioni in particular.[11] The deep concern with the problem of form shared by the most advanced artists in Munich must have made a deep impression on the young Kirchner.

The tardy impressionism of the Munich Secessionists, however, repelled Kirchner because of its shallowness.

Their pictures were dull both in design and execution, the subjects quite uninteresting, and it was quite obvious that the public was bored. Indoors hung the anaemic, bloodless, lifeless studio daubs and outside life, noisy and colorful, pulsated in the sun.[12]

The type of painting he saw there—it was then called modern—could never, Kirchner believed, be an expression of the time. It had no universal qualities because it by-passed the sources of life. The artists lacked imagination, and failed to perceive the real life of their time. Kirchner, as he wrote later, "had the audacious idea of renewing German Art."[13] He was encouraged in this endeavor by his early impression of Dürer and by the great experience of seeing Rembrandt's drawings in the Munich Cabinet of Engravings.

They taught me how to arrest a movement in a few bold lines. I practised this wherever I went. At home and elsewhere I made larger drawings from memory, catching the passing moment and finding new forms in the swift ecstasy of this work, which, without being true to nature, expressed everything I wanted to express in a bigger and clearer way.[14]

Kirchner was convinced that art must be an expression of life itself and not a background for living. His historical studies had made him aware that Greek vase painting, Roman murals, the art of the South Seas, and Byzantine and medieval art were formed by and expressed the essences of their respective lives and cultures. This, he felt, must be the aim of the new generation of painters.[15] He wanted his painting to be a vital image of the life of his time, the result of a creative imagination stimulated by the realities of its environment. He wanted to do paintings, he later wrote, similar in feeling to Walt Whitman's *Leaves of Grass,* "the book which became his best friend."[16]

Rembrandt had done much to influence Kirchner's line; a small exhibition of neoimpressionist painting similarly affected his color. He saw paintings by Seurat, Signac, and Luce, and became interested in theories of pure, spectrum colors. He began to study the color theories of Helmholtz, Rood, and Newton; he made experiments in pointillist painting, but soon arrived at an opposite conclusion from that of the pointillists. His pointillist paintings seemed gray and colorless to him. When he read Goethe's color theories in the *Farbenlehre,* he was particularly impressed by the observations on the afterimage; he began to feel that if the eye produced complementary colors, their use in painting was quite superfluous. However, only much later—in his Berlin period—did Kirchner abandon complementaries in favor of adjacent colors.

In 1904 an exhibit of neoimpressionist painting was organized in Munich by the artist group Phalanx, of which Kandinsky had been president since 1902. This show, the tenth Phalanx exhibition,[17] included a series of paintings by Signac and work by Flandrin, Guerin, Laprade, Toulouse-Lautrec, Theodor von Rysselberghe, and Felix Vallotton.[18] It may be assumed that Kirchner saw their exhibit.[19] This would mean that he became familiar with work by Vallotton and Toulouse-Lautrec in 1904. The question remains, however, whether he had seen their work earlier.

An extremely interesting woodcut by Kirchner, *Head of a Girl* (fig. 4), is dated 1898–1900 by Walter Kern.[20] It is certainly one of Kirchner's

Figure 4.   ERNST LUDWIG KIRCHNER   Head of a Girl
ca. 1898–1900   Woodcut

earliest works, since it does not yet have either the specific jagged or curvilinear forms, both of which occur in his later work. This woodcut is close to Vallotton, first of all in the striking pattern of black and white. The black serves negatively as the background and simultaneously as a positive part of the girl's costume, hair, and mouth without any line of demarcation among the functions. Beyond that, the manner in which the head is placed against the black background and within the plane recalls Felix Vallotton's woodcut portraits of the 1890's.

If the dating 1898–1900 is correct, Kirchner may either have become familiar with Vallotton's work at an earlier period or arrived quite independently at similar forms from the same general Jugendstil basis. The positive-negative interrelationship of black and white—the recognition of the void as a quantity in the picture—was generally used by Jugendstil artists. There

might be a third possibility: that the undated print is considerably later, and was done around 1904. This would bear out his own statement, which does not acknowledge any prints before 1900: "Around about 1900 the graphic work of Kirchner begins. He begins with the woodcut." [21]

Kirchner's own dating and documentation, however, are frequently unreliable. Often he predates his work; at other times he refuses to acknowledge it at all. Stylistic analysis must discount the late dating, when the print is compared with Kirchner's much bolder woodcuts of 1905 and 1906.

Although his woodcuts grow out of Jugendstil, Kirchner's early painting clearly shows impressionist and neoimpressionist influences. A *Self-Portrait* (pl. 22), done in 1904 at the end of Kirchner's neoimpressionist period, probably in Munich or right after his return to Dresden that year, still shows comparatively little independence. His painting at this time was quite unrelated to his graphic art; this *Self-Portrait* is built up in terms of light color, using a neoimpressionist palette. Instead of the dot or dab, however, Kirchner works with a larger, more vital brush stroke, which is loaded with energy and which is similar to the painting of the Fauves—especially Vlaminck—at the same period. There was, to be sure, a small Matisse exhibit at the Munich Artists' Association in 1904, but only drawings by Matisse were shown. It is necessary to find the root somewhere else, perhaps in sketches by neoimpressionist painters, which are less scientifically constructed than their finished paintings, as well as in the work of van Gogh. The Munich Artists' Association held an exhibition of Cézanne, van Gogh, and Gauguin in 1904, and these artists were also treated quite thoroughly in Meier-Graefe's *Entwicklungsgeschichte der modernen Kunst,* published in the same year. There is little doubt that the work of these painters began to be regarded attentively by the advanced painters in Germany from that time onward.

Kirchner continued to draw and make woodcuts extensively, and it was the highly disciplined craft of the woodcut that really simplified his style, as can be seen in the *Still Life* (pl. 23) [22] (1902—i.e., two years earlier than the *Self-Portrait*). This color woodcut, in yellow ocher, gray-green, and a pinkish red, consists of large and definite planes contoured by jagged lines. Particularly interesting are the undulating stripes of the jar and the relationship of transparent green and yellow planes of the glass.

The scratching, scraping, and cutting into the wood block, with the resulting contrast of large areas, brought Kirchner to a more largely conceived form. From the very beginning, Kirchner would transfer his drawings to the block with a few quick lines and then cut for long periods of time, so that the final outcome only vaguely approximated the original drawing.[23]

While still in Munich, Kirchner also made his first experiments in wood sculpture, extending, as he said, the woodcut into three dimensions in order to arrive at the more definite closed form of sculpture.[24]

In the spring of 1904 Kirchner returned to Dresden to resume his architectural studies. There he soon met the three other young architectural students who shared his aims and who were soon to form the first group of

German expressionist painters: Fritz Bleyl, Erich Heckel, and Karl Schmidt-Rottluff.

Kirchner began his *Chronik der Brücke:* "In the year 1902 the painters Bleyl and Kirchner met in Dresden. Heckel came to them through his brother, a friend of Kirchner. Heckel brought Schmidt-Rottluff along, whom he knew from Chemnitz. They came together in Kirchner's studio to work there." [25] This document, written in 1913, seems to be only partly correct. As mentioned above, Kirchner frequently predated his own work, and similar alterations of fact probably occurred in his written documentation. All available evidence shows the artists met in 1904, although Kirchner had known Bleyl from 1902.

FRITZ BLEYL

Fritz Bleyl was doing woodcuts at the time. These were in the rather popular turn-of-the-century manner of wood engravings, similar to earlier work in England, with considerable Jugendstil influences. A print, *Cityscape,* about 1903 (fig. 5), again recalls Vallotton in its variegated pattern of black and

Figure 5.   FRITZ BLEYL   Cityscape   ca. 1903   Woodcut

white. The blacks and whites are, however, considerably more interspersed than in Kirchner's woodcuts, and where Kirchner and Vallotton were primarily interested in the creation of a two-dimensional effect, Bleyl is much more concerned with the illusion of space. The black-and-white pattern is broken up to give the effect of light on the trees, the cobblestones, the shutters on the houses, and the roofs. This woodcut is actually closely related to impressionist prints.

Bleyl cannot rightly be considered an expressionist, and he remained aloof from the community spirit that soon prevailed among the other artists. Kirchner's close friendship with Bleyl gave impetus to his personal development, but his meeting with Heckel in 1904 was much more important for the gestation of the movement.

ERICH HECKEL

Gustav Schiefler described the young Heckel, a man of slight build and stooped posture who gave the impression of delicate health, as a well-educated individual of extreme sensitivity and great restraint.[26] Sensitiveness and restraint are descriptive of his work also. Theodor Däubler, one of the chief representatives of German expressionist prose, poetry, and criticism, frequently spoke of the asceticism of the Brücke—a description hardly applicable to the primitive force of a Nolde or a Schmidt-Rottluff or to the sensuous quality of Pechstein's work, but certainly characterizing some of Kirchner's early productions and a succinct expression of Heckel's style. In the period under consideration, Heckel developed a lyrical, refined form.

Erich Heckel was born in 1883 into a middle-class family in Döbeln, near Chemnitz. From 1897 to 1904 he attended the Realgymnasium in Chemnitz. He was a few classes below Kirchner, who was a classmate of his brother's and whom he knew slightly there. Erich Heckel met Schmidt-Rottluff, around 1903, and they became friends on the basis of their mutual preoccupation with painting and poetry.[27]

Unlike Kirchner, Heckel and Schmidt-Rottluff had no academic training. They were self-taught—a fact of which they were emphatically proud. Heckel's acquaintance with the works of the past came through his own observation. When he arrived in Dresden as an architectural student in 1904, he was as impressed by the painting he saw in the Gemäldegalerie as he was by the charm of the city itself. He spoke[28] of the powerful impact of Poussin's brilliant, fully saturated whites, blues, and reds. Even Rembrandt seemed pale in comparison, although Heckel loved his etchings as well as those of Seghers. He admired Holbein, Dürer, Cranach, Antonello da Messina, and Titian.

His greatest experiences were Vermeer's *Girl Reading at the Open Window* and *The Matchmaker*. In the latter he admired the broad treatment of color, the scarlet red of the man's coat adjacent to the lemon yellow of the girl's jacket—both applied in broad, daring masses. Heckel felt the "constructed art of the plane"[29] in Vermeer, and came to acknowledge a great debt to the master. The content of *The Matchmaker* was also highly significant for him: the prostitute seemed to him and his friends a most honorable individual because of her frank defiance of bourgeois society and her clear affirmation of sex as the driving force of life.

In addition to the paintings in the Gemäldegalerie, Heckel mentions his early appreciation of Egyptian wood sculpture and the "South Sea carvings in the ethnographic museum." [30]

Heckel, at that time extremely catholic in his taste, was scornful of most of the modern painting he saw. He found Corinth and Slevogt "superficial and disagreeable," and thoroughly rejected Klinger's false pathos. He even felt that paintings by Hodler, shown in an international exhibition,[31] were too literary and intellectual.[32]

With these artistic experiences behind him, Heckel began to do his first paintings, wood sculpture, and woodcuts in 1904.[33]

KARL SCHMIDT-ROTTLUFF

If Heckel was the lyricist of the group, Schmidt-Rottluff was its passionate eulogist. Schiefler said that when Schmidt-Rottluff came to see him in 1906, he was a strong young man with a rough-cut face, someone who had obviously undergone a difficult youth and was still suffering from its inner tensions.

Karl Schmidt was born in 1884 in Rottluff near Chemnitz, and soon adopted the name of his birthplace. From 1897 to 1905 he attended the gymnasium in Chemnitz, and, as mentioned above, became a friend of Heckel around 1903. The two men remained close friends throughout the years of the Brücke, the struggles in prewar Berlin, the first World War, the acknowledgment after the war, the suppression by the Nazis, and the final renewed recognition and appointment to academic positions after the second World War.

There was little art activity in Chemnitz around the turn of the century —no museum or art school, only the local Kunstverein, which opened its solid doors twice a week.[34] Here Schmidt-Rottluff began to paint his first oils while he was still going to the gymnasium. He does not evaluate these early attempts too highly: "I began painting in oil while still in high school, but pictures which I am able to consider as my own beginning, date only from 1905." [35] Heckel, however, considers his friend's earliest work of much greater importance: "It is difficult to determine what each of us brought to the others in stimulation, because it was reciprocal and often in common . . . but it is certain that Schmidt-Rottluff brought the glowing and pure color from Chemnitz." [36] Except for a few water colors in the collection of his brother, none of these early paintings are still in existence, and it is thus difficult to ascertain whether Schmidt-Rottluff underestimated his own attempts or whether Heckel exaggerates the first contributions of his friend.

Schmidt-Rottluff met Kirchner briefly in 1904, but did not arrive at the Technische Hochschule in Dresden until 1905. Evidently Kirchner, older than Heckel and Schmidt-Rottluff by three and four years, respectively, also matured artistically earlier than his associates. Schmidt-Rottluff points out that although he is self-taught in all techniques, Kirchner helped stimulate him to do his first woodcuts.[37]

Nothing could better illustrate the double origin of expressionism from impressionism and Jugendstil than two early woodcuts by Schmidt-Rottluff. The *Cityscape* (fig. 6) is clearly impressionist in its handling of light in the trees, roofs, and street, as well as in its unlimited extension into space. Yet about a year later and in the same medium, Schmidt-Rottluff did the remark-

Figure 6.   KARL SCHMIDT-ROTTLUFF
Cityscape   ca. 1904   Woodcut

able *Woman with Hat* (fig. 7) in rather abstract areas of black and white with a minimum amount of breakup in the pattern. The shape and line are quite independent of subject matter—for example, the strange, flamelike form of the forward-shooting hat. The space arrangement is far from being impressionist, as the figure is thrust toward the spectator by a solid white against the almost pure black in the background. This effect is enhanced by the slightly inclined white diagonal, suggesting a shoreline or road in the distance, which further pushes the figure out of the picture plane.

Although this print recalls both Munch and Toulouse-Lautrec, the prints, posters, and trade-marks published in journals such as *Die Kunst für Alle* and *Deutsche Kunst und Dekoration* indicate that the influence of these

Figure 7.
KARL SCHMIDT-ROTTLUFF
Woman with Hat 1905
Woodcut

artists had spread far enough by this time so that a familiarity with their actual works would not have been necessary.

FORMATION OF THE BRÜCKE

When the four architectural students turned from architecture to painting, they acted in exact contrast to the previous generation, in which the representatives of the Jugendstil—Henry van de Velde, Otto Eckmann, Peter Behrens, August Endell, and many others—relinquished painting for architecture and the applied arts. Both Jugendstil and expressionism were manifestations of youthful force and freshness, a liberation from historicism and the staleness of the academy—movements for the renovation of art. Both movements were thoroughly opposed to the *l'art pour l'art* point of view. Jugendstil turned to the arts of use, to architecture, to the crafts and industrial design of all varieties. This new group of young artists in Dresden believed in creative self-expression as the road to a basic rejuvenation of life in all its aspects.

These young artists not only wanted to live as complete lives as possible, but to penetrate in a new way directly to the essence of things. From the very beginning, expressionist prose, poetry, and criticism spoke of pure being, the "Urform," the revelation of the pulse beat of life, art as the expression of inner necessity.

These men came together, not on pragmatic issues, but out of a great optimism, a positive and intuitive attitude toward art and life in general. The young artists were repelled by the lack of passion and commitment in the art with which they were surrounded.

The Brücke rejected: the finished and correct formalism of the academies; the flat, linear, and abstract decoration of Jugendstil, which seemed like meaningless ornament to them; and the pleasing color sensations of impressionism. They looked at nature in an attempt to fix its most essential characteristics in terms of their own immediate reactions. They seemed to be searching for an intuitive expression, which they felt lay somewhere between imaginative and descriptive art. The result of this instinctive approach was an emphatic painting that, although often exaggeratedly emotional, resulted in some pictorial statements hardly equaled in the annals of modern art.

The artists had first gathered in Kirchner's furnished room, but soon Heckel was able to rent and rebuild an empty butcher shop on the Berlinerstrasse in Friedrichstadt, Dresden's workers' quarters. This workshop, according to Heckel,[38] had several advantages: it was cheap, it was on the ground floor, did not have "the indirect cold light of the northern exposure of most artists' studios," and was well suited to the cutting and carving of wood, which the artists began to practice at this time. Its location in the working district helped the group definitely to detach itself from its own bourgeois background, which its members so thoroughly rejected.[39]

Here they lived and worked together with exorbitant intensity, discussing their artistic problems, severely criticizing each other's work, being far more embroiled in the excitement of creation than concerned with the finished product. Schiefler, one of the first great patrons of the artists and the man who did the definitive print catalogs of Munch, Nolde, and Kirchner, described their Bohemian life,[40] the dark, "artistic" atmosphere where they slept during the day, worked at night, and lived on coffee, cake, and cigarettes.

The furniture of the place—benches, stools, and chests—was carved by the artists themselves, eliminating, in the Jugendstil tradition, the old distinction between fine and applied art. Their canvases, frequently painted on both sides, were hung on the walls (or piled on the floor) along with their murals and painted burlap and batiks. Their wood carvings stood in the corners.[41] A spirit of communal living and working prevailed: often signatures were omitted, and pictures painted by one artist were cut in wood by another.

During the first few years of mutual stimulation and affirmation, based on very similar concepts and aims, the work of the Brücke became increasingly similar, so that it is at times incredibly difficult to distinguish the work of one artist from that of another. In Dresden the anonymous guild workshop of the twentieth century, which van Gogh had wished to establish in his own time in Arles, was a reality for a few years. This is the reason why the more individualistic Emil Nolde withdrew from the group soon after having joined it. This mutual stimulation was also of greatest value to the evolution of their art, for it was in the years immediately after the inception of the Brücke that most of the painters did their really important work.

Only a few examples of this early work are now extant.[42] After both sides of the canvas were painted, the artist would often re-use the same surfaces. The cheapest paper or cloth was used for the prints, and there was little time to pull more than a handful of proofs from a single wood block. Seized with new inspirations, the artists felt they had to find formal expression immediately.

Their thoughts were entered in an unpublished manuscript, "Odi Profanum," which also contained drawings. The title, derived from Horace's *Odi profanum vulgus,* expresses their scorn "not for the common masses, not for the masses in the social sense, but for the bigoted and philistine bourgeoisie, solidified in its biased tradition." [43] Unfortunately, this important document has disappeared.

Typical of the feverish activity of the artists is this anecdote, told by Schiefler about Heckel:

As a possession he had secured for himself a stone and he told how, during the night, driven by the inspirations of his fantasy, he would jump from his bed in order to commit the visions of his inner eye to the stone, then etch it, make a few prints, and again grind it off the stone, so that it would be ready to receive new designs.[44]

EARLY INFLUENCES

The men worked in many media and materials: painting, drawing, etching, lithography, wood carving, and—perhaps most important—the woodcut. Inspirations and influences in this largely self-taught group were derived from many nonacademic sources and then shared by the whole group of artists. Kirchner, of course, had shown enthusiasm for early German art at the time of his Nürnberg trip in 1889. There he found paradigms for the direct woodcut, which he revived "under the inspiration of the old prints in Nürnberg." [45]

Heckel also had an early interest in the late medieval German woodcut. It is true that the technique of the expressionist woodcut is largely a reversion to that of the early German woodcutters, who designed and cut their blocks and then printed the edition by hand. Whereas the fifteenth-century German woodcut is primarily linear, the expressionist woodcut, also influenced by the work of the Japanese, attempted a more planar structure than

Figure 8. FELIX VALLOTTON Portrait of Schumann 1893 Woodcut

the earlier German work. It is worth noting in this connection that a Japanese woodcut appears on the wall of the Brücke studio in Dresden's Friedrichstadt in an early photograph of the room.[46]

More directly was the influence of Felix Vallotton's bold juxtaposition of large black-and-white surfaces. Vallotton's earliest woodcuts date from 1891 (*Portrait of Verlaine*). His woodcut portrait of Robert Schumann (1893) (fig. 8)—erroneously entitled *A. Schumann*—was published in the first volume of *Pan* in 1895. Three years later Meier-Graefe published Vallotton's woodcuts. Kirchner probably saw work by Vallotton in the Munich Phalanx exhibition of 1904.

Most important are Munch's explorations of the natural texture of the wood with his simple and rough cutting tools. According to Gustav Hartlaub: "It is the knife of Munch, which in contradiction to all classical idealism and Renaissance taste first spoke its own peculiar barbaric dialect in rough wood."[47]

It is most unlikely that anyone in Germany was familiar with Gauguin's very rare color woodcuts at this time.[48]

The efforts of the Brücke painters in the woodcut medium not only belonged to their most important accomplishments, but were also decisive in the development of their style in painting.

Although it would seem that Munch and van Gogh influenced the Brücke artists in their formative years, an early familiarity with the work of these two men has been specifically denied by some Brücke painters and their spokesmen.

Paul Ferdinand Schmidt, one of the most significant critics and patrons of the expressionist movement, maintained in an article on Heckel in 1920: "As things stood, he encountered Munch, Van Gogh, Matisse only much later when his own style had long been stabilized."[49] Similarly, Heckel dates his acquaintance with these painters rather late: "I encountered works by Munch presumably around 1908 or 1909; at about the same time paintings by Van Gogh."[50] Heckel further said that if they had known Munch's work, they would surely have invited him to participate in their early exhibition.[51] It is possible,[52] however, that such an invitation actually did take place and was rejected by Munch.

Schmidt-Rottluff dates his knowledge of van Gogh and Munch as about 1906, but—perhaps correctly—does not acknowledge an early debt to these masters. "Works by Van Gogh and Munch were probably to be seen in Dresden around 1906. I was not able to do much with them at that time."[53]

Writing about the early days of the Brücke, Pechstein commented to Georg Biermann in 1919: "We recognized our similar yearning, our similar enthusiasms for the Van Goghs and Munchs which we had seen. For the latter Kirchner was most ardent. . . ."[54] Kirchner, however, absolutely denied having seen any work by Munch in his early Dresden period, and it is even rumored that he indulged in spurts of anger when the Norwegian's name was mentioned.

In a recent letter Max Pechstein became quite specific about the date when he saw works by Munch and van Gogh. "Pictures by Munch and Van Gogh I saw . . . in 1906." [55] Emil Nolde has always admitted his knowledge of these painters. He mentioned them in his autobiographies: "I saw in Munich as early as 1898 his [van Gogh's] 'Self Portrait' with the cloth over the severed ear. Knowing nothing about him, I said innocently: 'A little crazy!' " [56] Although the statements by the artists themselves are conflicting, there is not only the strong internal evidence of their woodcuts and paintings to indicate the effect of Munch and van Gogh, but also the fact that work by the two masters was easily available to them. The Galerie Arnold in Dresden was certainly frequented by the Brücke painters. There they discovered Nolde and Amiet, whom they invited to membership. In 1905 the Galerie Arnold had an exhibition of van Gogh paintings. [57]

The violence of van Gogh's expression must have made an enormous impression on the young Dresden painters. They saw in van Gogh's work a breakup of the old, established forms in a vehement brush stroke, agitated line, symbolic color. They became aware of his empathy with, and animation of, subject matter, which was to find further development in their own identifications. The ecstatic expression of a personal symbolism, leading to a subjective unity of form and content, made van Gogh of the greatest importance to the expressionists. Soon German writers on expressionism were to make constant references to van Gogh as one of the principal sources of the movement:

Inspired by a strong internal force, he did not paint nature but himself within nature, which can only be understood as a reflection of his psyche. With the fire of his own convulsive invention he shaped his world, which, bare of all material elements, must be seen as a part of his tempestuously pulsating blood. His stylistic means consist of a strong line and enhanced color, by which he proves himself also stylistically the immediate predecessor of the modern art of expression. [58]

Worringer, whose theories on art were basic to expressionist esthetics, saw in expressionism a new independence from mere sense perception and a breakthrough to God. He considered it parallel to the spiritual art of the Gothic, and said about modern expressionism: "A great new direction deriving from van Gogh, an artistic manifestation, potent in mystic expression" (pl. 24). [59]

The problem of Munch, the other principal precursor of expressionist painting, is similar to that of van Gogh. It is true that his great initial impact on Germany occurred much earlier—in 1892 at the Berlin Artists' Association—and it resulted in the foundation of the Berlin Secession, [60] so very different in aim and make-up from the group of Dresden artists. But Munch continued to exhibit regularly with the Berlin Secession as well as at Cassirer's, and by 1905–1906 prints by Munch were probably in many collections in Germany. The Norwegian painter actually spent a good deal of time in Saxony and Thuringia at this very time. In 1903 he was in Leipzig, in 1904 in Weimar, and in 1905 he came to Chemnitz to paint portraits of Dr. Esche and his family. [61] Further, the second volume of the widely circulated *Kunst und Künstler* (1904) had an article on the paintings Munch had just done for his first major patron, Dr. Max Linde, as well as on the paintings and prints by Munch in Dr. Linde's collection.[62] Altogether, thirteen reproductions of works by Munch appeared in the same volume of *Kunst und Künstler*.[63]

After the first World War this connection, especially between Munch and the Brücke, became increasingly recognized. In 1920 J. B. Neumann, leading art dealer of the group almost from its inception, arranged an exhibition of graphic works at the Kunsthalle in Bremen: "Munch und die Künstler der Brücke." Emil Waldmann points out in the introduction to the catalog that the young group saw in Munch its ancestor and was exceedingly close to him in its beginning years.

In recent years the acquaintance with, if not the influence of, Munch and van Gogh on the first work of the Brücke has become widely accepted.[64] Erwin Petermann has recently summed up the evidence:

The first works [Kirchner's], especially the large pastels and drawings, but also the early woodcuts, denied by himself, show the derivation from Jugendstil and the dependence on the commanding figure of Edvard Munch. The woodcut style comes from Vallotton. The parallel to the early Kandinsky is clear.[65]

Perhaps as important as the contemporary work of van Gogh or Munch was the discovery of tribal art. In the Ethnological Collection in the Zwinger in Dresden, Kirchner became aware of the esthetic value of African and South Sea sculpture and thought he found in it a parallel to his own creation. This probably occurred before Vlaminck's independent findings in Paris.[66] Heckel was especially impressed by South Sea sculpture; Schmidt-Rottluff became interested in tribal, especially African, sculpture only much later:

African sculpture was to be seen in the ethnographic department of the Zwinger. I must unfortunately admit that at that time I did not have very much understanding for it. As a painter I had at that time just recognized that nature knows no contour, no plastic form—only color. This changed later on.[67]

Pechstein confirmed that Schmidt-Rottluff did not share their predilection for the exotic in the beginning.[68] Pechstein, however, was greatly impressed by primitive work—a fascination that ultimately led him to travel to the South Sea islands: "I visited the Ethnographic Museum in Dresden and was spellbound by the South Sea carvings and African sculpture."[69] Under these various inspirations and in mutual stimulation, the four artists formally banded together in 1905,[70] and accepted Schmidt-Rottluff's suggestion for a name—"Brücke": "the bridge, which would attract all the revolutionary and surging elements."[71]

VIII

The Expansion of the Brücke

The year 1906 was a year of expansion and promulgation. Enough of a foundation had been laid that the Brücke felt competent to admit more members without losing its identity, and four new painters were added to the original four. This was also the year of the first public exhibition and the publishing of the manifesto of the Brücke as well as of the first of the series of annual print portfolios distributed to the new lay membership.

In January, Emil Nolde held an exhibition of his most recent work at the Galerie Arnold in Dresden, which fascinated the members of the Brücke. Here, they felt, was a man who, independent of them, struggled with similar problems toward similar expression. They asked him to join:

Dresden, 4. Feb. 06

Permit me to speak right out: The artists' group "Brücke" of Dresden would consider it a great honor to greet you as a member. To be sure—you will know as little of the Brücke as we knew of you before your exhibition at Arnold. Now, one of the aims of the Brücke is to attract all the revolutionary and surging elements— that is what the name, Brücke, signifies. The group in addition annually arranges several exhibitions, which travel through Germany, so that the individual artist is relieved from business activity. A further goal is the creation of our own exhibition space—for the time being, only wishful thinking because the funds are still lacking. Now, dear Mr. Nolde, think what you will, we want herewith to pay our tribute to your tempests of color.

With sincerity and homage,

The painters' group, Brücke
per Karl Schmidt [1]

Nolde gladly abandoned his self-imposed isolation on the island of Alsen; after Schmidt-Rottluff visited him there in the summer, he came to live in Dresden intermittently for almost two years and became an active member of the group.

EMIL NOLDE

Emil Nolde (1867–1956) was considerably older than the original Brücke painters, and was also much further advanced in his work by 1906 than they were. Nolde not only exerted an important influence on the Brücke, but was also one of the most significant representatives of the whole expressionist movement.

He came from the north German plains on the edge of the sea; the part of Germany that, although it had produced writers like Friedrich Hebbel and Theodor Storm and painters like Asmus Jacob Carstens—the late descendant of Michelangelo and forerunner of neoclassic artists—had heretofore lain apart from the mainstream of cultural development. Three important twentieth-century artists came from this northern sea country: Christian Rohlfs, Ernst Barlach, and Emil Nolde.

Emil Hansen was born in Nolde on the German-Danish border in 1867 (he began to sign his paintings "Nolde" about 1904). He was three years younger than Munch and, like the Norwegian, he painted impressionist pictures before he found his own style. Yet Nolde did not begin as an impressionist. Like medieval or Renaissance artists, he began his career learning a craft: from 1884 to 1888 he was apprenticed in Sauermann's furniture factory in Flensburg. There he gained important knowledge and a feeling for material that prepared him for a direct, craftsmanlike approach to his graphic work and were also partly responsible for the expert quality of his oil painting. After a brief period as a commercial draftsman in Karlsruhe and Berlin, he was appointed to a minor teaching position in St. Gallen, where he remained from 1892 to 1898. Coming from the northern plains, he was overwhelmed by the power of the Alps; in an early painting, *Mountain Giants* (1896–1897), he personified the Alps as ribald old men, similar to the trolls that encrust the ceramic steins of Bavaria.

To support himself he published pictures of the mountains as enormous, grotesque heads on postcards, and also had these reproduced in the periodical *Jugend*. For a time he earned an excellent income from this venture. In these weird caricatures are a lively observation and an unusual aptitude for exaggeration. Their humor is raw and violent; the humor disappeared from his later work, but the violence remained. In Switzerland—and not unconnected with his expression on the picture postcards—Nolde discovered for himself the significance of Hodler. He began to understand that Hodler's symbolism, through which the older painter gave form to the underlying fundamental values of human experience, was in essence distortion for the sake of expression:

The picture [*Mountain Giants*] went to the annual exhibition in Munich in 1896. Hodler's picture "Night," which established his fame, was also there. But my "Mountain Giants" was soon returned, rejected. . . . In those days there was a general and stormy derision and ridicule about each of Hodler's pictures. "And his colors are as ugly as can be possible!" What help was my contradiction and my firm conviction that his sinuous, pushing, wry bodies are part of the character of the mountain folk, just as the firs on the mountain slopes are gnarled and grown oddly.[2]

Nolde soon realized, however, that he needed more formal training as a painter. He left St. Gallen for Munich in 1898 to enter the Munich Academy, but was refused admission by Franz von Stuck. Perhaps Stuck, who in his teaching emphasized drawing almost to the complete exclusion of color, felt that Nolde's seemingly instinctive drive toward color expression did not fit him for the Munich Academy. In Munich he spent much time looking at the masters in the Alte Pinakothek and saw the large Marées paintings in Schleissheim Castle. He was soon attracted to the work of Adolf Hoelzel, who approached art primarily as a problem of form and color, and who was not, like Stuck, preoccupied with the literary, story-telling element.

Thus Nolde, in 1899, became the first of the significant series of German painters to come under Hoelzel's influence. Under the master's guidance Nolde made the most interesting formal analyses of paintings by Goya, Constable, Watts, Whistler, Millet, Menzel, Böcklin, and Zorn,[3] in which he successfully attempted to penetrate to the basic laws of pictorial composition.

Hoelzel's scientific approach, however, did not suit Nolde, who was basically a mystic. Although Nolde was willing to acknowledge his debt to Hoelzel, he could not remain with him. Following are typical verbal expressions of the two painters: "Those who have the greatest ability and sensitivity say: art is science, such as Leonardo, Dürer, Delacroix, etc." [4] "He [the artist] does not believe in science, it is only half the story. . . ." [5]

Hoelzel had proclaimed very early that the solution of formal problems, rather than the observation of nature, leads to the work of art. Nolde, in his own way, also rejected the careful copying of nature. While studying under Hoelzel in Dachau, he formulated his principle of distance: "The further one removes oneself from nature and still remains natural, the greater the art." [6]

In 1899 Nolde continued on to Paris to the Académie Julian where he worked under Toni Robert-Fleuri and Lefevre. He was much impressed by Delacroix, Millet, Rodin, Degas, and especially by Manet's "bright beauty" and Daumier's "dramatic grandeur." Perhaps most important in view of his *Last Supper* (1909) is his remark about his love for "Rembrandt's small and wondrous Emmaus picture" in the Louvre.[7] At the same time he fully eschewed what seemed to him the superficiality of the impressionists: "The sweetness, often sugariness in the paintings by Renoir, Monet and Pissarro did not meet with my harsher taste, but their art, because it meets popular taste, is the elected darling of the world." [8]

The following year he had a brief meeting with Clara Westhof and Paula Modersohn-Becker in Paris.[9] Soon afterward, yearning for his own northern country, he left for Germany.

Nolde returned to his own country in 1900 and, after brief visits to Berlin, Copenhagen, and Flensburg, settled on the island of Alsen in the North Sea. The still lifes, garden pictures, landscapes, and seascapes he painted during these formative years appear at first glance to be closely related to the impressionist style of the time. His palette, very dark originally, had brightened, and light and air entered his pictures. Yet these paintings have little of the pleasant and charming appeal of the impressionists. The expressive language of color fascinated Nolde, and he seemed almost as obsessed with a longing for light and sunshine as van Gogh. "I was interested from the very beginning in the characteristics of color, from its tenderness to its strength—especially in cold and warm colors. I love their purity, and shunned all mixture of cold and warm colors, which mixture always becomes muddy and kills the light." [10] Nolde's benefactor and biographer Max Sauerlandt spoke of the painter's preference for "hot" colors, how the glow of the bright colors of his garden and flower pieces makes them burn, and how even the brightest impressionist paintings seem pale and faded when put next to one of Nolde's. [11]

Nolde subordinated all other pictorial elements to color. What Munch had accomplished with line, Nolde did with color. It was no longer employed primarily for its representational value or for its decorative quality, but was more symbolic and expressive. Nolde always retained contact with nature, but he seemed to anticipate Kandinsky's later concepts of the spiritual value of pure color as an expression of human emotion. Nolde said that he often considered himself only a medium through which color could exercise its powerful effect on canvas. Like Kandinsky, he wrote emotionally of color:

Colors, the materials of the painter: colors in their own lives, weeping and laughing, dream and bliss, hot and sacred, like love songs and the erotic, like songs and glorious chorals! Colors in vibration, pealing like silver bells and clanging like bronze bells, proclaiming happiness, passion and love, soul, blood and death. [12]

In 1904–1905 Nolde took a trip to Italy. Feeling stifled by the weight of the past and the pressure of tradition, [13] he went to the extreme south and spent most of his time in Taormina. Later he was to sympathize with the futurists, who fought against the suffocating domination of the centuries. [14] Italy also failed to cure his ill wife Ada. He brought her back to the lonely island of Alsen.

He spoke of his great admiration and love for the works of van Gogh, Gauguin, and Munch at this time. These were the men, he felt, who must be understood and who—unlike the impressionists in Berlin—pointed down the right road. [15] Inspired, rather than influenced, by them, Nolde felt even greater urgency to continue as individualistic a development as possible. In Alsen he began to shut himself off from the world—an isolation that was to break only at certain intervals when he would try desperately to find the support and comradeship of other young painters.

Nolde had only two friends and patrons in those early days: Karl Osthaus, of the Folkwang Museum; and Gustav Schiefler, who had early recognized the importance of Nolde's graphic effort. Nolde speaks with rare admiration of Osthaus the collector, whom he went to see in Hagen. The two men, sharing from the first a common admiration for van Gogh, also entered into an extremely fruitful relationship of artist and patron.

The Folkwang Museum in Hagen was like a sign in the sky for the young artists and art scholars in western Germany. There they saw an ideal, which appeared to them like a guiding example. Karl Ernst Osthaus stood—with rare energy and strong, combative drive—as the champion of modern concepts in architecture and art, and he manifested it with enthusiasm in his newly-founded museum.[16]

In the winter of 1905–1906 Nolde and his wife settled in the nearby medieval city of Soest, where Christian Rohlfs came to see them:

We sat together at dinner and spoke about various things, but neither talked much. Never perhaps has so little been said about problems of art between two painters. But we looked at each other—I at that dear human being, he at me—and we understood each other without many words, and so it has remained for life.[17]

In 1906 he left Hagen to go to Berlin, where his *Harvest* had been accepted by the Berlin Secession. The jury of the Secession that year showed a great interest in the young generation. Beckmann, Nauen, Purrmann, Jawlensky, and Kandinsky were also among the admitted painters. But Nolde had never heard of these other young painters, unknown like himself, and did not meet them. He was thoroughly disgusted, however, by the pretense and ostentation of the opening and the boisterous behavior of the Secession leaders: Liebermann, Slevogt, Corinth, Leistikow, their dealers Bruno and Paul Cassirer, and the patrons and bankers who also put in an appearance.

During the summer of 1906 Nolde had his first one-man show at Fritz Gurlitt in Berlin. His canvases at the time were mostly sunny landscapes, bright in color and with a thick, impasto application of paint. They recall the painting of the neoimpressionists but the dot is much larger, is applied with greater vigor and gusto, and the whole form is much less controlled. One of the earliest comments on Nolde appeared in *Die Kunst für Alle*: "From Monet and Van Gogh a Schleswig painter has developed a style of painting for himself in which a strong color effect and brilliance cannot be denied. The results, however, are only conditionally satisfying. His desire is much greater than his accomplishment." [18]

Nolde then continued on to Hamburg and to his meeting with Gustav Schiefler, of whom he was first to hear simply as "a gentleman in Hamburg" but who was to be significant for his future.

Both Nolde and Schiefler refer to this first encounter in their autobiographies. Nolde wrote:

. . . there would be a gentleman in Hamburg who would be interested in "such things" [Nolde's quotation marks]. I should go to him.

We stood there: the door was opened. "Please sit down!"—we confronted Gustav Schiefler. . . . He took hold of the prints, sensitively as has to be, one after another, all of them, and he looked at them again with interest and with love, in a way we had not seen before.[19]

And Schiefler: "In the summer of 1906 Emil Nolde was announced to me through the *Commertsche Kunstsammlung:* 'he would paint similarly to Munch.' I replied that I did not care for such people." [20] But Schiefler bought some of Nolde's highly imaginative etchings, and a long friendship followed, which led to Schiefler's great patronage of Nolde, his definitive catalog, Nolde's meeting with Munch ("Our meeting was not an especially happy one, or even very interesting. It has remained a single encounter." [21]), and Schiefler's continued stimulation of Nolde as a print maker.

Nolde's etching technique at the time was extraordinary. Schiefler spoke of an "asphalt technique, similar to aquatint." [22] Nolde actually combined line etching, dry point, and soft-ground etching much like the intaglio of the mid-twentieth-century print makers of Stanley Hayter's group. These etchings do not have the dynamic excitement of his slightly later work, but show an undercurrent of symbolism that keeps recurring in Nolde's work at almost regular intervals. In etchings such as *Joy of Life, Brutal Force, The Petit Bourgeois, The Little Jumping Jack* (all 1904), he burlesques ordinary middle-class life with diabolic irony. *The Little Jumping Jack* shows a well-fed, middle-aged woman wearing a ridiculous, feathered hat and holding a little jumping jack who peeks sadly down his long, pointed nose. *The Petit Bourgeois* pictures a group of four or five men in long white coats sticking their heads into the air with smug, conceited expressions.

Soon Nolde was to find a fusion between the imaginative concepts of his drawings, water-color sketches, and etchings, on the one hand, and the greatly intensified color and rather ordinary subject matter of paintings such as *Harvest,* on the other. This fusion was perhaps the most important single event in his career as a painter.

Schmidt-Rottluff wrote about Nolde's "tempests of color," [23] but it was above all the quality of fantasy as well as remarkable technique in his etchings that seem to have captivated Kirchner: ". . . his fantastic style bringing a new feature to 'Brücke.' He enriched our exhibitions with his interesting etching technique and learned how we worked with the woodcut." [24]

The use of brilliant color—this time in the work of another artist—was again the direct cause of an addition to the group: Max Pechstein.

MAX PECHSTEIN

Max Pechstein (1881–1955) had been commissioned in the late spring of 1906 to paint the ceiling decoration for the Saxon pavilion of the Dresden Arts and Crafts Exhibition. He had just completed a spontaneous painting of a brilliant red tulip bed, a painting in which he seemed to forget all about his academic training. He decided to transfer this painting onto the ceiling: rough and unfinished but jubilantly red. Returning to the gallery a few days later, he found to his horror that his red was watered down with enough grayish-white to subdue it thoroughly. He had not been consulted, and the job was complete, the scaffolding removed. Pechstein stood there cursing indignantly, when suddenly, according to his story, he found a slight young man standing next to him and sympathizing. Erich Heckel proceeded to tell Pechstein about the Brücke and introduced him to Kirchner and Schmidt-Rottluff, whereupon it was generally agreed that Pechstein should become a member of the group.[25]

Pechstein, a man of a most affirmative character and elementary power, a painter whose strength and shortcomings rested in his decisive action and lack of contemplation, came from a working-class background in the industrial city of Zwickau in Saxony, where his father was a textile worker.

He took his first drawing lessons at ten and soon began to draw with passion, sketching the Saxonian countryside during his walks. Drawing to Pechstein was not an expression of the intellect. Rather, it meant a physical expression of his visual and motor senses. He made an analogy between his early drawing and previous fist fights. "Now I drew as wildly during my tramps as I had fought before." [26]

Leaving school at fifteen in 1896, he became an apprentice to a local painter in Zwickau. After completing his four-year apprenticeship in 1900, he set out for the Saxon capital like a journeyman of the past. There he found a position as assistant to painter-decorators and spent his time on flower designs and ornamentations of all sorts and for all purposes.

In the fall of 1900 he entered the Dresden School for Arts and Crafts, living—in the bohemian tradition—on bread while studying art. In the spring of 1902 he transferred to the Dresden Academy and was accepted by Otto Gussmann's atelier, where he went through the regular curriculum of drawing from plaster casts and executing still life and ornamental designs. He remained a student at the academy until 1906 and supported himself by all sorts of commercial commissions. Osborn said [27] that Pechstein disliked this activity and wished only to be a free painter, but during this time he acquired extraordinary skill and dexterity, which accounts for the great ease of execution in his later work.

His first great inspiration as an artist was probably the van Goghs he saw at the Galerie Arnold in 1905.[28] In their originality and nonconformity, these paintings seemed to be painted by a man driven by a demon of violence and ecstasy. In a recent letter Pechstein also stressed his fondness in this period for Cranach, early German woodcuts, and for exotic art.[29]

Pechstein's first prints—woodcuts—date from 1905 or 1906,[30] but no woodcuts by Pechstein from 1905 seem now to be extant. He was essentially a painter, and color was his direct means of expression. His prints—with some important exceptions—were mostly quick notations for paintings. Both new members of the Brücke, Pechstein and Nolde, were to participate in the first public exhibition held in the fall of 1906.

THE FIRST BRÜCKE EXHIBITION

Heckel, meanwhile, had interrupted his architectural studies and found employment as a draftsman in the office of Wilhelm Kreis, a successful architect then at work on the design of the Deutsche Kunstgewerbeausstellung (Dresden, 1906). Kreis had also been commissioned to build a showroom for Seifert, a manufacturer of lampshades and light fixtures in Löbtau.[31] Heckel, who executed the actual work, thought that the large sample room could quite well be used as a gallery. The Brücke considered the arrangement of exhibitions for its membership as one of its major tasks, as Schmidt-Rottluff had pointed out in his letter to Nolde. But there were no funds to pay the rent for exhibition space, and no museum, Kunstverein, secession, or private gallery wanted to show their work. Heckel therefore persuaded the manufacturer that he could find no better use for his empty walls and that the planned exhibition would be of mutual benefit.

Oils were hung on the walls; water colors, prints, and drawings were displayed in specially designed showcases; wood sculpture was placed on hand-carved pedestals. Thus, in a conservative factory building, in a room that seemed exceedingly low because of the hanging, eye-diverting lamps of an emphatically bourgeois taste, the first and historic Brücke exhibition was held.[32]

The event was publicized in the city by an aggressive poster designed by Kirchner. Under large, crude letters—"K. G. BRÜCKE"—that form an integral part of the design, a nude figure, with a small body and enormous head, juts diagonally like a large check mark across the rectangular space. The sex of the little girl—Fränzi—is strongly emphasized by the indistinct object she holds over the pubic area and by the highly exaggerated angles of her body. This three-color lithograph in black, yellow, and red must have been an effective poster because of its shock value.[33]

Few people came to the sample-room exhibition. The lampshade salesmen found the art work rather distracting; the few artists, art experts, and critics who did come felt threatened by this display, and clamored about insane art. The important exception was a review in the *Dresdner Neueste Nachrichten* by Paul Fechter, who spoke out with some courage in favor of a rising new movement in art.

The Brücke did not publish catalogs of its exhibitions until 1910, but there are fragments of a manuscript for a catalog by Kirchner for this first show.[34] These fragments indicate that the participants were: Kirchner, Bleyl, Heckel, Schmidt-Rottluff, Nolde, and Pechstein. There is no indication of the size or content of the exhibition. We can judge only from the work the artists did at the time.

BRÜCKE PAINTINGS AND PRINTS, 1905–1906

Kirchner's *River Boat near Dresden* (1905) (pl. 146) is bold, where the earlier *Deciduous Forest* (1904) (pl. 25) is hesitant. The rather impressionistic treatment in the earlier painting is replaced by rich, startling color areas. The contemplative mood has given way to excitement caused by the intense and arbitrary colors. The houses in the background are bright spots against a blue sky, resembling contemporary Fauve painting, but much broader

areas of color occur in the foreground. The boat on the right is a dark
Prussian blue form, interrupted by red ribbons. The large mysterious
shape itself is as compelling as its strong color.

Just as great is the contrast between Kirchner's *Self-Portrait at Dawn*,
(pl. 26) (a lithograph of 1906) and earlier lithographs. Here he made
full use of the textural possibilities of the medium, achieving an almost
infinite variety of tone values and a great richness of ornamental lines. The
eyes and mouth—slitlike, upturned curves and gashes—resemble each
other, as they do the general sinuous movement of forms merging together
throughout the composition. This print seems impossible without knowledge of Munch: not only because of the cursive, Munch-like line, but also
because of the content of the picture. There is the same preoccupation with
sex and the evocation of the dream image: the brooding, intense male face
against the barely indicated female body.

Figure 9.   ERICH HECKEL   Nude   1906   Woodcut

Heckel may have been represented by some such work as *Grazing Horses,*[35] a painting of five horses at different angles nibbling in a meadow stems from the impressionist tradition. However, the forms have become more definite: the horses are clearly outlined against the landscape background, and the body of each horse has become a definite color plane. The brush stroke is broader, and color is applied in much larger areas. The drawing and composition of this painting are not very interesting—the horses line up in a monotonous horizontal in the foreground—but this painting indicates the beginnings of Heckel's concern with light and color. "The things and objects do not speak as much through their form or drawing as through the expression of color, i.e., the peculiar selection of color tensions." [36]

Heckel's graphic work was considerably advanced over his painting at this early time, and only his prints give some indication of his great esthetic experience in discovering Grünewald in 1905, when he saw the Aschaffenburg *Pietà*.[37]

A woodcut of a nude (about 1906) (fig. 9) gives an indication of Heckel's graphic work at the time of the first Brücke exhibition: large planes are outlined by long, continuous, attenuated curves.[38] This print is imbued also with the dramatic, self-conscious accusation and despair so often found in Heckel's later work. The skull-like head, the sagging breasts, and the flayed body add to the feeling of morbidity and suffering. The background looks like a wooden wall from which chips are peeling off. At this same time Heckel spent much time at wood carving,[39] and it seems certain that he exhibited several pieces of sculpture in the first Brücke exhibition.

Schmidt-Rottluff was then in the process of doing a series of lithographs, still impressionist in the handling of form but superb in the mastery of technique. *Court Church, Dresden* (pl. 27) is related to *Cityscape* (fig. 6), a woodcut of 1903, but a remarkable development has taken place. The swift, easy lines for building, people, and sky, and the striking composition of the large black building on the left contrasted to the area of rapid gray lines on the right, make this print a masterpiece of impressionist lithography.

Typical of Schmidt-Rottluff's painting at that time is a river landscape, *On the Peisse* (1906),[40] which has remained in his own collection. It is rather bright in color, and immediately recalls the neoimpressionist technique except that it consists of innumerable small strokes rather than dots and is much less careful in its execution. It is more directly related to Kirchner's self-portrait of about 1904. When Schmidt-Rottluff was asked about the similarity of this painting to neoimpressionist work, he maintained that this was accidental, that he had intended to work with a larger and broader brush stroke but had not been able to succeed in doing so because of the highly absorbent canvas at his disposal.[41] This painting also differs from pointillist paintings in its freer and bolder personal expression.

On the Peisse was painted at the time when most of the Brücke artists were finding their own individual styles. Will Grohmann, in his essay on Emil Nolde, spoke of the "breakthrough toward visual form in 1906."[42] This is the year in which Nolde found himself, perhaps partly because of some recognition and the fruitful give-and-take companionship in Dresden.

The extremely important first figure composition in his new style, *The Free Spirit,* was completed at this time. As in his slightly earlier oil, he used brilliant color to build up the composition, and this is now combined with the symbolism that heretofore had been found only in his graphic work. The background still consists of loose blue dabs of color, but the four tall, thin figures are large planes of color. On the left the bright red figure of the zealot raises his arms in imploring adoration. Next to him the free-thinker, standing firmly with his wrists crossed, faces the spectator as though secure in his belief. This figure is orange and in strong contrast to the green mocker at his side, who points his finger with a frightened sneer. On the far left stands a fourth figure in blue—a cool, cynical spectator. The "free spirit" is not much larger than the other figures, yet Nolde has made him seem to tower above them in complete self-reliance with the others in dependent attitudes.

This painting is symptomatic of the turn from landscape to figure painting in Germany in the first decade of the century. It also expresses Nolde's own free thought, and points toward his unorthodox religious works of a few years later.

Pechstein now began to paint his series of nudes—a eulogy to women—which has played such an important part in his life work. These are not the slender women of Kirchner or Heckel's haggard creatures, but vigorous, voluptuous females. Pechstein joined with all the Brücke artists in an *épater le bourgeois* spirit in revolt against conventional beauty, among other conventions. He also produced his first woodcuts at this time.

PORTFOLIOS AND PUBLICATIONS

In spite of high hopes, the exhibition in the lampshade factory had not put the painters in touch with the public. They then published the first of their annual portfolios—now rare incunabula of twentieth-century art.[43] These portfolios were distributed among the small nonprofessional membership, who for the modest membership fee of at first twelve, then twenty-five, marks received each year a portfolio of original prints, a membership card (also an original print), as well as annual reports, frequently illustrated.

The portfolios were exceedingly modest, usually containing only three prints and later an additional print for the cover. The 1906 portfolio consisted of three woodcuts, one each by Bleyl, Heckel, and Kirchner. About twenty copies were printed. Bleyl also designed the layout of the title page as well as the index, and he contributed the design for the letterhead and envelopes of the group.

Also in 1906 Kirchner wrote the program of the group, which he cut in wood and printed by hand (fig. 10), his typography recalling William

Morris' title page of the Kelmscott Chaucer. This, too, was probably distributed to the nonprofessional membership:

With faith in development and in a new generation of creators and appreciators we call together all youth. As youth, we carry the future and want to create for ourselves freedom of life and of movement against the long-established older forces. Everyone who with directness and authenticity conveys that which drives him to creation, belongs to us.[44]

Figure 10.   ERNST LUDWIG KIRCHNER
Manifesto of Künstlergruppe Brücke   1906
Woodcut

Increasingly the painters worked from models in the common studio. This can be seen from their paintings and prints of the time. They met for discussion at the Café Central, and frequently visited Nolde's studio. Nolde, although he now lived in Dresden, remained comparatively aloof from their common endeavors.

NEW MEMBERS

Before the year was over, two more artists were drawn into the group: the Finnish painter Axel Gallén-Kallela and the Swiss Cuno Amiet.

Axel Gallén-Kallela (born 1865) had received his early academic training in Helsingfors and then at the Académie Julian in Paris, where he was more impressed by the work of Bastien-Lepage than by Bouguereau. The genre and landscape pictures he painted in Paris in the late 'eighties have a serene, silvery, *plein-air* quality similar to Bastien-Lepage. He exhibited work of this kind in the Paris Salons of 1888 and 1889.

When Gallén returned to Finland in 1890, his work began to change: the brush stroke became freer, his color planes broader, and his contour lines more definite and forceful. Perhaps most important, his motifs changed from Finnish genre pictures and landscapes to Finnish mythology and folk legend. In 1892 he executed the first of a long series of triptychs and frescoes of the ancient Finnish Kalevala, which he continued far into the twentieth century.

Some of his mythological paintings were first seen in Germany in 1895 when the Baroccio gallery in Berlin arranged a show of Gallén and Munch.[45] Gallén soon became a contributor to the Jugendstil organ, *Pan*. In 1900 he received a gold medal at the Paris world's fair for his Kalevala frescoes on the dome of Saarinen's Finnish pavilion. In 1903 he was the featured guest artist at an exhibition of the Phalanx group in Munich.[46]

Gallén's use of motifs of the ancient heroes and legendary Finnish deities occurred simultaneously with a change in his former naturalistic style. His style became charged with a dramatic tension that made him the leader of the romantic trend in Finnish painting [47] and caused the Brücke painters to admire his work and to invite this famous painter to participate in their exhibitions.

Cuno Amiet was asked to join the Brücke in connection with an exhibition of his work at the Galerie Arnold. His personal participation in the group seems to have been limited to his contribution of a woodcut to the 1907 portfolio, and the work of the Brücke artists had little influence on his own. His membership is never mentioned in any of the monographs and articles on him.

His influence on the development of the Brücke, however, must have been considerable: Amiet brought them the direct message of Gauguin, of Hodler, and of his own work in Fauve-like color.

Amiet was born in Solothurn, Switzerland, in 1868, and had his first training with the realist painter Frank Buchser. Like many Swiss-German artists, he went to Munich to study; he was at the academy from 1886 to 1888. He continued on to Paris to become a student of Bouguereau and Tony Robert-Fleuri at the Académie Julian in 1888. In 1892 Amiet went to Pont-Aven into a community of artists entirely unkown to him: "There was a strange art, never seen before. The dining room of the inn was papered with pictures by painters whose names I had never read. Laval, Moret, Gauguin, Sérusier—bright, clear objectivity." [48]

He did not meet Gauguin himself, who had already left Brittany, but he was close to O'Connor, Séguin, and Emile Bernard. The latter told him of Gauguin and van Gogh. Amiet was impressed by the lithographs of Daumier which he saw in Pont-Aven, and by reproductions of Giotto, Botticelli, and Ghirlandaio.

He was at Pont-Aven in 1892 and 1893; his pictures became lighter, his light soft and diffuse. He relinquished the realistic local color he had been using for soft, subtle color harmonies in *Breton Washerwoman* (1893), which is built up of large, two-dimensional elements. *The Sick Boy* (1895) is still symbolist in form, with its flat color areas, sharply outlined contours, and over-all decorative aspect.

Soon after his return to Switzerland in 1893, Amiet came under Hodler's personal influence. In search of independence he resisted Hodler's invitation to join him in Geneva, but he began to work in clear-cut silhouettes and to move his figures into definite relationships with the frame. Linear rhythms were paramount in Hodler's work, but Amiet continued to work in terms of his strong color. By 1899, in his important *Richesses du Soir,* he is indeed very close to Hodler with the five Swiss peasant women in parallel movement. Even the name was given to the picture by Hodler, but Amiet asserted his individuality in the use of rich, saturated colors.

At the turn of the century Amiet came close to the pointillist approach of his older compatriot Segantini. He worked with long strokes of complementary colors placed next to one another. By 1905 he was painting in large, flat, brilliant planes combined with an arabesque line; these canvases show a definite independent parallel development to Fauvism in Paris.

Amiet was never in personal contact with the Dresden painters, and his art always remained much closer to nature than theirs. He was not only "ahead of us with his large planes of color," [49] but because of his own background he was able to help the Brücke evolve from a provincial group of German artists to a movement of European importance.

IX

Development of the Brücke from 1907 to 1910

The period from 1907 to 1910 was one of steady development, not so much for the artists individually but rather for them as a group. In twos and threes they left the city for the nearby countryside or for the more distant North Sea or Baltic. Their purpose was to study nature at first hand and the human body moving in natural surroundings.

MORITZBURG

The free human body was of paramount concern to them—not the un-dressed model drawn to scale in the academies. Having realized that studio models were not usually nude, but merely undressed and naked, and since they wanted to study the human body moving freely and unconsciously in its nudity, they spent several weeks with a number of women companions nude in the forests, bathing, living in huts or tents.[1] Yet they wanted more than an objective study of the human body in action. They were prompted by a desire to achieve new strength through a close link with the sources of nature—an impulse found contemporaneously in the German youth movement and in the nudist cult. It was a worship of the freely mov-ing human body as a part of the total complex of nature. Groups like the Wandervögel and movements such as the Freiluftbewegung and Nackt-kultur were widespread and popular among the younger generation, who were in revolt against the urban restrictions of the period and rejected the confinement of the body in the corset as much as the confinement of the spirit in a Prussian school system.[2]

The naked figure had loomed paramount in importance to Lovis Corinth and his group in the previous generation: "Robust female nudes in a style that combined Rubensian eroticism with Teutonic gruffness."[3] The draw-ings, prints, and paintings of the Brücke painters unified the nude human figure with the landscape. This absorption of the figure into nature was carried to a point where hands or feet of the nudes often became indistinguishable from the surrounding foliage. This union of man and nature had already been expressed in Hodler's paintings—for example, *Fusion with the Cosmos*—but with the Brücke it was less studied, less stylized, and became instead spontaneous and energetic.[4]

Schmidt-Rottluff had started the move away from the city when he visited Nolde on the island of Alsen in the summer of 1906. The following year he and Heckel went to the Dangast moor country in Oldenburg; Kirchner began going to Moritzburg in 1906. In 1907 Pechstein joined Kirchner in Goppeln, in the Moritzburg lake district near Dresden. Moritzburg became the Argenteuil of the Brücke, and it was here especially that the painters developed their theories of the unity of man and nature. Schmidt-Rottluff spent every summer in Dangast between 1907 and 1912. Heckel joined Kirchner in Moritzburg in the summers of 1908, 1909, and 1910. Pechstein, who had spent the summer of 1909 in almost complete isolation in the small fishing village of Nidden on the Kurische Nehrung in East Prussia, was back with them in Moritzburg in 1910, the last summer in which productive group activity took place. In 1912 Kirchner and Heckel went to the island of Fehmarn, where the former returned to paint in 1913 and 1914.

Even more than in the studio in the city, a style evolved at Moritzburg—frequently called the "first Brücke style"—characterized by shouting colors instead of soft harmonies, by hard, pointed, splintered forms, and by large, sharply contrasting planes of pure color. The contour, which impressionism had almost entirely rejected, was reintroduced, but more as the border of the color plane than as the outline of the object.

Nature presented the immediate stimulus but was never imitated. Instead, the expression of a concept of nature by means of absolute color—including pure white and pure black—and a strongly emphasized contour became increasingly important.

EXHIBITIONS, 1906–1907

In the winter of 1906–1907 a second Brücke exhibition took place, but only of graphic works. This small exhibit included a group of woodcuts by a new artist invited to participate: Wassily Kandinsky.[5] Kandinsky, who had been living in Paris and evolving his own version of Fauvism, worked with intense color as well as with line. The immediate cause of his participation in the Brücke show was perhaps his visit to Dresden at the time. This was probably the first direct contact of the Brücke with the most recent developments in painting in Paris and Munich.

Even more noteworthy, however, was an exhibition in the Salon Richter in Dresden in the fall of 1907. This was no factory building, but a real salon (and Pragerstrasse was Dresden's rue de la paix) large, silent rooms with heavy, expensive furniture, lit by skylights, then smothered with rugs and wall coverings. In these chambers, saturated with bourgeois taste, the Brücke hoisted the banner of revolt. They might as well have raised it over the roof of the royal residence—the result was a violent rejection.[6]

PORTFOLIOS, 1907–1912

The group continued to publish and distribute its annual portfolios. Proud of its new members, it published a woodcut each by Amiet and Gallén-Kallela, an etching by Nolde, and a lithograph by Schmidt-Rottluff to make up the portfolio of 1907. The following year the portfolio consisted entirely of woodcuts; Pechstein, as well as Kirchner and Heckel, was asked to contribute. Beginning in 1909 the annual portfolios were devoted to the work of one individual artist, while another made a woodcut for the cover. The portfolio for 1909 featured the work of Schmidt-Rottluff, with Kirchner providing the cover; that for 1910 contained work by Kirchner and a cover by Heckel. Heckel's work appeared in 1911, with a cover by Pechstein. Pechstein was responsible for the last portfolio, published in 1912, with a cover done by Otto Mueller, who had joined the group two years previously. For 1913 the publication of the *Chronik der Brücke* was planned, with contributions from each of the artists. This was to become the immediate cause of the dissolution of the group.[7]

KIRCHNER'S DEVELOPMENT

The early Moritzburg style is well exemplified in a color woodcut by Kirchner, *Three Bathers,*[8] taken from three color blocks: black, blue, and green. The female figures—one sitting, two walking—are a brilliant royal blue on a green ground. Most of the background is a jagged black shape that tends to flatten out the picture space, leaving an extremely narrow platform for the figures. On the left is a small white space, denoting distance, but here again black and green geometric shapes destroy the three-dimensional illusion. The shape of the serrated black form is as abstract as the unbroken blue of the nude figures.

The previous generation had painted nudes that either dissolved in an all-embracing light or posed as charmingly self-contained creatures of high breeding. Kirchner offered the spectator primitive, naked women moving to awkward rhythms. The distortions in these figures, the blue bodies, and the faceless heads are by no means arbitrary, but create the picture's mood and dominate the landscape of which they are a part. Neither light nor air is in this landscape; shading occurs at only one point: to emphasize the breasts. Erotic content was a dominant interest of Kirchner and the Brücke painters at this period.

Kirchner felt that the woodcut was essential to his development as a painter, and that the technical manipulation of the block released powers in him that could not grow through the much easier techniques of drawing and painting.[9] His woodcut style is often several years advanced over his style in painting, especially during this early period.

The cutting and gouging of the block led Kirchner to wood sculpture, which he had begun as early as 1900. The roughly carved primitive figures, with a strongly tactile, plastic quality, betray the sometimes too direct influence of African sculpture.

Kirchner felt that his work in the woodcut and wood carving helped him to achieve the closed form for which he was striving, but he continued to record his immediate impressions by quick line renderings. Kirchner's drawing—his most sensitive medium—is often the key to his prints or paintings. In his drawings he reached the desired intensity of expression with the greatest economy of means.

Kirchner's close relationship to the natural world was essential to his work. He always drew his subject matter from nature and external impressions, but he did not reproduce the optical illusion, as the impressionists had done. Instead, he brought his own fantasy and personal experience into play to give an incisive form to the original inspiration; indeed, he considered inspiration from nature the source of artistic expression. He insisted on the importance of a synthesis of careful observation of nature and free expression of the imagination. Taking cover behind his nom de plume, he spoke with no lack of self-esteem about the means he chose to achieve it:

Kirchner grew to recognize that a new form, created from intensive study of nature with the aid of imagination, had a much stronger effect than naturalistic representation. He developed the hieroglyph and enriched modern art thereby with an important means of expression, as Seurat in his time invented the division of color and Cézanne the system of cylinder, cone and sphere.[10]

This hieroglyph, a line that merely implies or suggests reality rather than representing it, seems akin to abstract calligraphic handwriting. Kirchner's network of linear abbreviations results in a coherence in terms of the objects represented: bathers, landscapes, cabaret and street scenes.[11]

Kirchner's street scenes are quick and vivid drawings of fleeting movements of people and objects he sketched on his walks through the city. The edges of the sheet of paper and the blank spaces are as important in the total drawing as the executed area itself. His lines—both chaotic and constrained in the beginning—become a consciously controlled network of angular tensions by 1906. He was aware of the junglelike character of the city, of the threatening streets, buildings, bridges, the mechanical movement of the people.

In Dresden, and later in Berlin, he became imbued with a tremendous enthusiasm for the multiple spectacle of metropolitan life. The impressionists, to be sure, had discovered the city as a motif for the painter, but for them the boulevard was merely a gay visual sensation, the people dancing particles of color. Toulouse-Lautrec and Munch began to express the human meaning of urban life, but it remained for Kirchner first to give form to the speed and rhythm of the big city. Unlike the futurists, he did not sing the praises of a mechanized city, because he felt that urban man in his cafés, night clubs, and cabarets was a puppet of a mechanized society.

The first important painting of a long series of the same motif is *Street* (1907) in the Museum of Modern Art (pl. 28). The fleeting impression of people moving down a city street is permanent and forcefully organized. A number of figures, painted in brash colors, thrust themselves forward at the spectator. This is actually a very unpleasant picture. The colors—pink, Chinese red, green, chartreuse, blue, and black—are used to shock the spectator into a sudden awareness. Fiery orange outlines around large blue, chartreuse, and pink areas make for an exciting and troublesome contrast. Figures seem to walk threateningly out of the picture plane. Space is turned steeply upward by a distortion of perspective that goes back to van Gogh, Toulouse-Lautrec, and Munch. The effect is greatly increased by the advancing pavement, a large, empty area of pink extending from the lower left and taking up an extensive part of the large picture. The red streetcar is perpendicular to the picture plane, and advancing figures are cut off only by the frame. The line is still the sinuous Jugendstil line apparent in his lithograph *Self-Portrait at Dawn*. It is an abstract line, leading its own cursive life and used at times to delineate several contours simultaneously or to create a fantastic shape.

Certain derivations are clearly indicated in this early Kirchner painting: The frontal figures and the general mood of the picture are related to Munch; the green faces recall Toulouse-Lautrec; the upturned space and the cursive line are still a part of the general turn-of-the-century style.

This painting at one time hung next to a Vlaminck landscape of 1908 in the Museum of Modern Art,[12] thereby offering an excellent opportunity to compare the Fauve and the Brücke styles. In the Fauve painting, combinations of clashing colors are also used, applied with a similar thick brush stroke, raised in places for purposes of emphasis. Yet in Vlaminck's painting the colors do not clash; there is no void like the pink area in the Kirchner; there are no burning outlines and no threatened human beings threatening the spectator. Vlaminck's Fauve landscape is pleasant decoration, in contrast to Kirchner's terrifying construction of a world in which each person is a member of a "lonely crowd," in which he seems to be neither an individual nor a member of a community, but a large and frightening robot that is part of a mass of robots.

Self-Portrait with Model (1907) (pl. 29) is extremely interesting from the point of view of construction. In the left foreground the artist in a boldly striped robe of orange and blue pushes himself toward the spectator. This self-conscious figure heavily overloads the picture on the left while at some depth on the right a half-undressed model is seated on a red divan. The whole picture is flattened out by the red curtain behind Kirchner and the shocking-pink rectangle in the upper right. The painter's position with relation to the rest of the picture plane is startling, and suggests that it was painted in front of a mirror.

Kirchner later overpainted this canvas, as he did with so many of his paintings. During the overpainting he eliminated some of the details, made his formerly rather curvilinear outlines more angular, and created a more generalized, bolder impression as well as one of even greater flatness. The self-consciousness of his earlier *Self-Portrait at Dawn* is still most evident, as is his stress on the almond-shaped eyes, here making an interesting horizontal tension in the sensuous face. Because of the expressions in the faces and the fact that Kirchner and his model are half undressed, the painting again has definite erotic implications.

Kirchner's concern with composition and color led him to paint the fascinating portrait of *Dodo and Her Brother* (1909) (pl. 147).[13] The figures of the man and woman are squeezed into a narrow, awkward space; the male figure, pressing against the canvas edge at top and side, is the more crammed of the two, and looks like a doll wedged into a tight box. The dominant dark blue of the figure and its thick, light blue outline help to give the figure the appearance of a paper cutout and keep it relegated to the rear plane. This is contrasted to the high-keyed yellow gown of Kirchner's model Dodo, who moves onto the spectator like the figures in *Street*. Indeed, as in *Street*, the excitement of the painting is primarily in color—in the man's green face, in the green flounces of the woman's sleeves, the pinks of her enormous hat, fan, and shoes, and the blood red of the tilted floor. The woman's black-gloved arms, meeting at right angles across the front of her dress, become independent units floating in their pink borders.

The curving forms in the portrait recall Kirchner's Jugendstil roots. The Brücke membership card, an etching of 1908, shows even stronger rudiments of Jugendstil. Kirchner continued to be active as a print maker during these last Dresden years. He always allowed the material to determine the print, or rather chose the print technique in terms of the desired result. The woodcuts have a hard strength of form: a powerful contrast of black and white or clearly defined flat color planes (fig. 11). In his prints of urban life, for example, he used the woodcut for scenes of bright daylight or night scenes in the sharp glare of electric bulbs; for his city scenes of foggy weather and views through windows, he preferred the etching. His etchings are closest to his drawings. He would take the copper plate along on his ramblings through the city and scratch down his first impressions. "Rich in temperamental calligraphy and versatile in its motifs, the etchings are like the diary of a painter." [14] Yet there are also carefully evolved etchings in which Kirchner investigated various additional intaglio techniques, especially aquatint and dry point.

In his lithographs Kirchner is, as in all his print work, conscious of his material: the peculiar textural effects of the stone. By means of the texture of the stone he achieves deep blacks and silky grays and the richest variety of values. Whereas he thought in terms of lines in his drawings and etchings, he turned to the plane in lithography. Several of his prints reached the public in the Brücke portfolio of 1910.

Edwin Redslob, eminent art critic and historian and the commissioner of art during the Weimar Republic, agrees with the constantly mounting literature on Kirchner that he was "the most intense and strongest tem-

Figure 11.   ERNST LUDWIG KIRCHNER   Head of Schmidt-Rottluff   1909   Woodcut
Title page for Brücke portfolio of 1909

perament" [15] among his group. Kirchner's leadership of the Brücke was then, however, disputable, and his later claim to such leadership was a main reason for the breakdown of the group.

HECKEL'S DEVELOPMENT

Heckel, meanwhile, was continuing his work as a print maker. In his series for Oscar Wilde's *The Ballad of Reading Gaol,* the decorative-linear ornament persists, as it does in the frame decoration of *Old Woman* (1907) (fig. 12). The *Old Woman* has an emaciated female body with the strange

Figure 12.   ERICH HECKEL
Old Woman   1907   Woodcut

face of a young man and sickly-looking, pendulous breasts. The nipples are abnormally enlarged, and seem to stare out of the figure like eyes. The roundness of the nipples is repeated in two white disks below. The jagged planes create a strong pattern of black and white.

This same contrast of black and white appears in his primitivistic woodcut *Standing Nude* (1908) (pl. 30). Temporarily Heckel has given up the pointed, angular Brücke forms for ovoid shapes in the nude's head, arm, belly, and thighs. The whole flat composition is a relationship of irregular, white, ovoid shapes against flat black planes. The influence of African sculpture is clearly evident in this woman's Negroid features and in the sculptural quality attained by means of the startling juxtaposition of black and white areas. The Brücke artist reflects the erotic quality of some African work by emphasizing the protruding belly, thick thighs, and sexual organs.

She seems to have a halo, but, unlike woodcuts and paintings by Gauguin, this does not necessarily imply the glorification of the primitive in Christian terms. The ugly and distorted woman is far from idealized. The halo could be interpreted as the sanctification of quiet suffering, but its purpose may simply be a formal consideration: to emphasize the head and to vary the background.

Similar in its black-and-white contrasts but very different in feeling is *Sailboat,* a woodcut of 1907. The ship is being blown across the water with great force. It does not stand out—not being at all sculptural in quality, like the *Standing Nude*—but is an integral part of the black-and-white ribbons of movement over the sea. Abstractly shaped cloud formations move through the sky in the wild, free convolutions of expressionism, no longer in the stylized curves of Jugendstil. This woodcut is also of great interest because of its similarity to the etchings of Hamburg harbor that Nolde did three years later.

Remnants of Jugendstil line, however, are still apparent in Heckel's *Village Ball* (1908) (pl. 148), particularly in the dark contours of the drapes and of the chaperones sitting along the wall. The entire painting recalls, in fact, Toulouse-Lautrec's *Moulin de la Galette* in subject as well as in composition. The major difference, however, is that the Heckel painting lacks Lautrec's subtlety of pictorial shorthand and is much cruder, almost primitive. Paint is applied thinly, and fragments of the canvas are even left blank. The strokes are straight and either horizontal or vertical within a given area. Speaking about his early work, Heckel mentioned his difficulties with the viscous paint as it came from the tube. Having had no art training, not even in the mixing of paint, he simply applied the paint in straight brush strokes, one next to the other, thereby achieving a definite rhythm throughout the canvas, which pleased him.[16]

The young Heckel must have been delighted with the impudence of juxtaposing the flowerlike blue and pink dresses with the blatant crimson curtains and the yellow-orange floor. This amusing contrast helps express the essential inconsistency of a village ball where peasants ape the gentry and the blue-gowned belle twirls woodenly in the arms of her bearlike partner.

Heckel spent the spring of 1909 in Italy, but seems to have been little affected by this journey. In the years after this trip, he reached his maturity and produced the most important work of his career.

SCHMIDT-ROTTLUFF'S PERIOD OF TRANSITION

The contrast between impressionism and expressionism seemed enormous during the period now under discussion. Expressionism was not only a different style of painting, but an altogether new way of living—"a return to mysticism and religion," "a turning inward," "a violent expression of racial memories," "a purposeful control and construction of form," or, on the other hand, "a passive release of inner necessities." Yet today it can

be fully realized that expressionism grew out of the movements that preceded it, as surrealist poetry almost imperceptibly grew from symbolist
verse.

Schmidt-Rottluff's *Windy Day* (1907) (pl. 31) is an excellent example
of the transitional period the artist experienced in the first decade of the
century. Schmidt-Rottluff considered this his first important painting.[17]
Compared to his earlier work (and to impressionist painting), everything
has become more emphatic. The colors are applied in large areas, and have
grown more brilliant; their contrasts are enhanced further; forms are
greatly simplified. Space is created by color rather than by perspective. A
broad brush stroke creates dense textures.

The simplification of form in *Windy Day* is carried much further in
Estate in Dangast (1910) (pl. 149). The artist no longer sees the landscape
in terms of reflected light, but rather he imposes his own sense of design
on "the corner of nature"; the temperament has become more important
than the visual experience. Shadows are no longer broken fragments of
pigment but thick running streams of color flowing in a willful pattern that
has little if any relationship to actual appearances. Similarly Schmidt-
Rottluff has reduced his color scheme to simple Fauve-like colors of red,
blue, green, yellow, and magenta—probably taken directly from the tube.
This use of forthright color, definite pattern, and lack of details gives the
painting the intensely emotional impact that is the hallmark of expressionist work.

Schmidt-Rottluff continued his interest in the woodcut as well as
lithography during this period. A woodcut, like *Head of a Man* (1909),[18]
relinquishes all interest in detail. There is only a powerfully convoluting
line that is more interesting in its own movement than in its function as a
contour. The lithographs from this period are more painterly and fluid, and
the artist evidently used etching acid in the treatment of the stone.[19]

These early lithographs by Schmidt-Rottluff often resemble prints by
Munch, but the Norwegian artist was deeply shaken when he first saw them
at the home of Gustav Schiefler. When the collector showed him the prints,
just sent to him from Dresden, Munch was silent for a time and then exclaimed: "Gott soll uns schützen, wir gehen schweren Zeiten entgegen
[God help us, we are heading toward difficult times]."[20] Munch was affected by them as symptoms of a sick society. Schiefler himself appreciated
their quality and bought several.

Schmidt-Rottluff's production of woodcuts was so impressive by 1909
that a Brücke portfolio was devoted solely to him. Kirchner contributed a
portrait of Schmidt-Rottluff in woodcut for the title page (fig. 11).[21]

BLEYL'S DEPARTURE FROM THE GROUP

Fritz Bleyl too was doing some interesting linoleum cuts and woodcuts in
this period. Three linoleum cuts, printed in purple ink and belonging
quite definitely to the earliest Brücke style, are found in Kirchner's sketch-

book of 1906, together with some sketches for book ornamentation by Bleyl.[22] One of his last known works is again a woodcut, *Girl* (1908) (fig. 13). This technically excellent print is still in the graphic style of flowing light and dark patterns of the turn of the century. Bleyl's technique has become refined, but he has clearly not kept pace with the increasingly expressive simplification of the other Brücke painters. His connections with

Figure 13.   FRITZ BLEYL   Girl   1908   Woodcut

the group were very loose by this time, and in 1909 he resigned from the Brücke to devote himself entirely to the practice and teaching of architecture.[23]

PECHSTEIN'S DEVELOPMENT

Pechstein, like the other members of the group, did much work in graphics at this time. His prints, however, generally do not have the expressive power of the other Brücke print makers. Like Schmidt-Rottluff he was turning away from an early impressionism, but these attempts, although interesting for their boldness of line and black-and-white pattern, seem to penetrate little beyond the surface. Pechstein was primarily a painter, and his energetic temperament seemed to resist the discipline and limitation of the print-making techniques. He received a 1,000-mark study stipend for his painting at the annual competition of the Dresden art academy in 1906.[24]

When Pechstein went to Italy the following year, he was drawn to early Italian art as the closest parallel to his own endeavors, much as the Nava-renes had been attracted to Raphael. "Chiefly looking, examining and thoroughly enjoying, I found my own striving confirmed by the primi-tives." [25] When asked who the "primitives" were that Pechstein meant in this letter of 1919, the artist wrote: "In 1907 I was most strongly in-fluenced by Giotto during my first Italian trip, as well as by Etruscan

Figure 14. MAX PECHSTEIN Italian Landscape 1907 Woodcut

sculpture and the early Etruscan landscape painting in the Vatican library in Rome." [26] From his later work, it could be assumed that it was painting as an integral part of the wall that impressed him so greatly on his Italian trip, as well as the use of color for symbolism instead of to indicate nuances of light and air.

His woodcut *Italian Landscape* (1907) (fig. 14) shows his easy flow of line even in this resistant medium. Most of the block has been cut away to yield the large areas of white in this print. It is an almost naïve statement of the landscape, conforming to his taste for the primitive.

Pechstein returned from Italy by way of Paris, where he made this wood-cut. According to his biographer Max Osborn, Pechstein was fascinated in Paris by "primitive art," the sculpture at St. Denis and in the Musée Cluny, and the tribal art on view at the Trocadero. He met Kees van

Dongen and drew him into the Brücke. Pechstein must have been fully aware of the work of other Fauves, including Matisse,[27] at this time. Indeed, it seems very difficult to imagine that Pechstein met Kees van Dongen and remained oblivious to the work done by the entire Fauve group. Yet this very position is maintained by Heckel:

Much that is incorrect has been written about "Brücke" . . . like the influence which the Fauves were supposed to have exerted on us. Pechstein was in Paris in 1908. When he returned he told us of the work of Kees van Dongen, whom we thereupon invited to an exhibition. . . . Obviously Matisse was not known at that time in the circles into which Pechstein accidentally came in Paris; had we known anything about him, we would surely have invited him, although his pictorial intentions had only a few points of contact with ours.[28]

Pechstein's own answer indicates at least a familiarity with the Fauves. According to his letter, he had no contact with Purrmann, Moll, Grossmann—that is, with the Café Dôme group who made up most of the Matisse school in 1907 and 1908. But he goes on to say: "I had to resolve the impressions of the French Fauves." [29]

His *Portrait of a Girl* (1908) (pl. 33) suggests the experience of Paris. Compared with the painting of the other Brücke artists and with his own earlier work, it shows a new elegance, an ease and charm that are in great contrast to the self-conscious intensity of the Dresden painters. The palette has brightened into light pastel colors. The speckles of light in figure and background lend the picture much of its vivacity, as does the light blue contour. The gay light and colors are appropriate to the good-natured coquette, whose blouse slips coyly off one shoulder. The brush stroke within the clearly outlined contours is still rather impressionist in this picture. Only two years later, in the *Woman* he exhibited in the New Secession in 1910, is a Fauve influence clearly evident.

Returning from abroad, Pechstein went to Berlin in the summer of 1908 and settled there permanently in the following winter. He was the first of the Brücke painters to make the important move from the provincial capital of Dresden to the modern, turbulent metropolis. Pechstein's active, exuberant personality was captivated by the dynamic life of the great urban center. In spite of prolonged periods in the Baltic and the trip to the South Seas, Berlin remained the core of his life and his work.

In the summer of 1909 Pechstein showed three paintings in the annual exhibition of the Secession: *Yellow Tulips, Landscape,* and *The Yellow Cloth. Yellow Tulips* and the *Landscape* were widely acclaimed and even sold. The former reminded the critics of Cézanne and Matisse; the latter, of van Gogh. Both were brilliant in color, decorative in total effect.

Many of Pechstein's paintings, drawings, woodcuts, and lithographs from this period do not show this same control, and are rather slovenly in execution. His work from this time often leaves an impression of something too quickly done, almost ready-made in its effect. Part of his difficulty seems to have been that he created under the immediate inspiration of life, without being able to communicate forcefully and without stopping to consider problems of form. He described artistic creation as analogous to child-bearing: "When you draw seek God within you; do not say 'I will' but 'So be it.' . . . The work arises! No task! Painful and joyful is the exultation of giving birth." [30]

It was possible for Pechstein, however, to achieve a triumph in *Indian and Woman* (1910) (pl. 150). An Indian in brilliant colors is seated on a drum in front of a mirror that reflects his profile, resulting in a double image of the figure. On a lower frontal plane is a nude whose sinuous lines create a remarkable contrast to the male figure and the straight, vertically rising lines of the mirror. Her curves are echoed in the top of the mirror and in the abstract design that occupies the right quarter of the painting. Strong color is the essential element of the composition, with bright red, green, and yellow dominating. Each color seems to carry out a design of its own. There is the yellow motif of the woman, frame of the mirror, and design on the right. This is contrasted to the dominant red color of the back wall, the Indian and his reflection, which pulls the back wall toward the frontal planes, continues in the diagonal strip toward the lower right, and is echoed in small areas of the woman. A mottled green expands on the floor, surrounding the woman, and is picked up in the mirror reflection. A royal blue creates its own space on the right wall, where it is preponderate.

The very subject of the Indian reveals Pechstein's romantic desire for an earth-bound life and art. He felt the need to counteract urban life, and in the summer of 1909 he went for the first time to Nidden on the Kurische Nehrung, in the highest dunes of East Prussia's Baltic coast. There in this almost forgotten human settlement he found fishermen who still lived a truly primitive life in rhythm with nature. There Pechstein painted the sea, the shore, the dunes, the breaking waves, and the endless planes of sea and sky. He also painted the men who worked the sea, the constant fight between sea and man, which determined the rhythm of life. He kept returning to Nidden for many summers, and his paintings began to lose impressionist vestiges and to become harder in modeling, more striking in color, and more powerful in decorative simplification, as in the magnificent *Beach at Nidden* (1911) (pl. 151), where nature has become a springboard for the artist's fantasy. This is no longer a scene at the Baltic, but a vigorous image taking place on the less specific shores of a fertile invention.

KEES VAN DONGEN

Pechstein had been most impressed during his trip to Paris by Kees van Dongen. Pechstein told his friends about van Dongen, who, he felt, was working in the same direction, and "whom we thereupon invited to an exhibition. He sent graphic works." [31]

Kees van Dongen (born 1877) had come to Paris from Rotterdam in 1897. His Dutch windmills and the later Normandy beach scenes, in the Salon des Indépendants of 1904, were still painted in an impressionist manner. By the following year, however, he had turned to working in larger surfaces of contrasting colors when he exhibited with Matisse, Manguin, Marquet, Vlaminck, Derain, and Rouault in the Salon d'Automne of 1905 and became associated with the Fauves. By 1907—probably even earlier— he was living in the Bateau-lavoir in the center of the *avant-garde* group of Montmartre: "The Dutchman van Dongen, who arrived in Paris in 1897, was probably the first to take a studio in the Bateau-lavoir." [32] The poets Pierre Reverdy, Max Jacob, and André Salmon, the painters Picasso and Juan Gris, and many of lesser fame took studios in the same building; most of the advanced artists lived close by and kept in constant contact with one another.

Although not an innovator, van Dongen adapted the pure color and audacious line of Fauvism to the portraiture of sensuous women. He was fascinated by the make-up and artifice of women on the more glittering fringes of proper society. He painted the brilliance of their jewels and lamé cloth in his pictures of dancers, actresses, and demimondaines.

Certain paintings by van Dongen from this period are strongly reminiscent of Brücke work:

. . . it was his belonging to the Paris "Fauves," his closeness to Matisse and Dufy, probably also simply his being Dutch, which recommended him [to the expressionists]. There is in these early works of the Dutchman gone Parisian a strength of line and a bravura in color dissonances which made him eligible for the German Expressionists.[33]

His *Portrait of a Woman* (about 1907) (pl. 34) is certainly similar to Kirchner's work. Kees here worked with large color planes—in the Chinese red blouse with its bold blue-and-ocher flower pattern, in the deep black hair, the ocher background, and the light flesh—giving the painting a very vivid appearance. These color planes, clearly delineated with dark outlines, are still somewhat broken up, more impressionist in the handling of color than in Kirchner's contemporary *Fränzi Seated* (1907).[34] Kirchner's painting, clearly derived from his own work in the woodcut, is even bolder in its flat color planes. Van Dongen's use of shading corresponds more to the optical appearance, whereas Kirchner uses arbitrary spots of darker colors to create an interesting pattern. The two paintings also resemble each other in their unusually large, almond-shaped eyes, which add to the intensity of expression in both.

Kees van Dongen may have become a member of the Brücke in 1908, but he remained on the periphery of the Dresden group. His work was not included in any of the Brücke portfolios, and he was represented in the exhibitions only with prints and water colors.

Another painter who was asked to exhibit with the group in this period was Franz Nölken (1884–1918). He was "a talented young man from Hamburg," [35] who soon went on to Paris to work close to Matisse. Like Kees van Dongen, Nölken never became an integral member of the group.

NEW SECESSION

In the spring of 1910 Pechstein again submitted work to the Berlin Secession, but the old guard, beginning to worry about its former courage, rejected him together with a large number of other advanced artists.

Since the withdrawal, under Liebermann's leadership, of a group of progressive artists from the Verein Berliner Künstler in protest against the closing of the Munch exhibition in 1892,[36] the Secession, founded in 1899, had been a liberal artists' organization. It was never a radical group by any means, but rather an elite of well-known artists. Hodler exhibited in the first show of the Secession in its own luxurious quarters in 1899, and Marées first reached a larger segment of the German public in the exhibition of 1900. Munch was featured with his *Frieze of Life* in 1902, and Toulouse-Lautrec and Cézanne in the following year. In 1906 new names —including Beckmann, Nauen, Nolde, Kandinsky, Jawlensky—showed the openness of the group to the younger generation. Barlach was appointed to the board in 1908. Then reactionary forces made themselves felt, and most of the progressive artists were excluded from the 1910 exhibition.

In protest the rejected artists banded together and opened their own "Salon des Refusées" in the Gemälde-Galerie Maximilian Macht, concurrently with the Berlin Secession.[37] The group, under Pechstein's leadership and with Sauermann as business manager, called itself the New Secession. The exhibit was composed of 56 works by 27 artists, including two paintings each by Kirchner, Heckel, and Schmidt-Rottluff, as well as four by Pechstein.[38]

The exhibition, judging from the reproductions in the catalog, was a medley of postimpressionist painting. The influence of Gauguin and the Nabis seems predominant, but an academic genre "machine" was hung with a Cézannesque still life by César Klein; Melzer and Segal were represented with pointillist paintings. Pechstein's voluptuous *Woman* was extremely close to Matisse, and Schmidt-Rottluff's *Still Life* was still an example of his enhanced impressionism. Kirchner's *Lady before the Mirror* and Heckel's *New Houses* were probably the most advanced and most personal expressions in the exhibition.

Trust, in the newly founded *Sturm*, voiced his opinion that the New Secession would be successful because the painters simplified and popularized for the German public the art of van Gogh, Gauguin, Hodler, Klimt, and Matisse, and that "divine inspiration has become acceptable human mannerism." [39] Curt Glaser, in *Die Kunst*, went into greater detail in his review. He saw Gauguin, van Gogh, and Munch as the standard bearers of the new generation, and agreed that the young painters were still dependent on the precursors. He also saw the beginning of a new art, in which color and composition were most strongly emphasized. Both critics pointed to Pechstein as the most talented painter of the group. Karl Scheffler, editor of the Secessionist *Kunst und Künstler*, on the other hand, spoke of the complete lack of talent in this exhibition, "so that one can by no means take issue with the rejection from the *Sezession.* . . . Significant and personal artists would probably not rise from the group of these youngest decorators." [40] Max Osborn, in *Kunstchronik,* noticed a "whole series of forceful and original talents," and also mentioned the influence of Cézanne, Gauguin, van Gogh, Matisse, and Munch on the young Germans. [41]

Quite suddenly the younger German artists thus came to the attention of the public. Some of the public's reaction, to be sure, was even more negative than Scheffler's review. The *Kunstchronik* also reported that people were found spitting at the paintings, and that a thick, rusty nail was found stuck in Pechstein's *Woman.* [42] Most of the critics, however negative they felt about the group, considered Pechstein the greatest talent and leader of the New Secession. [43]

Soon after the first exhibition the New Secession arranged a second one, this time of graphics, in the fall of 1910. In addition to the artists who had participated in the first exhibition, Rudolf Grossmann and Emil Nolde took part in the second show. This was quickly followed by a third show in the spring of 1911, which brought the Munich group into the first real contact with the north German painters. Marc, Kandinsky, and Jawlensky participated in the third show. Nolde realized the importance of this first coming together of the new trends in German art: "Never again during the following twenty years were such excellent works by our young artists brought together in such a concentrated fashion." [44]

Until this time the regular members of the Brücke had exhibited only as a closed group. Since their two early exhibitions in Dresden—at the lampshade factory and the Salon Richter—they had held small exhibitions of paintings and graphics in the major art centers of north and west Germany, especially in the Rhineland, and also in Denmark, Sweden, and Switzerland. Although they occupied a room of their own at the New Secession, they believed that continued isolation was necessary to keep their aims pure. They also felt that many members of the New Secession lacked talent, and they soon resigned in unison. The New Secession arranged its fourth exhibit in April, 1912. This was an exhibition of prints and drawings, and the New Secessionists César Klein, Bengen, Melzer, and Tappert [45] were joined by August Macke and Wilhelm Morgner. [46] This was the last show of the New Secession, which could not long outlast the withdrawal of the Brücke members. In his review for *Die Kunst* (formerly *Die Kunst für Alle*), Curt Glaser said that the exhibiting body had "lost its best forces." [47]

OTTO MUELLER

Otto Mueller (1874–1930) resigned with the Brücke artists. He had shown one canvas at the first exhibition of the New Secession: *Bathers,* a painting of a nude woman on the beach—rather close to Ludwig von Hofmann's work, but much more conscious in its handling of color and form.

This canvas appealed greatly to the Brücke artists who had come to Berlin. It had none of the flamboyant, explosive quality often associated with German expressionism; instead, like all Mueller's work, it was restrained, gentle, even passive. This motif of bathers was to recur for the rest of his brief life. The angular, almost fleshless figures managed to convey a soft and sensual appeal, and the mood never really changed from a bucolic romanticism.

Mueller, the last painter to join the Brücke, was born in Liebau, a small city in the Riesengebirge in Silesia. His mother, it is believed, was the child of a gypsy, and was brought up in and adopted by the Hauptmann family as a cousin of Carl and Gerhart Hauptmann. His career as an artist started in an apprenticeship to a lithographer in Görlitz, and in 1895 he was at the Art Academy in Dresden. He studied painting and was friendly with the revolutionary writers' circle around Carl and Gerhart Hauptmann, then reaching the first climax of their success. The painter, involved in his early ferment, is the hero of Carl Hauptmann's novel, *Einhart der Lächler.*

Unhappy about the dogmatic teaching at the academy, Mueller left Dresden in 1898, several years before his companions-to-be of the Brücke had arrived there, and secluded himself for a decade in solitude in the Silesian mountains. Interestingly enough, the mythological nudes—such as his *Cleopatra* or *Lucretia*—from this period are remarkably close to the work of Franz von Stuck, not only in subject matter but also in their manner of painting and in composition. It is possible that Mueller actually was in Munich for a brief time during this obscure ten-year period.

When he returned from his isolation and went to Berlin in 1908 he seemed to have formed his own style and technique, as is evidenced in his painting *Two Nudes on the Grass.* He had rediscovered the peculiar qualities of distemper, which medium permitted the unified application of liquid paint in thin layers over large planes. He was thus able to attain an effect like fresco, even tapestry. Kirchner, in the *Chronik der Brücke,* said simply: "He introduced us to the fascination of distemper technique." [48]

This new technique was extremely important, because it helped all the painters to get away from the pastose tenacity of oil and the method of applying paint in thick blotches, and to start painting in the large planes that they had already worked into their woodcuts. The medium seemed especially appropriate to Heckel's style, and he continued to explore its possibilities for many decades.

In addition, Mueller's enthusiasm for Cranach and German Renaissance painting as well as the "sensuous harmony of his life with his work made Mueller a natural member of Brücke." [49]

In the summer of 1910 Mueller and his new friend Kirchner went on a trip to Bohemia. In Prague they met the *avant-garde* artists Emil Filla and Bohumil Kubišta, who were already executing semicubist pictures. An interesting exchange of ideas among the four painters resulted in an exhibition of Brücke paintings and sculpture in Prague under the sponsorship of the Association Manes and reproductions of Brücke work in its review

Volné Smery (Free Trends), as well as in a peripheral membership of Kubiŝta in the Brücke.

THE BRÜCKE EXHIBITION OF 1910

Mueller was still a guest exhibitor in the important Brücke exhibition at the Galerie Arnold in Dresden in 1910. Amiet, Heckel, Kirchner, Pechstein, and Schmidt-Rottluff were also represented. This was the first time that a catalog was published for a Brücke exhibition, and it remains one of the most illuminating documents of the early Brücke style.[50] All the lettering in the catalog was done by the woodcut process, presumably by Kirchner (fig. 15). There is a complete listing of the exhibited works,[51] as well as a brief statement about the activities of the Brücke since its foundation —erroneously predated to 1903.[52] Most interesting are the eighteen woodcuts that form part of the catalog.

Katalog ————————
zur Ausstellung der K. G.
„Brücke" ————————
in Galerie Arnold ————
Dresden • Schloßstraße
September 1910 ————

Figure 15.   Title page, Brücke exhibition catalog,
Galerie Arnold, Dresden, 1910

The group character of the Brücke is especially in evidence in this catalog. One artist frequently made a woodcut of the painting of another, permitting little individuality of his own to show itself. Heckel explained that the reason for this procedure was not a conscious desire for anonymity, but rather a feeling that a more original work would result in this manner than if the painter himself would make a graphic reproduction of his painting.[53] The catalog contained paintings by Kirchner cut in wood by Heckel, Schmidt-Rottluff, or Pechstein, paintings by Pechstein repeated in woodcut by Kirchner and Heckel, and so on. Stylistically the woodcuts are similar, being done in broad but jagged and angular planes of definite blacks and definite whites, executed in a rough, almost savage, woodcut technique.

The frontispiece is a woodcut of Fränzi by Heckel done after Kirchner's color poster for the first Brücke exhibition of 1906 (fig. 16).[54] Rather typical is the figure composition cut by Kirchner after a painting by Heckel (fig. 17). A naked man and woman are in a pose that, although not clearly defined, is suggestive of an approach to coition. The woman is seductive; the man seems less enthusiastic. The bodies are highly distorted—the woman's body is shaped rather like a turnip and is much smaller in scale than that of the man. There is no modeling in depth, and both figures are entirely in a frontal plane; there is some indication of depth behind them on the upper right. The decorative border design on top is probably derived from Oceanic batik work; both it and the legend on the bottom form an integral part of the total design.

Figure 16. ERICH HECKEL Fränzi 1910 Woodcut after poster by Kirchner Frontispiece of Brücke exhibition catalog, Galerie Arnold, Dresden, 1910

Schmidt-Rottluff's view of a building (fig. 18), cut in wood by himself, is stronger and more powerful than his earlier woodcuts, as for example, *Court Church, Dresden* (1906). Enigmatic shapes of powerful blacks and whites are not determined by natural appearances but by the requirement of the woodcut. The spectator is fully aware of the cutting and gouging operation, of the material and the tools.

It is worth noting that Amiet's woodcut *On the Lake* is also very much in the Brücke style in its angular forms and strong opposition of black-and-white areas.

The subject matter throughout the catalog consists of landscapes, sea-scapes, houses, bathers, scenes at the circus, carnival, and racetrack, portraits, human figures. The figures are seen at close range: the spectator is directly confronted with their large and distorted features.

Part of the catalog is a list—cut in wood in Kirchner's hand-hewn Gothic lettering—of the sixty-eight nonprofessional members of the Brücke, mostly in Saxony, Thuringia, the Rhineland, Hamburg (with some twenty mem-

Figure 17. ERNST LUDWIG KIRCHNER Man and
Woman 1910 Woodcut after painting by Heckel

bers), Switzerland, and Sweden. The members, where occupations are given, are primarily professional people. Art historians and critics are nota-bly absent; the only museum curator is Paul Ferdinand Schmidt, of the print room at the Kaiser Friedrich Museum in Magdeburg, who had been buying graphic works of the Brücke since 1905. Gussmann of the Dresden Academy is also listed among the members of the group in 1910, and among the outstanding patrons appear Rosa Schapire and Gustav Schiefler (both from Hamburg).

This exhibition traveled from the Galerie Arnold to the Grand Ducal Museum in Weimar. The next—and largest—Brücke exhibition took place in all the galleries of Fritz Gurlitt in Berlin in April, 1911. By this time most of the Brücke artists had already moved from Dresden to Berlin, driven by lack of recognition, sales, commissions—and food. Berlin seemed to promise all these things. It was in Berlin in the next decade that all the Brücke artists reached the climax of their careers.

Figure 18. KARL SCHMIDT-ROTTLUFF View of a Building with Tower 1910 Woodcut

X

Emil Nolde, 1907-1912

Emil Nolde resigned from the Brücke in the summer of 1907, only a year and a half after having joined.[1] The immediate reason, according to his autobiography, was a series of insulting letters from Schmidt-Rottluff, who had spent the previous summer with Nolde at Alsen. This tension was interpreted differently by Schmidt-Rottluff: "We were immensely pleased about our meeting with Nolde. As young Saxons we were very violent in our criticism of each other, while Nolde was restrained and probably felt uncomfortable. Unfortunately he soon left 'Brücke' again."[2] Nolde felt under pressure because of the conflicts, both personal and artistic, that were inherent in belonging to the closely knit group. He also objected to the similarity developing among the young artists, which left few distinguishing characteristics in their work.

Nolde was probably justified in leaving the group. For the other artists —including Kirchner—the following few years were still a period of groping and early development in which mutual stimulation was essential. The older Nolde was now reaching the climax of his career as a painter. Much earlier than the younger artists, he decided that each had to fight his own battles. He never wanted to be classed with any group, and did not even consider himself an expressionist: "Intellectuals and literati call me an Expressionist; I do not like this narrow classification. A German artist, that I am."[3]

Returning to the solitary Alsen, Nolde continued to paint garden and flower pieces for some time. His motifs never varied much, and certain ones were treated fifteen and twenty times with the greatest perseverance to bring them to full maturity. In his garden pictures of 1907 and 1908 the object—a bed of flowers or an individual flower—is no longer a function of the environment as in his early semi-impressionist pictures; instead, the object has become individualized and much more subjective: it is now the carrier of the painter's own dynamic emotion expressed in pure, symbolic color. Typical is his brilliantly painted *Flower Garden* (pl. 32) of 1907.

Nolde had begun to etch in 1904, but the Brücke artists soon introduced him to the woodcut. His own early training as a wood carver soon enabled him to master the technique. His first woodcut series of 1906 went far beyond his painting, and showed the direction his art was to take. He gave the freest rein to his mystical imagination in these woodcuts, as in the fantastic *Girl with Large Bird* (fig. 19).[4]

Figure 19.   EMIL NOLDE   Girl with Large Bird   1906   Woodcut

He shows an ability to wrest her secrets from nature as well as to enunciate the demonism and witchery of his dreams and visions, expressed in a highly unclassical and, as it were, Low German dialect. He is . . . the most inventive and most versatile German graphic artist of our time.[5]

Nolde's religious paintings, which he began in 1909, were anticipated by his woodcut series. The paintings constitute a climax in German expressionist work, and are related to the Brücke style in their violence of form and content. The first, and in many respects the most effective, was *The Last Supper* (pl. 35).

Throughout his autobiography prevails the deepest religious feeling, from a near Christ identification in his early years [6] to his sudden need for religious self-expression through painting: "I followed an irresistible desire for a representation of the deepest spirituality, religion and fervor, without much will, knowledge or deliberation." [7]

Longing for a primitive religiosity close to magic, he did not follow the well-known iconography of earlier renditions of the motifs when choosing religious subjects; he gave form and color to the vivid concepts of his own people and childhood fantasies, setting forth religious feelings of doom and transcendent spirituality. Nolde expressed what was really an emotional outburst mainly through color. The event was communicated by the dramatic contrast of colors: warm against cold, light against dark, pale against strong.

This visualization by means of color, according to Max Sauerlandt, is the major element that distinguishes Nolde's religious paintings from the religious art of the immediate past: "It is this which gives Nolde's biblical paintings the unmistakable character which removes them far from all religious art of the nineteenth century and permits them to appear related not in form but in emotion to the deepest which the early Middle Ages have created in stained glass and to the art of the seventeenth century." [8]

Color is undoubtedly the most important element in Nolde's art, but there are also other factors to be considered. In *The Last Supper* the illusion of the third dimension is destroyed by the crowded figures, utterly confined, pressing toward the center—the head of Christ. The whole painting has two movements: one pushing toward the center; the other, releasing—or rather exploding—the original thrust and making it burst beyond the frame. The gesture too is in keeping with the general spiritual and mystic content of Nolde's painting. Instead of the dramatic situation of Christ's exclamation in Leonardo's mural ("One of ye shall betray Me"), Nolde shows Christ offering the Eucharistic wine, thereby conveying the impression of self-sacrifice.

The Last Supper was followed, in 1909 and 1910, by the *Pentecost,* the *Derision of Christ, Christ among the Children, The Wise and Foolish Virgins, Joseph's Dream, Christ in Bethany,* and a number of others. In *Christ among the Children* (pl. 36) Nolde again does not present the Saviour with classical dignity or conventional pietism. Christ looms up as an overpowering diagonal shape and is seen from the back. This rear view gives His action an unusual appearance of naturalism. He is bent in a tender gesture of enclosure, and embraces one of the brightly painted little children. His form symbolically separates the light area of the children that were brought to Him for blessing from "His disciples [who] rebuked those that brought them" (Mark 10:13), who occupy the dark areas on the left. Admiration and astonishment are seen on the faces of the apostles; the children have expressions of eager gaiety. As in most of Nolde's paintings, a heavy impasto color has been applied boldly and sketchily, which enhances the emotional quality of the painting.

Less ambitious in size or composition is *Eve,* also painted in 1910 (pl. 37). His Eve is a thin, nude, awkward, bewildered young girl. In great contrast to the confident mother-of-mankind concept, Nolde has painted a personal image of original sin in this tall adolescent. She is shaped like a flame, an impression heightened by her fiery red hair. Her body is generalized, with lean arms hanging from her uncoördinated trunk. Her feet, pointing to the side of an otherwise frontal figure, add to the ungainliness of the girl; the deadly color of her flesh increases her ugliness. Her figure is placed against a jungle background in which a clear azure predominates, a color that is caught again and intensified in tone in her eyes, to give them a startling look of anxiety.

Nolde has described the religious doubts that assailed him at that time and their solution through his work on the canvases. He had rejected all religious dogma, but found his way back to what he felt was the spirit of the Bible through a mystical empathy that he experienced while painting religious scenes. G. F. Hartlaub, who had hoped to see in expressionism the emergence of a great new religious art, found in Nolde the manifestation of man's contemporary attitude to religion: "An era which succeeds in pictorializing the life of Christ and the apostles with passionate vision, as Nolde did, has not ceased to experience these events; on the contrary, it feels them as intense problems. But it is just as certain that the Christian church, liberal or orthodox, will never know what to do with a Nolde." [9]

It was not only the Church that objected to Nolde's religious paintings. In 1910 Max Sauerlandt bought *The Last Supper* for the museum in Halle, of which he was director at the time. This was probably the first so-called expressionist painting purchased by a German public museum. Wilhelm von Bode, Germany's acknowledged arbiter of taste, felt called upon to interfere: "His feeling for art, which barely reached a cognizance of Liebermann's portraits, rebelled against the boldness and intellectual independence which such a young upstart dared to display. He ascended the throne of Zeus and released a thundering curse of anathema upon the transgressor." [10]

Nolde was exhibiting now in many parts of Germany. The same jury that rejected work by the Brücke artists refused Nolde's *Pentecost* for the Berlin Secession of 1910.[11] Nolde's case was actually outrageous. His work had been accepted by the Secession since 1906, and he had been a member of that organization since 1907. The other rejected artists organized the New Secession. Nolde wrote a furious criticism of Max Liebermann, president of the Berlin Secession, in which he accused him of dictatorial methods as well as of bad and repetitive painting. He sent this strongly worded letter to Karl Scheffler, editor of *Kunst und Künstler,* as well as to other men of importance, including Liebermann himself. Scheffler published it together with an editorial antagonistic to Nolde and an announcement of his expulsion from the Berlin Secession for publicly insulting its president.[12]

A constant and often vociferous fight resulted between Nolde on the one hand and the Berlin Secession and the German art dealers on the other. Nolde, always a strong believer in theories of racial superiority and the need for a national German art revival,[13] was frequently guilty of employing openly anti-Semitic attacks against Liebermann and Paul Cassirer, who were leaders of the Berlin Secession, as a means of venting his bitterness toward them; he also decried cubist and constructivist paintings as being of Jewish origin, because he disliked them.[14] It was by no means accidental that Nolde became one of the charter members of the Nazi party in North Schleswig at its foundation in 1920.[15]

Suffering from indignation, Nolde had not taken part in the first exhibition of the New Secession, but he did send a fine new series of etchings to its second show in the autumn of 1910. What he had accomplished the year before in painting, he now achieved in etching, climaxing in the series of *Hamburg Harbor*.

The *Hamburg Harbor* series is not so fantastic in content as the earlier prints. By this time Nolde was thoroughly excited by the real life of the port: the barges, tenders, and tugs. He used steel instead of copper plates, at first because they were cheaper, then because he became fascinated with the toughness and hardness of the steel plate. Frequently combining etching and dry point, he incised hard, brittle lines into the surface. Double biting seems to have been used for his deepest lines. With great sureness he scraped and scratched into the plate, capturing the whole atmosphere of the harbor. There is a certain resemblance between these etchings and earlier woodcuts of the sea by Erich Heckel; Nolde's prints, with their complex technique, are infinitely richer in line and much more exciting as graphic works. In addition they show a more complete understanding of and insight into the variegated life of the harbor. In these etchings he brought to the industrial scene the same legendary vision that had succeeded earlier with his paintings of religious themes.

By 1910, when his graphic works numbered about two hundred, he had a large exhibition at Commeter in Hamburg. The show opened with a eulogy of Nolde by Botho Graef, the Jena archaeologist who had the rare faculty of recognizing the best art of his time. Jena owes its great Hodler murals to him, and immediately after the war he was to be among the first to recognize Kirchner's stature. Nolde's print exhibition was a success, and Gustav Schiefler decided to write a definitive catalog of his graphic work up to 1910.[16]

Before Schiefler's catalog appeared, Nolde had turned to the religious motif in his etchings. As in his painting, a simplification occurred, with the richness of surface in his earlier etchings making way for larger, more basic forms in the new series of etchings, which include *Christ and the Adulteress, Christ among the Scribes, Saul and David, Solomon and His Wives,* and *Joseph and His Brothers.*

ENSOR AND THE INFLUENCE OF TRIBAL ART

Nolde was to find another source of inspiration by delving into primitive art. He began sketching in the ethnological museums around 1910, and was immediately fascinated by the vehement, expressive character of much exotic and primitive art. There he found forms similar to his own in directness, in feeling for tactile form, and in frequent use of grotesque expressions. Tribal art, with its impression of primeval force, was to concern him for a considerable period. One of the first manifestations of this theme in his art was *Masks* (1911) (pl. 38), which also showed the impact of another important influence on Nolde and on German expressionism as a whole.

Nolde was traveling in the Low Countries in the summer of 1911, looking with renewed interest at Rembrandts and van Goghs, when he decided to visit James Ensor at Ostend. Ensor's work was known only to a relatively small number of individuals in Germany, among whom were Alfred Kubin and Paul Klee. Nolde, however, was the first young German painter to establish direct contact with the master of Ostend, who himself had come so close to expressionist painting and was to exert considerable influence on the Germans.

In the 'eighties and 'nineties Ensor had been a very prominent member of Les XX and La Libre Esthètique, but his general antagonism to society finally led him to retire to his native Ostend. There he settled above his mother's souvenir shop full of sea shells, puppets, live parrots, and carnival masks. For a counterpart to the shop below, he crowded his studio with all sorts of knickknacks and trinkets, dolls and marionettes, curios, glass beads, shells, vases, faded lace fabrics, and artificial flowers. It must have looked like a surrealist concept of a Victorian parlor. Visitors described it as reminding them of a mixture of Oriental bazaar, palmist's studio, and horror cabinet. In this weird setting James Ensor created his most important work and received his guests.

The masks cluttering Ensor's studio, typical of those worn in Belgium on Mardi Gras, began to enter his paintings about 1883. These masks helped him express his scorn of society; with their use he was to revenge himself on the citizens who sneered at his work. His grim affection showed preference for doctors, magistrates, bankers, and gendarmes: the pillars of society. He dressed them in masks depicting their platitudinous airs, stupidity, avarice, and pretense. He took the spectator into gambling houses and brothels, and his morbid fancy added the participation of death to these macabre frolics. The etching *Death Pursues the Herd of Mankind* actually comes close to drawings by schizophrenics. Apparently he needed such an outlet for his suffering from and contempt for people. Ensor's consciousness of mass psychoses and his anxiety over mass catastrophe were to recur in Germany in the painting of Ludwig Meidner and the poetry of Georg Heym.

The content of Ensor's religious painting differs completely from Nolde's. In place of Nolde's highly subjective experience of faith in God, Ensor formulates a bitter accusation of his fellow men. His *Entry of Christ into Brussels* (1888) is a huge canvas in the brightest colors combined with great freedom and applied in wild, slashing or swirling strokes. There is extreme confusion in the compact crowd, the tight and menacing ranks of advancing masks and grimacing faces. Christ's figure on the donkey in the background all but disappears. Similar to Dostoevski's famous passage in *The Brothers Karamazov* (published ten years earlier), this is a depiction of the welcome given to the returning Christ—but Ensor does not burn his Christ. More sarcastic than Dostoevski, Ensor makes this an opportunity for a great fair in which all the city gathers in the public square, raises its banners, shouts its slogans, and publicizes its products—completely neglecting, or overwhelming, Christ in the process.

At about this time Ensor painted his strangely visionary *Tribulations of St. Anthony,* the most significant work of his now in America. When it was acquired by the Museum of Modern Art, Alfred Barr called attention to its relation to German expressionist painting: "Ensor's 'St. Anthony' of 1887 surpasses even the late works of Van Gogh and Gauguin in pointing the way to the spontaneous abstract expressionism of Kandinsky a quarter of a century later and the unfettered humor and fantasy of Klee. . . ." [17]

Ensor was one of the significant precursors of German expressionism, but the contrast between his work and that of the expressionist movement is perhaps as important as the similarities. Nowhere is the contrast more apparent than in a comparison of a detail from his *Entry of Christ into Brussels* (pl. 152) with Nolde's *Masks,* which was influenced by the former.

Ensor's style was formulated in the period of impressionism. In the 'eighties he acquired a light, luminous palette that is as indebted to Turner as it is to the French impressionists. He combined this bright color with delicate line and precise draftsmanship into carefully controlled compositions. His interpretation of a diseased mankind did not rely on formal elements, however, but almost entirely on the masks, which burlesque man with diabolic satire.

Nolde, on the other hand, evokes a feeling of terror in *Masks,* not only by his representation of their grotesque shapes, but by his rich, symbolic color, by the angular forms in some of the masks contrasted with almost disintegrating contours in others, and by the much greater place the painter's own fantasy has played in this much less literary painting. In place of Ensor's bitter cynicism, Nolde's masks seem to be attempting to evoke magic connotations.

Nolde continued to be preoccupied with tribal art forms. In 1912, for the introduction to a book on primitive art,[18] he wrote about the greater value of primitive art when contrasted to the so-called perfection of the Greeks and Raphael. Characteristically, he included the medieval sculpture of Naumburg, Magdeburg, and Bamberg among the art of the primitives, and emphasized their freshness as resulting from work in terms of the material. The following year he went to the South Seas. There he believed he would come closer to the sources of creative activity, which to him was closely related to magic and religion.

The Christian religious motif was still uppermost in Nolde's work in 1912 when he created an altarpiece of the life of Christ, a great nine-panel polyptych in the German medieval tradition of the Life and the Passion with the Crucifixion as the center panel. He considered this the most complete expression of his genius, but in the frescolike monumentality of the work, its form and its color, the painting—as Sauerlandt has pointed out [19]

—grew beyond the stage of mere explosive self-expression to become a valid religious symbol.

In the same year he painted the triptych *The Life of St. Mary of Egypt* (pl. 39), which evokes an atmosphere of general insurgence by its gestures and rhythms and—above all—by its blazing red and yellow. The left panel shows the sinful life of Mary of Egypt, the central panel her conversion as she falls violently to her knees before the image of the Virgin, the right panel her death in the presence of St. Zosimus and the lion.

The painting, with the brilliantly yellow, too-ripe body of Maria Aegyptica in the left panel and her sensuous prayer in a religious trance in the center, indicates more than any other expressionist work the very intimate connection between the ecstatic religiosity and the extreme eroticism of these artists. It can readily be seen why Protestant as well as Catholic clergy did not approve of the emotional frenzy of Nolde's religious paintings. When some of the large triptychs and altarpieces were exhibited in the Katharinenkirche of Lübeck in the winter of 1921–1922, a reviewer wrote that only here, where they became a part of the large total structure and where their brilliant colors were muted by the dimness of the church, did they achieve their full effect. Here the colors, which might look brash on the wall of a museum, were able to take on the full and deep glow they were meant to possess.[20]

Nolde's most impressive works were not to be restricted to his big, splashingly colored canvases. The small woodcut *Prophet* (1912) (fig. 20) is as powerful in its way as the large painting. *Prophet* is startling at first glance because of the large areas of black, but the areas left white are actually those chiefly emphasized. Broken by black lines one-half or one inch in thickness, these white areas are largely concentrated in the center of the picture. The white areas—the gaunt cheekbones, the retina of the right eye, the closed lower lip, the high, sloping bony forehead—besides being in the formal center of the picture, are very effective symbols traditionally associated with the prophet. Like a legendary mask, this disembodied head floats into the picture frame and gives the print some of the dramatic intensity of an ikon.

Religious painting was to remain one of Nolde's primary motifs. He often returned to the same subjects as in *Become Ye as Little Children* (pl. 40) as late as 1929. Christ is no longer in a natural pose of embracing the children, but He is conceived as a severe, almost frontal figure in the hieratic gesture of blessing. The spectator's eye follows along the vertical form of the child and focuses on the eye of Christ and His arm, which seem to be illuminated from below. Nolde has reversed the composition from the earlier version,[21] with the disciples appearing on the right and the children on the left. The apostles have masklike faces; the one in the rear is closely related to Oceanic sculpture. The central figure itself is a mystic and incorporeal blond Christ who seems far more a demon of natural forces than part of Christian iconography.

Figure 20. EMIL NOLDE Prophet 1912 Woodcut

The emotional fervor and intense conviction of the earlier phase has given way to a religious painting, more stylized in form and more symbolic in meaning.

Nolde, after his separation from the Brücke, achieved true originality as a colorist and print maker. Being the oldest member of the group, he was perhaps the first of the German expressionists to reach an active, dynamic form that erased visual complexity in favor of barbaric, emotive form. His most important work was a series of religious paintings that manifested the restless and irrational seeking for a new faith—a longing for the divine in which emphatic affirmation conflicted with constant doubt. His colors became violent and symbolic; he combined the logical with the illogical to form fresh, imaginative visual relationships that often shake the observer into a new state of emotional awareness. He gave expression to the consciousness of world crisis and fervent hope for renewal that is characteristic of the entire expressionist movement.

XI

The Brücke Painters in Berlin

Paris and London had for centuries been centers of cultural activity. Germany, however, had no such single focal point. Instead, largely because of the late political unification of the country, Germany had a number of smaller traditional cultural centers. Dresden, Munich, and—beyond the German borders—Vienna were of particular importance for the development of expressionism; the Rhineland also made a unique contribution.

Berlin had grown into a cultural center of considerable significance after the unification of Germany in 1871. Here the imperial court and the Prussian army resided. Here was the center of German commerce and business.

The new capital of the Reich showed the beginnings of growth into a cultural center for the entire country. First performances of revolutionary plays by Ibsen, Strindberg, and Hauptmann had put Berlin in the forefront of the development of new theater. Max Reinhardt, called to Berlin from Vienna, converted the traditional stage into a magic world of symbols. Replacing the scene painter with the "stage architect," he created a stage "at once tribune, pulpit and altar." [1] Writers from all over Germany settled in Berlin. Painters came, and the Berlin Secession assumed a position of leadership in German art and grew into the rallying point for German impressionists. The galleries of progressive art dealers, such as Paul and Bruno Cassirer, Alfred Flechtheim, and later Fritz Gurlitt, J. B. Neumann, and Herwath Walden, became meeting places for appreciators and collectors of modern German and foreign art. Artists and intellectuals of all descriptions lived in an environment mingling Prussian respectability with Bohemian cosmopolitanism. The name of the café where many of these people congregated—Grössenwahn (Megalomania)—is typical of the self-conscious cynicism of Berlin's Bohemia.

The city offered a much stronger stimulus to the Brücke artists than provincial Dresden, as well as a better market. After Pechstein settled in Berlin in 1908, the other Brücke painters followed him, so that by 1911 they were all there. They rallied together in the spring of 1910 with the establishment of the New Secession in response to the refusal by the old Berlin Secession to show the work of the *avant-garde,* and the first exhibition of the New Secession at the Galerie Macht brought the painters to the attention of Berlin for the first time. The Brücke members continued their connection with the New Secession until the autumn of 1911, when they resigned in unison from that body [2] and prepared for the large Brücke exhibition at the Galerie Fritz Gurlitt in the spring of 1912.

Gurlitt, the first dealer to handle the Brücke artists in Berlin, gave them a first, although rather small, exhibit early in 1911. In the same year small exhibits of Brücke paintings and graphic art were held in Danzig, Schwerin, Lübeck, Düren, München-Gladbach, as well as at the Folkwang Museum in Hagen. The most important show of the year, however, was the one at the Galerie Arnold in Dresden (see chap. ix).

The Brücke painters also contributed to the new Berlin periodical *Der Sturm.* This periodical, founded by Herwath Walden in March, 1910, was at first primarily a weekly for literature and criticism, but soon included the visual arts as well. At first Kokoschka was the only artist featured in the journal, but after Max Pechstein's frontispiece of the issue of January 21, 1911, the Brücke painters were frequently called upon to submit drawings and woodcuts for reproduction in the magazine. Between January, 1911, and the spring of 1912, when Walden became more interested in the work of the Blaue Reiter and the futurists, the Brücke artists—Pechstein, Kirchner, Schmidt-Rottluff, Heckel, and Nolde—were responsible for most of the visual material in *Der Sturm.* Walden, however, never sponsored an exhibition of the Brücke.

In the fall of 1911 Kirchner and Pechstein also founded the MUIM Institute,[3] of which they became co-directors. The MUIM Institute announced courses of instruction in painting, graphics, sculpture, tapestry, glass, and metal, as well as "painting in relationship to architecture." This instruction in new media used new approaches (figs. 21, 22). During the summer, *plein-air* painting from the nude model was to take place by the sea. Art appreciation was to be taught through discussion of the new artistic aims and their relationship to modern life.[4] Kirchner's and Pechstein's reputation was not yet established, however, and very few students registered for instruction. The institute was advertised regularly in *Der Sturm* until the summer of 1912, when Kirchner went to Fehmarn and Pechstein to the Baltic coast of East Prussia.

In 1912 Schmidt-Rottluff asked his close friend Lyonel Feininger to join the Brücke.[5] Feininger, however, had just embarked on a new road under the influence of cubism and, feeling that he must continue to develop in his own manner, declined Schmidt-Rottluff's invitation.

The important exhibition at the Galerie Fritz Gurlitt opened in April, 1912. This show, at a well-known modern art gallery, finally brought the painters into the limelight. The press could no longer ignore the Brücke; further, reviews were not entirely unfavorable. Many of the critics in the art journals *Die Kunst, Kunstchronik, Kunst und Künstler,* and *Cicerone* commented favorably on Pechstein, whom they called a highly talented painter for whom the expressive possibilities of form and color were more important than the representation of nature. Pechstein was at that time

Figure 21.   ERNST LUDWIG KIRCHNER
Cover for prospectus of MUIM Institute   1911

generally considered the leader of the Brücke; the comments on Kirchner, Heckel, and Mueller were much less favorable, and Schmidt-Rottluff's arbitrary distortions antagonized the critics.

The Gurlitt exhibition was followed by another large show of the Brücke at Commeter in Hamburg. This show included twelve paintings each by

MUIM-**INSTITUT**
Leiter:
M. Pechstein und E. L. Kirchner

Moderner Unterricht
in Malerei, Graphik, Plastik
Teppich-, Glas-, Metall-Arbeit
:   Malerei   :
in Verbindung mit Architektur

••••••

Unterricht mit neuen Mitteln auf neue Art. Skizzieren nach dem Leben, verbunden mit Komposition.   Unterricht im Institut oder Atelier des Einzelnen. Institut tagsüber zur Verfügung. Im Sommer Freilichtakt an der See. Fördernde Korrektur aus der Eigenart des Einzelnen heraus. _____

Das neuzeitliche Leben ist der Ausgangspunkt des Schaffens.   Die Konversation gibt Einblick in die neuen Kunstbestrebungen.

••••••••

Anleitung zum Verständnis und Anregung durch Anschauung und Erleben (auch für Nichtausübende).

Eintritt jederzeit   1 Monat 60 M.
_____   ½ Monat 40 M.

Unterricht im Atelier des Einzelnen
1 Monat 100 M. — 6 Monate 500 M.

Auskunft und Anmeldung
Wilmersdorf, Durlacher Straße 14, II.
Montag und Sonnabend 12 bis 1 Uhr

Figure 22.   Prospectus of MUIM Institute   1911

Schmidt-Rotluff and Heckel, ten by Kirchner, eight by Mueller, two by Amiet, as well as a large number of drawings, graphics, and sculptured pieces by Heckel and Kirchner. Pechstein's work was absent from the Hamburg exhibition because he had already severed connections with the group.

Commeter published a catalog with woodcuts by the artists. Kirchner's *Dancers* (fig. 23) [6] shows his development toward a steadily more jagged,

Figure 23. ERNST LUDWIG KIRCHNER Dancers 1912
Woodcut from Brücke exhibition catalog, Galerie Commeter,
Hamburg, 1912

angular line. The eye is carried immediately to the white area between the woman's legs, from which the legs exercise an arrowlike pull in opposite directions. The whole composition can be seen as consisting of a repeated V-pattern in various scales: the woman's legs, the small triangular patterns on her dress, the man's tailcoat, his feet—even the total arrangement of the figures on the plane. The obvious defiance of convention in this most erotic picture seems as important as the form itself.

Mueller's woodcut *Bathers* (fig. 24) is much calmer in mood. There is a very simply conceived contrast of black (for the ground, the outlines, the intimation of waves, and the frame) to white (for the bodies and the water). The shapes of the figures are much more graceful and gentle than in Kirchner's woodcut; the pattern is pleasant in its quiet rhythm and symmetrical arrangement. The erotic subject matter lacks the provocative anxieties apparent in Kirchner's picture. The contrast between these two woodcuts is reflected in the individual artistic personalities of Kirchner and Mueller to a considerable extent. This, incidentally, is one of the few woodcuts ever executed by Otto Mueller; technically, it is similar to the woodcuts of Kirchner and the other Brücke artists. Mueller preferred the softer technique of lithography, in which he became a master.

Figure 24.   OTTO MUELLER   Bathers   1912   Woodcut from Brücke exhibition catalog, Galerie Commeter, Hamburg, 1912

PECHSTEIN

Pechstein was achieving considerable success and was thought of as the leader of the new artists because his work was facile and easily understood. In April, 1912, he was given a retrospective exhibition at the Kunsthalle of Mannheim, which was followed by large one-man shows in Magdeburg and at Thannhauser in Munich, at J. B. Neumann's Graphisches Kabinet (which had been opened in Berlin in 1911), and early in 1913 by a large retrospective at Gurlitt. Everywhere his work was acclaimed as a sure and spontaneous statement by the leader of the Brücke and the New Secession. Schmidt's criticism—"the limit of Pechstein's talent seems to be in his inability to find full agreement between the spontaneous freshness of optical experience and the considered form demanded by a painting" [7]—was in the minority.

Typical of Pechstein's work at that time is the color lithograph *Dancing by the Lake* (1912) (pl. 41). It seems to have the spontaneity and freshness of his earlier work, like *Beach at Nidden* of 1911, but the spectator may wonder whether much of this is not actually contrived. The dancing figures are too reminiscent of Matisse, who had a large exhibition at Cassirer in Berlin in 1909.[8] The superimposition of the three tiers of light and dark curves, making a mound in the foreground and recalling similar uses in Chinese painting, seems to have little relationship to the rest of the picture. Earlier in 1912 a large exhibition of East Asiatic art took place in the Berlin Academy.

Similarly under the influence of Matisse and the Fauves, yet without the sensitivity of the French, is Pechstein's painting *Under the Trees* (1913) (pl. 42). He used an almost academic motif—a series of studies of the female figure in movement—but he has added vigorous life to the movement by distorting the muscular bodies, by his swirling line and van Gogh-like brush stroke, and by his use of brilliant color. He has painted the romping women with extreme oversimplification to achieve an effect almost of violence.

During 1913 two articles on Pechstein appeared in the important *Cicerone*,[9] which published no other articles on living artists that year. Soon a series of monographs on Pechstein was published,[10] many years before any other member of the Brücke group received similar recognition.

SCHMIDT-ROTTLUFF

Schmidt-Rottluff's work was much more difficult to comprehend, mainly because he was concerned with complex problems of form rather than with easy solutions. A painting like *Lofthus* (pl. 43), painted in 1911 during his trip to Norway, shows the considerable change that has taken place in his work after the harbor scene of the previous year. The agitated, staccato effect of the earlier painting has given way to a slower movement, a more sonorous harmony. Instead of the violent interaction of Fauve colors, Schmidt-Rottluff now uses broad planes of saturated color, delineated by black-and-red lines. This would give the painting a stained-glass effect, if the rough texture of the canvas, emphasized by the artist's application of the pigment, did not stress the fact that this is a painting. *Lofthus* is severely ordered, bringing to mind Schmidt-Rottluff's earlier training as an architect. The picture is built up with unmixed orange, green, and blue colors, and also with the structural planes of the roofs and walls in the foreground. If the earlier painting was obviously related to Fauvism, this may be perhaps compared to cubism. Writing about Schmidt-Rottluff's work of that time, Alfred Hentzen said: "The axes form themselves into planes in severe and immovable order. One is reminded of the severe style of the contemporary cubists in Paris, to whom there existed no external relationship. The inner necessity of artistic development prescribed similar roads here as there."[11]

Rising Moon (1912) (pl. 153) is also a strongly structured painting, but here the organization of colors, shapes, and space follows the dictates of the artist's feelings. Everything has now become part of a violent thrust, and the observer is confronted with a compelling and threatening landscape. The colors—the orange moon in the apple green sky, the blue houses, the magenta mountain, the brown path, and the almost black cart—are part of this emotional structure, as are the steep, upward-striving triangles. There is no longer any similarity between the actual colors of the objects and the painted colors on the canvas. Colors as well as shapes seem much more deeply felt than in *Lofthus,* and are woven together into an imaginative unity of great pictorial richness and romantic drama.

HECKEL

Heckel, like Mueller, Pechstein, and Schmidt-Rottluff, was concerned with painting the human body in the open air. In *Bathers* (1912 or 1913) (pl. 44) [12] he used the same motif as in his *Landscape with Bathers* (1910), now in the Busch-Reisinger Museum at Harvard University. The paint here is applied in strokes and splashes. When painting water, Heckel was not interested in catching the impression of flickering reflections, but "wanted to paint the way one would knit." [13] He therefore used blue lines for blue, and the white of the canvas itself for his whites. He carefully avoided any suggestion of modeling, and animated his landscape with spindly figures; the lake and the island are vertical planes parallel to the picture plane itself. It is interesting to note that although Schmidt-Rottluff's brush stroke has broadened considerably by this time, Heckel's landscape with bathers consists of much smaller color areas than his previous painting of the same motif. His lines have become more pointed and sharper, and the whole painting seems much more nervous and tense as well as quicker in its movement. Most important perhaps—especially for Heckel's later development—is the fact that the element of light has entered his landscapes and has become a decisive factor.

At the same time Heckel was preoccupied with the human figure. He painted melancholy people with meager bodies and overlarge heads. These figures were pressed into inadequate spaces, thereby giving an impression of restriction and hampered movement. He painted clowns, prostitutes, trapeze artists, musicians, and dancers, but they seemed incapable of free action. In his incisive monograph on Heckel, Ludwig Thormaehlen interpreted Heckel's human beings as tools of masks in which the mask has absorbed the person and the person has sacrificed himself to the mask. [14]

A fairly typical example is the *Head of a Woman* (pl. 45) in strict profile, gazing into space. The head is starkly outlined, and the decidedly curved line carries the emotional content. The carefully drawn head is contrasted to the rest of the body and to the protecting hand with which she grasps her own shoulder. The sharp line and the shading creating the gaunt-ness of cheeks, chin, and mouth as well as the intense eye convey an impression of brooding worry.

A similar emotional content exists in the triptych *To the Sick Woman* (completed in 1913) (pl. 46), one of Heckel's most significant works. In the center an anemic, evidently troubled woman is resting on a bed, which extends into the left panel, where an emaciated, ghostly person with the angularity of a piece of African sculpture looks out at the spectator. The right panel, in which the bed is also continued, is given over primarily to heavy, yellow sunflowers, whose slender stems seem hardly able to sustain their big blossoms. The triptych is also called *Convalescence:* the woman may be interpreted as recovering from a long sickness, and the figure in the left panel may symbolize her during the climax of the illness. Perhaps this triptych—like the similar *Head of a Woman*—can be interpreted as an expression of the sensation of crisis, of which the German intellectuals were so acutely aware in the years before the war. Heckel himself has implied that such an interpretation may be correct.[15]

In 1913 Heckel also painted the *Glass Day* (pl. 154). Light, which was important to Heckel before this, here has become his supreme formal means of expression. Form is broken down in terms of light planes. This breakup into transparent planes of light transforms his surface into crystalline blue transparencies, enhanced by triangular orange forms. The woman in the foreground looks solid and plastic, like a piece of African wood carving, and rocks and water seem shattered into jagged pieces. This effect of fission is ameliorated by the rocks in the immediate foreground, which are still quite solid, and by the cliff in the left background, which is less crystalline and more earthlike in appearance.

The use of directional lines in this painting may indicate an influence of the futurists, who had their first exhibition in Berlin at Der Sturm in the spring of 1912. The transparent planes of color and the attention to light rays suggest a relationship to Delaunay as well as to Marc and Macke; these features occur also in the painting of Heckel's friend Lyonel Feininger at approximately the same time.

Heckel, with his peculiar sensitivity to light and light refraction, has made a unique contribution in this painting. Instead of representing earth and water, he communicates a sense of the structure of a crystal, which is his image of earth and water.

KIRCHNER

By about 1911 the Brücke painters had found their individual forms of expression. How different, for example, Kirchner's *Nude with Hat* (1911) (pl. 47) is from Heckel's *Head of a Woman*. Kirchner's line is still round and smooth, not sharp and angular. His erotic nude is certainly also in complete contrast to Heckel's ascetic women.

Nude with Hat is made up primarily of smoothly curved lines of shoul-

der, arms, breast, face, and hat. These curves can be characterized further
as wide, slow, and easy, and they set up a repeat pattern that is responsible
for the sensuality of the painting. The almost transparent light, the flesh
color, and the blue background establish a lively mood. Attention is focused on the woman's right eye by the dark purple of the hat as well as
by its brim, which is the most emphatic line in the picture. She peers
through the brim of her hat in a provocative and aggressive manner. If at
first this nude recalls nudes by Matisse, an important contrast soon appears
between the pleasant sexuality of a Matisse nude, usually passive, amused
and inviting, and Kirchner's aggressive *Nude with Hat* or *Portrait of a
Woman* (pl. 155),[16] which "at that time represented his ideal of physical
beauty." [17]

The *Lady with Hat* (pl. 48) [18] (1912) represents perhaps one of the
most decisive changes in the development of the artist. The long, smooth,
flowing line has been replaced by a line that is quick, hatched, sharp, and
broken. Color, which had been only an important additive factor before,
has become basic to the construction of the painting. The brush stroke is
left visible, and its quick, short strokes build up the form. There is less
outline, less modeling. The shapes have been laid out on the canvas with
this nervous brush stroke, and the effect is largely that of a flat pattern.
The brush stroke immediately recalls the gouging of the wood block, and
much that Kirchner had developed in his profuse activity as a woodcutter
has here been transferred to the painting medium. The whole painting
vibrates with the excitement of the quick hatch marks, which are retained
within the outline of the narrow chest and head of the woman but explode
outward in the feather of her hat.

The *Dancer* (pl. 156) of the same year uses a similar vibration of hatch
marks. The single figure of a dancing girl twirls on bare boards before a
plain wall, against which has been draped a blue curtain. The long, tapered,
sensitive fingers of her right hand stand out strongly against the blue background; the other hand extends as flat as paper. The dancer's legs taper like
pencils to the points of the toes. The face is extremely simplified, with large
almond-shaped cavities for the eyes. Perhaps because of similar stimulation
from African sources, this face seems related to the earlier precubist heads
by Picasso; years later Jawlensky arrived at similar results. The dancer's
green skirt sweeps out like a fan in an S-curve. The curve is counteracted
on its horizontal axis by the vertically oriented curve of the body itself, so
that an equilibrium or balance is established, bringing the rapid movement
to a standstill. Kirchner does not observe the dancer in an unguarded moment, as Degas had done, but confronts the spectator with her immediate
presence. The movement is rather stiff, and the dancer recalls a sculptured
figurine or a doll. This dancing girl is not an individual, but rather a representation of the "Dancer," and recalls the universal characters of the expressionist playwrights—the "Man," the "Mother," the "Beggar"—rather
than a detailed observation of individual characteristics. Nevertheless, this
very fact is part of an innate contradiction in expressionist thought—the

great emphasis on unbounded individual expression on the one hand, and the establishment of a representative group norm on the other.

A typical landscape of this important and fruitful year—1912—for Kirchner is *Houses in Fehmarn* (pl. 157). The scene is viewed from above; there is the barest indication of a foreground—a quick movement into space, which is then shut off. These compositional devices recall Cézanne, and lead to the assumption that Kirchner at that time was familiar with late Cézanne landscapes.[19] Two buildings on the sides of the picture are placed at sharp diagonals. The village square is in the center of the picture, and the back is closed off with a row of houses and heavily foliated trees. The building on the left is a church whose provincial baroque façade and modest bell cupola, seen from the back and side, are an interesting diversion of curves in a picture that consists primarily of straight, angular lines. The eye reads this picture from the left to right, primarily because of the implied reverse perspective of the house on the right. This form is stopped from falling out of the picture plane by the tree trunk, which leans in at an angle and helps to keep the painting in its self-imposed frame. It is important for the general effect of the picture that the houses in the back also form a slight diagonal. The colors—primarily greens, yellows, and blues—convey an extraordinary richness and warmth that are reminiscent of van Gogh's Arles period. The broken hatch marks of the brush stroke are one reason for dating this painting as 1912; another is the compositional resemblance to Cézanne. Early in 1912 Kirchner worked on murals as decoration for the chapel in the Sonderbund exhibition in Cologne, and had an excellent opportunity to study the twenty-six paintings by Cézanne that were an important part of the exhibition.

Most of Kirchner's energy at this time went into an attempt to understand and formulate his reactions to the city. He seems to have loved city life but was also frightened by it. He wrote about the loneliest times in his life when he was driven to walk restlessly in the streets. In his explanatory notes to his woodcuts for *Peter Schlemihl*,[20] he talked about his undefined hopes in loneliness, when he looked for a god among men but was unable to find one, and how his solitude was only increased by the pulsating life of the city. He then described how the resultant fear needed expression, which he found in painting the rhythm of the men walking through the city streets—thousands of people with individual faces, all in the unreal color of electric light.

Kirchner made a great many drawings to capture these impressions (pl. 49). He was specifically interested in recording the emotional, not the visual, sensation of city life, and he comprehended the presence of man as an important part of the total impression.

The Street (1913) (pl. 50) is one of the most important paintings of a long series on the city. It is related to the *Street* of 1907, but the change in style from the curvilinear earlier treatment to the swift, jagged brush stroke of linear hatch mark in the later work is significant. Three people—two women and a man—are in the center of the picture. Behind them mills an indefinite number of people. All are in city dress, giving the effect of supersophistication, increased by their pointed forms in both body and dress. At the right a gentleman, grasping his cane behind him, leans forward to look into a shop window. Behind him, just left of center, two women with large feathered hats and fur collars turn to each other. There is an interesting psychological rhythm of attention: the man looks in the window, the central woman turns left to the woman by her side, who in turn looks across to the man and the window. Everything is pointed: shoes, coats, collars, hat brims, hands, noses, ears, and the figures themselves. All forms give the impression of sliding down from the picture plane toward the spectator, largely because of the uptilted perspective of the painting and the diagonal running through the picture. These diagonals also create action in a picture that would otherwise be static. The people themselves perform quiet tasks: looking in windows, walking, chatting. But the lines are so sharp, diametrically opposed, and harsh—jabbing into the picture space, plunging out again—that they transmit a quality of unusual excitement to this ordinary scene. The same effect is produced by the immediate contrast of light and dark: the bright furs and light hat, the light skin tones, the dark clothes, the light sidewalk and window, the dark automobile with its white tires—a sign of the machine age—in the background. Kirchner has reinterpreted a perfectly ordinary scene, has given it a highly personal form and has communicated it with extraordinary success.

THE "CHRONIK DER BRÜCKE" AND COLLAPSE

The work done by the Brücke artists in 1912 and 1913 was no longer characterized by a fairly uniform style, like their earlier endeavors. Each individual artist had found a personal means of expression. This by itself, as well as the broader basis of the Berlin art world and the many new artistic stimuli, weakened the coherence of the group.

The last Brücke portfolio was published in 1912, and included three prints by Pechstein (one etching, one lithograph, and one woodcut) and a woodcut cover by Mueller. This portfolio was never distributed to the membership.[21] One reason for this nondistribution was Pechstein's leaving the Brücke at that time. According to Kirchner's *Chronik der Brücke*, Pechstein was expelled for exhibiting by himself in the Berlin Secession, thereby breaking faith with a decision of the group to show their work only jointly.[22] According to Pechstein's own statement, he withdrew because of Kirchner's too personal judgments about the group.[23]

For 1913 the artists had planned to publish a chronicle of the movement. This was to be a joint expression of the group: a history, a visual statement of the work, and a manifesto. Each member was to participate. The *Chronik* was to contain prints by each of the artists and photographs by Kirchner of their paintings, who was also to write the text.

The text, however, did not correspond to the estimation of the facts as seen by Schmidt-Rottluff, Mueller and myself and was opposed to our concept which rejected the programmatic, so that we decided not to publish the *Chronik*. Each one received his prints and a part of the text. Kirchner later cut the title page with the four portraits and assembled a few copies in Switzerland, of which you have been able to acquire one for the Kestner-Museum.[24]

Figure 25.   ERNST LUDWIG KIRCHNER   Title page of "Chronik der Brücke" 1913 Woodcut

The *Chronik* is a rather personal statement by Kirchner, and each extant copy differs from the others as to content. The copy in the print room of Zentralinstitut für Kunstgeschichte in Munich has seventy-four pages, and measures $52 \times 68\frac{1}{2}$ cm. It contains the following:

Title page, printed in red, with lettering cut in wood by Kirchner and portraits of Kirchner, Heckel, Schmidt-Rottluff, and Mueller (fig. 25).

Table of contents. This is inaccurate when compared with the actual compilation of the Munich chronicle.

Text of the actual *Chronik* with marginal woodcuts: two each by Kirchner, Schmidt-Rottluff, and Heckel.[25]

List of the "Friends of the Brücke," and a list of the "Members of the Brücke."

Several photographs taken by Kirchner and pasted into the book. These dark photographs seem to have been taken at the Brücke exhibition at Gurlitt in Berlin.

Kirchner's essay "Über die Malerei." Here he said that exact representation is now the task of photography, and that painting "is the art which represents a sense experience on the two-dimensional plane." He also said that, although order is seen in the finished work, there can be no rules in art.

Photographs of paintings by:

Amiet: 1 painting (landscape)

Heckel: 8 paintings (landscapes, figure pieces, bathers)

Kirchner: 4 paintings (heads, nudes, city scenes)

Mueller: 7 paintings (nudes, lake scenes)

Schmidt-Rottluff: 4 paintings (self-portrait, landscapes, nudes)

Kirchner's essay, "Über die Graphik." The key sentence of this brief essay is: "The motivation for the graphic arts is the artist's desire to communicate the manual aspect of his personality through mechanical means."

Seventeen lithographs and woodcuts (originals) by Amiet, Heckel, Kirchner, Mueller, and Schmidt-Rottluff (fig. 26).[26]

Figure 26.   ERNST LUDWIG KIRCHNER   Head of Otto Mueller   1913
Color Woodcut

Kirchner's editing of the *Chronik der Brücke* and its repudiation by the other members of the group were the immediate causes of the dissolution of the group. Probably the maturity that the individual members had achieved in the Berlin years was at the root of their rejection of Kirchner's continued leadership. Each then went his own path, according to his individual desires.

Kirchner himself became antagonistic toward his former associates. He refused to take part in the exhibitions of the former Brücke members that were arranged by Karl Nierendorf and by J. B. Neumann in the 1920's. In spite of his bitterness, however, he painted from memory a most remarkable group portrait—*The Painters of the Brücke* (pl. 51)—of Mueller, Kirchner, Heckel, and Schmidt-Rottluff, when he lived alone at "Wildboden" in the mountains near Davos. The other Brücke painters, however, remained friends, and certain clear parallels can be traced—especially in the development of Heckel, Pechstein, and Schmidt-Rottluff.

PART FOUR

Expressionist Trends in Vienna

XII

The Vienna Secession, Klimt, and Schiele

The development of expressionism in Austria was an inherent part of the history of German expressionism. The separation of the two countries is political; the cultural relations between them are exceedingly close. Oskar Kokoschka, leader of expressionism in Vienna in his early years, later became one of the principal exponents of that movement in Germany. Egon Schiele was recognized in Germany long before he achieved recognition in his native Austria.

Vienna itself is of great importance in any consideration of expressionism, because of the different currents that merged there and specifically influenced the movement. Vienna's geographic position on the Danube made it a major trading post between eastern and western Europe. The Habsburg Empire of Francis Joseph embraced a great variety of national ethnic groups: Germans, Hungarians, Czechs, Slovaks, Rumanians, Slovenes, Serbs, Poles, Italians, Greeks, Ruthenians, gypsies. There were even more languages than nationality groups: although German was the language of the official bureaucracy, people in Vienna spoke also Czech, Yiddish, or French, depending on national, religious, or class status. Roman Catholicism was the official state religion, but the empire had many severe Czech Protestant churches, synagogues, Greek Orthodox churches, and even mosques in the southeastern provinces. During the final stages of the decay of Habsburg rule, imperial pomp was celebrated in an elaborate eighteenth-century manner, in the "City of Festivals," while the ordinary populace sought a more relaxed enjoyment in the Prater and the Vienna Woods.

The Industrial Revolution was late in coming to Austria-Hungary. Taking advantage of the rich mineral resources—especially those in the Bohemian provinces—the Austrian middle class eventually shifted increasingly toward industrialization. By the 1890's, in a rapid growth of wealth and power, Austria was nearly as industrial as Germany, France, and England.

The monarchy was beset with many problems arising from the increasing conflict of the nationalities and the mounting tension between classes.

Now the growing, prosperous Viennese bourgeoisie wished to establish itself on a par with those of the western nations, not only economically but also culturally. The meteoric rise to power of a middle class in what had formerly been largely feudal territory took place concurrently with an important development in most aspects of cultural activity.

Toward the end of the nineteenth century men asserted their faith in the significance of external reality. Mach and his followers investigated the problem of relationships between mental and physical phenomena on the basis of the phenomenal world and within the limits of scientific thinking, and positivist philosophy came close to being a theoretical science. A generation later, Sigmund Freud, himself emerging from a background of scientific research in clinical neurology, delved into hitherto unexplored realms of the human mind. In 1900 he published *The Interpretation of Dreams,* which contains what he felt were his most valuable discoveries.[1] By analysis of the dream, man can, according to Freud, gain conscious access to his unconscious wishes, which an overcivilized society forces him to conceal. Estranged by civilization and social convention, man is forced to repress his true desires; this repression plunges him into the anxieties and neuroses of modern times. Freud's theories—his penetration beyond man's self-deception to the unconscious self and his interpretation of art as the successful sublimation of the libido toward creative pursuits—are highly important for an understanding of the art of his time.

Austria's great traditional art—music—now turned toward "expressionism" in the atonality of Schönberg and the spasmodic eruptions of Béla Bartók's powerful early compositions. The Viennese theater, with its tradition of pomp, music, and visual excitement, gave rise to Max Reinhardt's stage design. In literature Arthur Schnitzler pinpointed the decadent life of the *fin de siècle* Viennese in a brilliant series of plays and novels, enveloping his accusations in a diaphonous veil of satire. Karl Kraus attacked the Austrian bourgeoisie with incisive analysis and biting irony in his periodical *Die Fackel* and in the strongly pacifist play *Die Letzten Tage der Menschheit.* Peter Altenberg wrote highly sensitive impressionist prose poetry. Hugo von Hofmannsthal turned toward a new romanticism with the melancholy evocation of the past in his lyric poetry. Unsuccessful in his attempt to escape from a cruel present, von Hofmannsthal frequently chose a passive surrender, made palatable to his supersensitive personality by the incantation of exquisite moods. At times, as in the libretto for Richard Strauss' *Elektra,* he reached a Dionysiac outburst of the inner self, like the expressionist writers. Franz Werfel, in the next generation, concerned himself with the problem of man's relationship to God and the liberation of the soul, and with the expressionist search for the "new man" in the "new community." Kokoschka's plays were concerned with the eternal man-woman conflict expressed through nonrational and instinctive primordial urges.

In the same period a new approach to the history of art, relating it closely to the history of culture, was developed by a group of Viennese art historians, foremost of whom were Franz Wickhoff, Alois Riegl, and Max Dvořák. Young critics were receptive to the new movement, and Hermann Bahr became one of its spokesmen. Arthur Roessler of the *Arbeiter Zeitung* became Egon Schiele's patron; Hans Tietze, the art historian, was one of the earliest supporters of Kokoschka.

In this era of general cultural activity the visual arts in Austria underwent a vigorous revival, giving birth to forms more in keeping with the new social, economic, and cultural conditions of the country. It is interesting, however, that these forms emphasized the decadence of the culture.

THE VIENNA SECESSION

In 1897, nineteen leading artists of Austria organized the Vienna Secession (officially called the Vereinigung Bildender Künstler Österreichs). In January, 1898, they published the first issue of their organ *Ver Sacrum*. Hermann Bahr, one of the editors of this publication, pointed out the important difference between the Vienna Secession and the earlier Secessions in Berlin and Munich. In the German cities the younger artists opposed the old tradition with their own new concepts of esthetic form, but in Vienna there was no tradition in the plastic arts.

Here in Vienna we do not fight for or against tradition, because we do not have any. There can be no struggle between the new and the old art, since the old art is nonexistent. We do not fight about a development or change in art, but for art itself, for the right to create artistically. . . . It is not the struggle between two concepts of art, but between art and peddling.[2]

Bahr added, as if he had known beforehand the fate of Oskar Kokoschka, the most important product of this revival: "One must know how to make oneself hated. The Viennese respects only those people whom he despises. . . . The Viennese painters will have to show whether or not they know how to be agitators. This is the meaning of our Secession." [3]

A survey of Austrian painting in the second half of the nineteenth century shows that Bahr was quite justified in his scorn for the lack of tradition. Vienna, like a provincial city, followed far behind western Europe. When impressionism was at its climax, painters like Pettenkofen or Emil Jakob Schindler depicted the Austrian and Hungarian landscapes and their people in the manner of the Barbizon painters.

Hans Makart's (1840–1884) style was not at all original, but was largely derived from Delaroche, Piloty, and Lenbach, and then further aggrandized. He is responsible for huge academic machines, such as the *Plague in Florence* or *The Entry of Charles V into Antwerp,* and was commissioned to execute decorative works of vast dimensions and glowing colors —extremely ornate, sensational pieces. His big paintings of victory processions enjoyed the greatest popularity in the 'seventies and 'eighties when he was the arbiter of Viennese taste; the Makart bouquet and Makart hat were stand-bys of Viennese *décor*.

More interesting were the large history paintings by Anton Romako (1834–1889), done in brilliantly glowing color with a baroque fervor and in an impressionist technique that seem more closely related to the eighteenth-century painters Guardi and Maulpertsch than to the impressionists themselves. Romako was the only recent artist whom Kokoschka credited with having made a deep impression on him.[4]

This love for sumptuousness and lavish ornament remained an important element, and became an immediate source of the Viennese version of the international Art Nouveau movement, which was known in Vienna by its most revolutionary name: "Secessionstil." Art Nouveau seems to have reached its most bizarre extremes in Vienna: the Viennese preference for the audacious and exotic had manifested itself twenty years earlier in the popularity of Makart, who "imported soft eastern cushions . . . and bedecked everything with carpets, Indian shawls and Persian textiles."[5]

At the International Exposition in Paris in 1900—in one of the high peaks of the Art Nouveau movement—the Austrian pavilion, designed by Hoffmann and Olbrich, stood out for its ornaments, its freely applied luxury, its use of expensive and exquisite materials. A typical reaction to the pavilion is the following excerpt from a review by Arsène Alexandre in the *Figaro Illustré:*

Nowhere have the new ideas of decoration been so favorably received as in Austria; and it must be admitted that her artists have made the most of them by adapting these novel formulae to suit the spirit of the race, which we, for our part, have not succeeded in doing as yet.[6]

The fact that by 1900 the imperial government of Austria was represented by the Secessionists indicates that the agitators of three years earlier had achieved a phenomenal success. This was largely the result of the efforts of three extremely talented young architects, designers, and decorators: Josef Maria Olbrich, Koloman Moser, and Josef Hoffmann. These men took the lead in the new arts and crafts movement in Vienna, and succeeded in persuading Vienna's older architect Otto Wagner to join the Secession in 1899.

Many indications pointed to success for the new style. Wagner had been appointed professor of architecture at the Vienna Academy in 1894. From his chair, as well as in his highly important book, *Moderne Architektur,* he taught that artistic creation must spring from its only possible source: contemporary life. Attacking historicism (and he himself had formerly built Renaissance revival buildings), he stated his firm belief in new principles of construction and in the use of new materials in keeping with a technological age. Arthur von Scala, director of the Austrian Museum for Art and Industry, began publishing *Kunst und Kunsthandwerk* in 1897, which became one of the most important organs of Art Nouveau in Austria although it never went to the extremes of the Secession publication *Ver Sacrum.*

Vienna suddenly emerged from its cultural provincialism to become a center of the new art movement. The membership list published in the first issue of *Ver Sacrum* in January, 1898, includes the honorary as well as resident members, and gives clear evidence of the cosmopolitan atmosphere of the group: Carrière, Paris; W. Crane, London; L. Dill, Munich; A. Hölzel, Dachau; M. Klinger, Leipzig; M. Liebermann, Berlin; F. Mackensen, Worpswede; C. Meunier, Brussels; Puvis de Chavannes, Paris; A. Rodin, Paris; Segantini, Seglio de Van Bregaglio; Lucien Simon, Paris; F. von Stuck, Munich; and Fritz von Uhde, Munich. Although this list is surprising as much for its strange omissions as for its rather haphazard combination, it does include many of the outstanding European artists of various trends, and helps to explain the reasons for the international quality of the new style. Rudolf Alt, a painter and etcher of traditional landscapes and cityscapes, served as honorary president. But the president of the Secession and one of its most active leaders was Klimt.

GUSTAV KLIMT

Gustav Klimt was born in one of Vienna's suburbs in 1862, and received a traditional academic training at the Vienna Kunstgewerbeschule. Makart's pretentious paintings were then at the height of their popularity among the fashionable Viennese on the Ringstrasse; he shared his glory only with Anselm Feuerbach, who had recently completed a ceiling fresco at the academy —*The Fall of the Titans,* a large neobaroque piece of decoration.

Klimt's own talent clearly tended toward decorative painting, and with his brother Ernst Klimt and Franz Matsche he executed large decorative commissions in the accepted style. These were usually murals and curtains for theaters in Vienna, Reichenberg, Fiume, and Karlsbad. Gustav Klimt's early work differs from that of Makart and the artists of the previous generation primarily in its unconcern with historical anecdote, in its greater emphasis on linear organization, and in a composition largely in terms of verticals and horizontals. Instead of continuing Vienna's baroque tradition, Klimt drew from archaic Greek vase painting, late Byzantine mosaics, and Japanese prints.

About 1895 he became acquainted for the first time with contemporary western art, and for a brief period painted some impressionist pictures, probably under the direct influence of Theodor von Hörmann, Austria's leading impressionist painter. Not until 1897 and the foundation of the Secession did Klimt come into a distinctive style of his own.

Among the foreign painters, it is difficult to say who had the greatest influence on Klimt. Schmalenbach, in his treatment of Jugendstil, said: "Klimt's style would be unthinkable without the influence of Toorop and Minne." [7] The importance of Toorop was reiterated by Gustav Glück; [8]

another Klimt biographer said that Khnopff was primarily responsible for
the change in style of Klimt and the Secession group in general.[9] A number
of artists tending toward a linear symbolism—names such as Burne-Jones,
Rops, Beardsley, and Stuck come to mind, in addition to those already mentioned—seem to have been responsible for Klimt's new "exaggerated sensual
sensations." [10] The result was that Klimt's painting became *Secessionsstil*
preëminently.

The leading Viennese painter, famous well beyond the border of his own country,
was then Gustav Klimt, an artist so typical of *art nouveau* that a more characteristic
example of that international style could hardly be found. If *art nouveau* was an
art of the surface—and a beautifully ornamented surface—of flowing curves and
delicate figures, of ephemeral beauty and rich ornamentation, or poetical, sometimes
symbolic subject, a feminine and decadent art—Klimt was its quintessence.[11]

Although this definition takes into account only one aspect—the decorative
—of Art Nouveau, it largely characterizes its Viennese corollary: *Secessionsstil*. However, it must be stated that Klimt also had ambitions toward
monumental mural decoration.

At this time Klimt turned toward a very personal eroticism. His drawings frequently included Lesbian scenes; he drew nudes in suggestive
poses, with particular emphasis on pelvis, pubic hair, breasts. In his paintings he added lustrous skin colors to the slim, angular bodies of his sensuous
young women, and set them off against a richly ornamented background;
often he applied real gold and silver to his canvases. He was probably inspired by Byzantine art in this application of metal to the picture plane,
but he also anticipated its use in the modern collage. In many respects
Klimt was the bridge between the old and the new—a function that was
clearly recognized by the stage designer Josef Urban, who was also leader of
the Viennese artists' organization, the Hagenbund: "His [Klimt's] greatest contribution to modern painting lies in the fact that he served as a bridge
between two styles—impressionism and expressionism, and found his supreme power in the combination of both." [12]

During the late 'nineties Klimt was in great demand as a portrait painter
of Viennese ladies. In these portraits he was by no means concerned with
the personality of the sitters—most of them had rather vapid facial expressions; rather, he turned them into highly ornamental society types. The
elaborate costumes of his ephemeral ladies became a part of the flat design
of the background; the more definitely modeled head and hands are likely
to stand out in disconcerting contrast.

His late portrait of Frederica Beer (1916) (pl. 52) essentially continued
his earlier adapted style of portraiture, except that Oriental decoration has
here become an absorbing preoccupation. The figure does not rest firmly
on the ground, but her feet hover over the flat carpet in the manner of
Byzantine reliefs; the elaborate *décor* of the woman's garments melts almost
imperceptibly into the Chinese wall hanging of the background. In striking

contrast, a very realistically conceived portrait head stands out against the decorative ensemble of the rest of the painting.

In his later landscapes and flower pieces he similarly strove toward purely ornamental values, and completely filled the picture space with a linear, carpetlike pattern of strong color. Representational elements were interwoven with freely invented geometric ornaments, and the whole canvas was executed with a festive ornateness suggestive of the handicraft products of the other Secessionists.

In 1900 Klimt was commissioned to execute allegorical paintings of the faculties of philosophy, medicine, and jurisprudence for the University of Vienna. This was a chance to attempt achievement of the Art Nouveau ideal of unified total decoration. Throngs of people circulate before allegorical figures of Love and Hygeia in *Philosophy* and *Medicine,* respectively. The slightly later *Jurisprudence* (1903) is simplified toward two-dimensionality and stylized to a geometric, mosaiclike tightness of composition. These paintings show perhaps most clearly the attempt by one of Art Nouveau's finest painters to achieve monumental decoration and—conversely—his inability to get beyond arts-and-crafts embellishment. The exhibition of these murals caused a vociferous protest from both public and university administration, resulting in the artist's withdrawal of the paintings.[13]

After this experience Klimt withdrew from public life, but continued to work vigorously in his small studio house surrounded by the huge flower garden he had painted so frequently. This studio was filled not only with his own work but also with a large collection of exotic art. "Around the rooms were hung in close proximity Japanese woodcuts and two large Chinese paintings. On the floor lay Negro sculptures, in the corner by the window stood a red and black Japanese armor."[14]

In 1902 Klimt executed another monumental decoration. At the time Vienna was enthralled with Klinger's bombastic Beethoven statue (*cf.* pl. 4). Josef Hoffmann built a temple to house it in Olbrich's Secession building, and Klimt did an allegorical frieze in the temple symbolizing mankind's yearning for release from the sinister powers of sin. This mural made a tremendous impression on the younger painters in Vienna, and Schiele considered it the climax of Klimt's work.[15]

In the same year the Vienna Secessionists were instrumental in the foundation of the Wiener Werkstätten under Josef Hoffmann's direction, an organization of designers and craftsmen who were interested in greater functionalism in the Viennese arts-and-crafts movement. Hoffmann himself showed a tendency to simplify the planar surface in his quietly elegant Palais Stoclet of 1905 in Brussels.

In the arts-and-crafts spirit, Hoffmann asked Klimt to design a large mosaic decoration. To stress the value of the wall as wall, Hoffmann frames his plain white surfaces with a heavy gold border. Similarly, there is no longer any three-dimensional illusion in Klimt's mural. The three motifs

—tree of life, dancer, and lovers embracing—are subordinated to a flat, ornamental structure of triangles, ovals, curves, volutes, and free arabesques. Klimt has here arrived at a restrained emotional expression through geometric form. His talent, which had always tended toward the decorative, found perhaps its fullest expression in this abstract surface decoration of glowing color. The designs were executed in a mosaic of glass and semiprecious stones, majolica, white marble, metal, and enamel; the overworked cliché of "Oriental splendor" describes them with some justification.

The Stoclet frieze determined Klimt's style for the remainder of his career. *The Kiss* (1908) (pl. 53), with its abstract mosaic pattern,[16] followed the same trend. The sensual quality of his work is maintained in the sinuous contours and brilliant array of glowing colors. His concern with symbolism appears in the spiral ornament on the woman's garment and the dominant rectangle on the man's robe. The amoeba shape of the group recurs in, among other things, the less severely outlined "free form" of the 1930's.

When Klimt died, a victim of the influenza epidemic of 1918, his symbolic decoration was no longer in the vanguard of pictorial expression. Younger Viennese painters, like Schiele and Kokoschka, had gone far beyond the style Klimt helped create. "It was for an intermediary like Gustav Klimt to clean the atmosphere and clear the ground on which . . . the autochthonous art of a painter like Oskar Kokoschka could take root."[17]

Because of his highly personal style Klimt had no pupils, but both Schiele and Kokoschka held him in the deepest admiration. The other important influence on Austrian painting in the first few years of the decade was the Secession's exhibition of Ferdinand Hodler in the winter of 1903–1904.

FERDINAND HODLER'S INFLUENCE IN VIENNA

Josef Hoffmann built galleries in the most elegant *Secessionsstil* for this exhibit. Hodler shared honors with Edvard Munch and Hans von Marées as the most important invited guest, but it was Hodler who was acclaimed master of the new form. Hodler's influence was decisive for the whole younger generation of German painters. Nolde became aware of Hodler's importance during his stay in Switzerland in the 1890's. Kirchner, much inspired by the Swiss master some twenty years later, acknowledged his debt in the form of a magnificent color woodcut portrait of Hodler. Fritz Burger, in his influential books,[18] considered Hodler next to Cézanne as the cornerstone of twentieth-century art. Hodler is mentioned in the context of the early expressionist movement in Vienna because it was there that his rhythmically drawn, definite outlines, his tight structure and strong symbolism had the most significant effect.

In his symbolism Hodler never resorts to the multitude of literary images of his Swiss-German predecessor Arnold Böcklin. Instead, he stresses the evocative quality of his formal relationships. He divides his composition severely into verticals and horizontals, or distributes forms over a two-dimensional picture plane, so that everything seems to revolve around a central core. Color is never used to combine forms but always to separate and distinguish them clearly, and he employs his vivid line for the same purpose. Hodler simplifies his figures and their garments to the utmost, eliminating everything that is accessory, transitory, or accidental. The landscape background is void of all naturalistic space concepts, and is used as a foil to set off the rhythmic movement of his figures. This measured rhythmic movement or "eurythmy" is the very essence of his paintings: "The interrelationship of the harmony of the form-rhythm of nature with the rhythm of emotion: this I call Eurythmy." [19]

In Hodler's painting *Eurythmy* (1895) (pl. 54a), the significance of old age is interpreted with great simplicity. Five old men are advancing from infinity and walking into infinity in a rhythmic movement comparable to that in the Ravenna mosaics or in the modern dance. Their path is a metaphor of the eternal law that leads them on. The gestures and bearing of his figures are similar.

Hodler saw in nature a constant repetition, which he called "parallelism." According to his philosophy of parallelism, each individual appearance of the real world is a primary force. This force eternally produces forms, necessarily similar to one another, that always express the same universal law.

In Hodler's *Admired Youth* (1903–1904) (pl. 54b),[20] three women—spaced at regular intervals—create a repeated rhythm. They walk in a severely restricted picture plane. Together they form a segment of an arch pointing toward the nude youth in the lower right, who stands upright in a frontal position. Again parallelism is clearly expressed. Hodler was concerned, not with diversity, but with universality and unity: "We know and we all feel in certain moments that that which unifies us human beings is stronger than that which separates us." [21] C. Loosli has emphasized the important social significance inherent in Hodler's visualization of the idea of human solidarity.[22] Hodler conceived of a brotherhood of man, similar to Schiller's ideas in "Ode to Joy," used by Beethoven in the Ninth Symphony.

Hodler's ideas were close to those of the generation of German painters that followed him. Hodler achieved his expressive content by indirect means, whereby the positions of his models and their gestures and movement were distorted to express the mood the artist wanted to convey. Hodler, as Paul Klee felt,[23] was masterful in the representation of man and his actions, but he was no painter. Color, light and shade, and texture have little place in his work—it was his symbolism that made Hodler of such extraordinary importance in the first decade of the century. The figure in Hodler's painting is, as in a play, the intermediary between the artist's idea and the spectator.

The first Austrian painter to come under Hodler's influence was Egger-Lienz (1868–1926), who belonged to Klimt's generation. In his powerful, sometimes almost brutal, scenes of Alpine people, man takes on the gnarled appearance of the mountain pines and rock formation. (This same use of a semipersonification is also found in much of Hodler's work.) Egger-Lienz's line does not have Klimt's subtle sophistication, but is rough-hewn. His figures are massive symbols of strength executed in Hodler's flat, linear, rhythmic manner. Although Egger-Lienz is in many aspects close to the expressionists, his external symbolism of the motif betrays his adherence to the older Jugendstil generation. Schiele or Kokoschka no longer used an apparatus of allegory to communicate their experience.

EGON SCHIELE

Egon Schiele (1890–1918), belonging to the expressionist generation succeeding Egger-Lienz, was also to experience Hodler's influence. He probably did not see the great Hodler exhibition that was held in Vienna at the time when he, a boy of thirteen, was attending the old monastery school at Klosterneuburg. But many of Hodler's paintings entered Carl Renninghaus' collection, where Schiele was to become familiar with them. The first important influence on Schiele was, however, the work of Klimt.

Schiele, born in the small, middle-class town of Tulln on the Danube, and schooled in Klosterneuburg, arrived at the Art Academy of Vienna in 1906. The sixteen-year-old boy was considered a child prodigy by his academic teachers, but by 1908 he had broken with the academy in an attempt to find a more personal style. This was also the year in which he held his first public showing, an exhibition sponsored by the Catholic authorities in Klosterneuburg. Although these earliest paintings by Schiele show some definite influence of Klimt and the Secessionists and a break with academic tradition, they are by no means as advanced or revolutionary as the work with which Kokoschka shocked the public that year at the Vienna Kunstschau. Schiele, younger by four years, is discussed before Kokoschka because the stylistic development is considered more important than strict chronology, and Schiele's more stylized, linear work still appears transitional.

In 1909 the Kunstschau of the previous year was repeated, to give the modern Austrian painters an opportunity to exhibit, since the Secession gallery had closed. The Kunstschau was international in scope, including work by van Gogh, Gauguin, Vallotton, Bonnard, Vuillard, Matisse, Minne, Toorop, Munch, Liebermann, and Corinth. Among the Viennese painters Klimt drew the greatest admiration and Kokoschka the greatest antagonism. Klimt, who had met Schiele earlier that year, invited the young painter to participate in the show. Schiele sent four paintings, which were almost as controversial as Kokoschka's. The critic Arthur Roessler remarked on his extraordinary talent, and became not only Schiele's patron and spokesman but also his closest friend. Typical of Schiele's work exhibited at the 1909 Kunstschau was a landscape that combined impressionist freshness of color with the stylized surface decoration of the Secessionists.

In this period Schiele came very much under Klimt's influence. Schiele's work is highly decorative; his landscapes are built up in horizontal strips or arranged in flat, mosaiclike patterns; and at all times the line is the dominant element. Schiele is, above all, a graphic artist and draftsman. Color in his oils and water colors is often intense, and may possess symbolic meaning; but the color is applied afterward, handled in a draftsmanlike manner, emphasizing and clarifying his delineatory structure.

By 1910 Schiele's work had achieved a good deal of independence. At this time he and a number of similarly oriented Viennese artists founded a new organization: the Neukunstgruppe Wien. The group exhibited in the Salon Pisco in Vienna; perhaps the most important work shown was Schiele's *The Self-Seer* (pl. 55), painted that year.

The expressive force of line, lack of space, and concern with symbolism certainly recall Klimt, but "the spiny, thorny, angular, Gothic character of Schiele's forms, their acrid aspect, their withered surfaces mark them as the very antipodes of a world of culture and luxury." [24] Klimt's decorations are never involved in the same introspection and self-doubt. Similar as Schiele's work may at first seem to that of his spiritual master, the great difference is between the joy of the nineteenth-century artist and the doubt, suffering, and emotional tension of the twentieth-century painter.

In *The Self-Seer* the background is not decorated, but consists of stagelike drapery; the figures stand out against the light that emerges through a cleftlike opening in the darkness. The Jugendstil line has become hardened, angular, and rough. The former elegance of slender figures is replaced by ugly, undeveloped bodies with enlarged joints and greatly emphasized, overlarge heads and hands. The space in which these enigmatic figures exist is undefined; their gestures seem meaningful—but of what? Is it a desire for self-revelation or a concealment of the self behind a mask? The relationship between the dual aspects of the figure is left ambiguous. The painting shows a state of severe anxiety and an attempt at self-analysis—further emphasized by its title: *The Self-Seer*.[25] The adolescent bodies seem exhausted with overindulgence. There is an emphasis on their nudity and on sex, accentuated by the very absence of genitalia. The painting is indeed a product of autoeroticism. The hair is given a most unusual treatment; its virility seems to be a substitution for the castration of the body, which is further emphasized by the missing or hidden arm. Schiele painted himself with an undeveloped body and an adult face; his self-image is a sardonic expression of consciousness of the intellect.

"Seeing" in this sense was the essence of art for Schiele. In the aphoristic language typical of his verbal statements, he said: "The painter is not yet the artist; it is the spirit which has created art. . . . The painter too can look. But to see is a great deal more." [26]

Schiele, like Klimt before him, was concerned with the erotic in art, but in the younger painter this concern bordered on obsession. Where Klimt masked his involvement behind nineteenth-century allegories and evasions, Schiele openly stated—even overstated—his fancies and frustrations. Many of his almost pornographic drawings and water colors are exceedingly gruesome, surpassing Lautrec, Beardsley, and even Rops. His drawings of erotica finally caused his imprisonment without charge by a narrow-minded provincial court in 1912. During his twenty-four days in prison Schiele produced a series of some of his most sensitive drawings and water colors. His incarceration remains a symptom of his constant conflict with bourgeois society.[27]

Schiele's work continued to show numerous direct influences—it could be called eclectic if it did not have his personal flavor of intense emotion. His *Room of the Artist in Neulengbach* (1911) (pl. 56) strikingly resembles van Gogh's *Bedroom in Arles,* even to the arrangement of the furniture in the room. The point of view is from above, to give greater verticality to the painting. Certain objects, however, like the shelves and the night table, are rendered from other angles, making a highly distorted perspective. The emphasis on the head, which was so strong in *The Self-Seer,* is here symbolized by the pillow that occupies half the bed. The spectator constantly feels that Schiele had a need to control his impulses by the intellect.[28] Whereas van Gogh's bedroom had three openings, one window, and two doors, Schiele's is totally closed. Seeking complete isolation, he leaves no outlet to the outside world. He places everything he needs for frugal living in this barren and ascetic room. There, in an affirmation of the self, he finds it necessary to sign his name on the rising floor three times in large, self-conscious letters.

The emphasis on a large empty space is related to the Jugendstil concern with voids, but in Schiele's work it suggests a desolate mood considerably stronger than the sentimental loneliness pervading much Jugendstil work. Forty years later, similar linear forms evoking a similar emotion of despair appear in the work of the French painter Bernard Buffet.

When Schiele exhibited his work in the large Hagenbund exhibition of 1911, the public was so preoccupied with its angry disapproval of Kokoschka that it took little cognizance of Schiele's paintings. Only much later did Schiele gain recognition in Austria. Between 1911 and the outbreak of the war in 1914, however, he showed in Munich, Düsseldorf, Hamburg, Rome, Paris, and Brussels, thus establishing an important international reputation.

Hodler's influence on Schiele appears strongest around 1912 in a painting like *Sunrise* (pl. 57). In this painting Schiele used, not only Hodler's motif of the repetition of a symbolic object clearly outlined against the open sky, but also his rhythmic, linear unity of composition and his expressive drawing and firm contours. The foliage creates linear Jugendstil patterns, but the prismatic rays of the sun suggest semicubist elements to be found from time to time in Schiele's work.

A similar interest in the possibilities of linear and planar pattern motivates *The Bridge* of 1913 (pl. 158). The series of overlapping planes constituting the strikingly foreshortened bridge are themselves constructed of an intricate linear webwork in the understructure and a delicate open framework above. This emphatic contrast is repeated in other modes: the complicated organization of the bridge is counteracted by the large, smooth planes and softly contoured forms in the right half of the picture, and the moderate tones of buff and ocher are suddenly interrupted by the brightly painted barge—a unique, almost playful manipulation of somber color.

Schiele's *Girl in Green Stockings* (1914) (pl. 58), an excellent example of his work near the beginning of the war, displays his fondness for strange positions, bold foreshortening of the human body, and overlapping forms. The water color is typical in its linear derivation, and shows the artist's increasing interest in abstract geometric forms—it seems to be composed with a compass. Prominent is his use of interlocking curves that fit into each other and serve more than one purpose. Benesch [29] has observed correctly that the circular arches of the eyebrows also define the nose ridge, and that the curve of the jaw coincides with the ellipsis of the collar bone. Convexities answer concavities. The body itself is not unified, but built up of linear fragments: head, rump, joints, stockings. Color is again an afterthought, and serves the free, expressive quality of the line. It, too, has become removed from optical reality. Green, red, purple, and ocher are splashed over the figure to bring out the appearance of disintegration in the body of the girl. She is obviously meant to be both erotically suggestive and disgusting, and combines a rather masculine figure with pronounced feminine characteristics. In pictures like this Schiele became independent of his various sources, and found his own medium of expression based primarily on a linear rhythm that delineated his emotional anxieties.

Soon after his marriage in 1915 Schiele was drafted into the Austrian army. A thorough individualist and a highly sensitive person, he hated the very thought of the war. Though he continued working, his output necessarily became fragmentary and there was no possibility for important artistic growth. However, a development from his linear abstraction of 1914 toward greater freedom of expression and a more uninhibited flow of line is clearly noticeable.

Real recognition came to him during the war. The Berlin publication *Die Aktion,* organ of the activist (rationalist) wing of the expressionist movement, devoted the pictorial part of one issue (September, 1916) entirely to Egon Schiele, familiarizing Berlin artists with his work. The same year two portfolios of his drawings were published in Vienna. In March, 1918, the Secession gave him a retrospective one-man show that proved an enormous success. When Gustav Klimt succumbed to the influenza epidemic a month later, Schiele was immediately chosen leader of the young and progressive artists of Vienna in their new organization, the Klimtgruppe.

In 1918 Schiele painted his weird, magnetic *Portrait of Paris von Guetersloh* (pl. 59). This canvas—in spite of its looser brush stroke, its richly worked, Kokoschka-like surface—has a great deal in common with *The Self-Seer,* done eight years earlier when he was in the first stages of artistic development. As in *The Self-Seer,* the basic element is line, which not only delineates the form but in its zigzag angularity causes much of the nervously emotional appearance of the sitter. Von Guetersloh's pose is rigidly frontal. He seems to be in a hypnotic trance or about to hynotize the spectator, an effect that is enhanced by the large, fixed eyes and the upraised hands—the palm of one turned outward, the palm of the other inward, toward himself. Only the painter von Guetersloh is important. There is a suggestion of the chair in which he sits, but the background has been reduced to a nimbuslike radiation and emphasis around his figure. Here the paint has been applied with impulsive, dynamic strokes, strangely foretelling the working method of the New York abstractionists of the 1940's.

At this very apex of his career Schiele himself fell victim to the influenza epidemic, and died three days after his wife in October, 1918.

When Schiele died, the twenty-eight-year-old artist had already achieved a truly independent stature. Perhaps his subjective creations, highly disturbed yet definitely under his mental and emotional control, are to be evaluated as more than a mere "link between the decorative qualities of Klimt and the seemingly spontaneous calligraphy of Kokoschka." [30]

XIII
Oskar Kokoschka, 1905-1910

By the time Schiele died—so soon after having gained public recognition in Vienna—Oskar Kokoschka's stature as an artist was widely acknowledged. Although he was only thirty-two, two important monographs had already been devoted to him.[1] In addition to having done about a hundred paintings, he had completed six plays—four of which had been performed—as well as a large number of articles and some criticism. Generally recognized as one of the leaders of German expressionism, he was even appointed to a professorship at the Dresden Academy of Fine Arts.[2] But a visual as well as a political revolution had been necessary to make this acknowledgment of Kokoschka a possibility. The appointment of this radical artist to the old academy of Dresden is symptomatic of the victory of expressionism in postwar Germany.

Almost from the beginning, Kokoschka was not only a most individualistic artist but a highly finished one also. Although he studied at the School for Arts and Crafts and later instructed there, Kokoschka was actually self-taught.[3]

When Kokoschka first appeared before the public with his exhibitions at the Kunstschau of 1908 and 1909, he encountered a violence of reaction that is rare even in the annals of modern art. From these very first exhibitions—and this is why he was so "shocking"—he showed an independent, original style. Many historians of modern art have puzzled over the problem of the derivation of Kokoschka's painting, especially of his penetrating early portraits, which are in many ways the very essence of expressionism. "Kokoschka's style, like that of Edvard Munch, is decorative and expressionist from the very beginning."[4] But why? Kokoschka's personality always inclined to rebellion and protest, but why would his opposition to romantic academic painting take the particular shape it did?

He himself has told us very little; it is possible only to mention the known early influences, and to analyze his first work in the light of what is known about it and in terms of the internal content of the work itself.

Kokoschka's father was a highly skilled craftsman, a goldsmith trained in the old tradition in Prague. His craft was out of place in the new industrial society of Austria, where he had gone. His traditional snuffboxes and jewelry—completely at variance with fashionable Art Nouveau styles—were no longer in demand, so that the fortunes of the Kokoschka family declined to the level of impoverishment. Kokoschka himself wrote: "The introduction of shoddy methods of production, the rise of new, purely commercial values, destroyed the craftsman's human dignity and brought direct suffering to my father. From him I learned to endure poverty rather than work slavishly at distasteful work." [5]

From an early age Kokoschka felt at odds with society, but his father was also able to transmit something else: he was a learned, literary man who infused his children with love for the writers of the Enlightenment from Comenius to Lessing. Kokoschka's mother, of peasant stock, brought him an appreciation and understanding of nature, and interesting overtones from her reputation for "second sight."

Arriving in Vienna when he was quite young, Kokoschka spent much of his time in the ethnological collections, where he admired South Sea masks, Japanese woodcuts, and all sorts of exotic cult images while ignoring the famous painting collections.

The European painter whom he thoroughly appreciated was Anton Franz Maulpertsch, probably for his turbulent baroque rhythm, the seemingly arbitrary use of brilliant color, his free imagination, and the visionary qualities of his work. Among recent painters Anton Romako, with his neobaroque frescoes, most impressed Kokoschka.

In many ways the key to Kokoschka's painting is the Austrian baroque tradition, which seems to have continued in his work. Kokoschka was born in 1886 in Pöchlarn on the Danube near the magnificent baroque monastery of Melk, and most of his life was to be spent in Vienna, Dresden, Prague, Salzburg—cities permeated with baroque traditions. He felt himself a part of this environment, and his lifelong admiration for the seventeenth-century pedagogue Comenius is a part of this identification. "It was the Baroque inheritance I took over, unconsciously still. Just as it offered itself to my dazzled eyes as a boy singing in choir in the Austrian cathedrals, I saw the wall paintings of Gran, the Kremser Schmidt, and of the outspoken extremist amongst them, Maulpertsch. . . ." [6] Throughout his life he expressed a longing for the baroque, which he considered the last manifestation of humanist culture and human dignity before mechanization set in: "The lover of Baroque art recognizes today that during that period men desired nothing more or less than the realization of the prophesied paradise." [7] But there is nothing neobaroque in Kokoschka's work. This is not a revival, but similar basic emotions that show themselves in wild fantasy, violent rolling and rocking effects, indistinct merging of forms, undulating line, and a painterly approach to color.

The link with this national style of Austria is basic to the derivation and development of Kokoschka's work. It may be the reason why he has been able to achieve stature as an artist, going far beyond expressionism as a trend or style in twentieth-century painting. The lack of a principle of form was always the weakness of the German expressionists; Kokoschka had the advantage of Maulpertsch and the Austrian baroque, which he could renew in the idiom of his own time.[8]

The baroque tradition is still submerged in Kokoschka's earliest drawings, done in 1907 while he was a student and assistant teacher at the School for Arts and Crafts. These pen or pencil sketches from the nude model are shorthand characterizations in contour with little detail. The line does not flow easily, as in Klimt, whom Kokoschka greatly admired at this time; it is abrupt, inarticulate, and somewhat awkward, and is used chiefly as a rather naïve expression of the warm attractiveness of full-breasted, maternal bodies or the dejection of angular figures.

From the time of his earliest drawings, Kokoschka's work can be seen as a documentation of his own process of individuation. He shocked the Kunstschau of 1908 with his first self-portrait, a polychrome head in clay (pl. 60).[9] This self-portrait is in many ways a key to Kokoschka's early work, in spite of the fact that it is sculpture, a medium that he evidently used in 1907 several months before turning to oil and then discarded. Clearly a painter's sculpture, the self-portrait lacks a true feeling for three-dimensional volume, for the clay is laid on in daubs like paint. At the same time it is a very accomplished work, amazingly so for a first attempt. The frequent statement that Kokoschka began as a skilled artist is certainly justified by an analysis of this sculpture. Further, its romantic expression and its form of bumps and hollows show that the young Kokoschka was receptive to Rodin, whose work had been shown by the Vienna Secession for about a decade.

One of Kokoschka's first important works was this self-portrait. He was twenty-one years old at the time, but he saw himself as a much older man in a state of derangement. His face is bony, gaunt, and almost old with its deep wrinkles and gasping mouth. He is a man assailed by fears and anxieties, drawing back from the world—not toward self-isolation, but rather into a self-conscious hostility.

The same exhibition also included a series of decorative panels by Kokoschka, *Die Traumtragenden* (*The Dream Bearers*), which was bought by the Wiener Werkstätte but has since been lost. Paul Westheim suggested that these panels probably resembled the illustrations to *Die träumenden Knaben* (*The Dreaming Boys*),[10] a book commissioned by the Wiener Werkstätte and published in 1908.[11] Kokoschka had both written and illustrated this richly imaginative fairy tale, which was intended for children but which became a record of his own experiences. With little regard for composition he crammed the pages with symbols of his own sensations. There is little coherence in space or time; as in the medieval illuminations, sun and moon appear simultaneously; size relationship seems to be determined arbitrarily by the artist.

Unlike the clay self-portrait, the human beings in *The Dreaming Boys* are far from violent. They have the gentleness of innocent fairy-tale figures. Kokoschka's illustrations are not the expression of a rude awakening; they are replete with the dreams of adolescence, but in this dream the lean boys and girls seem lost and insecure in their Garden of Eden. The great variety of images is subordinated to a flat, over-all pattern. The book contains eight lithographs, in black, blue, green, yellow, and red.[12] The harmonious arrangement of pairs of complementaries—green and red, yellow and blue—as well as the decorative pattern effect, clearly shows the Jugendstil derivation; not by accident was the book dedicated to Gustav Klimt. Instead of the exquisitely refined subtleties of Klimt's ornament, Kokoschka's color prints are much closer to the popular Austrian ornate and naïve peasant art, with its flat areas of color and simplified design, which was achieving a wide vogue at that time.

The young boy in the last of the lithographs (pl. 61a) is evidently derived quite directly from Ferdinand Hodler's *The Admired Youth* (pl. 54b). Kokoschka did not share Hodler's positive optimism and idealized concept of nature and man. Kokoschka's concept of man is that of a puzzling, inconsistent, frantic creature. Yet in these eight color illustrations for *The Dreaming Boys* he does evoke the image of an ideal world in which human beings and natural forms are intimately interwoven. For a short time Kokoschka worked under the spell of both Klimt and Hodler, but soon was to probe deeper as a painter than either into the anxieties of his fellow human beings.

Hodler was one of the first to become aware of the work of the young Kokoschka, whom he evidently met on one of his trips to Vienna: "Hodler told of a newly discovered Viennese child prodigy, who was painter, draftsman and poet at the same time." [13] Joseph Lux, reviewing the Kunstschau for the Jugendstil publication *Deutsche Kunst und Dekoration*, compared Kokoschka to Rimbaud, "who wrote astonishing verses at seventeen," and found Rimbaud's "drunken, unrestrained verses related to the color intoxications of Kokoschka's puberty legends." [14] Kokoschka was almost as active in poetry as he was in painting, and had completed two verse plays by 1908: *Sphinx und Strohmann* and *Mörder, Hoffnung der Frauen*.[15] These plays combined original concepts with a new, frequently obscure use of language. Far from the fairy-tale ideal of *The Dreaming Boys,* their theme is the eternal conflict between man and woman, which results in the final irrational victory of woman over man. The conflict is expressed through symbolic characters and choruses, exalted language, and cruel, irrational actions. The antigrammatical attitude of expressionist literature had its beginnings in Kokoschka's *Mörder, Hoffnung der Frauen.* Samuel and Thomas, in their excellent treatise on expressionist literature, refer to Kokoschka as "the first expressionist writer, who distorted language radically in 1907: omissions of parts of sentences, arbitrary word order." [16]

At the time of the Kunstschau of 1908 it would still have been difficult to say toward which field of creative expression Kokoschka would develop. His exhibitions and his plays had outraged the citizenry of Vienna, and

Kokoschka became the center of a heated public controversy, which also brought him to the attention of, and acceptance by, the powerful Viennese *avant-garde*.

Adolf Loos was the first to recognize Kokoschka's great talent. Loos, a firm exponent of functional architecture—the very concepts of modern architectural design for use begin with Adolf Loos and his battles against Jugendstil ornament in the late 'nineties—also recognized the validity of creative expression in painting.[17]

Loos introduced Kokoschka to other leading Viennese intellectuals: the poet Peter Altenberg, the writer Karl Kraus, the actor Reinhold, the art historians Hans and Erica Tietze, became his friends and his models. The new world of the intellectual fascinated him; he, the painter, felt impelled to grasp it by painting its image: the face of the intellectual himself. This Kokoschka saw as restless and anxious—the face of a man who could, for example, explain the reality of existence but was unable to deal with it, who may be frightened by it because he understood it so well. In each of this long series of portraits the artist's own concept was expressed through a remarkable understanding of the sitter.[18]

Paul Westheim, Hans Heilmaier, and Leopold Zahn have attempted to give psychological explanations of these portraits by observing that Kokoschka's first great experience was with death—that of his brother when Kokoschka was five.[19] Kokoschka himself has said nothing about the effect this experience had on his development, and it is by no means necessary to seek an explanation of his profound pessimism in this particular event. When Kokoschka painted these portraits he was the object of general ridicule: he had been dismissed from his position, was poverty-stricken, and was able to gain the recognition of only a small group of intellectuals who themselves were rejected by the citizenry whom they scorned in turn. Vienna was quite aware of the decay of its culture—indeed, it was fashionable to enjoy the decadence in a continuation of the best *fin de siècle* manner. Perhaps it was an exciting sensation to be close to the end. Kokoschka too felt this decadence, but did not see it playfully. Recently he commented on his early portraits: "My early black portraits arose in Vienna before the World War; the people lived in security yet they were all afraid. I felt this through their cultivated form of living which was still derived from the Baroque; I painted them in their anxiety and pain."[20]

Edith Hoffmann has given a fairly complete account of the early portraits—the "black portraits," as the artist himself referred to them. These can be clearly divided into the dark and linear portraits painted between 1907 and 1910 in Vienna and Switzerland and those of a looser, more pictorial and frequently more symbolic nature done in Berlin and Vienna between 1910 and 1914.

In the winter of 1907–1908 Kokoschka spent much of his time as a house guest of Oskar Reichel, one of his early patrons and collectors. In return for the hospitality Kokoschka painted his *Still Life* [21] for Dr. Reichel, an almost black painting combining a turtle, a mouse, an axolotl, a skinned lamb, a brown jug, and a flowering hyacinth. This strange array of objects is set into an exceedingly narrow space and painted in the darkest values. The arbitrary highlighting of certain areas—such as the skull of the lamb, the threatening little rodent, and the flowering plant—gives an eerie and morbid effect that establishes a link between the *fin de siècle* generation's enjoyment of decadence and the surrealists. In motif this still life stands almost alone in Kokoschka's early work.

Immediately he decided to paint Oskar Reichel's son, who was sick in bed at the time. The painter spent little time at the boy's bedside, but painted his *Portrait of a Boy* (1908) (pl. 61b) almost entirely from memory.[22] This portrait, one of Kokoschka's earliest, has a simple composition, resembling a parallelogram. It is rather flat, but the slight twist of the figure—one hand behind his head, the other opened in a grasping gesture in the immediate foreground—gives a certain feeling of space. The boy looks like a young dancer; even his costume—a blue blouse, which Hans Reichel never owned—is like a leotard. The dark blue of the blouse seems to merge with the neutral background; face and hands are emphasized by their pallid color. This very sparing use of color conveys the impression of an anemic, sensitive boy, who might be the end of a long, highly pedigreed line. Hanno Buddenbrook or Tonio Kröger might look like this.[23] The hands of the boy are thin, curved, and opened; the left one seems to have stiffened in a clawing pose.[24] The eyes are deep-set and large, one significantly larger and more plastic than the other to emphasize the sensitivity of the child. This emphasis on eyes and hands is evident in a long series of Kokoschka's portraits.

Perhaps slightly earlier than the *Portrait of a Boy* is the portrait of the actor Reinhold, called *The Trance Player* (pl. 62a).[25] Unlike his other "black" portraits of this period, *The Trance Player* is light in color and almost impressionist in its broken brush stroke. The actor, against a bright background of light grays, blues, and pinks, has a pink face and hands, and wears an indistinct, dark suit. He is characterized by a high forehead, long wavy hair, a pudgy neck, and a highly sensitive and pleading facial expression. Most important are two extraordinary characteristics: excessively long, heavy-lidded, light eyes and an enormous, powerfully tensed left hand. The long, red-rimmed eyes hold the spectator. In an otherwise fairly ordinary face they are striking, and call the attention back again and again because of their very strangeness. Their half-closed appearance makes them seem mysterious, secret—above all, unusual. If it were not for the white shirt and blue tie—a blue that picks up the blue of the eyes—the spectator would not move his glance from the eyes. The arrow-shaped shirt and tie point downward to the big hand, which seems to strike chords on the strings of a musical instrument. The four plucking fingers are thick and huge—not at all those of a typical instrumental musician. Attached to the body of this plump-faced man with the exotic eyes, these fingers suggest incongruities—they suggest power also. This weird little man compels with his powerful hand—here he has a kind of magic. What an astonishing result for a "first oil painting"!

In Kokoschka's plays, written at the same time, he used nameless characters—such as the Man and the Woman—as Strindberg had done, perhaps recalling the universality for which Hodler was striving. But in his portraits Kokoschka transformed his sitters into highly individualized figures whose magnetism lies not so much in a timeless universality as in their very individuality. I cannot agree with Hoffmann's statement that *The Trance Player* "is illustrative of Kokoschka's tendency to transform familiar individuals into fundamental human types." [26] Rather, these portraits attract the spectator's attention because of their difference and strangeness, not only from the rest of the world but from one another. The subjects of the portraits may all have large, shadowed eyes, tensed hands, and skin painted in colors to suggest corruption, but each faces us with his own peculiar characteristics—or those the painter chose to give him, expressing the premium placed on individuality, on difference, on personal identity. Yet the artist's own self is also projected into these portraits.

Approximately a year later Kokoschka painted his first double portrait: of the art historians Hans and Erica Tietze (1909) (pl. 159). The painter solves the difficult problem presented by any double portrait by placing the two figures at right angles to each other and concentrating the spectator's interest on a kind of dialogue between the hands. The hands form a truncated triangle leading the eye to the space between the two figures, then to the expressive faces of the two individuals, and back again to arms and hands. Color has become more vital now. The canvas is alive with irridescent pigment into which small figures and lines have been scratched. These "seem to form a whole organic world in themselves, foreshadowing in fact some creations by Paul Klee, who, years later, found in similar images both the subject matter and the formal starting point of whole pictures." [27] Against this background, and at times merging with it, appear the two figures. The woman—in frontal pose, monolithic, almost inert, in form and expression—recalls the Roman encaustic mummy portraits from Egypt; the man—outgoing, demanding response, gesturing with his heavy large hands—is the active force against her passivity. The most exciting passage in this painting is perhaps the tension created by Tietze's two gesturing hands.

In 1909 Kokoschka painted a portrait of Adolf Loos: a pointed observation, done rapidly and fluidly with a high, flickering light to emphasize essential elements. Interestingly enough, the portrait of his closest friend, patron, and protector is much less psychologically searching and more objective and detached (cf. fig. 28). [28]

Kokoschka did a striking portrait of the court tailor Ebenstein, in exchange for the fashionable clothes Kokoschka needed for Loos' invitations to court balls. Of the poet Peter Altenberg, Kokoschka executed a moving portrait of a desperate, overwrought man, a helpless figure coming forward with hands reaching out in supplication and with eyes distorted by fear.

The excited line, the asymmetric eyes, and the frightened expression are repeated in most of the early portraits, which are therefore not entirely free of mannerism. The same is also true of the great sixteenth-century mannerists themselves.[29] The historical study of mannerism was just about to begin at this time.

Only one of this series of portraits—*The Trance Player*—was sent to the Second International Kunstschau in 1909. This exhibition was considerably broader in scope than that of the previous year; it contained, among other things, the first public showing of Schiele's work.

Hodler, Loos, and Tietze expressed their admiration for Kokoschka's painting, but the Viennese public was highly affronted by it. Kokoschka, now frequently referred to as the *Bürgerschreck,* was further to alarm Vienna by the performance of his plays *Sphinx und Strohmann* and *Hoffnung der Frauen* at the open-air theater of the Kunstschau. A public scandal resulted from these performances, and Adolf Loos—who had become Kokoschka's guardian angel by this time—after intervening on the artist's behalf with the police, decided that the time had come for Kokoschka to get away from Vienna.

Late in 1909 Loos took Kokoschka with him to Switzerland. For years Kokoschka had known only city life, and had been fascinated by urbanites; now suddenly his eyes opened to the grandeur of mountain landscapes.

Winter Landscape, Dent du Midi (1909) (pl. 62b) was his first step in the direction of landscape painting, later to become his principal activity for several decades. This landscape is arranged in four receding planes. Closest to the observer are representations of sleigh and dog, done in a primitive, childlike manner. Behind this plane are the precisely outlined trees reminiscent of Breughel's winter landscapes. The third plane is formed by low hills, followed by the hazy mountains. All these parallel layers are unified on the right by a sharply foreshortened area. The sun over the mountains is a yellow ball embedded in fog and mist. The whole distant area, in its haziness as well as the light hues and thin application of pigment, recalls Turner's late landscapes. Kokoschka, however, contrasts this haziness with the clarity of the objects in the foreground.

In Switzerland, Kokoschka painted Loos' wife in a tuberculosis sanitarium, and became fascinated by the patients he saw enduring intellectual as well as physical suffering. His portraits painted early in 1910 show the same interest in disease and death that formed the catalytic agent for Thomas Mann's study of a disintegrating society in *The Magic Mountain.*[30]

Count Verona seems both mentally deformed and physically decayed. *The Duchess of Rohan-Montesquieu,* emaciated and hyperintellectual, presents a strange reversion to an earlier, thoroughly flat style. The linear pattern of the carefully posed figure shows a calculated relationship to the long and narrow frame. Its excessive stylization, especially of the elongated hands, may indicate less personal commitment on the part of the artist.

Kokoschka must have been deeply involved in the portrait he did of Auguste Forel (pl. 63) early in 1910. Loos brought the two men together, either by letter [31] or through personal introduction,[32] to have "the greatest artist of the future" paint the portrait of "the most famous scholar in the world." [33] Kokoschka spent several weeks with the Forel family, but

Auguste Forel was not interested in sitting for the painter. He had little understanding of modern painting; a convinced atheist, he was reluctant to "have his soul painted." [34] The scientific work of the psychiatrist and entomologist was not to be disturbed; Kokoschka had to observe him at work or during naps in the evening. The painter, affected by the presence of a great and incisive mind, felt that his task was to give a visual equivalent of the scholar's mental power. Here were eyes that were accustomed to seeing behind the outer appearance of objects, and hands infinitely skilled in the laboratory. The old man's wrinkles seemed to the painter "like documents of a life's experiment." [35] The completed painting was rejected by Forel and his family. They said that it was not a good likeness of the scholar, who did not look as old as Kokoschka's portrait would have him; the face seemed overtired, the hair was faded, the right eye blind, the hands strangely constricted.

Much has been said about Kokoschka's psychological insight, his "second sight," his painting of the "inner life," his premonition—especially in the early portraits. He is said to have painted his models as they actually appeared twenty years later. Karl Gruber, a personal friend of Forel's, recently said that only about four months after Kokoschka painted this portrait, Forel suffered a stroke that paralyzed the right half of his body, especially the right hand and eye. The right hand drooped; the left hand assumed the very gesture as seen in the picture; the right eye appeared dim. The deep sadness of existence was stamped in his face, exactly as in the portrait.[36]

Kokoschka returned to Vienna after his visit with Forel, but he was restless and went on to Munich. There, instead of forming contacts with the *avant-garde* Bavarian and Russian painters, he became acquainted with Gustav Meyrink, the imaginative writer of fantastic prose. After a few weeks he returned to Vienna, where he met Herwath Walden. Writer, journalist, composer, and critic, Walden was in the process of establishing *Der Sturm*—both journal and gallery—nucleus of new expressionist creations in all the arts in the fruitful years in Berlin before, during, and after the first World War. Kokoschka became the first illustrator of *Der Sturm*.

The Portrait of Mrs. K. (ca. 1911) (pl. 64) dates from this period of transition.[37] The face is more carefully modeled and more individualized than the rest of the body, showing the persistence of the Klimt influence. Color and light play a more important role in this portrait than in earlier ones. A criss-cross web of lines relates the figure to its background. But the danger of mannerism is now evident, especially in the long, thin, emaciated hands—now a stylistic characteristic of Kokoschka's portraits. Here the thin, supersensitive hands seem to clash with the highly competent and somewhat prosaic face.

During the prewar years in Berlin and Vienna, Kokoschka found a new approach to pigment, to brush work, to the use of light and dramatic movement—toward a most individual twentieth-century style. Wilhelm Hausenstein called it "baroque expressionism," [38] indicating that a bridge between the eighteenth and twentieth centuries was possible.

PART FIVE

The Development of Expressionism
in Munich

XIV

Munich at the Turn of the Century:
Kandinsky's Beginnings

At the end of the nineteenth century, Munich had an artistic life of extraordinary activity and variety.

Franz von Lenbach, still exceedingly powerful in his old age, represented the official art sponsored by the court of the Wittelsbachs. He had painted innumerable state portraits, not only of Bismarck, but also of the celebrated men of a whole generation: Kaiser Wilhelm I, Kaiser Wilhelm II, Pope Leo XIII, Moltke, Helmholtz, Gladstone, Wagner, Mommsen. His reign over the Munich school was passed on to Friedrich August von Kaulbach, who attempted to continue the former's eclectic tradition. "Everyone went through his atelier that could lay claim in Munich to being elegant, rich and beautiful." [1]

Outside the official circles Leibl, the outstanding representative of the realism of the 'seventies and 'eighties, was still painting the simple, robust Bavarian peasants in his retreat in Aibling. Although Leibl never taught, he became an enormous influence on a whole generation of men including Thoma, Trübner, Schuch, Alt, Albert von Keller, Zügel, the whole Munich Secession group, as well as the painters of Neu-Dachau.

The artists who severed themselves from their older colleagues in Munich in 1892 were the first to adopt the name "Secession." Opposed to the officialdom of Lenbach and Kaulbach, they opened their ranks to the realists of the Leibl tradition, as well as to the impressionist generation that followed. During the 'nineties Slevogt, Corinth, and Uhde achieved great prominence in Munich.

Simultaneously many of the Munich painters turned to applied design, in keeping with the Jugendstil movement, and much Jugendstil form entered the painting of men like Franz von Stuck. Jugendstil reached its climax in Munich with the great exhibition in the Glaspalast in 1897. [2] The Bavarian capital was the most fertile ground for this movement, because here a concern with formal considerations became increasingly dominant. It was here that Julius Meier-Graefe succeeded in arranging an important retrospective exhibition of Hans von Marées in 1891, which led to the rediscovery of Marées' painting in terms of formal organization. Two years later Marées' old friend Adolf von Hildebrand published his influential book *The Problem of Form in Painting and Sculpture;* Hildebrand continued in his own sculpture to resist the powerful influence of Rodin's dissolution of closed sculptural form. Paintings by Munch were exhibited at the Glaspalast in 1893; in 1897 Hodler held his first German exhibition there and received a medal for his painting *Night.* At the university, Furtwängler and Wölfflin stressed the formal aspects of works of art in their seminars on classical archaeology and Renaissance and baroque painting; in 1898 August Endell, himself a student of Theodor Lipps, formulated an early theory of abstract art.

The trend toward the emphasis on form in painting may also have been responsible for the fact that painters concerned primarily with purely optical impressions left Munich at this time. Lovis Corinth moved to Berlin in 1900, and Max Slevogt followed in 1901.

Wassily Kandinsky (1866–1940) arrived in Munich from Moscow in 1896. He moved into a small studio in Schwabing, a cosmopolitan center of culture, beer, and bohemian life in the north section of Munich. There writers, composers, artists, and would-be artists from Russia, Hungary, Austria, Italy, England, America—even from Prussia, but few from Bavaria —gathered together in the Café Stefany, the Cabaret Simplicissimus, or in their own bohemian studios. They might even venture to the more respectable Café Luitpold to rub elbows with Rainer Maria Rilke; Wedekind, the leader of the literary vanguard; Heinrich Mann, exponent of liberalism and an important link with the culture across the Rhine; or with the young Thomas Mann.

If the majority of Schwabing's bohemians never got around to writing or painting because they were so busy making their lives into personal works of art—if they followed the cult of individuality to the point of conformity and confused artificiality with art—they yet engendered an artistically exciting atmosphere, which in its turn helped stimulate a new movement in painting. This movement was primarily the joint effort of Russian and German artists.

KANDINSKY, 1896–1901

Kandinsky, a man of exceedingly broad training and experience, was to become the leader of this group. He came to Munich at the age of thirty, "leaving Moscow and, as I thought, all uncongenial and compulsory toil behind me. Stretching before me, I could see the joyous prospect of dedicating myself to the work of my choice." [3]

When Kandinsky refused an appointment at the University of Dorpat in 1896 to come to Munich, he had behind him a long period of training for a career in jurisprudence and political economy, lengthy ethnological and anthropological studies and field work among primitive Russian folk groups, a background in musical education, and a comprehensive study of the physical sciences.

This exceedingly varied but thorough background was a firm basis for his later development as painter, esthetician, and thinker. He was able, for example, to draw parallels between Russian rural law and art: "According to this principle [law 'according to the man'], the basis for the verdict is not sought for in the official, physical action of the crime alone, but also in the quality of inner motivation, arising in the soul and spirit of the accused. How close this comes to the very foundations of art!" [4]

His mind never seemed to be directed toward a purely rational approach. He was concerned neither with the practical side of political economy nor with the positivist aspect of the natural sciences. His bent was clearly metaphysical and mystical from the beginning. In his student days at the University of Moscow he was primarily "interested in the field of Non-Objective Thought." [5] In his studies of science, his whole belief in a rational world was completely shaken by the "disintegration of the atom":

This discovery struck me with terrific impact, comparable to that of the end of the world. In the twinkling of an eye, the mighty arches of science lay shattered before me. All things became flimsy, with no strength or certainty. I would hardly have been surprised if the stones would have risen in the air and disappeared. [6]

Throughout his life he increasingly doubted the ability of science or of the intellect to cope with "true"—that is, intuitive—reality. This concern with a more abstract reality of the soul and the spirit—the "spiritual in art"—was closely related to the earlier movements of symbolism and Jugendstil and was to become basic not only for the development of expressionism but for much of the rest of twentieth-century painting. To the artists of the next generation Kandinsky was "the great initiator of abstract painting, whose theoretical work represents the beginning of a new art history which, as he [Kandinsky] states, 'in its consequent development will grow beyond the frontier of painting and, in fact, art in general.'" [7]

His receptivity to color was the key to this development, not only from the time, when comparatively late in life he felt the "inner necessity" to become a painter, but indeed from the outset. His autobiography does not begin with the memory of objects, events, or people, but: "The first colors which impressed me were—a light juicy green, white, black, carmine-red, and yellow ochre." [8] The story of his life is primarily the story of color impressions received in earliest childhood and through adolescence. A gondola ride at night in Venice when he was a child is recalled in terms of "black lack-lustre water, a long black boat with a terrible black box." [9] He describes the sunset over Moscow as an experience of heavenly color music that causes his soul to vibrate; his vision of it is kaleidoscopic—a "choir of colors"—of which he writes in florid language: certainly a verbal parallel to the visual expression of color improvisations that he painted at the time *Rückblicke* was written.

The colors of the sunset over Moscow remained a crucial experience. There was also the unforgettable "emotion that I experienced on first seeing the fresh paint coming out of the tube," [10] when he bought his first oil paints at thirteen: "The impressions of colors strewn over the palette: of colors—alive, waiting, as yet unseen and hidden in their little tubes—all this acquired for me an inner spiritual life and meaning." [11]

The experience of music became one of color: "It was in 'Lohengrin' that I felt the supreme incarnation and interpretation of this vision through music. The violins, deep basses and, most of all, the wind instruments, created for me the full image and power of the evening hour." [12] Later this experience led him to his important experiments in "total stage composition" and his theory of synesthesia. He first saw paintings by Rembrandt [13] in 1889, when he came upon them in the Hermitage of St. Petersburg, and was profoundly impressed by the "vibrating color tones." Before leaving Russia for Munich he saw Monet's haystacks at an exhibition in Moscow, an event that was "to influence me strongly in my future life." [14] At first he had great difficulty in recognizing objects in the picture, but then "deep inside of me, there was born the first faint doubt as to the importance of an 'object' as the necessary element in painting." [15] Color remained the key to his painting as well as to his esthetics. Much later, graphic expression—point, line, and plane—found equal status with color in his visual vocabulary.

At first Kandinsky felt the need of receiving instruction as a painter. In Munich he entered the private studio of Anton Azbé (1859–1905) to work from the model. Very little is remembered of Azbé, but at the turn of the century he was internationally known and attracted many students, of whom he demanded that they should see their study as a coherent whole rather than as separate details. Kandinsky referred to his first teacher's "generosity and kindness" and called him a "talented artist and a man of rare spiritual qualities." [16] Although in his youth a great future had been predicted for his talent, Azbé never came into his own as an artist. He became very popular with the Russian art students who came to Munich at the turn of the century, perhaps because of his own Slavic ancestry or because of the fact that he taught many people gratuitously. When he died in 1905, however, only a brief obituary appeared in the *Kunstchronik*: "Teacher of many now recognized artists, he himself was of almost proverbial modesty and never came to fame himself. A man of selfless devotion his effect was great on his pupils and friends. As a human being he was one of the most original and best-known artistic personalities of Munich." [17]

In Azbé's studio Kandinsky first met Alexey von Jawlensky, who had arrived in Munich the same year from St. Petersburg together with Marianne von Werefkin (Werefkina) and two other Russian painters.[18] A few years later David and Vladimir Burliuk were to enter Azbé's atelier. The acquaintance of Kandinsky and Jawlensky in this studio developed into a long-lasting friendship between the two Russian painters; a decade later both were instrumental in founding the New Artists' Association, and almost thirty years later they collaborated with Feininger and Klee in the "Blue Four."

Jawlensky's early work consists largely of still life employing colors similar to those found in Russian ikons and folk art; this affinity constantly grew stronger in his painting.

Kandinsky, meanwhile, much more at home with color than with drawing, decided that he needed instruction in draftsmanship: "At that time Franz Stuck was the foremost German draughtsman, and so it was to him that I finally took some of my studio works." [19]

After failing the academy entrance examination and waiting for a year, Kandinsky was admitted to Stuck's painting class in 1900. He early recognized his teacher's insensitivity to color, but he also admitted owing a great debt to Stuck. Stuck was a man who approached art with affection and sincerity, and was endowed with genuine imagination, which unfortunately was to run dry in succeeding years. He was an excellent drawing master, and—perhaps most important—he taught Kandinsky to exercise discipline and work seriously at completing a painting. "It is with gratitude that I remember that year in his class, though I must say that some of the things they perpetrated there in the name of art were quite beyond belief." [20]

PHALANX

In 1901 Kandinsky was instrumental in founding the artists' club Phalanx, which was "to further common interest by close coöperation. Above all it wants to help overcome the difficulties which young artists encounter in getting their work exhibited." [21] According to the same brief notice, Phalanx had plans for a permanent exhibition building for the work of its members and invited guests. In the following year the group insisted that entries be submitted without signatures to anonymous juries, to eliminate all possibilities of favoritism. [22]

Late in the autumn of 1901 Phalanx held its first public exhibition of painting, sculpture, graphics, and architectural design, but met with almost no notice. The list of names of the exhibiting members—Hecker (vice-president), Freytag (secretary), Hoch, Salzmann, Meeser—is most unimpressive; although Kandinsky's paintings at that time were not masterpieces, it is not surprising that he was elected to the presidency of the organization. [23]

Kandinsky designed the poster for the first exhibition of the group, and it serves as an excellent example of his early style, which is very much what might be expected of a painter coming from Russia, with the revival of its folk art, to the center of Jugendstil activity. [24] Elements of both are present in this poster, a flat and decorative color woodcut (pl. 65). The lettering, built up in blocks of color, consists of decorative, curvilinear elements that are an integral part of the page, as in the book designs of Eckmann and Obrist or in the title pages of *Jugend, Pan,* and *Simplicissimus.* The picture itself consists of three parts, vertically divided by decorative columns. Two Roman lancers in richly ornamented armor, symbolizing the phalanx formation, advance to the left in the central panel. On the right, fallen warriors lie on a highly abstract battlefield; on the left is a landscape with an encampment surmounted by a medieval castle. Elements of perspective are totally eliminated, and space is created by the relationship of positive and negative forms. The columns, for example, are the white of the paper itself, but appear in an advanced plane because of the heavy black outlines surrounding them. These same black outlines, however, invade the white shape to form the abacus of the columns, so that positive and negative elements are constantly reversed. Similarly the faces and helmets of the warriors, the tents, castle, parts of shields and lances consist merely of outlined negative white space. This idea of making a simple, uniform background serve multiple spatial functions creates space tension and is characteristic of a great deal of Jugendstil design. It occurs again in the earliest graphic work of the Brücke artists, such as Schmidt-Rottluff's *Woman with Hat* (1903) (fig. 7), and it is found in Kokoschka's color lithographs to *Die träumenden Knaben* (1908) (pl. 61a), which also resemble the Phalanx poster in their decorative fairy-tale detail.

Kandinsky's concern with the relationship of black and white—here used for a tension between near and distant planes—had also caused his immediate response to Rembrandt. This concern seems to have had even greater psychological reasons: "All my life, pure black and white paints have aroused in me strong and totally opposite emotions." [25] "White is not without reason taken to symbolize joy and spotless purity, and black, grief and death." [26]

Kandinsky's paintings of this period—his Russian market squares and scenes from Russian fairy tales, his gentle ladies in medieval costume walking through parks with pages—are very similar in style to the Phalanx poster. Although Mme Nina Kandinsky, who has divided Kandinsky's work into nine major periods, calls his painting before 1900 "Realist" and that from 1900 to 1906 "Impressionist," [27] the painter actually worked in an astonishing variety of styles during this time. Much of his work was strongly influenced neither by realism nor by impressionism, but rather by Jugendstil. In 1902 he began making woodcuts—in color as well as black and white—with large, clear-cut, highly stylized areas in the Jugendstil manner. Some of his paintings also frequently resemble decorative theater sets.

The Sluice (1902) (pl. 66),[28] one of his finest paintings of these years, deviates from this style most considerably. This landscape might be considered an impressionist picture, for the experience of impressionism had taught him to dissolve three-dimensional values. Kandinsky applies his pigment very thickly where he feels a demand for large blobs of color, but in other areas the canvas itself shows through only a thin layer. The brush stroke, however, is much larger than in impressionist painting, and the color richly glowing. The golden yellow of the willow tree on the left is contrasted to the three dark pines in the center with their multifarious somber tones of blue, olive, and brown. The yellow is taken up again in the tree on the right, which recalls the intense color and brush work of Monticelli or even van Gogh. The sky is mostly a light blue, and the embankment a juicy green; the walk is flesh-colored, and a definite white shape—perhaps a boat landing—appears in the center of the painting. Yet all these—even the broad flatly painted area of the bank—are broken up into a multitude of colors and strokes. A lady with a blue hoop skirt walks slowly down the path in the color fantasy. Perhaps most magnificent are the colors in the mirror surface of the water, with yellow flowers floating on the reflection and a glorious transparency in the lower left-hand corner. A high-keyed reflection, it is the most startling part of the whole painting, and offers a glimpse of what Kandinsky later was to accomplish. The whole painting is highly romantic in mood: although soft and contemplative, it has a tranquility that has been compressed into an intense and lyrical statement.

When Kandinsky went to Rothenburg in 1902, he was fascinated by the medieval town with its gates, moats, narrow houses, and steep roofs. Like the impressionists, he felt that he needed sunshine to paint, but he did not complete his painting in *plein-air*.

Only once in the whole week, and then for not more than half an hour, did the sun break through the clouds. . . . Only one picture did I bring back from that trip, and that I did from memory already after my return to Munich. It is "The Ancient Town" and is filled with sunshine, while the roofs are of the most vividly flaming red I could achieve.[29]

In *Ancient Town* (pl. 67) [30] the colors are bold and are applied in considerably larger areas: the dabs of colors are even larger than those used by Signac, and come very close to Fauve technique. At the same time a strong feeling for structure is evident: towers and roofs are simplified into sharply cut facets, the large clumps of trees into spheroid structures; the interest in the fork of the road in the foreground is centered on the possibilities of right-angular relationships. The geometric forms of the buildings could have developed into cubist interpretations if he had had such inclinations.

Kandinsky's experimentation with color began to be noticed by the critics at this time. A review of the second Phalanx exhibition said:

Wassily Kandinsky, the original Russian colorist, who paints purely and entirely for the sake of color, displays all kinds of colorist fireworks and uses the most varied techniques: oil, tempera, lacquer—the latter unfortunately succeeding so well that the picture can no longer be seen.[31]

Kandinsky had twelve paintings and prints in the second Phalanx exhibition. His close relationship to the Jugendstil painters at the time is indicated by the participation of Peter Behrens, Rudolf Bosselt, Hans Christiansen, Patriz Huber, and many other minor Jugendstil artists. It is particularly interesting, however, that Ludwig von Hofmann exhibited as a guest artist. Von Hofmann's idyllic, harmonious landscapes, peopled with a supernatural race, must have appeared like the measured Apollonian counterpart to Stuck's Dionysiac Olympus—indeed, they came close to Hildebrand's classic idealizations. Von Hofmann attempted to achieve a rhythmic, monumental restraint in painting that might be a pictorial parallel to the poetry of his spiritual master Stefan George. Kandinsky was a close friend of the "Georgianer" Karl Wolfskehl at the time, and there can be no doubt that Stefan George's emphasis on formal structure found much admiration in the Munich vanguard.

Later that year Albert Weissgerber (1878–1915) was invited to exhibit with the members of Phalanx,[32] and he showed work of a completely different character. Weissgerber turned at that time from his decorative illustrations for *Jugend* toward religious subject matter. Where von Hofmann's rhythm has a restraint recalling Puvis de Chavannes, Weissgerber's work seems overdynamic, almost frenetic in its activity.

At the same exhibition Axel Gallén-Kallela, the Finnish painter, who was being acclaimed for his strongly decorative Kalevala frescoes, was represented with several canvases. Four years later Gallén-Kallela was asked to exhibit with the Brücke in Dresden. Kandinsky found much acclaim at this time and was elected to membership in the Berlin Secession [33] and in the Deutsche Künstlerbund. In 1902 he also opened his own school of painting and drawing, called the Phalanxschule, in Munich.

One of Kandinsky's first pupils at the Phalanxschule was Gabriele Münter (born 1877), whose life and artistic career were to become closely interwoven with Kandinsky's for more than a decade. Gabriele Münter, born in Berlin, had spent two years in America, where her father had lived and her mother had been born. Returning to Germany in 1900, she continued in Munich the art study she had begun earlier in Düsseldorf. After studying with Angelo Jank, the Jugendstil painter and draftsman of horses, she became one of the few students of the Phalanx School.

In the spring of 1903 Kandinsky and Münter traveled to Rapallo on the Italian Riviera, and then continued on to Tunisia to visit the old city of Kairuan. Returning to Munich, Kandinsky organized the seventh Phalanx exhibition, with which the group attained international significance by showing sixteen paintings by Claude Monet, who was still considered extremely modern in Germany. Kandinsky was represented by six canvases.

The following year, 1904, marked Kandinsky's first real public success. He had been to Paris in 1889 and 1892, but now, accompanied by Münter, he went there as a successful painter. The catalog of the Salon d'Automne (October–November) of that year lists eighteen items by Wassily Kandinsky. He also exhibited in St. Petersburg, Moscow, Odessa, Cracow, Warsaw, Rome, Hamburg, Wiesbaden, and at the Berlin Secession; he was included in the Grosse Kunstausstellung in Dresden as well as in a show at the Galerie Richter.[34]

Typical of Kandinsky's work during this period is *Der Blaue Reiter* (1903) (pl. 68a)—a painting that later, almost accidentally, gave the name to Kandinsky's association with Franz Marc. The palette is quite impressionist, but the choice of colors—the blue rider on a white stallion against a large green expanse—is certainly symbolist, as is the subject matter itself. The stylization of trees and white clouds and the conscious repetition of shape—such as the movement of the cloud, repeating the movement of the rider—show the impact of the symbolists. The brush stroke, however, is not carefully calculated; on the contrary, it is exceedingly free and spontaneous.

For the ninth Phalanx exhibition in January, 1904, Kandinsky invited the draftsman Alfred Kubin to participate. Kubin, who was to exhibit frequently with Kandinsky in the future, became a cofounder of the New Artists' Association and later an associate of the Blaue Reiter; yet in style he remained completely different from the other artists. Where the others were concerned with color, Kubin was interested only in graphic media; when they moved toward nonobjective form, Kubin continued his creation of weird monstrosities. In the ninth Phalanx exhibition Kubin showed twenty-four drawings of strange, specterlike shapes and fearful images; Kandinsky was represented by thirteen canvases that combined his narrative and descriptive interests with brilliant color.

The ninth Phalanx exhibition was followed shortly by another show of great importance for the developments in Munich. This, the tenth exhibition of the group, included Signac, Flandrin, Laprade, Guerin, and van Rysselberghe, as well as Toulouse-Lautrec and Vallotton.[35] Paintings by Signac and Seurat had been seen before, and their theories were known and widely discussed in Germany since the publication of Signac's essay *D'Eugène Delacroix au néo-impressionnisme*.[36] However, this exhibition included what was undoubtedly the largest number of neoimpressionist works seen in Germany up to this time. Ernst Ludwig Kirchner, who was in Munich at this time, admitted the influence of neoimpressionist color.[37] In Kandinsky's work a definite change toward the use of pure color dates from this period. Later, however, he was to evolve his own color theories, considerably at variance with the scientific attitude of the pointillists.

The last Phalanx exhibit was held at the Galerie Helbing in 1904. This was an exhibition devoted to graphic work, and Kandinsky was now the featured artist. Interestingly enough, the reviewer in *Die Kunst* recognized neoimpressionist tone values in Kandinsky's prints, and also suggested the artist's debt to Vallotton, Whistler, and the Japanese woodcut.[38]

EARLY DEVELOPMENT TOWARD ABSTRACT EXPRESSIONISM

Kandinsky's woodcuts at that time were largely concerned with the effects of black-white relationships; they worked from dark to light much like the earlier graphic works, such as the first Phalanx poster. At this time he used a black mirror to achieve his particular dark effects.

He continued to explore the black-white, negative-positive relationship.

In *Promenade* half of the woman's face merges completely with the background. The continuous flowing line recalls Munch and Jugendstil, as does Kandinsky's desire to treat the wood block clearly as such. The hard, angular lines and the contrasting patches of black and white plainly show that they have been cut into a block of wood. At the same time Kandinsky's pattern is considerably more abstract than most of the work of the time. His aim seems to have been similar to that stated by a critic who reproduced several of his woodcuts in an article on the revival of the graphic arts in Munich: "The graphic arts are not an effort toward truth to nature, but a longing for subjective expression." [39]

Kandinsky's experiments with the woodcut helped him to master linear elements and showed a preoccupation with black and white. His great concern with color came again to the fore during his stay in Sévres near Paris, where he and Münter remained from the spring of 1906 to the following spring. According to Gabriele Münter, they met none of the important painters personally, but they saw pictures by Gauguin, Matisse, Picasso, Rouault, and Rousseau. They were fascinated by Gauguin's and Rouault's strong color; entranced by Rousseau's naïveté, they bought several of his canvases, which were later reproduced in *Der Blaue Reiter*. [40]

In his own work Kandinsky applied color more thickly and with greater freedom, much in the manner of the Fauves. His early Jugendstil formalizations loosened up, his narrative interest disappeared. Sometimes he completed a painting out-of-doors in the impressionist manner, or in this period of experimentation he used color for its own expressive value very much in the style of Matisse and Vlaminck. He participated in the Salon d'Automne of 1905, and showed twenty works in the Salon of 1906. [41] He must actually have been in touch with the Fauves, because he exhibited six of his paintings with them in the twenty-third Salon des Artistes Indépendents in 1907.

In the winter of 1906–1907 Kandinsky also participated in the second Brücke exhibition, of graphic works, in Dresden; these prints give evidence of the new freedom he had gained in France.

Kandinsky returned to Munich by way of Berlin and Dresden in 1907. In the summer of 1908 he and Gabriele Münter discovered Murnau, a charming old village in the foothills of the Bavarian Alps, as an ideal place to live and work.

His paintings *Church at Froschhausen* (pl. 160) and *Street in Murnau* (pl. 161) of 1908 are typical examples of the work—almost exclusively landscapes—that Kandinsky did at this time. In the former, a charming small canvas, color has been applied in slablike areas, and each brush stroke remains clearly visible. The sharply emphasized light and dark planes, alternating across the picture plane in variations of blue, green, yellow, and pink, give the surface a flashing, neon-lit character very curious in a village scene.

The same aspect of unreality—or of another quite unreal reality—appears in *Street in Murnau,* where the peculiar high angle of vision severely limits a distant space illusion. A sweeping concave plane of gable roofs on the lower right leads the eye to a multicolored street shooting diagonally up into the picture plane, which is abruptly shut off by church and mountains. The brush stroke is similar to that in *Church at Froschhausen*. Certain areas are highly stressed by brilliant color: the orange dormer window on the left, the vividly yellow house on the right. As in Fauve painting, there is very little correlation between factual local color and the color used in the picture: the street consists of purple, green, pink, brown, and blue; the houses are tan and green, purple and yellow. Composition, handling of space, and application of color are all very close to Fauve painting, but the palette is richer and darker, the colors luminescent rather than brilliant, the resulting mood somber and ominous rather than exuberant.

Similar in feeling and intense in color is Münter's *Landscape with Monk* (1909),[42] in which each shape is surrounded with definite black outlines. When asked about the derivation of the dark contour, Münter pointed out that she and Kandinsky wished to get away from naturalistic painting, that they were concerned with shape as shape, that they found affirmation of this in the work which Jawlensky was doing when he stayed with them in 1908 and 1909.[43] Jawlensky had been working with Matisse in 1907, and had adopted much of the Frenchman's use of color as an expressive, emotional element. Kandinsky admired Matisse above all other living French painters at that time.[44] Jawlensky's landscapes of 1908 are astonishing in the bold application of deep color and in the overlapping flat areas surrounded by strong, dark outlines.

More important than contemporary work were the discoveries by Kandinsky and Münter of Bavarian behind-glass paintings, many of which could be found in the peasants' houses around Murnau. These pictures were first drawn with definite outlines and then filled in with color. "And we tried to achieve similar effects by working in a like manner."[45]

In Kandinsky's landscapes there was now a clear, almost conscious progression toward abstraction, with color acting as the expressive and evocative element. He even began giving his paintings "abstract" titles, as Whistler had done before him. The first of these interestingly enough borrows from the realm of music: *The White Sound* (1908). The relationship of vision and sound—color and music—was to occupy him for the rest of his life.

The doubt as to the importance of the object in painting, first raised by his experience with Monet, grew slowly into the deliberate assertion that the object only detracts from the direct sense experience of color and line. Perhaps most important in this development was one particular experience he had in Munich about this time:

I was returning, immersed in thought, from my sketching, when on opening the studio door, I was suddenly confronted by a picture of indescribable and incandescent loveliness. Bewildered I stopped, staring at it. The painting lacked all subject, depicted no identifiable object and was entirely composed of bright color-patches. Finally I approached closer and, only then, recognized it for what it really was—my own painting, standing on its side on the easel. . . . One thing became clear to me—that objectiveness, the depiction of objects, needed no place in my paintings, and was indeed harmful to them.[46]

Even after he had recognized this, he found that the final step toward painting removed from the object was not an easy one. Though he had "reached, both intuitively and intellectually, the simple solution—that the goal and aims of nature are essentially and basically different from those of art, also that both are equally great, and therefore, equally strong," [47] the final formulation of this insight in plastic terms was wrought with dangers of which he was fully aware.

If we begin at once to break the bonds that bind us to nature and to devote our- selves purely to combination of pure color and independent form, we shall produce works which are mere geometric decoration, resembling something like a necktie or a carpet. Beauty of form and color is not sufficient aim by itself, despite the asser- tions of pure aesthetes or even of naturalists obsessed with the idea of "beauty." It is because our painting is still at an elementary stage that we are so little able to be moved by wholly autonomous color and form composition. The nerve vibrations are there (as we feel when confronted by applied art), but they get no further than the nerves because the corresponding vibrations of the spirit which they call forth are weak. When we remember, however, that spiritual experience is quicken- ing, that positive science, the firmest basis of human thought, is tottering, that dis- solution of matter is imminent, we have reason to hope that the hour of pure composition is not far away. The first stage has arrived.[48]

The artist, he felt, must do a great deal more than manipulate form. He must have a message to convey, and this message must be the expression of his innermost emotion.

This was to become the goal of the Blaue Reiter group, the movement of abstract expressionism [49] that had its beginnings in Munich between 1910 and 1914. There was still another reason why Kandinsky, who saw his aims so clearly, could not implement them immediately; he stated it years later in a letter to Hilla Rebay: "I could not immediately come to 'pure abstraction' because at that time I was all alone in the world." [50] Kan- dinsky was helped in his search by meeting Wilhelm Worringer, who had just published his influential *Abstraction and Empathy*. He needed also the inspiration of other artists. Since he possessed the qualities of spiritual and intellectual leadership, a group of painters seceded with him from the Munich Secession in January, 1909, to form the "New Artists' Association."

XV

The New Artists' Association

A series of highly important exhibitions occurred in Munich in the first decade of the twentieth century. Exhibits of Marées, Munch, and Hodler were followed in 1904 by a significant show of works by Cézanne, Gauguin, and van Gogh at the Munich Kunstverein.[1] The same year Matisse displayed some drawings at the Kunstverein, and in 1907 Cassirer arranged a large exhibition of Matisse paintings. The Phalanx exhibitions of *avant-garde* art were followed by a large Secession show of Bonnard, Roussel, Vuillard, and Vallotton in 1908. The private galleries of Brackl, Zimmermann, and Thannhauser presented constantly changing shows of modern work—interspersed, to be sure, with conservative offerings.

The whole field of Munich's artistic reference was widened in 1909 and again in 1910 by two great Oriental exhibits. The first—of Chinese, Japanese, and Korean art—included work from the T'ang dynasty to the nineteenth century.[2] The second—of Mohammedan art—was exhaustive in its display of carefully chosen work from Persia, India, Syria, and other Middle Eastern countries.[3] These shows, presenting art with very different concepts from those of the West, created a new awareness of greater visual possibilities, and helped considerably in increasing receptivity to new esthetic impressions.

FIRST EXHIBITION, 1909

The Munich Secession, which had set the example for the German Secession movement, had become conservative in its exhibition policies by the end of the first decade of the century. In the fall of 1909 a number of more advanced painters resigned from the Secession: the Russians Kandinsky, Jawlensky, and Werefkina; the Bohemian Alfred Kubin; Gabriele Münter from Berlin; two artists from Karlsruhe, Alexander Kanoldt and Adolf Erbslöh, the latter American-born.[4] Together they formed the New Artists' Association of Munich. Later, when they also included French painters in their exhibits, they were denounced by Munich critics, not only for their "abstruse mysteries" and "pathological forms," but also for daring to call themselves a Munich group:

The beautiful and artistically renowned name of Munich has to serve as shingle for a society of artists of mixed Slavic and Latin elements. Furthermore they are hostile towards the Munich tradition in the arts. . . . There is not *one* Munich painter among them. How dare they call themselves a Munich group? They neither work nor feel "münchnerisch." [5]

The members of the New Artists' Association of Munich were not only widely varied as to cultural background; there was absolutely no similarity in style among the violent color explosions of a Kandinsky, the carefully structured compositions of a Kanoldt, and the eerie linear drawings of a Kubin. The only unifying element was in their opposition to the official art of Munich.

Kandinsky's *Improvisation No. 3* (1909) (pl. 68b) [6] shares with the earlier painting *Der Blaue Reiter* the subject matter of man on horseback. The ancient image of man as rider was frequently treated by Kandinsky for a whole decade. Kenneth Lindsay is able to trace it in the painter's so-called nonobjective work, and said that he "apparently found in the image of the horseman the symbol of inspired human endeavor." [7]

A comparison between the two paintings—five years apart—gives a revealing insight into the artist's development. The still illusionistic space of the earlier picture has been abandoned. The composition is built up in planes parallel to the picture plane, and the most advancing color—a cadmium yellow—is used for the wall of a house in the background. The small, dappled brush stroke of the earlier picture has given way to a much heavier application of pigment. Light, which in *Der Blaue Reiter* still appeared natural, is now a function of the pigment itself. Shapes, which were recognizably defined in 1903 as trees, hills, and clouds, have now become ambiguous. Clouds, horse, rider, and building, in resembling the shapes of shrubs and trees, create a new, organic unity of color and brush stroke. The rhythm too has changed completely. This is no longer a horseman galloping through the land, but a rider who must slowly and deliberately fight the elements. He advances, however: the rearing figure of horse and rider stops the lines and colors that sweep down against him from the upper right section of the painting. Thus color, line, plane, and brush stroke have all become more immediately suggestive.

Alexey von Jawlensky (1864–1941) achieved similar effects with his rich color outlined by heavy, black contours. The oldest member of the group, he was born in Torschok near Twer in Russia. As a member of the minor Russian aristocracy, he went to military school. He had already become an officer in the Imperial Russian Guard when, after spending his Sundays in the Tretiakoff Gallery in Moscow, he decided to give up his military career to become a painter. He gained admission to the St. Petersburg Academy of Fine Arts, and studied under the celebrated leader of the Russian realist school Ilya Repin.

Jawlensky was soon thoroughly disappointed with his academic training in St. Petersburg, and in 1896 he and Werefkina left for Munich. There in Azbé's studio he made his first acquaintance with Kandinsky.

His early, semirealistic style changed under the Jugendstil influence of Munich. In the first decade of the century he was highly receptive to—indeed sought out—a great many influences: Cézanne, van Gogh, Hodler, Gauguin, and later Matisse, as well as Near Eastern art, old German wood sculpture, and his own Russo-Byzantine tradition. He traveled in Russia, Germany, and France. He was recognized relatively early and was invited to show at the Munich Secession in 1903, whereupon Corinth asked him to participate in the exhibition of the Berlin Secession. The following year his work was seen in the Paris Salon d'Automne as well as in St. Petersburg.

A trip to Brittany and Provence in 1905 helped him greatly in developing expressive form and symbolic color. Then, in 1907, Jawlensky worked in Matisse's studio for a short period; he owes his large, bold, contrasting color surfaces, as well as the dark contour lines, to the Fauve painter. Jawlensky's line never attains the dynamic activity of Matisse's; it is a more passive line, which encloses the rich color areas of the landscapes and heads of 1909. On the other hand, a painting like *White Feathers* (pl. 69a) [8]— a portrait of the Russian dancer Sacharoff—is still closely related to Jugendstil work in its interaction of black-and-white areas that keep intruding on each other and constantly alter their spatial relationship.

Jawlensky's close friend Marianne von Werefkin (1870–1938) was not nearly so open to influences, but worked in a highly personal manner, doing *gouaches* of a literary nature that frequently have a superreal quality. "Like confessions in a diary," [9] she catches quick, transitory moods, but beyond mere narrative she creates rhythmic arrangements by large, strongly outlined color planes that cut into each other.

Alfred Kubin (born 1877), in complete contrast to the other painters who were so much concerned with color, was a draftsman and print maker. He was born in Bohemia, then still a part of the Austrian Empire, in 1877, and came to Munich in 1898. His father was an army officer who failed to understand his son's sensibilities; his mother died when he was ten. His whole early development, as revealed in his autobiography *Sansara*, [10] was a repetition of traumatic experiences. After failing school, he went to the Industrial Art School at Salzburg, then into apprenticeship with an uncle who was a photographer in Klagenfurt. He wrote of early suicide attempts at his mother's grave and a complete nervous breakdown after three months in the army.

Kubin arrived in Munich in 1898, in the midst of its period of artistic fermentation. His academic study with Schmitt-Reutte at the academy meant little to him. He expressed the greatest admiration for Klinger—indeed, his discovery of Klinger apparently carried him into a prolonged state of trauma.

Kubin managed to find some release by transferring into linear forms the fantasies that agitated his imagination. His tortured drawings and lithographs seem automatic in their lack of self-consciousness, yet they show an uncanny feeling for composition. His stark, gruesome distortions are the result of a very observant eye and extremely fine draftsmanship, which implies conscious control. His human beings are like ugly specters, and express his feeling of the threat of existence. Typical of his early period is *Crushing* (*Das Erdrückende*) (1903) (pl. 69b).[11] Here a soft animal, half fish and half reptile, is about to crush a little man who balances on the edge of an abyss—there is no hope of escape. The whole thing is doubly gruesome because the beast is a huge enlargement of a small, harmless-looking creature.

The subject matter seems frequently to be derived from dream images; there are also illustrations to Dostoevski, Poe, Verlaine, and de Nerval, as well as to his own expressionist writings like *Die andere Seite*.[12] Everything expresses destruction, resignation to inevitable catastrophe, or unpleasantly grotesque humor. His work has been referred to as the "abortion of a morbid fantasy." It is a modern dance of death.

Kubin's style is personal, but is related to the turn-of-the-century decadence. At the turn of the century "the names of Goya, Beardsley and Rops were on everybody's lips in the studios and cafés." [13] Beardsley's influence is quite evident in *Mme la Décadence* (1900)—a painting of a woman with a long beard emerging from her pelvic area, which is partly concealed by an ermine skirt. Her headdress is a stylized, Oriental-looking affair; she rests one foot on a coffin, and a human head reposes on a plate in a corner of the small room.

His famous series *War* (completed in 1903) differs significantly from Stuck's contemporary paintings of the same subject. Where Stuck's paintings have a gruesome pseudo-classical beauty, Kubin's drawings evidence the more direct power of his vision—these images have a personal passion.

In 1903, the same year in which he exhibited jointly with Kandinsky in Phalanx, Kubin found his first patron, who bought forty-eight drawings and financed his first portfolio. This gave the artist enough courage and money to get married, but his young bride died after only a year of marriage.

During a trip to Paris in 1905 he met Odilon Redon, and at about this time he turned from literary imagery toward a more direct symbolism. He gained greater control of his imagination as well as of formal problems, but his drawings remained thoroughly pessimistic. The detailed, realistic treatment of the most horrible situations recalls Kafka.[14] After 1905 he began his fantastic biological series: pictures of amoeba and mollusks in which he combined microscopic observation with dream images, and revealed uncanny light effects.

A completely personal style like Kubin's could exercise little influence on other artists. Yet there is a resemblance between his work and the quick, diffuse line of Klee's early drawings. Klee too showed a liking for the fantastic and macabre, but an image that formed a threat to Kubin would be treated with humor by Klee.

Whereas Kubin seemed to visualize the world in a constant state of disintegration, Alexander Kanoldt (1881–1947) was concerned with revealing its structure. Kanoldt was born in Karlsruhe, the son of the landscapist Edmund Kanoldt. He attended the Arts and Crafts School and then the Academy in Karlsruhe and came to Munich in 1908. He was instrumental in the foundation of the New Artists' Association in 1909, and even acted as its secretary.[15]

Kanoldt began as an academic painter, but loosened under the impact of impressionism. Perhaps his most significant experience during his development as an artist was an exhibition of postimpressionist French painting in Karlsruhe in 1906, which included work by Cézanne and Signac as well as Seurat's *Grande Jatte*. Kanoldt's work almost immediately became more structural; although at first he used a pointillist method, he soon applied his color in broader areas.

By 1909 Kanoldt had completed his first series of houses, towns, and villages, which are canvases built up with large, angular planes and compact cubic forms. The solid, bare plane of the wall in his cities evokes a certain loneliness—these are unpeopled, stereometric structures. His solidity and balanced form suggest a classical heritage: Kanoldt's father had received his training from Friedrich Preller, who in turn was close to Carl Rottmann and Josef Anton Koch. Alexander Kanoldt spent much time in Italy, where his work, especially the series done in S. Gimigniano, was strongly appreciated by de Chirico, Carrà, and Morandi as a prototype of Valori Plastici (pl. 70).[16]

Adolf Erbslöh (1881–1947), although born in New York, also spent his formative years in Karlsruhe. He came to Munich in 1904, where he was the most traditional member of the group developing most slowly and most carefully.

A painting such as *Tennis Court* (pl. 71),[17] although painted one year after the formation of the New Artists' Association, gives an excellent idea of his work at the time. He contrasts the wide, empty space of the light tennis court with the crowded masses of trees, which quickly limit the illusion of depth. The round shapes of the trees are repeated in the round parasol of the woman acting as a *repoussoir* in the immediate foreground; the two round forms are separated from each other by the tennis nets, which cleave diagonally into the picture and create a major division, leaving an open space on the lower right. The colors are deep and resonant, and emphasize the contrast of light and dark. His palette of saturated colors, in which greens and reds seem to dominate, and the definite, dark outline of his masses show a clear influence coming from Kandinsky, Jawlensky, and Münter; his concern with structural build-up indicates the proximity to Kanoldt. Erbslöh was the most eclectic member of the group.

Being a man of some wealth as well as taste, Erbslöh also became a collector, and some important pieces by Picasso and Delaunay [18] as well as work by the associates of the New Artists' Association—including the later members Vladimir von Bechtejeff and Pierre Girieud—are on his estate in Irschenhausen near Munich.

While preparations were being made for the first exhibition of the New

Artists' Association, to be held in the new exhibition rooms of the Moderne Galerie Thannhauser in the rococo Palais Arco in Munich's Theatinerstrasse, additional artists joined the group.

In terms of later accomplishments, Karl Hofer (1878–1955) was the most significant addition. Hofer also came from Karlsruhe, where he studied in Hans Thoma's class at the academy for two years. The first strong impressions on the young Hofer were Thoma's calm landscapes and Böcklin's romantic allegories. After completing his academic training Hofer went to Rome, where he remained from 1905 until 1908, sharing his studio with the sculptor Hermann Haller. There Hofer came under the influence of the *Deutschrömer* tradition, and admired the work of Hans von Marées. His own early work of large nudes, constructed with solid plasticity and posing in solitude against an indefinite landscape background, shows Marées' powerful influence. His painting *Two Women* (1907) (pl. 72) displays his academic attention to the careful structure of solid bodies as well as his sensitivity to clear composition and a preference for subtle color nuances.

Hofer left Rome in 1908 and went to Paris, where he hoped to develop further and to learn from Cézanne's forceful line structure. His connection with expressionist groups, even the form-conscious New Artists' Association, could be of only short duration, as his own tendency had always been toward a more objective and perhaps classical form. He exhibited with the association in their initial show of 1909, but soon resigned from the group.

Paul Baum (1859–1932) was also for a very brief time a member of the group. Baum began painting landscapes in the dark palette of the Weimar Academy, but an early removal to Paris and Brussels introduced him to impressionism and neoimpressionism. He went to the south of France and North Africa, where he experienced the bright light and glowing color of the sun-drenched southern landscape. Returning to Germany, he became the leading exponent of neoimpressionism beyond the Rhine, although the basic concepts and composition of his landscapes were to remain essentially a continuation of the tradition-bound style of the Weimar Academy.

Erma Barrera-Bossi was the third woman artist to join the New Artists' Association. Her work, though somewhat amateurish, is interesting for its freshness of observation, unusual composition, and rich saturation of colors.

Both Vladimir von Bechtejeff and Moissey Kogan had come to Munich from Russia during the first decade of the century. Von Bechtejeff (born 1878), like Jawlensky, had turned to painting from a career as a Russian army officer. He had traveled extensively through France, Italy, and Spain. "The experience of El Greco, the impressions of Marées and Puvis revealed to him his true task: ideal figure composition on an heroic scale." [19] Von Bechtejeff tried to achieve a harmonious integration of human forms and natural forces, using large color planes and gently curving lines. He strove toward a mural quality, but his work hardly ever transcends stylized decoration.

Moissey Kogan (1879–1942) had achieved a reputation for his medals, plaquettes, gem cutting, and his fine terra cotta figurines. Turning toward sculpture, he sent reliefs and busts to the first exhibition of the group. These were stylized nudes of an archaistic, primitive quality, closed in their linear form and showing a clear influence from Maillol. In 1910 Kogan moved to Paris, and was accepted by Maillol as one of the most talented members of the younger generation.

In addition to these visual artists, the Russian dancer Alexander Sacharoff supported the New Artists' Association by becoming a member.

These then were the artists who opened the first exhibition of the Neue Künstlervereinigung München on December 1, 1909. There were ten painters, one sculptor, and one exclusively graphic artist among them, as well as three lay members. About half the group were Russians. Some of the artists, like Kandinsky and Jawlensky, had already achieved recognition; others, like Werefkina or Münter, were still unknown.

Kandinsky designed the poster (pl. 73) for this exhibition, as he had done for the earlier Phalanx show. In this poster all literary allusion is absent: large planes of color have little differentiation within themselves, and contrast sharply with each other. Everything is considerably simplified when compared with the earlier Jugendstil poster. The entire exhibition tended toward simplification.

As might be expected, the show was not favorably received by either the Munich public or the art critics. The reviewer for *Cicerone* (probably Uhde-Bernays) said correctly that Hofer had been influenced by Marées, and that there was some talent in Baum and Erbslöh. As for the rest of the artists, he was certain that the whole show must be a "carnival hoax during Advent." [20] The critic for the Munich journal *Die Kunst* saw esoteric translations of Gauguin, Cézanne, Munch, and van Gogh—no individuality, but merely facile, sensational paintings. He felt that it was "much better to look at Purtscher's animal pictures or Felber's Venetian paintings," also on view at the Moderne Galerie. [21]

SECOND EXHIBITION, 1910

The members of the New Artists' Association, however, turned neither to painting animals nor to painting Venice, but made preparations for a second and much larger show. They were joined at this time by two French painters: Pierre Girieud and Le Fauconnier.

Pierre Girieud (1874–1940), originally from Marseilles, had promising beginnings as a painter. He had interesting one-man shows at Weill in Paris in 1902 and at Kahnweiler's in 1907. By 1910 his style, fairly close to the religious symbolism of Maurice Denis and developed under the influence of Gauguin and the symbolists, had well crystallized. He painted religious and mythological subjects in clear, cool colors, and was mostly concerned with definite, slowly flowing contours. Although some of his work is appealing, Girieud never fulfilled his early promise.

The entrance of Le Fauconnier (1881–1946) into the Munich group was of the greatest importance to the development of both French and German painting of the twentieth century, although this fact has been entirely overlooked by all publications on the subject thus far.

Born near Le Havre, Henri Le Fauconnier came to Paris at twenty and studied at the Académie Julian. His paintings in the early years of the century were impressionist, but he became interested in firm structural elements and geometric forms during his one-year stay at Plaumonach in Brittany in 1908. In 1909 he returned to Paris, and was close to Gleizes and Delaunay as well as to Severini and the futurists. According to evidence recently made available by Amédée Ozenfant, Le Fauconnier was important in the early history of cubism, especially as an influence on Fernand Léger. This was Apollinaire's original opinion, according to the galley proof of his *Les Peintres Cubistes.*[22]

Le Fauconnier was already painting pictures like L'Abondance [pl. 74], which prefigured that infinite number of compositions painted all over the world during the last thirty-eight years; that category of seminaturalistic Cubism, based upon nature and architecture: a very different sort of Cubism from that to be found in the ornamental variations of Picasso and Braque.[23]

L'Abondance, as well as one of Le Fauconnier's landscapes, was reproduced two years later in Kandinsky's and Marc's *Der Blaue Reiter.*[24] Le Fauconnier used cubist analysis of form and space for a new three-dimensional approach, which Apollinaire calls "physical cubism": "The painter-physicist who created this trend is Le Fauconnier." [25]

This particular trend in cubism, referred to by Apollinaire as "not a pure art," [26] was most important to the German developments. In his article on contemporary trends in French painting in *Der Blaue Reiter,* Roger Allard mentioned Metzinger and Le Fauconnier before any of the other cubist painters.[27] Le Fauconnier's forms, based upon a structural concept of nature and reintroducing the elements of color and light, were much closer to the aims of the German painters than the more cerebral forms of analytical cubism "which have become meaningless as a goal for the 'wild ones' of Germany." [28]

Conversely, Le Fauconnier's association with the German painters brought a new and important stimulus to France. He turned from "physical cubism" toward a form that was at the same time more subjective, more realistic, and closely related to Northern expressionism. In 1912 he achieved an influential position as director of the Académie de la Palette. Alix and Gromaire were among his pupils there; they and the other so-called French expressionists—de la Patellière, Fautrier, and Goerg—were strongly influenced by him. Bernard Dorival recognized this, but in his attempt to prove that French expressionism was an autonomous French movement, he overlooked Le Fauconnier's early connections with Germany: "Beginning in 1912 he [Le Fauconnier] becomes an Expressionist and engages his disciples to follow him in this path. French Expressionism was born, and was born from our Cubism." [29]

After joining the New Artists' Association, Le Fauconnier retained his connections with Germany. His first one-man show was held at the Folk-wang Museum in Hagen in 1912,[30] followed by an important retrospective exhibition at the Galerie Gurlitt in Berlin in 1913.[31]

In Munich preparations were being made for the second exhibition of the New Artists' Association while the first show was "circulated to many cities of Germany and Switzerland. Everywhere it encountered opposition, yet everywhere there were also some friends who . . . found stimulation in it."[32]

The second exhibition of the New Artists' Association opened at the Neue Galerie Thannhauser in September, 1910. In addition to the German, Russian, and French members, many more artists were invited to participate as guests. It was the first exhibit held anywhere in which the international scope of the modern movement could be estimated, and it gave rise to more great international shows, like the Cologne Sonderbund of 1912 and the New York Armory Show of 1913.

The impact of cubism was felt most strongly. In addition to Le Fauconnier, Picasso and Braque participated in the show with three and four paintings respectively. Other painters also showed the strong influence of cubism. Derain exhibited his classically constructed landscapes of his Cagnes period. Vlaminck's still lifes become more geometric, showing the impact of the new movement—especially that of Cézanne. Rouault's style had reached a solidity of glowing dark color areas outlined by heavy black lines expressing deep humanity and pathos. Rouault was represented by three paintings, and the introduction to the catalog of his first one-man show held at Druet in Paris in 1910 was translated for the catalog of this show. Van Dongen showed his boldly outlined, audacious women.

Picasso's color drawing *Head of a Woman* (1909), now in the Art Institute of Chicago (pl. 75), is illustrated in the catalog of the second exhibition of the New Artists' Association.[33] This head, influenced by ancient Iberian and African sculpture, has a definite sculptural structure, but volumes are flattened into planes, and forms break down into simplified geometric figures. It by no means follows the objective or scientific reasoning claimed for it by some German critics of cubism; the human head has been taken apart structurally and reassembled according to the artist's highly personal conception. In this particular head, moreover, there is great emphasis also on facial expression: the diamond-shaped planes of the eyes, from which linear beams radiate; the sculptured nose, with its long, sharply defined white plane on the side; the interpenetration of facial planes, which seem to push and pull. The face itself is extraordinarily long, and the sharply defined features give the head a rough-hewn appearance. The shapes of the head and its integral parts carry the emotive power. Color is reduced to sober earth tones, and almost disappears. Surface values are removed to reveal the essential structure.

The Munich painters were familiar with the early stages of cubism. Although they rejected the formal character, which they believed too intellectual, theoretical, and nonsensual in some cubism paintings, they were under the constant impact of the influence of works like Picasso's *Head of a Woman,* Le Fauconnier's *L'Abondance,* and the landscapes of Braque and Derain.

Cubism had already exercised a strong influence on many Russian painters. This impact was most clearly seen in the heads and landscapes sent by the two brothers David Burliuk (born 1882) and Vladimir Burliuk (*ca.* 1880–1917), then living in Kherson in southern Russia. The two Burliuks had studied at the St. Petersburg Academy around the turn of the century and with Azbé in Munich from 1903 to 1904. They continued their studies in Paris and then returned to Russia. They exhibited with Mir Iskusstva, the most advanced group of Russian artists, and were part of the Russian artistic vanguard that was thoroughly familiar with the new expression in art and literature all over Europe. Their reputation had grown so that "in the autumn of 1910 Kandinsky came to see him [David Burliuk] in Odessa and invited him, with his brother Vladimir, to take part in an important exhibition which 'Der Blaue Reiter' in Munich was organizing." [34]

The Burliuks not only exhibited their cubist pictures, but also helped formulate the new art theories in the catalog of the exhibition, pointing out that the new artistic forms were both deeply national and universal and expressing their affinity to Manet, Cézanne, Gauguin, van Gogh, Derain, Le Fauconnier, Matisse, and Picasso. [35]

The catalog contained five articles. Le Fauconnier's abstruse essay "Das Kuntswerk" was not aided by an obscure translation, evidently done by Kandinsky. This was followed by the Burliuk statement. A manifesto by Kandinsky defined the language of art as the communication between man and man concerning the superhuman. Redon, who incidentally did not exhibit in the show, said that his art was "expressive, suggestive and intimate" and emphasized the significance of the dream image. The translation of the introduction to the catalog of the Rouault exhibition at Druet in 1910 concluded the catalog's textual matter.

In addition to the artists mentioned, many others participated in this important exhibition. There were four color drawings by Eugen Kahler (1882–1911), a highly individualistic young artist from Prague whose rich and sensitive imagery of an exotic world appealed greatly to the Munich artists. Two years later, after his premature death, he was given a eulogy in *Der Blaue Reiter.* [36] Besides the Russian artists who were part of the first exhibition and the Burliuks, several other painters from Russia participated, including Wassily Denissof, Alexander Mogilewsky, and Seraphim Sudbinin. The sculpture in the exhibition was amazingly conservative when compared with the painting: Kogan was joined this time by three German sculptors, Hermann Haller, Bernhard Hoetger, and Edwin Scharff, none of whom were innovators in sculptural form.

Jawlensky, represented with eleven paintings, had the largest number of works in the exhibition. He had recently begun his series of monumental heads. In these, as well as in his landscapes, he had given up the last remnants of the neoimpressionist *tache;* he worked primarily with a thick, dark contour and a striking pattern of light and dark areas, as is apparent in the *Floating Cloud* (1910) (pl. 76a). In this painting, shapes are precisely delineated; the triangular forms of the pine trees marching up the hill are an almost regular repetition of the pointed shapes of the mountain chain beyond and above them. A series of clearly defined planes of foreground, middle ground, and background are parallel to the picture plane, but are compressed into a narrow, stagelike area.

Gabriele Münter was represented by seven paintings. The similarity of her work to that of Jawlensky has already been indicated. *Landscape with White Wall* (1919) (pl. 76b) is a typical example of this similarity. But it must be added that in this painting Münter has made a more interesting use of juxtaposed geometric shapes and an even more clearly defined delineation of forms than in the contemporary Jawlensky painting: the large planes of dark blue mountain, black and green trees, white wall, pink and green houses are not only outlined clearly but create a space of rhythmic movement. The harmony of color is closely related to the rhythm of the shapes. The quick, jagged line of the reddish cloud, for example, is in great opposition to the calm form of the contour of the dark blue mountain.

In contrast to the balanced calmness of the landscapes of Jawlensky and Münter, Kandinsky's work in this exhibition is characterized by emotional violence. In order to see his development most clearly, three further examples of the horse-and-rider motif will be considered.

Composition No. 2 (pl. 77) [37] was painted early in 1910. The horseman rides again with great speed through the landscape, but there seems to be less feeling of threat and anxiety than in *Improvisation 3.* Objective content is further reduced. The painting is gay, because of a brilliant array of bright colors that whirl together in a chaotic rhythm. The rider himself has become less important. The total rhythm is essential; this is created by the colors, by the ambiguous shapes that are still connected with the world of appearances. There are humanlike forms in all sorts of attitudes—lying down, standing in ranks, communing with one another, a playing child—but everything is ambivalent, full of a variety of possibilities. Shadows and substance become interchangeable. The relationship of colors and forms is one of enormous activity—there is hardly a place where the eye can rest.

Kandinsky's paintings, discarding natural objects, were soon to consist of violently whirling color movements. He was to do without "natural forms," which "make boundaries which often are impediments to this expression." [38] But the time for this final step had not yet arrived.

In the summer of 1910 he painted his *Improvisation No. 12—The Rider* (pl. 78). The man on horseback is more immediately recognizable in his stance opposing evidently threatening forces, which sweep down from the upper right. The whole effect has become one of great tension. The rider seems to thrust himself into danger. The observer is brought into immediate proximity with the figure. All extraneous detail has been eliminated. There is just one image: the central turning figure of horse and rider, attacked but rising to meet the attack of hostile forces. Color, shapes, contrast of light and dark, combine to effect this central focus. There is little connection with the empirical world, but rather an expression of the subjective world of personal experience.

This painting is again an "improvisation" rather than a "composition." Kandinsky distinguishes between three different categories in his own painting:

An impression is a direct impression of nature, expressed in purely pictorial form.

An improvisation is a largely unconscious, spontaneous expression of inner character, non-material nature.

The composition is an expression of a slowly formed inner feeling, tested and worked over repeatedly and almost pedantically. Reason, consciousness, purpose, play an overwhelming part. But of calculation nothing appears: only feeling.[39]

When the Munich public was confronted with this first international exposition of twentieth-century art, its reaction generally was one of derisive opposition. The following excerpt from a review in Munich's leading daily implies much about the intelligence and critical ability of the anonymous reviewer:

There are only two possible ways to explain this absurd exhibition: either one assumes that the majority of the members and guests of the Association are incurably insane, or else that one deals here with brazen bluffers who know the desire for sensation of our time only too well and are trying to make use of this boom. For my part, I tend toward the latter opinion—in spite of holy assurances to the contrary; yet I am willing to accept the former out of the goodness of my heart.[40]

The writer of this review, anticipating later criticism of modern art in Germany, would undoubtedly have agreed that this was "degenerate art." Many years later Kandinsky, recalling the response to this exhibition, wrote about it: "The press demanded the immediate close of this 'anarchist' (the term 'marxist' was then not yet in vogue) exhibition, composed of foreigners dangerous to the ancient Bavarian culture. It emphasized that the Russian artists were especially dangerous: Dostoevski with his 'all is permitted.'"[41]

Only a few voices were heard in defense of the new group. Among them were Hugo von Tschudi, the enlightened director of the Bavarian State Collections who, because of his nonacademic views, had only recently been dismissed from his curatorship in Berlin; Otto Fischer, an art historian who actually became a member; and the Munich painter Franz Marc, who defended the association in print and was the last painter to join, in January, 1911.

BREAKUP AND THIRD EXHIBITION, 1911

The group was attacked not only from the outside; an inner split became increasingly inevitable between the more conservative group, centered in Erbslöh and Kanoldt, and the more radical painters under Kandinsky's leadership.

Marc, who by the summer of 1911, had become a close friend of both Kandinsky and Macke, wrote to the latter in August:

Kandinsky and I clearly foresee that the next jury, late in the fall, will cause a horrible controversy and now or the following time a split, i.e. an exit of one or the other party. The question is which one will remain. We do not want to abandon the Association, but incapable members will have to get out.[42]

The opposing party, to be sure, had its own opinion. Otto Fischer, who was to become its spokesman, wrote in his brief history of the association in 1912: "Several members insisted on acceptance of their works without submitting to a jury, the others stood for severe judgment and rejections. Therefore Kandinsky, Kubin, Marc and Gabriele Münter declared their exit from the Association."[43]

There is no indication, however, that the group of four opposed a jury. Nor was Wilhelm Hausenstein correct when he said: "The Association broke up in 1911 over the question of programmatic non-objectivity demanded by Kandinsky."[44] Far from it—Kandinsky, as will be pointed out later, believed in any type of form as long as it followed what he called "inner necessity," and was severely opposed to any programmatic demands.

The true reason for the split, which occurred in December, 1911, was a great difference of esthetic ideology. The group around Kanoldt, Erbslöh, and Fischer opposed the freedom of expression that Kandinsky and Marc demanded. Fischer very pointedly said:

A painting is not solely expression, but also representation. It does not express the soul directly, but the soul in terms of the object. A painting without object is senseless. . . . These are fallacies of empty fanatics and impostors. These confused individuals may talk about the spiritual—but spirit makes for clarity, not confusion. A few colors and dabs, a few lines and notches are by no means art. . . .[45]

Kandinsky, on the other hand, believed in the greatest freedom of expression. "Everything is at the artist's disposal. Today is one of freedom such as characterizes great germinative periods."[46] Far from prescribing nonobjectivity, he saw two "poles" of forms: "(1) the great abstraction, (2) the great realism. These two poles open up two roads, which eventually will lead to the same end."[47]

The immediate cause of the split was the rejection by the jury of Kandinsky's rather abstract *Last Judgment,* allegedly because of its large size. Kandinsky, Marc, Münter, and Kubin then left the association. Jawlensky and Werefkina, although in agreement with them, remained members.

The third exhibition of the association opened at the Galerie Thannhauser on December 4, 1911. This by no means great international show included works by Vladimir von Bechtejeff, Erma Barrera-Bossi, Adolf Erbslöh, Pierre Girieud, Alexey von Jawlensky, Alexander Kanoldt, Moissey Kogan, Alexander Mogilewsky, and Marianne von Werefkin.

This exhibition received scant public notice. In November, 1912, Otto Fischer published his *Das Neue Bild*,[48] to bring the group before the public as well as to serve as a refutation to *Der Blaue Reiter,* published earlier that year by Kandinsky and Marc. Fischer said in this book that the New Artists' Association was presently engaged in preparing for its fourth exhibition. This, however, never materialized. The group had evidently served its purpose in rallying the advanced painters and giving them an opportunity to exhibit.

In December, 1911, immediately after the four artists seceded from the association, Franz Marc went to work on an arrangement for a show to be held simultaneously with the association's exhibition. In a letter to his brother, Marc wrote:

The dice have been cast. Kandinsky and I . . . have left the Association. . . . Now we have to fight further! The editorship of *Der Blaue Reiter* will now be the starting point for new exhibitions. I think it is well this way. We will seek to be the center of the new movement. As for the Association—it can take over the role of the *Scholle*.[49]

XVI

Der Blaue Reiter I

Franz Marc (1880–1916) was chiefly responsible for the organization of the first Blaue Reiter exhibition, which opened on December 18, 1911, in two rooms of the Moderne Galerie Thannhauser adjoining the rooms of the third exhibition of the New Artists' Association.

FRANZ MARC

The son of a minor landscape and genre painter in Munich, Marc received a full academic training. In 1900 he began to study at the Munich Academy of Art under Gabriel Hackl and Wilhelm Diez. Even at the beginning he preferred strong color to the heavy gray tone painting of his teachers. In his resentment of the effect of academic instruction on his generation, he later said: "The wasteland of nineteenth century art was our nursery." [1]

Marc's earliest pictures are heavy, lonely, moody landscapes, flatly painted and lacking in aerial perspective. Already they indicate a visual experience of form in flat successive planes rather than in three-dimensional bodies. But by and large his landscapes and portraits from this period are no more outstanding than some of the better work done by the traditional Munich artists.

A trip to Paris and Brittany in 1903 brought a new brightness and vigor into his painting. It is not certain whether he was acquainted with the work of the impressionists at that time, but a quick sketch, like his *Café Chantant* (1903)—an immediate impression caught in a few dabs of India ink— indicates such familiarity.

Apparently gaiety could not long subsist. Marc returned to Munich and a long period of searching; even the titles of his drawings—*The Dead Sparrow, Death Playing the Violin, Head of the Dead Horse, Dying Deer* —give evidence of his melancholy frame of mind. The animal was already assuming an important place as his subject, although the human figure, especially the drawing of the nude, still occupied much of his effort. He was confirmed in his interest in the animal by his friendship with the Swiss animal painter Jean Bloé Niestlé (1884–1942), whose portrait (1906) (pl. 79a) shows Marc's deeply mournful state of mind as well as his sensitivity to his subject. The execution of this charcoal portrait is still in the traditional manner.

At this time (*ca.* 1904–1907) Marc was also interested in the work of the artists' group Scholle. The attempt of the Scholle to create a new style by combining decorative, stylizing Jugendstil elements with *plein-air* painting usually resulted in dull, sentimental, but not unpleasant, posterlike pictures. The clearly drawn contour, planar quality, concern with form and color for their own sake, and the structural composition of their paintings proved to be an important transition for Marc as well as for so many other expressionists in the passage from a rather descriptive to a more conceptual art. Although nonrepresentational elements were still used primarily for purposes of decoration, rather than for the expression of a deeper content, the experience of Jugendstil did much to liberate form from subject matter.

Another trip to Paris helped Marc further in finding his own métier. He left Munich on Easter, 1907, the night of his ill-starred first marriage. He wanted to "bring his hovering and frightened soul to rest in front of the wondrous works of van Gogh." [2] He went to see the work of the impressionists in the Luxembourg; his diary and letters speak of a great turning point in his art, caused by his becoming acquainted with impressionism. Marc was also greatly interested in the Japanese woodcuts he saw in Paris and brought some back to Munich with him. Although he was struck with the impressionists' solution of color, light, and free composition, and with the handling of planes and contour in the Japanese woodcut, he did almost no painting during his stay in Paris except for a few sketches, which show a loosening brush stroke and lightening palette. Marc could never accept the impressionist style as his own: he felt that the new problems of his time called for an altogether different approach toward meaningful art. A letter from Paris told of his admiration of the work he had seen there, but also spoke of his own desire to find the "inner truth of things" and to "express the life of the dream."

When Marc returned from his second trip to Paris, he concerned himself primarily with the most meticulous study of the anatomy of animals. He sketched from nature and in the zoölogical gardens, and studied bone structure in natural history museums. Between 1907 and 1910 he was actually able to earn a partial living as a teacher of anatomy. This exacting study of the animal body was the necessary framework for his later interpretations. His most important lithographs and his animal sculpture in wax and bronze date from 1908 and 1909.

Deer among the Reeds (*ca.* 1908) (pl. 79b) shows his understanding of a rhythm created by the movement of the animal in nature. He wrote to his publisher Reinhard Piper in December, 1908:

I try to intensify my sensitivity for the organic rhythm of all things; I seek pantheist empathy with the vibration and flow of the blood of nature—in the trees, in the animals, in the air. . . . I see no happier medium for the *"Animalization"* of art, as I would like to call it, than the animal picture. . . .[3]

The light palette and impressionist brush stroke of *Deer among the Reeds* did not satisfy Marc. He sought for a color that would be as strongly symbolic as the concave-convex rhythmical line of this painting. In 1910 he painted a few pointillist pictures only to realize that this technique too was not what he desired. Other studies of the same year, very bold in color, show a Fauvist influence. The Mohammedan exhibition of 1910, with its brilliantly colored Oriental textiles, showed Marc the magnificent possibilities of color. But he had to find his own way: he worked unceasingly on the problem of color for his first large animal composition, often only to destroy the results of months of hard labor.

At this time Marc saw the exploitation of the possibilities of color as a means of expression directly communicable to the emotions in the work of the painters of the New Artists' Association, especially Kandinsky. This liberating influence of Kandinsky's was often declared in Marc's own statements and has recently been reaffirmed by his widow:

The greatest impulse occurred through the encounter of the pictures of the *Neue Künstlervereinigung München*, whose center was Kandinsky. It was as if suddenly through this onslaught, strong forces were liberated, which had been held back by his inhibitions. Through the experience of Kandinsky it seems that the scales fell from his eyes and he soon realized the reason why his paintings did not have a unified effect. He wrote at this time: "Everything had then been on an organic basis, only not color." [4]

Marc's search for the free use of meaningful color was further aided by his meeting with August Macke in January, 1910. Macke's own early development will be discussed later, but it is necessary to emphasize that the young Rhenish painter had by this time already a most extraordinary sensitivity and feeling for luminous color. Alois Schardt said in his excellent monograph on Marc:

He was soon linked in friendship to August Macke. The latter, considerably younger, was more optimistic by nature and achieved artistic expression with less effort. This ease was exceedingly beneficial for Franz Marc. In addition, Macke had at that time already solved the problem of color . . . with which Marc still had to struggle violently. [5]

This new treatment of color was important, because it was necessary for the Munich painters—as it had been previously for the artists of the Brücke and the Fauves—that color in painting be liberated from the world of appearance and that it achieve by itself the strongest emotional effect. This, they felt, was possible if color was used independently and in large areas of definite relationships. Marc eventually was to go as far as any of the painters of his generation in delving into the symbolism of color, which he used chiefly to explore animal life. After a considerable time and a great deal of experimentation, he found a fitting synthesis of his line studies and his feeling for color. For more than three years he worked at Sindelsdorf, a small village in Upper Bavaria, on only a few large paintings in an attempt to find a solution for the expression of one particular motif of the horse in landscape. At the time of his first exhibition at the Galerie Brackl in Munich in January, 1910, he received much praise and a fair amount of public success, but he had in no way reached his goal.

Toward the end of 1910 Marc painted his magnificent *Horse in Landscape* (pl. 162). Here he has achieved a complete unity of form and color, and the painting has all the freshness of first discovery. A red horse is seen from the back staring into a broad landscape. The relationship of the animal to its environment is expressed by the positive form of the red horse against the negative form of the wide yellow space; the hills in the background seem to repeat the lines of the horse.

Similar, though lacking some of the direct freshness of the earlier painting, is the *Red Horses* (1911) (pl. 80). The observer is again conscious that Marc's horses seem freed of all human domination or even relationship. Horses by Manet or Degas were trained, well-disciplined animals, objects of human amusement or sport. Marc's horses are free and untamed, moving swiftly in the enjoyment of their life or standing together in close harmony with the surrounding landscape.

Marc considered color and form more abstractly in order the better to demonstrate his feeling of identification with nature: his horses are red, blue, or sometimes yellow, depending upon the emotion he felt and intended to convey; bulls are black or white, cows are a golden yellow. In a letter to Macke, Marc referred to the masculine quality of blue and the passionate quality of red. Yet Marc never described his metaphysics of color symbolism as did Kandinsky; for Marc, each color was a metaphorical "equivalent" by means of which he wanted to penetrate beyond visual reality:

Art is metaphysical . . . it will free itself from man's purposes and desires. We will no longer paint the forest or the horse as they please us or appear to us, but as they really are, as the forest or the horse feel themselves—their absolute being— which lives behind the appearance which we see. We will be successful in so far as we can succeed in overcoming the traditional "logic" of millennia with artistic creativity. There are art forms which are abstract, which can never be proven by human knowledge. These forms have always existed, but were always obscured by human knowledge and desire. The faith in art itself was lacking, but we shall build it: it lives on the "other side." [6]

He actually wished, then, to paint the animal as it feels itself and as it sees the world.

Is there a more mysterious idea for the artist than the conception of how nature may be mirrored in the eye of the animal? How does a horse see the world, or an eagle, or a deer, or a dog? How poor and how soulless is our convention of placing animals in a landscape which belongs to our eyes, instead of penetrating into the soul of the animal in order to imagine his perception? [7]

Marc's *Yellow Cow* (1911) (pl. 81), the most significant of the four paintings he entered in the first Blaue Reiter exhibition, shows a large cow bounding jubilantly through a hilly landscape. The cow is not particularly stylized in form, but its color is remarkable to say the least: a defiant yellow with two large blue markings. Neither is the surrounding countryside real in appearance: the trees are poles; the hills are bumps; the earth is blue and orange, purple and yellow—in short, a carnival landscape with a cow that acts enchanted. The animal does not determine the form of the landscape, but neither does the countryside determine the form of the animal. The curve of a ravine repeats in reverse the arch of the cow's tail; the forms of the hills correspond to the forms of its udders and the taut curve of its belly; the tree trunks balance in angle and match in shape the rigid thrust of the animal's legs as it drives its hooves into the turf. The manner of interpretation recalls the similes in the twenty-ninth Psalm: "The voice of the Lord breaketh the cedars; yea, the Lord breaketh the cedars of Lebanon. He maketh them also to skip like a calf; Lebanon and Sirion like a young unicorn." [8] Color and shape and rhythm in the world outside not only answer color and shape and rhythm in the cow's body, but are made to do so with unusual emphasis. Although the spectator still knows where the landscape ends and the animal begins, he is made to understand the thesis that "Each animal is the embodiment of a cosmic rhythm." [9]

KANDINSKY'S FIRST NONOBJECTIVE PAINTINGS

The importance of Kandinsky's liberating influence on Franz Marc has already been pointed out. The Russian painter himself had taken the step toward so-called nonobjective painting, a category to which two out of three pictures in the first Blaue Reiter exhibition can be assigned. For almost a decade Kandinsky had worked toward this goal, and in 1910 he achieved the first tentative result in the form of a water color in which otherwise disparate forms were organized in a whirling rhythm of color (pl. 82). The first series of large nonobjective paintings was done during the following year.

Nonobjective pictures may have been painted before Kandinsky's water color of 1910 and his more ambitious impressions, improvisations, and compositions of 1911. Possibly the earliest nonobjective paintings by Kupka and Picabia were done not much later. Delaunay painted his nonobjective *Color Disks* in 1912. Recently it has been maintained that the self-taught Lithuanian artist M. K. Čiurlionis painted nonobjective pictures between 1905 and 1910.[10] The reproductions included in Rannit's articles on Čiurlionis are, however, highly symbolic abstractions, verging on the fantastic work by Kubin, Redon, or some surrealists. Representational elements also play a greater part in Picabia's paintings of 1912 than in Kandinsky's paintings of 1911. The American painter Arthur Dove may have painted abstractions as early as 1910, but he remained essentially a lyric landscape painter. In Stuttgart Adolf Hoelzel made attempts at nonobjective paintings in 1911, but, as his biographer Hans Hildebrandt said, "this fact by no means detracts from the great Russian's contribution in calling to life the movement of non-objective painting." [11] Whereas for Hoelzel nonfigurative painting was merely experimentation in additional possibilities, Kandinsky raised nonobjectivity to the "basic principle of his total pictorial creation." [12]

Kandinsky formulated his ideas of nonobjective painting over an extended period of time. Notes for *Concerning the Spiritual in Art* date back to 1901, although the book was completed in 1910. He still expressed many doubts about the possibilities of the new art, and was constantly aware of the dangers. But, believing that his era was at the "spiritual turning point" in most aspects of the human mind and spirit, he saw ahead to the immediate future, when the artist can create forms based on his own emotions rather than on a relation to the visual appearance of objects. "In general nowadays we are still by and large bound to external nature and must find our forms in her. (Purely abstract paintings are still rare.) The only question is, how are we to do it? In other words, how far may we go in altering her forms and colors?" [13] He then replied to his question: "We may go as far as the artist is able to carry his emotion; and once more we see how immense is the need for cultivating this emotion." [14]

Kandinsky frequently expressed his debt to those modern painters whom he considered, in one way or another, as his precursors: Monet, Rossetti, Böcklin, Segantini, van Gogh, Hodler, Cézanne, Matisse, Carrière, and Whistler. Finally, just before the Blaue Reiter period, Kandinsky critically examined cubism. He admired it for seeking to "develop the constructive forms of the epoch," [15] but felt that it was only a transitory form. It "demonstrates how natural forms are subordinated to constructive purposes and what inessential hindrances these realistic forms are. A transition is cubism, in which natural form, by being forcibly subjected to constructional ends, becomes an impediment." [16] Cubism placed a predominant value on form rather than on free expression of the inner necessity that alone can create complete beauty: "That is beautiful which is produced by internal necessity, which springs from the soul." [17]

In this vein he painted *Trojka* (1911) (pl. 83), which creates a highly emotional rhythm. This rhythm is indeed the most essential part of the painting. A fast-swinging whiplash line sets up the basic movement. Smaller lines add to the feeling of great speed, like the small lines in the team of horses—lines that move against one another and set up a forward pushing and pulling motion. This very quick movement of the carriage, below the Russian village on the left, is in contrast to the slower and more mysterious feeling of alarm engendered by the "hill men" on the right. The two are separated by the flower—as large as the hill—that creates a visual center in the painting from which elements fly off in all directions in a centrifugal movement. [18]

At the same time the horse-and-rider motif still occupied Kandinsky.

He painted *Lyrisches* (1911) (pl. 84), which may be considered his final statement of this leitmotiv, now becoming a symbol of dynamic movement. The tension evident in *Trojka* is heightened even further in *Lyrisches*. Kandinsky has stripped his earlier concepts of man on horseback to the barest essentials, and the great economy of means makes this painting look almost like a drawing. Horse and horseman have been released from the struggle that occupied them in earlier paintings. Complications have been resolved as the rider speeds ahead with easy assurance.

In *Composition No. 4* (1911) (pl. 85), a painting typical of Kandinsky's earliest nonobjective work, the energetic lines in the upper left may still recall the horseman motif, as Kenneth Lindsay maintained in his careful tracing of the theme.[19] Certain elements of this painting are related to objects in nature: the two vertical lines in the center may be projected as a tree trunk; the form behind them appears to be a boulder; and a deep gorge leading toward an arch may be seen at the left. Kandinsky himself had something to say about the painting: "Mutual harmony of quiet masses, contrast of indistinct and clearly defined forms, preponderance of the sound of color over the sound of form, dissolution, etc."[20] An illusion of three-dimensional space is created primarily by the series of irregular planes. The vertical lines in the center act as a *repoussoir;* the eye follows the diagonal shapes moving off to the right. A boulderlike element occupying the middle space is modeled with a variety of hues and values and has a dark outline that gives it a rounded, plastic appearance. On the right the eye is pushed toward a jagged and angular line resembling the outline of a mountain and belonging to a plane farther back than the boulder. Behind it are two almost vertical cone-shaped objects. In the center a black, notched line behind the boulderlike shape resembles the outline of a transparent plane and moves the eye far back toward an indistinct area. On the left a convulsive movement of lines of various thicknesses suggests the shapes of needles, combs, and boomerangs, all leading the eye down toward a great arch that rises over a round form. A definite rhythm is set up in the painting: it is quick on the left, where small, thin lines jet out briefly but become more leisurely; sweeping on the right, where the divided diagonal shapes seem to move more slowly and deliberately toward the distant plane.

The colors, both gay and somber, are intense throughout, and—as Kandinsky himself said—may or may not adhere to contours. They easily change their values, their saturation, and their textures, and help to create what seems to be the chief tension in the painting: the movement among the arch on the left, the boulderlike shape in the center, and the divided diagonal on the right—all three centered in the vertical black lines in the center which inaugurate the rhythm.

Although *Trojka, Lyrisches,* and *Composition No. 4* were not in the first Blaue Reiter exhibition, the three Kandinsky paintings that were there—*Composition No. 5, Improvisation No. 22,* and *Impression: Moscow* (all 1911)—were similar in style to the three pictures discussed here.

A hand-colored sketch for *Composition No. 4* was included in the *Blaue Reiter* almanac the following year.

THE FIRST BLAUE REITER EXHIBITION AND INVITED ARTISTS

The group "Der Blaue Reiter" consisted strictly speaking of only Kandinsky and Marc, who were fully responsible for the first exhibition held at Thannhauser in December, 1911. The name of the organization is derived from the title of the almanac on which the two artists had been working since April, 1911. Kandinsky originally thought of calling the almanac *Die Kette;* [21] Marc thought of *Blaue Blätter.*[22] The idea of using the same name for the exhibiting body as for the publication may have been derived from a similar usage several years earlier by the Moscow group *Mir Iskusstva.*

The artists who participated in the Blaue Reiter exhibition were invited by Kandinsky and Marc: Henri Rousseau, Paris; A. Bloch, Munich; D. Burliuk, Moscow; V. Burliuk, Crimea; H. Campendonk, Sindelsdorf; Robert Delaunay, Paris; E. Epstein, Paris; E. Kahler, Prague; A. Macke, Bonn; G. Münter, Munich; J. B. Niestlé, Sindelsdorf; A. Schönberg, Berlin.

The Blaue Reiter was neither a school nor a movement. Nolde's criticism of the Brücke—that the work of its artists was confusingly similar—could never apply to the Blaue Reiter, who stated as their motto on the title page of their first exhibition catalog: "We do not seek to propagandize a *single* precise and special form in this small exhibition, but we aim to show in the *variety* of represented forms how the artist's inner desire results in manifold forms." [23]

The vitality of the group was strengthened and stimulated by its diversity, and the artists were more concerned with the mental approach than with the forms through which they expressed this spirit. By contrast with the multiformity of expression of the Blaue Reiter, cubism and futurism were almost "school" movements.

The first exhibition included Kandinsky's early nonobjective paintings, animal pictures by Franz Marc, and paintings by the group that was living close to Franz Marc in Sindelsdorf, a little town in the foothills of the Bavarian Alps. Like the impressionists—if for different reasons—these painters wanted to get away from the city and live close to nature. Marc settled in the small Bavarian village in 1910, and was joined almost immediately by his old friend Niestlé, who also had a canvas in the exhibition. August Macke, who had been living in nearby Tegernsee from 1909 to 1910, visited Marc in Sindelsdorf in September, 1911. Heinrich Campendonk, whose work Marc and Kandinsky had seen almost accidentally, was invited by Marc to join him; Campendonk moved to Sindelsdorf from his native Krefeld in October, 1911, and remained there until the outbreak of the war in 1914.

August Macke (1887–1914) influenced Marc's development as a colorist, but perhaps his young, carefree, positive personality and frank enjoyment of life were as important in his association with Marc. Unlike so many of his colleagues, Macke was not a theorist but solely a painter—perhaps because he worked freely, without mental turmoil or conflict with external forces, as though the creative process was the natural use of his energies in a harmonious world.[24]

Macke, who was born in Westphalia, began his training at the Düsseldorf Academy, later transferring to the Arts and Crafts School. His most important early influences seem to have been paintings by Böcklin and Hodler, which he saw during trips to Switzerland; much more effective for his own development was the slightly later first acquaintance with Manet, who, he writes: "has so much poetry, that he does not need to convert his women into naiads." [25] Bernhard Koehler, a wealthy Berlin manufacturer who was later the important patron of the Blaue Reiter, took Macke to Paris in 1907 to see the famous Carrière retrospective exhibition; Macke's great experience in Paris was, however, the impressionists, especially Renoir.

Returning to Germany, Macke decided to study with Germany's famous impressionist Lovis Corinth, but when he got to Berlin he was considerably more interested in the modern French paintings in the National Gallery. He spent less than a year with Corinth. In the spring of 1908 he made a second trip to Italy; in the same summer Koehler invited Macke to join him a second time in Paris, in order to rely on the painter's judgment and taste for the purchase of modern French paintings for Koehler's growing collection. Following Macke's advice, Koehler bought not only important impressionist paintings but also two pictures by Seurat; they met Fénéon, and saw *La Grande Jatte* and *Le Cahut* in his house.[26]

The influence of impressionism and neoimpressionism is clearly evident in Macke's painting *Sunny Garden* (1908) (pl. 86). It is quite unified in its high tone value; its brush stroke is pointillist, leaving parts of the canvas blank.

After a year in the army and a third trip to Paris, Macke moved from Bonn to Tegernsee in Upper Bavaria. Here he painted a long series of landscapes, figure paintings, still life. His work became much richer in color, definite in contour, simple in form. Frequently he went to nearby Munich, where, in February, 1910, he saw the Matisse exhibit. This exhibit was the dominating influence of this period, and had an important effect on his whole development. But the young painter was still open to a great variety of influences. It was his special gift to be able to expose himself to a great many, often contradictory, influences, and to transform them into his own personal idiom. In January, 1910, Macke met Franz Marc, who became his most intimate friend.

Marc introduced Macke to the painters of the New Artists' Association, Munich: Kandinsky, Jawlensky, Werefkina. For a short time Macke was part of the group; he even painted very much like Marc and Kandinsky, as in his *Storm* (1911) (pl. 87),[27] the one painting by Macke that incidentally was valued most highly by the two Blaue Reiter painters. Painted in the "style" of Marc, *Storm* has little of Macke's own individuality. His symbolic-abstract paintings, like *Storm* and *Indians*,[28] remain an exception in his work.

Although Macke contributed an article to the Blaue Reiter almanac, he objected to the preoccupation with theory and form. Seeing the second exhibition of the Association, he wrote: "Kandinsky, Bechtejeff and Erbslöh all have gigantic artistic sensitivity. But their means of expression are too large for what they wish to say. . . . Because of this the human element is lacking. They strive, I think, too much for form."[29] Macke was primarily a painter; Marc, on the other hand, believed that ideas could be more important than painting. Macke developed as an important artist only after his Blaue Reiter period. This was true also of Campendonk, the other Rhenish artist who exhibited with the group.

Heinrich Campendonk was born in 1889 in Krefeld. His training included a fruitful apprenticeship with Thorn-Prikker, whose decorative stained-glass designs were an important part of the Jugendstil movement. Campendonk worked in a similar style when assisting with the murals of the Osnabrück Cathedral. Thorn-Prikker, it must be remembered, had also painted semiabstract symbolist pictures like *The Bride* (pl. 18) as early as 1892, and this freedom of expression was to have important repercussions in Campendonk's own work.

Campendonk was working "in complete solitude in Krefeld" when his paintings "were seen accidentally by Kandinsky and Franz Marc. Marc asked the artist to come to Sindelsdorf in Upper Bavaria, where he moved in October, 1911."[30] At first the influence of the Blaue Reiter was inescapable, and Campendonk consciously followed Marc, although with his own gay imagination and sense of color he could not become a mere imitator. A picture like the *Jumping Horse* (1911),[31] one of two paintings in the first Blaue Reiter exhibition, is under Marc's domination. Later Campendonk, like Macke, developed a style that was very much his own, but for him too the contact with the Blaue Reiter was to be a great liberating influence.

The American-born painter Albert Bloch (born 1881) was represented by six paintings in the exhibition, including the *Harlequin with Three Pierrots* (1911) (pl. 88), now in the Art Institute of Chicago. Bloch was born and educated in St. Louis, and then went to New York and Paris, but it was in Munich that he found the greatest artistic kinship. There he was captivated by Marc's painting and Kandinsky's mind. Some forty years later he wrote about his experience:

What wonder, then, that an obscure newcomer like me, still in his twenties, who had until then shown only an occasional picture or two at the jury-shows of the Berlin and Munich Secessions, should feel delighted and flattered to be asked by two such men to join them in their planned enterprise of *Der blaue Reiter,* which in itself interested me very little, despite my awareness (or suspicion) that the group or rather the team of Marc and Kandinsky was to make Central European art history.[32]

Bloch's work from his most productive Munich period shows a wealth of imagery, and seems to use the entire scale of colors. His *Harlequin with Three Pierrots* shows clowns dancing on clouds surrounded by a splash of fireworks or confetti. Space is completely imaginary and indefinite. The whole composition is unified by a wavy, over-all rhythm. Describing other, similar paintings of his, he said: "I think it strikes a note of *pure fun,* of unbridled extravagance and folly. When I speak of doing these things in a spirit of fun, of romping frolicsomeness, I do not mean, of course, that I have set out consciously or purposely to be funny. As with all my pictures, the clowns are the expression of a mood." [33]

Albert Bloch returned to the United States in 1921 and, after a year's teaching at the Academy of Fine Arts in Chicago, became director of the Department of Drawing and Painting at the University of Kansas in Lawrence, a position he held from 1923 until his retirement in 1947.

Gabriele Münter also had six paintings in the exhibition, some of which were much less austere in mood than the *Landscape with White Wall* (1910). Her *Still Life with Queen* (1912) (pl. 89) [34] is typical of her highly personal vision of the world at this time. In this painting she uses a light pastel palette in which blues, yellows, and pinks predominate. The flowers, drawn with arabesque lines, come apart to reveal the visionary "queen," a floating doll, modeled and costumed by Alexander Sacharoff, [35] the famous Russian dancer and a member of the New Artists' Association. The light, incorporeal colors of the doll contrast to the heavier, more representational and earthy colors of the flowers. The whole painting has an almost surrealist effect in its combination of the real still life and the imaginary figure, and is similar in style to the somewhat more somber *Still Life* (1911) reproduced in the catalog of the first Blaue Reiter exhibition.

Vladimir Burliuk sent two paintings from Russia: an imaginary landscape and a *Portrait Study* (1911), [36] formed of facets that indicate how strongly he had been influenced by cubism. David Burliuk's *Head* (1911), [37] on the other hand, is a transparent, two-dimensional outline, transversed by large areas of color that have absolutely no reference to the face itself. Eugen Kahler of Prague, who had just died at the age of twenty-nine, was represented by two paintings of dream visions.

Arnold Schönberg (1874–1951) not only contributed an article [38] and a song [39] to the Blaue Reiter almanac, but was also invited to send three paintings to the first Blaue Reiter exhibition. Schönberg had painted a good deal between 1907 and 1910, and had an exhibition of his work at the Galerie Hugo Heller in Vienna in the autumn of 1910. [40] Kandinsky, becoming an immediate admirer of the nonacademic quality and childlike directness of these pictures, published an article on them in the first book on Schönberg, [41] *Die Bilder,* and praised the composer's efforts to set down his subjective emotions in permanent form.

Kandinsky's interest in Schönberg's primitive directness may be related to the former's great admiration for Henri Rousseau. Kandinsky considered Rousseau the father of the new realism and his own counterpart in modern painting. Kandinsky referred to Rousseau in speaking of the "great realism" as one of the poles of contemporary art.[42] Rousseau, he felt, arrived at his similarly pure emotional stage in painting not by abstraction but by a naïve and total immersion in the reality of the object. Rousseau's unpretentious, emotional directness was similarly unconcerned with traditional formal values, and his form was almost wholly the result of his own imagination.

Kandinsky had bought six paintings by Rousseau during his stay in Paris in 1906–1907 and brought them back to Munich. Two of these were shown in the first Blaue Reiter exhibition, and all were reproduced in the almanac, as against three pictures by Kandinsky and two by Marc. Rousseau had a formative influence on the entire Munich group. In a letter to Robert Delaunay, Marc wrote on March 11, 1913: "The douanier Rousseau is the only one whose art often haunts me. I constantly attempt to understand how he painted his marvelous pictures. I try to identify myself with the inner state of this venerable painter, that is to say, with a state of great love."[43]

ROBERT DELAUNAY AND HIS INFLUENCE

Robert Delaunay (1885–1941), who exhibited five paintings at the first Blaue Reiter show, also had been a great admirer of Henri Rousseau. "He introduced the Douanier to his mother who described her travels in India and inspired the famous painting 'La Charmeuse de serpents' which she commissioned."[44] Delaunay did not exhibit in Paris until the Salon des Indépendents of 1911. There Kandinsky's friend the painter Elizabeth Epstein [45] saw several of Delaunay's canvases in the famous Room 41 along with the most recent work by Le Fauconnier, Léger, Gleizes, and Metzinger. When she described Delaunay's work to Kandinsky, the latter asked Delaunay to contribute to the Blaue Reiter exhibition. Delaunay responded by sending four paintings and one drawing.

Delaunay was of central importance to the Munich painters: his color was always the determining factor in his work, whereas cubism was almost accidental to it. His need for bright color seems to have been extraordinarily intense.[46]

After experimentation in neoimpressionism and cubism, and thorough familiarization with Cézanne, Delaunay in 1909 began his series of the ambulatory at St. Séverin (pl. 90). As in other cubist paintings of the time, the picture seems to advance outward from the picture plane toward the observer. The quick succession of steep, diagonal lines, the variation in value, and the intricate treatment of the arches—all create a rapid rhythm in the picture. The color is still rather somber. One painting of St. Séverin was in the first Blaue Reiter show; it was bought by Adolf Erbslöh, and was reproduced in the Blaue Reiter almanac.

In 1910 Delaunay began his second great series: the towers—chiefly the Eiffel Tower, but also the tower of the Cathedral of Laon. Here he adds color rhythm to the cubist vocabulary. In the Eiffel Tower series he works with overlapping and partly transparent cubist planes, but these have become planes of pure color. A simultaneity of color and light sensations is achieved by a leaping, swinging movement of angular, prismatic planes. Great height, power, and strength, plus the implicit danger of collapse, are integral parts of his artistic vision in this series.[47]

In 1911 Delaunay began a number of abstract views of the city, seen through his open windows. There is now little depth or perspective, but luminous color overflows all limitations of space. His friend Apollinaire coined the term "Orphism" for these highly abstract works, which inspired his poem *Les Fenêtres:*

> La fenêtre s'ouvre comme une orange
> Le beau fruit de la lumière.

Two paintings of this series were in the first Blaue Reiter exhibition, and one was reproduced in the almanac. These views (pl. 163) recall the paintings of Seurat. Like Seurat, Delaunay works with harmonious areas of color and goes beyond the limitations of the frame; but where Seurat hollowed out the canvas, Delaunay adheres to the two-dimensional aspect of the canvas. He dissolves his motif of the city into flickering small color planes in the shapes of squares, triangles, rhomboids, and trapezoids that interpenetrate each other, achieving a kaleidoscopic play of pure, spectral colors.

These paintings were of the greatest importance in the further development of Marc, Macke, and Klee, who also endeavored to use pure color as a structural element. Later in 1912 Marc, Macke, and Klee went to see Delaunay in Paris. Klee then translated Delaunay's article "Sur la lumière" and published it in *Der Sturm,*[48] and an extensive and fruitful exchange of ideas resulted between Delaunay and the German painters.

In January, 1913, Delaunay and Apollinaire traveled to Berlin—with a stopover at Macke's in Bonn—to attend the Delaunay exhibition arranged by Walden in the Sturm galleries.[49] Delaunay exhibited with the Blaue Reiter, and Apollinaire lectured to the German public. It is incorrect to assume, however, that, after giving an all-important stimulus to the Blaue Reiter group, Delaunay had nothing more to say;[50] instead, as was true with Le Fauconnier, it was a matter of reciprocal influences. Following Kandinsky's lead, Delaunay began to eliminate subject matter from his painting, maintaining that "color alone is both form and subject," and occupied himself with circular and infinite color rhythms.[51]

The first and most significant Blaue Reiter exhibit closed in Munich in January, 1912, after which it toured Germany, sponsored by Macke's friend Bernhard Koehler. At the end of January, it opened in Cologne; in March, Herwath Walden, editor of the review *Der Sturm,* showed it in his newly opened gallery, where it was the first of many Sturm exhibitions.

XVII

Der Blaue Reiter II

Winter and spring of 1912 were probably the most active periods of the Blaue Reiter. January marked not only the close of the first exhibition at Thannhauser, but also the publication of Kandinsky's *Concerning the Spiritual in Art,* the first edition of which was so quickly sold that a second edition was published by Piper in Munich in April. The same spring Piper published the all-important almanac *Der Blaue Reiter* as well as *Klänge,*[1] Kandinsky's book of prose poems and woodcuts.

THE SECOND EXHIBITION

The first Blaue Reiter exhibition had moved on to Berlin in March when the second exhibition opened at the gallery of Hans Goltz in Munich. This exhibit was limited to graphic arts and water colors, but the more than three hundred items came from an extraordinary variety of sources. In 1910, during an exhibition of the New Secession in Berlin, there had still been no contact between the new trends in painting within various parts of Germany. Nolde was riding with another artist on a streetcar in Berlin and "speaking more than usual about our young, budding art. 'What are the names?' he said, somewhat excitedly. 'Kirchner, Schmidt-Rottluff, Heckel, Otto Mueller, Pechstein,' I said. He knew nothing of them as I knew nothing of the concurrent young Munich artists: Marc, Erbslöh, Kanoldt, and the Russians, Kandinsky and Jawlensky. . . ."[2]

In the second Blaue Reiter exhibit Nolde was represented with seventeen graphic works. Kirchner sent thirty-three drawings, etchings, lithographs, and woodcuts; Heckel, twenty-eight prints and drawings; Mueller, fourteen items; Pechstein was represented with the largest number—thirty-eight water colors, drawings, and prints.

The Blaue Reiter members themselves were not only considerably more modest, but, being more deliberate in their work, probably never had the vast amount of material on hand that their northern friends made available.

Kandinsky showed twelve water colors; Franz Marc, five animal studies; Gabriele Münter, August Macke, and Albert Bloch, several studies, drawings, and water colors.

France was represented with prints and drawings of the leading cubists: Braque, Derain, de la Fresnaye, Picasso. Delaunay was surprisingly absent from this exhibition. Other French painters included were Robert Lotiron, Paul Vera, and Maurice Vlaminck.

A number of new Russian names appeared in the exhibition catalog: Nathalie Gontcharova, Michael Larionoff, and Kasimir Malevich. The Blaue Reiter, like its predecessor, the New Artists' Association, had the ability to attract the newest trends in painting, no matter where they occurred. Larionoff (born 1881) had probably just written the *Rayonist Manifesto* (dated 1912, but published in 1913),[3] which set forth a philosophy of abstract art, closely related to futurism (Marinetti had been to Moscow in 1910), that stressed color relationship as of paramount importance in painting.

Kasimir Malevich (1878–1935) founded the suprematist movement in Moscow in 1913. In the same year he exhibited a plain white square on a black background and spoke of the supreme emotion engendered by the absence of objects.

The Russian painters who had exhibited earlier in Munich had been greatly inspired by the outstanding collections of Morosoff and Stchoukine, representing recent French painting; the Russian nonobjectivists were influenced by Russia's own leading painter—Kandinsky. Kandinsky had published the important "Letters from Munich" in the Russian art magazine *Apollon* in 1909 and 1910. His article "Content and Form" was published in Odessa in *Salon 2* in connection with a large international exhibition in 1910–1911; in December, 1911, Kandinsky's still unpublished manuscript "Concerning the Spiritual in Art" "was presented to the Congress of Russian Artists held in St. Petersburg. This book was printed in its entirety in Russian the following year." [4]

There seems to be little doubt that the movements of rayonism, suprematism, as well as the slightly later constructivism, felt the impact of Kandinsky. Whether or not Kandinsky's own postwar style was in turn influenced by these Russian movements is still a moot question that may very well demand an affirmative answer.

The second Blaue Reiter exhibition not only represented its own members, the Brücke, the cubists, the rayonists, the suprematists, and nineteenth-century popular Russian woodcuts, but also a newly founded group of Swiss painters: Der Moderne Bund.

"Der Moderne Bund is an association of Swiss artists, who seek expression of their personalities in a greatly widened realm of art, the realm of Expressionism," [5] wrote Paul Klee, who had been one of its members, in a review of an exhibition of the group in Zürich. This exhibition included eight paintings by Kandinsky, work by Marc, Münter, Amiet, Matisse, and two cubists: Le Fauconnier and Delaunay. Cubism, according to Klee, was "a special branch of Expressionism." [6] Klee's review contained also one of the earliest definitions of expressionism: a form of artistic expression in which a long period can elapse between the moment of perception and the actual painting, in which several impressions can be combined or rejected in the final composition, and in which the constructive element of art is heightened and emphasized.

The Moderne Bund had been founded in Weggis, Switzerland, by Hans Arp, Wilhelm Gimmi, Walter Helbig, Oscar Lüthy, and D. Rossiné in 1911, and the first exhibition of the group took place in a Lucerne hotel in the summer of that year. Paul Klee joined the group, and all the artists except Rossiné were included in the second Blaue Reiter show. Klee himself was represented by seventeen drawings and *gouaches*. After the large exhibition in Zürich in the summer of 1912, the Moderne Bund continued to exist for some time. Perhaps after the model of the Brücke, it had a lay as well as professional membership, and published portfolios of graphic work for distribution among the lay members. [7]

PAUL KLEE

Klee had settled in Munich in 1906. As the art and literary correspondent of the Swiss review *Die Alpen,* he also wrote about the second Blaue Reiter exhibition, in which he himself was included: "The dealer [Hans Goltz] is taking a risk as the 'first on the street' to exhibit Cubist art in his show window. This is considered by the passersby as typically *schwabingisch*. Picasso, Derain, and Braque as *'schwabinger Freunderln'*—what a pretty thought." [8]

Although Klee had not been an original member of the Blaue Reiter, his later close association with Kandinsky and his stature as one of the leading painters of the twentieth century merit a discussion of his early development in this framework.

Paul Klee (1879–1940) was born in a suburb of Bern. He grew up in a predominantly musical atmosphere: his father, who was German-born and came from a long line of master organists, taught music in Bern and was an outstanding musicologist; his mother, whose background was also musical, encouraged these same inclinations in Klee. By the age of ten Klee was already playing the violin in an orchestra. He continued playing in concerts in Bern, and remained an excellent amateur for the rest of his life, playing chamber music in his homes in Munich, Weimar, and Dessau. His performances of Bach and Mozart are said to have combined the greatest precision with unusual sensitivity.

Klee began to paint when he was about ten, under the inspiration of his maternal grandmother, who painted ornamental flower pieces. At a very early age he seemed aware of the value of his imaginative and artistic inclinations, and wanted to devote himself fully to the dream-fantasies that seemed so important to him. "But aside from these sensible occupations, I

had to graduate from the humanistic Gymnasium which became more painful to me every year." [9]

Having completed his formal education, Klee went to Munich for the
first time in 1898 and began to study painting with the painter Knirr, who
encouraged his talents. After two years—he was twenty-one at the time—
he had definitely made up his mind to become a painter rather than a
musician.

I work, that I can say with assurance, day and night, in order to digest everything
which offers itself to me and then, if possible, I try to recreate it as a work of art.
I am no longer a hermit or dreamer, but take part in everything I can; I open my
eyes widely and grasp what is to be grasped. That is a necessity for a painter who
wants to formulate life in the most intimate connection with the dear earth. I have
become a real painter. Not an inkling of wavering—but I am very certain that I
am born for painting, not for music. [10]

Klee, like Kandinsky and Marc, was undoubtedly stimulated by the
new and vital approaches to visual form that stirred Munich in the first
decade of the century, when the abstract form of Jugendstil had begun to
replace the moody landscape painting of the Dachau school.

Klee was admitted to Stuck's class at the academy in 1900. He received
severe formal training in figure drawing and, like Kandinsky, was stimulated by the teacher's imaginative powers. Kandinsky was also studying
with Stuck that year, but there is no indication that the two young painters
met at the time. Although Klee learned much about drawing with Stuck,
he learned little about painting; it was many years before he found any
close relationship to the world of color.

In 1901 he went on a study trip to Italy with his friend the Swiss sculptor Hermann Haller. In Italy his eyes opened to the great cultures of the past.
He spoke of "finding a paradise in ancient art," of the great impression
made on him by Michelangelo, and the even greater effect of the early
Christian mosaics. Strangely enough, he discovered the Gothic in Florence,
and "the Baroque startled me." [11]

All aspects of life fascinated the young artist. His friend and dealer Karl
Nierendorf wrote about Klee's

visit to the famous Aquarium at Naples, probably the only existing at the time. In
a darkened room the unearthly world of the ocean appeared behind glass windows,
close enough to make one feel the breath and the life of this monstrous fauna and
weirdly demonic flora. How fascinating to watch a flower's transformation into an
animal and to discover a rock to be a turtle or an old mossy fish. Klee was struck to
meet in tangible form phantoms and apparitions he had envisioned as a child and
which had impelled his imagination toward creative endeavor. [12]

Enriched by his Italian experience, Klee returned to Bern, where for
several years he worked slowly and carefully in a constant, conscious effort
to find his own style by starting again from the very beginning. In Italy
he had realized how much had been done in the past, and he conceived his

task to be not the playing of clever new tricks—which he felt was expected of him—but the making of a small and humble beginning constantly restrained by sincerity of intention.[13]

Klee spent much time in reading; his tastes included Poe, Gogol, Dostoevski, E. T. A. Hoffmann, Baudelaire, and the French symbolists. A similar preference for the symbolic and fantastic manifested itself in his tastes in past and contemporary art. At the Munich Cabinet of Engravings he saw the works of Beardsley and the visionary engravings of Blake. The form as well as the content of Goya's *Caprichos* aroused his admiration. Probably on a brief trip to Paris in 1905 Klee familiarized himself with Redon; two years later he was introduced to the grotesque world of Ensor, which made a lasting impression on him.[14] It has often been said that Klee's art is so completely unique that it is impossible to speak of antecedents and influences. Yet the inspirations from other artists throughout his entire development do become evident from careful analysis of his work. His earliest works show the influence of early German Renaissance woodcuts and engravings, and of quattrocento Italian drawings.

The volume of his work from this period in Bern is exceedingly small: Klee completed only seventeen etchings in the six years from 1901 to 1906; there are some drawings but no paintings. These early etchings give an inkling of his later and mature work, of his constant attempt to balance fantasy and reality within a deliberate structure; yet they were still basically naturalistic treatments of allegorical subjects. His actual work had by no means caught up with his much more abstract theoretical ideas, as expressed in a letter to Hans Bloesch:

Plastic art never begins with a poetic mood or with an idea, but with the construction of one or more figures, with the harmonious accord of several colors or tone values, or with the evaluation of space relationships, etc. Whether or not an idea is added makes absolutely no difference; it can be, but does not have to be.[15]

Conversely, although he was fully aware of the significance of form, his series of early etchings is much concerned with literary subject matter. The titles—*Virgin in the Tree; Two Men, Supposing Each Other in a Higher Position, Meet; Perseus; Victory of Wit over Suffering; Crown Mania; The Hero with the Wing*—indicate both the satirical content and the importance of subject matter. These are no direct studies from nature, but grotesque exaggerations and caricatured distortions. Certain influences from the art of the past are evident, and James Thrall Soby has pointed out the unmistakable similarity between Klee's *Virgin in the Tree* and Pisanello's *Allegory of Luxury*.[16] It may actually have been the experience of these early Italian drawings to which Klee referred when he spoke of the discovery of the Gothic in Florence.

The tortuous curves and flat, two-dimensional space of an etching like *Crown Mania (Kronennarr)* of 1904 (pl. 91) make it very much part of the Jugendstil of the time. Its ironic content, its literary interest in decadence, its indication of emotion by means of theatrical gesture—all bring it even closer to that movement. Klee also communicates his message of social satire by representing the obscenely naked, plucked-chicken-like "monarchist" as sticking his buttocks up into the air, bending over blindly before the haloed crown, and teetering on the edge of a gaping abyss—a telling comment on the Prussian virtue of blind obedience to authority. Klee was to battle such conventions through every subsequent picture that left his hand, until he was finally driven from his adopted land thirty years later. He soon overcame the macabre atmosphere and obvious satirical quality of his early work. Instead of contenting himself with poking fun at the Philistine and destroying the masks behind which Philistinism hides, he demanded, by means of his work, the most thorough reëxamination of social and personal values. And this he did by his complete mastery of the various possibilities of line, chiaroscuro, and color—or "measure, weight and quality," as he referred to them later in his published lecture *On Modern Art*.[17]

An exhibition of ten of his etchings in a large show at the Munich Secession brought Klee back to Munich in 1906. Attracted by the manifold cultural activities of that city, he decided to remain. He saw important exhibitions of the "classic" impressionists, and of van Gogh, Cézanne, and Matisse. The influence of each of these can be seen in his pen-and-wash drawings from this period. Under the inspiration of the impressionists he discarded his earlier allegories and worked directly from nature, loosening his pen stroke to catch a quick impression of atmosphere and landscape by means of a rapid, vibrating line—as in the ink drawing *Willikofun* (1909) (pl. 92a). But far from being impressionist, Klee's individual perception was clearly evident in the little wriggles or miniature lines which take on a life of their own. From the same period, certain pen-and-ink studies are strongly reminiscent of van Gogh's vigorous circular brush stroke. Klee began to add color to his work at this time; some of his paintings clearly show familiarity with the distortion of shapes, the negation of linear perspective, and the free use of color by Matisse. In several water colors he applies his pigment in flat, related areas in the manner of Cézanne. Even before the Cézanne exhibit in Munich in 1909, Klee became increasingly conscious of the significance of structure. "How far one goes beyond the scaffolding is voluntary. The scaffolding by itself may exert a visual effect which is deeper than that of surface by itself."[18]

The results of this early period are still not of great importance in themselves, but Klee had found his direction: a free, highly imaginative improvisation based on a definite, disciplined structure.

By October, 1910, he had finished a sufficient body of work for his first one-man show in the Bern Museum. This exhibition then traveled to Basel, Winterthur, and Zürich, and was shown at the Moderne Galerie Thannhauser in Munich in the fall of 1911. His *Scaffolding Is Being Loaded* (1910) (pl. 92b)[19] dates from this period. The total composition is much more structural than in his earlier landscapes. The spectator is still confronted with a quick impression, yet this is now evoked by almost geometric planes. In this wash drawing, Klee makes the most of the effect created by the movement of a fine pen across rough paper, which is largely responsible for the joggling, nervous, constantly active line.

When a point moves and becomes a line, it requires time. Also when a line becomes a plane. The same is true of the movement of planes into spaces. Does a picture come into being all at once? No, it is constructed piece by piece, just like a house. . . .[20]

The exhibition in Munich immediately attracted the attention of the members of the New Artists' Association. Alfred Kubin, especially, saw in Klee a great affinity to his own work, and went to see the young painter to ask him for one of his drawings. At that time there was considerable similarity between the work of the two graphic artists, and a mutual influence resulted from their acquaintance. Yet the difference between Kubin's macabre visions and Klee's quiet, understanding humor seems much more significant than the similarities. Kubin confronts a hostile world with cynical antagonism. Klee, having much deeper insight, shows *The Mocker Mocked.* He wrote about Kubin in his diary in 1915: "He stopped half-way. He longed for the crystalline but was unable to free himself from the tenacious clay of the world of appearance." [21]

Klee's illustrations for *Candide* (1911) [22] are superficially similar to Kubin. Voltaire's characters have been transformed into frightening insects: they look like praying mantises. Yet the element of wit had been introduced: the gestures of the insects betraying their trite foibles are thoroughly human. Like Voltaire, Klee has used exaggeration and distortion to poke fun at the humanity with whom he deeply sympathizes.

Kubin bought some of Klee's drawings and brought them to Kandinsky's attention. Klee had already met August Macke at the home of Louis Moillet in the summer of 1911, and he now came into close personal relation with Marc and Kandinsky. Their work was an affirmation of Klee's own ideas. There he saw the bold beginnings of a new art in which form was the result of the expression of human feeling. He wrote about his admiration for these artists in a review for *Die Alpen:*

Among the private galleries, Thannhauser has again attracted my attention by its [third] exhibition of the New Association and the still more radical secession, called Der Blaue Reiter . . . the most daring of them here is Kandinsky, who is also an active writer.[23]

Although Klee's work was to find forms different from those of Kandinsky and Marc, he felt himself to be in basic agreement with their esthetic theories about the spiritual essence of art. Kandinsky's influence as the great liberator was as significant for Klee as it was for Marc and so many other painters. But, although he became a close friend of Marc and Kandinsky, Klee's part in the Blaue Reiter remained that of a junior colleague. In 1936 Kandinsky wrote:

I admire Klee very much and consider him one of today's greatest painters, but in the far off time when I was doing *Der Blaue Reiter,* Klee was at the beginning of his development. Nevertheless I very much liked the little drawings which he was doing then, and I reproduced one of these drawings in *Der Blaue Reiter*. This was the full extent of his participation in the book.[24]

Klee's whimsical landscape *Residential Section* (1912) (pl. 93), although remarkable for its childlike freshness of concept, is only a minor work by comparison with Kandinsky's nonobjective compositions of 1912, Marc's major animal compositions, or Delaunay's powerful explorations of color relationships.

Sensing the renewal of art in the new painting in Munich, which had been able to shake loose the ballast of a "tradition which was choked with sand" and "presented the epitome of fatigue," Klee "saluted those men working together on the coming reformation." [25]

THE BLAUE REITER ALMANAC

In the Blaue Reiter almanac [26] Klee is represented only by a small drawing, *Stonecutters,* similar in style to *Scaffolding* (1910).

As early as 1910 Franz Marc wished to articulate the aim of modern art and its relationship to art forms of the past in a periodical to be called *Blaue Blätter*. Kandinsky had similar intentions, and said that, after completing the manuscript of *Concerning the Spiritual in Art* at the end of 1910,

. . . my desire matured to edit a book (a kind of almanac) in which only artists were to participate as authors. I dreamt primarily of painters and musicians. The corrupt distinction of one art from another, furthermore, of "Art" from folk art and children's art, from "ethnology"—all these firmly built walls rising between forms which in my eyes seem so closely related, indeed frequently identical; briefly the synthetic relationship of art left me no peace.[27]

Slowly the idea took shape. During 1911 Marc and Kandinsky worked constantly to assemble the visual material and to collect and edit manuscripts. R. Piper, the Munich publisher, worked with the editors. Bernhard Koehler helped finance the project. For the pictures to be included in the volume, Franz Marc made arrangements with the Brücke painters, now living in Berlin and still unknown in Europe. Originally Max Pechstein had promised to send a manuscript on the New Secession. Macke helped with the material on primitive and tribal art,[28] and contributed the article "Die Masken." Kandinsky took responsibility for the Russian material.

In spite of a desire to reject all traditions ("Traditions are beautiful— to create—not to follow" [29]), Marc and Kandinsky realized that their feeling about their own creativity was related to the past. They tried to establish ties with all art that neither submitted to convention nor copied nature. They hoped to find altogether new solutions in their own work, and —as an afterthought—welcomed related solutions as a confirmation of their efforts:

We went with a divining-rod through the art of the past and the present. We showed only that art which lives untouched by the constraint of convention. Our devoted love was extended to all artistic expression which is born out of itself, lives on its own merit and does not walk with the crutches of custom. Wherever we have seen a crevice in the crust of convention, we have called attention to it, because we have hoped for a force underneath, which will someday come to light.[30]

This search for the unconventional and the fresh might explain the otherwise arbitrary selection of the 141 illustrations: Bavarian glass paintings, Bavarian and Russian votive pictures, medieval art (manuscript illuminations, woodcuts, Gothic sculpture, late medieval painting, ivories, tapestries, mosaics), Chinese popular paintings and masks, Japanese ink drawings and woodcuts, Egyptian shadow-play figures, African masks, a Benin bronze, pre-Columbian sculpture and textiles, Malayan and Easter Island sculpture, and children's drawings (pl. 94).

Among the moderns were included the artists who exhibited in the Blaue Reiter exhibitions,[31] most of the Brücke artists,[32] as well as Kokoschka, and Gauguin, Cézanne, van Gogh, and Rousseau—evidently considered the most significant masters of the immediate past. Contemporary French painters represented were Matisse, Picasso, Delaunay, Le Fauconnier, and Girieud. From the "Great Masters," Kandinsky and Marc chose only a woodcut by Hans Baldung-Grien and a painting by El Greco.

Much of the primitive, medieval, and folk art actually showed no lack of convention, but merely represented conventions different from the classical Renaissance tradition. The group felt, however, that in primitive art all consideration of external forms was renounced for the full expression of internal truths. It is highly important that here—for the first time—children's drawings were included on the same basis as "fine art." Approximately half the illustrations are examples of primitive, tribal, and folk art.

My idea then was to show, for instance, that the difference between "official" art and "ethnographic" art had no *raison d'être;* that the pernicious custom of not seeing the internal organic root of art under the varying exterior forms ought to end —at the universal door of human behavior. Likewise the differences among children's art, "amateur" art and academically trained art: the force of expression and a common principle prevailed over the slight differences between "finished" and "unfinished" form.[33]

The affinity of the Blaue Reiter to primitive and exotic art was expressed by such contrapositions as Kandinsky's *Lyrisches* and a popular German nineteenth-century illustration, Kirchner and Borneo sculpture, Campendonk and Bavarian behind-glass painting, Burliuk and Russian folk art, Delaunay and El Greco, Gauguin and archaic Greek sculpture, van Gogh and a Japanese woodcut. This affinity was also expressed verbally in many articles in the book. The following passage from Macke's essay is typical: "To create forms means to live. Are not the children who construct directly from the secrets of their emotions more creative than the imitators of Greek form? Are not the savages artists, who have their own form, strong as the form of thunder?"[34]

Programmatic essays were interwoven with the illustrations. In the three introductory articles Franz Marc discussed the problems and tasks facing the modern artist and spoke of the essential qualities of the new art. The most significant article in the book was an essay by Kandinsky on the problem of form, "Über die Formfrage."

Kandinsky also included his essay on stage composition, "Über Bühnenkomposition." Here he took issue with the "external effects" of the traditional stage in drama, opera, and ballet, and proposed a new stage directed toward the evocation of man's innermost soul vibrations through new combinations of music, dance, and color. His own composition, "Der Gelbe Klang," making use of synesthesia and directed toward the "total stage" of the future, was also included in the volume. Kandinsky also contributed a eulogy on Eugen Kahler. He had become aware of the work of the Russians, and had translated David Burliuk's article on the new movement in Russia "Die Wilden Russlands."

Roger Allard's essay "Die Kennzeichen der Erneuerung in der Malerei" analyzed the contemporary situation in French art, primarily in terms of cubism. There was an interesting discussion about the development of Delaunay's style by Erwin von Busse.

Interspersed throughout the volume were four articles on modern music. Arnold Schönberg, also represented by two drawings, contributed an article on the relationship of composition and text in music, "Das Verhältnis zum Text," in which he said that music was abstract and must be entirely free of textual matter or literary allusions. Thomas von Hartmann made the same claim for music that Kandinsky did for painting by stating in "Über die Anarchie in der Musik" that "all is permitted" and that the composer must not be hampered by questions of form. N. Kulbin's essay "Die freie Musik" took a similar stand. In the same framework Sbanjer analyzed Scriabin's "Prometheus." An appendix contained three lieder by Arnold Schönberg,[35] Alban Berg,[36] and Anton von Webern.[37]

Essentially the book was a declaration of the artistic ideas of the young expressionist painters and musicians. It achieved an almost immediate popularity so that the 1,500 copies of the first edition were soon sold. Marc's articles "Die Wilden Deutschlands"—discussing the three most vigorous modern movements in German art: the Brücke, the New Artists' Association, and the New Secession—and "Geistige Güter"—in which he stressed his admiration for El Greco, Cézanne, and Picasso, plus the contributions made by Meier-Graefe and von Tschudi—were reprinted in the Berlin periodical *Pan* together with Schönberg's "Verhältnis zum Text."[38]

In 1914 Piper published a second edition, of about six thousand copies, of *Der Blaue Reiter*. This 1914 edition is identical to the earlier one, except for the addition of a brief introduction by each of the editors.

The reception of the book encouraged the editors to continue with their original plan of bringing out an annual almanac "to awaken the realization and understanding of the spiritual essence of all things."[39] The second volume was to go beyond the boundaries of the first. Scholars and scientists in various fields of endeavor were to be included as well as artists and musicians. The editors hoped to come to a synthesis of art and science: "Encouraged we made plans for another book, which was to re-unite the forces of artists and scholars. To find the common root of art and science was then our dream which demanded an immediate realization. But the war put an end to these dreams." [40]

This was Kandinsky's account in 1936. But evidently it was not only the war that brought an end to the Blaue Reiter publication. Ludwig Grote has recently published a letter in which Kandinsky announced to his friend and co-editor as early as March, 1914, that he could no longer work on the book:

Since our last conversation I've noticed that when I awake at night, I very often think not of my work but of the volume. But since my work occupies me at the present time with particular intensity, the consequences for me of this dispersion are bound to be unfortunate, for I would do either one or the other only half-heartedly.[41]

Kandinsky the painter had to return to painting. But before the war he had been largely responsible for *Der Blaue Reiter,* and had written the important essay "Über die Formfrage" included in it, as well as *Concerning the Spiritual in Art.* Hugo Zehder, his first biographer, felt that these statements were of even greater historical importance than Kandinsky's paintings:

Probably no book on modern painting, no manifesto, has achieved similar significance, or has exercised such a great influence on the development of modern painting itself. It is a fact that most of the painters who today paint à la Kandinsky, have never seen one of his paintings face to face, but surely his books; and there is hardly an artist among the "Expressionists" who does not somehow instinctively acknowledge his writings, when it is a matter of the "inner sound" of color or the principle of forming according to "inner necessity." [42]

XVIII

Esthetic Theories of Wassily Kandinsky

The artistic purpose of the Blaue Reiter movement was most thoroughly articulated in Kandinsky's theoretical writings, especially the two essays, *Concerning the Spiritual in Art* and "Über die Formfrage," published in *Der Blaue Reiter*. Although these essays, which both appeared in 1912,[1] are largely based on earlier esthetic theory, they constitute almost a programmatic manifesto for the expressionist generation:

If *Der Blaue Reiter,* published by R. Piper, is taken together with Kandinsky's supplement, *Das Geistige in der Kunst,* as a unity, then this double volume is just as much *the* book of the pre-war years, as Hildebrand's *Problem der Form* was *the* book of the turn of the century. The separation of the two generations is already made clear in the title, which emphasizes form in the one and spirit in the other.[2]

Kandinsky's particular didactic style makes his writings difficult to read and analyze. Kenneth Lindsay, in his study of Kandinsky's theories, described Kandinsky's peculiar literary style as follows:

Characteristic of Kandinsky's writing is the technique of breaking up the given topic into opposites or alternatives. These opposites or alternatives usually follow directly after the posing of the problem and are numbered. Often they suggest further sets of opposites and alternatives. The sequence of thought is flexible, sometimes abrupt and cross-tracking, and frequently associative. The dominating relativity of the thought process contrasts strongly with the conclusions, which are often positively stated.[3]

THE REJECTION OF MATERIAL REALITY

Kandinsky was always strongly predisposed toward sense impressions. In his autobiography he indicates that he experienced objects, events—even music—primarily in terms of color; he did not conceive of color in its physical and material aspects, but rather in its emotional effect. During his scientific studies he lost faith in the rational scientific method and felt that reality could be fully comprehended only by means of creative intuition.

Kandinsky was not alone in his rejection of positivism and pragmatism at the turn of the century. His doubt of the ultimate possibilities of quantitative analysis was shared by many philosophers, not only by neo-Hegelian idealists. His philosophy found perhaps its closest parallel in the thinking of Henri Bergson, who taught that true reality can be grasped only through artistic intuition, which he contrasted to intellectual conception. The intellect, according to Bergson, is man's tool for rational action, but "art, whether it be painting or sculpture, poetry or music, has no other object than to brush aside the utilitarian symbols, the conventional and socially accepted generalities, in short everything that veils reality from us, in order to bring us face to face with reality itself." [4]

"The twentieth century has in its first third taken up a position of reaction against classic rationalism and intellectualism." [5] Even in the pure sciences the value of the intuitive as against the purely experimental was stressed during the early part of the twentieth century, so that by 1925 Werner Heisenberg was able to formulate the "Principle of Uncertainty." According to this principle, there is a limit to the precision with which we can observe nature scientifically. This did not mean a return to metaphysics, but it indicated the inherent limitations of quantitative observation.

The concept that matter was not eternally fixed, but could be transmuted into energy, was also of great interest to the artists in their attempt to liberate themselves from servitude to the material world. Franz Marc, aware of the developments in scientific thought, hoped to find, behind the curtain of appearances, the "true reality":

I am beginning more and more to see behind or, to put it better, through things, to see behind them something which they conceal, for the most part cunningly, with their outward appearance by hoodwinking man with a façade which is quite different from what it actually covers. Of course, from the point of view of physics this is an old story. . . . The scientific interpretation has powerfully transformed the human mind; it has caused the greatest type-change we have so far lived to see. Art is indisputably pursuing the same course, in its own way, certainly; and the problem, our problem, is to discover the way. [6]

Similarly, Kandinsky was "struck with terrific impact" by the discovery of the disintegration of the atom. [7] As early as his first encounter in Moscow with the paintings by Monet, he felt that the material object was not a necessary element in his painting: "I had the impression that here painting itself comes into the foreground; I wondered if it would not be possible to go further in this direction. From then on I looked at the art of ikons with different eyes; it meant that I had 'got eyes' for the abstract in art." [8] Later he wrote: "The impossibility and, in art, the purposelessness of copying an object, the desire to make the object express itself, are the beginnings of leading the artist away from 'literary' color to artistic, i.e. pictorial aims." [9]

Agreeing with earlier writers, such as the symbolists van de Velde and Endell, Kandinsky and Marc felt that art must express the spirit, but that in order to accomplish this task it must be dematerialized. Of necessity, this meant creating a new art form.

Kandinsky wished to forsake objective reality not only for philosophic reasons; psychological reasons, it seems, also played their part. Speaking about his period of study at the Munich Art Academy, Kandinsky wrote: "The naked body, its lines and movement, sometimes interested me, but often merely repelled me. Some poses in particular were repugnant to me, and I had to force myself to copy them. I could breathe freely only when I was out of the studio door and in the street once again." [10]

Franz Marc, when turning toward nonobjective painting shortly before his death, gave a similar reason: "Very early in life I found man ugly; the animal seemed to me more beautiful and cleaner, but even in it I discovered so much that was repelling and ugly that my art instinctively and by inner force became more schematic and abstract." [11]

Significantly, the human body, which is an almost universal motif in the art forms of most cultures, is here eschewed as subject matter. It is true that the art of the West emphasized the nonhuman aspects during the nineteenth century, when painters turned their attention to still life and landscape. The conscious rejection of the human form is, however, certainly fraught with significance. A psychological interpretation of the reasons for this response would be a highly rewarding task, especially as it might result in a more profound understanding of the nonobjective artist and his work. Such an analysis, however, goes beyond the framework of this book.

From the point of view of the history of esthetics it is also interesting that Kandinsky's rejection of the forms of nature occurred at approximately the same time as Worringer's publication *Abstraction and Empathy,* which advances the theory that the cause for abstraction is man's wish to withdraw from the world or his antagonism toward it. [12]

Kandinsky and Marc gave no further reasons for their retreat from natural and human forms. [13] Kandinsky said in his autobiography that he often preferred to leave the studio to follow his own dreams and visions. Returning from a walk one day, he had the experience of seeing one of his paintings in an unusual position, which made it clear to him that the representation of nature was superfluous in his art. [14] His experience shows the importance of the element of distance in the esthetic experience, as stated by Edward Bullough in 1912: "The sudden view of things from their reverse, usually unnoticed, side, comes upon us as a revelation, and such revelations are precisely those of art." [15]

Kandinsky felt, however, that he could not immediately turn to "concrete" or "absolute" painting. In a letter to Hilla Rebay [16] he said that at that time he was still alone in the realization that painting ultimately must discard the object. A long struggle for increasing abstraction from nature was still necessary. In 1910 he was still saying: "Today the artist cannot progress exclusively with purely abstract forms, as these forms are not sufficiently precise. Limiting oneself to the unprecise, it deprives one of possibilities, excluding the purely human and therefore, weakening the power of expression." [17]

But he was already pointing out at that time, that the abstract idea was constantly gaining ground, and Kandinsky predicted that the final predominance of the abstract would be inevitable. He said that the choice of subjects must originate from the inner necessity of the artist, and that material, or objective, form might be more or less superfluous. He insisted that the artist must be given complete freedom to express himself according to the "principle of inner necessity." He looked hopefully to the future: "When the possibility of speaking through artistic means will be developed, it will become superfluous to borrow from the exterior world for spiritual expression." [18]

In 1910 Kandinsky executed his first abstract work: a water color. The first large nonobjective oil dates from 1911; throughout 1912 he did both objective and "concrete" paintings. After 1912 there were very few objective works. His art had become completely free from nature; like music, its meaning was now meant to be inherent in the work itself and independent of external objects.

Kandinsky distinguished what he called "objective" art from "concrete" art by distinguishing between the means chosen by the artist. In objective art both artistic and natural elements are used, resulting in "mixed" art; in concrete art exclusively artistic means are used, resulting in "pure" art. [19] In a short article, published in 1935, he gave a lucid example of this distinction:

There is an essential difference between a line and a fish. And that is that the fish can swim, can eat and be eaten. It has the capacities of which the line is deprived. These capacities of the fish are necessary extras for the fish itself and for the kitchen, but not for the painting. And so, not being necessary they are superfluous. That is why I like the line better than the fish—at least in my painting. [20]

The element of representation was thus rejected by Kandinsky for his art. He insisted that a picture's quality lay in what is usually called form— its lines, shapes, colors, planes—without reference to anything outside the canvas. But here was an apparent contradiction in Kandinsky's theory, because he—like expressionist theoreticians in general—did not believe that a picture must be evaluated from its formal aspects. Kandinsky and the expressionists did not agree with "formalists" like Roger Fry, who believed that the esthetic emotion was essentially an emotion about form. Seeing Kandinsky's first abstractions, Fry concerned himself only with their form: ". . . one finds that . . . the improvisations become more definite, more logical and more closely knit in structure, more surprisingly beautiful in their color oppositions, more exact in their equilibrium." [21]

Kandinsky took strong issue with this theory. In his esthetics the formal aspect of a work of art was as unimportant as its representational quality.

THE INSIGNIFICANCE OF FORM

Form, to Kandinsky, was nothing but the outward expression of the artist's inner needs. Form is matter, and the artist is involved in a constant struggle against materialism. Kandinsky's words are reminiscent of medieval thought: "It is the spirit that rules over matter, and not the other way around." [22]

The artist should not seek salvation in form, Kandinsky warned in his essay "Über die Formfrage," because form is only an expression of content and is entirely dependent on the innermost spirit. It is this spirit that chooses form from the storehouse of matter, and it always chooses the form most expressive of itself. Content always creates its own appropriate form. Form may be chosen from anywhere between the two extreme poles: the great abstraction and the great realism. Kandinsky then proceeded to prove that these opposites, the abstract and the realistic, are actually identical, and that form is therefore an insignificant concern to the artist: In the "great realism" (as exemplified in the art of Henri Rousseau) the external-artistic element of painting is discarded, and the content—the inner feeling of the object—is brought forth primitively and "purely" through the representation of the simple, rough object. Artistic purpose is expressed directly because the painting is not burdened with formal problems. The content is now strongest because it is divested of external and academic concepts of beauty. Kandinsky preferred this "great realism" (also found in children's drawings) to the use of distortion, which always aroused literary associations. [23]

Since the "great abstraction" excludes "real" objects, the content is embodied in nonobjective form. Thus the "inner sound" of the picture is most clearly manifest. The scaffolding of the object has been removed, as in realism the scaffolding of beauty has been discarded. In both cases the artist arrives at the spiritual content itself.

The greatest external differentiation becomes the greatest internal identity:

$$\text{Realism} = \text{Abstraction}$$
$$\text{Abstraction} = \text{Realism} \text{ [24]}$$

The hypothesis that the minimum of abstraction can have the most abstract effect—and vice versa—is based by Kandinsky on an esthetic law, which he postulates: A quantitative decrease can be equal to a qualitative increase—2 plus 1 can be less than 2 minus 1 in esthetics. A dot of color, for example, may lose in its *effect* of intensity if its *actual* intensity is increased. [25] The pragmatic function of a form and its sentient meaning are dissimilar, yet abstraction and realism are identical.

Kandinsky cited several examples to prove this thesis. A hyphen, for instance, is of practical value and significance in its context. If this hyphen is taken out of its practical-purposeful context and put on canvas, and if it is not used there to fulfill any practical purpose at all—such as the delineation of an object—it then becomes nothing but a line; it is completely liberated from signification and abstracted from all its meaning as a syntactical sign; it is the abstract line itself. At the same time, however, it has also become most real, because now it is no longer a sign but the real line—the object itself.

It may be argued that Kandinsky used a very narrow definition of both the abstract and the realistic, and that the line may be a great deal more realistic and more meaningful as a sign (such as a hyphen) in its context than it is as a line only. It is a valid objection to say that this identity of the abstract and the real holds true only in this verbal analogy, and that Kandinsky did not present logical proof. Kandinsky, however, was not concerned with the correctness of intellectual thought, or with the proof of his spiritual values. He admitted: "I have always turned to reason and intellect least of all." [26]

He concluded his analysis of form by saying: "In principle there is no problem of form." [27] The artist who expresses his "soul vibrations" can use any form he wants. Formal rules in esthetics are not only impossible but a great stumbling block to the free expression of spiritual value. It is the duty of the artist to fight against these rules to clear the way for free expression. In the history of art, artists were often bogged down by matter and could not see beyond the formal. The nineteenth century was such a period, in which men failed to see the spirit in art as they failed to see it in religion. But to seek art and yet be satisfied with form is equivalent to the contentment with the idol in the quest for God. Form is dead unless it is expressive of content. There cannot be a symbol without expressive value.

In his introduction to the second edition of *Der Blaue Reiter,* Kandinsky said that the aim of the book was "to show by means of examples, practical arrangement and theoretical proof, that the problem of form is secondary in art, that art is above all a matter of content." [28]

Kandinsky understood his own time as the beginning of a new spiritual age when the abstract spirit was taking possession of the human spirit.[29] Artists would increasingly recognize the insignificance of form per se and realize its relativity, its true meaning as nothing but "the outward expression of inner meaning."

ART THE AFFIRMATION OF THE SPIRIT

In Kandinsky's esthetics the form and representational aspects of art have no importance by themselves, but are meaningful only as they express the artist's innermost feelings. Only through the expression of the artist's inner emotion can he transmit understanding of true spiritual reality itself. The only "infallible guide" that can carry the artist to "great heights" is the *principle of internal necessity* (Kandinsky's italics). This concept of internal necessity is the core and the basis of Kandinsky's esthetic theory, and becomes a highly significant element in expressionist criticism in general.

Kandinsky believed that a period of spiritual revolution—which he called the "spiritual turning point"—was approaching. He perceived indications of this period of transition in many cultural manifestations. In the field of religion, for example, theosophy was attempting to counteract the materialist evil. In the Theosophical Society, "one of the most important spiritual movements," [30] man was seeking to approach the problem of the spirit by the way of inner enlightenment. In the realm of literature, Kandinsky cited Maeterlinck as

. . . perhaps one of the first prophets, one of the first reporters and clairvoyants of the *décadence*. . . . Maeterlinck creates his atmosphere principally by artistic means. His material machinery . . . really plays a symbolic role and helps to give the inner note. . . . The apt use of a word (in its poetical sense), its repetition, twice, three times, or even more frequently, according to the need of the poem, will not only tend to intensify the internal structure but also bring out unsuspected spiritual properties in the word itself.[31]

By using pure sound for the most immediate effect upon the reader or listener, the writer depends upon prelanguage signs—that is, sounds that, like music, do not depend upon language for their meaning. This level of signification was also the basis of Kandinsky's nonobjective painting. In music, Kandinsky pointed to Schönberg's panchromatic scheme, which advocates the full renunciation of functional harmonious progression and traditional form and accepts only the means that lead the composer to the most uncompromising self-expression: "His music leads us to where musical experience is a matter not of the ear, but of the soul—and from this point begins the music of the future." [32] Kandinsky thought of music as an emancipated art; further, music had the quality of time extension, and was most effective in inspiring spiritual emotion in the listener. Painting, although still largely dependent upon natural form, was showing similar signs of emancipation. Picasso's breakdown of volumes and Matisse's free use of color for its own sake were manifestations of the turning point toward a spiritual art.[33]

How would the artist achieve full spiritual harmony in his composition? Kandinsky said that the painter had two basic means at his disposal—form and color—and that there was always an unavoidable mutual relationship between them.

In Kandinsky's prewar writings he did not come forth with a thorough analysis of forms as he did later in his systematic *Point and Line to Plane,* yet he was already saying: "Form alone, even though abstract and geometrical, has its internal resonance, a spiritual entity whose properties are identical with the form. A triangle . . . is such an entity, with its particular spiritual perfume." [34]

Color is the most powerful medium in the hand of the painter. It has a psychic as well as a physical effect upon the observer. It can influence his tactile, olfactory, and especially aural senses, as well as his visual sense; chromotherapy has shown that "red light stimulates and excites the heart, while blue light can cause temporary paralysis." [35] Color is the artist's means of influencing the human soul. Its meaning is expressed metaphorically by Kandinsky: "Color is the keyboard, the eyes are the hammers, the soul is the piano with many strings. The artist is the hand that plays, touching one key or another purposively, to cause vibrations of the soul." [36]

Kandinsky then proceeded to develop an elaborate explanation of the psychic effect of color. This contrasts to the more scientific color theories of Helmholtz, Rood, Chevreul, and Signac, and closely approaches the psychological color theory of Goethe and metaphysics of color of Philipp Otto Runge. Like his romanticist predecessor, Kandinsky believed that color could directly influence the human soul.[37]

Blue is the heavenly color. It retreats from the spectator, moving toward its own center; it beckons to the infinite, arousing a longing for purity and the supersensuous. Light blue is like the sound of the flute; dark blue has the sound of the cello.

Yellow is the color of the earth. It has no profound meaning; it seems to spread out from its own center and to advance to the spectator from the canvas. It has the shrill sound of a canary or of a brass horn, and is often associated with the sour taste of lemon.

Green is the mixture of blue and yellow. The concentricity of blue nullifies the eccentricity of yellow. It is passive and static, and can be compared to the so-called "bourgeoisie"—self-satisfied, fat, and healthy. In music it is best represented by the placid, long-drawn middle tones of the violin.

White, which was not considered a color by the impressionists, has the spiritual meaning of a color. It is the symbol of a world void of all material quality and substance—it is the color of beginning. It is the "sound" of the earth during the white period of the Ice Age.

Black is like eternal silence. It is without hope. It signifies termination, and is therefore the color of mourning.

By the symbolic use of colors combined "according to their spiritual significance" the artist can finally achieve a great composition: "Color itself offers contrapuntal possibilities and, when combined with design, may lead to the great pictorial counterpoint, where also painting achieves composition, and where pure art is in the service of the divine." [38]

Kandinsky's color symbolism is in no way based upon physical laws of color or upon the psychology of color vision. "All these statements are the results of empirical feeling, and are not based on exact science." [39] This may even explain his own inconsistencies—such as his statement in *Concerning the Spiritual in Art* that "red light stimulates and excites the heart," [40] contradicted by his assertion that "red . . . has brought about a state of partial paralysis." [41]

Specific colors call forth different associations in people as well as cultures. Specific reactions to specific colors have never been proved experimentally. Max Raphael, in his book *Von Monet bis Picasso,* said that colors have had altogether different meanings for those individuals most occupied with them. Yellow, for example, signified the earth for Leonardo; had gay, happy connotations for Goethe; meant friendliness to Kant, and heavenly splendor to van Gogh; suggested the night to Gauguin, and aggressiveness to Kandinsky.[42] Yellow symbolizes jealousy in German usage, an emotion associated with green in English idiom.

Kandinsky did not attempt to set down scientific rules for color associations. He merely indicated his own personal associations:

It is very clear that all I have said of these simple colors is very provisional and general, and so are the feelings (joy, grief, etc.) which have been quoted as parallels to the colors. For these feelings are only material expressions of the soul. Shades of color, like those of sound, are of a much finer texture and awaken in the soul emotions too fine to be expressed in prose.[43]

In his second significant book, *Point and Line to Plane: A Contribution to the Analysis of the Pictorial Elements*, Kandinsky presented his grammar of line, forms, and space, as he had done with his color theory in *Concerning the Spiritual in Art*.

The task of the painter, according to Kandinsky, is to achieve the maximum effect by bringing his media, color, and form into orderly and expressive composition. Each art has its own language, and each artist—painter, sculptor, architect, writer, or composer—must work in his specific medium and bring it to the expression of greatest inner significance. But once painting, for example, is divested of the crutch of natural form and becomes completely abstract, the pure law of pictorial construction can be discovered. Then it will be found that pure painting is closely related *internally* to pure music or pure poetry.

SYNTHESIS OF THE ARTS

Kandinsky pointed out that human beings, because of individual differences, differ in the type of art expression to which they are most receptive —for some it is musical form, for others painting or literature. The artist can also achieve esthetic effects in sensory fields not limited to his own medium. Kandinsky was much interested, for example, in Scriabin's experiments with sound-color combinations. The reënforcement of one art form with another by means of synesthesia greatly increases the final esthetic effect upon the receptor. The greatest effect can be obtained by the synthesis of all the arts in one "monumental art," which was the ultimate end of Kandinsky's esthetics.

Kandinsky here continued the nineteenth-century tradition—from Herder to Wagner—with its desire for a union of all arts. A synthesis of the arts is possible, because at a basic level all artistic means are identical in their inner meaning—ultimately the external differences will become insignificant, and the internal identity of all artistic expression will be disclosed. Each art form causes a certain "complex of soul vibrations." The aim of the synthesis of art forms is the refinement of the soul through the sumtotal of these complexes.

Kandinsky's "Über Bühnenkomposition"[44] and "Schematic Plan of Studies and Work of the Institute of Art Culture"[45] outlined the possible steps to be taken for the achievement of "monumental art." Present-day drama, opera, ballet are as criticized as the plastic arts. A greater internal unity can be achieved by discarding external factors in "stage composition" [46]—particularly plot, external relationship, and external unity. Kandinsky experimented with such a composition: *Der Gelbe Klang*.[47] He attempted to combine music, the movement of dancers and of objects, the sound of the human voice (without being confined by word or language meanings), and the effect of color tone (after experiments by Scriabin).

Kandinsky admitted that his "stage composition" was weak but believed the principle to be valid. It is necessary to remember that we are still at the very beginning of the great abstract period in art. Materialism still has its grasp on modern activity, and is not as yet completely vanquished. But the new, "the spiritual in art," already manifests itself in most fields of creativity.

Kandinsky made his first attempt at the realization of a synthesis of the arts when he founded the Institute of Art Culture in Moscow in 1920, a comprehensive institute for the study and development of the arts and sciences. Kandinsky was active in this organization as vice-president for about a year; then political pressure forced his resignation, and he found a similar field of activity in the Bauhaus in Weimar, which he joined in 1922.

THE DIRECT COMMUNICATION OF VISUAL ELEMENTS

Expressionism, which began by shifting emphasis from the object to be painted to the artist's own subjective interpretation, reached in Kandinsky the total negation of the object. In this respect he was of great inspiration to succeeding artists. The final phase of expressionism also became the beginning of an altogether new artistic concept: nonobjective painting. Kandinsky was heralded by the following generation as the innovator of nonobjective painting, even by painters whose own direction was completely different:

I know of nothing more real than the painting of Kandinsky—nor anything more true and nothing more beautiful. A painting by Kandinsky gives no image of earthly life—it is life itself. If one painter deserves the name "creator," it is he. He organizes matter as matter was organized, otherwise the Universe would not exist. He opened a window to look inside the All. Some day Kandinsky will be the best known and best loved by men.[48]

In his rejection of the representational aspects of art, Kandinsky cleared the way for new values in art. By experimenting with the possibility of an expressive—rather than a formalistic—art in the nonobjective idiom, he threw out a challenge that performed a most valuable function in the history of modern art. Through his activity as an esthetician as well as a painter, he wrote a series of books that clearly articulated his ideas and became as influential in the history of modern painting as his paintings did.

Kandinsky's esthetic theory emphasized, among other things, the precept that the elements of painting—lines and colors and their combinations—evoke emotional associations in the observer. This precept was basic to expressionism, although not original with the expressionist movement. Much of this precept was implied in romanticist esthetics, and was clearly stated in the theory of empathy; it was expressed differently in Paul Signac's theory of neoimpressionism, and recurred in Bergson's *Essai sur les données immédiates de la conscience;* [49] it was a significant part of symbolism and its corollary Jugendstil, and was reiterated by such men as Gauguin, Denis, Sérusier, Walter Crane, and Endell.

Kandinsky's essays are exceedingly important because they were written by the man who was the innovator of nonobjective painting. In the total absence of representational objects, the plastic elements were to become sole carriers of the artist's message—which is probably why he felt called upon to express verbally what he had done in his painting through the intuition of "inner necessity."

In the analysis of Kandinsky's color theory it was pointed out that no direct parallels can be established between the artist's statement and the observer's response. Both projections rest on highly personal and subjective factors, and do not differ greatly from music. It has, for example, been shown that the major and minor modes are by no means endowed with characteristics that call forth identical reactions in different listeners [50]—much depends upon previous experience and training.

As Kandinsky indicated, prose cannot express the shades of emotion awakened by sound and color. Each person may verbalize differently about the experience of a work of art, and his verbalization may be at great variance with that of the artist. Yet direct communication can take place on a primary visual (preverbal) level before either spectator or artist articulates. It is toward this level of communication that the art of Kandinsky and other expressionists was directed. For in art, "things that cannot be stated may nonetheless be *shown*—understood, symbolized and presented to our direct apprehension." [51]

PART SIX

The Prewar Years

XIX

Controversies about the Modern Movement and Its Affirmation in the Sonderbund

In the first decade of the twentieth century the attitude of the German public toward the new developments in art generally ranged only between apathy and ridicule. The established artists, however, felt a threat to their vested interest, and began to take a stand against the younger generation. The Berlin Secession, which had invited Nolde, Kandinsky, and Jawlensky to its 1907 exhibition, rejected the work of the *avant-garde* artists in 1910, leading to the formation of the New Secession.[1] Nolde, who had been a member of the Berlin Secession since 1907, was expelled from it in the course of a vociferous argument in 1910.[2] The following year a vehement controversy within the leadership of the Secession led to the resignation of its president, Liebermann, and to the election in his place of Corinth, who at that time was most outspokenly opposed to the new style. Liebermann accepted the title of honorary president, but Beckmann and Slevogt resigned from the board. The 1911 exhibition showed young French artists, but the door was barred to the Germans, a condition that prevailed through the following year.

Another crisis occurred early in 1913. The impact of the International Exhibition of Modern Art, sponsored by the Sonderbund and held in Cologne, was sufficient to defeat the reactionary group in the powerful Secession for a brief period. Corinth was defeated, and Paul Cassirer the art dealer was elected to the presidency. Cézanne and van Gogh were among the featured artists of the Secession's exhibition that year; Kirchner, Heckel, Schmidt-Rottluff, Pechstein, and Kokoschka were invited to submit work. The new board's liberal attitude led to the final schism of the Secession in the fall of 1913. The more progressive majority resigned under Liebermann's leadership, and Barlach, Pechstein, and Beckmann were among the board members of the new "Free Secession." The minority, forming under Corinth's directorship the so-called "Rump Secession," continued in its ultra-conservative way for a few more years.

THE PROTEST DEUTSCHER KÜNSTLER

As soon as a few forward-looking museum directors—like Osthaus in Hagen, Lichtwark in Hamburg, Tschudi in Munich, Sauerlandt in Halle, and Paul F. Schmidt in the print room in Magdeburg—began to show interest in the work of the young German and French generation, and even went so far as to buy some of their work, members of the older generation felt a direct threat to their livelihood. Carl Vinnen became the spokesman of these disgruntled artists, and wrote the *Protest deutscher Künstler*.[3] This was published in Jena by Diederichs, one of the leading publishers in Germany, and was signed by 120 artists and critics, with "fortunately almost no art historians among the signers." [4] Wilhelm Trübner, an artist of great prestige, was among the subscribers, but most were obscure or soon to become so.

The *Protest,* a mixture of chauvinism and self-pity, claimed that a powerful organization of Paris and Berlin art dealers, supported by interested critics, forced the German people to buy French art at exorbitant prices, leaving little funds for, or interest in, native art. It maintained, further, that influential museum directors and critics in Germany gave unwarranted praise not only to young French artists, who themselves were working against their own fine national traditions, but also to young German artists imitating these renegade Frenchmen. In the true spirit of mercantilism, Vinnen found it most alarming that the import of paintings into Germany was greater than the export. The pamphlet concluded with dire prophecies as to the future of German art.

Almost immediately the Munich collector Alfred Walter Heymel edited a counterstatement,[5] including articles by most prominent individuals in the German art world—Paul Cassirer, Lichtwark, Pauli, Swarzensky, Liebermann, Slevogt, Corinth, Klimt, van de Velde, and Worringer—all indicating that German academism would by no means prevent interest in French innovations, that it would in fact push the young German artists only further toward Paris. Even Emil Nolde, although a stalwart German nationalist, took strong issue with the Vinnen group, and asserted that in the previous century only France had shown that a great, independent new art could arise out of the past.

THE BECKMANN-MARC CONTROVERSY

Max Beckmann (1884–1950) was at the time perhaps the most successful young painter in Germany. The son of a prosperous flour merchant in Leipzig, he had received his training at the conservative academy of Weimar during the first years of the century. The very strongest early influence on his work came from Hans von Marées, whose heroic romanticism of subject matter left a strong impact on him. On an important study trip to Paris he was especially impressed by the work of Piero della Francesca, Signorelli, and Rembrandt, but perhaps most strongly by the *Pietà d'Avignon,* which he saw at an exhibition of French primitive art in 1903.

Attracted by the vigor and liveliness of the Berlin art world, Beckmann moved there late in 1904. His *Young Men by the Sea* (1905) (pl. 95a) certainly shows Marées' influence, and is rather conventional in composition and form. This painting brought him to immediate public attention when it was bought by the Weimar Museum in 1906—an unprecedented success for a painter in his early twenties—and he was awarded the prize of a study trip to Florence.

In 1906 Beckmann was admitted to membership in the Berlin Secession, and his annual exhibitions received most favorable criticism. At this time he met Munch, who felt that Beckmann was capable of more significant work than academic figure compositions; [6] Beckmann, however, preferred to continue working in an academic style somewhat invigorated by Corinth-like gusto. He painted melodramatic reportage of great catastrophes, such as the Messina earthquake (1910) and the sinking of the *Titanic* (1912) (pl. 95b), or mythological and Biblical scenes. His effort at this time then was to give clear, tangible form to significant events of a cataclysmic nature.

In 1911, when Beckmann held his first large exhibition in Frankfurt, Karl Scheffler, spokesman for the Secessionists, lauded him as one of the most promising young artists in Germany.[7] The Frankfurt exhibition was followed by a large retrospective in Magdeburg in 1912, where Paul F. Schmidt saw in his work "a grand synthesis of the pathos of Rubens, the light of Rembrandt, and the brushstroke of the Impressionists." [8] The following year, in connection with a major exhibition of no less than fifty paintings at Paul Cassirer's, a monograph appeared on Beckmann,[9] by this time considered a leader of the young generation of German painters. In spite of the general acclaim, however, the reviewer in *Cicerone* pointed out quite correctly that the monograph was premature, that Beckmann had not yet found his final means of expression and that his present work was overestimated. He noted that Beckmann was a painter who owed his form and perception to impressionism and who was trying to go beyond impressionism toward his own fusion of form and expression, but that his purpose still suffered from an inadequacy of means.[10]

In 1913 Beckmann did indeed undergo a transformation in style that eventually led him to his mature form. It is not surprising that in 1912, although certainly not adhering to Vinnen's group, he joined the voices of reaction. His objection was provoked by a statement made by Franz Marc in *Pan* emphasizing the great contribution that France had made to the development of modern painting. Marc singled out van Gogh, Gauguin, Seurat, Cézanne, and Matisse, and said that the young artists were progressing still further in assembling around Picasso, "the logical executor of Cézanne in whose magic work the ideas of Cubism were latent." [11]

Today we search behind the veil of appearances for the hidden things in nature which seem to us more important than the discoveries of the Impressionists. . . . We seek and we paint the inner, spiritual side of nature, and we do this not out of whim and caprice for the novel, but because we *see* this other side, as in former times they saw suddenly purple shadows and objects veiled in ether.[12]

Marc stated in conclusion that the new movement in art, although greatly indebted to French artists, was not Parisian but European and that quality, not nationality, should be the decisive standard in art.

Almost immediately Beckmann answered:

There is something which repeats itself in all good art, that is artistic sensuousness, combined with artistic objectivity toward the things represented. If that is abandoned, one arrives involuntarily in the realm of handicraft. I too want to speak about quality. Quality as I understand it. That is the feeling for the peach-colored glimmer of the skin, for the gleam of a nail, for the artistic-sensuous, for the softness of the skin, for the gradated depth of space. Not only the plane but also depth. And then above all, the appeal of the material. The surface of the oil pigment, when I think of Rembrandt, Leibl, Cézanne, or the spirited structure of the line of Hals.[13]

Marc retorted to this statement in an article in *Pan,* calling his reply "Anti-Beckmann":

No, Mr. Beckmann, quality does not lie in the gleam of a nail, or the beautiful surface of the oil pigment. Quality signifies the inner greatness of the work, that which distinguishes it from the works of imitators and small minds. Leibl's works have quality, the works of his followers usually do not, because the spirit is lacking. . . .[14]

Later, after Beckmann had become one of the vanguard of modern art in Germany, he fought against the powers he had earlier supported. Ultimately he was to agree with Marc's concept rather than with his own earlier point of view: "What I want to show in my work is the idea which hides itself behind so-called reality. I am seeking for the bridge which leads from the visible to the invisible." [15]

In 1912, however, the strongest answer to the doubts about the validity of a new art form, as well as the most significant affirmation of the value of foreign influences, was the great International Exhibition of the Sonderbund, comprising almost six hundred paintings and demonstrating the truly international character of modern art and its derivations. Among the truly important German painters of the period, only Franz Marc and Max Beckmann were absent from this show—the latter because his work was too conservative to allow him to receive an invitation from the board, and the former because he withdrew his five paintings, feeling that the selections of the jury were not advanced enough.

FIRST YEARS OF THE SONDERBUND, 1908–1911

The Cologne exhibition of 1912 was actually the final undertaking of a small group of Düsseldorf artists and friends of art whose initial ambitions had been far more humble.

The Sonderbund was started in Düsseldorf in 1908 as a part of the prevalent Secession movement. The original seven members who severed connections with the entrenched academists of Düsseldorf were Julius Bretz, Max Clarenbach, August Deusser, Walter Ophey, Alfred and Otto Sohn-Rethel, and Wilhelm Schmurr. To lend prestige to the group, Max Liebermann was made an honorary member. Their first modest exhibition was held in Düsseldorf in 1909. The following year the Sonderbund planned a much more important show in which it tried to include some of the most outstanding French and German painters. Liebermann was guest of honor, but various modern French movements were also represented: neoimpressionism with Cross and Signac; the Nabis with Bonnard, Vuillard, and Roussel; and the former Fauves with work by Matisse, Friesz, Derain, Vlaminck, as well as earlier work by Braque. The Munich group was represented by Jawlensky and three of Kandinsky's "indefinable color orgies." [16]

Color held the center of interest at the 1910 Sonderbund exhibition. A *Denkschrift* was published, devoted to an investigation of recent color theories and their application in painting, particularly French painting. In these articles, dealing with "colorism," there are frequent discussions of the rhythm of color and the synesthetic relationship of color to music. [17]

In 1911 the Sonderbund arranged an exhibition in Düsseldorf similar in scope to that of the previous year. Again the French painters were featured, because the young Düsseldorf group saw in the work of the French "the most highly developed art forms in our time, of which all German masters, who are capable of sincere artistic responsibility, must take cognizance." [18] A reviewer took issue with this statement, and claimed that the work of French painters exhibited in the show was held in storage by famous Paris dealers to sell to German snobs. He protested that of 147 pieces, 101 were French.

The young French painters represented in the 1911 Sonderbund exhibition—Braque, Derain, van Dongen, Friesz, Guerin, Vlaminck, and Picasso —were designated as "expressionists" in this review by G. Howe. [19] This is one of the first times that the term was used in criticism; it was evidently coined to emphasize the contrast of Fauvism to the previous impressionism. "Expressionism" occurred first as a prevalent critical term, or as the name of a movement, in the reviews of the twenty-second exhibition of the Berlin Secession, held slightly earlier in 1911. [20] The term, however, was not adopted by the French painters themselves; it was soon used in Germany as a general term to describe *all* modern pictorial expression, including cubism and futurism as well as the work of the Brücke and the Munich group. Only later was the term appropriated by the Germans to describe their own specific artistic endeavors.

THE INTERNATIONAL EXHIBITION OF THE SONDERBUND, COLOGNE, 1912

While the third exhibition of the Sonderbund was still in progress, plans were being made for a great international show (fig. 27) to provide a complete survey of contemporary painting, sculpture, and the crafts, as well as to demonstrate their immediate derivations from the masters of postimpressionism. Richard Reiche, director of the museum in Barmen and director of the Sonderbund, said:

This year's fourth exhibition of the Sonderbund wishes to give a survey of the present state of the youngest movement in painting, which has come to the fore after the Naturalism of atmosphere and the Impressionism of movement. This movement strives for a simplification and enhancement of forms of expression, a new rhythm and color as well as decorative and monumental formulation. The exhibition attempts to give a survey of this movement, which has been called Expressionism.[21]

Figure 27.   Announcement of Internationale Ausstellung des Sonderbundes, 1912

At first the International Exhibition was planned for the Palace of Arts in Düsseldorf, but because of pressure from the academy the group was refused this space. Then the lord mayor of Cologne and his city council put the large Cologne Kunsthalle as well as a fund of 25,000 marks at the disposal of the Sonderbund. To bring this major undertaking to a successful conclusion the board included: Carl Ernst Osthaus, owner of the Folkwang Museum in Hagen, as president; Reiche, as director; Alfred Flechtheim, the prominent art dealer, as treasurer; Herbert Eulenberg, the noted author, as literary advisor; a large number of painters, directors, and museum curators in the Rhineland; and members of the Cologne City Council. Leading industrialists, government officials, university professors, and prominent intellectuals in all fields of knowledge were members of the honorary council.

Perhaps most important was the "Working Committee" itself, which included museum directors, city councilmen, art dealers (like Bernheim Jeune of Paris and Paul Cassirer of Berlin), art historians (like Hans Tietze of Vienna), and painters (like August Macke).

The jury consisted of two painters (August Deusser and Max Clarenbach, both charter members of the Sonderbund) and two museum directors (Alfred Hagelstange of the Wallraf-Richarts Museum of Cologne, and Richard Reiche of the Barmen Museum). The fact that many of the most prominent individuals in the German art world, as well as significant people from other walks of life, stood behind this undertaking made it impossible to decry it as a quirk of the *avant-garde* or a usurpation of German funds by scheming Paris dealers.

The Working Committee commissioned Jan Thorn-Prikker to execute stained glass windows with scenes from the life of Christ for a chapellike room in a central location among the twenty-five major exhibition rooms. Thorn-Prikker did these windows in a rectilinear, stylized manner, simplifying much of the involved symbolism of his earlier work. Kirchner and Heckel were commissioned to decorate the chapel itself with murals painted on jute. This was the first important mural commission awarded to Brücke artists, and was a distinction they had always hoped to receive. No clear photographs of this decoration are extant; in a recent article Paul F. Schmidt remarked that he remembered the murals as not having been thoroughly successful, because the talent of both painters was better suited to work on a smaller scale and was of a more intimate nature.[22]

Bathers, one of the two canvases that Kirchner had in the Sonderbund exhibition, indicates a clear trend toward the decorative in his work in 1912.

The exhibition, from May 25 until September 30, 1912, included twenty-five galleries of paintings, the chapel, and four rooms of crafts arranged by the West German Guild for the Applied Arts, an organization loosely connected with the Sonderbund. Altogether, 577 paintings by 160 artists from nine countries were shown.[23] Fifty-seven pieces of sculpture were interspersed with the paintings throughout the galleries. All the work was modern except, significantly, several El Greco paintings among the van Gogh and Picasso canvases.

The first five galleries were devoted to a large retrospective exhibition honoring Vincent van Gogh and comprising 125 of his paintings. Van Gogh was considered the central personality in the modern movement. Paul F. Schmidt wrote: "With Van Gogh the new era in art begins. All that the artists now are concerned with is either implied or fulfilled in his work."[24]

Ten years later Karl Jaspers presented his investigation into the psychopathology of art and artists, and made an interesting statement about the work of van Gogh compared with the more recent work by the younger men:

In this exhibition in Cologne in 1912 Expressionist art, which was strangely monotonous and came from all Europe, was to be seen around the magnificent Van Goghs.

One frequently felt that Van Gogh was sublimely the only artist mad against his will among so many who wished to be mad, but were only all too healthy.[25]

Jaspers then voiced a warning against a new period in which artists felt it necessary to identify themselves consciously with the psychotic as they also imitated the exotic and the infantile. In this essay, which dealt with Strindberg, Swedenborg, Hölderlin, as well as with van Gogh, Jaspers pointed out that now the schizophrenic personality—he attempted to prove that the four men all suffered from schizophrenia—had become the archetype of the creative artist, because he could give man a glimpse into the realm of the absolute for which everyone was searching.

Jaspers showed quite correctly that the prewar period was sensitive to the art of neurotics, but the same era was most certainly also responsive to the exceedingly well-disciplined painting of Cézanne, who was represented by twenty-six oils and water colors in the gallery adjoining the van Gogh retrospective at the Sonderbund. Schmidt said that Cézanne looked like an "old master next to Van Gogh," and went on to observe that Cézanne's full impact was still to come and that thus far only Picasso, and to a lesser extent Kokoschka, had really understood Cézanne.[26]

Ludwig Coellen—in an important book, *Die neue Malerei,*[27] written and published in connection with the Sonderbund exhibition—felt that Cézanne went beyond van Gogh in many respects. Van Gogh's space and his relationship of objects to each other and the total picture space were still impressionist in its formulation, whereas Cézanne's space engagement pointed toward the expressionists.[28]

In a room next to the van Gogh exhibition, the third of the important retrospective showings consisted of twenty-five paintings by Gauguin, largely from his Tahiti period. Coellen, who consistently drew parallels between the new painting and romanticism, said: "Unlike the old Romantics who found their imaginary world in their own fantasy, Gauguin found it more objectively in Tahiti." [29] Coellen admired the linear, rhythmic flow of Gauguin's painting and compared him to Hodler: "Where Hodler is monumental, Gauguin is idyllic." [30]

An exhibition of neoimpressionism, comprising seventeen paintings and water colors by Henri Cross and eighteen by Paul Signac, was included "in order to conclude the chain of relationships which connect modern painting with the art of the last classics of the past." [31]

One room had sixteen paintings by Picasso, including not only those from the blue and rose periods like *Actor,*[32] but also important cubist paintings like the *Girl with Violin* and the *Mandolin Player* (1911). The advanced critics saw in Picasso the "leading painter of his time, the only one worthy of Cézanne and continuing his work." [33] Schmidt said that his cubist paintings were difficult to understand, that they went to the limit of liberation from the object; if at first they looked like intellectual exercises, they were actually derived from inner necessity.[34]

Braque, represented with seven paintings, was mistaken for a weak imitator in Schmidt's review. Coellen, who had not been familiar with the earlier work of the Brücke, believed that he found ornament derived from Picasso and cubism in Kirchner's and Heckel's mural and in the stained glass by Thorn-Prikker.[35] Coellen was convinced that Picasso had found the basic form and constructive law of new pictorial expression.[36]

In addition to Signac, Picasso, and Braque, a large number of significant living French painters had been invited to participate in the Sonderbund exhibition. They included: Pierre Bonnard, Maurice Denis, André Derain, Othon Friesz, Pierre Girieud, Auguste Herbin, Marie Laurencin, Henri Matisse, Aristide Maillol, Henri Manguin, Albert Marquet, Maurice de Vlaminck, and Edouard Vuillard.

Among the paintings reproduced in the catalog is Girieud's *Three Marys* (pl. 96),[37] interesting for its symbolism of line, repeat rhythm, and pattern. Girieud, who had been a member of the Munich New Artists' Association, still enjoyed considerable recognition in Germany at that time, where he, rather than Maurice Denis, was understood to be the leader of the French symbolist group.

Seven Dutch painters were included, among whom were Kees van Dongen [38] and Piet Mondrian, who is listed in the catalog as having entered a drawing of a hyacinth.

Switzerland was represented with ten painters, including Amiet, who showed his rhythmical composition *Apple Harvest,* and Hodler with his bold, hierarchic *William Tell.*

Among the thirteen Hungarian artists, Jules Pascin had two paintings of young ladies—one of which had already been seen in the Berlin Secession exhibit of 1911.

Norway, in addition to a general gallery, had a large retrospective exhibition of Edvard Munch, whose thirty-two entries ranged in scope from his symbolist-Jugendstil *Madonna* (1895) (pl. 97) [39] to the much more sober and quiet portrait of the author Jappe Nilssen (1909) (pl. 98).[40] To the Germans the impact of Munch was second in importance only to that of van Gogh. The depth of psychological penetration and the frightening pessimism of his earlier work came close to the artistic purpose of a large number of German painters, many of whom had never before seen such a comprehensive display of the Norwegian's work. Munch, guest of honor of the show, accompanied his paintings to Cologne and found much greater admiration for his early painting than for his more recent achievements.

. . . the drastic and systematic distortions and the abrupt opposition of strong colors which give many Expressionist paintings their quality of intense animation were very unlike his work. . . . He was pleased and surprised at the emphasis given him, and he was struck by the difference between himself and the new generation. "Here the wildest things in Europe are collected—I am quite faded and classic," he wrote his friend Jappe Nilssen.[41]

Kirchner's and Heckel's chapel was situated between the Norwegian and the Austrian galleries. Austria was represented by a dozen painters, including the Czech cubists and friends of the Brücke, Emil Filla and

Bohumil Kubišta. Egon Schiele exhibited three paintings. including the *Self-Seer* (discussed in chap. xii).[42] Kokoschka had six paintings. They ranged from the portrait of the actor Reinhold, *The Trance Player,* which was one of his earliest portraits,[43] and the magnificent early alpine landscape *Dent du Midi* (1909),[44] to his *Sposalizio* (1912),[45] a tender, symbolic double portrait of two intimate friends of the painter. In many of the reviews Kokoschka was singled out as one of the most promising and talented young painters in Europe; Paul F. Schmidt compared him to Grünewald,[46] and even Emil Nolde wrote about Kokoschka's beautiful landscape at the Sonderbund in his autobiography.[47]

The German section, of 4 galleries, 73 painters, and 149 works, mixed conservative and rather tedious painting (like the retrospective exhibition of August Deusser) with the most radical work in the whole exhibition. The German galleries offered an excellent cross section of the work of the younger generation. Only some of the groups and names can be mentioned in this context; among the original members of the Sonderbund, Julius Bretz, Max Clarenbach, Walter Ophey, and Alfred Sohn-Rethel had work in the exhibition.

In addition, there was a rather large number of Rhenish painters, including Heinrich Nauen with six entries. Nauen (1880–1940) was born in Krefeld, received his early training at the Düsseldorf Academy, then studied with Knirr in Munich and Kalckreuth in Stuttgart. He had been a member of the assembly of young artists, the First Group of Laethem-St. Martin (Georges Minne, Gustave van de Woestijne, and Albert Servaes), from 1902 to 1905. His peasants, landscapes, and flower pieces at the Sonderbund exhibition used a simplified linear structure and brilliant color. While the Sonderbund exhibition was in progress, Nauen began the most important work of his life: the six large murals at the Castle Drove in the Eifel. Among these the *Battle of the Amazons* and the *Pietà* show best his rhythmically flowing stylized forms. The close affinity of the group of Nauen's St. John and the Virgin in the *Pietà* to his experience of Grünewald's *Crucifixion* in Colmar has already been pointed out.[48]

New among the Rhenish painters was Helmuth Macke (1891–1936), a cousin of August Macke. Helmuth Macke had studied with Thorn-Prikker at the Krefeld School of Arts and Crafts and with Nauen, and was later well acquainted with Campendonk and August Macke, who brought him to Sindelsdorf in 1910. From there he went to Berlin in 1911, and established a direct connection between the Munich group and the Brücke early in 1912.[49] Although his own work is eclectic, Helmuth Macke served a function as a catalyst among the German painters of his generation.

The Sonderbund exhibition included also paintings by Rudolf Grossmann, Rudolf Levy, Hans Purrmann, and Albert Weissgerber, all of whom had in 1906 been students of Matisse in Paris. They continued to work with a refined taste that forms an interesting contrast to the drastic styles of so many of the expressionists.

Emil Nolde's two paintings in the exhibition included one of his recent masks. In his autobiography Nolde told of the marvelous experience that the exhibition seems to have been for him; he also objected violently to the power exercised by the dealers and their special treatment of the French.[50]

All the Brücke painters were represented. Kirchner's *Bathers* (pl. 99) had discarded the quick hatch-mark technique of the previous year, and was painted in large, rounded shapes; even modeling was used to achieve greater plasticity in the forms. Kirchner was to return to his angular elongation the following year, but now for a brief period, perhaps because of his mural commission or the experience of Cézanne, he worked in this manner of more deliberate composition and formulation. Among Heckel's entries was the *Forest Pond,* a picture very similar to his *Bathers* of the same year.[51]

Especially interesting among the Brücke canvases was Mueller's single entry: *Bathing Women* (pl. 100).[52] His triangular, elongated shapes and jagged lines are close to the style of the Brücke in general, but the mood that Mueller creates—this mild dream of a new arcadia—is entirely different from the general intensity of Brücke work. It is strange to find this revival of a pastoral romanticism suddenly interrupting the violent struggles of the expressionist movement. In Mueller's unassuming work, the same motifs recur constantly with only minor variations: slender bathers, quiet horses at pasture, and—later—gypsies sitting contemplatively in the dusk. The surge of excitement so characteristic of expressionism seems to emanate from his work only as a strong sensuality. A gentle rhythm and a soft lyricism that never become too sweet pervade his painting. Pigments are applied thinly, and seem to be interwoven; the white of the canvas itself serves as the white of the picture. Furthermore, the rough surface quality is retained to give the picture its own texture effects. Little attention is paid to three-dimensional illusion.

The effect of large, flat, mural painting was always Mueller's aim. He was particularly interested in Egyptian painting as well as in the simplicity of Egyptian art in general: "The chief aim of my endeavors is to express the sensations of man and landscape with greatest possible simplicity; my model, in purely technical matters also, was and still is the art of the ancient Egyptians." [53]

Mueller's desire for simplicity results in an almost symmetrical balance in his compositions, which are frequently based on simple triangles (*Bathing Women*) or on rectangles. For Mueller the transition to simpler and perhaps more formal composition during the more form-conscious postwar period might have seemed a natural and expected development, yet he had even less in common with the "New Objectivity" of the 1920's than with the turbulence of the early expressionist era.

The Brücke already had followers by 1912: a number of painters working in Berlin who adopted much of the form that the Brücke painters had developed, and who were associated with them for a brief time in the New Secession. A number of these artists—such as César Klein, Moritz Melzer, and Georg Tappert—were included in the Sonderbund exhibition.

One of the most interesting young artists in the Cologne exhibition was Wilhelm Morgner, whose work will be discussed in a later chapter.[54]

Finally, both the Blaue Reiter and the New Artists' Association exhibited—among the latter, von Bechtejeff, Erbslöh, Kanoldt, and Jawlensky.

Jawlensky's *Infanta* (1912) (pl. 164) has departed a considerable distance from the Jugendstil of *White Feathers* from three years earlier. Instead of the concentration on continuous, curving line and emphatic contrast of light and dark patterns almost to the exclusion of other interests, *Infanta* employs its brilliant colors and vigorous brush work to outline a facial type. The sinuous curve has become a wiggle—a line that is almost curly. With a Matisse-like playfulness it defines smaller color areas more immediately related to the attributes of his sitter as a type: the glowing pompoms at her ears, the enormous eyes, the provocative, doll-like mouth, and egg-shaped Spanish jaw. But Jawlensky was still moving toward the concretization of a form that would be less dependent upon the intrusions of individual humanity. The *Spanish Woman* of the same year (pl. 165), with her eyes like wedges of lapis and her purple mouth, has solidified from a type into the painted idol of a type. The figure is quite wooden, and the fact that the eyebrows and the configurations and shadows of the face are all defined with the same green does nothing to lessen this effect of the graven image. These colors are the iconography. This solidity of form and emphasis on specific shapes—such as the eyes—by means of resonant color ultimately led Jawlensky to the extremely simplified symbol of the head in the postwar period.

Kandinsky was represented with two paintings, one of which—*Improvisation No. 21a*—was nonobjective. Paul Klee submitted four drawings to the exhibition; August Macke, who had been on the Working Committee, had five paintings in the show.

Franz Marc is also listed in the catalog with five works—including the important *Yellow Horses, Tiger* (pl. 166a),[55] and *Two Cats* (pl. 166b)[56] —but Marc withdrew his work to protest the manner in which entries for the exhibition were selected.[57] By this time Marc had experienced the first influence of cubist form. He had seen cubist exhibits in Munich and had met Delaunay in Paris in 1912. Much of this new influence, leading to an interlacing of transparent forms, took time to develop into the specific form of Marc's late work. Early in 1912 his form underwent considerable stylization and mannerism; simultaneously his compositions became much more tight and definite. *Tiger* and *Cats,* paintings often considered among Marc's finest achievements, can be regarded as transitions from the free-flowing, organic rhythm of *Red Horses* to the tight, crystalline structure of the paintings (like the *Tower of Blue Horses*) that were to be seen in the next great international art exhibition in Germany: the First German Autumn Salon, sponsored by *Der Sturm* in Berlin in the fall of 1913.

The Cologne exhibition was the last one held by the Sonderbund. Soon after the show closed, the organizing group dissolved. Nolde blamed the dealers: "The exhibition in Cologne was so great an event that the dealers in Berlin acted very enviously and knew how to defeat the young and proud *Sonderbund*." [58] Actually, internal and organizational difficulties led to the dissolution, but fortunately only after the work of the great international show had been completed. "The exhibition became the proclamation of the century. Its significance and even its sensation—understood rightly—were never surpassed, at least in Germany, and hardly ever reached again." [59]

After the dissolution of the Sonderbund the young Rhenish painters participated in one more important exhibition: the Rhenish Expressionists, sponsored by the Galerie Friedrich Cohen in Bonn. The group, changed somewhat since the previous year, now included Heinrich Campendonk, Paul Seehaus, Max Ernst (both the latter under August Macke's influence at the time), Nauen, Helmuth Macke, and others. Soon a new organization—Das Junge Rheinland—absorbed some of the organizational responsibilities of the former Sonderbund but never became internationally or even nationally significant.

The Sonderbund exhibition was the direct model for the International Exhibition of Modern Art given under the auspices of the Association of American Painters and Sculptors—later to be known as the Armory Show —in New York. Walt Kuhn, one of the organizers and secretary of the association, said: "Later in the midst of a painting trip in Nova Scotia I received from him [Arthur B. Davies, president of the organization] by mail the catalogue of the 'Sonderbund' Exhibition then current in Cologne, Germany, together with a brief note, stating, 'I wish we could have a show like this.' " [60] Kuhn decided to sail immediately for Cologne to survey the exhibition:

The Cologne Exhibition, housed in a temporary building, had been well conceived and executed, in fact it became in a measure the model of what we finally did in New York. It contained a grand display of Cézannes and Van Goghs, including also a good representation of the leading living modernists in France. The show had languished through half the summer, much maligned by the citizens, but toward the end burst forth as a great success with big attendance and many sales.

I arrived in town on the last day of the exhibition. . . . I met the sculptor Lehmbruck and secured some of his sculpture, also works by Munch, the Norwegian, and many others through the courtesy of the show's management. [61]

The Armory Show was not the only sequel to the Sonderbund. J. B. Neumann, who was ultimately to introduce German expressionism to the United States, directed his Graphisches Kabinett in Berlin "to be a kind of permanent continuation on a smaller scale of the International Exhibition of the Sonderbund in Cologne." [62]

Perhaps most important, the Sonderbund exhibition was followed by another significant exposition of modern art held in Germany: First German Autumn Salon, organized by Herwath Walden of *Der Sturm* in September, 1913. Not as comprehensive as the Sonderbund exhibition, this later show put much greater emphasis on the *avant-garde*.

XX

Der Sturm

In 1924 Lothar Schreyer, a collaborator on *Der Sturm,* pointed out [1] that the Sturm—periodical, publishing house, gallery, school, theater, and all its other related facets—was not an organization of artists, not a bolshevik band, not a capitalist cartel, not a clique of Jews, and not an exclusive club, but rather that "Der Sturm ist Herwath Walden." [2]

Walden was a "critic, artist, prophet and—business man." [3] He was also an impressario, a great publicist and propagator of novel ideas; he was a man who, through his own prodigious energy and enthusiasm and the hydra-headed organization he created, became the catalyst of the modern movement and the focal point of expressionism—a term that he made popular. In retrospect it seems that excellence in art was less important to Walden than provocativeness, difference, and novelty, but at least for a number of years during the prewar period his choice luckily coincided with the truly significant currents in art. [4]

In January, 1910, when Walden was dismissed as editor of the theater magazine *Der neue Weg* for his too radical ideas, a strong letter of protest was signed by Peter Altenberg, Hermann Bahr, Peter Behrens, Max Brod, Richard Dehmel, Elizabeth Förster-Nietzsche, Arno Holz, Detlev von Liliencron, Heinrich Mann, Julius Meier-Graefe, Alfred Mombert, Hermann Multhesius, René Schickele, and Henry van de Velde among others. With this ensemble of famous defenders trumpeting moral support, Walden immediately started his own publication, *Der Sturm,* the first issue of which appeared in March, 1910.

In its earliest phase *Der Sturm* was a weekly periodical devoted primarily to literature and criticism; during the first year it was published in both Berlin and Vienna. Its first article, by Viennese poet and journalist Karl Kraus, contained a statement prophetic of Dadaist thought: "The world becomes more rational every day which naturally renders its utter stupidity more and more conspicuous." [5]

This literary weekly, with a circulation of about thirty thousand copies, attracted many of the leading writers of the period, including Strindberg, Döblin, Dehmel, Brod, Altenberg, Loos, Kraus, Heinrich Mann, Wedekind, and Else Lasker-Schüler, the poet, who was Walden's first wife.

Coming from the theater and concerned with its more literary aspects, Walden was at first comparatively little interested in the visual arts. In the second issue, in fact, an article by J. A. Lux expressed complete pessimism about the existing state and future of art in a technological age. True art is an expression of the divine, the metaphysical, and has no place in an age of reason; capitalism and democracy are its enemies. Today we may live by moral values, but there is no place in our lives for mysticism and religion, and no single artist who has gone beyond the discoveries of impressionism. "Art is dead." [6] This attitude in *Der Sturm* soon changed. The visual arts were introduced with an illustration by Liebermann, and soon Kokoschka provided regular illustrations.

KOKOSCHKA AND DER STURM

Walden met Kokoschka through Adolf Loos in Vienna in the spring of 1910, and took the young artist to Berlin with him on the basis of a contract to furnish illustrations for the periodical. Kokoschka's contributions in

Figure 28.   OSKAR KOKOSCHKA   Portrait of Adolf Loos   1910
Drawing

the beginning were mostly portrait sketches. The incisive portrait of Adolf Loos (1910) (fig. 28) indicates how well the artist, only twenty-four years old at the time, understood the nature and possibilities of line. He used the peculiar qualities of line, as he had previously used the peculiar quality of pigment, to produce a sketch at once expressive of the characters of the sitter and of the painter.

Slightly later Kokoschka published a portrait drawing of his new patron, Herwath Walden (fig. 29). The character of the "pseudo-genius" [7] is fully expressed by Kokoschka's handling of line and shape. Most important in the drawing is the contrast between forehead and lower part of the face. The enormous expanse of bare skull, with which the artist seems to

Figure 29.   OSKAR KOKOSCHKA   Portrait of
Herwath Walden   1910   Drawing

indicate the importance of the man's intellect, is strongly emphasized by a heavy line drawn around the upper part of the forehead; the forehead itself is left bare except for a few short repeat lines, stressing the void areas. This area is in contrast to the lower part of the picture, filled with a multitude of small, busy lines moving at every angle between eyebrows and receding chin and coming to a focal point in the eye sockets and the heavy, round glasses. Kokoschka's concern with morbidity and the corruption of the flesh is here evident in the cracked lips, the wiggling line of the jawbone—recalling a caterpillar—and the wrinkled neck.

A year later Kokoschka published his striking drawing of Yvette Guilbert in *Der Sturm* (fig. 30). Mlle Guilbert had aged considerably since Toulouse-Lautrec's time, and Kokoschka's essentially tragic approach enhances this change. The sly, long, almond-shaped eyes in Lautrec's pictures have grown large, sunken, and sad. Her pug nose, which looked amusing in Lautrec, is now a bulbous projection balanced by the tensely backward-moving bun, where intricate lines interweave haphazardly.

Kokoschka also published his play *Mörder, Hoffnung der Frauen* [8] in *Der Sturm,* as well as illustrations for the play.[9] These savage drawings, with their barbaric expressiveness and the double faces incorporating both profile and full face, may be compared with work by Picasso in the 1930's, though this formal device of the dual face was much more fully explored in its evocative possibilities by Picasso.

Figure 30. OSKAR KOKOSCHKA Portrait of Yvette Guilbert 1911 Drawing

Once Kokoschka had come to Berlin, a city much more open to progressive art forms than Vienna was, he began to gain recognition. Paul Cassirer offered him an exhibition in June, 1910, where Kokoschka had an opportunity to show his whole series of portraits, his faces of attrition, and his masks of the rarefied, the refined, and the decadent. Success was by no means assured, but he was now under the patronage not only of an eccentric and bohemian editor but at the same time under the sponsorship of the most respected modern art dealer in Berlin. This first meeting between Kokoschka and Cassirer was to lead to a most fertile collaboration, with Cassirer sending Kokoschka half around the globe to paint a modern *orbus pictus* after the war and before the eventual break between the two. The exhibition at Cassirer's was immediately followed by an invitation from Osthaus to show Kokoschka's portraits at the Folkwang Museum in Hagen in September, 1910. The following month Walden appointed Kokoschka the Vienna editor of *Der Sturm.*

In Vienna, where the Hagenbund organized a major one-man show for him in February, 1911, Kokoschka met with even greater public condemnation than he had previously. He returned to Berlin and continued to contribute to *Der Sturm* during 1911; he now was to share honors with the painters of the Brücke, whom Walden was just discovering. This "partnership" broadened his view. During his first stay in Berlin he had become familiar with the Brücke artists and the expressionist movement. He liked and admired the work of Nolde, Kirchner, Heckel, and Pechstein, although their influence on him was largely a confirmation of his own direction. Although Kokoschka had much in common with the Brücke artists, he was always too individualistic to affiliate himself; he did, however, exhibit with them in the New Secession in 1911.

COLLABORATION WITH THE BRÜCKE

Significantly, Pechstein was the first among the Brücke to be included in *Der Sturm;* his buxom females contrasted strangely to Kokoschka's neurotic, emaciated types. In the spring of 1911 Nolde became a contributor to *Der Sturm,* to be followed by Kirchner, Heckel, and Schmidt-Rottluff. Walden printed their woodcuts or reproduced their drawings. *Der Sturm* carried full-page advertisements of the exhibitions of the New Secession while they were in progress; as soon as Kirchner and Pechstein founded the MUIM Institute, the new school was announced and advertised in Walden's journal.

Figure 31.   ERNST LUDWIG KIRCHNER   The Ball   1911   Woodcut

Kirchner was by far the most frequent art contributor to *Der Sturm* during the period of active collaboration between Walden and the Brücke in 1911 and early 1912. Typical of the work he submitted as well as of his own development is the woodcut *The Ball* (fig. 31). Kirchner creates an interesting space relationship by representing a cross section of a cabaret wide open to the spectator's view, with dancers on the lower floor and a couple seated at a table in the upper story. The wedge shapes of black and white are only the barest indications of people; their purpose is essentially decorative.

Kirchner's woodcut *Summer* (fig. 32) shows a big nude seated in the foreground, occupying the total vertical space of the picture; a large, not clearly defined but phallic-shaped object is at the side; and another nude is lying on a deck chair in the background. The picture shows the

Figure 32.   ERNST LUDWIG KIRCHNER   Summer   1911   Woodcut

strong influence of Melanesian art, especially in the decoration of the object on the right; the influence of primitive art had increased since the early impact of Oceanic and African sculpture in the Ethnological Museum in Dresden.

Soon Walden began to publish work by other artists who quickly adopted the Brücke style: Moritz Melzer, A. Segal, Ludwig Kainer, and César Klein. But in 1912 Walden slowly started to withdraw his attention from this group as he discovered the Munich painters of Der Blaue Reiter, the futurists, and later the cubists.

"EXPRESSIONISTS"

During 1911, while the painters of the Brücke, their disciples, and Kokoschka were being featured in *Der Sturm,* the term "expressionist" made its first of frequent appearances in the journal, although it was not yet applied to these artists.

Der Sturm did not coin either "expressionist" or "expressionism," but it popularized both terms. *Der Sturm* became the semiofficial spokesman of expressionism, a movement that included almost anyone whom Walden and his circle liked and publicized at any given time. Soon the term became descriptive simply of artistic quality as seen by Walden: "We call the art of this century Expressionism, in order to distinguish it from what is not art. We are thoroughly familiar with the fact that artists of previous centuries also sought expression. Only they did not know how to formulate it." [10]

The original derivation of the term "expressionism" is still not known. The French painter Julien-August Hervé exhibited eight paintings, which he called *expressionismes*,[11] in the Salon des Indépendants of 1901. But the term did not then take root. During the first decade of the century Matisse frequently spoke to his students—particularly the German painters Grossmann, Purrmann, Levi, and Moll—of the importance of *expression,* but was always quick to add a second word: *sensibilité.* The expressive quality Matisse had in mind was to be revealed in his own decorative compositions of carefully related elements. Theodor Däubler recalled, however, that the word *expressionisme* was used first by Matisse and that Vauxcelles was the first to publish the term.[12] It is possible that the man who christened Fauvism and cubism was also responsible for the term "expressionism."

In Germany the term suddenly appeared in relation to French painters and their exhibit in the Berlin Secession of 1911. It occurred almost simultaneously in the reviews of this particular section of the exhibit in most of the German art periodicals.[13]

The term first appeared in *Der Sturm* in reference to the same group of Fauve painters in the Secession exhibit. Walter Heymann, then the art reviewer for the magazine, published a series of four articles about the twenty-second exhibition of the Secession. Heymann was by no means the type of *avant-garde* critic usually associated with Walden. In the first of this series of articles Heymann admitted that Fritz von Uhde compromised with the past, but he admired Liebermann above all measure: "Nobody, I think, has come so close to Rembrandt as the best of the German Impressionists. He looks at us from this self-portrait, done in relief, fully glowing . . . transfigured by light." [14] In the last of the series Heymann spoke of the expressionists as being primarily under the influence of van Gogh and Hodler. He described the French painters Marquet, Vlaminck, Derain, Doucet, Friesz, Braquet [*sic*], and Puy as men of average artistic talent who went wild with the fanaticism of theory, and he took issue with the jury for not including native talents who belonged to this group—particularly Pechstein and Melzer.[15]

The word "expressionist" was then used in an important essay by Worringer, in which he delivered his own answer to Vinnen's *Protest deutscher*

Künstler.[16] In this key article Worringer related the new endeavors of the "synthetists and expressionists" in Paris to primitive art, and maintained that their form was not a sudden fad but a historical necessity. It is a return to primitive and elemental form conditioned by the time, and naturally misunderstood by those who detect in primitive art nothing more than a lack of ability and who point with false pride to the evolution and progress of art in Europe. Worringer explained, however—in keeping with his previous statements in *Abstraction and Empathy*—that primitive and abstract forms were not determined by lack of ability but by a different artistic purpose. The young artist of the day, he continued, sought his inspiration in this elemental primitive source. He tried to break with the illusionist art of the Renaissance, because he felt more affinity with the mystic vision of primitive art than with the rational perception of the Western tradition. Taking issue with the *Protest* in particular, Worringer encouraged museums to continue buying new, experimental art, and suggested that they should make history rather than being archives of the past.

During the latter part of 1911 *Der Sturm,* following Worringer's important essay, devoted an increasing amount of its space to art criticism. A highly perceptive article on Hodler, together with a drawing by the Swiss artist, was published in the weekly.[17] Paintings by Kandinsky, shown by the New Secession, were referred to as "the purest works of art." [18] August L. Mayer's monograph on El Greco was most favorably reviewed; El Greco was called "probably the first painter who did not wish to feign nature." [19] All the covers of the magazine had woodcuts by the Brücke artists and painters working in a related style.

In January, 1912, Walden published "Die Expressionisten," by Paul Ferdinand Schmidt, briefly outlining the development of this new movement:

Cézanne taught the simplification of tone values, Gauguin the effect of the plane, and Van Gogh added the flaming luminosity of color. Maurice Denis, Vuillard and Bonnard attempted to prepare a planar simplification in the grand style, but they lacked persuasive expression. This was found by the Teutons of the north and south, Munch and Hodler.[20]

Schmidt said that there was no school of expressionism, that there was little relationship between Pechstein, Puy, Vlaminck, Herbin, and Nolde, and that "the common name is the product of a dilemma—it signifies little." [21] They were tied together by their concern with truth rather than verisimilitude, by their strong accents on plane, color, and space for the sake of the immediate evocative power of these elements.

In March, 1912, months after the appearance of this article, Walden decided, in connection with the one-hundredth issue of *Der Sturm,* to arrange the first Sturm exhibition. He invited the "expressionists" to participate—the term still implying the contemporary French group, primarily Fauves. In addition, Ferdinand Hodler, Oskar Kokoschka, Edvard Munch, and a mediocre sculptor—Franz Flaum—were included. To this combination Walden added a large selection of the first Blaue Reiter exhibition, which had just been exhibited in Cologne. But even before he became really concerned with the work and the esthetic ideas of Marc and Kandinsky, Walden made a new discovery and introduced the futurists to Germany.

INTRODUCTION OF FUTURISM INTO GERMANY

In March, 1912, two years after its first publication at the Teatro Chiarella in Turin, Walden published the "Technical Manifesto of Futurist Painting," signed by Giacomo Balla, Umberto Boccioni, Carlo Carrà, Luigi Russolo, and Gino Severini.[22] The manifesto, phrased in the language of their spiritual father, F. T. Marinetti, glorified originality and demanded that artists blast to fragments the fetters of the past. The present—indeed, the future—was advocated. The result was to be an art of the twentieth century eulogizing the machine and devoted to speed. According to the manifesto, it was the task of the modern artist to translate the fast, confused, dynamic sensations of modern life and the speed of its rhythm into visual form:

. . . everything moves, everything runs, everything is being rapidly transformed. Given the continuation of the image on the retina, objects in movement multiply themselves like vibrations launched into the space which they traverse. Thus a trotting horse has not four legs but twenty and their movements are triangular.[23]

Art, then, was to express the dynamic movement of the world, and the sensitivity of the artist could resolve it into a series of vibrating waves. "They said that they sensed molecular movements, and that in their plastic imagination they saw that very atomic movement which philosophy suspected and science demonstrated."[24]

The constant motion of all matter was to be expressed by "simultaneity." Boccioni and Soffici gave very complex explanations of that concept, but the term simply meant the simultaneous representation of various aspects of an object, including the sensations that the objects call forth in the mind of the artists. It was not enough to represent a man's face: the artist had to relate it to the total environment and all the motions constantly occurring. "The bus falls upon the buildings which it passes and the buildings on their part simultaneously fall upon the bus and melt with it."[25]

The futurist painters felt, further, that painting could no longer be a matter of passive contemplation for the observer, but that the painter must make sure that his work conjured up an immediate experience that transposed the spectator into the very center of the work.

In addition to what Marinetti called *passéism,* the futurists counted both harmony and good taste in their catalog of anathemas. The futurist manifesto declared that art criticism was useless and ought to be abolished. They said they were proud of being called fools. Yet they seem to have been prophetic in demanding the destruction of the materiality of forms through movement and light.

Most artists in the various movements of twentieth-century art occasionally published verbalizations of their ideas for the sake of clarification or publicity, but the futurists made a special point of manifestoes and of seeking the strongest possible limelight. In February, 1909, F. T. Marinetti released the highly revolutionary "Futurist Manifesto" in *Figaro*, the most respected daily of the Paris bourgeoisie. This provocative statement maintained that a racing car was more beautiful than the Nike of Samothrace,[26] and included a metaphorical statement to the effect that the axis of an automobile's steering wheel continued to the center of the earth. Marinetti also praised war, militarism, and patriotism, and censured museums, libraries, and women. This manifesto appeared in *Der Sturm* immediately after its publication of the "Technical Manifesto of Futurist Painting." [27] These manifestoes were followed in the succeeding issue by an announcement of the second Sturm exhibition—"The Futurists"—and a statement by the futurist painters to the German public.[28] The painters explained "without boasting" that this was the most important exhibition of Italian painting ever shown in Germany. They said that their French contemporaries—men like Picasso, Braque, Derain, Metzinger, Le Fauconnier, Gleizes, Léger, and Lhote—painting only a static world, honored the tradition of Poussin, Ingres, and Corot; the futurists wanted to express the simultaneity of states of mind. The statement continued by saying that the French also mistakenly ignored the importance of subject matter; the futurists, in the forefront of European painting, were deeply involved with the subject.

Although the futurists announced the destruction of harmony in art, Walden next published Kandinsky's "Language of Form and Color" [29] (chap. vi of *Concerning the Spiritual in Art*). Although Kandinsky was in agreement with the futurist attempt to abolish the materiality of forms, he proposed a new harmony in art based on the force of internal necessity.

For the remainder of 1912 *Der Sturm* printed reproductions of paintings by Boccioni, and published postcards of his works as well as of Russolo's and Severini's. The novelist Alfred Döblin wrote a critical review of the futurist exhibition, in which he explained that the space in a futurist painting is distinct from Cartesian space and that the painter has not two dimensions at his disposal but as many as his imagination permits.[30] Later Franz Marc, now a frequent contributor of articles to *Der Sturm*, wrote his eulogy of futurism:

The connoisseurs speak of "peinture" like the dog-breeders of pedigrees. This they may still find in Picasso but not in the Futurists. . . . When a window is opened, the total noise of the street, the movements and materiality of the objects outside enter the room. . . . Carrà, Boccioni and Severini will become milestones in the history of modern art. We will yet envy Italy for its sons and hang their works in our galleries.[31]

The impact of futurism was felt by Marc, and appeared in his work. Earlier, however, Marc had also experienced a definite influence from cubism—not through Picasso, but through Delaunay.

Late in the summer of 1912 Marc, Maria Marc, and August Macke went to Paris to visit Delaunay, whose use of prismatic forms and refracting color made an immediate and lasting impression. Where previously Marc's animals existed in the landscape, they now became a structural part of it, interwoven with and absorbed in nature itself—a cosmos of which they were a symbol. Nolde noticed this change as early as the New Secession exhibition of 1912:

Franz Marc had painted his simple groups of deer and animals without any tendency toward mannerism; now he became almost suddenly constructive, cubistic, almost to the unrecognizability of the animals represented. Was this the new emerging time? These great configurations of rays, curvatures, lines and prismatic colors? [32]

A painting like *The Bewitched Mill,* painted late in 1912 (pl. 101), shows unmistakably the introduction of both cubist and futurist shapes

Figure 33.   FRANZ MARC   Riding School   1913   Woodcut

and the use of transparent and prismatic color planes. The design has become more angular and the composition much tighter than in his earlier work. The rotating motion of the red wheel on the left is counterbalanced by the movement of the white waterfall; dropping vertically through the center of the picture, the waterfall is answered by the rectangular shapes on the right. The brilliant and imaginative colors enhance the subject matter and lend it much of its fairy-tale effect.

This period in Marc's career as an artist must be called transitional, in the sense that he still assimilated a variety of influences. *The Bewitched Mill* is redolent of Delaunay's open windows; the woodcut *Riding School* (fig. 33), done during the same winter, shows rather more influence from futurism. The horse and rider are dynamically bound to their environment by futurist "force lines." The futurists—especially Boccioni— used these force lines to break up objects and to link forms simultaneously, in order to indicate velocity of movement, as in Boccioni's *Dynamism of a Football Player* (1913) (pl. 167). These force lines, appearing again in Marc's *Riding School,* do not allow the spectator to contemplate this picture, but impel him to take part in the dynamic movement of the interlinked forces.

Marc was the first to express his admiration for futurist painting, but critics also soon realized the impact of futurism on one of Germany's leading expressionists. In connection with a retrospective exhibit for Gino Severini held by Der Sturm in August, 1913, Adolf Behne said: "Merely the fact that such a sincere and fine artist as Franz Marc took over Futurist elements in his paintings must convince even the greatest skeptic of the stimulative value and the artistic significance of Futurism." [33]

The Severini exhibition was the sixteenth show held by Der Sturm and was followed by the First German Autumn Salon in September, 1913.

STURM EXHIBITIONS, 1912–1913

1. (March–April, 1912): Hodler, Munch, Kokoschka, Flaum, "Expressionists," Der Blaue Reiter.
   The term "Expressionists" is here still used for the French artists coming from Fauvism.
2. Futurists.
3. French Graphic Arts.
   This exhibition included primarily Picasso, Herbin, and Gauguin. It was probably the first time Gauguin's color woodcuts were shown in Germany.
4. German Expressionists: Marc, Kandinsky, Bloch, Jawlensky, Münter, Werefkina.
   This is the first usage of the term "German Expressionists," then applied by Walden exclusively to the Blaue Reiter group.
5. French Expressionists: Braque, Derain, Friesz, Herbin, Laurencin, Vlaminck.
6. Belgian Expressionists: James Ensor and Ryk Wouters. This was the first Ensor exhibition in Germany. Wouters (1882–1916) was a Flemish painter working in the Fauve style. Later the term "Belgian," or rather "Flemish," Expressionism was applied to a

younger group, particularly Constant Permeke, Gustave de Smet, Frits van den Berghe, Jean Brusselmans, and Edgard Tytgat.

7. Kandinsky.

    An essay by Kandinsky, "Über Kunstverstehen," [34] in which he discusses the dangers of man's fear of new experiences as well as his eager pursuit of novelty for its own sake. Six original woodcuts by Kandinsky dating from 1906, 1907, 1909, and 1910 were published in conjunction with the exhibition and article.

8. Die Pathetiker: Ludwig Meidner and Jacob Steinhardt.

    Meidner, one of the most interesting painters of the second generation of German expressionism, will be discussed in some detail in a later chapter. This was his first exhibition, as well as Steinhardt's first. The latter became a leading painter and print maker in Israel.

9. Campendonk, Jan Gauguin, A. Segal.

10. New Secession.

    This exhibition, held late in the autumn of 1912, no longer had the participation of the Brücke artists. Although the members of the Brücke frequently contributed drawings and woodcuts to *Der Sturm*, they never exhibited in the galleries.

11. Gabriele Münter.

12. Robert Delaunay and Ardengo Soffici.

    Soffici had joined the futurist group late and brought a strong French influence to the movement. Delaunay, a close friend of the Blaue Reiter, traveled together with Apollinaire to Berlin for the opening of this exhibition. On their way they stopped with August Macke in Bonn in January, 1913. Apollinaire published his article "Realité, peinture pure" in connection with this exhibition. [35] Here he emphasized the debt the contemporary painters of pure light and color, especially Delaunay, owed to Seurat. A similar observation was made by the critic who reviewed the exhibition for *Pan*. [36]

    Delaunay's own article, "Sur la lumière," translated by Paul Klee, appeared in *Der Sturm*. [37] Here Delaunay maintains that art must free itself from the object and from all descriptive and literary implications. Its task is to give expression and form to the manifold rhythms and harmonies of color and to raise light to plastic independence.

    Another significant article about Delaunay's conquest of perspective, by Paul Bommersheim, was published; in this the critic distinguishes between two kinds of movement: the mechanistic and static movement and object to object relationship of perspective, as against the vitalistic, dynamic movement in which the object relates to the total, fluid space as realized in the work of Robert Delaunay. [38]

13. Alfred Reth.
    Reth was a Hungarian painter who had come to Berlin from Paris and an early association with Picasso, Gris, and their friends at the Bateau-lavoir.
14. Franz Marc.
15. *Der moderne Bund/Schweiz.*
    This included Arp, Gimmi, Helbig, Huber, Klee, Lüthy, Pfister.
16. Gino Severini.

    In the fall of 1913, while Walden held the *Erster deutscher Herbstsalon*—the First German Autumn Salon—at Potsdamerstrasse 75, he continued the smaller exhibitions at the home office of *Der Sturm:*
17. Alexander Archipenko.
    Archipenko was one of the important discoveries of Walden. This was his first exhibition in Germany.
18. *Skupina,* Prague.
    Paintings, sculpture, and architecture by Czech artists.
19. Cubists.

    The year 1913 ended with the following two exhibitions:
20. Albert Bloch.
21. August Macke.

22. Der Blaue Reiter.
    This was the first Sturm exhibition in 1914 and the last joint exhibit of Der Blaue Reiter. It repeated to a considerable extent the first Blaue Reiter show, even to the actual work shown, such as Kandinsky's *Composition No. 5,* Marc's *Yellow Cow,* Bloch's *Harlequins,* Campendonk's *Jumping Horse.* Several artists included in the original exhibition, such as Henri Rousseau, Delaunay, Niestlé, and Schönberg were now absent; certain additions were made by Walden: Klee and Werefkina as well as Heckel, Kirchner, and Pechstein. It is particularly interesting that three of the original Brücke artists were included in this Blaue Reiter show. The individual artists grew apart, but the movements or groups began to merge. Franz Marc wrote a brief foreword to the catalog for this exhibition, and Kandinsky's essay "Über Kunstverstehen" was reprinted. The plates in the catalog are reprints from the almanac, *Der Blaue Reiter.*

WALDEN AS THE CHAMPION OF HIS ARTISTS

During this whole period Walden was primarily concerned with promoting the futurists and the Blaue Reiter. When Marc decided to withdraw his work from the Sonderbund exhibition in Cologne, Walden exhibited it together with withdrawn and rejected paintings by Kandinsky, Bloch, Jawlensky, Münter, and Werefkina (fourth Sturm exhibition). At the same time Franz Marc published a series of articles in *Der Sturm* in which he voiced his displeasure with most public exhibitions.

In March, 1913, Kandinsky had a one-man show in Hamburg, which resulted in a vicious review by one Kurt Küchler, who called the work arrogant, bungling, impudent, debauched, and insane.[39] Walden immediately took up the cudgels: he attacked Küchler and his paper, reprinted the review and proceeded to muster a defense for Kandinsky. He published letters by Apollinaire, Hausenstein, Kokoschka, Dehmel, Osthaus, Hanns Swarzensky, Fritz Burger, and issued a letter signed by a most astonishing array of leading artists from Germany, France, Russia, and Italy.[40]

Walden also became the legal protector of his artists. When the Herbstsalon opened in September, 1913, he acted as attorney for both Marc and Kandinsky. Marc had brought suit against *Kunst und Künstler* for reproducing his work without his permission; Walden preferred charges against a critic for stating that "Kandinsky has adhered to the Futurist trends in art entirely for business reasons." [41] These lawsuits, always settled outside of court, helped publicize the artists and of course kept Walden's name in the newspapers.

XXI

First German Autumn Salon

The Berlin Secession had planned to hold an "autumn salon" in Berlin in the fall of 1913, to be modeled after the Paris Salon d'Automne. However, the split that occurred in the administration in the summer of that year made any such activity impossible; encouraged by the financial support of Bernhard Koehler, Walden immediately took it upon himself to sponsor such an undertaking. The purpose was to "present a survey of the creative art in all countries," [1] which to Walden meant the most *avant-garde* artists and movements. He traveled with meteoric speed through most European art centers from Budapest to Paris. He was able to assemble 366 paintings and pieces of sculpture by some 90 artists from 15 countries, including the Asian and American continents. This was to be the last of the significant international exhibitions of contemporary art held in Germany before World War I. Many of the artists represented in the Sonderbund were absent from the Herbstsalon, but many new ones were added. The general tendency in painting went strongly in the direction of abstraction. Among the "precursors" of modern art, Walden limited himself to a memorial exhibition of twenty-two pictures by Rousseau, who was considered the father of the new trends. [2] The more important artists represented in the Herbstsalon were:

FRANCE:	Marc Chagall	Robert Delaunay
	Sonia Delaunay	Albert Gleizes
	Fernand Léger	Louis Marcoussis
	Jean Metzinger	Francis Picabia
ITALY:	Giacomo Balla	Umberto Boccioni
	Carlo Carrà	Luigi Russolo
	Gino Severini	Ardengo Soffici
RUSSIA:	David Burliuk	Vladimir Burliuk
	Natalie Gontcharova	N. Kulbin
	Michael Larionoff	Alexander Mogilewsky
AUSTRIA:	Oskar Kokoschka	

HOLLAND: Five artists including Jacoba van Heemskerck and Piet Mondrian

SWITZERLAND: Members of the *Moderne Bund,* including Paul Klee (22 pictures) and Louis Moilliet

UNITED STATES: Albert Bloch (Munich)   Lyonel Feininger (Berlin)
P. H. Bruce (Paris)   Marsden Hartley (New York)

GERMANY: Among the Munich group around Der Blaue Reiter:

Vladimir von Bechtejeff   Heinrich Campendonk
Alexej von Jawlensky   Wassily Kandinsky
Alfred Kubin   August Macke
Franz Marc   Gabriele Münter
Marianne von Werefkin

Among the younger generation:

Hans Arp   Willi Baumeister
Max Ernst   Hellmuth Macke
P. A. Seehaus   Jacob Steinhardt

There were also works by five contemporary Czech artists, Turkish paintings, Russian peasant art, Indian paintings, and Japanese and Chinese rice pictures. The most important sculpture of the exhibition was sent by Archipenko from Paris and by Boccioni from Milan.

The catalog lists some of the most distinguished works done during 1913, the culminating year in the history of early-twentieth-century art: Balla's *Dog on Leash,* Boccioni's *Unique Forms of Continuity in Space,* Delaunay's *Disques Soleils,* Léger's *Woman in Blue,* Kandinsky's *Composition No. 6,* and Marc's *Fate of the Beasts* and *Tower of Blue Horses.*

THE BLAUE REITER PAINTERS

Franz Marc was now at the height of his powers. Among the seven canvases in the exhibition were the three that are generally considered his finest. *The Tower of Blue Horses* (1913) (pl. 102) [3] is even more tightly knit in its composition than *The Bewitched Mill.* The movements of the heads and bodies of the horses in their rhythmical repetition suggest the successive movements of a single animal in a futurist painting or a later stroboscopic photograph. *The Tower of Blue Horses* is based on the rectangle; instead of the predominant downward movement of *The Bewitched Mill,* everything here strives upward. This vertical force is created chiefly by means of color, which changes from the fully saturated blue at the bottom to the delicate vermilion in the rainbow on top. The blue of the horses has a transparency that is reminiscent of stained glass, as is the structural form of the painting: circles, triangles, prisms, and rhomboids. The sickle of the moon appears on the chest of the horse in the foreground—the heraldic animal of the Blue Horseman has been lifted from the earth to some transcendental region.

Two more explicitly troubled paintings from the same year were in the Herbstsalon. *Fate of the Beasts* (1913) (pl. 168), [4] perhaps also related to the prevailing apprehensions of war, portrays a total, inescapable catastrophe. Hard, arrowlike diagonals intersect to shoot across the canvas. Trees bleed and descend in a cosmic cataclysm. The pony running from the whinnying mother plunges toward the falling tree. Foxes, noses pointing the wind, stand curiously together at the root of a gigantic tree. On the lower left two boars seem to root in the earth to hide. Above are green horses, one of them running into the red danger; in the center a blue deer sacrificially lifts its neck to the crushing trunk and carries the meaning of the painting. Marc originally called this painting *And All Being Became Flaming Suffering,* but Paul Klee suggested the now accepted title.[5] The interrelationship of forms is carried to its greatest effectiveness: angular abstract shapes become animals, and animals turn into abstractions. Marc, when receiving a reproduction of *Fate of the Beasts* during the war in 1915, expressed astonishment at his own sense of approaching ruin:

Koehler wrote to me today on a Sturm postcard reproducing my "Tierschicksale." I was greatly struck and excited at its sight. It is like a premonition of this war, horrible and stirring; I can hardly conceive that I painted this! . . . It is artistically logical to paint such paintings before the war, not as dumb memory after the war; then we must paint constructive pictures denoting the future.[6]

A similar cataclysm prevails in *The Unhappy Tyrol* (pl. 103). Again there are broken luminous color planes with jagged edges, and the strong diagonal of a barren, falling tree predominates. The colors are red, black, and gray, like fire, smoke, and cinders. Objects—such as huts, trees, sun, and mountain peaks—are merely intimated. The content is expressed almost solely through the tension of transparent color planes. A year after the painting was completed, Marc asked to have it returned, and he added— evidently with renewed faith—the contour of a Virgin and Child in the shape of a Bavarian wood carving.

Marc—like Kandinsky, Kokoschka, Meidner, and Nolde—seems to have had intimations of approaching disaster:

The closer the time of the outbreak of the Great War approached, the more clearly the work of the most aware artists reveals a breaking and bursting of form, a calamity of content. Some people believe that the threatening tempest announced itself to awakened souls; one fact is evident in such creations: the European spirit had turned from innocent and naive hedonism to a dark anguish and often helplessness before the horrible event occurred.[7]

Kandinsky's *Improvisation No. 30* (1913) (pl. 104) [8] shows a similar premonition of war. In a letter to Arthur Jerome Eddy, the Chicago lawyer, critic, writer, and collector who bought the painting, Kandinsky wrote:

The presence of the cannons in the picture could probably be explained by the constant war talk that had been going on throughout the year. But I did not intend to give a representation of war; to do so would have required different pictorial means; besides such tasks do not interest me. . . .[9]

The designation "cannons," Kandinsky explained, was for his own use only and was by no means intended to convey the contents of the picture.[10]

Essentially this painting is similar to *Composition No. 4.*[11] Certain objects from the actual world are still included in the painted world. The fluid, shifting, turbulent movement in a variety of directions is created primarily by the independence of the color areas from the linear structure. As in most of Kandinsky's paintings from the prewar era, the color areas go their way quite unrelated to the paths of the lines. Kandinsky gave a brief analysis of the painting in the letter to Eddy. Pointing out that the cannons were not part of the content of the work, he continued:

These contents are indeed what the spectator *lives* or *feels* while under the effect of the *form and color combinations* of the picture. This picture is nearly in the shape of a cross. The centre—somewhat below the middle—is formed by a large, irregular blue plane. (The blue color in itself counteracts the impression caused by the cannons!) Below this centre there is a muddy-gray, ragged second centre almost equal in importance to the first one. The four centres extending the oblique cross into the corners of the picture are heavier than the two centres, especially heavier than the first, and they vary from each other in characteristics, in lines, contours, and colors.

Thus the picture becomes lighter or looser in the centre, and heavier or tighter towards the corners.

The scheme of the construction is thus toned down, even made invisible for many, by the looseness of the forms. Larger or smaller remains of *objectivity* (the cannons for instance) produce in the spectator the secondary tone which objects call forth in all who feel.[12]

Yet this was one of the last paintings by Kandinsky in which natural objects indicating his point of departure are left visible to the observer.

In *The Black Arc* (pl. 169) of the preceding year, reference to the external world is actually more remote; to be sure, the red disk in the upper left is like a sun, and the blue shape may recall a torso. But the large red-magenta form that dominates the surface is like nothing in outer reality. It may *remind* the spectator of an outsized insect with a stabbing stinger or of a robot, but these are images arising from his own subterranean layers; Kandinsky is responsible for them only to the extent that he creates a threatening image sheerly by means of line, plane, position, and color.

Yet the painter has created a mood. In his violent white world, swept by lines and shapes, the warm and cool colors conflict, the withdrawing and aggressive forms meet in battle. To speak of a premonition of war is too hasty in this case, and at any rate superfluous. This is more than an omen of a specific event—it is an expression of the violence of an entire era.

Although Jawlensky was not one of the original members of Der Blaue Reiter, he was a close friend of both Kandinsky and Klee and became loosely associated with the Blaue Reiter circle. Jawlensky restricted himself at this time almost entirely to a study of heads. The hierarchic implications of the frontality of *Spanish Woman* (1912) (pl. 165) are fully developed in the austere *Sibyl* (1913) (pl. 170). Much like the primitive artist, Jawlensky proceeded by an additive process: the almond-shaped eyes, the vertical strip of the nose, the horizontal block of the mouth. All this is framed in a decorative wreath of hair. The colors are darker—varying intensities of earth tones. In this startlingly successful synthesis of emotional depth and decorative form, he suggested a devious return to those everyday images of his youth: the severe ikons of the Orthodox Church.

August Macke had been as actively engaged in the preparation of the Herbstsalon as in the Sonderbund exhibition the previous year. He even helped with the distribution of posters for the show,[13] in which he included eight of his recent paintings.

After Macke had experienced the impact of Marc and Kandinsky in 1911 and 1912—apparent in his *The Storm* (1911)—he came under the influence of cubism at the Sonderbund exhibition. For Macke, who had earlier shown such astonishing understanding of Cézanne, cubism meant an affirmation of his own interest in formal structure for the sake of expressing and communicating optical sensation. Interested in the cubists' treatment of plane and space, he found in Delaunay a combination of cubist structure with another element of painting important to him as an expressionist: color. Macke, like Delaunay, affirmed that "to find the space-creating energy of color must be our highest aim." [14] His very friendship with Delaunay at this time was extremely important for his own development; Delaunay asked Macke in June, 1912, to accept one of his recent paintings as a token of appreciation.[15]

Macke also carefully analyzed the meaning of futurist painting in terms of its dramatization of time and movement. In 1913 he wrote to Bernhard Koehler: "Recently it became especially clear to me that in painting space does not stand by itself, but that space and time are inseparable." [16]

At the time of the Autumn Salon, Macke's style was by no means unified. *Bathing Girls* (1913) (pl. 105) shows the impact of futurism and of Delaunay translated into the joyful grace characteristic of Macke's work. Macke relates the bathing girls to their wooded environment by circular and elliptical shapes. Like Delaunay, he has provided a frame within a frame: the trees, the plants, and the woman in the right foreground form a framing device through which the observer views three nude women standing among leafy trees. Looking over the shoulder of the woman in the right foreground, the observer is even further removed from the event. Light plays an extraordinary part in this painting: it creates a bright pool in the dark forest, similar to the glade in the romantic novel, and in it Macke reveals the bathing girls like a carefully kept secret. But his use of light is not only romantic; it is structurally revelatory also, in that all forms are seen in terms of the angles and planes that are struck by light.

Sunny Path (1913) (pl. 171) is not so broken up by light. Instead the light is all-pervasive, glowing through this joyously happy painting and turning it into a shimmering surface in which the complementaries green and orange are dominant. The color planes, no longer cut sharply apart, are larger; the brush stroke is richer and more heavily applied. The picture is conceived mainly in terms of crossing diagonals, with the sunlit path and rail extending to the frame. Unlike the observer's experience in viewing

Bathing Girls he is now immediately on the threshold of the scene: the lady and her little boy walk toward him from the center of the painting; the elegant couple has paused to gaze down into the blue pool. Like the bathing girls, the figures are by no means aware of being watched; turning their graceful backs to the spectator to contemplate the water, they themselves become part of the permeating light.

Gabriele Münter's *Man in the Armchair* (1913) (pl. 106), on the other hand, faces squarely out of the picture. Individual elements are combined as in her earlier landscapes, in a slow, studied series of shapes and planes to build up a unified, fairly closed composition. Even the humor has a studied effect: the square face before the seemingly interminable series of square-framed pictures on the wall; the man's pose, with half of him uncompromisingly front view and the other half turned to the side with equal determination. Over and over the rectangle repeats itself in solid light and dark shapes throughout the room. Light and dark areas are carefully juxtaposed, with the trousers balancing the light shirt across the dark chair back and the light door area. Even the solid, square shapes are carefully contrasted to the jumble of odd, mostly unidentifiable, irregularly shaped objects on the table. The man in the armchair is Paul Klee, sitting in his Munich studio.

Klee was represented with fourteen drawings and eight water colors in the Herbstsalon. Next to the heroic canvases of Marc, Kandinsky, Delaunay, and Boccioni, Klee's drawings must have looked tiny and unassuming. Indeed, modesty of scale was an essential part of his work. Much earlier Klee had set out to discover a "tiny, formal motive"; now apparently he felt he was accomplishing work "upon which he could really build":

It is a great difficulty and great necessity to have to start with the smallest. I want to be as though new-born, knowing nothing, absolutely nothing, about Europe; ignoring poets and fashions, to be almost primitive. Then I want to do something very modest; to work out by myself a tiny, formal motive, one that my pencil will be able to hold without any technique. One favorable moment is enough. The little thing is easily and concisely set down. It's already done! It was a tiny but real affair, and some day, through the repetition of such small but original deeds, there will come one work upon which I can really build.[17]

Klee's drawing *Rejection* (1913) (pl. 107a) is still in the expressive linear style of the *Candide* illustrations of 1911; his people still resemble insects with an apparently nonhuman number of arms and legs. Klee here abandons all shading and, to achieve greater subtlety, works entirely by means of freely moving line. The people, seeming to float or to be suspended in water, are a closed group, forming a circle that rejects intrusion. As in so much of Klee's work the title is needed for the most complete understanding of the work. Klee's symbols are not always readily communicable, probably because they are highly personal and, avoiding all clichés, seem thoroughly unfamiliar. Klee once said that he had to create symbols to reassure his mind.

Klee, with an introduction from Kandinsky, went to see Delaunay in

Paris in the spring of 1912, a few months before Marc and Macke visited the French painter. At the same time Klee also met Picasso, Braque, Le Fauconnier, and Apollinaire. In Paris, Klee saw further affirmation of what he first discovered among the Munich artists: the nonrepresentational use of light, space, and color. But the French artists applied greater discipline: either in the planimetric concept of the cubists or in Delaunay's color dynamism. For Klee, as for the other Munich artists, Delaunay became the major influence during his most formative period. Delaunay's concept of color in a space-time continuum [18] was to become of particular importance to Paul Klee, who conceived of the world as in the process of genesis and metamorphosis rather than of being.

Flower Path (1913) (pl. 108) [19] clearly shows Delaunay's influence on Klee in its use of prismatic color planes. Whereas Delaunay uses light and transparent colors, Klee works in deep, full, saturated color—juicy green, warm browns, and brick reds—in this delightful abstraction of the colors and forms of lush vegetation in early springtime.

At the same time the influence of the futurists is also visible in Klee's work. In 1918 *Der Sturm* published a picture book of drawings Klee had done between 1913 and 1915. These are highly imaginative pieces in which he attempts to express the simultaneity of thought and movement solely by line. *Suicide on the Bridge* (1913) (pl. 107b) shows a little man, with a big top hat, on a fragile bridge. A large clock in the linear framework of the bridge indicates the decisive hour; weird faces and cogwheels surround the clock. Klee seems to indicate the simultaneous states of the man's mind, including the premonition of the big splash to be caused by his drop into the water.

Campendonk had settled in Sindelsdorf and was working closely with Franz Marc. In 1913 he also studied cubism, as is evidenced by his *Harlequin and Columbine* (1913) (pl. 109). This painting is not only related to cubism in its reduction of natural forms to semigeometric planes, but it is also more specifically related to Picasso in its mood of nostalgia. The figures, much like the clowns and acrobats of Picasso's rose period, are isolated in a dream world in which their abortive attempts to establish contact only emphasize their solitude. The cubist stylization by Campendonk, however, ameliorates the often desolate mood evoked by Picasso. *Harlequin and Columbine,* with its harmonious color relationships, is a work of considerable charm that forecasts the ubiquitous decorative modernism in painting since the first World War.

THE END OF DER STURM

In spite of much adverse criticism by the conservative press, the Autumn Salon was such an enormous success that Walden decided to sponsor further exhibitions. He now began circulating exhibits, in the course of which he sent the most advanced paintings to small German towns that had never seen anything more startling than the paintings of their local Kunstvereins.

These exhibits also traveled far afield from Germany. In February, 1914, Der Sturm had traveling shows not only in Hamburg, Leipzig, Halle, Giessen, and Fürth, but also in London, Helsinki, Agram, and Tokyo. During the year other cities were added: Magdeburg, Marburg, Erlangen, Stuttgart, Hannover, Eisenach, Frankfurt, Trondheim, and Geneva.

Walden continued his monthly exhibits at Sturm headquarters, showing among others van Heemskerck, Werefkina, Klee, Chagall, Gleizes, Metzinger, Duchamp-Villon, Villon, Campendonk, and Marc.

The outbreak of the war meant the curtailment of publication. The magazine, which had started as a weekly and which began appearing biweekly in April, 1913, was published as a monthly after July, 1914. But Walden's activities continued without abatement: he published postcards of his artists and gave them the widest distribution; he published large color reproductions as well as original woodcuts; starting with de luxe portfolios of work by Kandinsky and Kokoschka in February, 1914, he began bringing out portfolios of his artists.

In 1916 Walden started the Sturmabende, which enjoyed great popularity among the Berlin intellectuals during and after the war. Frequent meetings were devoted to lectures on art, discussions, poetry readings, and recitals. This type of salon soon spread to other German cities and abroad, and within a few years Sturmabende were held in Budapest, Amsterdam, Oslo, Göteborg, The Hague, Copenhagen, Paris, and Vienna.

In 1916 also the magazine announced the advent of the newly founded Sturmschule, which was to provide training in stage design, acting, elocution, painting, poetry, and music. Rudolf Bauer, Rudolf Blümer, Heinrich Campendonk, Jacoba van Heemskerck, Paul Klee, Georg Muche, Gabriele Münter, Lothar Schreyer, and Herwath Walden were listed on the faculty of the Sturm school, but it remains very doubtful that Campendonk, Klee, or Münter ever taught there.

In 1917 an experimental expressionist theater, the Sturmbühne, was founded under the joint direction of Lothar Schreyer and Herwath Walden.

In the meantime, *Der Sturm* continued to publish portfolios and picture books. In 1913 Walden published Kandinsky's autobiography *Rückblicke*, and *Der Sturm* brought out Apollinaire's *Les Peintres cubistes* only a few months after its original publication by Eugenè Figuière in Paris. Soon thereafter Walden and Figuière established a reciprocal publishing arrangement. In addition, *Der Sturm* brought out poetry, plays, essays, short stories —even musical compositions by the versatile Walden.

After the war Walden edited and wrote a series of books on modern art, most important among which were: *Expressionismus—Die Kunstwende* (1918); *Die neue Malerie* (1919); *Einblick in Kunst—Expressionismus, Futurismus, Kubismus* (1924).

By the end of the war Der Sturm had become the center of the modern movement in the arts in Berlin, but in spite of its widespread activities it did not long remain in this commanding position. Walden continued to sponsor new and important younger artists—Max Ernst, Georg Muche,

Kurt Schwitters, and Laszlo Moholy-Nagy—but for the most part he concentrated his publicizing efforts on second-rate artists such as Rudolf Bauer, Nell Walden, Lothar Schreyer, William Wauer, Oswald Herzog, Maria Uhden, and Hilla von Rebay. The important artists, however, whom he had originally represented left him one by one.

As other periodicals (such as Paul Westheim's *Kunstblatt*) and other galleries (such as Cassirer, Gurlitt, Möller, and Neumann) increasingly stole the limelight, Walden's influence waned and he began devoting most of his magazine to sarcastic attacks on his colleagues and competitors. By 1924 the monthly *Der Sturm* had become a quarterly; the various other activities—the theater, the evenings, the school—had been discontinued. Finally the magazine itself grew preoccupied with problems of health and Walden's rather esoteric brand of utopian socialism. Walden left for the Soviet Union early in 1933, where he published articles on modern art and society in the Moscow periodical *Das Wort* in 1937 and 1939.[20]

XXII

The Expressionist Movement Expands

The expressionist movement reached its qualitative culmination in the years immediately before the first World War and its popular climax shortly after. Many artists who were not connected with the original groups in Dresden, Vienna, and Munich later became a part of the expressionist movement.

CHRISTIAN ROHLFS

Rohlfs (1849–1938) developed slowly and almost entirely on his own, passing through many stages and metamorphoses to arrive finally at a personal expressionist form and recognition as the "old master" of modern painting in Germany. Born in 1849, Rohlfs was at least a generation older than Kirchner and Marc (both born in 1880), considerably the senior of Nolde (born 1867) and Kandinsky (born 1866), older even than van Gogh (born 1853) or Munch (born 1863), and contemporary of Liebermann (born 1847) in Germany and Gauguin (born 1848) in France. His background, like Nolde's, was the ancient peasantry of Holstein—the northernmost area of Germany between the Baltic and the North Sea. Rohlfs himself would probably have worked on the family land if he had not been incapacitated by leg injuries at an early age. After the first manifestations of his artistic talent, he was sent off to art school by his family on the advice of the well-known writer Theodor Storm.

Rohlfs went to study in Berlin and from there to the Weimar Art School. In the early years of the nineteenth century in Goethe's time Weimar had been a focal point of European cultural activity, but in the 1870's it was almost as far removed from the mainstream of art as Rohlfs' native village in Holstein. The brief attempt by the grand duke to establish a new art center there in 1860 had proved unsuccessful; when Rohlfs arrived in 1873, even the Barbizon School had not yet made its mark.

Rohlfs won the grand duke's patronage, which meant a roof over his head and enough funds for paints and canvases but a strict adherence to the academic dictum. Yet even in Rohlfs' early work it is possible to perceive a difference from the paintings of his fellow artists—men such as Karl Buchholz and Carl Gussow. Rohlfs' paintings are more modest, and tend less toward the narrative and the genre. Using a limited palette and working closely from nature, he did studies of most careful organization. His landscapes of the 'eighties have definite structure and rhythmic composition. About 1890, however, his work became loose and free. Through his study and formulation of the effects of air and atmosphere, he came to an increasingly painterly dissolution of form and arrived at results similar to impressionism.

The effects of light and color were less important to Rohlfs than the treatment of atmosphere. This led him to the complete dissolution of form into subtle nuances of gray, as in *March Morning on the Ilm* of 1894 (pl. 110), three years before his first acquaintance with the work of Monet in Weimar.[1] His experience in seeing three paintings by Monet, however, reaffirmed his tendency toward dissolution of form, and at the same time suggested to Rohlfs the use of a brighter and lighter palette.

After twenty-five years of slow, deliberate working and self-denial of his own endowments, Rohlfs had found a free style of expression. The revolutionary impressionist form, however, did not find the approval of the academy, and he lost his post at Weimar in 1900.

The following year Henry van de Velde "discovered" Rohlfs and suggested to Karl Osthaus that Rohlfs be appointed as art consultant at the Folkwang Museum in Hagen. Osthaus, an enthusiast of French impressionism and postimpressionism and a great patron of the arts, had just started the Folkwang Museum, which was to become such a significant focal point of twentieth-century art in Germany. Here Rohlfs first became familiar with the work of the neoimpressionists. Interested in their dissection of color, he set himself similar problems, first in water color then in oil. His initial pointillist paintings, like *Landscape near Weimar* (1902) (pl. 111), are rather schematic and studied in their mosaic arrangement, strongly reminiscent of Cross.

Soon Rohlfs began to learn of other trends in modern art. Most important was the van Gogh exhibition in the Folkwang Museum in 1902. Here he saw a use of color and brush stroke, as well as a concept of painting, entirely new to him—all of which were to be of the greatest consequence for his own development.

Rohlfs was now working in *Soest* near Hagen. There, in the winter of 1905–1906, he met Emil Nolde, whose attitude gave a moral support to the older painter's quest for an honest personal style. Nolde indicated to Rohlfs the direction in which the younger generation was turning, and found in Rohlfs and Osthaus two of the first supporters of his work.[2]

In 1910 Rohlfs decided to leave Hagen and the Folkwang Museum: there was too great a difference between the cultured, sophisticated Karl Osthaus, primarily concerned with the exploration of his esthetic ideas, and the earthy Rohlfs, who seemed to care for little beyond the development of his own sensations. Rohlfs was attracted to Munich, which enjoyed the reputation of a great art center, but on arrival he found himself at odds with this official art world where Franz von Stuck stood for the most radical trends. (Kandinsky and Marc and their circle were still working in comparative obscurity and did not come to the attention of the visiting artist.) Rohlfs went on to the Tyrol and the Bavarian forests, where he did some magnificent landscapes in strong colors and free lines. *Beeches in Autumn* (1910) (pl. 112) is a powerful painting that demonstrates the strong impact of van Gogh: the verticality of the central trunk, supported by the other two trees, forms a clear structure against the swirling wave movement of brilliant colors of the foliage.

By 1912 Rohlfs was back in Hagen in his former capacity in residence at the Folkwang Museum; when the museum moved to Essen after Osthaus' death, Rohlfs went with it. Now in his sixties he began to experience the real unfolding of his creative talents. A truly rare phenomenon in the history of modern art, Rohlfs did his most significant paintings in his old age. In his work and life at this time—he was seventy years old when he married in 1919—he manifested the vigor of a young man. Crossing the threshold to a form of expression in which the emotional or mental concept was more important than visual perception, he stepped into the forefront of the young artists in Germany and became a leader of the new movement.

After about 1910 Rohlfs had abandoned the viscosity of the oil pigment to work in tempera, water color, complex graphic techniques, and embroidery. His *Dancers* (1913) (pl. 113) is a first indication of the extraordinary transparencies he achieved in his late work. He had freed himself entirely from impressionism as earlier he had freed himself from the academy; he felt that there was more to painting than a representation of optical light reflections. This kind of naturalism was an error in interpretation, he believed, since the sensations of light and color had their origin within man —thus the task of the painter was really the projection onto the canvas of inner sensations. The colors of these dancers against a cool, white background have an eerie, transparent glow that sets the basic mood of the painting.

The outbreak of the war inspired his tempera *War* (1914) (pl. 114), in which war is symbolized by a brutish man grasping a club and yelling into empty space. He is about to trample upon a collapsing woman. The color has glowing transparencies emphasized by the bloody red spots prevailing throughout the painting.

During the war, there was a long pause in his work.

The events of the time are so uncommon, that they crush everything and only peace can bring back quiet and a gathering of strength. . . . It seems impossible to me to consider now the small trivia of one's own life, while the peoples and lands of Europe are being shattered.[3]

When he turned again to painting after the war, he returned to the theme of Soest and its towers. Color has now become the predominant element, subservient neither to idea nor to composition, but creating its own form and concepts. In his postwar paintings of Soest, like the *St. Patroklus* (1918) (pl. 115), a pulsating color is the constructive element. The color creates the volumes and the movement in space, which oscillates in and out of the picture plane. Gravity is gone, and only directional energy is expressed. The steeple of the early Gothic church bursts through the surrounding roofs to pierce clouds and sky. These Soest paintings, with their uprising, flamelike lines and emotional, glowing colors, are perhaps the essence of the expressionist concept of the Gothic.

A comparison between this series of Rohlfs' Soest paintings and Delaunay's series of St. Séverin (1909–1910) (pl. 90) illustrates the similarities as well as differences between German expressionism and the closest the French have come to it. Delaunay's paintings, which had such an influence on the Munich group of Der Blaue Reiter, are also presentations of the Gothic church as it effects us emotionally rather than as it looks objectively. Delaunay and Rohlfs are both primarily colorists, but Delaunay develops a new concept of perspective according to cubist analysis of form. He is much more concerned with the structural element, both in the Gothic arch and in his own painting, than Rohlfs, who releases his whole emphasis for a somewhat less well articulated emotional statement.

When Rohlfs turned again to painting the year the war ended, it was with a series of fine canvases, among them a beautiful and curious *Self-Portrait* (pl. 172), in which he seems more concerned with rendering the insubstantiality of his aging frame than in manifesting its presence. The body is but a continuation of the delicately luminous background, separated from it by merely a dark outline, so that the surrounding atmosphere penetrates the body, making it virtually nonexistent, or rather merging the physical form with its environment. Indeed, he has stressed, rather than mass, the energy of light. In contrast, the massive head looks as if it were carved in wood; as the only solid object in the portrait, it seems to emphasize the transcendence of the mind over the body. It is one of Yeats' "Monuments of unaging intellect."

LYONEL FEININGER

The precision of Feininger's (1871–1956) painting and the clarity of his structure are only distantly related to the seething forms of the expressionists. "To find a close parallel to Feininger among authentically German painters one must go back a hundred years to Caspar David Friedrich, the great romantic painter of Gothic ruins and Baltic horizons. Of modern German artists only Franz Marc bears some resemblance." [4]

In 1912 Feininger was asked by Schmidt-Rottluff [5] to join the Brücke, and in 1913 he followed Marc's invitation to exhibit with the Blaue Reiter at Walden's First German Autumn Salon. Like the artists of the Blaue Reiter, Feininger had learned a great deal from Delaunay and the cubists, and like them he created his own personal formulations. In a letter written in 1917 Feininger considered himself an expressionist, and defined expressionism as the most individual expression of which the artist is capable, as the formulation of his inner visions and his personal statement of the great and painful nostalgia for order.[6]

Feininger's love for formal order has always been the principal motivation for his work—not only in painting but also in music:

Music has always been the first influence in my life, Bach before all others. . . . Without music I cannot see myself as a painter—although [he writes elsewhere] I could never attempt to express the one in the other as many have done. Polyphony, paired with delight in mechanical construction, went far to shape my creative bias.[7]

Feininger shared his strong interest in music with Kandinsky (who based his theory of painting to a great extent on musical theory) and with Klee (who was an excellent pianist and loved Mozart as Feininger did Bach). Klee and Feininger frequently performed music together, as a matter of fact, when they both taught at the Bauhaus after the war.

Feininger was born in New York in 1871, of parents who were both professional musicians. He began playing the violin in concerts at the age of twelve. Among early impressions that became important in his life and work were locomotives and trains, the construction of the elevated lines, ships on the Hudson River.[8]

His interest in the visual arts was not considerable. However, when he was taken to the Metropolitan Museum, he was impressed primarily by the bright and beautiful color and the representation of architecture in Gothic painting.[9] An aunt spoke to him about Hogarth's "line of beauty"; this baffled him, because he felt that the straight line and right angle were more beautiful.[10]

In 1887 Feininger sailed to Germany to study music in Hamburg. Instead of enrolling in the conservatory, he attended the Kunstgewerbeschule to study painting and continued at Calarossi in Paris from 1892 to 1893. In 1893 he settled in Berlin, where except for visits to Paris in 1906–1907 and in 1911 he remained until 1919, when he became the first painter to be asked by Walter Gropius to join the Bauhaus.

Until 1907 Feininger worked primarily as a cartoonist, contributing his drawings to the German humor magazines *Ulk* and *Lustige Blätter,* as well as the Parisian *Le Témoin.* In 1906–1907 he did comic strips for the *Chicago Tribune* ("The Kin-der-Kids," "Wee Willie Winkie's World").[11]

Feininger turned to easel painting and, attempting to work like Monet and Liebermann, went out-of-doors to paint in the style of the time. During his second stay in Paris in 1906–1907, he became friendly with Oskar Moll, a pupil of Matisse and a man who worked in a manner considerably different from that of the impressionists. Slowly Feininger turned to working in his own "primitive" way, as he had done cartoons and caricatures and had made figures like those in shooting galleries.[12] His cartoons give an indication of this later work. Using inverted perspective, he drew huge, angular people who rise far above the buildings (for *Le Témoin*) or animated trees, trains, ships, and clouds with childlike whimsy (for "Wee Willie Winkie's World").

In Feininger's early paintings and drawings, odd, stovepipe-shaped figures rush along narrow streets or stalk under viaducts. Space is severely crowded; everything—people, houses, streets—is narrow and steep. The artist is still a humorist, painting or drawing grotesques, but he now infuses his tall figures with a new kind of satire. In their eighteenth-century costumes these figures seem ill at ease in a world they never made. Like *Gulliver's Travels,* these pictures combine various levels of meaning—the appearance of a child's imagination with sophisticated social allusions.

But problems of form became increasingly important to Feininger. As early as 1907 he wrote:

I visualize quite different values of light form—different possibilities of translation than heretofore—but it seems nearly impossible to free oneself from the accepted reality of nature. That which is seen optically has to go through the process of *transformation* and *crystallization* to become a picture.[13]

The question of space became fundamental, and the void spaces as important as the solid forms. "He made the space-creating forces beyond the individual forms the basis of his composition."[14] Realizing that "there is no foreground and background but a continuity of interlacing relationships,"[15] he abandoned the conventional system of perspective. Because of this concern with the phenomena of space, he arrived at a space structure in his painting similar to that of the cubists, although evidently still independent of Paris.[16]

In 1911 he returned to Paris, where five of his paintings were exhibited at the Salon des Indépendents and where he became familiar with Robert Delaunay and his work. Returning to Zehlendorf near Berlin, Feininger attempted to simplify his forms in a more direct manner. Only then did he establish real contact with his German contemporaries—especially Schmidt-Rottluff, who invited him to join the Brücke in 1912. At that time he also met Heckel, Mueller, Pechstein, and Kubin. The latter grew to be a close friend, and caused Franz Marc to invite Feininger to exhibit with the Blaue Reiter at Walden's Autumn Salon. In 1909, 1910, and 1911 Feininger had shown at the exhibitions of the Berlin Secession.

Church, one of four Feininger paintings exhibited at the Herbstsalon, consists of precise diagonals creating planes of color and light. The actual planes of the church, the other buildings, and the sky are shattered into cubist transparencies and opacities that seem to rise rapidly toward a culminating point at the steeple of the church. The dynamic quality recalls Delaunay, but Feininger's color has not yet achieved the formal meaning of Delaunay's nor his own later crystalline clarity.

Harbor (1915) (pl. 117) is more clearly reasoned in terms of planar structure. The forms are broken apart by light, and the painting seems less charged emotionally. Whereas the breakup of forms in *Church* was still external to the picture world, in *Harbor* it seems to be a part of an intrinsic, coherent whole. Again a variation from light to dark values, as well as colors, occurs within a single plane, which is modulated from transparency to opacity and causes the eye to constantly shift and partake of the dynamic movement of ascension and descent within a homogeneous surface.

Feininger's development can be seen even more clearly by comparing *Church* (1913) with the same subject, *Zirchow VI* (1916) (pl. 116). Now the whole organization is resolved. The lower part, with the repeat wedge forms recalling the futurist usage to symbolize rapid movement, is contrasted to the light, thrusting tower, which Schardt has called "a symbol of man's striving toward security and freedom." [17]

Paintings like *Harbor* or *Zirchow* no longer show any clear distinction between voids and solids; instead, they interpenetrate to create a crystalline order, in which chlorine greens and steel blues predominate. He has transformed the tangible world into a world of light: "I don't believe Feininger thinks or builds in terms of architecture. Those straight lines are rays. They are not architectural, they are optical." [18] Yet Feininger's fragile planes of light do form transparent structure not unlike modern architecture's use of glass. With constancy of purpose he gave linear forms to his perception of ships at sea, dreamlike shorelines, medieval churches, and the narrow streets and towers of Manhattan. His emphasis on purity of structure was an important foil to the German expressionists' denunciation of form for the sake of self-disclosure, especially during the war and postwar era. After his return to America, in the 1930's, he was able to fulfill a peculiarly similar role in relation to the "abstract Expressionists," especially in the era after the second World War.

LUDWIG MEIDNER

The buildings in Meidner's cities also burst apart. In place of Feininger's careful rearrangement of their structure in terms of light planes or Rohlfs' abrogation of gravity by means of color and energy, Meidner's more literary imagination turned to actual or envisaged catastrophes: earthquakes, pestilence, war.

Ludwig Meidner was born in 1884 in a small Silesian town in a section "which has never brought forth a painter or poet." [19] After an early decision to become a painter and a certain amount of encouragement from Franz von Stuck, to whom he had sent some romantic drawings of ghosts and forests, he entered the Breslau Academy in 1903.

In 1905 he arrived in Berlin, where he earned a poor living doing fashion illustrations. He then traveled to Paris, "our true home, the tender and soft beloved, the center of the intellectual world and beauty on earth." [20] There he admired Cézanne and van Gogh, as he had formerly esteemed Marées. Manet was his favorite artist, "the most magnificent master of the last century." [21] He also befriended Modigliani.

Meidner returned to Berlin in 1907, where he painted day and night, sometimes with almost hysterical energy, creating distorted portraits and ecstatic, cramped, passionate pictures of vast catastrophes. In 1912 he was instrumental in the foundation of Die Pathetiker with Jacob Steinhardt and Richard Janthur; the group exhibited at Der Sturm for the first time in the autumn of that year.

George Grosz, who arrived in Berlin in 1912, wrote of Meidner at the time:

Meidner was co-founder of a Berlin group called "Die Pathetiker." His style was Expressionist and he painted with great vigor. His paintings were dedicated for the most part to poets. He would work all night long by candle light, because the gas light was too uncertain and burned too faintly. He would draw Old Testament prophets with a scroll-pen on large sheets of paper. He also delighted in painting his friends. One night he painted me too. He worked passionately, his breast heaving as if he were going through some great emotional crisis. Suddenly the easel collapsed, throwing the board, paper and all onto the slag pile. The dust rose in billows and I was seized with a violent fit of sneezing. Not so Meidner. He pounced on the fallen board and continued to draw on the floor, completely unmindful of the catastrophe.[22]

In 1912 Meidner began a series of paintings of cataclysms, exemplified by his *Burning City* (1913) (pl. 118). The earth bursts apart in heaving planes, the buildings topple, and small, squirming, frightened figures scramble about. The explosive chaos of the scene is enhanced by the color—dark brown and dark blues, highlighted by bright reds and greens—as well as by the distorted perspective and the spaces moving in a variety of directions. There is a suggestion of futurist influences in the repetition of the parallel ranks of forms in the center and the upper left, but especially in the dynamic violence of the painting. The distorted, compressed forms forecast similar uses of space in the postwar period, as in the film *The Cabinet of Dr. Caligari*—strongly influenced by the paintings of Meidner, Feininger, and Kubin. It crops up again also in the apocalyptic visions of Chaim Soutine, who also works with similar impasto textures.

Meidner repeated the scene of *Burning City* in a number of similar paintings, including the back of that canvas in the Morton May Collection in St. Louis. In the same period he completed *In Expectation of Judgment* (1912), *Cholera* (1913), *Apocalyptic Landscape* (1912–1913), *I and the City* (1913), as well as the lithograph *Street Impressions* (1915). These are intoxicated visions of despair, and can be interpreted as premonitions of the great war with its shellings and bombardments of cities. Meidner seems to have suffered from a disturbing combination of delight and misgivings when he painted these apocalyptic landscapes: "I am dragged through such nights! Colors flutter around my soul. The soul smiles on the point of the brush and sings of my pastose forests with the chorus of the clouds. The heat surges about me, hot songs wish to emerge from me—a horrible force ruminates in my breast." [23]

Meidner appears as a very disturbed individual in his *Self-Portrait* of

1916 (pl. 119). In its undulating baroque forms, dramatic use of light and shade, and psychological distortion, this portrait is reminiscent of Kokoschka portraits of 1908 and of Soutine portraits of the 1920's. Pigment is applied heavily, and the color is dark throughout the Meidner portrait; an excitedly twisting line creates a pinched and squeezed masklike physiognomy. For Meidner the human face was "a reflection of heavenly glory and more frequently a battlefield of bloody rage." [24] In his highly expressionist use of language Meidner admonished the artist to "crowd together the wrinkled brow, root of the nose and the eyes, to dig like a mole into the inexplicable ground of the pupil and the white of the eye and never to rest until the soul of the sitter has been wedded to the artist in a covenant of pathos." [25]

Meidner continued working in this way—giving vent to ecstatic visions verbally (for example, in his *Septemberschrei* of 1919) as well as in painting; because he lacked formal discipline and a versatile imagination, his work in the postwar decades was overtaken by mannerisms.

WILHELM MORGNER

Wilhelm Morgner (1891–1917) was able to work only a few years before he died, but in that brief time he achieved a remarkably disciplined clarity and order in his work and was one of the first nonobjective painters in Germany. He was born in Soest, and his only early contact with painting was his boyhood experience of watching old Rohlfs paint a landscape. In 1908 he went to Worpswede to study with Georg Tappert, a latecomer to the artists' colony. Morgner undoubtedly received inspiration from the Worpswede painters, but the moody sentimentalism of the regionalist group could not satisfy his own unsentimental purposes. Returning to Soest, he did his first important drawings and paintings in 1910, three years before he was forced by conscription to stop working. His work from 1910, undoubtedly influenced by Hodler, shows an acute power of observation and a most remarkable talent. He worked from nature on portraits, combining a detailed realism with unusual sensitivity.

In 1911 the young painter visited Berlin, where the many evidences of new trends in painting liberated him from academic conventions and infused him with the courage to find his own mode of expression after his return to Soest. Although he never affiliated himself with any of the advanced groups of painters in Berlin, he exhibited with them in the fourth exhibition of the New Secession in the spring of 1912 and was represented in the Sonderbund in the summer of that year.

It seems contradictory to speak of early and late work by Wilhelm Morgner, whose really creative span lasted only three years, but a considerable development is noticeable during that period. Typical of his work in 1911 is *Woman with Brown Wheelbarrow* (pl. 120) in the horizontal division of the canvas into two parts, with the protagonist cutting from the lower into the upper part. The painting is arranged in parallel planes and rhythmic lines created by the definite brush strokes. The brush stroke is influenced by neoimpressionism, but recalls even more paintings by van Gogh during his Paris period. The motif is also related to the early van Gogh and to Millet, but Morgner lacks van Gogh's expressive power and Millet's sentiment and is much more concerned with formal decoration. All his brush strokes are arranged so that they create a series of circles concentric to the central point of importance, which, interestingly enough, is not the woman but the burden she is carrying; her figure is emphasized as the sole vertical axis.

A concern with planar structure and rhythmic line, problems that actually derived from Jugendstil, was uppermost in Morgner's mind. He was also strongly interested in the applied arts, and many of his paintings were made as designs for embroideries executed by his sister. From this point of departure Morgner arrived at nonobjective painting early in 1912—that is, almost at the same time that Kandinsky did.

The tempera painting *Ornamental Composition* (1912) (pl. 121a) can be understood as a direct development from *Woman with Brown Wheelbarrow* in its interest in the rhythmically decorative possibilities of concentric circles and planar arrangement of radiating disks. The disparate organization of the painting actually adds to its vitality, and it is immediately reminiscent of Delaunay's "simultaneous compositions," like *Les Disques Soleils* or *Hommage à Bleriot*. However, *Les Disques Soleils* dates from 1913, and *Hommage à Bleriot* was painted in the following year— two years after Morgner's *Ornamental Composition*. This is not to suggest that Delaunay might have been in any way familiar with the rather obscure work by Morgner in Soest in Westphalia, but rather that the common basis of neoimpressionism and symbolism—Jugendstil and its concomitant liberation of formal means—could lead to similar results in Soest and in Paris. The qualitative difference—the fact that Delaunay's brilliant color gives a dynamic quality to his work that is lacking in the rather flat composition by Morgner—must also be taken into consideration, but seems of secondary importance in this context.

Morgner continued working in the nonobjective vein. His tempera *Adoration* (1912) (pl. 121b) has only the faintest relationship to representational forms. The circular organization noted in his earlier paintings is still present, but forms have become much more fluid and less choppy. His space is still two-dimensional, but there is now a greater suggestion of depth. This painting is closely related to Kandinsky's work of the time in its dramatic relationship of color and line—even in the comblike forms reoccurring in this painting.

It is difficult to ascertain whether Morgner reached this stage independently or whether he was familiar with Kandinsky's work, which had just begun to be seen in Germany. Harald Seiler, in a recent evaluation of Morgner, said: "Morgner arrived simultaneously and completely independently at total abstraction." [26] Although this assumption is possibly correct, it is even more likely that Morgner first saw Kandinsky's *Im-*

provisation No. 21a at the Sonderbund exhibition in the summer of 1912, or a similar work by Kandinsky, before painting *Adoration*. This was the first of a series of religious paintings by Morgner—most of which were considerably less abstract—and was followed by *Assumption, Ecce Homo, Crucifixion,* and *Deposition*.

The turn toward the religious is as little surprising with Morgner as the turn to Non-Objective art, if one stops to realize that both Expressionism with its revival of the religious motif in art and the Non-Objective art of line and plane have their common root in Jugendstil.[27]

Morgner painted representational, frequently religious works interchangeably with nonrepresentational works, until he was suddenly drafted into the army in 1913. While serving in the army he was able to accomplish only occasional water colors and pen drawings of the Polish, Serbian, and French countrysides and their people—very simple statements of superb craftsmanship.

In 1917 Morgner, having left only a fragment of a very promising career, was reported missing in action on the western front.

MAX BECKMANN

Beckmann's opposition to the painting of his less conservative contemporaries and his controversy with Franz Marc have been discussed in an earlier chapter.[28] It was also pointed out that Beckmann was to undergo a major transformation of style in the years immediately preceding the war, and that this was propelled further by his war experience.

Beckmann has never wished to be classified with the expressionists [29] or to be considered as a part of any group or movement. He worked alone and without association after leaving the Berlin Secession in 1911; although he was a supporter of the socialist trends in the Weimar Republic, he felt that "the greatest danger which threatens mankind is collectivism." [30]

Yet Beckmann—in his later work, in which he created his own highly subjective world of human symbolism—must be considered with the expressionist movement. Westheim, one of the leading critics of expressionism, wrote in 1923:

It has once been said about Beckmann that his work is true Expressionism. I can explain little with the word "Expressionism"; it is too equivocal, it is interpreted too dissimilarly. But it seems to me [he continued facetiously although with a grain of truth], as if here the designation would be truly suitable; if there had been no Beckmann, Expressionism would have had to invent him.[31]

Beckmann's *Self-Portrait* of 1912 (pl. 122), the same year as his large canvas *The Sinking of the Titanic* (pl. 95b), is painted in the pastose style of the Berlin Secessionists. His modeling from light to dark, the relationship of bust to background, the impressionist—or rather Hals-like—brush stroke, are all in the early style that had brought him such acclaim in Germany. In retrospect, however, compared with the large series of searching self-portraits that so often set the stage for his other paintings, this early work betrays Beckmann's continuing concept of himself as brutal and romantic at the same time. He saw himself as a stocky, squarish, powerful man, and communicated this impression by the square shape of the head, the thin, determined mouth, the humorless expression. The soft brush stroke in this early painting is not consonant with its interpretation of character.

Beckmann's prints, even more than his self-portraits, frequently anticipate his changes in style. *The Division of the Cloak* (pl. 123), a lithograph executed in 1911 from a series on the New Testament, also indicates his interest in the use of light and dark for the sake of shading and modeling. Light is used dramatically and effectively. His space still adheres largely to a system of linear perspective, but the figures of Christ on the left and the standing soldier on the right loom up largely and seem to push the figures of the gamblers downward and outward, severely limiting the narrow stage. Further, Beckmann uses, tentatively still, a strange and arbitrary engagement in space to show various figures—the gamblers as against the standing soldier—from different vantage points. The bestial quality of his characters, even the choice of subject, strikes that note of deep pessimism that is a persistent trait in Beckmann's work.

Ulrikusstrasse, a lithograph of 1912, probably indicates his first real concern with the objective reality of the city. He here confronts the spectator with a naked prostitute in Hamburg's red light district. In its quickly rendered network of lines as well as in its subject matter, this lithograph suggests similar renditions by Rouault; Beckmann, however, did not yet possess Rouault's strong power of image formation.

In 1913 Beckmann painted *The Street* (pl. 124), a teeming city crowd with a self-conscious self-portrait in the center. In this painting, as Perry Rathbone suggested, "the casual composition with its prismatic color is not without the ingratiating pictorialism dear to the French Impressionists." [32]

Beckmann's *Street* was painted in the same year as Kirchner's *The Street* (pl. 50); a comparison of the two paintings shows that, in contrast to the older Kirchner, Beckmann had made only tentative attempts toward the development of his own idiom.

When war broke out Beckmann enlisted as a medical corpsman, and was sent almost immediately close to the firing line in Belgium. He was forced to stop painting, but found release by drawing, lithography, and etching. He wrote from the front: "My will to live is at present stronger than ever, although I have already experienced great horror and have seemed to die myself with the others several times. But the oftener one dies the more intensively one lives; I have drawn—that is what keeps one from death and from danger." [33]

In Belgium Beckmann met Heckel, who was also in the medical corps, and began to simplify his figure compositions and to strive toward a more disciplined, more tangible form.

A great deal has been written about the effect of the war on Beckmann's development as an artist, but nothing could show this more clearly than a comparison between the first and third (final) states of the dry point *Der Krankenträger (Carrying the Wounded)* (1914) (pls. 125, 126). In the first state the head of the wounded man is reminiscent of a conventional head of Christ, and his bandage and hair recall a crown of thorns. At first glance the dry point could be taken for a representation of the Good Samaritan. This is not true of the final state. Here all vestiges of romanticized conception and mannered execution are abandoned in favor of a more objective and simpler treatment. In the face of the carnage of war the former sentimentality apparently became useless to the artist. He phrased his new artistic purpose in another letter from the field hospital: "I hope to become gradually simpler, more concentrated in effect. But I know that I shall never abandon the full, the round, the quality of pulsating life . . . no arabesque, no calligraphy, but full plastic form." [34] Meier-Graefe commented on the restraint and contraction in Beckmann's art at this time: "His discipline was a wild castigation of his former Impressionism and suppressed unmercifully the vestiges of Corinth and Munch. It was not a fusion of two trends in art, but a decision between action and contemplation, between life and art." [35]

Beckmann was a casualty of the war in 1915, and was taken to Frankfurt for hospitalization and recuperation. In Frankfurt, where he was to remain for two decades, he began carefully studying the art of the late Middle Ages. He mentioned his love for Grünewald, whose Isenheim Altarpiece he had seen as early as 1903, and he also considered Bosch among the greatest masters.[36] Beckmann's biographer Wilhelm Hausenstein also suggested a relationship to Jörg Ratgeb, Veit Stoss, and Hans Holbein the Elder.[37]

After a period of slow recovery and small productivity as a painter, in 1917 Beckmann finished his significant canvas *Christ and the Woman Taken in Adultery* (pl. 127), which embodies many of the pronounced changes in his style. The former melodrama is completely abandoned, as is conventional perspective. His space is exceedingly shallow, and he presents his figures as actors on a stage. This psychological distance is increased by presenting the top half of the painting from below and the bottom half from above. This is a device found in fifteenth-century German painting, such as Multscher's Wurzach Altarpiece, but it bears the closest resemblance to Hans Hirtz's panels of the Passion of Christ in the Karlsruhe Museum. Although this treatment of space prohibits the observer's entrance into the picture, the presence of the figures becomes all the more compelling. The tactile figures themselves create their space, which recedes and advances with them in a zigzag movement and relates them intimately to the picture plane. The figures are crowded together, yet no human contact seems possible between them. In contrast to the brutish face of the men and passive countenance of the kneeling woman, Christ's face expresses dominating intellectual capacity with its high forehead and look of thoughtful detachment. There is also a telling contrast of hands between the three main figures. The adultress kneeling at His feet, a woman combining traits of a little girl with those of full adulthood, seems concerned only with herself and the imminent peril and prays to Christ's sheltering presence. The sneering soldier on the right points to the scene but looks in the opposite direction. His eyes are closed, like those of the adultress. Other figures are almost completely in hiding or turn their backs; the observer is allowed to look into the eyes of only one character: the man with the troubled, gaping-mouthed face behind the fence.

This painting, besides being significant for its formal arrangement, is noteworthy in that it, together with the *Battenberg Family* of 1915, introduces Beckmann's world, with its persistent anxiety about the lack of meaningful human relationships and its questions as to the reasons for existence:

For the Ego is the great veiled mystery of the world. Hume and Herbert Spencer studied its various conceptions but were not able in the end to discover the truth. I believe in it and in its eternal immutable form. Its path is, in some strange and peculiar manner, our path. And for this reason I am immersed in the phenomenon of the Individual, the so-called whole Individual, and I try in every way to explain and present it. What are you? What am I? Those are the questions that constantly persecute and torment me and perhaps also play some part in my art.[38]

Beckmann seems to have felt that he had to know himself in order to penetrate ever more deeply into man's inner life. He painted more self-portraits than any other twentieth-century artist. His *Self-Portrait* of 1919 (pl. 128) shows the radical change that has taken place in his work since the *Self-Portrait* of 1912 (pl. 122). The former hesitancy has given way to a definite and resolute style. The hard line of the dry point fits Beckmann's strong square face better than did the softer tones. In place of the impressionist portrait, there is now a boldly expressionist statement —personal, severe, and aggressive in every line and almost frightening in its bold simplicity of black and white. This is the artist as a forthright human being, the man who has experienced the war and who continues to live and work in spite of the butchery he has experienced. His eyes have become large, his expression has become set, and he presents his face with a realism or verism that is almost unique in the art of the twentieth century —although, to be sure, this is the harsh and disillusioned countenance of the postwar world.

Christ and the Woman Taken in Adultery and the cruel painting of murder, *The Night* (1918–1919)—paintings with crowded "mannerist" space and involved symbolism—forecast another major aspect of his work in the ensuing thirty years. His large figure compositions and his nine great triptychs are enigmatic; Beckmann, like William Butler Yeats, created his own myths—personal, complex, and ambiguous. As Beckmann grew more fully convinced of the existential tragedy of human life and the rigid determinism behind human behavior, his space, his symbols, and the total imagery of his world increased persistently in their complexity and fullness of statement.

XXIII

Journeys to Exotic Countries

Gauguin, who wrote to his daughter, "You will always find nourishing milk in the primitive arts, but I doubt if you will find it in the arts of ripe civilizations," [1] and who left Paris for Brittany and then for Tahiti and finally the Marquesas, became the model for German painters who also disdained the over-refinement of European civilization and looked for rejuvenation among primitive cultures.

Children's art, too, was recognized as clearly distinct from adult standards. After Ricci's *L'Arte dei Bambini* [2] was translated into German in 1906 the specific expression of the child began to be recognized as such, especially by the art teacher Franz Cizek, who was a member of the Vienna Secession and a friend of Klimt, Schiele, and Kokoschka. In *Der Blaue Reiter* children's art was for the first time included on the same level with other artistic expressions, including a great variety of aboriginal art. In 1915 Carl Einstein published an important book on African sculpture, [3] and several years later this interest in direct, untutored expression spread to the art of the insane. [4]

The search by many painters from Gauguin to the surrealists for roots in the art of primitive tribes, peasant and folk cultures, as well as of children, has been investigated by Robert Goldwater. [5] Goldwater stressed the important difference between true aboriginal art and sophisticated European art that sought a new inspiration in it; he called the former "primitive," and the latter "primitivistic."

Primitive art, in the judgment of the German expressionist generation, was an unspoiled expression of inner emotion. According to the English anthropologist G. A. Stevens,

Primitive art is the most pure, most sincere form of art there can be, partly because it is deeply inspired by religious ideas and spiritual experience, and partly because it is entirely unselfconscious as art; there are no tricks which can be acquired by the unworthy, and no technical exercises which can masquerade as works of inspiration. [6]

EMIL NOLDE

When Gauguin spoke about "primitive art," he was referring to the art of the Persians, Egyptians, and Cambodians. He was also familiar with Aztec sculpture and with Polynesian art. Kirchner [7] found later "in the ethnographic museum . . . a parallel to his own creation in African negro sculpture and Oceanic beam carving." [8] This was in Dresden in 1904, the year the Brücke was founded. Tribal art was definitely one of the major sources for the art of the Brücke, and even now fine examples of Cameroon sculpture, collected in the Dresden years, are to be found in Schmidt-Rottluff's apartment in Berlin-Dahlem. The influence of African and Oceanic sculpture on the Brücke painters was generalized rather than specific, and their works are never ethnological documents. Only occasionally, as in the woodcut *Summer* (fig. 32), which Kirchner did for *Der Sturm,* is it possible to recognize the definite provenance—here, Melanesia—of an object.

Nolde's acquaintance with the Brücke artists first familiarized him with primitive art. For a long time he had felt drawn toward the elemental quality of primitive and non-European art. In the first volume of his autobiography he spoke of his admiration for the art of the Egyptians and Assyrians, which struck him with "mystic power" when he first saw it around 1900. Still, he felt that it was outside the pale; then

. . . the following decade brought understanding and liberation; I encountered Indian, Chinese, Persian art, the primitive, strange products of the Mexicans, and those of the aborigines. These were no longer curiosities as they were called by the professionals; no, we raised them to what they are: the strange, rugged, aboriginal and popular art of the savages. [9]

Taking issue with ethnologists and museum officials, he said: "The science of ethnography, however, considers us still as troublesome intruders, because we love sense perception more than sole knowledge." [10] In 1913 he welcomed an opportunity to take part in an anthropological expedition to the South Seas.

Before leaving Europe, however, Nolde painted pictures of war and the destruction of war through what he later called prophetic vision: "Immediately, in the midst of deepest peace, as if being forced, my war pictures originated. 'War' riding cruelly over land and over people, and the 'cavalry picture,' in which the Frenchman cuts down the German." [11] Thus, like Kandinsky, Marc, and Meidner, Nolde was affected by the anxieties that prevailed in 1913. The painting *War,* in its vigorous brush stroke, and its dynamic, wild forms, even in its colors, recalls Delacroix's animal hunts. The soldiers are mounted on galloping horses, and swing their sabers as they trample on masklike faces that strew the ground. These faces, with their tendency toward caricature, are related not only to Nolde's masks of the same period (pl. 38) but also to the very personifications of mountains. Nolde's concept of war, as expressed in this painting, is that of a savage carnival of horrors.

Late in the spring Nolde left Germany with the Külz-Leber anthropological expedition for the German possessions in the Pacific islands. The group traveled through European Russia, Siberia, China, Japan, and the Philippines to the Bismarck Archipelago. He wrote about his hatred for imperialism and its evil influence. He found China and the Philippines spoiled by European and American missionaries, imperialists, and officials—men who lacked understanding of the value of native cultures. "We live in an evil era, in which the white race brings the inhabitants of the whole earth into servitude." [12]

Nolde was profoundly stirred by the life of the natives in the South Seas. "The natives are a magnificent people insofar as they have not already been spoiled by contact with the civilization of the white man." [13] He discussed his esteem for primitive art:

Why is it that we artists are so entranced by the primitive expression of the savages? . . . With the material in his hand, between his fingers, the savage creates his work. The expressed purpose is desire for and love of creation. The absolute originality, the intense, frequently grotesque expression of strength and life in the simplest possible form—that could be the factor which gives us so much joy. [14]

Nolde spent about six months in the islands, absorbing the primitive culture which, he felt, was similar to the original state of life in his own north Germany; he hoped to recapture something parallel to his "racial memory." He had gone to the South Seas, not because he was disgusted with civilization or spurred by a Rousseau-like romanticism, as Gauguin had done before him. These feelings may have been in part responsible for his trip, but he felt primarily a strong affinity with the art of the savages and wanted to search their primordial forms for the very sources of art. [15]

Nolde found in the South Seas a genuineness in life and art that he believed had been lost in Europe. His letters said that he had never been able to work so well or so much at the prodding of inspiration. [16] Although he actually painted little during his stay in the islands, he made innumerable pencil and water-color sketches, as he had done on his trip through the Asian continent.

Surprised by the declaration of war, the expedition had to return to Germany by way of Java and Burma. At Suez the British seized their baggage, including Nolde's sketches, which were not recovered until 1921, [17] when his series of South Sea and Siberian paintings had long been completed from memory.

South Sea Dancers (1915) (pl. 129) attempts to recapture the rhythm of the native dance. The solid, circular forms of the squatting women on the left foreground are juxtaposed to the angular dancer on the right. Burning, saturated colors are still predominant, but compared with Nolde's prewar work this painting is quiet, restrained, and balanced.

Two Russians (1915) (pl. 173)—a broadly painted canvas in blue-greens, tans, and browns—is carefully worked out in the relationship of the heads to the frame. Their size seems even greater by virtue of being crammed into the narrow, rectangular space; and one effect of the picture is that of a close-up snapshot. The strong contrast between the faces suggests a sharp delineation of character. The squashed and flattened physiognomy on the left may suit our stereotype of the more shrewd and watchful, but the narrow eyes and ragged beards and the cautious mutual inclination of the heads unites the pair inseparably. Nolde painted a series of Russian peasants at this time, pictures that seem to stem from his own blood-and-soil mystique, the rejuvenating force that comes from man's close relationship with the land.

Precisely this desire for a return to the soil and Nolde's nostalgia for primitive culture and its magic rites were the motivating forces for his great religious cycle, his primitivistic masks, his journey to the South Seas, and his final isolation on the North Sea island of Alsen and in Seebüll in northern Schleswig, where he painted solemn, impassioned still lifes and landscapes like *Marsh Landscape* (1916) (pl. 174). Here the spectator is pulled along the winding path through brown, green, and purple marsh country toward the center where a brilliant yellow glows like a vat of liquid metal.

These later paintings, from about 1916 to the present, bring Nolde closer to interpreting his own life and the expression of that belief in a primordial instinct, whose impelling force he experienced for so long a lifetime.

MAX PECHSTEIN

In 1913 Pechstein left Germany, where he was considered by many to be the leader of the young German painters, and went on his third trip to Italy. This time, however, he avoided the large cities and artistic centers and stayed at Monterosso al Mare, a small fishing village on the Gulf of Genoa. This for him was a southern counterpart to the silent fishing villages on the shores of the Baltic, where he had spent his summers since 1909. In the southern climate Pechstein's form became clarified, and the greater contrast of light and shade urged him toward a more emphatic treatment of structure, as in the canvas *Monterosso* (1913) (pl. 131a). His colors are brighter and intensified, with light greens and purples appearing for the first time. This painting and similar ones from the same period have been compared by Pechstein's biographer Max Osborn with the later work of the Italian contributors to *valori plastici,*[18] because of the stress on the severity of structure.

Soon Pechstein, like Gauguin before him, felt the urgency to go further in a search for the primitive beginnings of man, art, and life. He expected to find an equivalent to his own vital energy and sensual impulses among native tribes. After long plans he sailed early in 1914 from Genoa by way of the Suez Canal, Ceylon, India, China, and the Philippines to the island of Palau, at that time a German colony east of the Philippines. He recorded his impressions in his *Palau Diary*, a combination of verbal and pictorial sketches. He was overawed by the tropical vegetation, the virgin forests, the beautiful coastlines, the brilliance of the sun, the exotic colors of the sea and the coral reefs, and the almost miraculous quality of the tropical night. But his greatest admiration was reserved for the native population and the integration of life with the sympathetic forces of nature.

After a few months Pechstein, too, was caught unawares by the war: the Japanese occupied the island, captured the artist and his wife, and shipped them to Nagasaki, where they were set free. Embarking for Manila by way of Shanghai, they reached San Francisco in the early spring of 1915.

Pechstein said: "After a stay of three months I was thoroughly fed-up with life in the neutral country of the dollar. The yearning for home constantly became stronger and the urge more demanding. I had to stop sitting around idly and without purpose in a foreign country while at home all forces and senses served the fatherland." [19] Finding a job as a coal stoker on an American vessel in New York and enduring all kinds of difficulties, he was able to return to Germany in the autumn of 1915. He enlisted in the German army, and served with many misgivings and severe disillusionment until 1917.

Returning to Berlin, Pechstein began working on his Palau paintings, partly from sketches, partly from memory. These were summarized in the *Palau Triptych* (1917) (pl. 131b), which represents natives ashore and in canoes in a rhythmical arrangement of parallel movements and gestures. Unfortunately Pechstein's spontaneity, which was his real strength, is lost in this final statement of his journey. Consequently, and in spite of its expressionist palette, the triptych is rather stiff and artificial.

He sought to capture a primitive atmosphere by rejecting all academic technical refinements, and using vigorous brush strokes in unmixed colours. It is possible that this technique was influenced by the polychrome decoration of the native carvings, but otherwise Pechstein's art, like Gauguin's, retained its essential European character, though it cannot be compared with it for quality.[20]

Some of Pechstein's early vigor is still preserved in scenes from the Baltic, painted in 1917 and the following years. Generally, however, Pechstein's work after the Palau journey—which Adolf Jannasch calls the "zenith of his life" [21]—lost much of its former interest and strength, possibly because of its loss of tension. Pechstein became calmer, less eager to startle the common citizen; yet the robustness, the sensual quality, and the expression of his own vital energy, which had done so much to popularize the ideals of his more reticent and uncompromising companions, were also lost in his later productions. Frequently he turned to stylized decoration; for example, the stained glass windows and mosaics for Wolfgang Gurlitt in Berlin (1917) and the windows for the International Labor Office in Geneva (1926).

When Pechstein rejected his early, revolutionary style, he was, unfortunately, unable to grasp a formal, structural expression to serve as a fitting successor to what had gone before. His work in the 'twenties as a member of the Prussian Art Academy has few of the good qualities of his previous efforts.

AUGUST MACKE AND PAUL KLEE

The *Blaue Reiter* almanac indicates the familiarity of the artists with a greater diversity of primitive and exotic arts than the north German painters had. Macke, in his essay "Die Masken," had dealt with many of them, and used examples of Mayan, Alaskan, Cameroon, and Melanesian art to serve as illustrations.

On the first page of *Concerning the Spiritual in Art,* Kandinsky pays tribute to primitive art:

When there is . . . a similarity of inner direction in an entire moral and spiritual milieu, a similarity of ideals, . . . of "inner mood" between one period and another, the logical consequence will be a revival of the external forms which served to express those insights in the earlier age. This may account partially for our sympathy and affinity with and our comprehension of the work of the primitives. Like ourselves, these pure artists sought to express only inner and essential feelings in their works; in this process they ignored as a matter of course the fortuitous.[22]

Kandinsky had studied the ethnology of the primitive Russian tribes in the Vologda district in northeastern Russia; traveling there in 1889, he had received some of his deepest impressions from the peasants in this region. Later, after he had moved to Munich, he visited Tunisia and the ancient desert city of Kairuan in 1903, but the impressions of North Africa were considerably less important in his work. His trip to North Africa and its Moslem civilization in search of new inspiration was of course hardly new. Nineteenth-century French painting abounds with Orientalism, as evidenced by only some of the artists who journeyed to Algeria, Egypt, and the Near East: Delacroix, Decamps, Champmartin, Gleyre, Fromentin, Horace Vernet. Most of these painters worked in a style to which the twentieth-century German artists felt diametrically opposed. The latter showed little interest in exotic subject matter. If Macke, Klee, and Moilliet did follow in their footsteps, it may be considered largely incidental; they went to North Africa for entirely different reasons, and no cult of Orientalism ensued.[23]

August Macke, Paul Klee, and Louis Moilliet met in Marseille to sail for Tunisia late in March, 1914. Before going on this journey Macke had painted his *Girl with Fishbowl* (1914) (pl. 132), in which he uses interlocking prisms of color similar to those in *Bathing Girls* of the previous year. These color areas, now more brilliant than ever, have become defined into pieces of ceramic or colored stone that shape the precious bowl in the lower right. The background is formed by a similar affirmation of tactile color prisms; the girl herself is a contrast to them because of her soft outlines and muted color. Like the figures in his previous paintings, she seems absorbed in her own tranquillity. Her face is uncharacterized, lending her figure a more universal meaning.

In a desire to penetrate "beyond our accustomed present and past," [24] Macke joined Klee, whose maternal ancestors—according to a modern legend—had come from North Africa. They reached Kairuan in April, 1914. Wilhelm Hausenstein, who used Klee's journey to Tunisia as the basis for a most perceptive book on Klee and his contemporaries, described Kairuan as

. . . the capital of one of the provinces of Tunisia. Kairuan is situated between salt marshes in the middle of a wide plain. Kairuan is surrounded by a red tiled wall, which is thirty feet high, contains five gates and is crowned at intervals with round towers. Kairuan has a citadel and about a hundred mosques and monasteries. The jewel of the religious buildings is the Obka mosque, which was built in the year 827 and is decorated with four hundred and twenty antique columns. The twenty-five thousand inhabitants of Kairuan and its dependent villages work carpets and leather ware, especially slippers, hammer out copper vessels and distill oil of roses. [25]

The red-tiled wall, the gates and towers, the columns of the mosques, perhaps even the oil of roses—all find abundant expression in Klee's later paintings though constantly transformed by his imagination. Klee's *View of St. Germain* (1914) (pl. 133), one of the many water colors produced in Tunisia, indicates how light and color have now become a part of his vocabulary. In the view of a suburb of Kairuan, lavender houses with blue gables are set into a bright yellow and green countryside flooded with sunlight. The triangular forms of the houses are repeated in the shapes of the mountains, and echoed reversely by the clouds. The bright tints create an atmosphere of gaiety; the almost abstract patchwork of colored triangles creates the space.

The vivid atmosphere of North Africa was the final decisive sensation that Klee needed to find his own individual approach to the free use of color. A slow, deliberate process, taking about fifteen years, led from simple line to chiaroscuro and finally to color. On April 16, 1914, the thirty-five-year-old artist made the following entry in his diary: "I feel a deep and mild penetration and I become certain, without trying. Color has claimed me. I need no longer run after it. It has claimed me once and for all, that I know. This is the meaning of this happiest hour: I and color are one. I am a painter." [26]

Klee was already in his thirties before he understood the full value of color, but after that

he opened up for us the world of color in a richness such as no artist of any period has possessed. While the majority of painters know only a single color melody—most suited to their personality—Klee's color melodies are inexhaustible. He has at his disposal every tonal scale, from the softest to the most violent, from the brightest to the darkest. Each time one is struck with the musical sensitivity with which he sets one color against another. [27]

Kairuan must indeed be considered a major turning point in Klee's career. Much of this sensitivity to color was undoubtedly inherent in his personality; added to this was the strong impact of North Africa, with its light and its color. But after a long and careful study of the development of both Klee and Macke and their work at this period, I must agree with Vriesen [28] and others that Macke had considerable influence on Klee's new relationship to color.

Macke, eight years Klee's junior, had begun as a colorist. Whereas Klee derived primarily from Jugendstil, Macke drew from impressionism; whereas both painters were close to Delaunay, it was Macke who adapted Delaunay's color relationships several years before the trip to Tunisia. Macke's water color *Tunis: Bright House* (1914) (pl. 175), certainly similar to Klee's water colors in its treatment of color, relates much more directly to Macke's own earlier work than Klee's does to his. Like Klee's *View of St. Germain,* Macke's painting is built up of areas of transparent water color that communicate the brightness of light and clarity of air of the North African spring scene. Macke's light is even clearer than the more saturated tones of Klee. The predominance of geometric form as a compositional motif appears in both paintings—especially in Macke's, which is built up of color rectangles. Macke's painting is also more clearly balanced in its space than Klee's; Klee's color patchwork creates an all-over pattern of shifting planes, but Macke's blocks of color create a two-dimensional mosaic-like surface. Like an impressionist painter, Macke has captured a moment of particular light, but he uses the cubist vocabulary to express it.

For Klee, Kairuan was a starting point; for Macke, it was almost the end. Macke returned to Bonn; before being drafted into the army but after the outbreak of the war, he painted *Farewell* (1914) (pl. 134). Macke had stated to his mother-in-law that he believed that he would not return from the war, because he would be sure to be picked off since he was so tall.[29] In *Farewell* men, women, and children wander aimlessly through a space that again is given form by planes of color. Their faces are left featureless, but the attitudes of these tubular figures are somber or anxious. Drab colors are substituted for his usually lively palette. Soon after the completion of this painting, Macke was conscripted and immediately sent to the front, where he was killed in September, 1914, at the age of twenty-seven.

Macke's friends praised above all his innovations in color:

We painters know well that with the extinction of his harmonies, color in German art must fade several tones. It will have a blunter and dryer sound. Among all of us, he has given color the brightest and purest sound, as clear and light as his whole being has been. Certainly, Germany today has no conception of how much it owes to this young, dead painter, how much he has effected and succeeded in. . . . But his work has now been halted without consolation, without return.[30]

The general criticism was less sympathetic:

Macke belonged to the group which liked to call itself "Expressionist" and considered itself the carrier of a new artistic development. . . . Macke was still in his mid-twenties, and would have had time to find his way, after the Munich Russians have been forever—we hope—exiled from Germany by the war. But Macke could no longer experience this liberation.[31]

Klee returned from Tunisia, and continued to work in a style closely related to that of Kairuan. His *South Wind in Marc's Garden* (1915) (pl. 176) is built up of large patches of water color smoothly blocked out and overlaid in some of the toothlike and rectangular shapes that he had used in *View of St. Germain.* The color—though now the warmly pale or somber tones of a northern spring—is again determined by environment and atmosphere. The *Föhn,* a south wind peculiar to the northern slopes of the Alps, creates an atmosphere in which far-distant objects seem to float into one's backyard, destroying the illusion of aerial perspective. This optical phenomenon was an ideal motif for Klee's sensibility, which often tended to weave three-dimensional space into an activated two-dimensional surface.

At this time Klee not only explored the visual aspect of the mountain as a triangle, but also delved into the heart of the structure itself. In *Opened Mountain* (1914) (pl. 135) cones rotate around their hubs, turning perpendicularly as well as parallel to the picture plane. The artist has stripped movement to planes of force, comparable to the futurists' "lines of force." Klee called this painting *Opened Mountain* perhaps because it suggested to him the primal forces responsible for the mountain formation or the actual crystalline formation itself. To Klee art, besides being the interpretation of nature and of human emotion, is the very likeness of creation.[32]

During the postwar era Klee made some of the most significant contributions to pictorial expression. *South Wind in Marc's Garden* is an example of his concern with the visual world; *Opened Mountain,* with the forces of creation. *House-Tree* (1918) (pl. 136), as fanciful as his early etchings but without their caustic, morbid mood, now uses preverbal symbols to suggest the imaginative process of the unconscious mind.

An analysis of Klee's major work of the later period, anticipated in the pictures just discussed, goes far beyond the scope of this book. Klee himself, however, has made important statements about his artistic purpose:

Art is a symbol of creation. It is an example, much as the earth exemplifies the cosmos. The liberation of the elements, their grouping into complex categories, the analysis and reconstruction of a totality from many simultaneous sides, visual polyphony, the achievement of rest through the equilibrium of movement—all these are important problems of form, decisive for artistic communication, but they are still not art in the highest realm. In the highest realm the mysterious begins, and the intellect is woefully extinguished.[33]

Creation to Klee meant genesis. Since "motion underlies all stages of becoming," [34] he created visual means for the expression of genesis and metamorphosis, creation and change. He, like the expressionists, was obsessed with the creative act, but he never adopted their idiom. Unlike most of the expressionist painters, Klee was not occupied merely with the state of his own mind, nor did he express an explosive image of an unresolved conflict with society. During the time in which Max Beckmann penetrated to an interpretation of the meaning of man and his relationships, Klee was concerned with the world itself—not merely with the world as his senses perceived it. He considered the present state of things as only a momentary and accidental arrangement, and occupied himself with a visual formulation of the world as it might once have been or as though it were in the process of becoming something quite different.

XXIV

1914 and After

The expressionists shared a concern with the visual projection of their emotional experiences, and attempted to find means of conjuring up strong emotional responses in the spectator; yet it is impossible to speak of an expressionist style. The element that the painters held in common was the cultivation of their own sensations and subjectively expressive means, and this very emphasis on the subjective defied the appearance of a unified style.

The final prewar statements of Nolde, Pechstein, Macke, and Klee were discussed in the previous chapter, and the work by artists not connected with specific groups—Rohlfs, Feininger, Meidner, Morgner, and Beckmann—has been mentioned. Comparatively little unity of style has been observed. At the time of the outbreak of the war many of the painters had reached their qualitative climax and perhaps their point of greatest individuality. It will be the task of this chapter to continue discussing the extremely varied work by a number of important painters with whose previous production the reader is familiar.

ERNST LUDWIG KIRCHNER

Early in 1914, as a result of his decorative work for the chapel of the Sonderbund exhibition in Cologne in 1912, Kirchner was called back to Cologne to design an exhibition of art in the tobacco trade (Die Kunst im Tabakgewerbe) at the exposition of the Werkbund. He was commissioned also to perform a similar task for the central gallery at the exhibition in Karlsruhe the following year. The war, however, intervened, making this impossible.

During the final prewar period Kirchner spent his winters in Berlin, painting with almost feverish energy, recording his impressions of people in the streets, cabarets, brothels, the circus. His summers from 1912 to 1914 were spent on the island of Fehmarn, where he concentrated primarily on finding more and more simplified methods of expressing the movement of the nude body in a natural setting. The outlines of the bodies become increasingly unified with those of the landscape, a union which is reinforced by the use of color.[1]

Kirchner appears as an emaciated but forceful young man in his *Self-Portrait,* painted in the winter of 1913–1914 (pl. 137). The hatch-mark brush stroke, which was never more evident, is most responsible for this impression. Forms are exceedingly angular: the goatee, the lips, nose, eyes, ears, collar, hair—even the indication of shadows. There is now a complete unity of angular brush stroke and angular form. This angularity has led to the triangular form as the module for this painting. The eyes, reversing the curvature of the mouth, seem set into a sculptured head. Kirchner's painting at this time was strongly influenced by his own work as a wood carver and by his woodcuts. The whole painting has the appearance of being carved in wood; its stiffness, sharpness of contour, and angularity suggest the manipulation of the carving knife or gouge.

Kirchner's concept of himself with protruding eyes, sensual and cynical mouth, high forehead, disarranged hair, and pencil-thin eyebrows is certainly a romantic notion, which is accomplished by the emotional, swift, harried execution of the picture.

After the declaration of war Kirchner was inducted into the army and was trained in Halle for the artillery. An extremely sensitive and excitable individual, he experienced severe physical and mental depressions during his period of training.[2] *Soldiers in the Shower Room* (1915) (pl. 138) is a visual expression of the constraint and coercion he felt in the army: a large number of undressed young men, pressed into a tiny room, take showers under the surveillance of an officer barking orders. The soldiers seem to need to assume their elongated forms even to fit into the shower room.

Much more forthright in its bitter condemnation of the military is the *Self-Portrait as Soldier* (1915) (pl. 139). Kirchner painted himself in a blue army uniform complete with cap, very close to the front of the picture plane and rather to the left. The most startling thing about the figure is the amputated red stump of his right arm, which he holds up before the viewer. Instead of wearing the eager, intense look of the previous self-portrait, Kirchner now stares expressionlessly. The eyes, lacking pupil or iris, are hollow like the eye sockets of a statue from which the jewels have been plundered. Wild hair, mustache, and goatee are gone; the head beneath the cap looks shaved. The face is thin and drawn. A cigarette hangs from the lips. In the background, just right of center, is the full front figure of a nude woman, seen from the thighs up—again the juxtaposition of self to the woman-model symbol. In the amputated wrist stumps, Kirchner declares not only the dreaded possibility of actual physical destruction or impairment, but the real "amputation" of his talents during the period of war. He cannot paint—he is completely handicapped in his life as an artist. The pink speckled swash in the left background might be a canvas. The nude woman contrasted to his amputated hands can stand either for the obvious symbol of sexual impotence or—more generally—for the frustration of his entire creative life. This portrait is much harder than *Self-Portrait at Dawn,* a lithograph done nine years earlier. Though he has retained a similar symbolism, he has discarded the early, fluid, Jugendstil contours, and substituted jagged edges and a broken, angular line of hatch-marks. His symbolism, too, is plainer, less ambiguous. His style at this point indicates a trend toward magic realism or new objectivity, which became an important force in Germany after the war. But for Kirchner it was only a trend—he was not to develop in this direction.

Kirchner's war service led to a complete physical and mental breakdown. Through the intervention of his commanding officer Hans Fehr,[3] a former lay member of the Brücke and a close friend of Nolde's, Kirchner was released from the army, and entered a sanitarium in Königstein in the Taunus, where restful living slowly restored his health. He was soon able to paint frescoes, very much in the style of the Fehmarn canvases, in the stairhall of the hospital. In this early period of recovery he also executed the color woodcuts for Chamisso's *Peter Schlemihl.*

In 1917 Kirchner left Germany for Switzerland. Still unable to work and live on his own, he followed the advice of Henry van de Velde and placed himself in a rest home in Kreuzlingen. He was finally discharged in 1918, the year in which he held a major exhibition in the Kunsthaus of Zürich. He found a lonely mountain retreat, the "Wildboden," above the village of Frauenkirch near Davos. He was spellbound by the Alps, by the form and power of the mountain world, and by the quiet and dignified people—a world so completely different from the pulsating and neurotic life of the city as he had known it.

Again the woodcut enabled him to express the new experience. His *Swiss Peasant* (1917) (fig. 34) shows his new relationship to the world of nature and mountains, a relationship as intimate as his previous empathy with the urban environment. He is aware of a single rhythm in this world. In this woodcut individual parts, such as the cow and the head of the man, repeat the angular form of the huts and mountain peaks. The man's eyes radiate wrinkles like the rays of a sun; these lines emphasize and create the texture of the wood block. The difference in scale between the oversized head in the foreground and the mountain background may be derived from the somewhat earlier German experiments in photomontage. The composition is unified by the repetition of shapes and the hatch work used for the rendition of inanimate as well as animate forms.

Color and form slowly lose their urgent, problematic quality and provocative incongruity in Kirchner's paintings, which become simplified, clearer, and more monumental. His great landscapes of the early 1920's derive from the artist's intimacy with nature. Then, around 1928, Kirchner's work experienced a considerable stylistic change toward a form related to Picasso's postcubist work. During his life in the Swiss mountains, from 1917 until his suicide in 1938, Kirchner had a most productive period. He left, besides a large number of canvases, about two thousand woodcuts, lithographs, and etchings—the most impressive graphic work of the first

Figure 34.   ERNST LUDWIG KIRCHNER   Swiss Peasant   1917   Woodcut

half of the twentieth century. In his prints and in his paintings he continued to search for the hieroglyph that would describe the experience of reality.

ERICH HECKEL

Heckel, who had collaborated with Kirchner on the murals for the Sonderbund chapel, again worked next to him at the Cologne Werkbund exhibition of 1914, where he executed the decoration of the Felmann galleries. In 1915 he volunteered for war service in the medical corps.

Figure 35.   ERICH HECKEL   Crouching Woman   1914   Woodcut

By the outbreak of the war Heckel had developed considerably as a print maker as well as a painter. Heckel's evolution was perhaps more homogeneous than that of many of his friends. His woodcut *Crouching Woman* (fig. 35) dates from about a year later than his painting *Glass Day*. It shows a clear development from earlier woodcuts, and is related in feeling to the *Head of a Woman* of 1912 (pl. 45). Much as before, he offers the spectator a haggard woman with drooping breasts and eyelike nipples. But since the *Standing Nude* of 1908 (pl. 30) he has become a master of the woodcutting technique. *Crouching Woman* is a strong, well-balanced contrast of broad black and white areas. The narrow, inhibited gesture of the woman is well suited to the small space she occupies. She is crowded into the frame; even the window presses her in further instead of opening up the space. The white plane around her head is closed down by the surrounding black area.

During the war Heckel served in Flanders. There he met Beckmann, Permeke, and Ensor, the latter becoming a lifelong friend and mentor to him. He made drawings, etchings, woodcuts, and lithographs of wounded soldiers—moving expressions of human suffering. His motifs of physical and mental impairment, desolation, and suicide are not revolutionary denunciations of social conditions, like the later drawings by George Grosz, but are attempts to express the universality of human suffering. When he makes use of the broadly planar form of many Brücke woodcuts, as in *Crouching Woman,* he endows it with a deeply human feeling. Yet sometimes his artistic form seems to lag behind his artistic purpose. His scenes of human anguish are not so convincing as, for example, Munch's treatments of similar subject matter. Heckel, a man of extraordinary intellectual and analytical power, at times lacked spontaneity of expression, and seems to have been held back by either his intellectuality or his romanticism.

In 1915 Heckel painted his *Ostende Madonna* on a piece of sailcloth for a soldier. This poetic vision of the Virgin, probably his best-known painting, has been called the only twentieth-century painting of the Madonna of real validity.[4]

After the war his painting underwent a basic change: it became less subjective and disturbing, and attempted to achieve an objective quality without any necessary relationship to the artist's emotional experience. His landscapes took on their own rhythm, and his people were conceived of as living peacefully in a natural environment. Again he painted bathers, but the former asceticism changed to a representation of women and children enjoying their outdoor activities. Some of his best postwar work was in water color, in which he used cool, contrasting colors. There, as well as in his late work, he painted fresh, sunlit landscapes extending to far distances.

KARL SCHMIDT-ROTTLUFF

It is fascinating to follow Schmidt-Rottluff's development from his early impressionist technique (*Windy Day,* 1907) through his Fauve-like use of color (*Estate in Dangast,* 1910) toward constantly more concise and definite form (*Rising Moon,* 1913). Like many of his comrades, he was guided toward this greater attention to linear structure primarily by his experiment in the woodcut. Before 1910 he had been active in almost all

graphic media, but later he found the woodcut the most fitting material
to express his new formal conceptions. As early as 1910 Wilhelm Niemeyer
wrote in the *Denkschrift des Sonderbundes:*

Nolde before him, and Heckel, Kirchner and Pechstein have worked simultaneously
in the same direction as woodcutters, both graphically and sculpturally. None of
them, however, has occupied himself with this technique with such exclusiveness,
energy, and therefore with an ability fully adequate for the material as Schmidt-
Rottluff, whose art, even his painting, really strives toward wood sculpture.[5]

Schmidt-Rottluff continued working in the woodcut during the prewar
years, but was unable to work consistently during his period of active service
on the eastern front. At the end of the war, and now very strongly influenced by a greater understanding of and affinity with African sculpture, he
took his final, most consequential step in a series of woodcuts on religious
themes. Between 1917 and 1919 he made twenty woodcuts on New Testament subjects. The quality of the wood itself had never been more important to him as a determining factor. Human beings—bodies, faces, and

Figure 36.   KARL SCHMIDT-ROTTLUFF   Road to Emmaus   1918   Woodcut

hands—are cut into the wood in a way most obviously to emphasize a series
of rigid gestures and movements. In Nolde's woodcuts there are still tone
gradations and round forms. In Schmidt-Rottluff's there is only the complete contrast of black to white planes, of sharp ridges and wedges to spikes.
   One of these religious woodcuts is the *Road to Emmaus* (1918) (fig.
36). The two apostles walk with lowered lids beside the tall, hierarchic

figure of Jesus through a landscape filled with the long shadows of late afternoon—"it is toward evening, and the day is far spent." [6] But if this woodcut is successful in its conveyance of a mystic religiosity, it is not because it is a careful depiction of the event, as reported in Luke,[7] but because of the sharply expressive character of each element. The setting sun looks more like a comet that has come out of Christ's halo. The lines between it and the halo form a strong tension between left and right in the picture. The road is a smooth, definite white path, in contrast to the black areas around it and the jagged rocks bordering it. The trees are strange, sharp forms—more like cacti than trees—with no hint of foliage or softness about them: it is a stage landscape, and every element of it is hard, even cruel. The humble, attentive figures of the disciples, though sharply outlined too, contrast in attitude to the character of this countryside and to the figure of Christ, which is like an ikon. His hand is raised in blessing, and His eyes stare out fixedly: one with a white pupil, one a solid black spot. Besides commanding the spectator's eye by virtue of the tension between them and their very oddity, the eyes may well be intended to symbolize the Christian duality of black and white, right and wrong. The apostles' eyelids are lowered, not only because "their eyes were holden," but symbolically because they are blind as well as meek before the wisdom of Jesus, whose eyes see all.

Much of Schmidt-Rottluff's work with angular planes was transposed from the woodcut to painting, as in the *Self-Portrait with Hat* of 1920 (pl. 140), also undoubtedly influenced by cubism and African sculpture. The strong, angular planes seem at times almost to be cut with a hatchet. His violent color sense is retained, and the head looks "hewn" into slabs of vivid color that are in constant tension in the picture space. Everything is disciplined into a scaffolding of color planes that impinge upon one another or are separated by definite, black demarcation lines. The position of the head, tilted in its frame, surprises the spectator with its sudden appearance. A comparison between this and Kirchner's *Self-Portrait* of a few years earlier shows the differences within the Brücke group.

In the 1920's Schmidt-Rottluff begins to soften his hard outlines and to turn toward a more picturesque gentleness, following a development not unlike that of Pechstein and Heckel. The almost barbaric simplification of his linear abstractions disappears in favor of a new proximity to life and nature in which color and light have again assumed a paramount place.

WASSILY KANDINSKY

The proximity to visual reality and the representation of the sensations called forth by this reality were essential to the Brücke painters, whereas Kandinsky's "inner necessity" demanded the rejection of representationalism. The "inner sound" takes the place of optic experience. Kandinsky, the "abstract expressionist" painter, no longer carries on a dialogue with the external world but only with his own personal conflicts and their solutions.

In *Composition 1914* (pl. 177) a dynamic flood of colors and shapes pours over the canvas in furious movement. Space is no longer tangible or rational, but has become disembodied; it derives from a series of intricately overlapping, interweaving planes, digging into depth toward a distant vista. Even many of the lines, especially the thickly shaded ones, are actually the edges of invisible planes that successively lead the eye toward the distant view on the upper margin of the canvas. Abstract forms vaguely suggesting a landscape had been used by Kandinsky for a number of years, but he has now deliberately turned from warm to cool color:

Beginning early in 1914 I felt a desire for the "tranquillity which is a little cold." I did not want to be rigid, but cold, cold enough. Sometimes even with a glacial coldness. To reverse, so to speak, those Chinese cakes which are glowing hot and hide a piece of ice inside. I wanted, on the contrary (and I like it still), burning power in an icy chalice.[8]

Composition 1914 is by no means carefully balanced into a pictorial harmony like a cubist painting. The lack of balance, the dynamic activity, and the all-over movement of this painting could be compared to the undisciplined and "barbarian" element in Celtic art. Kandinsky, however, felt a need for a greater firmness of structure. Contemporary with the "cooling" of his palette, he began experimenting with geometric form. As early as 1913 he used a compass for circular forms in the preparatory drawing for *Kleine Freuden,*[9] thus indicating his future interest in the artistic possibilities of these geometric shapes.

The war forced Kandinsky, a Russian citizen, to leave Germany, and also stifled his enormous productivity of the prewar years. Between 1910 and 1915 he had painted more than one hundred canvases; in the following five years he completed only twenty-eight.

After a brief stay in Switzerland and Sweden, Kandinsky returned to his native Moscow. The revolution over, he became a member of the art section of the People's Commissariat for Popular Culture and a professor at the Academy of Fine Arts. In 1919 he was appointed a director of the Museum of Pictorial Culture; in 1921 he became a founder and vice-president of the Academy of Artistic Sciences, for which he had hopes of realizing his plans to synthesize the arts and sciences. His theoretical work and interest in and early experimentation with geometric forms were a major stimulus to the rise of suprematism and constructivism in Russia. Kandinsky in turn was probably influenced by the work of Gabo and Pevsner, whom he first met in Moscow in 1919.

Because of the conservative pressure of Soviet cultural politics, Kandinsky left Moscow for Berlin in 1921. In the summer of 1922 he was appointed professor at the Bauhaus in Weimar. There his work continued in its trend toward greater precision and deliberate construction. He investigated the pictorial possibilities of the triangle, the square, and the circle, and the relationship of these figures to primary colors. His interest in the possibilities of scientific and analytical examination of form was stated in his last important book, *Punkt und Linie zu Fläche,* published by the Bauhaus in 1928. In the 'thirties his form changed again toward a freer, biomorphic style until he finally evolved a language of space, movement, and color that, while retaining strict control of form, also returned to the personal factor of his earlier work. Like Klee, Kandinsky had come to an understanding that geometry too was only one of many means, and that art like nature creates form for its own ends in a world where everything is both tangible and intangible, physical fact and subjective symbol.

FRANZ MARC

Franz Marc was always ready to admit the great debt he owed to Kandinsky, especially in the free use of color. In his final paintings Marc followed Kandinsky in an almost complete departure from the object. This final step, however, grew out of Marc's own development, and followed his own needs and aims. As early as 1908 he spoke of seeking a "pantheistic empathy with the vibration and flow of the blood of nature." [10] In *Fate of the Beasts* (1913) he came close to the formulation of such a pantheistic view of the organic world.

The relationship of the expressionist movement, especially the Blaue Reiter, to the romanticists has been mentioned earlier.[11] Perhaps it is most striking in the case of Franz Marc, who, like Runge or Friedrich or Novalis, was concerned with finding formal expression for the secret life of the creatures of nature.[12] Marc's work in the winter of 1913–1914, as evidenced in a painting such as *Cattle in Landscape,* in the Detroit Institute of Arts, perhaps approaches this pantheism even closer. Forms and colors are transparent, and pervade each other. Trees, plants, and cattle, splintered by the rays of the sun or suffused with its glow, are joined in an interpenetrating, kaleidoscopic unity of color and form.

Many factors were responsible for Marc's increasing abstraction. His repulsion at the ugliness of man and, eventually, at even that of the animal has been cited.[13] Again as with Kandinsky, Marc had an interest in the abstract reasoning of the pure sciences.[14] Religion, too, Marc felt, was dematerialized and therefore strengthened by the destruction of the idol. To the symbolism of religion and the cognition of science Marc added the visual penetration of the artist, who must be almost primarily concerned with the breakdown of matter and the search for life-giving energy. One road in this search for the inner core of matter, which is at the disposal of the artist, is abstraction: "that deep desire of modern seekers to express the generally valid and unifying by means of the abstract." [15] As a painter, he used color and form to dismantle the material and the objective and to help create the world of the spirit.

In the spring of 1914 Marc painted a series of abstract paintings: *Gay Forms, Fighting Forms, Playing Forms, Broken Forms.* With Marc's departure from the object there is also a change in style from the angularity of sharp, splintered shapes to the curvilinear shapes of *Fighting Forms* (pl. 178). Here the movement is circular; although these "fighting forms" seem to be engaged in combat with each other, they display no hostility toward the spectator, perhaps because of their smoothly rounded shapes.

Fighting Forms was one of Marc's last canvases. The war made it impossible for him to continue painting. As a soldier, he was limited to the pencil and the sketchbook; nevertheless, he continued his search for an all-inclusive world picture, as in his small pencil drawing *Arsenal for Creation* (1915). These last paintings and drawings were considered by the artist to be experiments toward a new form in which he hoped to create an organic, dynamic reality that would recognize only spirit, energy, and flux. Marc's further development was tragically halted by his death near Verdun on March 4, 1916, at the age of thirty-six.

HEINRICH CAMPENDONK

When the Rhenish painter Heinrich Campendonk came to live in Bavaria, he saw peasant votive pictures painted under glass. Fascinated by this naïve, forceful expression, he tried to re-create—not imitate—the spirit, technique, and subject matter of folk art. He settled among the Bavarian peasants and lived on their farms for many years, first in Sindelsdorf, and then, after being discharged from the army in 1916, in Seeshaupt, on Lake Starnberg. Aided by his strong sense of color, he soon mastered the technique of under-glass painting. After the death of Marc and Macke, who had exerted such a strong influence on his work, Campendonk carried on many of their forms and concepts and at the same time was deeply occupied with the problems of cubism (pl. 109). It was actually only after his return from the war that he became an important painter in his own right.

Campendonk's subject matter consists of the most elementary objects of country life—farmers and their wives, their cattle and fowl—but he dismembers this ordinary world and reassembles it into a magic, dreamlike place, as in *Pastoral Scene* (*ca.* 1920) (pl. 141). Campendonk attempts here to approach the naïveté of Rousseau or children's drawings even more than Bavarian peasant art. His animals are stylized in the simplest possible terms; so are his trees, buildings—even his moon. The nude in the left middle ground is very Rousseau-like in appearance, even to her stylized hairdo. The picture plane is kept flat to increase this primitivistic appearance. Yet Campendonk has actually produced a highly sophisticated work—an understanding of its derivations in primitive and children's art is imperative for its full appreciation. His space is complex, in spite of its apparent flatness. Considerable depth is achieved by the thick overlapping of forms in the center, which pushes the eye forward and out of the canvas; the long, empty space at either side of this cluster of trees, animals, and people creates a recession in space. This recession is, however, again arbitrarily stopped by the buildings on either side. Another important aspect of this painting is its ambiguous symbolism. The spectator is forced to ask questions. Is the animal in the right background an elk or a horse? Are the crosses on the buildings the bars of windows, or are they actually crosses indicating churches? What is implied by the nudity of the figures? Why does the woman in the foreground squat so stiffly and awkwardly, and what is the meaning of her forlorn expression? Above all, what is the relationship between the various figures and objects? Campendonk has established a formal unity of patterns, color, and overlapping planes. As in the pictures that inspired him, the arrangement of the figures is according to their importance, and objects are painted in their broadest, simplest, and most significant aspects. But he leaves the spectator to question the implications of the relationships of these seemingly disparate elements. The animals wander in different directions; the people seem to have no interest in one another or in the animals, the trees, the grass, the houses, or the moon.

By means of his extremely personal symbolism, Campendonk has created an idyllic, evocative world that defies rational explanation. As early as 1921 Georg Biermann pointed out that among European artists Campendonk was most closely related to Marc Chagall,[16] probably with reference to the mysterious symbolism that each artist employed.

Campendonk abandoned country life in 1920 to travel to Italy, where he studied the mosaics in Ravenna and the frescoes of Giotto and Fra Angelico. In 1922 he returned to his native Krefeld to accept a position at the School of Fine Arts. In Krefeld, as well as in his later activities at the Düsseldorf Academy (1926–1933) and at the Rijsakademie van Beeldende Kunsten in Amsterdam (since 1933), he has turned increasingly toward the applied arts: stage design, textile design, and stained glass.

OSKAR KOKOSCHKA

Kokoschka's close affinity to the baroque tradition, indicated in an earlier chapter,[17] is especially apparent in the portraits and symbolic compositions he painted after returning to Vienna just before 1914. The sharp lines of his earlier portraits are now replaced with more fluid forms, as in *Brother and Sister* (1914) (pl. 142a). Paint is applied with quick, wavelike movements; the brush work looks more pastose, and has become more essentially important. Color, though still subdued, is now a determining element in the formal organization. *Brother and Sister,* in its somber colors and in the attitudes of its sitters, in the children's curving, empty hands resting loosely in their laps, expresses a certain mood of brooding resignation. The boy, who remarkably resembles a self-portrait, looks off aimlessly to one side; the boyish sister gazes out without much expectation. Yet the mood has changed slightly from Kokoschka's earlier paintings: the children are interpreted neither as tensely nor as languidly self-dramatizing. Their listlessness is closely related to the softer, rounder outlines that have taken the place of Kokoschka's former angularity. The painting is both animated and unified by the flickering highlights on the rich, variegated surfaces of the girl's face and pinafore and the head of the boy.

Increasingly the psychological portrait gives way to daring, more symbolic compositions in Kokoschka's work, like the double portrait of himself and his friend in an intimate dance. This portrait not only indicates his close and fruitful friendship with Alma Mahler, one of the great women of the modern era, but—much more successfully than his plays, with their nameless characters and symbolic statements—also symbolizes the relationship of man to woman in a more general way. Similarly his magnificent composition *The Tempest* (1914) (pl. 179) translates his response to the strength and power of love into a visual symbol. The painter and his beloved, lying together in a boat or large shell, are swept along in a rotating movement by the elementary forces of wind and water in a fantastic, deep blue landscape. Dynamic movement pervades the painting. "*The Tempest* is in every sense a baroque picture; the couple are shrouded in swirling mists of another world, their unreal bark floating in space. Its color is cool and subdued, the painting itself fluid." [18]

The Tempest was Kokoschka's last great painting before the war. Before volunteering for service in the cavalry, however, he painted another important canvas: *The Knight Errant* (1915) (pl. 142b), which is again a self-portrait, this time of Kokoschka as a wounded soldier. He lies on the ground almost alone in a weird landscape reminiscent of the landscape background of the prostrate Christ in the *Pietà* predella of Grünewald's Isenheim altarpiece. A small figure of death rides down from the sky, and a strange female figure crouches sleepily on the right as though unenthusiastically awaiting rescue. The range of colors is limited by a domination of deep blues, and an undulating rhythm is achieved with the dynamic brush stroke. A year later Kokoschka was severely wounded on the battlefield:

Strongly pacifist and humanitarian by nature, he was determined not to kill, and military regimentation, to a man who had fretted under the restrictions of normal civilian life, was intolerable. Within a year he had been wounded gravely. He was ambushed during a reconnaissance patrol on the Eastern front, shot in the head, bayoneted in a lung and captured by the Russians. [19]

The following years, spent recuperating in a Swedish hospital and then in becoming a central figure of postwar expressionism in Dresden—where, unable to follow normal human pursuits and relationships, he became known as the "mad Kokoschka" [20]—were a period in which he felt the need for a more emphatically structural form. In the early 'twenties he worked with large areas of vivid colors, organized into more solid relationships in such pictures as the Dresden landscapes and *The Slave* (1920) (pl. 180). [21] In *The Slave* the artist has abandoned his earlier emphasis on linear movement to explore the possibilities of the color patch. In place of the whorling baroque lines of a painting like *The Tempest,* he has now achieved an openness of form essentially characteristic of the baroque. The large and monumental woman in the foreground is not delineated by an outline of any sort, but consists entirely of color areas that, as in stained glass windows, have become autonomous carriers of emotion.

The sexual overtones are to a considerable extent suggested by the hot red tones of the woman's body and the man's garments set against a jewel green background of related value. The male figure, again resembling Kokoschka, whose hand pulls hesitantly at the curtain while his large sad eyes bore into the room, is a wizened, little clown—a parody of the master type; his fruitful-looking slave is so enormous that, even kneeling, she greatly dominates him in size. The enfolding irony—the full comment on the relationship—is provided by their attitudes. Hers is one of listless waiting, a mild remoteness that is not supine but simply uninterested. She might be thinking of something else, and in her thoughtful resignation she bears a certain resemblance to the brooding stillness of Kokoschka's earlier *Brother and Sister*. Yet while the woman still waits, the man—a grown-up little clown—haunts us with his desire, so sadly insistent as to be sinister. He is disharmonious, a misfit, a twentieth-century clown whose foster brothers trail across the canvases of Picasso and Rouault.

In 1924 Kokoschka suddenly left Dresden and his position at the academy. He set out to paint the cities of Europe, North Africa, and the Near East. His work became more closely related to the whole European tradition of landscape painting, but he captured the total atmosphere of each city as few painters had done before him.

Again I have lent expression to the sensations of the time, by painting landscapes from the *vue des oiseaux,* from the highest building, from the tallest mountain and in as many countries as possible. I have travelled in these years in order to conquer the world which has so long been kept from me and into which I was born as a citizen.[22]

Yet this "citizen of the world" was forced by the Nazis to leave his native Austria shortly after his return in the early 'thirties. He went to Prague, but again had to flee Czechoslovakia and continued on to work and live in England.

Kokoschka's brilliant landscapes of the 'twenties are stylistically related to impressionism; his paintings of the 'thirties, sincere in their conviction, are sometimes labored in their symbolism. Since the end of the second World War Kokoschka has worked with a remarkable boldness of spatial structure, bright, vibrant color, and a sweeping baroque movement. In some of his best recent landscapes and portraits he combines his early intuitive penetration with his later interest in the beauty of color and light, so that the result looks almost like the synthesis of mental and sensual vision that Hermann Bahr saw in the baroque and hoped to see return in a post-expressionist era.

XXV

Conclusion

When the war ended in November, 1918, Marc, Macke, and Schiele were dead. Kokoschka was recuperating in Dresden [1] from severe injuries. Kirchner was hospitalized in Switzerland. Kandinsky, as well as a number of other "Munich Russians," had returned to his native country. The close communication of the expressionist painters with their French contemporaries had been disrupted. The original groups, Die Brücke and Der Blaue Reiter, had long since ceased to exist. Many of the artists who had banded together to give the original impulse to the movement now worked isolated from each other—from Nolde's retreat on Germany's northern boundary to Campendonk's near the southern frontier.

The war and expressionist thought seemed to be fellow symptoms of the same sickness—not in the sense of the futurists' glorification of militarism, but as the war revealed with cruel clarity the very conditions of life that gave rise to expressionism and against which artists and writers had protested so vehemently. The despair, violence, and suffering expressed in much of expressionism became a daily experience in more than four years of bloodshed.

With the end of the war, and in spite of the dispersal of the artists, expressionism suddenly found itself an accepted art form. Certain of its inherent pacifist propensities tended to ally it with the peace movement. Its search for universal forms and its sponsorship of great international exhibitions corresponded to the then prevalent dreams of a united Europe and a brotherhood of man; its intoxication with the idea of a community of artists corresponded to the plans for new social utopias pronounced throughout Germany in the last years of the war and in the period immediately following the revolution of 1918.

In November, 1918, the Novembergruppe was formed in Berlin, more or less under the leadership of Max Pechstein and César Klein. Intended as a close alliance between the expressionist artists and the socialist state, it became a focal point of cultural life in Berlin immediately after the war.

The Novembergruppe established Workers' Councils for Art and concerned itself with the place of the artist in the new society—the responsibilities to be assumed by artist, public, and state. Suggestions for a fusion of a utopian socialism and expressionist forms appeared in the pamphlet *An Alle Künstler*.[2] Max Pechstein had designed the cover: a man standing against a background of flames raises his right arm and points with his other hand to his own glowing heart. This figure was meant as a symbol of man's fervent dedication to reconstruction after the conflagration. The pamphlet, written by many people, contained a "Call to Socialism" by Meidner, who defined socialism as "justice, liberty and love of man—the divine order in the world."[3] Pechstein attacked the academies and museums as storehouses of tradition, and called upon the artist to break the chains of the past and to take his place as an active participant in the shaping of the new society: "We desire to achieve through the socialist republic not only the recovery of the conditions of art, but also the beginning of a unified artistic era for our time."[4] Pechstein considered art a duty for the people and, urging a close relationship between arts and crafts, voiced his belief that the training of *all* people in the crafts will lead toward this new artistic era.

Kurt Eisner, then head of the short-lived Soviet Republic of Bavaria, took a similar stand from the point of view of the new state.[5] Other expressionist artists—César Klein, Richter-Berlin, Feininger, and Tappert among them—contributed graphic work to the pamphlet.

The hope for a new unity of art, crafts, architecture, and city planning within the socialist state is summarized in the book *Ja! Stimmen des Arbeitsrates für Kunst in Berlin*. Published in November, 1919,[6] this book contained articles by: painters, such as Schmidt-Rottluff, Campendonk, Melzer, and Tappert; architects, including Obrist, Gropius, Bruno and Max Taut; critics, such as Adolf Behne, Karl Ernst Osthaus, and W. R. Valentiner. Included in the more than one hundred signators were the art dealers Paul Cassirer and Alfred Flechtheim and the painters Feininger, Heckel, Meidner, Mueller, Nauen, Nolde, and Pechstein.

Competing with Der Sturm, the Novembergruppe promoted what it considered to be modern art, but was more concerned with mass media of communication. It not only sponsored composers like Berg, Hindemith, and Weill, but concerned itself with city planning, arranged for radio broadcasts, and supported Viking Eggeling and Hans Richter in their first experiments in the abstract film in 1920 and 1921. The Novembergruppe also propagandized for artistic anonymity.

Similar groups emphasizing the creative arts in the new social framework started in various German cities: Gruppe 1919 in Dresden, Der Wurf in Bielefeld, Gruppe Rih in Karlsruhe. All these organizations believed that a new kind of art education, beginning in early childhood and continuing through adult life, was essential, and many of their activities were focused on educational ends.

The most ambitious educational undertaking, combining the arts and crafts, was the union of the Weimar Art Academy with the Weimar School of Arts and Crafts under the original sponsorship of the Grand Duke of Saxe-Weimar and the direction of Walter Gropius as the Staatliches Bauhaus Weimar. The original aims of this institution are stated clearly in its first proclamation:

The complete building is the final aim of the visual arts. Their noblest function was once the decoration of buildings. Today they exist in isolation, from which they can be rescued only through the conscious, coöperative effort of all craftsmen. Architects, painters and sculptors must recognize anew the composite character of a building as an entity. Only then will work be imbued with an architectonic spirit which it has lost as "salon art."

Architects, sculptors, painters, we must all turn to the crafts.

Art is not a "profession." There is no essential difference between the artist and the craftsman. The artist is an exalted craftsman. . . . Proficiency in the craft is essential to every artist. Therein lies a source of creative imagination.

Let us create a new guild of craftsmen, without the class distinctions which raise an arrogant barrier between craftsman and artist. Together let us conceive and create the new building of the future, which will embrace architecture and sculpture and painting in one unity and which will rise one day toward heaven from the hands of a million workers like the crystal symbol of a new faith.[7]

The newly formed Bauhaus was closely related to the medieval Bauhütte, the corporation of artists and craftsmen working on the cathedrals. The proclamation itself was fittingly illustrated with a woodcut by Lyonel Feininger representing a Gothic church within the points of a constellation (fig. 37).

Feininger was the first painter on the Bauhaus staff, soon to be joined by artists working in a great variety of styles:[8] Georg Muche and Lothar Schreyer were formerly associated with Der Sturm; Johannes Itten and Oskar Schlemmer came from Hoelzel. Kandinsky and Klee, and finally in 1923 the constructivist Laszlo Moholy-Nagy, were perhaps the most important appointments.

In its attempt to break the isolation of the artist, whose function was considered to be that of an anonymous worker for functional design, the Bauhaus stood opposed to the emphasis on the personal expression of a subjective world by the expressionists. In many ways the Bauhaus was founded on certain principles that Jugendstil had articulated at the turn of the century. Gropius was in fact suggested as director by Henry van de Velde, his predecessor as head of the School of Arts and Crafts and architect of the building.[9]

Other trends made themselves felt in the German art world. In many ways the very opposite pole of the functionalism of the Bauhaus was the complete permissiveness of Dada, making itself widely seen and loudly heard in postwar Germany: in Cologne (Arp, Ernst), in Berlin (Hülsenbeck, Franz Jung, Mehring, Baader, Grosz), in Hannover (Schwitters). Yet the close friendship between Schwitters and Moholy-Nagy, both initially influenced by expressionism, and the fairly direct relation between

Arp's Dadaist constructions and Kandinsky's forms indicate the many cross-fertilizing currents in postwar Germany.

George Grosz (born 1893) had briefly been a member of the Dadaist group:

> . . . I was the "Propagandada." My job was to invent slogans to promote our cause. Not that any of us knew what Dadaism actually was. It could be almost anything: a void, a new wisdom, a new brand of Mother Sill's pills against seasickness, a sedative, a stimulant. It was everything and yet nothing.[10]

Figure 37. LYONEL FEININGER Woodcut from the first Bauhaus proclamation, 1919

Grosz soon turned toward more definite expression in pungent drawing and lithographs that were bitter social commentaries and powerful accusations of the ruling classes. His superrealism in confronting the observer with the most ghastly aspects of reality and his utmost precision of line were soon found also in the work of Otto Dix and, temporarily, Max Beckmann. Certain other artists of this generation—born in the late 'eighties and 'nineties—turned to an objective realism and the exactitude of static form. Especially important was the Munich group around Alexander Kanoldt, formerly associated with the New Artists' Association of Munich: Karl Mense, Georg Schrimpf, and Davringhausen. These artists painted in various media with a dry, hard realism in an attempt to exclude individual feeling. Much of this painting is characterized by a clinical exactness that often evokes a shock in the observer because of the painter's precise dissection of forms normally taken for granted. This attempt at veracity, of taking objects for themselves on their material basis, must be seen as a reaction to the distortions by the previous generation. It occurred contemporaneously with the temporary stabilization of the German political and economic situation in the mid-'twenties.

Gustav Hartlaub, director of the Mannheim Kunsthalle, labeled these painters—Grosz, Dix, Scholz, Beckmann, Kanoldt, Mense, Schrimpf, and Davringhausen—as Neue Sachlichkeit in 1924, and assembled an exhibition of this group the following year. The term "Neue Sachlichkeit" (new objectivity) has been in usage in Germany since that time to designate the German corollary of the postwar trend also known as verism and magic realism.[11] Hartlaub characterized it as a period of calm resignation or bitter cynicism after a period of exuberant hope. Many of these painters reacted to the mechanization of the time as did the young constructivists and the Bauhaus group. Instead of attempting to use the machine, however, the "new objectivists" painted canvases in which they offered angular, smooth, mechanistic interpretations of an objective world.

Simultaneous with all these new trends, expressionist painting became popular with the wider public that supported it by purchases. The art market flourished, especially because savings and securities had become worthless in the inflation; since there was not enough art to go around, new art was constantly being produced.[12]

As expressionist painting was publicized in the papers, magazines,[13] galleries, museums, and in a steadily growing array of books and monographs, the public became increasingly responsive to what had at last really become a style. Some of the painters working in this manner were highly talented; others merely enjoyed a particular wave of fashion. Certain names among this second generation recur often in the journals and exhibition catalogs: Karl Caspar, Hans Drexel, Josef Eberz, Konrad Felixmüller, Walter Gramatté, Franz Heckendorf, Willy Jaeckel, Max Kaus, César Klein, Karl Kluth, Moritz Melzer, E. Mollenhauser, Max Oppenheimer (Mopp), Richter-Berlin, P. A. Seehaus, Hermann Stemmler, Stanislas Stückgold, Georg Tappert, Maria Uhden, Max Unold, Erich Waske.

All too frequently the dramatic quality of the first generation was now a theatrical gesture, the intensity was a matter of mere energy, the anguish and suffering were sensationalism. Expressionism in its early stages was often an ecstatic self-expression of an inner need; this, by its very nature, could not persist for a long period of time. As pointed out earlier, new forms of artistic expression, largely influenced by expressionism, took its place.

The repetition of expressionist forms in the postwar period had little but popular value.

Meanwhile the older expressionist painters had grown respectable. Feininger, Kandinsky, and Klee were professors at the state-supported Bauhaus. The Berlin Secession came under the direction of the expressionists when Schmidt-Rottluff was elected president in 1919 (Liebermann moved up to become president of the Prussian Academy of Fine Arts in 1920). Kokoschka, once the ostracized "Bürgerschreck," was appointed professor at the Dresden Academy about 1919: [14]

The revolution of 1918 produced as one of its first remarkable effects in the field of public art matters, the instatement of Kokoschka, the insurgent, as professor at the Dresden Academy. It was a weird experience to walk past plaster casts, through the tedious halls of this institution, and then suddenly to step into Kokoschka's workshop with its most unusual pictures of an altogether original chromatic quality. [15]

Max Beckmann had received an appointment at the Frankfurt Academy as early as 1916. Otto Mueller became professor at the Breslau Academy in 1919. Campendonk was called to the Krefeld School of Fine Arts in 1923 and to the long-established Düsseldorf Academy in 1926, where he was joined by Paul Klee in 1930. Pechstein accepted his election to the Prussian Academy of Fine Arts in 1922. Schmidt-Rottluff, who taught at the German Academy in Rome in 1930, was the last Brücke artist to become a member of the former august body in 1931.

A number of these painters turned toward more traditional forms of expression at this time, when they found that their private symbolism could not lead them toward a new universal iconography as they had hoped. The very important attitude of rebellion could not be maintained in the face of success and recognition.

One probable explanation for expressionism's loss of vitality after the war is its very success. Its popular acceptance and consequent crystallization in the work of minor artists would perhaps not have affected the inventiveness of some of its major painters and their followers as it did if the movement itself had not grown accustomed to flourishing on opposition. "In the previous discussions of so-called Expressionism it has been overlooked above all that this style of our time was engendered by rebels," [16] Kokoschka wrote recently.

In its beginnings expressionism was an exceedingly revolutionary movement with socially disruptive overtones, particularly erotic ones. This was in the post-Victorian era. But in the 'twenties many of the free-thinking notions of the expressionist painters were accepted, if not approved of, by most of the well-to-do bourgeoisie. Sexual equality was touted; heroines of movies and popular novels began to fling their chemises, along with caution, to the winds.

The situation facing expressionism was roughly comparable to that facing a revolutionary when the revolution is over and its objectives partly accomplished, partly unattainable. He quiets down, or is liquidated, or becomes accepted. All this happened to expressionism. With some of the reasons for its rebellion gone, its voice was stilled; to a large degree its spontaneity suffered thereby.

Wilhelm Worringer, whose essay *Abstraction and Empathy* had been a theoretical basis of abstract expressionist painting, was among the first to declare that expressionism was losing its vitality and betraying its weaknesses. Only one year after writing an essay in which he stressed the significant contribution of expressionism,[17] he gave vent to his disappointment with the movement in a lecture delivered in Munich in November, 1920.[18] Tracing the decrease of the social function of the artist since the baroque, he declared that expressionism had been the last struggle against the vacuity and meaninglessness of art, but that it was now a vain attempt in which "men in hopeless solitude wished to find a community. . . . Agitated revelations, visionary flashes of light have been handsomely framed, declared permanent, and degraded to peaceful wall decorations."[19] The revelation was fictitious; its form had become an accepted style, and the movement was now reaching a stage of mannerism. Worringer admonished the artist to be humble rather than conceited enough to imagine himself as the lone carrier of a new culture. Paraphrasing Spengler, whose first volume of *The Decline of the West* had already been published, Worringer maintained that art can only be peripheral in a scientific, industrialized civilization.

Carl Georg Heise had founded the expressionist publication *Genius* in 1919, but discontinued this important periodical in 1921. "The time of propaganda has passed . . . the work of the pioneers has been taken up by the publicists; the new art has become fashionable."[20] Heise thought that the period demanded a more searching criticism possible only from a clear, historical analysis. Later, in 1925, he announced the death of expressionism as a movement: "The new form of a spiritual attitude and its artistic expression, all that which we have become accustomed to calling expressionism in art and life, that is to say, the drive toward a transevaluation of the elements of a no longer feasible Weltanschauung in our century, disintegrates. Expressionism has become a fashion."[21] Heise put part of the blame on the art historians and critics, who, in praising the expressionist forms beyond all measure, had helped to stifle its further development. Some of the artists like Nolde, Kirchner, and Kokoschka, he believed, would continue to grow, but the movement itself had withered away.

Hans Tietze, once the champion of Kokoschka, made a similar pronouncement in a lecture in 1924: "Expressionism is dead . . . but those elements which were able to die have never been truly alive."[22] Gustav Hartlaub, who in 1919 had affirmed his belief in a renewal of religious faith through a new art form, now admitted his disappointment with expressionism. He judged the dispassionate cynicisms of new objectivity as betokening the most vital movement of a disillusioned era.

In 1925 Franz Roh published his book, *Nach-Expressionismus*,[23] in which he defined the new movement and proposed a scheme of opposites:

EXPRESSIONISM	POSTEXPRESSIONISM
ecstatic object	sober object
object is suppressed	object is clarified
dynamic	static
loud	quiet
diagonal and acute angles predominate	right angles parallel to the frame predominate
monumental	miniature
warm	cool
thick pigment	thin pigment
summary execution	careful execution . . .[24]

Roh considered postexpressionism a broad European movement, and discussed the recent work of the following men as being among its representatives: Picasso, Derain, Carrà, de Chirico, Severini, Miró, and the Germans Schrimpf, Mense, Davringhausen, Kanoldt, Dix, Grosz, Scholz, and Ernst.

The approach to realism—whether it is called magic realism, verism, or new objectivity—proposed a controlled certainty that had little firm foundation in the intellectual, spiritual, and moral limbo of Germany between the wars. New objectivity is now considered a precursor of surrealism, which in turn, like so many trends in the art of the second quarter of the twentieth century, showed elements found in expressionism itself.

Expressionism had long ceased to exist as a vital artistic manifestation in its original form when the National Socialists outlawed expressionist painting, exhibited it in the Degenerate Art Exhibitions of 1937, prohibited artists like Nolde [25] and Schmidt-Rottluff from painting, and forced others into starvation or exile. It might be suggested that the disappointment of German intellectuals over the failure of expressionism in art, literature, theater, and film to achieve the mission of a renewal of society led to a resigned disillusion that may well have contributed to their acceptance of a nihilist philosophy.

Appendix A

Chronik der Brücke

In the year 1902 the painters Bleyl and Kirchner met in Dresden. Heckel came to them through his brother, a friend of Kirchner. Heckel brought Schmidt-Rottluff along, whom he knew from Chemnitz. They came together in Kirchner's studio to work there. Here they found the opportunity to study the nude—the basis of all visual art—in its natural freedom. From drawing on this basis resulted the desire, common to all, to derive inspiration for work from life itself, and to submit to direct experience. In a book, *Odi profanum,* each individual drew and wrote down his ideas, and in this way they made it possible to compare their distinctive features. So they grew, very naturally, into a group which came to be called "Brücke." One inspired the other. From southern Germany Kirchner brought the woodcut, which he had revived under the inspiration of the old prints in Nürnberg. Heckel carved wooden figures. Kirchner enriched this technique with polychromy and sought the rhythm of closed form in pewter casting and in stone. Schmidt-Rottluff made the first lithographs on stone. The first exhibition of the group took place on its own premises in Dresden; it was given no recognition. Dresden, however, yielded much inspiration through its scenic charm and old culture. Here "Brücke" also found its first art-historical corroboration in Cranach, Beham and other medieval German masters. During an exhibit of Amiet in Dresden he was appointed to membership in the group. In 1905 Nolde followed, his fantastic style bringing a new feature to "Brücke." He enriched our exhibitions with his interesting etching technique and learned how we worked with the woodcut. On his invitation Schmidt-Rottluff went with him to Alsen, and later Schmidt-Rottluff and Heckel went to Dangast. The brisk air of the North Sea brought forth a monumental Impressionism, especially in Schmidt-Rottluff. During this time, in Dresden, Kirchner continued to work in closed composition and in the ethnographic museum found a parallel to his own creation in African negro sculpture and in Oceanic beam carvings. The desire to free himself from academic sterility led Pechstein to join "Brücke." Kirchner and Pechstein went to Gollverode, to work there together. An exhibition of "Brücke," including its new members, took place in the Salon Richter in Dresden and made a great impression on the young artists of Dresden. Heckel and Kirchner attempted to bring the new painting and its exhibition space into harmony. Kirchner furnished the rooms with murals and batiks, on which Heckel had worked with him. In 1907 Nolde resigned from "Brücke"; Heckel and Kirchner went to the Moritzburg lakes, in order to study the nude in the open air; Schmidt-Rottluff worked in Dangast on the completion of his color rhythm; Heckel travelled to Italy and brought back with him the inspiration of Etruscan art; Pechstein went to Berlin to work on a commission for decorations. He attempted to bring the new painting into the "Sezession." In Dresden Kirchner studied the hand printing of lithography. Bleyl, who had gone into teaching, left "Brücke" in 1909. Pechstein went to Dangast to join Heckel. During the same year both of them came to Kirchner at Moritzburg in order to do studies of the nude in the lake environment. In 1910 the "Neue Sezession" was organized after the rejection of younger German painters by the old "Sezession." In order to support Pechstein's position in the "Neue Sezession" Heckel, Kirchner and Schmidt-Rottluff also became members. In the first exhibition of the "Neue Sezession" they met Mueller. In his studio they saw Cranach's "Venus," which they themselves had always esteemed very highly. The sensuous harmony of his life with his work made Mueller a natural member of "Brücke." He introduced us to the fascination of distemper technique. In order to keep their endeavors pure the members of "Brücke" resigned from membership in the "Neue Sezession." They exchanged promises to exhibit only jointly in the "Sezession." Then followed an exhibit of "Brücke" in the entire gallery of the art salon, Gurlitt. Pechstein broke the confidence of the group by becoming a member of the "Sezession," and was expelled from "Brücke." The "Sonderbund" invited "Brücke" to join its Cologne exhibition of 1912, and commissioned Heckel and Kirchner to decorate and paint the chapel of the exhibition rooms. The majority of the members of "Brücke" is now in Berlin. "Brücke" has retained here its intrinsic character. From its internal coherence it radiates the new values of artistic creation to the modern artistic production throughout Germany. Uninfluenced by contemporary movements of cubism, futurism, etc., it fights for a human culture, the soil of all real art. "Brücke" owes its present position in the art world to these goals.[1]

E. L. Kirchner

Appendix B

Chief Periodicals Dealing with the German Expressionist Movement

Die Aktion, ed. Franz Pfemfert, Berlin, 1911–33.
Der Anbruch, ed. J. B. Neumann, Berlin, 1917–22.
Der Ararat, ed. Galerie Goltz, Munich, 1919–21.
Artlover, ed. J. B. Neumann, New York, 1926–37.
Die Bildenden Künste, ed. Victor Fleischer, Vienna, 1916–22.
Der Bildermann, ed. Paul Cassirer, Berlin, 1916.
Cicerone, ed. Georg Biermann, Leipzig, 1909–30.
Die Fackel, ed. Karl Kraus, Vienna, 1908–36.
Feuer, Weimar, 1919–21.
Genius, ed. Carl Georg Heise, Munich, 1919–21.
Jahrbuch der jungen Kunst, ed. Georg Biermann, Leipzig, 1920–24.
Kündung, eds. W. Niemeyer and Rosa Schapire, Hamburg, 1921.
Deutsche Kunst und Dekoration, publ. and ed. Alexander Koch, Darmstadt, 1897–
   1932.
Die Kunst, publ. F. Bruckmann, Munich, 1899–1937.
Kunst und Künstler, publ. Bruno Cassirer, ed. Karl Scheffler, Berlin, 1903–33.
Das Kunstblatt, ed. Paul Westheim, Weimar, Potsdam, Berlin, 1917–32.
Museum der Gegenwart, publication of German museum for contemporary art,
   Berlin, 1930–33.
Neue Blätter fur Kunst und Dichtung, ed. Hugo Zehder, Dresden, 1918–20.
Pan, publ. and ed. Paul Cassirer, Berlin, 1911–12.
Der Querschnitt, ed. H. von Wedderkopp, Berlin, 1921–36.
Der Sturm, publ. and ed. Herwath Walden, Berlin, 1910–32.
Zeitecho, "Ein Kriegstagebuch der Künstler," Munich, 1914–18.
Das Wort, Moscow, 1936–40.
Zeitschrift für Bildende Kunst, publ. E. A. Seemann, Leipzig, 1866–1932.

Appendix C

List of Most Important German and Foreign Participants in the Major Group Exhibitions

CODE

NKV	Neue Künstlervereinigung
SEC.	Secession
DBR	Der Blaue Reiter
EDH	Erster deutscher Herbstsalon
I	First Exhibition
II	Second Exhibition
III	Third Exhibition

Note: The futurists exhibiting in the *Erster deutscher Herbstsalon* were: Balla, Boccioni, Carrà, Russolo, Severini, and Soffici.

	BERLIN SEC. Summer 1905	BRÜCKE I *Dresden* Fall 1906	BRÜCKE II *Dresden* Winter 1906–07	NKV I *Munich* Winter 1909–10	NEW SEC I *Berlin* Spring 1910	BRÜCKE *Dresden, Gal. Arnold* Spring 1910
AMIET			*			*
BECKMANN	*					
BLEYL		*	*			
BLOCH						
D. BURLIUK						
CAMPENDONK						
CHAGALL						
DELAUNAY						
FEININGER						
HECKEL		*	*		*	*
HODLER						
HOFER				*		
JAWLENSKY	*			*		
KANDINSKY	*		*	*		
KANOLDT				*		
KIRCHNER		*	*		*	
KLEE						
KOKOSCHKA						
KUBIN				*		
LE FAUCONNIER						
MACKE						
MARC						
MODERSOHN-BECKER						
MORGNER						
MUELLER					*	*
MÜNTER				*		
MUNCH	*					
NAUEN	*					
NOLDE	*	*	*			
PECHSTEIN		*	*		*	*
PICASSO						
ROUSSEAU						
SCHIELE						
SCHMIDT-ROTTLUFF		*	*		*	*
VAN DONGEN						*
THE FUTURISTS						

NKV II Munich Winter 1910–11	NEW SEC. III Berlin Spring 1911	DBR I Munich Winter 1911–12	DBR II Munich Spring 1912	SONDERBUND Cologne Summer 1912	EDH – DER STURM Berlin Fall 1913	
				*		AMIET
						BECKMANN
						BLEYL
		*	*	*	*	BLOCH
*		*			*	D. BURLIUK
		*			*	CAMPENDONK
					*	CHAGALL
		*			*	DELAUNAY
					*	FEININGER
	*		*	*		HECKEL
				*		HODLER
				*		HOFER
*	*			*	*	JAWLENSKY
*	*	*	*	*	*	KANDINSKY
*				*		KANOLDT
	*		*	*		KIRCHNER
			*	*	*	KLEE
				*	*	KOKOSCHKA
*					*	KUBIN
*						LE FAUCONNIER
		*	*	*	*	MACKE
		*	*	*	*	MARC
				*		MODERSOHN-BECKER
			*	*		MORGNER
	*		*	*		MUELLER
*		*	*		*	MÜNTER
				*		MUNCH
				*		NAUEN
			*	*		NOLDE
	*		*	*		PECHSTEIN
*			*	*		PICASSO
		*			*	ROUSSEAU
				*		SCHIELE
				*		SCHMIDT-ROTTLUFF
*				*		VAN DONGEN
					*	THE FUTURISTS

NOTES

CHAPTER I

1. Gottfried Semper, *Der Stil in den technischen und tektonischen Künsten oder praktische Aesthetic* (Munich, 1878).
2. *Ibid.*, vol. I, *Textile Kunst*, p. 7.
3. *Ibid.*, p. 299.
4. Oskar Sommer, *Gottfried Semper: Vortrag gehalten in den Versammlungen des Architekten- und Ingeniuer-Verein, Frankfurt a/M., 1885* (Berlin, 1886), p. 7.
5. Conrad Fiedler to Adolf Hildebrand, December, 1875, quoted in Hans Eckstein (ed.), *Konrad Fiedler, Vom Wesen der Kunst* (Munich, 1942), p. 203.
6. *Ibid.*, p. 153.
7. *Ibid.*, p. 119.
8. Fiedler, in Victor Hammer (ed.), *Nine Aphorisms from the Notebooks of Conrad Fiedler* (Aurora, N. Y., 1941), p. 7.
9. Fiedler, in Eckstein, *op. cit.*, pp. 151–152.
10. *Ibid.*, p. 119.
11. *Ibid.*, p. 140.
12. Fiedler, quoted in H. Schaefer-Simmern, *The Unfolding of Artistic Activity* (Berkeley and Los Angeles, 1950), p. xi.
13. Adolf Hildebrand, *The Problem of Form in Painting and Sculpture,* translated by Max Meyer and Robert M. Ogden (New York, 1907), p. 14.
14. *Ibid.*, pp. 11–12.
15. *Ibid.*, p. 19.
16. Heinrich Wölfflin, "Adolf von Hildebrand," *Kunst und Künstler,* XVI (1918), 19.
17. Thieme-Becker (ed.), "Adolf von Hildebrand," *Allgemeines Lexikon der bildenden Künstler,* vol. XVII (Leipzig, 1924).
18. Wölfflin, *op. cit.*, 13–14.
19. Robert Vischer, *Das optische Formgefühl. Ein Beitrag zur Ästhetik* (Leipzig, 1873).
20. Theodor Lipps, *Aesthetik, Psychologie des Schönen in der Kunst,* vol. I, *Grundlegung der Aesthetik* (Hamburg, 1903), p. 207.

21. Vernon Lee, *Beauty and Ugliness* (London, 1912), p. 53.
22. Paul Signac, "D'Eugène Delacroix au néo-impressionisme," *Pan,* IV (1898), 55–62.
23. Henry van de Velde in 1902, quoted in Carola Giedion-Welcker, *Paul Klee* (New York, 1952), p. 63.
24. Walter Crane, *Ideals in Art* (London, 1905).
25. Paul Sérusier, *ABC de la peinture* (Paris, 1950).
26. Albert Gleizes and Jean Metzinger, *Du Cubisme* (Paris, 1912).
27. Wassily Kandinsky, *Punkt und Linie zur Fläche,* Bauhaus Book no. 9 (Munich, 1926).
28. Paul Klee, *Pädagogisches Skizzenbuch,* Bauhaus Book no. 2 (Munich, 1925).
29. Hermann Bahr, *Expressionismus* (Munich, 1919), p. 70.
30. The meaning of Riegl's "Kunstwillen" is better expressed as "artistic purpose" than by its usual translation as "will to art."
31. Paul Frankl, *Das System der Kunstwissenschaft* (Brünn, 1938), p. 999.
32. Alois Riegl, *Spätrömische Kunstindustrie* (1st published, 1901) (Vienna, 1927), p. 9.
33. Wilhelm Worringer, *Abstraktion und Einfühlung* (1st published, 1908); English edition, *Abstraction and Empathy* (London, 1953).
34. Worringer, *Form Problems of the Gothic* (New York, 1918), p. 21.
35. Worringer, *Abstraction and Empathy,* p. 14.
36. The other book is Kandinsky's *Concerning the Spiritual in Art.*
37. Franz Marc, "Die konstruktiven Ideen der neuen Malerei," *Pan,* II (1911–1912), 530. This weekly periodical *Pan,* published by Cassirer from 1911 to 1912, shares only the name with the earlier quarterly *Pan,* published by Otto Julius Bierbaum and Julius Meier-Graefe in Berlin from 1895–1900.
38. Worringer, "Kritische Gedanken zur neuen Kunst," *Genius,* II (1919), 230. Only two years after writing this essay, Worringer was one of the first critics

to announce the "end of Expressionism," because of the poor response of modern society to the budding revival of spiritual art. *Künstlerische Zeitfragen* (Munich, 1921). Cf. chapter xxv.

39. Hans Tietze, "Der deutsche Expressionismus," lecture given in Vienna in 1924, published in Tietze, *Lebendige Kunstwissenschaft* (Vienna, 1925), p. 24. The Viennese art historian Hans Tietze, an early patron of Kokoschka, was also one of the first spokesmen of the expressionist movement, although his statements were always more guarded and conservative than Worringer's.

40. See chapter xviii.

41. Fritz Burger, *Einführung in die moderne Kunst,* 1915; Herwath Walden, *Expressionismus,* 1918; Hermann Bahr, *Expressionismus,* 1919; Gustav Hartlaub, *Kunst und Religion,* 1919; Wilhelm Hausenstein, *Über Expressionismus in der Malerei,* 1919; Joachim Kirchner, *Die Voraussetzungen des Expressionismus,* 1919; Theodor Däubler, *Im Kampf um die moderne Kunst,* 1920; Eckart von Sydow, *Die deutsche expressionistische Kultur und Malerei,* 1920; Paul Fechter, *Der Expressionismus,* 1920; Franz Landsberger, *Impressionismus und Expressionismus,* 1920; Georg Marzynsky, *Die Methode des Expressionismus,* 1921; Oskar Pfister, *Expressionism in Art,* 1922; and Max Deri, *Naturalismus, Idealismus, Expressionismus,* 1922.

42. Riegl was an art historian little concerned with contemporary creative activity. The Vienna school of art history, which included Franz Wickhoff and Max Dvořák, had an altogether new approach to the history of art as universal history.

43. Bahr, *op. cit.,* pp. 104–105.

44. *Ibid.,* pp. 111–112.

45. *Ibid.,* p. 115.

46. Kasimir Edschmidt, *Das Bücherdekameron* (Berlin, 1923).

47. Klee, *Schöpferische Konfession* (Berlin, 1920). See chapter xxiii.

CHAPTER II

1. Wilhelm Worringer, "Art Questions of the Day," *Monthly Criterion* (Aug., 1927).

2. Worringer, *Form Problems of the Gothic* (New York [1918]), p. 77.

3. *Ibid.,* p. 84.

4. *Ibid.,* pp. 77, 83.

5. *Ibid.*

6. Karl Scheffler, *Die europäische Kunst im neunzehnten Jahrhundert* (Berlin, 1927), vol. II, p. 212.

7. Scheffler, *Der Geist der Gotik* (Leipzig, 1925).

8. *Ibid.,* p. 39.

9. *Ibid.,* pp. 106–107.

10. Scheffler, *Deutsche Kunst* (Berlin, 1915), pp. 93–94.

11. Heinrich Wölfflin, *Die Bamberger Apokalypse* (Munich, 1920).

12. *Ibid.,* p. 6.

13. *Ibid.,* pp. 13–14.

14. "Die Bamberger Apokalypse, herausgegeben von Heinrich Wölfflin," *Kunstblatt,* III (Dec., 1919).

15. Wölfflin, *Italien und das deutsche Kunstgefühl* (Munich, 1931).

16. See chapter vi.

17. Paul Westheim, *Das Holzschnittbuch* (Berlin, 1921), p. 186.

18. Max Friedländer, "Das Schicksal des Holzschnitts," *Die neue Rundschau,* XXX (1919), 1001–1005.

19. Willi Wolfradt, "Holschnitte von Gerhard Marks," *Kunstblatt,* VII (1923), 141.

20. E. L. Kirchner, in Peter Selz, "E. L. Kirchner's 'Chronik der Brücke,'" *College Art Journal,* X (1950), 50. See Appendix A.

21. *Ibid.,* p. 51.

22. Kirchner, quoted in Westheim, *Künstlerbekenntnisse* (Berlin [1923]), p. 232.

23. Max Sauerlandt, *Die Kunst der letzten dreissig Jahre,* lecture delivered in 1933 (Hamburg, 1948), p. 117.

24. Heinrich Alfred Schmidt, *Die Gemälde und Zeichnungen von Matthias Grünewald* (Strasbourg, 1907–1911).

25. Adolf Frey, *Arnold Böcklin* (Stuttgart, 1903), pp. 215, 245, 281.

26. J.-K. Huysmans, "Les Grünewalds du Musée de Colmar," *Trois primitifs* (Paris, 1905). Huysmans wrote about Grünewald first in his novel *Là Bas* (Paris, 1891).

27. Max Liebermann, *in* Uhde Bernays (ed.), *Künstlerbriefe über Kunst* (Dresden, 1926), p. 649.

28. Statement by Max Beckmann, personal interview, Chicago, Jan., 1948.

29. Ludwig Meidner, *Septemberschrei* (Berlin, 1919).

30. Max Deri, *Naturalismus, Idealismus, Expressionismus* (Leipzig, 1922), p. 73.

31. Paul F. Schmidt, "Die internationale Ausstellung des Sonderbundes in Köln," *Zeitschrift für Bildende Kunst,* N.F., XXIII (1912), 234.

32. Paul Fechter, *Der Expressionismus* (Munich, 1920), pp. 32–33.

33. G. F. Hartlaub, "Die Kunst und die neue Gnosis," *Kunstblatt,* vol. I (1917); and *Kunst und Religion* (Leipzig, 1919).

34. Wilhelm Hausenstein, *Über Expressionismus in der Malerei* (Berlin, 1919).

35. Worringer, *Künstlerische Zeitfragen*. Cf. chapter xxv.

36. Carl Einstein, *Die Kunst des 20. Jahrhunderts,* vol. XVI of *Propyläen Kunstgeschichte* (Berlin, 1926), pp. 105–106.

37. Richard Hamann, *Die deutsche Malerei vom Rokoko bis zum Expressionismus* (Leipzig, 1925), p. 458.

38. Novalis, *Schriften,* ed. Paul Kluckhohn (1928), vol. II, p. 98.

39. C. D. Friedrich, in Carus, *Friedrich der Landschaftsmaler* (Dresden, 1841), reprinted in *Genius,* II (1920), 88–90.

40. Marc, in *Pan* (March, 1912), published in connection with exhibition "Der Blaue Reiter" at the Thannhauser Gallery in Munich; translated by Peter Thoene (pseud.), *Modern German Art* (Harmondsworth, England, 1938), p. 62.

41. Wassily Kandinsky, "Text Artista," *Wassily Kandinsky Memorial* (New York, 1945), p. 63.

42. Kandinsky, "Über die Formfrage," in Wassily Kandinsky and Franz Marc (eds.), *Der Blaue Reiter* (Munich, 1912), p. 77.

43. Ludwig Coellen, *Die neue Malerei* (Munich, 1912), p. 21.

44. August L. Mayer, *Grünewald der Romantiker des Schmerzes* (Munich, n.d.).

45. P. F. Schmidt, "Erich Heckels Anfänge," *Zeitschrift für bildende Kunst,* LX (1920), 258.

46. Schmidt, "Romantik und Gegenwart," *Feuer,* III (1922), 225.

CHAPTER III

1. Max Schmidt, *Klinger* (Bielefeld und Leipzig, 1899).

2. *Ibid.,* p. 3.

3. Anselm Feuerbach, quoted in *German Art from the Fifteenth to the Twentieth Century,* exhibition catalog (Philadelphia, 1936–1937), p. 126.

4. Emil Nolde, *Das eigene Leben* (Berlin, 1931), p. 203.

5. Rudolf Schick, *Tagebuch-Aufzeichnungen aus den Jahren 1866, 1868, 1869 über Arnold Böcklin* (Berlin, 1901), p. 194.

6. Paul Clemen, *Contemporary German Art,* Introduction to exhibition catalog, Art Institute of Chicago (Berlin, 1908), p. 18.

7. Julius Meier-Graefe, *Der Fall Böcklin* (Stuttgart, 1905), p. 110.

8. Carl Schurz Memorial Foundation, *German Art from the Fifteenth to the Twentieth Century* (Philadelphia, 1936), p. 130.

9. Werner Weisbach, *Impressionismus,* vol. II (Berlin, 1911), pp. 279–280.

10. Meier-Graefe, *Hans von Marées* (Munich, 1910).

11. Franz Marc, "Zwei Bilder," in Kandinsky and Marc (eds.), *Der Blaue Reiter* (Munich, 1912), pp. 9–10.

12. Paul Fechter, *Der Expressionismus* (Munich, 1920), p. 22.

13. Joachim Kirchner, "Deutsche Meister des Dekorativ-Monumentalen Stils des 19. Jahrhunderts," *Deutsche Kunst und Dekoration,* XLVII (1921), 260.

14. Schmid, *op. cit.,* p. 11.

15. *Ibid.,* p. 124.

16. Otto Julius Bierbaum, *Stuck* (Bielefeld and Leipzig, 1899), p. 67.

17. Wilhelm Hausenstein, *Kunstgeschichte* (Berlin, 1927), p. 444.

18. See chapter xiv.

19. Hausenstein, *op. cit.,* p. 406.

20. Edwin Redslob, *Fünf Generationen* (Berlin, 1948), p. 27.

CHAPTER IV

1. The term "realism" is used in Courbet's meaning of the word, implying both a method of representation of verisimilitude and a social awareness.

2. Max Liebermann, "Die Phantasie in der Malerei" (1916), in *Gesammelte Schriften* (Berlin, 1922), p. 25.

3. Karl Scheffler, *Die europäische Kunst im neunzehnten Jahrdert,* p. 107.

4. Lovis Corinth, *Selbstbiographie* (Leipzig, 1926), p. 131. Corinth's chauvinistic attitude is revealed throughout this autobiography.

5. Julius Held, *Lovis Corinth,* catalog of retrospective exhibition (New York, 1950–1951) [p. 9].

6. Kirchner, in a letter to his brother, Hans Walter Kirchner, Oct. 10, 1937, "Aus nachgelassenen Briefen E. L. Kirchners," *Das Kunstwerk,* V (1951), 19–20.

7. Emile Zola, *Proudhon et Courbet, Oeuvres complètes* (Paris, 1927–1929).

8. Max Sauerlandt, *Die Kunst der letzten dreissig Jahre* (Hamburg, 1948), p. 49.

9. Berlin, Kronprinzen Palais, Neukastel (Palatinate), and Bremen, Ratskeller.

10. Carl Einstein, *Die Kunst des 20. Jahrhunderts* (Berlin, 1926), p. 102.

11. A typical example is the triptych *The Days of Our Years Are Threescore Years and Ten* (1898) in

the Bayerische Gemäldesammlungen, Munich.

12. See chapter vi.

13. J. P. Hodin, "Expressionism," *Horizon,* XIX (1949), 45–46.

14. Curt Glaser, "Die Geschichte der berliner Sezession," *Kunst und Künstler,* XXVI (1927), 16.

15. Liebermann, speech at the opening of the second exhibition of the Berlin Secession in 1900, quoted in *Gesammelte Schriften,* p. 157.

16. Glaser, *op. cit.,* p. 18.

17. Corinth, *op. cit.,* p. 149.

18. Liebermann, "Zehn Jahre Sezession," *op. cit.,* p. 274.

19. *Ibid.,* p. 272.

CHAPTER V

1. *"Scholle"* is best translated as "native soil."

2. Paul Clemen, *Contemporary German Art* (Berlin, 1908), pp. 29–30.

3. Hans Hildebrandt, introduction to catalog *Adolf Hoelzel,* retrospective exhibition on the anniversary of his hundredth birthday (Stuttgart [1953]) [p. 10].

4. Adolf Hoelzel, "Einige aphoristische Sätze," *Hoelzel und sein Kreis* (Stuttgart, 1916), p. 5.

5. Hoelzel, "Über künstlerische Ausdrucksmitte und deren Verhältnis zu Natur und Bild," *Die Kunst,* X (1905), 81–88, 106–113, 121–142.

6. See chapter xvi.

7. The large exhibition of paintings by Hoelzel and Dill at the Galerie Arnold in Dresden took place in 1901 before the Brücke painters had arrived in Dresden.

8. Hoelzel, quoted in Hildebrandt, *op. cit.* [p. 34].

9. Nora Wydenbruck, *Rilke: Man and Poet* (New York, 1950), p. 86.

10. Rainer Maria Rilke, *Worpswede* (Bielefeld and Leipzig, 1903), p. 27.

11. *Ibid.,* p. 45.

12. Hans Bethge, *Worpswede,* vol. XXXII of Richard Muther, *Die Kunst* (Berlin, 1907), p. 42.

13. See chapter xviii.

14. Rilke met Vogeler in Florence in 1897. Cf. Rainer Maria Rilke, "H. Vogeler," *Deutsche Kunst und Dekoration,* X (1902).

15. After World War I, Vogeler left Germany for the Soviet Union, where he is still active at the time of this writing.

16. Wydenbruck, *op. cit.,* p. 67.

17. Paula Modersohn-Becker, letter to Otto Modersohn, Paris, 1903, *in* S. D. Gallwitz (ed.), *Briefe und Tagebuchblätter von Paula Modersohn-Becker* (Linz, 1920), p. 204.

18. Modersohn-Becker, letter to Clara Rilke-Westhoff,

quoted in Rilke-Westhoff's contribution to Rolf Hetsch (ed.), *Paula Modersohn-Becker* (Berlin, 1932), p. 49.

19. Modersohn-Becker, letter to the artist's mother, 1907, quoted in Gallwitz, *op. cit.,* p. 256.

20. *Ibid.,* p. 192.

21. Rainer Maria Rilke, *Briefe an seinen Verleger,* vol. II (Berlin, 1949), p. 316.

22. Modersohn-Becker, letter to her family, Paris, 1900, *in* Gallwitz, *op. cit.,* p. 130.

CHAPTER VI

1. This discussion of the symbolist movement in literature is based for the most part on the original documents contained in Guy Michaud, *La Doctrine symboliste (Documents)* (Paris, 1947).

2. René Ghil, "Notre Ecole," *La Décadence,* no. 1 (Oct. 1, 1886), 7.

3. Stéphane Mallarmé, "Réponse à une enquête," *in* J. Huret, *Enquête sur l'evolution littéraire* (Paris), p. 60.

4. Mallarmé, *Ecrits pour l'art,* no. 1 (Jan. 7, 1887), 5.

5. Paul Valéry, "Lettre à Mallarmé," quoted in H. Mondor, *Vie de Mallarmé* (Paris, [1943]), p. 607.

6. Jean Royère, "Sur la poésie actuelle," *La Phalange* (Paris, 1910), p. 381.

7. Quoted in Michaud, *op. cit.,* p. 101.

8. Saint-Antoine, "Qu'est-ce que le symbolisme? (1894)," *ibid.,* pp. 48–50; Henri de Régnier, *Figures et caractères* (Paris, 1900), pp. 333–336; Paul Claudel, *Art Poétique* (Paris, 1904), pp. 151–153.

9. E. Raynaud, *in* Michaud, *op. cit.*

10. Maurice Denis, "Impressionnistes et symbolistes," *Théories* (Paris, 1920), p. 27.

11. Paul Gauguin, *in* Parjean de Rotonchamp, *Paul Gauguin* (Paris, 1904), p. 210.

12. Denis, "Notes sur la peinture religieuse," *op. cit.,* p. 33.

13. Paul Sérusier, *ABC de la peinture* (Paris, 1950), p. 33.

14. Sérusier, "Extracts de lettres à des élèves et notes de cours (1910–1912)," *ibid.,* p. 164.

15. Arthur Schopenhauer, *The World as Will and Idea,* in Thomas Mann (ed.), *The Living Thoughts of Schopenhauer* (New York, 1939), p. 90.

16. T. de Wyzewa, "L'Art wagnerien: la littérature," *Nos Maîtres* (Paris, 1886), pp. 45–50.

17. Huysmans was also one of the first modern critics to appreciate Grünewald. J.-K. Huysmans, *Là Bas* (Paris, 1891) and *Les Grünewalds du Musée de Colmar* (Paris, 1905).

18. Charles Chassé, *Le Mouvement symboliste dans l'art de XIX siècle* (Paris, 1947), p. 48.

19. Odilon Redon, *A soi-même; journal (1867–1915)* (Paris, 1922).

20. Max Beckmann, *On My Painting* (New York, 1941), p. 11.

21. Redon, quoted in Giedion-Welcker, *Paul Klee* (New York, 1952), p. 108.

22. Toorop exhibited a similar series of paintings in Munich in 1893, and exerted a considerable influence on German development.

23. Gustav Schiefler, *Edvard Munchs graphische Kunst* (Dresden, 1923), p. 2.

24. No mention of this connection is made in the most important analysis of Jugendstil published thus far: Fritz Schmalenbach's *Jugendstil* (Würzburg, 1935). Henry R. Lenning's *The Art Nouveau* (The Hague, 1951) overlooks it completely, and Clay Lancaster's otherwise excellent essay "Oriental Contributions to Art Nouveau," *Art Bulletin*, XXXIV (1952), 297–310, neglects to mention this relationship. It is briefly hinted at in N. Pevsner's *Pioneers of the Modern Movement* (London, 1936). Henry R. Hope's brilliant doctoral dissertation "The Sources of Art Nouveau" (Harvard University, Dec., 1942) has never been published. It is to be hoped that Hans Curjel's forthcoming comprehensive study of the art around 1900 will delve more deeply into this problem.

25. A reverse application of the close relationship of symbolism and Jugendstil art is submitted by Hans Curjel when he calls Rainer Maria Rilke in his early period "a typical art nouveau figure" ("Vom neunzehnten zum zwanzigsten Jahrhundert," *Um 1900*, exhibition catalog [Zurich, 1952], p. 17). Art nouveau was a manifestation of symbolism, not vice versa.

26. Schmalenbach, *op. cit.*, p. 26.

27. Ernst Haeckel's *Kunstformen in der Natur* (1899) is a highly important source for this group.

28. Henry van de Velde, "Prinzipielle Erklärungen," in *Kunstgewerbliche Laienpredigen* (Weimar, 1902), p. 188.

29. Van de Velde, *Die Renaissance im neuen Kunstgewerbe* [Leipzig, 1903], p. 104.

30. Van de Velde, "Prinzipielle Erklärungen," pp. 190–191.

31. *Van Nu en Straks* was a review of literature and the arts connected with the Flemish avant-garde, published from 1893 to 1901, first in Brussels and later in Antwerp. Among the artists who figure in its important first volume are Ensor, Meunier, Minne, Thorn-Prikker, Toorop, van de Velde, van Gogh, van Rysselberghe.

32. *Van Nu en Straks,* I (1893), 3, fig. 26.

33. *Ibid.*, fig. 27.

34. Schmalenbach, *op. cit.*, pp. 31–32.

35. The leading German Jugendstil periodicals were: Berlin: *Pan*, 1895–1900; *Die Insel*, 1900–1902. Munich: *Die Jugend*, 1896—; *Simplicissimus*, 1896 —; *Dekorative Kunst*, 1897–1929; *Kunst und Handwerk*, 1850–1932; *Die Kunst*, 1899—. Darmstadt: *Deutsche Kunst und Dekoration*, 1897–1924; *Innen-Dekoration*, 1890—. Vienna: *Ver Sacrum*, 1898–1899; *Kunst und Kunsthandwerk*, 1898–1921.

36. A partial table of contents is added at this point: Cover design by Stuck; excerpt from Nietzsche's *Thus Spake Zarathustra;* invocatory prose poem by Paul Scheerbart illustrated by Axel Gallen; hymn by Novalis; reproduction of Böcklin's *Dragonkiller;* poetry by Paul Verlaine and Stéphane Mallarmé (the latter with an illustration by Fernand Khnopff); a drinking song by Richard Dehmel; Vallotton's woodcut of Robert Schumann (original); an excerpt from Fontane's autobiography; appreciation of Dürer's woodcuts by W. von Seidlitz with reproductions of woodcuts; etching by Liebermann; a section on the crafts with a contribution by Wilhelm Bode; a news section on art, literature, the theater, and music in Europe.

37. *Transactions of the National Association for the Advancement of Art and Its Application to Industry* (Liverpool, 1888), p. 216.

38. *Les XX* was founded in 1884 with Ensor, Khnopff, Toorop, and van Rysselberghe among the charter members. Van de Velde became a member of the group in 1889 as did Rodin. This was the year in which Ensor's *Entry of Christ into Brussels* was the focus of attention.

39. Thorn-Prikker was also noted for his work in the design of furniture, batik, tapestry, and mosaic. In the same period Toulouse-Lautrec's posters and programs, or the posters designed by Cheret and Steinlen in Paris, also linked painting with applied design.

40. Otto Julius Bierbaum, *Deutsche Chansons (Brettl Lieder)*, pp. ix–x, quoted in Dika Newlin, *Bruckner, Mahler, Schönberg* (New York, 1947), p. 218. Counterinfluences between trends in literature and the visual arts around the turn of the century are frequent.

41. In America, Louis Sullivan could make a similar pronouncement as early as 1885 in a paper read to the convention of the Western Association of Architects in St. Louis: "Our art is for the day, suited to the day, and will also change as the day changes." "Characteristics and Tendencies of American Architecture." *Inland Architect and Builder*, VI (Nov., 1885), 58.

42. S. Bing, "L'Art Nouveau," *Architectural Record,* XII (Aug., 1912), 283.

43. "The most hidden, but also the most important constituent part of van de Velde's art is his tradition. . . . This tradition is with van de Velde as with all original and functional artists of the present the Rococo. . . . The Rococo was not, as is generally believed, the end and decadence of a brilliant art epoch, but it contained the first beginnings of a new style, which we can only now develop after it was suppressed by the noise of the world for over a hundred years. It takes attentive eyes to see the Rococo through the work of the moderns, especially van de Velde's, but once one has noticed it, it becomes irrepressible, and one is pleased that tradition is not lacking in modern architecture." Karl Scheffler, quoted in van de Velde, "Das Ornament als Symbol," *Die Renaissance im modernen Kunstgewerbe* (Leipzig, 1901), pp. 94–95.

44. Van de Velde, *ibid.,* pp. 65–66.

45. Lancaster, *op. cit.,* pp. 297–310.

46. Ernst Michalski, "Die entwicklungsgeschichtliche Bedeutung des Jugendstils," *Repertorium für Kunstwissenschaft,* XLVI (1925), 133–149.

47. See chapter vi.

48. Robert Breuer, "Batiks," *Kunst und Handwerk,* vol. LIV (1903–1904).

49. Van de Velde to Sigfried Giedion, *in* Sigfried Giedion, *Space, Time and Architecture* (Cambridge, Mass., 1946), p. 126.

50. Van de Velde, "Das Ornament als Symbol," pp. 92–93.

51. Similar statements were made in various places at the same time. In England, Lewis Day stressed the importance of machinery, steam power, and electricity as early as the 'eighties (Lewis F. Day, *Every Day Art* [London, 1882]). In the United States, Frank Lloyd Wright glorified the scientist, inventor, and engineer in his manifesto "The Arts and Crafts of the Machine," delivered in Chicago in 1903. In Austria, Otto Wagner's *Moderne Architektur* (Vienna, 1895) foresaw an architecture based on the new structural principles and contemporary materials.

52. Van de Velde, "Die Rolle der Ingenieure in der modernen Architektur," in *Die Renaissance im modernen Kunstgewerbe,* p. 111.

53. *Ibid.,* p. 110.

54. Van de Velde, "Geschichte der Renaissance im modernen Kunstgewerbe," in *Die Renaissance im modernen Kunstgewerbe,* p. 30.

55. August Endell, "Möglichkeit und Ziele einer neuen Architektur," *Deutsche Kunst und Dekoration,* I (1898), 141.

56. Schmalenbach, *op. cit.,* p. 61.

57. Bing, *op. cit.,* p. 281.

58. Destroyed by bombing in World War II.

59. *La Libre Esthètique* was a regrouping of the former *Les Vingt.*

60. Bradley exhibited with *La Libre Esthètique* in Brussels in its second show in 1894. Among the other invited artists were: William Morris, Walter Crane, Holman Hunt, M. Luce, Camille, Feliz, Georges and Lucien Pissarro, Vallotton, Max Klinger, and Ludwig von Hofmann.

61. Alexandre Benois, *The Russian School of Painting* (New York, 1916), p. 189.

62. Leon Bakst was to do a cover page for *Jugend* in 1903 (no. 43).

63. Translated as *The World of Art.* This is also the name of an association of Moscow artists.

64. Christian Brinton, preface to Benois, *op. cit.,* p. vi.

65. Van de Velde in the introduction to vol. IV, *Deutsche Kunst und Dekoration* (1900).

66. Bing, *op. cit.,* p. 283.

67. Adolf Loos, "Ornament und Verbrechen" (1908), in *Trotzdem* (Innsbruck, 1930), p. 89.

68. *Ibid.,* p. 82.

69. Usually translated as "objectivity," it also means "functionalism."

70. Was the neo-rococo of the Jugendstil replaced by a neo-neoclassicism or neo-Biedermeier? Endell's Elvira Studio recalls Cuvilliés' Amalienburg; Mies van der Rohe considers Schinkel his prototype.

71. The first issue of the *Dial,* published in 1889, was illustrated with woodcuts by Rickets and Shannon "printed from the wood to insure the greater sweetness of printing." John Rewald (ed.), Camille Pissarro, *Letters to His Son Lucien* (New York, 1943), p. 138.

72. Julius Meier-Graefe, *Félix Vallotton* (Berlin and Paris, 1898), p. 13. Cf. fig. 8.

73. "C'est à l'automne de 1894, à Pont-Aven, que Gauguin composa ses premières planches de bois d'apres des souvenirs des ses tableaux de Tahiti." Marcel Guérin, *L'Oeuvre gravé de Gauguin* (Paris, 1927), vol. I, pp. xiii–xiv.

74. As an intimate friend of Meier-Graefe, Vallotton's publisher in Berlin, Munch was undoubtedly familiar with Vallotton's work even before his 1896 trip to Paris.

75. Munch was certainly familiar with Gauguin's woodcuts when he made his first experiments in that medium in 1896. It is interesting that Munch's first woodcuts were actually colored.

76. Wilhelm Michel, "Münchner Graphik: Holzschnitt und Lithographie," *Deutsche Kunst und Dekoration,* XVI (1905), 437–457.

CHAPTER VII

1. Statement by Erich Heckel, personal interview, Hemmenhofen (Bodensee), Germany, Sept. 7, 1953.
2. Richard Müller's precise draftsmanship was an important influence on his two famous pupils George Grosz and Otto Dix.
3. Statement by Heckel, personal interview, Sept. 7, 1953.
4. W. von Seidlitz, "Dresdens junge Künstlerschaft," *Pan,* II (1896), 140.
5. E. L. Kirchner, "Anfänge und Ziel," *Kroniek van hedendaagesche Kunst en Kultur,* I (June, 1935), 5.
6. *Ibid.,* p. 6.
7. L. de Marsale, "Über Kirchners Graphik," *Genius,* III (1921), 251.
8. Kirchner, *op. cit.,* p. 7.
9. See chapter vi.
10. Zürich, Kunstgewerbemuseum.
11. Hans Curjel, "Konfrontationen," *Werk,* XXXIX (Dec., 1952), 382–388.
12. Kirchner, in a letter to Curt Valentin dated April 17, 1937, in *Ernst Ludwig Kirchner,* exhibition catalog (New York, 1952), p. 11.
13. *Ibid.*
14. *Ibid.,* pp. 11–12. The influence of Rembrandt's drawings and etchings on the early graphic work of the Brücke painters, especially Kirchner and Schmidt-Rottluff, is considerable.
15. Kirchner, "Anfänge und Ziel."
16. Kirchner, "Short Biography of Kirchner" (unpublished typewritten manuscript written by Kirchner in English around 1932). This manuscript, as well as a wealth of further original Kirchner documentation, is in the possession of Hans Bolliger, Bern, who has made it available to me.
17. See chapter xiv.
18. *Die Kunst,* IX (May, 1904), 388.
19. Kirchner, in letter to Valentin, April 17, 1937, in *Ernst Ludwig Kirchner,* p. 12; Kirchner, "Anfänge und Ziel," p. 5.
20. Walter Kern, "Un contributo allo studio dell'Expressionismo Tedesco," *La Biennale di Venezia,* No. 7 (1952), p. 24. Kern labeled this print a lithograph; it is a woodcut.
21. L. de Marsale, *op. cit.,* 252.
22. This woodcut, Schiefler 43, appeared in the Brücke portfolio of 1908.
23. It seems that Kirchner—and the other Brücke artists—learned a great deal about the qualities of paper from Kirchner's father, a paper chemist, who taught in that capacity at the Chemnitz crafts school. Heckel, letter to me, July 16, 1952.
24. Marsale, "Über die plastischen Arbeiten Kirchners," *Cicerone,* XVII (1925), 694–701.
25. Kirchner, quoted in Peter Selz, "E. L. Kirchner's 'Chronik der Brücke,'" *College Art Journal,* X (Fall, 1950), 50. See Appendix A.
26. Gustav Schiefler, *Meine Graphik-Sammlung* (Hamburg, 1927).
27. Erich Heckel, letter to me, July 16, 1952.
28. *Ibid.* Statement by Heckel, personal interview, Sept. 7, 1953.
29. Heckel, personal interview, Sept. 7, 1953.
30. *Ibid.*
31. Arranged by Gotthard Kühl, director of the Dresden Academy, 1904–1905.
32. Statement by Heckel, personal interview, Sept. 7, 1953.
33. Heckel did linoleum cuts, however, as early as 1903. *Ibid.*
34. Statement by Karl Schmidt-Rottluff, personal interview, Berlin-Dahlem, June 27, 1953.
35. Schmidt-Rottluff, in a letter to me, July 11, 1952.
36. Heckel, in a letter to me, July 16, 1952.
37. Schmidt-Rottluff, in a letter to me, July 11, 1952.
38. Heckel, personal interview, Sept. 7, 1953.
39. *Ibid.*
40. Schiefler, *op. cit.,* p. 51.
41. The subject matter of the burlap paintings and sculpture, according to a photograph of the studio, was highly erotic.
42. Paul F. Schmidt comments on their rarity as early as 1920. "Erich Heckels Anfänge," *Zeitschrift für bildende Kunst,* LV (1920), 262.
43. Wilhelm F. Arntz, "Die Künstlergruppe 'Brücke,' 1905–1913," *Paula Modersohn und die Maler der "Brücke,"* catalog (Bern, 1948), p. 7.
44. Schiefler, *op. cit.,* p. 49.
45. Kirchner, *in* Selz, *op. cit.,* p. 50.
46. Photograph in Heckel studio in possession of Hans Bolliger, Zürich.
47. G. F. Hartlaub, *Die Graphik des Expressionismus in Deutschland* (Stuttgart, 1947), p. 24.
48. Cf. chapter vi for a brief survey of the development of the modern woodcut.
49. Schmidt, *op. cit.,* 258.
50. Heckel, in a letter to me, July 16, 1952.
51. Statement by Heckel, personal interview, Sept. 7, 1953.
52. According to still unpublished material in the possession of Dr. Wentzel, Stuttgart. I have not seen this material, but have heard about its existence and contents from several reputable sources.
53. Schmidt-Rottluff, in a letter to me, July 11, 1952.
54. Pechstein, in a letter to Biermann, *in* Georg Biermann, *Max Pechstein* (Leipzig, 1920), p. 14.

55. Pechstein, in a letter to me, Sept. 23, 1952.

56. Nolde, *Jahre der Kämpfe* (Berlin, 1934), p. 163.

57. Max Sauerlandt, in his generally excellent treatment of the development of modern art, says erroneously: "The first painting by van Gogh appeared at the Berlin Secession only in the year 1908" (*Die Kunst der letzten 30 Jahre* [Berlin, 1935], p. 67). Van Gogh had been seen in Germany many times before this. The exhibition at the Galerie Arnold in Dresden in 1905 was actually the third van Gogh show in Germany. The first (Cézanne, van Gogh, Gauguin, Munch, Bonnard) was held in 1903 at the Berlin Secession; the second (Cézanne, van Gogh, Gauguin), in 1904 at the Munich Artists Association.

58. Joachim Kirchner, "Die Voraussetzungen des Expressionismus," *Monatshefte für Kunstwissenschaft*, XII (1919), 12.

59. Wilhelm Worringer, "Kritische Gedanken zur neuen Kunst," *Genius*, II (1920), 228.

60. See chapter iv.

61. *Edvard Munchs Brev*, letter 240 (Oslo, 1949), p. 196.

62. Emil Heilblut, "Die Sammlung Linde in Berlin," *Kunst und Künstler*, II (1904), 303–325; "Einige neuen Bildnisse von Edvard Munch," *ibid.*, pp. 488–492.

63. See Munch's painting of *Dr. Linde's Children*, 1904.

64. Arntz, *op. cit.*, p. 7; P. F. Schmidt, "Blütezeit der dresdner 'Brücke,'" *Aussaat*, II (1947), 50.

65. Erwin Petermann, in *E. L. Kirchner*, catalog (Stuttgart, 1948).

66. "Although it is useless to quibble over chronology it seems probable that Kirchner's discovery of African and Polynesian art in the Dresden Ethnological Museum in 1904 definitely precedes Vlaminck's discovery of Negro sculpture in Paris. What is more important is the fact that as soon as they had come upon primitive art the Germans did not turn it into a formal exercise such as cubism." Alfred H. Barr, *German Painting and Sculpture* (New York, 1931), p. 10.

67. Schmidt-Rottluff, in a letter to me, July 11, 1952.

68. Pechstein, in a letter to me, Sept. 23, 1952.

69. *Ibid.*

70. Although it occurred in the very recent past, the date for the establishment of the group has often been given wrongly. Edith Hoffmann gives it as early as 1902 in *Kokoschka: Life and Work* (Boston [1946]), p. 70. The first Brücke catalog for the exhibition at the Galerie Arnold in Dresden in 1910 erroneously dates the Brücke from 1903. This year was cited again by Carl Einstein in *Die Kunst des 20. Jahrhunderts*, p. 132, and is given as the date by Will Grohmann, as late as 1951, in "L'Expressionism," *Documents. Revue mensuelle des questions allemandes* (Offenbourg, 1951), p. 18. In his more recent book, *Bildende Kunst und Architektur* (Berlin, 1953), pp. 44, 504, Grohmann cites 1904 as the date for the formation of the Brücke. Other writers have suggested the late date of 1906 as the year in which the Brücke was established. Karl Woermann, *Geschichte der Kunst*, vol. VI, p. 491; Egon von Sydow, *Die deutsche expressionistische Kulstur und Malerei* (Berlin, 1920). It would have been impossible for the group to be formed before Schmidt-Rottluff, one of the charter members, arrived in Dresden in the spring of 1905, and it is certain that the group was well in existence when Nolde was asked to join in February, 1906 (see chapter viii). This evidence must eliminate earlier and later dates, and points toward the assumption that the group was formed officially and christened "Brücke" during the year 1905. This date was recently confirmed by Erich Heckel (letter to Alfred Hentzen, June 25, 1953, in *Brücke*, catalog of Brücke portfolios and graphic work [Hannover, 1953], p. 3, and interview with me, Sept. 7, 1953). It is corroborated in the following sources: Sauerlandt, *Die Kunst der letzten 30 Jahre* (Berlin, 1935), p. 147; Arntz, *op. cit.*, p. 7; Hans Bolliger, in Maurice Raynal *et al.*, *Matisse, Munch, Rouault*, pp. 77, 137, 145; Ludwig Grote, *Deutsche Kunst-Meisterwerke des 20. Jahrhunderts*, exhibition catalog (Lucerne, 1953), p. 18. P. F. Schmidt, *Geschichte der modernen Malerei* (Stuttgart, 1952), p. 169.

71. Schmidt-Rottluff, letter inviting Nolde to join Brücke, Feb., 1906, *in* Nolde, *Jahre der Kämpfe*, p. 90.

CHAPTER VIII

1. Emil Nolde, *Jahre der Kämpfe* (Berlin, 1934), pp. 90–91.

2. Nolde, *Das eigene Leben* (Berlin, 1931), pp. 103–104. This appreciation of Hodler is strangely absent in the second, enlarged edition of Nolde's autobiography (Flensburg, 1949), pp. 189–190.

3. *Ibid.*, pp. 209–216. The second (1949) edition is used for this and all the following references to this work.

4. Adolf Hoelzel, "Einige aphoristische Sätze," *Hölzel und sein Kreis* (Stuttgart, 1916), p. 3.

5. Nolde, in a letter of 1926, quoted in Schmidt, *Emil Nolde* (Leipzig, 1929), p. 16.

6. Nolde, *Das eigene Leben*, p. 207. Here Nolde comes surprisingly close to the esthetic theory of Edward

Bullough, the British psychologist and contemporary of Nolde's who formulated the "antimony of distance." Bullough warns against "over-distancing" and "under-distancing" as two common failings of art; the former results in "crude naturalism," the latter in "artificial idealism." The middle ground of "proper distancing," which Bullough sees as the proper realm for the esthetic response, seems to come close not only to Nolde's statement but also to his work, with its clear demarcation from the imitative realism that preceded it and the nonobjectivism of Hoelzel's later students. Edward Bullough, "Psychical Distance as a Factor in Art and an Aesthetic Principle," *British Journal of Psychology,* V (1912–1913), 87–118.

7. Nolde, *Das eigene Leben,* p. 239.

8. *Ibid.,* p. 240.

9. "During a noon hour I met two strange German girls. The one, Paula Becker, was small, questioning, vivid; the other, Klara Westhof, sculptress, was tall and restrained. I never saw either of them again. But not long thereafter the sculptress became the wife of the poet, Rainer Maria Rilke, and the woman painter the wife of the painter, Modersohn. During a few short years she painted simple and beautiful and humanly deeply-felt pictures. And then came early, difficult death." *Ibid.,* p. 246.

10. *Ibid.,* p. 222. Paul Sérusier makes an almost identical statement in his *ABC de la peinture* (Paris, 1950), p. 29: "It is not proper for the painter to mix the colors of the warm scale with those of the cold scale . . . in this way he will not have poor mixtures; no loss of light." Nolde's autobiography was first published in 1931; Sérusier's essay, in 1921.

11. Max Sauerlandt, *Emil Nolde* (Munich, 1921), p. 22.

12. Nolde, *Jahre der Kämpfe,* p. 181.

13. "Artistically the country gave me nothing. There were no previous years in which I worked as little and as badly. I was unable to carry out that which I intended and became incapable when confronted with the strange nature of the southern country." *Ibid.,* p. 62.

14. *Ibid.,* p. 120.

15. *Ibid.,* p. 71.

16. *Ibid.,* pp. 75–76.

17. *Ibid.,* p. 79.

18. Hans Rosenhagen, "Von Ausstellungen und Sammlungen," *Die Kunst,* XI (June, 1906), p. 406.

19. Nolde, *Jahre der Kämpfe,* p. 81.

20. Gustav Schiefler, *Meine Graphik-Sammlung* (Hamburg, 1927), p. 40.

21. Nolde, *Jahre der Kämpfe,* p. 87.

22. Schiefler, *op. cit.,* p. 40.

23. See p. 84.

24. E. L. Kirchner, quoted in Peter Selz, "E. L. Kirchner's 'Chronik der Brücke,'" *College Art Journal,* X (Fall, 1950), 50. See Appendix A.

25. Pechstein relates some of this in his letter to Biermann, in Georg Biermann, *Max Pechstein* (Leipzig, 1920), p. 14. The story is told in greater detail in Osborn's Pechstein biography: Max Osborn, *Max Pechstein* (Berlin, 1922), pp. 49–51.

26. Pechstein, in a letter to Biermann, *in* Biermann, *op. cit.,* p. 13.

27. Osborn, *op. cit.,* p. 40.

28. *Ibid.,* p. 52. Pechstein himself, as quoted above, dates his first acquaintance with van Gogh at 1906.

29. Pechstein, in a letter to me, Sept. 23, 1952.

30. Paul Fechter maintains in his definitive catalog of Pechstein's graphic work that he began as a print maker in 1906 under the tutelage of the Brücke artists. Paul Fechter, *Das graphische Werk Max Pechsteins* (Berlin, 1921), p. vii. Pechstein himself claims the earlier year. Max Pechstein, in an autobiographical note in Fritz Gurlitt, *Das graphische Jahr* (Berlin, 1921), p. 101; Pechstein, in a letter to me, Sept. 23, 1952: "1905 habe ich meine ersten Holzschnitte angefertigt als Autodidakt."

31. The factory, according to Heckel's own statement to the author, was in Löbtau near Dresden, not in Friedrichstadt as stated by Arntz. "Die Künstlergruppe 'Brücke,' 1905–1913," *Paula Modersohn und die Maler der "Brücke,"* catalog (Bern, 1948), p. 11.

32. *Ibid.,*

33. Probably the only copy of this poster still extant is in the collection of Dr. F. Bauer, Davos, Switzerland. Cf. fig. 16 for a later woodcut of this poster.

34. The fragment for the catalog of the first Brücke exhibition is in the possession of Erich Heckel. There is also a sketch for the cover of the planned catalog in a sketchbook of Kirchner's from 1906, now in the library of the Kunsthaus, Zürich.

35. This painting is dated 1906 by W. F. Arntz in *Paula Modersohn-Becker und die Maler der Brücke* (Bern, 1948). Even if Heckel's own dating of 1909 should prove to be correct, *Grazing Horses* is a good example of Heckel's early style.

36. Thormaehlen, *Erich Heckel* (Leipzig, 1931), p. 8.

37. Letter to me, July 16, 1952.

38. The earliest known woodcuts date from 1905, but he evidently began working in woodcut and linoleum cut considerably earlier. His graphic *œuvre* includes a total of about 360 woodcuts.

39. Interview with me, Hemmenhofen, Sept. 7, 1953. Some of his early wood sculptures are still in his personal collection.

40. Berlin, collection of the artist.

41. Statement by Schmidt-Rottluff, personal interview, Hochschule der Bildenden Künste, Berlin, June 28, 1953.

42. Will Grohmann, "Emil Nolde," *in* Thieme-Becker, *Allgemeines Lexikon der bildenden Künstler,* vol. XXV, p. 503.

43. The Kestner Museum in Hannover has perhaps the only complete set of these portfolios now in existence.

44. E. L. Kirchner, *Künstlergruppe Brücke Manifesto* (1906), fig. 10.

45. "Moderne Kunst," *Pan,* I (1895), 45.

46. *Die Kunst,* VII, 549.

47. Gallén-Kallela was a close friend of Jan Sibelius and painted a symbolic, visionary group portrait of himself, Sibelius, and other Finnish romanticists in *Symposon* of 1894.

48. Cuno Amiet, quoted in C. von Mandach, *Cuno Amiet und seine Schule,* exhibition (Bern, 1928).

49. Statement by Schmidt-Rottluff, personal interview, June 27, 1953.

CHAPTER IX

1. Gustav Schiefler, *Meine Graphik-Sammlung* (Hamburg, 1927), p. 50.

2. Heckel intimated this relationship in a personal interview, Sept. 7, 1953.

3. Charles S. Kessler, "Sun Worship and Anxiety," *Magazine of Art,* XLV (Nov., 1952), 306–307.

4. Slightly later, Franz Marc evolved a similar unification of humans or animals and landscape and carried it further.

5. Kandinsky, catalog of exhibitions (unpublished). Grateful acknowledgment is made to Mme Nina Kandinsky, Paris, for permitting me to see this manuscript. A complete list of exhibitions of Kandinsky's work is appended to Kenneth C. E. Lindsay, "An Examination of the Fundamental Theories of Kandinsky" (Ph.D. dissertation, University of Wisconsin, 1951).

6. Wilhelm F. Arntz, "Die Künstlergruppe 'Brücke,' 1905–1913," *Paula Modersohn und die Maler der "Brücke,"* catalog, (Bern, 1948), pp. 11–12.

7. See chapter xi.

8. Schiefler, no. FH128.

9. L. de Marsale, "Über Kirchners Graphik," *Genius,* III (1921), 250–263.

10. Marsale, "Über die plastischen Arbeiten Kirchners," *Cicerone,* XVII (1925), 695.

11. Cf. Eberhard Roters, "Ernst Ludwig Kirchners Begriff der 'Hieroglyphe' und die Bedeutung des graphischen Details," *Edwin Redslob zum 70 Geburtstag* (Festschrift), Berlin, 1955, pp. 332–346. Roters points out that Kirchner's style of hieroglyphics was developed *fully* only after 1915.

12. Summer, 1952.

13. This painting has been erroneously identified as a portrait of Heckel and his wife (cf. *College Art Journal,* XV [1955]; *Art News,* May, 1956). According to Erich Heckel himself, it is a portrait of Kirchner's model Dodo and her brother. Erich Heckel, letter to June-Marie Fink, Nov. 21, 1956.

14. Marsale, "Über Kirchners Graphik," 258.

15. Edwin Redslob, *Fünf Generationen* (Berlin, 1948).

16. Heckel, personal interview, Sept. 7, 1953.

17. Statement by Schmidt-Rottluff, personal interview, Berlin-Dahlem, June 27, 1953.

18. This head, certainly a portrait of Heckel, was in the Schmidt-Rottluff Brücke portfolio of 1909.

19. Schiefler, *op. cit.,* p. 47.

20. *Ibid.*

21. This portfolio, with a woodcut portrait of Schmidt-Rottluff by Kirchner on its cover (fig. 12), contains a Schmidt-Rottluff portrait lithograph of Heckel as well as a Dresden cityscape in litho (Sch. 57) and an etching of old Dresden houses (Sch. 9).

22. Kirchner, sketchbook, manuscript, in library of Kunsthaus, Zürich.

23. Heckel, in a letter to me, Aug. 16, 1952, and personal interview, Sept. 7, 1953.

24. "Personal und Atelier Nachrichten," *Die Kunst,* XI (1906), 408.

25. Pechstein in a letter to Biermann, *in* Georg Biermann, *Max Pechstein* (Leipzig, 1920), p. 14.

26. Pechstein, in a letter to me, Sept. 23, 1952.

27. This opinion is held by Wilhelm Hausenstein in his article on Pechstein. "One may add that just then the name, Henri Matisse, created a most magnetic atmosphere." "Max Pechstein," *Deutsche Kunst und Dekoration,* XLII (1918), 205–237.

28. Heckel, in a letter to me, Sept. 23, 1952. Schmidt-Rottluff's answer to this question (in a letter to me, July 11, 1952) simply makes no sense. He writes: "Modern Frenchmen, i.e., Impressionists, I came to see only after I had moved to Berlin—1911. About the Fauves one heard only much later—probably after 1920—and there was hardly anything to be seen."

29. Pechstein, in a letter to me, Sept. 23, 1952.

30. Pechstein, *in* Westheim, *Künstlerbekenntnisse* (Berlin, 1925), p. 240.

31. Heckel, in a letter to me, Aug. 16, 1952.

32. Maurice Reynal *et al., From Picasso to Surrealism* (Geneva, 1950), p. 20.

33. Ernst Scheyer, "Expressionism in Holland,"

Maandblad Voor Beeldende Kunsten (Dec., 1950), p. 293.

34. Basel, Nachlass Kirchner, reproduced in Reynal et al., *Matisse, Munch, Rouault* (Geneva, 1950), p. 83.

35. Schmidt-Rottluff, personal interview, Berlin-Dahlem, June 27, 1953.

36. See chapter iv.

37. The Berlin Secession opened in April, 1910; the New Secession, on May 10 of the same year.

38. Pechstein is also responsible for the nude *Diana* on the cover of the catalog. Artists represented in the first exhibition of the New Secession, 1910: Ahlers-Hestermann, Assendorpf, Bengen, Besteher, Bonnevie, Einbeck von Hairoth, Heckel, Helbig, Philipp Klein, César Klein, Kirchner, Lederer, Ledschnitzer, Melzer, Otto Mueller, Pechstein, Richter, Schlittgen, Schmidt-Rottluff, Schütz, Segal, Sigmund, Steinhardt, Tappert, Torstenson, Waske.

39. Trust, "Die neue sezession," *Sturm,* I (Oct., 1910), 255–256.

40. Karl Scheffler, "Berlin, Neue Sezession," *Kunst und Künstler,* VIII (July, 1910), 525.

41. Osborn, "Berliner Ausstellungen," *Kunstchronik,* XXI (May 13, 1910), 403.

42. *Kunstchronik,* XXI (June 24, 1910).

43. Sievers, in *Die Kunst,* XVII (March 28, 1911); and "Berliner Ausstellungen," *Kunstchronik,* XXIII (May 24, 1912).

44. Nolde, *Jahre der Kämpfe* (Berlin, 1934), pp. 193–194.

45. Glaser, *Die Kunst,* XVII (May 1, 1912), 361.

46. "Berliner Ausstellungen," *Kunstchronik,* XXIII (May 24, 1912).

47. Glaser, *op. cit.,* p. 361.

48. E. L. Kirchner, in Peter Selz, "E. L. Kirchner's 'Chronik der Brücke,'" *College Art Journal,* X (Fall, 1950), 51. See Appendix A.

49. *Ibid.*

50. I am grateful to Hans Bolliger, Zürich, for the microfilm of this catalog.

51. List of works in Exhibition of the Brücke, Dresden, Galerie Arnold, September, 1910:
Cuno Amiet, Oschwand, Switzerland—2 paintings.
E. Heckel, Dresden—10 paintings, 2 dry points, 3 lithos, 2 woodcuts, 3 drawings.
E. L. Kirchner, Dresden—10 paintings, 1 dry point, 1 litho, 2 color lithos, 2 color woodcuts, 5 drawings.
Max Pechstein, Berlin-Wilmersdorf—8 paintings, 5 lithos, 7 drawings.
Schmidt-Rottluff, Dangast—8 paintings, 9 woodcuts, 3 drawings.
Otto Mueller, Steglitz (guest)—2 paintings, 3 drawings.

52. There is also a listing of exhibitions held by Brücke members until this time, which includes Darmstadt, Hamburg, Düsseldorf, Berlin, Leipzig, as well as Switzerland, Sweden, and Denmark.

53. Statement by Heckel, in personal interview, Hemmenhofen, Bodensee, Sept. 7, 1953.

54. Cf. chapter viii.

CHAPTER X

1. E. Nolde, *Jahre der Kämpfe* (Berlin, 1934), p. 92. Although Emil Nolde resigned from the Brücke in 1907, his wife Ada was still a nonprofessional member of the group in 1910 and was listed as such in the membership list of the catalog of the Brücke exhibition at the Galerie Arnold. Heckel erroneously dates Nolde's separation at 1908. Heckel, in a letter to me, July 16, 1952.

2. Schmidt-Rottluff, in a letter to me, July 11, 1952.

3. Nolde, *op. cit.,* p. 182.

4. Three years later, Munch made a very similar print of a girl confronted by a huge animal—the lithograph *Omega and Bear,* part of the Omega series of 1909.

5. Hartlaub, *Die Graphik des Expressionismus in Deutschland* (Stuttgart, 1947), p. 28.

6. Nolde, *Das eigene Leben* (Berlin, 1931), pp. 49–50.

7. Nolde, *Jahre der Kämpfe,* p. 104.

8. Sauerlandt, *Emil Nolde* (Munich, 1921), p. 36.

9. Hartlaub, *Kunst und Religion* (Leipzig, 1919), pp. 88–89.

10. Paul F. Schmidt, "Blütezeit der Dresdner Brücke," *Aussaat,* II (1947), 52.

11. Liebermann on Nolde's *Pentecost:* "Wen det Bild ausjestellt wird, lege ick mein Amt nieder," quoted in Nolde, *Jahre der Kämpfe,* p. 141.

12. Karl Scheffler, "Erklärung," *Kunst und Künstler,* IX (Jan., 1911), 210–211.

13. Nolde, *Jahre der Kämpfe,* pp. 122–124, 170–171, 172–178, 195–196, 212, 215–216, 234.

14. *Ibid.,* p. 196.

15. Paul Ortwin Rave, *Kunstdiktatur im Dritten Reich* (Hamburg, 1949), p. 74.

16. The publication of the catalog, comprising 147 etchings, 31 lithographs, and 39 woodcuts, had to be postponed for a year because of Nolde's fiery attack on Liebermann and Scheffler in 1910.

17. Alfred H. Barr, "Ensor's St. Anthony," *Bulletin of the Museum of Modern Art,* IX (Oct., 1941), 5.

18. Nolde, *Jahre der Kämpfe,* pp. 172–173. This introduction was neither completed nor published.

19. Sauerlandt, *op. cit.,* p. 62.

20. With, "Nolde," *Feuer,* III (1921–1922), 147.

21. Cf. pl. 40.

CHAPTER XI

1. Richard Samuel and R. Hinton Thomas, *Expressionism in German Life, Literature and Theatre* (Cambridge, England, 1939), p. 67.

2. See chapter ix.

3. MUIM stands for "Moderner Untericht in Malerei."

4. From the prospectus of the MUIM Institute, figs. 21, 22.

5. Lyonel Feininger, in an interview with me, Cambridge, Mass., Aug. 11, 1952. Schmidt-Rottluff corroborated this information in an interview, Berlin, June, 1953.

6. I want to thank Mr. Hans Bolliger, Bern, for letting me study this catalog as well as other source material on the Brücke.

7. P. F. Schmidt, "Ausstellungen," *Der Cicerone,* IV (1912), 230.

8. Matisse's esthetic theories appeared at the same time in a German publication. Henri Matisse, "Notizen eines Malers," *Kunst und Künstler,* VII (1909), 335–347.

9. Hans Friedberger, "Zeichnungen von Max Pechstein," *Cicerone,* V (1913), 289–291; "Plastiken und neue Zeichnungen von Max Pechstein bei Gurlitt," *Cicerone,* V (1913), 760–762.

10. Walter Heymann, *Max Pechstein* (Munich, 1916); Georg Biermann, *Max Pechstein* (Leipzig, 1919); Max Osborn, *Max Pechstein* (Berlin, 1922).

11. Alfred Hentzen, *Karl Schmidt-Rottluff,* exhibition catalog (Hannover, 1952) [p. 5].

12. A water-color sketch for this painting in the City Art Museum of St. Louis is dated by the artist but it is difficult to decipher the date. It is possible that a previous 1913 dating has been altered by the painter to read 1912.

13. Heckel, in a personal interview, Hemmenhofen, Sept. 7, 1953.

14. Thormaehlen, *Erich Heckel* (Leipzig, 1931), p. 12.

15. Heckel, in an interview with me, Hemmenhofen, Sept. 7, 1953.

16. Pl. 155, *Portrait of a Woman* (1911), is one of the brilliant paintings of Kirchner's Berlin period.

17. Grohmann, *Das Werk Ernst Ludwig Kirchners* (Munich, 1926), p. 27.

18. Grohmann refers to this painting as *Sick Woman. Ibid.,* p. 56.

19. Cf. Cézanne's painting *Ferme à Montgeroult* (1899).

20. E. L. Kirchner, explanatory notes to "Peter Schlemihl," written in his notebook of 1918 (unpublished). Hans Bolliger, Zürich, who owns this notebook, has graciously permitted me to read and quote from it. The comments comprise a free paraphrasing.

21. Heckel, letter to Alfred Hentzen, June 25, 1953, printed in *Brücke,* catalog of Brücke portfolios and graphic work (Hannover, 1953) [p. 4].

22. E. L. Kirchner, *Chronik der Brücke:* "Pechstein broke the confidence of the group by becoming a member of the 'Sezession,' and was expelled from 'Brücke,' " *in* Peter Selz, "E. L. Kirchner's 'Chronik der Brücke,' " *College Art Journal,* X (Fall, 1950), 51. This statement by Kirchner was corroborated by Erich Heckel. Heckel, in an interview with me, Sept. 7, 1953.

23. Pechstein, in a letter to me, Sept. 23, 1952: "The Brücke broke because of Kirchner's too personal judgments. I withdrew."

24. Heckel, letter to Hentzen, *op. cit.* [p. 4].

25. See Appendix A for a complete translation of this important document.

26. Certain observations on the *Chronik* must be made: It is interesting, for example, that Amiet is represented with one painting in the reproduction section and with one print in the graphic section, both being in a style very different from the rest of the work. The inclusion of the Swiss painter here as well as in the later Brücke exhibition seems to have been a gesture of mutual friendship and respect. He really always remained on the periphery of the group. There are no contributions by Pechstein, who no longer belonged to the Brücke at the time. On page 40 of the Munich *Chronicle* is a color woodcut signed by Otto Mueller. This woodcut, in black, ocher, and brown, is a portrait head of Mueller, obviously done by Kirchner and *not* by Mueller. It is identical with Kirchner's *Head of Otto Mueller* listed in Gustav Schiefler's catalog. (Schiefler, *Das graphische Werk E. L. Kirchners bis 1924* [Berlin, 1926], p. 90. Sch. 220, 2d state [color]. Cf. fig. 26). The other known copy of the *Chronik der Brücke,* in the Kestner Museum, Hannover, differs considerably from the Munich version. The Hannover *Chronicle* contains neither the photographs of the paintings nor the original graphic work, and has only twenty-two pages instead of the forty-seven pages in the Munich version.

CHAPTER XII

1. Sigmund Freud, in the foreword to *The Interpretation of Dreams,* translated by A. A. Brill (New York, n.d.).

2. Hermann Bahr, "Secession," *Ver Sacrum,* I (Jan., 1898), 9–10.

3. Hermann Bahr, "Secession," *Ver Sacrum,* I (Jan., 1898), p. 13.

4. Edith Hoffmann, *Kokoschka: Life and Work* (Boston [1946]), p. 26.

5. W. Fred, "The Artists' Colony at Darmstadt," *Studio,* XXIV (1901), 24.

6. Alexandre, quoted by Fernand Khnopff, in "Josef Hoffmann—Architect and Decorator," *Studio,* XXII (1901), 261–266. Perhaps nothing could be more typical of the international aspect of art nouveau than this acclamation of the Austrian pavilion by a French critic quoted by a Belgian artist in an English publication.

7. Fritz Schmalenbach, *Jugendstil* (Würzburg, 1935), p. 58.

8. Gustav Glück, "Gustav Klimt," *Die Bildenden Künste,* II (1919), 13.

9. Max Eisler (ed.), *Gustav Klimt—An Aftermath* (Vienna, 1931), p. 7.

10. *Ibid.,* p. 8.

11. Hoffmann, *op. cit.,* p. 30.

12. Josef Urban, in *Bulletin of the Art Institute of Chicago,* XVI (Oct., 1922), 68.

13. *Medicine* was later bought by the state, but all three paintings were destroyed by fire in World War II.

14. Egon Schiele, quoted in Arthur Roessler, *Erinnerungen an Egon Schiele* (Vienna, 1922), pp. 50–51.

15. *Ibid.,* p. 51.

16. Exhibited at the Vienna Kunstschau of 1908.

17. Eisler, *op. cit.,* p. 5.

18. Fritz Burger, *Einführung in die moderne Kunst* (Berlin, 1917), and *Cézanne und Hodler* (Munich, 1920).

19. Ferdinand Hodler, *in* Hans Mühlestein, *Ferdinand Hodler* (Weimar, 1914), p. 259.

20. This painting was exhibited in the Secession show of 1903–1904.

21. Hodler, *in* Burger, *Cézanne und Hodler* (Munich, 1920), vol. I, p. 50.

22. C. Loosli, *Ferdinand Hodler* (Paris, 1931), and *Ferdinand Hodler, Leben Werk und Nachlass* (Zürich, 1919).

23. Paul Klee, "Kunst und Literatur des Auslands," *Die Alpen,* VI (1912), 243.

24. Otto Benesch, *Egon Schiele as a Draughtsman* (Vienna, [1950]), p. 5.

25. He repeated this motif of the self-seer in the following year with a painting now in the collection of Rudolf Leopold, Vienna.

26. Egon Schiele, quoted in Hans A. von Kleehoven, "Egon Schiele," *Das Kunstwerk,* V (1951), 22.

27. Arthur Roessler (ed.), *Egon Schiele im Gefängnis* (Vienna, 1922).

28. "The head is essentially the center for intellectual power, social dominance, and control of body impulses" (Karen Machower, *Personality Projection in the Drawing of the Human Figure* [Springfield, Ill., 1949], pp. 36–37). Disproportionately large heads occur frequently in expressionist painting. They are also very common in the drawings of children. Interesting studies of functional interpretations of the human figure have been undertaken by Karen Machower, F. L. Goodenough, and others. Machower points out that children often draw a large head to indicate a complete person and that "the head of the adult is the most important organ relating to the emotional security of the child" (*ibid.,* p. 39). Among adults this configuration is found in the work principally of frustrated intellectuals, inadequate males, and "the paranoid, narcissistic, intellectually righteous, and vain individual may draw a large head as an expression of his inflated ego" (*ibid.,* p. 38).

29. Benesch, *op. cit.,* p. 10.

30. Joseph von Sternberg, introduction to *Egon Schiele,* exhibition catalog (New York, 1948) [p. 3].

CHAPTER XIII

1. Paul Stefan, *Oskar Kokoschka: Dramen und Bilder* (Leipzig, 1913); Paul Westheim, *Oskar Kokoschka* (Potsdam-Berlin, 1918).

2. The date of this appointment is still doubtful. Westheim implies 1918; Kokoschka himself implies a date as late as 1920. Edith Hoffmann, *Kokoschka: Life and Work* (Boston [1946]), p. 151.

3. Most probably the immediate reason for Kokoschka's studying art was a scholarship he received to attend the Vienna School for Arts and Crafts. He had really wanted to study chemistry and was more interested at that time in chemical reactions than in the academic study of art.

4. Alfred Neumeyer, "Oskar Kokoschka," *Magazine of Art,* XXXVIII (1934), 261.

5. Kokoschka, quoted in Hoffmann, *op. cit.,* p. 22, *n.*

6. *Ibid.,* p. 33.

7. Kokoschka, "An Approach to the Baroque Art of Czechoslovakia," *Burlington Magazine,* LXXXI (1942), 264.

8. Cf. John Anthony Thwaites, "Personalismus in der Malerei," *Das Kunstwerk,* V (1951), 33.

9. Formerly owned by Adolf Loos and now located in a private collection in New York. This

very important work is frequently overlooked. Georgine Oeri, in an otherwise perceptive review of the Kokoschka exhibition in Basel in 1947, based her analysis of Kokoschka's early work on his inability to portray the self until 1914; she overlooked this earliest work as well as his painted self-portraits of 1912 and 1913. "Oskar Kokoschka," *Werk,* XXXIV (1947), Suppl., 54–55. Edith Hoffmann (*op. cit.,* p. 37) wrote in her biography that the "Self-portrait in plaster is only traceable in a reproduction (*Kunstblatt* [January, 1929], p. 17)"; she obviously had reference to the clay sculpture that appeared in the original in the Kokoschka exhibition at the Institute of Contemporary Art in Boston and is reproduced in James S. Plaut (ed.), *Oskar Kokoschka* (New York, 1948), p. 80.

10. Westheim, *op. cit.,* p. 20. This assumption agrees with Kokoschka's own recollection as quoted in Hoffmann, *op. cit.,* p. 37.

11. Only five or six copies were sold in 1908. The edition of 275 copies was later bought by Kurt Wolff who republished it in 1917.

12. Hoffmann (*op. cit.,* pp. 36, 39, 338) correctly refers to these prints as lithographs, as does Plaut, *op. cit.,* p. 87.

13. W. Wartmann, "Oskar Kokoschka," *Catalogue of the Kokoschka Exhibition* (Zürich, 1947), p. 3.

14. Joseph A. Lux, "Kunstschau-Wien 1908," *Deutsche Kunst und Dekoration,* XXIII (1909), 53.

15. *Sphinx und Strohmann,* first performed in Vienna in 1907. Later rewritten as *Hiob. Mörder, Hoffnung der Frauen,* originally entitled *Hoffnung der Frauen,* written in 1907 and first performed in the open-air show at the Vienna Kunstschau in July, 1909. This play, set to music by Paul Hindemith in 1920, was performed in Stuttgart as an opera in 1921 under Heinrich George's direction with constructivist sets by Oskar Schlemmer. The opera had a second production in Dresden in 1922 with Kokoschka's own stage design.

16. Richard Samuel and R. Hinton Thomas, *Expressionism in German Life, Literature and Theatre* (Cambridge, England, 1939), p. 160.

17. Loos' belief that architecture is a matter of technology and engineering and not of ornamentation, coupled with his admiration for free painting and Kokoschka, is really the immediate forerunner to the Bauhaus and its combination of functional design and the free teaching of Kandinsky and Klee. Future research may indicate that the connection between Loos and the Bauhaus is a direct one. Loos was a close friend of Alma Mahler's who soon became Kokoschka's friend and then Gropius' wife. According to Nina Kandinsky and the personal recollections of other individuals connected with the school, Alma Mahler was partly responsible for the early Bauhaus program.

18. Kokoschka has often been called the "Freud of painting." In Vienna it was often said: "He paints the dirt of one's soul."

19. Westheim, *op. cit.,* p. 13; Hans Heilmaier, *Kokoschka* (Paris, 1929), p. 4; Leopold Zahn, "Oskar Kokoschka," *Das Kunstwerk,* II (1948), 29–35.

20. Kokoschka, quoted in Zahn, *op. cit.,* p. 29.

21. Vienna, Österreichische Galerie.

22. Hans Maria Wingler in his recent monograph and oeuvre catalog of Kokoschka, *Oskar Kokoschka* (Vienna, 1956), listed these two paintings as having been painted "presumably in the 2nd half of the year 1909" (p. 295). Their stylistic characteristics, however, point to a slightly earlier dating. This assumption has been confirmed to me in a personal interview in Champaign, Illinois (March 15, 1953) with Dr. Hans Reichel. Dr. Reichel, the youthful subject for the *Portrait of a Boy,* recalls the time Kokoschka spent in the Reichel household.

23. Soon after it was painted, the portrait was called the *Blue Boy,* a name that has adhered to it since that time, probably because it so well emphasized the contrast between the *fin de siècle* world Kokoschka painted and Gainsborough's coolly elegant society.

24. Kokoschka painted this left hand very carefully from the model; he had the boy hold an orange in it. Later he painted over the orange.

25. This portrait of the actor who played the leading part in *Mörder, Hoffnung der Frauen* in 1908 has been dated by Edith Hoffmann as 1907–1908. H. M. Wingler agrees with this dating. Kokoschka himself dates it 1907, and believes it to be his first oil painting, as stated in Hoffmann's monograph (p. 51). It must certainly have been completed before the Kunstschau of 1909, as it was included in that exhibition. There is a good deal of disagreement about the dating of the early Kokoschka portraits, and the memory of the artist himself does not always appear to be completely accurate. Both Edith Hoffmann and H. M. Wingler have made careful studies of the chronology of Kokoschka's work, and these datings are generally accepted by the author in all cases where no new evidence has been found.

26. Hoffmann, *op. cit.,* p. 52.

27. Hoffmann, *op. cit.,* pp. 99–100.

28. Cf. Kokoschka's drawing of Loos for *Der Sturm,* I (1910), 141. Cf. fig. 28.

29. Neumeyer, *op. cit.,* p. 262.

30. It is hoped that a comparative study of Kokoschka and Mann—two survivors of humanism in twen-

tieth-century German painting and literature—may some day be undertaken. It is interesting in this connection that Mann hoped—in 1933—to ask Kokoschka, whom he greatly admired, to illustrate his *Joseph and His Brothers* (Mann, "Ein Maler—ein Dichter, Ein Brief," in Wolfgang Born, *Der Wiener Kunstwanderer,* I (Nov., 1933).

31. Hoffmann, *op. cit.,* p. 61.
32. Karl Gruber, "Zur Entstehung von Kokoschka's Forel-Bildnis," *Das Kunstwerk,* V (1951), 60–61.
33. Hoffmann, *op. cit.,* p. 61.
34. Gruber, *op. cit.,* p. 61.
35. Zahn, *op. cit.,* p. 31.
36. Gruber, *op. cit.,* p. 61.
37. Kokoschka now believes he painted this picture in 1912. The internal evidence of style, however, makes Edith Hoffmann's date, *ca.* 1910, much more acceptable.
38. Wilhelm Hausenstein, "Über Kokoschka," *Die Kunst,* XXXI (1926), 153–161.

CHAPTER XIV

1. Paul Clemen, *Contemporary German Art,* Introduction to exhibition catalog, Art Institute of Chicago (Berlin, 1908), p. 25.
2. See chapter vi.
3. Wassily Kandinsky, "Text Artista," *Wassily Kandinsky Memorial* (New York, 1945), p. 64. This autobiography was first written in 1913, and published under the title *Rückblicke* by *Der Sturm* in Berlin in the same year. In 1918 the artist translated it into Russian, and a revised and enlarged edition was published by the Department of the People's Commissariat of Education, Moscow. This last is the text that was translated into English by Boris Berg and published by the Guggenheim Foundation in 1945. It is the major source for material on Kandinsky's early life and for an understanding of the genesis of his art. In 1945 the Guggenheim Foundation also published a translation of the original German text (edited by Hilla Rebay) as "Retrospects by Wassily Kandinsky," in *Kandinsky* (New York, 1945).
4. *Ibid.,* p. 53.
5. *Ibid.*
6. *Ibid.,* p. 55. Kandinsky probably had reference to the discoveries of Rutherford in England.
7. Laszlo Moholy-Nagy, *Vision in Motion* (Chicago, 1947), p. 145.
8. Kandinsky, *Wassily Kandinsky Memorial,* p. 49.
9. *Ibid.*
10. *Ibid.,* p. 62.
11. *Ibid.,* p. 63.
12. *Ibid.,* p. 54.

13. In spite of evidence to the contrary, Mme Nina Kandinsky believes that Rembrandt is the only painter who ever influenced Kandinsky. Personal interview with Mme Kandinsky, Neuilly-sur-Seine, May, 1950.
14. Kandinsky, *op. cit.,* p. 49.
15. *Ibid.,* p. 54.
16. *Ibid.,* p. 65, *n.*
17. *Kunstchronik,* N.F., XVI (1905), 505.
18. D. Karowski and I. Graber.
19. Kandinsky, *op. cit.,* p. 66.
20. *Ibid.,* p. 67; cf. chapter iii above.
21. "Vermischtes," *Die Kunst,* VI (1901), 488.
22. "Von Ausstellungen und Sammlungen," *Die Kunst,* VII (1902), 22.
23. This was the first time Kandinsky exhibited his work to the public.
24. Kandinsky was rather close to the Jugendstil group and a friend of Olbrich's.
25. Kandinsky, *op. cit.,* p. 56.
26. Kandinsky, *Concerning the Spiritual in Art* (New York, 1947), p. 61. This book contains Kandinsky's fundamental theories of art. It was written over a period of ten years and first published in 1912 by Piper in Munich:—*Über das Geistige in der Kunst.* It was immediately widely accepted in art and literary circles as one of the sources of the movement in art and esthetics. It was also considered a manifesto of German expressionism and "absolute painting." Within the first year it went through three printings in Germany, and soon it was translated into many major languages, including the very influential Japanese translation. The first English translation was made by Michael Sadler and published in London in 1914 under the title *The Art of Spiritual Harmony.* The first American edition, *On the Spiritual in Art,* appeared in 1946, and was published by the Solomon R. Guggenheim Foundation, New York. This translation contained many errors. In 1947, Wittenborn, Schultz published a new edition, authorized by Mme Kandinsky and translated by Francis Golffing, Michael Harrison, and Ferdinand Ostertag. The Wittenborn translation, *Concerning the Spiritual in Art,* will be used here because it is much closer to the original text.
27. This division of his work has frequently been published: Nina Kandinsky, "Some Notes on the Development of Kandinsky's Painting," *in* Kandinsky, *Concerning the Spiritual in Art,* pp. 9–11; Nina Kandinsky, "Les periodes dans l'oeuvre de Kandinsky," in Max Bill *et al., Wassily Kandinsky* (Paris, 1951), p. 8; and Charles Estienne, *Kandinsky* (Paris, 1950), pp. 6–10.
28. This painting, now in the collection of Richard

Feigen, New York, was exhibited in the important Kandinsky show at Goltz in Munich in 1912.

29. Kandinsky, *Wassily Kandinsky Memorial*, p. 51.

30. This painting was exhibited in the Paris Salon d'Automne of 1906.

31. *Die Kunst*, VII (1902), 285.

32. *Ibid.*, 549–550

33. Hans Rosenhagen, "Die 5. Ausstellung der Berliner Secession," *Die Kunst*, VII (1902), 433–443.

34. The data on Kandinsky's exhibitions are taken largely from the complete list of exhibitions in the unpublished doctoral dissertation by Kenneth C. E. Lindsay, "An Examination of the Fundamental Theories of Wassily Kandinsky" (University of Wisconsin, 1951). Dr. Lindsay obtained most of his information from Kandinsky's own five House Catalogues, which are now in the possession of Mme Nina Kandinsky, and which this author has also seen. Acknowledgment is made to Dr. Lindsay for his many stimulating suggestions during discussions in Paris, Washington, Chicago, and New York.

35. *Kunstchronik*, XV (May 13, 1904), 413.

36. Published in *Pan* six years earlier in 1898, one year before its first publication in Paris; Signac, "Neoimpressionismus," *Pan*, IV (1898), 55–62. This is a short version of his essay.

37. See chapter vii.

38. "Von Ausstellungen und Sammlungen," *Die Kunst*, IX (1904), 408.

39. Wilhelm Michel, "Münchner Graphik," *Deutsche Kunst und Dekoration*, XVI (1905), 437.

40. Statement by Gabriele Münter in a personal interview, Murnau, Sept. 6, 1953. Cf. pl. 94.

41. Among Kandinsky's paintings of 1906 his series of the Parc de Saint Cloud stands out as most important. These paintings indicate Kandinsky's familiarity with the work of Matisse, who had just completed his *Joie de Vivre*. In an interview with Karl Nierendorf in 1937, Kandinsky acknowledged his debt to Matisse for his development toward nonobjective painting. (Kandinsky, *Essays über Kunst und Künstler*, [Teufen, Switzerland, 1955], pp. 202–203.) It must be kept in mind, however, that Kandinsky's "Fauve" style of 1906 is most intimately related to his own earlier work such as *The Sluice*.

42. Murnau, Germany, collection of Gabriele Münter.

43. Gabriele Münter, personal interview, Murnau, Sept. 6, 1953.

44. Kandinsky, "Letters from Munich," *Apollon*, II, VII, XI (1909–1910).

45. Münter, personal interview, Murnau, Sept. 6, 1953.

46. Kandinsky, *Wassily Kandinsky Memorial*, p. 61.

47. *Ibid.*, p. 51.

48. Kandinsky, *Concerning the Spiritual in Art*, pp. 67–68.

49. The term "abstract expressionism" used popularly for the abstractionists who had their nucleus in New York immediately following World War II is actually older in derivation. I find its first occurrence in Walden's *Der Sturm* in 1919 in an article by Oswald Herzog—himself an abstract painter—entitled "Der abstrakte Expressionismus" (*Der Sturm*, X [1919], 29). Herzog considers this form as "fulfilled expressionism" and equates it with life itself. He states that abstract expressionism, of which he considers himself an exponent, creates objects which are not taken from nature, but are related to nature through their rhythm. The following year Paul F. Schmidt first applied this term to Kandinsky in the preface to Hugo Zehder's monograph, *Wassily Kandinsky* (Dresden, 1920, pp. 2–3). I find no further usage of the term until 1929 when it occurs in a description of a lecture which Alfred H. Barr delivered at Wellesley College. One of his topics was "Kandinsky and Abstract Expressionism in Germany." Barr continued to refer to Kandinsky's style as "abstract expressionism" in Museum of Modern Art catalogs in 1929, 1932, 1934, and 1936. It is probably from this source that the term gained its wide currency.

50. Kandinsky, letter to Hilla Rebay, Jan. 16, 1937; *Wassily Kandinsky Memorial*, p. 98.

CHAPTER XV

1. *Die Kunst*, X (Oct., 1904), 46.

2. G. Graf-Pfaff, "Zur Ausstellung 'Japan und Ostasien,' München, 1909," *Münchner Jahrbuch der Bildenden Kunst*, IV (1909), 107–126. Kandinsky wrote an interesting and enthusiastic appreciation of the East Asiatic exhibition for the Moscow periodical, *Apollon*: "Letter from Munich," *Apollon*, II (1909), 17–20.

3. Ernst Köhnel, "Die Ausstellung Mohamedanischer Kunst, München, 1910," *ibid.*, V (1910), 209–251, and W. Kandinsky, "Letter from Munich," *Apollon*, XI (1910), 13–17.

4. There were also two non-artists in the original group: Heinrich Schnabel and Oskar Wittenstein.

5. G. J. W., "Von Ausstellungen," *Die Kunst*, XVI (1910–1911), 68–70.

6. Also called *Rider across the Bridge* and *Picture with Yellow Wall*. It is listed in Kandinsky's house catalog as No. 78. It may have been in Erbslöh's collection in Irschenhausen. Its present whereabouts is unknown.

7. Lindsay, "The Genesis and Meaning of the Cover

Design of the First *Blaue Reiter* Exhibition Catalog," *Art Bulletin*, XXXV (1953), 48.

8. This picture was in the first exhibition of the New Artists' Association.

9. Otto Fischer, *Das neue Bild* (Munich, 1912), p. 42.

10. Alfred Kubin, *Sansara* (Munich, 1913).

11. Reproduced in Arthur Holitscher, "Alfred Kubin," *Die Kunst*, VII (1903), 163.

12. Alfred Kubin, *Die andere Seite* (Munich, 1908).

13. Hermann Esswein, *Alfred Kubin* (Munich, 1911), p. 18.

14. Ludwig Grote believes that Kubin actually influenced Kafka. *Deutsche Kunst, Meisterwerke des 20. Jahrhunderts,* exhibition catalog (Lucerne, 1953), p. 23.

15. After the New Artists' Association ceased operating, Kanoldt became a founder of the Munich New Secession in 1913.

16. Hausenstein, in his article on "Kanoldt, Alexander," Thieme-Becker, *Allgemeines Lexikon der Bilden Künstler,* vol. XIX, pp. 534–535, and Sauerlandt, *Die Kunst der letzten 30 Jahre* (Berlin, 1935), p. 169.

17. Exhibited at the second exhibition of the New Artists' Association, in 1910.

18. Delaunay's *St. Séverin,* reproduced in *Der Blaue Reiter.*

19. Fischer, *op. cit.,* p. 27.

20. U-B, "Ausstellungen," *Cicerone,* II (1910), 30.

21. G. J. W., "Aus den Münchner Kunstsalons," *Die Kunst,* XV (1909–1910), 189–190.

22. Ozenfant, presentation of galley proofs of Apollinaire's *Les Peintres Cubistes,* section on Léger, in a letter to J. B. Neumann, in *First American Le Fauconnier Exhibition,* exhibition catalog (New York, Dec., 1948–Jan., 1949). Here Le Fauconnier's name is mentioned before Picasso's as a cubist source for Léger.

23. Ozenfant, *op. cit.* [p. 3].

24. Kandinsky and Marc (eds.), *Der Blaue Reiter* (Munich, 1912), pp. 37, 71.

25. Guillaume Apollinaire, *The Cubist Painters* (New York, 1949), p. 17.

26. *Ibid.*

27. Roger Allard, "Die Kennzeichen der Erneuerung in der Malerei," *in* Kandinsky and Marc, *op. cit.,* pp. 35–41.

28. Marc, "Die Wilden Deutschlands," *in* Kandinsky and Marc, *op. cit.,* p. 7.

29. Bernard Dorival, *Les Étapes de la peinture française contemporaine,* vol. III, *Depuis le cubisme* (Paris, 1946), p. 145.

30. Ozenfant, *op. cit.* [p. 14].

31. *Kunstchronik,* XXIV (April 11, 1913), 405.

32. Fischer, *op. cit.,* p. 22.

33. *Neue Künstlervereinigung München,* 2d exhibition catalog (Munich, 1911).

34. Katherine S. Dreier, *Burliuk* (New York, 1944), p. 55. Miss Dreier gives the correct place and date, but erroneously refers to the second exhibition of the New Artists' Association as the "Blaue Reiter" exhibit. The latter took place only in 1911.

35. *Neue Künstlervereinigung München,* 2d exhibition catalog.

36. Kandinsky and Marc, *op. cit.,* pp. 53–55.

37. This painting is erroneously labeled *Composition No. 35* in the Solomon R. Guggenheim Museum, New York, and in the publications of that museum.

38. Kandinsky, *Concerning the Spiritual in Art,* p. 73.

39. *Ibid.,* p. 77.

40. *Münchner Neueste Nachrichten,* September 10, 1910, quoted in Alois Schardt, *Franz Marc* (Berlin, 1936), p. 70.

41. Kandinsky, "Franz Marc," *Cahiers d'Art,* XI (1936), 273.

42. Marc to August Macke, Aug. 10, 1911, quoted in Grote, *Der Blaue Reiter,* p. 6.

43. Fischer, *op. cit.,* p. 23. Although not involved in the dispute, Le Fauconnier left the group at the same time.

44. Hausenstein, in Thieme-Becker, *op. cit.,* vol. XIX, p. 534.

45. Fischer, *op. cit.,* p. 15.

46. Kandinsky, *Concerning the Spiritual in Art,* p. 72.

47. Kandinsky, "Über die Formfrage," in Kandinsky and Marc, *op. cit.,* p. 82. Cf. chapter xviii.

48. Fischer, *op. cit.*

49. Marc, letter to his brother, December 3, 1911, in Klaus Lankheit, "Zur Geschichte des Blauen Reiters," *Cicerone* (1949, Heft 3), p. 112.

CHAPTER XVI

1. Franz Marc, *in* Herman Bünemann, Franz Marc, *Zeichnungen-Aquarelle* (Munich, 1948), p. 13.

2. Marc, quoted in Klaus Lankheit, "Franz Marc," exhibition catalog, *Franz Marc Aquarelle und Zeichnungen* (Munich, 1949–1950), p. 6.

3. Marc, *in* Lankheit, *Franz Marc* (Berlin, 1950), p. 18.

4. Maria Marc, "Maria Marc über Franz Marc," in *ibid.,* p. 73.

5. Alois Schardt, *Franz Marc* (Berlin, 1936), p. 68. There is a constantly growing literature on Franz Marc. Most of the monographs and essays, however, are only feeble attempts compared with Schardt's searching analysis. Schardt's book was published in Berlin in 1936, but immediately banned by the Nazi government. Most of the copies

of the book were reduced to pulp. A new edition of
this monograph is still to be hoped for.

6. Franz Marc, *Briefe, Aufzeichnungen und Aphorismen* (Berlin, 1920), vol. I, p. 121.

7. *Ibid.,* p. 123.

8. Psalms 29: 5, 6.

9. Theodor Däubler, "Franz Marc," *Die Neue Rundschau,* XXVII (1916), 564.

10. Aleksis Rannit, "M. K. Čiurlionis," *Das Kunstwerk,* I (1946–47), 46–48; "Un pittore astratto prima di Kandinsky," *La Biennale,* VIII (April, 1952). Čiurlionis' work is now in the Čiurlionis Gallery in Kaunas.

11. Hildebrandt, *Adolf Hoelzel* (Stuttgart [1952]) [p. 14].

12. *Ibid.*

13. Kandinsky, *Concerning the Spiritual in Art* (New York, 1947), p. 68.

14. *Ibid.,* p. 69.

15. *Ibid.,* p. 73.

16. *Ibid.*

17. *Ibid.,* p. 75.

18. It is strange to think of such a nonliteral painter as Kandinsky doing a canvas which in some ways is almost a literal interpretation of a famous passage in Russian literature, but *Trojka* bears a startling resemblance to the following lines from Gogol's *Dead Souls,* translated by George Reavey (London, 1942), pp. 308–309: "And is not a galloping troika like a mysterious force that has swept you away on its wings, so that you find yourself flying along, and everything else flying with you? The milestones fly past to meet you, the merchants in their carts are flying by, on each side of your forests of dark fir and pine trees are flying past to the thump of axes and the croaking of crows, the whole of the highway is flying on, no one knows where, into the receding distance; and there is a lurking terror in that glimmer of objects that keep flashing by rapidly and are gone before they can be identified. . . . Ah, you troika! Bird-like troika, who invented you? . . . Your driver . . . when he stands up, cracks his whip and starts up a song, then the horses rush like a hurricane, the spokes of the wheels spin in one smooth disk, and only the road shudders beneath them while some passerby cries out as he stops in alarm! And the troika is off and away, away!"

19. Lindsay, "The Genesis and Meaning of the Cover Design of the First *Blaue Reiter* Exhibition Catalog," *Art Bulletin,* XXXV (1953), 49.

20. Kandinsky, in Hugo Zehder, *Wassily Kandinsky* (Dresden, 1920), p. 49.

21. *The Chain.*

22. *Blue Leaves.* Cf. Schardt, *op. cit.,* p. 70. Kandinsky explains the derivation of the name simply enough as follows: "We invented the name at the coffee table in the garden at Sindelsdorf; we both loved blue, Marc also loved horses and I horsemen. So the name came by itself. And the enchanting coffee of Frau Maria Marc tasted even better." Kandinsky, "Der Blaue Reiter (Rückblick)," *Kunstblatt,* XIV (1930).

23. *Der Blaue Reiter,* catalog of 1st exhibition (Munich, 1911).

24. Gustav Vriesen, "Der Maler August Macke," *Westfalen,* XXX (1952), 33.

25. Macke, *in* Vriesen, *op. cit.,* p. 36.

26. Statement by Dr. W. Macke, in personal interview, Bonn, July 26, 1953.

27. This painting was one of three by Macke exhibited in the first Blaue Reiter exhibition and is reproduced in *Der Blaue Reiter* [p. 5]. Will Grohmann expresses doubt that Macke's *Storm* was really painted as early as 1911. Grohmann, *Bildende Kunst und Architektur* (Berlin, 1953), p. 149. The painting, however, is reproduced in the catalog of the first Blaue Reiter exhibit.

28. Bonn, Macke Nachlass (Dr. W. Macke). Also exhibited in the first Blaue Reiter show.

29. Macke, *in* Vriesen, *op. cit.,* p. 40.

30. Georg Biermann, *Heinrich Campendonk* (Leipzig, 1921), p. 15.

31. Kandinsky and Marc, *Der Blaue Reiter* (Munich, 1912) [p. 10].

32. Albert Bloch, letter to Edward A. Maser, published in *Albert Bloch,* catalog of retrospective exhibition, University of Kansas (Lawrence, Kansas, 1955).

33. Albert Bloch, quoted in Eddy, *Cubists and Post-Impressionists* (Chicago, 1914), pp. 201–203.

34. Chicago, Art Institute, Arthur Jerome Eddy Memorial Collection. This painting and the Albert Bloch are unfortunately never on exhibit at the Art Institute of Chicago.

35. Interview with Gabriele Münter, Murnau, Sept. 6, 1953.

36. Exhibited in the first Blaue Reiter exhibition; reproduced in Kandinsky and Marc, *op. cit.* [p. 15].

37. Exhibited in the first Blaue Reiter exhibition; reproduced in Kandinsky and Marc, *op. cit.* [p. 18].

38. Arnold Schönberg, "Das Verhältnis zum Text," *in* Kandinsky and Marc, *op. cit.,* pp. 27–33.

39. Arnold Schönberg, "Herzgewächse," text by M. Maeterlinck, *in* Kandinsky and Marc, *op. cit.,* musical supplement.

40. Dika Newlin, *Bruckner, Mahler, Schönberg* (New York, 1947), p. 250.

41. *Arnold Schönberg* (Munich, 1912).

42. Kandinsky, "Über die Formfrage," Kandinsky and Marc, *op. cit.,* pp. 74–100.

43. Marc to Delaunay, quoted in Bühnemann, *Franz Marc* (Munich, 1952), p. 42.

44. Hans Bolliger, "Biographical and Bibliographical Summaries," in Raynal *et al., History of Modern Painting,* vol. III, *From Picasso to Surrealism* (Geneva, 1950), p. 193.

45. Epstein herself was represented in the exhibition by two rather undistinguished paintings.

46. Statement by Sonia Delaunay, personal interview, Paris, May, 1950.

47. A painting of this series was in the exhibition, reproduced in the almanac, and bought by Bernhard Koehler.

48. *Der Sturm,* III (Jan., 1913).

49. See chapter xx.

50. John Anthony Thwaites, "Der Blaue Reiter: A Milestone in Europe," *Art Quarterly,* XIII (Winter, 1950), 15: "With the astounding effort of four years, Delaunay's invention was exhausted. Everything he had went into the Blaue Reiter period. He died as an artist twenty years before he did so as a man." Delaunay not only continued to do important work as a painter, but his influence did not stop with the Blaue Reiter exhibition. His feeling for rhythm and color gave the significant stimulus to the "Synchronism" of the Americans, Morgan Russel and Macdonald Wright, and became one of the major influences on the younger French generation —painters such as Bazaine and Manessier.

51. It is probable that Delaunay is responsible for the first nonobjective painting in France. This is maintained by Germain Bazin, who in his biographical notes to René Huyghe's *Les Contemporaines* (Paris, 1949) cites 1914 as the year in which Delaunay did the first nonobjective painting in France. This author is able to predate this by two years, since he has seen Delaunay's *Color Disk,* a completely nonobjective painting, dated 1912, in his Paris studio. It is possible, however, that Picabia and Kupka did nonobjective paintings in Paris before then.

CHAPTER XVII

1. Wassily Kandinsky, *Klänge* (Munich, 1912). Limited edition of 300 copies. (40 woodcuts in black and white, 12 color woodcuts.)

2. Nolde, *Jahre der Kämpfe* (Berlin, 1934), p. 140.

3. There is no documentation for the assertion that rayonism was started in 1909, as claimed by Larionoff and Gontcharova.

4. Lindsay, "The Genesis and Meaning of the Cover Design of the First *Blaue Reiter* Exhibition Catalog," *Art Bulletin,* XXXV (1953), p. 52.

5. Paul Klee, "Die Ausstellung des Modernen Bundes im Kunsthaus Zürich," *Die Alpen,* VI (Aug., 1912), 696.

6. *Ibid.,* p. 699.

7. *Ibid.,* p. 698. I am indebted to Hans Bolliger, Zürich, for information and documentation on the Moderne Bund.

8. Paul Klee, "Kunst und Literatur des Auslands," *Die Alpen,* VI (1912).

9. Paul Klee, "Autobiographische Notizen," *in* Klee Gessellschaft, *Paul Klee* (Bern, 1949), p. 3.

10. Klee, letter to his mother, Feb. 3, 1900, in *ibid.,* p. 5.

11. Klee, "Autobiographische Notizen," *ibid.,* p. 4.

12. Karl Nierendorf (ed.), *Paul Klee* (New York, 1941), p. 23.

13. Paul Klee, "Aufzeichnungen aus dem Tagebuch," *in* Leopold Zahn, *Paul Klee* (Potsdam, 1920), p. 26.

14. "It is perhaps useful to point out that toward 1907 Klee became familiar with the work of James Ensor through J. E. Sonderegger. Ensor played here once more his role as magnificent precursor" (George Marlier, "Paul Klee," *Cahiers de Belgique* [Feb., 1929], p. 78).

15. Klee, letter to Hans Bloesch, Sept. 30, 1903, in Klee Gesellschaft, *op. cit.,* p. 6.

16. James Thrall Soby, *The Prints of Paul Klee* (New York, 1945), p. iv.

17. Paul Klee, *Über die Moderne Kunst,* lecture in Jena, 1924; English translation: *On Modern Art* (London, 1947).

18. Klee, quoted in Werner Haftmann, *Paul Klee* (Munich, 1950), p. 30.

19. "Gerüst wird aufgeladen."

20. Paul Klee, "Schöpferische Konfession" (Berlin, 1920); translated by Mini Catlin and Greta Daniel as "Opinions on Creation," in *Paul Klee* (New York, 1945), pp. 11–12.

21. Klee, quoted in Haftmann, *op. cit.,* p. 33.

22. Voltaire, *Kandide,* with 26 illustrations by Paul Klee (Munich, 1920). Klee planned to do illustrations for *Candide* in 1906 and carried them out in 1911, but the book was not published until 1920. Kurt Wolff, the publisher, brought out an English edition (New York, 1944).

23. Klee, "Kunst und Literatur des Auslands," *Die Alpen,* VI (Jan., 1912), 302.

24. Kandinsky, letter to James Johnson Sweeney, 1936, quoted in Soby, *op. cit.,* p. viii.

25. Klee, excerpt from his journals, in Grohmann, *Bildende Kunst und Architektur* (Berlin, 1953), p. 433.

26. Advertisement of Blaue Reiter almanac, from catalog of Sonderbund exhibition, 1912. Pl. 94.

27. Kandinsky, "Der Blaue Reiter (Rückblick)," *Das Kunstblatt*, XIV (1930), 57. See also Kandinsky's letter to Marc in April, 1911, about his plans for the book: Klaus Lankheit, "Zur Geschichte des Blauen Reiters," *Cicerone* (1949, Heft 3), p. 110.

28. Most of the tribal art objects came from the Munich Ethnographic Museum.

29. Marc, "Aphorism Nr. 31," *Briefe, Aufzeichnungen . . .* , vol. I, p. 127. This aphorism was adapted later by Katherine Dreier and Marcel Duchamp as the motto of the Société Anonyme.

30. Marc, "Vorwort zur zweiten Auflage," *in* Kandinsky and Marc, *Der Blaue Reiter* (Munich, 1912) [p. vi].

31. Kandinsky, Marc, Arp, Bloch, Campendonk, Klee, Kubin, Macke, Marc, and Münter.

32. Heckel, Kirchner, Mueller, Pechstein, and Nolde.

33. Kandinsky, "Franz Marc," *Cahiers d'Art,* VII–X (Paris, 1936), 273–275.

34. Macke, "Die Masken," *in* Kandinsky and Marc, *op. cit.,* p. 22.

35. Arnold Schönberg, *Herzgewächse;* text by M. Maeterlinck.

36. Alban Berg, "Aus dem 'Glühenden' "; text by Alfred Mombert.

37. Anton von Webern, "Ihr tratet zu dem Herde," from *Jahr der Seele* by Stefan George.

38. "Der Blaue Reiter," *Pan*, II (June 13, 1912), 852–858.

39. Kandinsky, *Wassily Kandinsky Memorial* (New York, 1945), p. 71.

40. Kandinsky, "Franz Marc," *op. cit.,* p. 275.

41. Kandinsky, quoted in Grote, "Kandinsky, the Painter," Max Bill (ed.), *Wassily Kandinsky* (Paris and Boston, 1951), p. 160.

42. Hugo Zehder, *Wassily Kandinsky,* vol. I of Paul F. Schmidt (ed.), *Künstler der Gegenwart* (Dresden, 1920), p. 11. Zehder's opinion is shared by Hugo Ball, who considers the two "programmatic books" the foundation of the "later so degenerated Expressionism." Cf. Hugo Ball, *Die Flucht aus der Zeit* (Munich and Leipzig, 1927), p. 12.

CHAPTER XVIII

1. In 1926 Kandinsky published his most systematic treatise, *Punkt und Linie zur Fläche* as Bauhaus Book no. 9 (Munich, 1926). This book, translated as *Point and Line to Plane* by Howard Dearstyne and Hilla Rebay (New York, 1947), was written at the Bauhaus and elucidates most clearly Kandinsky's thinking during this later period. It falls, however, outside the realm of the present book.

2. Hans Hildebrandt, *Die Kunst des 19. und 20. Jahrhunderts* (Potsdam, 1924), p. 382.

3. Lindsay, "An Examination of the Fundamental Theories of Wassily Kandinsky," p. 40. Lindsay's dissertation is a considerably more complete and broader survey of Kandinsky's theories than I am attempting here. It raises many important issues; if Lindsay's interpretation seems at times too partial to the artist, its major importance rests in the incisive relationships he establishes between Kandinsky's theories and his paintings. While doing research in Kandinsky's studio in Neuilly-sur-Seine in the spring of 1950 I had adequate opportunity to compare my interpretations with those of Lindsay. In many ways our interpretations differ, especially as to the placing of emphasis. I am also greatly indebted to Klaus Brisch for many provocative ideas during our discussions in Cologne in the summer of 1953. Unfortunately I have not been able to consult his doctoral dissertation, "Wassily Kandinsky: Untersuchung zur Entstehung der gegenstandslosen Malerei" (University of Bonn, 1955).

4. Henri Bergson, *Laughter* (New York, 1911), p. 157.

5. Thomas Mann (ed.), *The Living Thoughts of Schopenhauer* (New York, 1939), p. 29.

6. Marc, diary entry, Christmas, 1914, *in* Thoene, *Modern German Art* (Harmondsworth, England, 1938), pp. 66–67.

7. Wassily Kandinsky, *Wassily Kandinsky Memorial* (New York, 1945), p. 55.

8. Kandinsky, *Notebooks,* quoted in Nina Kandinsky, "Some Notes on the Development of Kandinsky's Painting," *in* Kandinsky, *Concerning the Spiritual in Art* (New York, 1947), p. 10.

9. Kandinsky, *Concerning the Spiritual in Art*, p. 48.

10. Kandinsky, *Wassily Kandinsky Memorial*, p. 65.

11. Marc, letter, April 12, 1915, in *Briefe, Aufzeichnungen . . .* , II, 50. In this respect Kandinsky and the late Marc differed decidedly from Paul Klee, who was always concerned with creating symbols to interpret man and the forces of nature. "The naked body is an altogether suitable object. In art classes I have gradually learned something of it from every angle. But now I will no longer project some plan of it, but will proceed so that all its essentials, even those hidden by optical perspective, will appear upon the paper. And thus a little uncontested personal property has already been discovered, a style has been created." Paul Klee, June, 1902, "Extracts from the Journal of the Artist," *in*

Margaret Miller (ed.), *Paul Klee* (New York, 1945), pp. 8–9.

12. See chapter i.

13. In his chapter "Reality and Art," Lindsay deals only with conscious aesthetic reasons for Kandinsky's absolute painting. He does not analyze the underlying causes for this retreat from physical reality, nor does he mention the important statement of repulsion to the naked body that appeared in the artist's autobiography.

14. See chapter xiv.

15. Edward Bullough, "Psychical Distance as a Factor in Art and in Aesthetic Principle," *British Journal of Psychology,* V (1912–1913), pp. 87–118.

16. See chapter xiv.

17. Kandinsky, *On the Spiritual in Art* (New York, 1946), p. 48. It is necessary to quote the Guggenheim edition of *Über das Geistige in der Kunst* for this passage as it approximates most clearly the original German version. Additions made by the artist in 1914 are incorporated in the Wittenborn edition. These changes imply Kandinsky's later, more hopeful attitude toward pure abstraction. Cf. *Concerning the Spiritual in Art,* p. 48.

18. Kandinsky, *On the Spiritual in Art,* pp. 80–81.

19. Kandinsky, "Abstrakte Kunst," *Cicerone,* XVII (1925), 639–647.

20. Kandinsky, "Line and Fish," *Axis,* II (1935), 6.

21. Roger Fry in the *Nation* (Aug. 2, 1913), quoted in Arthur J. Eddy, *Cubists and Post-Impressionism* (Chicago, 1914), p. 117.

22. Kandinsky, *Wassily Kandinsky Memorial,* p. 64.

23. Lindsay points out correctly that "these opinions of his must be taken into consideration when he is labeled an 'expressionist.'" Lindsay, "An Examination of the Fundamental Theories of Wassily Kandinsky," [University of Wisconsin, 1951], p. 59. On the other hand, expressionist painting may make use of distortion, but to consider expressionism an art of distortion is a frequently encountered misconception.

24. Kandinsky, "Über die Formfrage," *in* Kandinsky and Marc, *Der Blaue Reiter* (Munich, 1912), p. 85.

25. *Ibid.,* p. 84.

26. Kandinsky, *Wassily Kandinsky Memorial,* p. 71.

27. Kandinsky, "Über die Formfrage," p. 88.

28. *Ibid.* [p. v].

29. This idea is very similar to Herder's theory of Inspiration. J. G. Herder, *Ideen zur Philosophie der Geschichte der Menschheit* (Leipzig, 1821). Here Herder maintained that cultural articulations were human manifestations of the Spirit, which came to man to use him as its organ of expression.

30. Kandinsky, *Concerning the Spiritual in Art,* p.

32. Kandinsky himself—as Lindsay has pointed out ("An Examination of the Fundamental Theories of Wassily Kandinsky," pp. 208–213)—was not a member of the Theosophical Society. He admired, however, the cosmology of Mme Blavatsky, which attempted to create a significant synthesis of Indian wisdom and Western civilization. The antimaterialistic concepts of the Theosophical movement attracted a good many artists and writers yearning for a new religious spirit in the early part of the century, including Piet Mondrian, Hans Arp, Hugo Ball, and William Butler Yeats.

31. Kandinsky, *Concerning the Spiritual in Art,* pp. 33–34.

32. *Ibid.,* p. 36.

33. *Ibid.,* p. 39.

34. *Ibid.,* p. 47.

35. *Ibid.,* p. 45.

36. *Ibid.*

37. The remarks about color are taken from "The Language of Form and Color," *ibid.,* chap. vi, pp. 45–67.

38. *Ibid.,* pp. 51–52.

39. *Ibid.,* p. 57, *n.*

40. See p. 229.

41. Kandinsky, *Wassily Kandinsky Memorial,* p. 75.

42. Max Raphael, *Von Monet bis Picasso* (Munich, 1919), p. 102.

43. Kandinsky, *Concerning the Spiritual in Art,* p. 63.

44. Kandinsky, "Über Bühnenkomposition," *in* Kandinsky and Marc, *op. cit.,* pp. 103–113.

45. Kandinsky, *Wassily Kandinsky Memorial,* pp. 75–87.

46. By "stage composition" ("Bühnenkomposition") Kandinsky referred to the totality of movement on the stage. The possibilities of a unity of the arts in the film were still far beyond consideration in 1912.

47. Kandinsky, "Der Gelbe Klang," *in* Kandinsky and Marc, *op. cit.,* pp. 119–131.

48. Diego Rivera, quoted in "Notes on the Life, Development and Last Years of Kandinsky," *in* Kandinsky, *Wassily Kandinsky Memorial,* p. 100.

49. Bergson, *Essai sur les données immédiates de la conscience* (Paris, 1904).

50. Christian P. Heinlein, "The Affective Characteristics of the Major and Minor Modes in Music" (dissertation, Johns Hopkins University, Baltimore, 1928); quoted in Lindsay, *op. cit.,* p. 104.

51. Suzanne K. Langer, "Art: The Symbol of Sentience," *New World Writing,* IV (New York, 1953), 54. This concept of art is by no means unique to expressionism, but is shared by many twentieth-century movements, including constructivism. "The constructive artist . . . has found the means and methods to make new images and

convey them as emotional manifestations in our everyday experience. This means that shapes, lines, colors, forms are not illusory nor are they abstractions, they are factual forces and their impact on our senses is as real as the impact on light or an electric shock." Naum Gabo, lecture at the Institute of Design, Chicago, March, 1948 (mimeographed).

CHAPTER XIX

1. See chapter ix.
2. See chapter x.
3. Carl Vinnen (ed.), *Protest deutscher Künstler* (Jena, 1911).
4. Hans Tietze, "Ein Protest deutscher Künstler," *Kunstchronik*, XX (May 19, 1911), 401.
5. Heymel (ed.), *Die Antwort auf den Protest deutscher Künstler* (Munich, 1911).
6. Benno Reifenberg, "Werke und Leben," *in* Reifenberg and Haustein, *Max Beckmann* (Munich, 1949), p. 12.
7. Scheffler, *Kunst und Künstler,* XI (Berlin, 1913), 297.
8. Schmidt, "Die Beckmann Ausstellung in Magdeburg," *Cicerone,* IV (1912), 314.
9. Hans Kaiser, *Max Beckmann,* vol. I of *Künstler unserer Zeit* (Berlin, 1913).
10. "Ausstellungen, Berlin," *Cicerone,* V (1913), 143.
11. Marc, "Die neue Malerei," *Pan,* II (1912), 469.
12. *Ibid.*
13. Beckmann, in *Pan,* II (1912), 485.
14. Marc, "Anti-Beckmann," *Pan,* II (1912), 556.
15. Beckmann, "On My Painting," a lecture delivered at New Burlington Gallery, London, July, 1938, quoted in *Max Beckmann,* exhibition catalog (New York, 1941), p. 4.
16. G. Howe, "Sonderbund-Ausstellung in Düsseldorf," *Die Kunst für Alle,* XXV (Aug., 1910), 571.
17. *Denkschrift des Sonderbundes* (Düsseldorf, 1910). Partial table of contents: "Spektralimpressionismus als Übergang zum Kolorismus," "Der koloristische Rhythmus der jungfranzösischen Kunst," "Malerische Impression und koloristischer Rhythmus," "Die Auflösung des Impressionismus zum musikalischen Kolorismus bei Paul Cézanne."
18. Sonderbund catalog (1911), quoted in G. Howe, "Ausstellung des Düsseldorfer Sonderbundes," *Die Kunst für Alle,* XXVI (June, 1911), 475.
19. *Ibid.,* p. 476.
20. See chapter xx.
21. R. Reiche, "Vorwort," *Internationale Kunst-Ausstellung des Sonderbundes westdeutscher Kunstfreunde und Künstler zu Cöln, 1912* (Cologne, 1912), p. 3.
22. P. F. Schmidt, "Blütezeit der Dresdner Brücke," *Aussaat,* II (1947), 52.
23. The Russian artists from Munich showed with the German group.
24. Schmidt, "Die Internationale Ausstellung des Sonderbundes in Köln, 1912," *Zeitschrift für Bildende Kunst,* N.F., XXIII (1912), 230.
25. Jaspers, *Strindberg und Van Gogh, Versuch einer Pathographischen Analyse unter Vergleichender Heranziehung von Swedenborg und Hölderlin* (Bern, 1922), p. 130.
26. Schmidt, *op. cit.,* p. 231.
27. Ludwig Coellen, *Die neue Malerei* (Munich, 1912).
28. *Ibid.,* pp. 39–44.
29. *Ibid.,* p. 61.
30. *Ibid.*
31. Reiche, *op. cit.,* p. 6.
32. Cf. Barr, *Picasso, Fifty Years of His Art* (New York, 1946), p. 33.
33. Schmidt, *op. cit.,* p. 232. Generally Germany in 1912 was not yet ready for the impact of cubism. Almost no one at the Sonderbund realized the full implication of cubist painting.
34. *Ibid.*
35. Coellen, *op. cit.,* p. 65.
36. *Ibid.,* p. 67.
37. Sonderbund catalog, entry no. 251.
38. Van Dongen, included among the French painters in the 1911 exhibition, was this time placed in a special Dutch gallery.
39. Sonderbund catalog, entry no. 523. The picture here reproduced, pl. 97, is a lithograph, similar to the painting, except for the added border design. It was done in the same year.
40. Sonderbund catalog, entry no. 550, pl. 98.
41. Frederick Deknatel, *Edvard Munch* (New York, 1950), p. 54.
42. Sonderbund catalog, entry no. 371; cf. pl. 55.
43. Sonderbund catalog, entry no. 360; cf. pl. 62a.
44. Sonderbund catalog, entry no. 363; cf. pl. 62b.
45. Sonderbund catalog, entry no. 359. Edith Hoffmann is doubtful about the date of this picture, and gives 1912 or 1913 as possible dates (*Kokoschka: Life and Work* [Boston (1946)], pp. 113, 300). The painting was in the Sonderbund exhibit of 1912, and must have been finished by that time.
46. Schmidt, *op. cit.,* p. 234.
47. Nolde, *Jahre der Kämpfe* (Berlin, 1934), p. 209.
48. See chapter ii; pl. 1a.
49. "Franz Marc sent Helmuth Macke from Sindelsdorf to Berlin with a letter addressed to the Brücke. Through Macke I met Dr. Kaesbach, an art historian who later, during the war, became my platoon

leader and knew James Ensor whom we visited in Ostende, and who became a close friend of mine during the war." Statement by Heckel, personal interview, Sept. 7, 1953.

50. Nolde, *op. cit.,* p. 212.

51. See chapter xi; pl. 44.

52. Sonderbund catalog, entry no. 462. Cf. pl. 100.

53. Otto Mueller, in *Catalogue of Otto Mueller Exhibition* (Berlin, 1919).

54. See chapter xxii.

55. Sonderbund catalog, entry no. 450. Cf. pl. 166*a*.

56. Sonderbund catalog, entry no. 453. Cf. pl. 166*b*.

57. Marc, "Ideen über Ausstellungen," *Der Sturm,* III (1912), 66, and "Zur Sache," *ibid.,* 79–80.

58. Nolde, *op. cit.,* p. 215.

59. Walter Holzhausen, *Bonn und der Rheinische Expressionismus,* exhibition catalog (Bonn, 1952) [pp. 3–4].

60. Walt Kuhn, *The Story of the Armory Show* (New York, 1938), p. 8.

61. *Ibid.,* p. 9.

62. "Graphisches Kabinett," *Der Sturm,* III (1912), 172. The Sonderbund exhibition was also the initial stimulus for Westheim's influential *Kunstblatt.* Westheim remembers that this exhibition was the great experience of the prewar years. "It suddenly presented the modern movement not in theory but in actuality." Interview with Paul Westheim, Mexico City, Aug., 1956.

CHAPTER XX

1. Lothar Schreyer, "Zur Geschichte des Sturm," *in* Walden, *Einblick in Kunst* (Berlin, 1924).

2. *Ibid.,* p. 168.

3. Eckart von Sydow, *Die deutsche expressionistische Kultur und Malerei* (Berlin, 1920), p. 151.

4. For a thorough, though by no means sympathetic, treatment of Herwath Walden, see the novel written about him, Hermann Essig, *Der Taifun* (Leipzig, 1919).

5. Karl Kraus, "Die Operette," *Der Sturm,* I (1910), 1.

6. J. A. Lux, "Kunst und Ethik," *ibid.,* 13–14.

7. Edith Hoffmann, *Kokoschka: Life and Work* (Boston [1946]), p. 78.

8. *Der Sturm,* I (1910), 155–156.

9. *Ibid.,* I (1910), 155, 163, 189.

10. Walden, "Kunst und Leben," *ibid.,* X (1919), 2.

11. Julius Elias, *Kunstblatt,* II (1918), 327.

12. Däubler, *Im Kampf um die moderne Kunst* (Berlin, 1920), pp. 41–42.

13. On May 5, 1911, Max Osborn wrote, for *Kunstchronik,* XXII (1911), 390: "The highly modern part is a gallery of the 'Expressionists,' as this group of *Salon d'automne* people calls itself in order to clearly indicate its difference from the older Impressionists. The room arouses indignation and laughter in Berlin. I admit that I don't know why. It is a group of young people who, on the shoulders of Cézanne and Gauguin, attempt to come to new solutions. Some are a little eccentric. Some are a little cracked. This is the way the joy of new innovation operates. Some, however, have extraordinary talent: Derain, Doucet, Manguin, Marquet, Puy, Vlaminck. I approve of this youth. They are not brutal and coarse, but show a real training, culture and sensibility and enlarge the frontiers of modern art." Two weeks later Sievers' review appeared: "France is represented with a group show in a special room of the 'Expressionists.' These are a number of young painters, mostly active in Paris. Their name signifies a program. They consider Impressionism vanquished. . . . They no longer want to reproduce an impression which they gain from nature, that is to say, paint naturalistically, but they want to express the impression which their observation exercises on their artistic imagination." Sievers, "Die XXII Ausstellung der Berliner Sezession," *Cicerone,* III (1911), 383. Karl Scheffler took issue with the newly coined name. "A group of young Frenchmen has been announced under the horribly stupid name, 'Expressionists.' This name is now being parroted by all its devotees, while others use it for cheap puns. About these painters, partly talented and fine—e.g., Manguin—and partly men who stubbornly adhere to sterile formulae, not much needs to be said as we intend to devote an article to them soon." Scheffler, "Berliner Sezession—die Zweiundzwanzigste Ausstellung," *Kunst und Künstler,* IX (1911), 486.

14. Walther Heymann, "Berliner Sezession, 1911," *Der Sturm,* II (1911), 504.

15. Heymann, *ibid.,* 543.

16. Worringer, "Zur Entwicklungsgeschichte der modernen Malerei, Die Antwort auf den Protest deutscher Kunstler," *Der Sturm,* II (1911), 597–598. According to Werner Rittich, "Kunsttheorie, Wortkunsttheorie und lyrische Wortkunst im 'Sturm'" (Greifswald, 1933), p. 10, and R. Samuel and H. Thomas, *Expressionism in German Life, Literature and the Theatre* (Cambridge, England, 1939), p. 10, this was the first appearance of the term "expressionism" in *Der Sturm.* Samuel and Thomas even believe that it was the first time the term was published in Germany. Heymann's review of the Berlin Secession, however, used the term in *Der Sturm* in the previous month, as pointed out

here. Osborn published his article on May 5, 1911, but even then the term may not have been entirely new.

17. Artur Weese, "Hodler und die Eurythmie," *Der Sturm,* II (1911), 660–661.

18. Ferdinand Kiss, "Neue Sezession," *ibid.,* 688.

19. Kiss, "El Greco," *ibid.,* 689.

20. Schmidt, "Die Expressionisten," *ibid.,* 734.

21. *Ibid.,* 735.

22. "Manifest der Futuristen," *ibid.,* 822–824.

23. From the "Manifesto of the Futurists," translated in Raynal *et al., From Picasso to Surrealism,* p. 83.

24. Rosa Trillo Clough, *Looking Back at Futurism* (New York, 1942), p. 99.

25. "Manifest der Futuristen," *op. cit.,* p. 823.

26. Interestingly enough, Boccioni's sculpture, *Unique Forms of Continuity in Space,* of 1913 combines features of both the racing car and the *Winged Victory* of Samothrace.

27. F. T. Marinetti, "Manifest des Futurismus," *Der Sturm,* II (1912), 828–829.

28. Boccioni, Carrà, *et al.,* "Futuristen," *Der Sturm,* III (1912), 3–4.

29. Kandinsky, "Formen und Farbensprache," *Der Sturm,* III (1912), 11–13.

30. Alfred Döblin, "Die Bilder der Futuristen," *Der Sturm,* III (1912), 41–42.

31. Marc, "Die Futuristen," *Der Sturm,* III (1912), 187.

32. Nolde, *Jahre der Kämpfe,* p. 150.

33. Adolf Behne, "Gino Severini," *Der Sturm,* IV (1913), 74.

34. Wassily Kandinsky, "Über Kunstverstehen," *Der Sturm,* III (1912), 157–158.

35. Apollinaire, "Realité, peinture pure," *ibid.,* 224–225.

36. Enzian, "Delaunay," *Pan,* III (1913), 463–465.

37. Robert Delaunay, "Uber das Licht," translated by Paul Klee, *Der Sturm,* III (1912), 255.

38. Paul Bommersheim, "Die Überwindung der Perspective und Robert Delaunay," *Der Sturm,* III (1912), 272–273.

39. Küchler, "Kandinsky," *Hamburger Fremdenblatt* (Feb. 15, 1913).

40. The protest letter defending Kandinsky was signed by Arp, Adolf Behne, V. von Bechtejeff, Campendonk, Delaunay, Max Deri, Döblin, Alfred Flechtheim, Gleizes, Jawlensky, Klee, Laurencin, Léger, Macke, Marc, Marinetti, Meidner, Schönberg, Werefkina, and others. "Für Kandinsky," *Der Sturm,* III (1912–1913), 288.

41. Walden, introduction to catalog, *Erster deutscher Herbstsalon* (Berlin, 1913), p. 8.

CHAPTER XXI

1. Walden, "Erster deutscher Herbstsalon," *Der Sturm,* IV (1913), 106.

2. "Ausstellungen," *Cicerone,* V (1913), 688–689.

3. This picture, "perhaps the most perfect fulfillment of all of German Expressionism" (H. Bünemann, "Das Tier in der Kunst von Franz Marc," *Kunst,* I [1948], 70), was lost in World War II. The German assumption that it was brought to the United States is most questionable.

4. This is Marc's most important extant painting. It was formerly in the Moritzburg Museum in Halle a.d. Saale, for which Dr. Alois Schardt had purchased it. Like so many masterpieces of expressionism, it was auctioned off as "degenerate art" by the Nazi government. It is now in the Basel Kunstmuseum.

5. Klee also restored and repaired the painting when the right section of the canvas was severely burned after Marc's death.

6. Marc, *Briefe, Aufzeichnungen* (Berlin, 1920), vol. I, p. 34.

7. Ludwig Justi, *Von Corinth bis Klee* (Berlin, 1931), p. 138.

8. Although this painting was not in the Herbstsalon, it was done at the same time as *Improvisation No. 31,* which as no. 183 of the catalog was one of the seven paintings and sketches by Kandinsky in that exhibition.

9. Kandinsky, letter to A. J. Eddy, quoted in Eddy, *Cubists and Post-Impressionism* (Chicago, 1914), p. 126.

10. Kandinsky's distinction between the object of the painting, which is only of personal interest to the artist, and the content, which is evoked by the disposition of the forms, is similar to earlier pronouncements by Whistler, such as those about his *Arrangement in Grey and Black.*

11. See chapter xvi.

12. Kandinsky, letter to Eddy, in Eddy, *op. cit.,* p. 126.

13. Gustav Vriesen, "Der Maler August Macke," *Westfalen,* XXX (1952), 43.

14. Delaunay, letter to Macke, quoted in *Bonn und der Rheinische Expressionismus* (Bonn, 1952) [p. 2].

15. Macke, letter, February 12, 1914, quoted in *August Macke,* exhibition catalog (New York, 1952), p. 7.

16. Macke to Koehler, 1913, *in* Westheim, *Künstlerbekenntnisse* (Berlin, 1925), p. 167.

17. Klee, notes from his diary, June, 1902, quoted in Robert Goldwater and Marco Treves, *Artists on Art* (New York, 1945), pp. 442–443.

18. Delaunay frequently expressed himself in these terms, according to Sonia Delaunay. Personal interview, Paris, 1950.

19. This painting was not in the Herbstsalon exhibition.

20. In 1954 Nell Walden and Lothar Schreyer brought out an interesting book of memoirs on H. Walden and *Der Sturm*. Nell Walden and Lothar Schreyer, *Der Sturm* (Baden-Baden, 1954).

CHAPTER XXII

1. Westheim, "Christian Rohlfs," *Für und Wider* (Potsdam, 1923), p. 130.

2. See chapter viii.

3. Christian Rohlfs, letter to Dr. Kaesbach, November 3, 1918, quoted in Gertrud Bender, "Christian Rohlfs, ein Mittler zwischen zwei Jahrhunderten," *Westfalen, XXX* (1952), 8.

4. Alfred Barr, "Lyonel Feininger—American Artist," in *Lyonel Feininger Marsden Hartley* exhibition catalog (New York, 1944), p. 11.

5. See chapter xi.

6. Feininger, letter, 1917; first published in *Kunstblatt* (1931) and republished in *Lyonel Feininger*, exhibition catalog (Hannover, 1932).

7. Feininger, quoted in Barr, *op. cit.*, p. 7.

8. *Ibid.*, pp. 7–8.

9. *Ibid.*, p. 8.

10. Statement by Feininger, personal interview, Cambridge, Mass., Aug. 11, 1952.

11. *Ibid.*

12. *Ibid.* I am greatly indebted to Feininger for his comprehensive statements in this interview.

13. Feininger, letter, quoted in Perry T. Rathbone, *Lyonel Feininger,* exhibition catalog (Detroit, Summer, 1941).

14. Alois J. Schardt, "Lyonel Feininger," in *Lyonel Feininger Marsden Hartley,* p. 14.

15. Statement by Feininger, personal interview, Aug. 11, 1952.

16. Perry T. Rathbone, in his introduction to the catalog of the Feininger exhibition at the Detroit Institute of Arts, said that Feininger became familiar with the "first exploits of the Cubists, Picasso and Braque, during his stay in Paris in 1907." The artist could not have seen any cubist paintings at the time—if any were to be seen. He saw the first cubist paintings in 1911, when he returned to Paris at the time five of his canvases were shown at the Salon des Indépendents. Like the Blaue Reiter painters, Feininger was most interested in Delaunay among the cubists.

17. Schardt, *op. cit.,* p. 17.

18. Walter Gropius, quoted in *The Work of Lyonel Feininger,* exhibition catalog (Cleveland, 1951), p. 13.

19. Meidner, "Mein Leben," *in* Lothar Brieger, *Ludwig Meidner* (Leipzig, 1919), p. 11.

20. *Ibid.,* 12.

21. *Ibid.*

22. George Grosz, *A Little Yes and Big No* (New York, 1946), pp. 213–214.

23. Ludwig Meidner, in *Almanach der neuen Jugend* (1917), quoted in Westheim, *op. cit.,* p. 108.

24. *Ibid.,* p. 106.

25. *Ibid.*

26. Harald Seiler, "Wilhelm Morgners Werk," *Westfalen, XXX* (1952), 63.

27. *Ibid.,* p. 66.

28. See chapter xix.

29. Statement by Beckmann, personal interview, Chicago, Jan. 18, 1948.

30. Beckmann, "Excerpts from the Writings of the Artist," *Max Beckmann,* exhibition catalog (St. Louis, 1948), p. 41.

31. Westheim, "Beckmann: Der Wahre Expressionismus," *op. cit.,* pp. 104–105.

32. Rathbone, *Max Beckmann,* p. 18.

33. Beckmann, in *Briefe im Kriege* (Berlin, 1916).

34. Beckmann, letter, quoted in Thwaites, "Max Beckmann—Notes for an Evaluation," *Art Quarterly* (Winter, 1951), p. 275.

35. Meier-Graefe, *Entwicklungsgeschichte der modernen Kunst,* III (Munich, 1920), 679.

36. Statement by Beckmann, personal interview, Chicago, Jan. 18, 1948.

37. Hausenstein, *in* Glaser *et al., Max Beckmann* (Munich, 1924), p. 69. The same author draws these comparisons in "Max Beckmann," *Die Kunst für Alle,* XLIV (1929), 161; "Max Beckmann," *Das Werk,* XXXIV (1947), 164; and Benno Reifenberg and Hausenstein, *Max Beckmann* (Munich, 1949), p. 35.

38. Beckmann, "Meine Theorie der Malerei," lecture, New Burlington Gallery, London, July, 1938, quoted in Beckmann, *On My Painting* (New York, 1941), p. 11.

CHAPTER XXIII

1. Gauguin, quoted in Robert Goldwater, *Primitivism in Modern Painting* (New York, 1938), p. 59.

2. C. Ricci, *L'Arte dei Bambini* (Bologna, 1887), translated into German as *Die Kinderkunst* (Leipzig, 1906).

3. Carl Einstein, *Negerplastik* (Munich, 1915).

4. Hans Prinzhorn, *Bildnerei der Geisteskranken* (Berlin, 1923). In this fundamental work on neurotic art, the author investigated the paintings of three hundred patients.

5. Goldwater, *op. cit.*

6. G. A. Stevens, "Educational Significance of Indigenous African Art," in Sir Michael Sadleir (ed.), *Arts and Crafts of West Africa* (Oxford, 1935), p. 13. Sadleir, one of Kandinsky's first patrons, translated Kandinsky's *Über das Geistige* as *Art of Spiritual Harmony* (London, 1914).

7. See chapter vii.

8. Kirchner, *Chronik der Brücke,* in Peter Selz, "E. L. Kirchner's 'Chronik der Brucke,'" X (Fall, 1950), 50.

9. Nolde, *Das eigene Leben* (Berlin, 1931), p. 265. Later in the second volume of his autobiography he returns to this point, militating against the isolation of non-European art in ethnological museums and stressing the specific value of primitive art, especially for the modern artist. Nolde, *Jahre der Kämpfe* (Berlin, 1934), p. 185.

10. Nolde, *Das eigene Leben,* p. 265.

11. Nolde, *Jahre der Kämpfe,* p. 185.

12. *Ibid.,* p. 242.

13. *Ibid.,* p. 240.

14. *Ibid.,* p. 173.

15. *Ibid.,* p. 178.

16. Nolde, letter, April, 1914, quoted in Sauerlandt, *Die Kunst der letzten 30 Jahre* (Berlin, 1935), p. 115.

17. *Ibid.,* p. 116.

18. Osborn, *Max Pechstein* (Berlin, 1922), p. 102.

19. Pechstein, quoted in *ibid.,* p. 136.

20. Leonhard Adam, *Primitive Art* (Harmondsworth, England, 1949), p. 227.

21. Adolf Jannasch, *Max Pechstein,* exhibition catalog (Berlin, 1952), p. 4.

22. Kandinsky, *Concerning the Spiritual in Art* (New York, 1947), pp. 23–24.

23. Max Slevogt, who went to Egypt in 1913, may still be considered as belonging to the earlier trends. The quick impressionistic improvisations of desert scenes, camels, and Bedouins, with which he returned from North Africa, indicated his primary interest in a search for new subject matter.

24. Macke, quoted in Vriesen, "Der Maler August Macke," *Westfalen,* XXX (1952), p. 47.

25. Hausenstein, *Kairuan, oder eine Geschichte vom Maler Klee und von der Kunst dieses Zeitalters* (Munich, 1921), p. 83; above quotation translated in Douglas Cooper, *Paul Klee* (Harmondsworth, England, 1949), pp. 9–10.

26. Klee, diary, April 16, 1914, quoted in Klee Gesellschaft, *Paul Klee* (Bern, 1949), p. 7.

27. Georg Schmidt, *Paul Klee* (Basel, 1946), p. 6.

28. Vriesen, "August Macke," in *August Macke,* exhibition catalog (New York, 1952), p. 8.

29. Statement by W. Macke, in a personal interview, Bonn, July 26, 1953.

30. Marc, diary entry, Hagéville, Oct. 25, 1914, *Briefe aus dem Feld* (Berlin, 1948), p. 168.

31. "Nekrologe," *Kunstchronik,* XXVI (1915), 58.

32. As early as 1912, in a review of an exhibition of painting by Amiet in Munich, Klee wrote: "The artist does not always want to reproduce the Lord . . . he wants to be the Lord himself" (Klee, "Literature und Kunst des Auslands," *Die Alpen,* VI [1912], 614).

33. Klee, *Schöpferische Konfession* (Berlin, 1920).

34. *Ibid.*

CHAPTER XXIV

1. Other former members of the Brücke, especially Heckel and Schmidt-Rottluff, were interested in the same problem of unification of man and environment, and used similar means for its achievement. Franz Marc and Campendonk, concentrating on the animal and using different formal means, were also still concerned with the representation of the natural form in its surroundings.

2. Hans Fehr, *Erinnerungen and Ernst Ludwig Kirchner* (Bern, 1955).

3. *Ibid.*

4. Hartlaub, *Kunst und Religion,* p. 91. The *Ostende Madonna* was destroyed by fire during World War II.

5. Niemeyer, *Denkschrift des Sonderbundes* (Cologne, 1910), p. 93.

6. Luke 24: 29.

7. Luke 24: 13–16.

8. Kandinsky, "Toile, vide, etc.," *Cahiers d'Art,* V–VI (1935), 117.

9. Lindsay reports this fact in his dissertation, "An Examination of the Fundamental Theories of Kandinsky," p. 152.

10. See chapter xvi.

11. See chapter ii.

12. Cf. Kurt Karl Eberlein, "Franz Marc und die Kunst unserer Zeit," *Genius,* III (1921), 173–179.

13. See chapter xviii.

14. See chapter xviii.

15. Marc, letter, April 18, 1915, in *Briefe aus dem Feld* (Berlin, 1948), p. 69.

16. Biermann, *Heinrich Campendonk* (Leipzig, 1921), p. 14.

17. See chapter xiii.
18. J. S. Plaut (ed.), *Oskar Kokoschka* (New York, 1948), p. 23.
19. *Ibid.,* p. 15.
20. Karen Michaelis, "Der tolle Kokoschka," *Kunstblatt,* II (1918), 361–366.
21. Kokoschka, in a letter, dated Jan. 5, 1954, to Catherine Filsinger of the City Art Museum of St. Louis, dates this painting 1918. It is, however, very different from the more stringy application of pastose paint that Kokoschka used at that time. Hans Maria Wingler, on the other hand, proposes the date 1923 for this painting (Wingler, *Oskar Kokoschka* [Salzburg, 1956], p. 311, fig. 161). It seems to me to be most closely related both in style and subject to his *Woman with Slave* of 1920.
22. Kokoschka, quoted in Hans Maria Wingler, "Kokoschkas Pädagosche Konzeption," *Kunstwerk-Schriften,* XXIII (1951), 46.

CHAPTER XXV

1. There had been a move on the part of the German imperial government to relieve certain artists from hazardous front-line service to paint pictures glorifying the war and its military leaders. The expressionist painters, considered dangerous and undesirable, were not included in this scheme. Flechtheim, "Mein Freund Nauen," *Feuer,* I (1919–1920), 34.
2. *An Alle Künstler* (Berlin, 1919).
3. *Ibid.,* p. 10.
4. Pechstein, "Was Wir Wollen," *ibid.,* p. 19.
5. Kurt Eisner, "Der soziliastische Staat und der Künstler," *ibid.*
6. *Ja! Stimmen des Arbeitsrates für Kunst in Berlin* (Berlin, 1919).
7. From the "First Proclamation of the Bauhaus," translated in Herbert Bayer, Walter Gropius, Ise Gropius, *Bauhaus, 1919–1928* (New York, 1938), p. 16.
8. Schmidt-Rottluff was among the first painters to be asked by Gropius to join the faculty of the Bauhaus.

He refused, but remained close friends with the Bauhaus artists, especially Feininger.
9. See chapter vi.
10. George Grosz, *A Little Yes and Big No* (New York, 1946), p. 184.
11. A similar development occurred at the same time in Italy. Carlo Carrà, formerly associated with the futurists, became a leader of the Valori-Plastici and published a monograph on Georg Schrimpf. Cf. Sauerlandt, *Die Kunst der letzten 30 Jahre* (Berlin, 1935), p. 168.
12. Westheim, "Der Kunstbetrieb," in *Für und Wider* (Potsdam, 1923), p. 32.
13. Cf. Appendix B. Paul Westheim's *Kunstblatt,* the most influential of the journals, had a circulation of about three thousand.
14. Cf. chapter xiii, note 2.
15. Ludwig Justi, *Von Corinth bis Klee* (Berlin, 1931), p. 141.
16. Kokoschka, "Vorrede," *Oskar Kokoschka,* exhibition catalog (Munich, 1950), p. 7.
17. See chapter i.
18. Worringer, lecture, Nov., 1920, to the *Deutsche Goethegesellschaft,* Munich, published as *Künstlerische Zeitfragen* (Munich, 1921).
19. *Ibid.,* pp. 16, 18.
20. Carl Georg Heise, "Zeitglosse und Beschluss," *Genius,* III (1921), 355.
21. Carl Georg Heise, "Die Forderung des Tages," *Kurt Wolff Almanach* (Leipzig, 1925), p. 6.
22. Tietze, lecture, Dec., 1924, in Vienna, published in *Lebendige Kunstwissenschaft* (Vienna, 1925), p. 44.
23. Franz Roh, *Nach-Expressionismus* (Leipzig, 1925).
24. *Ibid.,* pp. 119–120.
25. This in spite of Nolde's charter membership in the Nazi party. See chapter x.

APPENDIX A

1. This translation is part of Peter Selz, "E. L. Kirchner's 'Chronik der Brücke,' " *College Art Journal,* X (Fall, 1950), 50–56.

BIBLIOGRAPHY

(Among the vast number of publications dealing with German expressionism the following books, articles, and catalogs were most helpful. The items marked with an asterisk are primary bibliographical sources.)

Books

Ahlers-Hestermann, Friedrich. *Stilwende: Aufbruch der Jugend um 1900.* Berlin: Gebr. Mann, 1956.

Amiet, Cuno. *Über Kunst und Künstler.* Bern: Bernische Kunstgesellschaft, 1948.

Apollinaire, Guillaume. *Les Peintres Cubistes.* Paris: Eugène Figuière, 1913. (Translated as *The Cubist Painters.* New York: Wittenborn, Schultz, 1949.)

Apollonio, Umbro. *Die Brücke e la Cultura dell'Expressionismo.* Venice: Alfieri, Editorem, 1952.

Arbeitsrat für Kunst, Berlin. *Ja!* (Texts by Alloh, Behne, Belling, and others.) Berlin: Photographische Gesellschaft in Charlottenburg, 1919.

Armitage, Merle. *Five Essays on Klee.* (Includes essays by Merle Armitage, Clement Greenberg, Howard Devree, Nancy Wilson Ross, James Johnson Sweeney.) New York: Duell, Sloan & Pearce, 1950.

Arp, Hans, and El Lissitzky. *Die Kunstismen.* Zürich: E. Reutsch, 1925.

Bahr, Hermann. *Expressionismus.* Munich: Delphin Verlag, 1920.

Ball, Hugo. *Die Flucht aus der Zeit.* Munich-Leipzig: Duneker & Humblot, 1927.

*Barr, Alfred H., Jr. *German Painting and Sculpture.* New York: The Museum of Modern Art, 1931.

———. *Picasso, Fifty Years of His Art.* New York: The Museum of Modern Art, 1946.

Baumeister, Willi. *Das Unbekannte in der Kunst.* Stuttgart: Curt E. Schwab Verlagsgesselschaft, 1947.

Baur, Albert. *Cuno Amiet.* Basel: Holbein Verlag, 1943.

Bayer, Herbert, *et al. Bauhaus, 1919–28.* New York: The Museum of Modern Art, 1938.

Beckmann, Max. *Briefe im Kriege.* Berlin: Bruno Cassirer, 1916.

———. *On My Painting.* New York: Buchholz Gallery, 1941.

Benesch, Otto. *Egon Schiele as a Draughtsman.* Vienna: State Printing Office of Austria [1950].

Benois, Alexandre, The *Russian School of Painting.* New York: Alfred A. Knopf, 1956.

Bergson, Henri. *Essai sur les données immédiates de la conscience.* Paris: F. Alcan, 1889.

———. *Le Rire.* Paris: F. Alcan, 1900. (Translated as *Laughter.* New York: The Macmillan Company, 1911)

Bethge, Hans. *Worpswede.* (Vol. XXXII of *Die Kunst.*) (Edited by Richard Muther.) Berlin, 1907.

Bierbaum, Otto Julius. *Stuck.* Bielefeld and Leipzig: Knackfuss-Künstlermonographien, 1899.

Biermann, Georg. *Heinrich Campendonk.* (Vol. XVII of *Junge Kunst.*) Leipzig: Klinkhardt & Biermann, 1921.

———. *Max Pechstein* (Vol. I of *Junge Kunst.*) Leipzig: Klinkhardt & Biermann, 1919.

———. *Oskar Kokoschka.* (Vol. LII of *Junge Kunst.*) Leipzig: Klinkhardt & Biermann, 1929.

Bill, Max, *et al. Wassily Kandinsky.* Boston: Institute of Contemporary Art, 1951.

Blanshard, F. B. *Retreat from Likeness in the Theory of Painting.* New York: Columbia University Press, 1949.

Brieger, Lothar. *Ludwig Meidner.* (Vol. IV of *Junge Kunst.*) Leipzig: Klinkhardt & Biermann, 1919.

Brisch, Klaus. *Deutsche Graphik seit 1900.* Bergisch Gladbach: Joh. Heider [1956].

*Buchheim, Lothar-Günther. *Die Künstlergemeinschaft Brücke.* Feldafing: Buchheim Verlag, 1955.

————. *Max Beckmann.* Feldafing: Buchheim Verlag, 1954.

Bünemann, Hermann. *Franz Marc, Zeichnungen—Aquarelle.* Munich: F. Bruckmann, 1948.

Burger, Fritz. *Cézanne und Hodler.* (2 vols.) Munich: Delphin Verlag, 1920.

————. *Einführung in die moderne Kunst.* Handbuch der Kunstwissenschaft. Berlin-Neubabelsberg: Akademische Verlagsgesellschaft Athenaion, 1917.

Busch, Günter. *Paula Modersohn-Becker, Handzeichnungen.* Bremen: Angelsachsen Verlag, 1949.

Carrà, Carlo. *Georg Schrimpf.* Rome: Valori Plastici, 1924.

Chassé, Charles. *Le Mouvement Symboliste dans L'Art du XIX Siècle.* Paris: Libraire Floury, 1947.

Clough, Rosa Trillo. *Looking Back at Futurism.* New York: Columbia University Press, 1942.

Coellen, Ludwig. *Die neue Malerei.* Munich: E. W. Bonsels & Co., 1912.

Cooper, Douglas. *Paul Klee.* Harmondsworth, Middlesex: Penguin Books, 1949.

Corinth, Lovis. *Selbstbiographie.* Leipzig: S. Hirzel, 1926.

Corinth, Lovis, and Wilhelm Hausenstein. *Von Corinth und über Corinth.* Leipzig: E. A. Seemann, 1921.

Corrinth, Curt. *Potsdamer Platz.* (Illustrated by Paul Klee.) Munich: Georg Müller, 1920.

Courthion, Pierre. *Klee.* Paris: Fernand Hazan, 1953.

Crevel, René. *Paul Klee.* (Vol. XXXVIII of *Les Peintres Nouveaux.*) Paris: Gallimard, 1930.

Däubler, Theodor. *Im Kampf um die moderne Kunst.* (Vol. III of *Tribüne der Kunst und Zeit.*) (Edited by Kasimir Edschmidt.) Berlin: Erich Reiss Verlag, 1920.

————. *Der neue Standpunkt.* Leipzig: Insel Verlag, 1919.

Debrunner, Hugo. *Wir entdecken Kandinsky.* Zürich: Origo Verlag [1947].

*Deknatel, Frederick. *Edvard Munch.* New York: Chanticleer Press, 1950.

Denis, Maurice. *Théories.* Paris: Bibliothèque de l'Occident, 1913.

Deri, Max. *Naturalismus, Idealismus, Expressionismus.* Leipzig: E. A. Seemann, 1921.

————. *Die neue Malerei.* Munich: R. Piper & Co., 1913.

Documents. Revue Mensuelle des Questions Allemandes: "L'Art Allemande Contemporain." Offenbourg: Bureau Internationale de liaison et de documentation, 1951.

*Dorival, Bernard. *Les Etapes de la Peinture Française Contemporaine.* (3 vols.) Paris: Gallimard, 1946.

Dreier, Katherine S. *Burliuk.* New York: The Société Anonyme, Inc., 1944.

————. *Modern Art: Société Anonyme.* New York: The Société Anonyme, Inc., 1926.

————. *Western Art and the New Era.* New York: The Société Anonyme, Inc., 1923.

Eddy, Arthur J. *Cubists and Post-Impressionism.* Chicago: A. C. McClurg, 1914.

Edschmidt, Kasimir (pseud.). *Das Bücherdekameron.* Berlin: Erich Reiss Verlag, 1923.

————. (ed.) *Schöpferische Konfessionen.* Berlin: Erich Reiss Verlag, 1919.

————. *Über den Expressionismus in der Literatur und der neuen Malerei.* (Vol. I of *Tribüne der Kunst und Zeit.*) Berlin: Erich Reiss Verlag, 1919.

Ehrenstein, Albert. *Tubutsch.* (With twelve drawings by Oskar Kokoschka.) Leipzig: Insel Verlag, 1919.

Eichner, Johannes. *Gabriele Münter: Werke aus fünf Jahrzehnten.* Murnau: (privately published), 1952.

Einstein, Carl. *Die Kunst des 20. Jahrhunderts.* (Vol. XVI of *Propyläen-Kunstgeschichte.*) Berlin: Propyläen-Verlag, 1926.

————. *Negerplastik.* Munich: Kurt Wolff, 1920.

Eisler, Max (ed.). *Gustav Klimt—An Aftermath.* Vienna: Oesterr. Staatsdruckerei, 1931.

Essig, Hermann. *Der Taifun.* Leipzig: Kurt Wolff Verlag, 1919.

Esswein, Hermann. *Alfred Kubin. Der Künstler und sein Werk.* Munich: Georg Müller Verlag, 1911.

*Estienne, Charles. *Kandinsky.* Paris: Editions de Beaune, 1950.

Faistauer, Anton. *Neue Malerei in Oesterreich.* Betrachtungen eines Malers. Vienna: Amalthea-Verlag, 1922.

Fechter, Paul. *Der Expressionismus.* Munich: R. Piper, 1919.

————. *Das graphische Werk Max Pechsteins.* Berlin: F. Gurlitt, 1921.

Fehr, Hans. *Erinnerungen an Ernst Ludwig Kirchner.* Bern: Gutekunst & Klipstein, 1955.

Festschrift für Emil Nolde zum 60. Geburstag. (Contributions by Klee, Sauerlandt, Schiefler, *et al.*) Dresden: Neue Kunst Fides, 1927.

Fiedler, Conrad. *Nine Aphorisms from the Notebooks of Conrad Fiedler.* (Translated and selected by Victor Hammer.) Aurora, New York: Wells College Press, 1941.

————. *On Judging Works of Visual Art.* (Translated by Henry Schaefer-Simmern and Fulmer Mood.) Berkeley and Los Angeles: University of California Press, 1949.

————. *Der Ursprung der künstlerischen Thätigkeit.* Leipzig: Hirzel, 1887.

Fiedler, Conrad. *Vom Wesen der Kunst*. Munich: R. Piper, 1942.

Fischer, Otto. *Das neue Bild*. Munich: Delphin-Verlag, [1912].

Forel, Auguste. *Rückblick auf mein Leben*. Zürich: Europa-Verlag, 1935.

Frey, Adolf. *Arnold Böcklin*. Stuttgart: J. G. Cotta, 1903.

Gallwitz, S. D. *Briefe und Tagebuchblätter von Paula Modersohn-Becker*. Linz: Genius-Kurt Wolff Verlag, 1920.

Gauguin, Paul. *Avant et Après*. Leipzig: Kurt Wolff Verlag, 1918.

Geist, Hans Frederich. *Paul Klee*. Hamburg: Hauswedell Verlag, 1958.

Giedion-Welcker, Carola. *Paul Klee*. New York: The Viking Press, 1952.

Gilbert, Katherine E., and Helmut Kuhn. *A History of Esthetics*. Bloomington: Indiana University Press, 1953.

Glaser, Curt. *Edvard Munch*. Berlin: Bruno Cassirer, 1917.

———. *Die Graphik der Neuzeit*. Berlin: Bruno Cassirer, 1922–1923.

Glaser, Curt, et al. *Max Beckmann*. Munich: R. Piper, 1924.

Gleizes, Albert, and Jean Metzinger. *Du Cubisme*. Paris: Eugène Figuière, 1912.

Goldwater, Robert J. *Primitivism in Modern Painting*. New York: Harper and Brothers, 1938.

Goldwater, Robert J., and Marco Treves. *Artists on Art*. New York: Pantheon, 1945.

Gopel, Erhard. *Max Beckmann der Zeichner*. Munich: R. Piper Verlag, 1954.

*Grohmann, Will. *Bildende Kunst und Architektur*. (Vol. III of *Zwischen den beiden Kriegen*.) Berlin: Suhrkamp Verlag, 1953.

———. *The Drawings of Paul Klee*. New York: Curt Valentin, 1944.

*———. *Karl Schmidt-Rottluff*. Stuttgart: Kohlhammer Verlag, 1956.

———. *Paul Klee*. Paris: Editions Cahiers d'Art, 1929.

*———. *Paul Klee*. New York: Harry N. Abrams, 1954.

———. *Das Werk Ernst Ludwig Kirchners*. Munich: Kurt Wolff, 1926.

———. *Zeichnungen von Ernst Ludwig Kirchner*. Dresden: Verlag Ernst Arnold, 1925.

Grosz, George. *Das Gesicht der herrschenden Klasse*. Berlin: Malik Verlag, 1921.

———. *A Little Yes and a Big No*. New York: The Dial Press, 1946.

———. *Der Spiesser-Spiegel*. Dresden: Carl Reissner Verlag, 1932.

Grote, Ludwig. *Deutsche Kunst im 20. Jahrhundert*. Munich: Prestel Verlag, 1953.

Guerin, Marcel. *L'Oeuvre Gravé de Gauguin*. Paris: H. Floury, 1927.

Händler, Gerhard. *Deutsche Maler der Gegenwart*. Berlin: Rembrandt Verlag, 1956.

Haftmann, Werner. *Malerei im 20. Jahrhundert*. (Vol. I, 1954; Vol. II, Plates, 1955.) Munich: Prestel Verlag.

———. *Paul Klee: Wege bildnerischen Denkens*. Munich: Prestel Verlag, 1950. (American edition: *The Mind and Work of Paul Klee*. New York: Frederick A. Praeger, 1954.)

Hahnloser-Bühler, Hedy. *Felix Vallotton et ses amis*. Paris: Editions A. Sedrowski, 1936.

Hamann, R. *Die deutsche Malerei vom Rokoko bis zum Expressionismus*. Leipzig: G. B. Teubner, 1925.

*Hartlaub, G. F. *Die Graphik des Expressionismus in Deutschland*. Stuttgart: Gert Hatje, 1947.

———. *Kunst und Religion*. (Vol. II of *Das Neue Bild*.) (Edited by Carl Georg Heise.) Leipzig: Kurt Wolff Verlag, 1919.

———. *Die neue deutsche Graphik*. (Vol. XIV of *Tribüne der Zeit und Kunst*.) Berlin: Erich Reiss Verlag, 1920.

Hausenstein, Wilhelm. *Die bildende Kunst der Gegenwart*. Stuttgart and Berlin: Deutsche Verlagsanstalt, 1914.

———. *Kairuan oder Geschichte vom Maler Klee und von der Kunst dieses Zeitalters*. Munich: Kurt Wolff, 1921.

———. *Über Expressionismus in der Malerei*. (Vol. II of *Tribüne der Kunst und Zeit*.) (Edited by Kasimir Edschmidt.) Berlin: Erich Reiss Verlag, 1919.

Heilmaier, Hans. *Kokoschka*. (Les Artistes Nouveaux.) Paris: Ed. G. Crès & Cie, 1929.

Hetsch, Rolf (ed.). *Paula Modersohn-Becker*. Berlin: Rembrandt Verlag, 1932.

Hevesi, Ludwig. *Altkunst—Neukunst. Wien 1894 bis 1908*. Vienna: Verlag C. Konegen, 1909.

Heym, Georg. *Umbra Vitae*. (Forty-seven original woodcuts by Kirchner, also typography and cover.) Munich: Kurt Wolff, 1924.

Heymann, Walter. *Max Pechstein*. Munich: Piper & Co., 1916.

Hildebrand, Adolf. *The Problem of Form in Painting and Sculpture*. (Translated by Max Meyer and Robert M. Ogden.) New York, 1907.

Hildebrandt, Hans. *Der Expressionismus in der Malerei.* Stuttgart and Berlin: Deutsche Verlagsanstalt, 1919.

—————. *Die Kunst des 19. und 20. Jahrhunderts* (Handbuch der Kunstwissenschaft.) Wildpark-Potsdam: Akademische Verlagsgesellschaft Athenaion, 1931.

—————. *Krieg und Kunst.* Munich: Verlag R. Piper & Co., 1916.

Hindenmith, Paul. *Drei Opern-Einakter.* (Includes Kokoschka's "Mörder, Hoffnung der Frauen.") Mainz: Verlag B. Schott's Söhne, [1921].

Hodin, J. P. *The Dilemma of Being Modern.* London: Routledge, Kegan Paul, 1956.

*Hoffmann, Edith. *Kokoschka: Life and Work.* Boston: Boston Book and Art Shop, [1946].

Hoffmann, Rudolf (ed.). *Holzschnitte von Emil Nolde.* (Introduction by Werner Haftmann.) Bremen: Verlag Michael Hertz, 1947.

—————. *Radierungen von Emil Nolde.* (Introduction by Werner Haftmann.) Bremen: Verlag Michael Hertz, 1948.

Holzhausen, Walter. *August Macke.* Munich: F. Bruckmann, 1955.

*Huyghe, René. *Les Contemporaines.* Paris: Editions Pierre Tisné, 1949.

Huysmans, J. K. *Trois Primitifs.* Paris: A. Messein, 1905.

Im Kampf um die Kunst. Die Antwort auf den "Protest deutscher Kunstler." Munich: R. Piper, 1911.

Jannasch, Adolf. *Carl Hofer.* (Vol. I of *Kunst der Gegenwart.*) (Edited by Adolf Behne.) Potsdam: Eduard Stichnote, 1946.

Jaspers, Karl. *Strindberg und Van Gogh. Versuch einer pathographischen Analyse unter vergleichender Heranziehung von Swedenborg und Hölderlin.* Berne, 1922.

Justi, Ludwig. *Neue Kunst. Ein Führer zu den Gemälden der sogenannten Expressionisten in der National-Galerie.* Berlin: Julius Bard, 1921.

—————. *Von Corinth bis Klee.* Berlin: Julius Bard, 1931.

Kahnweiler, Daniel-Henry. *Klee.* Paris: Braun & Cie, 1950.

Kaiser, Hans. *Max Beckmann.* Berlin: Paul Cassirer, 1913.

Kandinsky, Wassily. *Essays über Kunst und Künstler.* (Edited by Max Bill.) Teufen (Switzerland): Verlag Arthur Niggli und Willy Verkauf, 1955.

—————. *Punkt und Linie zur Fläche.* (Vol. IX of *Bauhausbücher.*) Munich: Albert Langen, 1926. (Translated as *Point and Line to Plane.* New York:

Solomon R. Guggenheim Foundation, 1947.)

—————. *Rückblicke* (1901–1913). (Seventy-five reproductions with text.) Berlin: Sturm Verlag, 1913. (Translation of revised Russian edition as "Text Artista," in *Wassily Kandinsky Memorial.* New York: Solomon R. Guggenheim Foundation, 1945.)

—————. *Über das Geistige in der Kunst.* Munich: R. Piper, 1912. (English translations: *The Art of Spiritual Harmony.* [Translated by Sir Michael Sadleir.] London: Constable & Co., Ltd., 1914. *On the Spiritual in Art.* [Edited by Hilla Rebay.] New York: The Solomon R. Guggenheim Foundation, 1947. *Concerning the Spiritual in Art.* New York: Wittenborn, Schultz, Inc., 1947.)

Kandinsky, Wassily, and Franz Marc (eds.). *Der blaue Reiter.* Munich: R. Piper & Co., 1912.

Kern, Walter. *Gedanken und Aufsätze über Kunst.* Zürich: Oprecht, 1940.

Kestner Gesellschaft, Hannover. *James Ensor. Festschrift zur ersten deutschen Ensor-Ausstellung.* (Articles by Alexander Dorner, Herbert von Garvens-Garvensburg, Wilhelm Fraenger.) Hannover: Kestner Gesellschaft, 1927.

Klee, Paul. *Das Bildnerische Denken* (Jürg Spiller, ed.). Basel/Stuttgart: Benno Schwabe, 1956.

—————. *Pädagogisches Skizzenbuch.* (Vol. II of *Bauhausbücher.*) Munich: Albert Langen, 1925. (Translated as *Pedagogical Sketch Book* by Sybil Moholy-Nagy. New York: Frederick A. Praeger, 1953.)

—————. *Tagebücher 1898–1918.* Cologne: DuMont-Schauberg, 1957.

—————. *Über die Moderne Kunst.* (Lecture delivered in Jena, 1924.) Bern: Benteli, 1945. (Translated as *On Modern Art* by Paul Findlay. [Introduction by Herbert Reed.] London: Faber and Faber, 1948.)

Klee Gesellschaft, Bern. *Paul Klee.* Dokumente und Bilder aus den Jahren, 1896–1930. Bern: Benteli, 1949.

Klumpp, Hermann. *Abstrakion in der Malerei: Kandinsky, Feininger, Klee.* Berlin: Deutscher Kunst-Verlag, 1932.

Kokoschka, Oskar. *Dramen und Bilder.* (3 plays.) Introduction by Paul Stefan. Leipzig: Kurt Wolff, 1913.

—————. *Der Expressionismus Edvard Munchs.* Vienna-Linz-Munich: Gurlitt Verlag, 1953. (Translated as "Edvard Munch's Expressionism," *College Art Journal,* XII [1952–53], 312–320; XIII [1953–54], 15–18.)

—————. *Der gefesselte Kolumbus.* (Portfolio of lithographs by Kokoschka.) Berlin: Fritz Gurlitt, 1916.

Kokoschka, Oskar. *Hiob.* (Drama with lithographs by Kokoschka.) Berlin: Paul Cassirer, 1917.

———. *Menschenköpfe.* (Portfolio of drawings by Kokoschka.) Berlin: Der Sturm, 1916.

———. *Mörder, Hoffnung der Frauen.* (Illustrated by Kokoschka.) Berlin: Der Sturm, 1916.

———. *O Ewigkeit-Du Donnerwort. Worte der Kantate nach Johann Sebastian Bach.* (Portfolio of lithographs by Kokoschka.) Berlin: Fritz Gurlitt, 1916.

———. *Schriften 1907-1955.* (Edited by H. M. Wingler.) Munich: Verlag Albert Langen–Georg Müller, 1956.

———. *Die Träumenden Knaben.* (Poem.) Vienna: Verlag der Wiener Werkstätte, 1908; Leipzig: Kurt Wolff, 1913.

———. *Variationen über ein Thema.* (Portfolio of drawings by Kokoschka; introduction by Max Dvořák.) Vienna: Richard Lanyi, 1921.

———. *Zwanzig Zeichnungen.* (Portfolio of drawings by Kokoschka.) Berlin: Der Sturm, 1913.

Kracauer, Siegfried. *From Caligari to Hitler.* Princeton: Princeton University Press, 1947.

Kubin, Alfred. *Sansara.* Munich: Georg Müller, 1913.

Künstler, Gustav. *Egon Schiele als Graphiker.* Vienna: Amandus Edition, 1946.

Kuhn, Walt. *The Story of the Armory Show.* New York: Walt Kuhn, 1938.

Landsberger, Franz. *Impressionismus und Expressionismus.* Leipzig: Klinkhardt & Biermann, 1919.

Lankheit, Klaus. *Franz Marc.* Berlin: Konrad Lemmer, 1950.

Lasker-Schüler, Else. *Mein Herz.* Ein Liebesroman mit Bildern und wirklich lebenden Menschen. Munich: Verlag H. F. S. Bachmaier, 1912.

Lemmer, Konrad. *Max Pechstein und der Beginn des Expressionismus.* Berlin: Konrad Lemmer, 1949.

Lenning, Henry R. *The Art Nouveau.* The Hague: M. Nijhoff, 1951.

Leonhard, Kurt. *Augenschein und Inbegriff. Die Wandlungen der neuen Malerei.* Stuttgart: Deutsche Verlagsanstalt, 1953.

Liebermann, Max. *Gesammelte Schriften.* Berlin, 1922.

Lipps, Theodor. *Aesthetik, Psychologie des Schönen in der Kunst.* (Vol. I: *Grundlegung der Aesthetik.*) Hamburg and Leipzig: L. Voss, 1903–1906.

Loos, Adolf. *Trotzdem.* Innsbruck: Brenner-Verlag, 1931.

Loosli, C. *Ferdinand Hodler, Leben Werk und Nachlass.* Zürich: Rascher, 1919.

———. *Ferdinand Hodler.* (Les Artistes Nouveaux.) Paris: Ed. G. Crès, 1931.

Lorck, Carl von. *Expressionismus.* Einführung in die europäische Kunst des 20. Jahrhunderts. Lübeck: Dr. I. M. Wildner Verlag, 1947.

*Madsten, Stephan Tschudi. *Sources of Art Nouveau.* New York: George Wittenborn, 1955.

Marc, Franz. *Briefe, Aufzeichnungen und Aphorismen.* (2 vols.) Berlin: Paul Cassirer, 1920.

———. *Briefe aus dem Feld.* Berlin: Helmut Rauschenbusch Verlag, 1948.

———. *Skizzenbuch aus dem Felde.* (Edited by Klaus Lankheit.) Berlin: Gebrüder Mann, 1956.

Marc, Maria (ed.). *Franz Marc. Botschafen an den Prinzen Jussuff.* Munich: R. Piper, 1954.

Marinetti, Filippo. *Futurismo e fascismo.* Foligno, 1924.

———. *Marinetti e il futurismo.* Rome, Milan: Augustea, 1929.

Martini, Fritz. *Was War Expressionismus.* Deutung und Auswahl seiner Lyrik. Urach: Port Verlag, 1948.

Marzynski, Georg. *Die Methode des Expressionismus.* Leipzig: Klinkhardt & Biermann, 1921.

Masciotta, Michelangelo. *Kokoschka.* Florence: Del Turco Editore, 1949.

Meidner, Ludwig. *Septemberschrei.* Berlin: Paul Cassirer, 1920.

Meier-Graefe, Julius. *Entwicklungsgeschichte der modernen Kunst.* (3 vols.) Munich: R. Piper, 1920.

———. *Der Fall Böcklin.* Stuttgart: J. Hoffmann, 1905.

———. *Felix Vallotton.* Berlin and Paris: E. Sagot, 1898.

———. *Hans von Marées.* Munich and Leipzig: R. Piper & Co., 1909–1910.

———. *Der Vater.* Berlin: S. Fischer Verlag, 1932.

Michaud, Guy. *La Doctrine Symboliste (Documents).* Paris: Libraire Nizet, 1947.

Michel, Wilhelm. *Das Teufliche und Groteske in der Kunst.* Munich: R. Piper, 1917.

Mihan, George. *Looted Treasure. Germany's Raid on Art.* London: Alliance Press, 1944.

Moholy-Nagy, L. *Vision in Motion.* Chicago: Paul Theobald, 1947.

Nemitz, Fritz. *Deutsche Malerei der Gegenwart.* Munich: R. Piper, 1948.

Newlin, Dika. *Bruckner, Mahler, Schönberg.* New York: King's Crown Press, 1947.

Niemeyer, Wilhelm. *Denkschrift des Sonderbundes.* Cologne, 1910.

Nierendorf, Karl. *Paul Klee.* New York: Oxford University Press, 1941.

Nirenstein, Otto. *Egon Schiele: Persoenlichkeit und Werk.* (Catalogue raisonné.) Vienna: Paul Zsolnay, 1930.

Nolde, Emil. *Briefe aus den Jahren, 1894–1926.* (Edited by Max Sauerlandt.) Berlin: Furche Kunstverlag, 1927.

————. *Das Eigene Leben.* Berlin: Julius Bard, 1931. (2d ed. revised, Flensburg: Christian Wolff, 1949.)

————. *Jahre der Kämpfe.* Berlin: Julius Bard, 1934.

Novembergruppe Berlin. *An Alle Künstler.* (Anthology.) Berlin, 1919.

Osborn, Max. *Max Pechstein.* Berlin: Propylaeen Verlag, 1922.

Pauli, Gustav. *Paula Modersohn-Becker.* Leipzig: Kurt Wolff, 1919.

Paulsen, Wolfgang. *Expressionismus und Aktivismus.* (Dissertation, University of Bern.) Strassburg: Heitz & Co., 1934.

Pechstein, Max. *Reisebilder, Italien, Südsee. 50 Federzeichnungen auf Stein.* Berlin: Paul Cassirer, n.d.

————. *Das Vater Unser.* Berlin: Propylaeen Verlag, 1921.

Pevsner, Nikolaus. *Pioneers of the Modern Movement from William Morris to Walter Gropius.* London: Faber and Faber, 1936.

Pfister, Kurt. *Deutsche Graphiker der Gegenwart.* Leipzig: Klinkhardt & Biermann, 1920.

Picard, Max. *Expressionistische Bauernmalerei.* Munich: Delphin Verlag, 1915.

Platschek, Hans. *Oskar Kokoschka.* Buenos Aires: Editorial Poseidon, 1946.

Plaut, James S. (ed.). *Oskar Kokoschka.* New York: Chanticleer Press, 1948.

Prinzhorn, Hans. *Bildnerei der Geisteskranken.* Berlin: Julius Springer, 1923.

Przybyszewski, Stanislaw. *Das Werk von Edvard Munch.* Berlin: S. Fischer, 1894.

Quast, Rudolf. "Studien zur Geschichte der deutschen Kunstkritik des 19. Jahrhunderts." (Dissertation, Münster, 1936.)

Rader, Melvin (ed.). *A Modern Book of Esthetics.* New York: Henry Holt, 1935.

Raphael, Max. *Von Monet bis Picasso.* Munich: R. Piper, 1919.

Rave, Paul Ortwin. *Erich Heckel.* Leipzig: Volk und Buch Verlag, 1948.

————. *Kunstdiktatur im Dritten Reich.* Hamburg: Gebr. Mann., 1949.

*Raynal, Maurice, *et al.* *Matisse, Munch, Rouault.* (Vol. II of *History of Modern Painting.*) Geneva: Albert Skira, 1950.

*————. *From Picasso to Surrealism.* (Vol. III of *History of Modern Painting.*) Geneva: Albert Skira, 1950.

Read, Herbert. *Art Now.* New York: Harcourt Brace, 1934.

————. *Klee.* London: Faber & Faber, 1948.

————. *The Philosophy of Modern Art.* New York: Horizon Press, 1953.

Redon, Odilon. *A soi même.* (Journal, 1867–1915.) Paris: H. Floury, 1922.

Redslob, Edwin. *Fünf Generationen.* Berlin: Druckhaus Tempelhof, 1948.

Reifenberg, Benno, and Wilhelm Hausenstein. *Max Beckmann.* Munich: R. Piper, 1949.

Rewald, John. *The History of Impressionism.* New York: The Museum of Modern Art, 1946.

————. *Post-Impressionism.* New York: The Museum of Modern Art, 1956.

Riegl, Alois. *Spätrömische Kunstindustrie.* (First published in Vienna, 1901.) Vienna: Oesterr, Staatsdruckerei, 1927.

————. *Stilfragen.* Grundlegungen zur Geschichte der Ornamentik. Berlin: R. C. Schmidt, 1923.

Rilke, Rainer Maria. *Briefe an seinen Verleger.* (2 vols.) Wiesbaden: Insel-Verlag, 1949.

————. *Requiem für eine Freundin.* Leipzig: Insel Verlag, 1909.

————. *Worpswede.* Bielefeld und Leipzig: Knackfuss-Künstler-Monographien, 1903.

Rittich, Werner. "Kunsttheorie, Wortkunsttheorie und Wortkunst im 'Sturm.'" (Dissertation, Greifswald, 1933.)

Roessler, Arthur (ed.). *Egon Schiele im Gefängnis.* Vienna: Carl Konegen, 1922.

————. *Erinnerungen an Egon Schiele.* Vienna: Carl Konegen, 1922.

————. *Das graphische Werk Egon Schieles.* Vienna: Rikola Verlag, 1922.

————. *Kritische Fragmente. Aufsätze über österreichische Neukünstler.* Vienna: Verlag Richard Lanyi, 1918.

Rognoni, Luigi. *Expressionismo e dodecafonia. In appendice scritti di Arnold Schönberg, Alban Berg, Wassily Kandinsky.* Torino: G. Einaudi, 1954.

Roh, Franz. *Nach-Expressionismus.* Leipzig: Klinkhardt & Biermann, 1925.

Rohlfs, Christian. *Blätter aus Ascona.* (Introduction by Helene Rohlfs.) Munich: R. Piper Verlag, 1955.

Rotonchamp, Parjean de. *Paul Gauguin.* Paris: E. Druet, 1906.

Samuel, Richard, and Hinton R. Thomas. *Expressionism in German Life, Literature and the Theatre.* Cambridge, England: W. Heffer, 1939.

Sauerlandt, Max. *Emil Nolde.* Munich: Kurt Wolff, 1921.

————. *Die Kunst der letzten 30 Jahre.* Berlin: Rembrandt Verlag, 1935.

Schapire, Rosa. *Karl Schmidt-Rottluffs graphisches Werk bis 1923.* Berlin: Euphorion Verlag, 1924.

Schardt, Alois. *Franz Marc.* Berlin: Rembrandt Verlag, 1936.

Scheffler, Karl. *Deutsche Kunst.* Berlin: S. Fischer, 1917.

————. *Deutsche Maler und Zeichner im Neunzehnten Jahrhundert.* (2d ed. revised.) Leipzig: Insel-Verlag, 1911.

————. *Der Geist der Gotik.* Leipzig: Insel Verlag, 1925.

————. *Geschichte der europäischen Malerei vom Impressionismus bis zur Gegenwart.* Berlin: Verlag Bruno Cassirer, 1927.

————. *Talente.* Berlin: Bruno Cassirer, 1921.

Schick, Rudolf. *Tagebuch-Aufzeichnungen aus den Jahren 1866, 1868, 1869 über Arnold Böcklin.* Berlin: E. Fleischel & Co., 1901.

Schiefler, Gustav. *Edvard Munchs graphische Kunst.* Dresden: Arnold, 1923.

————. *Edvard Munch—Das graphische Werk.* Berlin: Euphorion Verlag, 1928.

————. *Das graphische Werk Emil Noldes bis 1910.* Berlin: Julius Bard, 1911.

————. *Das graphische Werk Emil Noldes 1910 bis 1925.* Berlin: Euphorion Verlag, 1927.

————. *Die Graphik E. L. Kirchners bis 1910.* Berlin: Euphorion Verlag, 1920.

————. *Das graphische Werk E. L. Kirchners bis 1924.* Berlin: Euphorion Verlag, 1926.

————. *Meine Graphik-Sammlung.* Hamburg: Gesellschaft der Bücherfreunde, 1927.

Schmalenbach, Fritz. *Jugenstil. Ein Beitrag zur Theorie und Geschichte der Flächenkunst.* Würzburg: K. Triltsch, 1935.

————. *Kunsthistorische Studien: Grundlinien des Frühexpressionismus.* Basel: Verlag Schudel, 1941.

————. *Neue Studien über Malerei des 19. und 20. Jahrhunderts.* Bern: Rota-Verlag, 1955.

Schmid, Max. *Klinger.* Bielefeld und Leipzig: Knackfuss-Künstler-Monographien, 1899.

Schmidt, Georg. *Paul Klee.* Basel: Holbein-Verlag, 1946.

Schmidt, Gerhard. *Neue Malerei in Oesterreich.* Vienna: Verlag Brüder Rosenbaum, 1956.

Schmidt, P. F. *Alfred Kubin.* (Vol. XLIV of *Junge Kunst.*) Leipzig: Klinkhardt & Biermann, 1924.

————. *Emil Nolde.* (Vol. LIII of *Junge Kunst.*) Leipzig: Klinkhardt & Biermann, 1929.

————. *Geschichte der modernen Malerei.* Stuttgart: Kohlhammer Verlag, 1952.

————. *Die Kunst der Gegenwart.* Berlin: Akademische Verlagsgesellschaft Athenaion, 1922.

Schreyer, Lothar. *Erinnerungen an Sturm und Bau-* *haus.* Munich: Albert Langen–Georg Müller, 1956.

Sedlmayr, Hans. *Die Revolution der modernen Kunst.* Hamburg: Rowohlt Verlag, 1955.

————. *Verlust der Mitte. Die bildende Kunst des 19. und 20. Jahrhunderts als Symptom und Symbol der Zeit.* Salzburg: Otto Müller Verlag, 1948.

Sellenthin, H. G. *Palau, Zeichnungen und Notizen aus der Südsee.* Feldafing: Buchheim Verlag, 1956.

Semper, Gottfried. *Der Stil in den technischen und tektonischen Künsten oder praktische Aesthetik.* Munich: F. Bruckmann, 1878–1879.

Serusier, Paul. *ABC de la peinture.* (First edition, Paris, 1921.) Paris: Libraire Floury, 1950.

Seuphor, M. *L'Art abstrait: ses origins, ses premiers maîtres.* Paris: Maeght, 1949.

Simon, Heinrich. *Max Beckmann.* (Vol. LVI of *Junge Kunst.*) Leipzig: Klinkhardt & Biermann, 1930.

————. *The Prints of Paul Klee.* New York: Curt Valentin, 1945.

Soffici, A. *Cubismo e futurismo.* Florence: Libreria della Voce, 1914.

Sydow, Eckhart von. *Die deutsche expressionistische Kultur und Malerei.* Berlin: Furche Kunstverlag, 1920.

Szittya, Emil. *Malerschicksale.* Hamburg: Johannes-Asmus-Verlag, 1925.

Thoene, Peter (pseud. for Peter Merin). *Modern German Art.* Harmondsworth: Penguin Books, 1938.

Thormaelen, Ludwig. *Erich Heckel.* (Vol. LVIII of *Junge Kunst.*) Leipzig: Klinkhardt & Biermann, 1931.

Tietze, Hans. *Deutsche Graphik der Gegenwart.* (Vol. XXXVII of *Bibliothek der Kunstgeschichte.*) Leipzig: E. A. Seemann, 1922.

Troeger, Eberhard. *Otto Mueller.* Freiburg: Crone & Co., 1949.

Uhde-Bernays (ed.). *Künstlerbriefe über Kunst.* Dresden: W. Jess, 1926.

Uphoff, Carl Emil. *Christian Rohlfs.* (Vol. XXXIV of *Junge Kunst.*) Leipzig: Klinkhardt & Biermann, 1923.

————. *Paula Modersohn-Becker.* (Vol. II of *Junge Kunst.*) Leipzig: Klinkhardt & Biermann, 1919.

Utitz, Emil. *Die Grundlagen der jüngsten Kunstbewegung.* Stuttgart: F. Enke, 1913.

————. *Die Kultur der Gegenwart.* Stuttgart: F. Enke, 1921.

————. *Die Überwindung des Expressionismus.* Stuttgart: F. Enke, 1927.

Valentiner, W. R. *Karl Schmidt-Rottluff.* (Vol. XVI of *Junge Kunst.*) Leipzig: Klinkhardt & Biermann, 1920.

Velde, Henry van de. *Kunstgewerbliche Laienpredigen.* Berlin: H. Seemann, 1902.

————. *Die Renaissance im modernen Kunstgewerbe.* Berlin: B. Cassirer, 1903.

————. *Zum neuen Stil.* Munich: R. Piper, 1955.

Venturi, Lionello. *Pittura contemporanea.* Milan: Hoepli Editore, 1947.

Vinnen, Carl (ed.). *Protest deutscher Künstler.* Jena: E. Diederich's, 1911.

Vischer, Robert. *Das optische Formgefühl. Ein Beitrag zur Aesthetik.* Leipzig, Stuttgart: Galler, 1873.

Voltaire, F. M. A. de *Kandide.* (With 26 drawings by Paul Klee, 1913.) Munich: Kurt Wolff, 1920.

*Vriesen, Gustav. *August Macke.* Stuttgart: Kohlhammer Verlag, 1953.

Walden, Herwath. *Einblick in Kunst.* Berlin: Der Sturm, 1917.

————. *Expressionismus.* Berlin: Der Sturm, 1918.

————. *Die neue Malerei.* Berlin: Der Sturm, 1919.

Walden, Nell, and Lothar Schreyer. *Der Sturm.* Ein Erinnerngsbuch an Herwath Walden und die Künstler aus dem Sturmkreis. Baden-Baden: Woldemar Klein, 1954.

Waldmann, Emil. *Die Kunst des Realismus und des Impressionismus.* (Vol. XV of Propylaen Kunstgeschichte.) Berlin: Propylaen-Verlag, 1927.

————. *Max Slevogt.* Berlin: Cassirer, 1923.

————. *La Peinture allemande contemporaine.* Paris: Ed. Crés, 1930.

Wedderkop, H. von. *Deutsche Graphik des Westens.* Weimar: Feuer Verlag, 1922.

————. *Paul Klee.* (Vol. XV of *Junge Kunst.*) Leipzig: Klinkhardt & Biermann, 1920.

*Weiler, Clemens. *Alexey von Jawlensky.* Wiesbaden: Limes Verlag, 1955.

Weisbach, Werner. *Impressionismus.* (2 vols.) Berlin: G. Grote'sche Verlagsbuchhandlung, 1911.

Wember, Paul. *Heinrich Nauen.* Düsseldorf: Verlag L. Schwann, 1948.

Westheim, Paul. *Für und Wider.* Potsdam: Kiepenheuer Verlag, 1923.

————. *Das Holzschnittbuch.* Potsdam: Kiepenheuer Verlag, 1921.

————. *Künstlerbekenntnisse.* Berlin: Ullstein Verlag, 1925.

————. *Oskar Kokoschka.* Potsdam-Berlin: Kiepenheuer Verlag, 1918.

————. *Oskar Kokoschka.* Berlin: Paul Cassirer, 1925.

Wild, Doris. *Moderne Malerei, Ihre Entwicklung seit dem Impressionismus.* Konstanz-Zürich: Europa Verlag, 1950.

Wingler, Hans Maria (ed.). *Der Blaue Reiter.* Feldafing: Buchheim Verlag, 1954.

————. *Der Sturm.* Feldafing: Buchheim Verlag, 1955.

————. *Die Brücke: Kunst im Aufbruch.* Feldafing: Buchheim Verlag, 1954.

————. *Ernst Ludwig Kirchner, Holzschnitte.* Feldafing: Buchheim Verlag, 1954.

————. *Künstler und Poeten. Bildniszeichnungen von Oskar Kokoschka.* Feldafing: Buchheim Verlag, 1954.

*————. *Oskar Kokoschka.* (Catalogue raisonné.) Salzburg: Galerie Welz, 1956.

————. *Oskar Kokoschka—Ein Lebensbild in zeitgenössischen Dokumenten.* Munich: Albert Langen–Georg Müller, 1956.

————. *Der Sturm.* Feldafing: Buchheim Verlag, 1955.

Winkler, Walter. *Psychologie der modernen Kunst.* Tübingen: Alma Mater Verlag, 1949.

Wölfflin, Heinrich. *Die Bamberger Apokalypse.* Munich: Kurt Wolff, 1920.

————. *Italien und des deutsche Kunstgefühl.* Munich: F. Bruckmann, 1931.

Wolfradt, Willi. *Lyonel Feininger.* (Vol. XLVII of *Junge Kunst.*) Leipzig: Klinkhardt & Biermann, 1924.

————. *Otto Dix.* (Vol. XLI of *Junge Kunst.*) Leipzig: Klinkhardt & Biermann, 1924.

Woltmann, Hans. *Worpswede.* Stade: Selbstverlag des Stader Geschichts und Heimatsverein, 1955.

Worringer, Wilhelm. *Abstraktion und Einfühlung.* (First published in 1908.) Munich: R. Piper, 1948. (English edition: *Abstraction and Empathy.* London: Routledge & Kegan Paul, 1953.)

————. *Formprobleme der Gotik.* (First published in 1910.) (English edition: *Form Problems of the Gothic.* New York: G. E. Stechert & Co., [1920].)

————. *Künstlerische Zeitfragen.* Munich: R. Piper, 1921.

————. *Problematik der Gegenwartskunst.* Munich: R. Piper, 1948.

Zahn, Leopold. *Paul Klee: Leben, Werk, Geist.* Potsdam: Kiepenheuer, 1920.

————. *Kleine Geschichte der modernen Kunst.* Frankfurt: Verlag das Goldene Vlies, 1956.

Zehder, Hugo. *Wassily Kandinsky.* (Vol. I of *Künstler der Gegenwart.*) (Edited by Paul Ferdinand Schmidt.) Dresden: Rudolf Kaemmerer Verlag, 1920.

Zeit-Echo. Ein Kriegstagebuch der Künstler. Munich: Goltzverlag, 1914–15.

Articles

Adler, Jankel. "Memories of Paul Klee," *Horizon*, VI (1942), 264–267.

Allard, Roger. "Die Kennzeichen der Erneuerung in der Malerei," *Der Blaue Reiter* (1912), 35–41.

Amyx, Clifford. "Max Beckmann: The Iconography of the Triptychs," *Kenyon Review*, XIII (1951), 610–623.

Apollinaire, Guillaume. "Notes," in *Il y a*. Paris: Messein, 1925.

———. "Realité peinture pure," *Der Sturm*, III (1912), 224–225.

Ashton, Dore. "Archtype Expressionist. Group of Nolde's Early Paintings at the Borgenicht Gallery." *Art Digest*, XXVIII (1954), 15.

Bahr, Hermann. "Secession," *Ver Sacrum*, I (1898), 9–10.

Behne, Adolf. "Paul Klee," *Die Weissen Blätter*, IV (1917), 167–169.

Bender, Ewald. "Deutsche Kunst um 1913," *Zeitschrift für Bildende Kunst*, N. F., XXIV (1912–1913), 287–304.

Bender, Gertrud. "Christian Rohlfs, ein Mittler zwischen zwei Jahrhunderten," *Westfalen*, XXX (1952), 1–30.

Biermann, Georg. "Oskar Kokoschka," *Cicerone*, XXI (1929), 19–24.

Bill, Max. "Paul Klee," *Das Werk*, XXVII (1940), 209–216.

Bing, S. "L'Art Nouveau," *The Architectural Record*, XII (1912), 283.

Bloesch, Hans. "Ein moderner Graphiker Paul Klee," *Die Alpen*, VI (1912), No. 5.

Boccioni, Carrà, *et al.* "Manifest der Futuristen," *Der Sturm*, III (1912), 822–824.

Born, Wolfgang. "Oskar Kokoschka and His Time," *Bulletin of the City Art Museum of St. Louis* (Dec., 1942), 32–34.

Brisch, Klaus. "Vassily Kandinsky," *Clima*, I (1950), 11–22.

Burchard, Ludwig. "Neue Bilderbücher," *Cicerone*, XI (1919), 276–278.

Carus. "Friedrich der Landschaftsmaler," *Genius*, II (1920), 88–94.

Coellen, Ludwig. "Der Formvorgang der expressionistischen Malerei," *Kunstblatt*, II (1918), 69–74.

Cohen, Walter. "August Macke," *Cicerone*, XIV (1922), 275.

Däubler, Theodor. "Emil Nolde," *Kunstblatt*, I (1917).

———. "Franz Marc," *Die Neue Rundschau*, XXVII (1916), 564–567.

———. "Paul Klee," *Kunstblatt*, II (1918), 24–27.

Delaunay, Robert. "Sur la lumière." Translated by Paul Klee: "Über das Licht," *Der Sturm*, III (1913), 255.

Deri, Max. "Die Kubisten und der Expressionismus," *Pan*, II (1912), 872–878.

Döblin, Alfred. "Die Bilder der Futuristen," *Der Sturm*, III (1912), 41–42.

Eberlein, Kurt Karl. "Franz Marc und die Kunst unserer Zeit," *Genius*, III (1921), 173–179.

Endell, August. "Möglichket und Ziele einer neuen Architektur," *Deutsche Kunst und Dekoration*, I (1898), 141.

Fechter, Paul. "Zu neuen Arbeiten Max Pechsteins," *Die Kunst*, XIV (1920), 219–232.

Fischer, Otto. "Die neueren Werke Max Beckmanns," *Museum der Gegenwart*, I (1930), 89–100.

Flechtheim, Alfred. "Mein Freund Nauen," *Feuer*, I (1919–1920), 34.

Friedberger, Hans. "Zeichnungen von Max Pechstein," *Cicerone*, V (1913), 289–291.

———. "Plastiken und neue Zeichnungen von Max Pechstein bei Gurlitt," *Cicerone*, V (1913), 760–762.

Friedländer, Max. "Das Schicksal des Holzschnitts," *Die neue Rundschau*, XXX (1919), 1001–1005.

Frimmel, Th. von. "Wiener Kunstbriefe: Die Jungen im Hagenbund," *Blätter für Gemäldekunde*, VI (1911), 173.

Gilles, "Matthias Grünewald," *Kunstblatt*, I (1917), 181–188.

Glaser, Curt. "Die Geschichte der Berliner Sezession," *Kunst und Künstler*, XXVI (1927), 14–20.

———. "Die neue Secession," *Die Kunst*, XIV (1909–1910), 448–452.

Glück, Gustav. "Gustav Klimt," *Die Bildenden Künste*, II (1919), 11–14.

Goll, Iwan. "Über Kubismus," *Kunstblatt*, IV (1920), 215–222.

Gosebruch, Ernst, "Erich Heckel Triptychon aus dem Jahre 1913," *Museum der Gegenwart*, I (1930), 30–34.

———. "Schmidt-Rottluff," *Genius*, II (1920), 5–20.

Gräf, Botho. "E. L. Kirchner," *Kunstblatt*, VII (1922), 65–80.

Grohmann, Will. "Paul Klee," *Cahiers d'Art*, III (1928), 295–302.

————. "Oskar Kokoschka," *Cicerone,* XVII (1925), 149–151.

————. "Wassily Kandinsky," *Cicerone,* XVI (1924), 887–898.

————. "Zeichnungen von Klimt, Kokoschka und Schiele," *Monatshefte für Bücherfreunde und Graphikensammler,* I (1925), 508–520.

Grossmann, Fritz. "Österreichische Malerei in der Zeit des Expressionismus," *Forum,* V (1935), 193.

Grosz, George, and John Heartfield. "Der Kunstlump," *Der Gegner,* I (1919), 48–56.

Grote, Ludwig. "Lyonel Feininger zum 60. Geburtstag," *Museum der Gegenwart,* II (1931), 41–49.

Gruber, Karl. "Zur Entstehung von Kokoschkas Forel Bildnis," *Das Kunstwerk,* V (1951), 60–61.

Grüner, Franz. "Oskar Kokoschka," *Die Fackel,* XII (1911), 18–23.

Haberfeld, Hugo. "Gustav Klimt," *Die Kunst,* XXV (1912), 173–178.

Haftmann, Werner. "Über das 'humanistische' bei Paul Klee," *Prisma,* No. 17 (1948), 31–32.

Hartlaub, G. F. "Die Kunst und die neue Gnosis," *Kunstblatt,* I (1917), 166–179.

Hausenstein, Wilhelm. "Ausstellungen. München," *Kunstchronik,* XXV (1913–1914), 603–606.

————. "Max Beckmann," *Der Querschnitt,* VIII (1928), 859–860.

————. "Max Beckmann," *Das Werk,* XXXIV (1947), 161–186.

————. "Max Pechstein," *Deutsche Kunst und Dekoration,* XLII [1918], 205–237.

————. "Über Kokoschka," *Die Kunst,* LIII (1926), 153–161.

Hayter, Stanley William. "Apostle of Empathy," *Magazine of Art,* XXXIX (1946), 126–130.

Heise, Carl Georg. "Emil Nolde, Wesen und Weg seiner religiösen Malerei," *Genius,* I (1919), 18–26.

————. "Die Forderung des Tages," *Kurt Wolff Almanach auf das Jahr, 1925,* p. 6.

————. "Franz Marcs Springende Pferde," *Genius,* I (1919), 218–220.

————. "Zeitglosse und Beschluss," *Genius,* III (1921), 355.

Henze, Anton. "Ernst Ludwig Kirchner und Carl Hagemann," *Das Kunstwerk,* IX (1955–1956), 9–15.

Herzog, Oswald. "Der abstrakte Expressionismus," *Der Sturm,* X (1919), 29.

Heymann, Walter. "Berliner Sezession," *Der Sturm,* II (1911), 503–504, 543.

Hildebrand, Adolf. "Zum Verständnis der Kunst Hans von Marées," *Deutsche Kunst und Dekoration,* XXIII (1909), 277–278.

Hodin, J. P. "Expressionism," *Horizon,* XIX (1949), 45–46.

————. "Munch and Expressionism," *Art News,* XLIX (1950), 26–29.

————. "Oskar Kokoschka. Die Krise der Kunst und der Expressionismus," *Der Monat,* II (1950), 651–657.

————. "Style and Personality. A Graphological Portrait of Oskar Kokoschka," *The Journal of Aesthetics and Art Criticism,* VI (1948), 209–225.

————. "Über künstlerische Ausdrücksmittel und deren Verhältnis zu Natur und Bild," *Die Kunst,* X (1905), 81–88, 106–113, 121–142.

Holitscher, Arthur. "Alfred Kubin," *Die Kunst,* VII (1903), 163.

Howe, G. "Ausstellung des Düsseldorfer Sonderbundes," *Die Kunst für Alle,* XXVI (1911), 475.

————. "Sonderbund-Ausstellung in Düsseldorf," *Die Kunst für Alle,* XXV (1910), 571.

Huelsenbeck, Richard. "Die dadaistische Bewegung," *Die Neue Rundschau,* XXXI (1920), 972–979.

Jollos, Waldemar. "Paul Klee," *Kunstblatt,* III (1919), 225–237.

Kandinsky, Wassily. "Abstrakte Kunst," *Cicerone,* XVII (1925), 639–647.

————. "Der Blaue Reiter: Rückblick," *Kunstblatt,* XIV (1930), 57–60.

————. "Franz Marc," *Cahiers d'Art,* XI (1936), 273–275.

————. "Letter from Munich," *Apollon,* Vols. II, IV, VII, VIII, XI (1909–1910).

————. "Line and Fish," *Axis,* II (1935), 6.

————. "Malerei als reine Kunst," *Der Sturm,* IV (1913), 98–99.

————. "Toile vide etc.," *Cahiers d'Art,* V–VI (1935), 113.

————. "Über die Formfrage," *Der Blaue Reiter,* (1912), 74–100.

————. "Über Kunstverstehen," *Der Sturm,* III (1912), 157–158.

Kauders, Hans. "Die religiöse Kunst der Gegenwart," *Kunstblatt,* II (1918), 180–183.

Kern, Walter. "Un contributo allo studio dell'Expressionismo Tedesco," *La Biennale di Venezia,* VII (1952), 23–28.

Kessler, Charles. "Sun Worship and Anxiety," *Magazine of Art,* XLV (1952), 304–312.

Khnopff, Fernand. "Josef Hoffmann—Architect and Decorator," *The Studio,* XXII (1901), 261–266.

Kirchner, E. L. "Anfänge und Ziel," *Kroniek van hedendaagesche Kunst en Kultur,* I (1935), 5–9.

————. "Die neue Kunst in Basel," *Kunstblatt,* X (1926), 321–329.

Kirchner, E. L. "Randglossen zum Aufsatz: Klee für Kinder," *Kunstblatt*, XII (1930), 154–156.

———. "Zur Rundfrage: 'Ein neuer Naturalismus,'" *Kunstblatt*, VI (1922), 375–376.

Kirchner, Hans Walter. "Aus nachgelassenen Briefen E. L. Kirchners," *Das Kunstwerk*, V (1951), 16–20.

Kirchner, Joachim. "Deutsche Meister des dekorativ-monumentalen Stils des 19. Jahrhunderts," *Deutsche Kunst und Dekoration*, XLVII (1921), 249–260.

———. "Die Voraussetzungen des Expressionismus," *Monatshefte für Kunstwissenschaft*, XII (1919), 8–13.

Klee, Paul. "Antwort auf eine Rundfrage an die Künstler: Über den Wert der Kritik," *Der Ararat*, II (1921), 130.

———. "Die Ausstellung des modernen Bundes im Kunsthaus Zürich," *Die Alpen*, VI (1912), 696–704.

———. "Exakter Versuch im Bereich der Kunst," *Bauhaus, Zeitschrift für Gestaltung*, II (1928), 17.

———. "Kunst und Literatur des Auslands," *Die Alpen*, VI (1912), 243, 302, 614.

Klein, Jerome. "The Line of Introversion," *The New Freeman*, I (1930), 88–89.

Kokoschka, Oskar. "An Approach to the Baroque Art of Czechoslovakia," *Burlington Magazine*, LXXXI (1942), 263–268.

———. "An die Einwohnerschaft Dresdens," *Der Ararat*, II (1920), 34.

———. "Aus meiner Jugendbiographie," *Der Wiener Kunstwanderer*, I (1933), No. 10.

———. "Der Fetisch" (letters) in Paul Westheim (ed.), *Künstlerbekenntnisse*. Berlin, Ullstein-Verlag (1925).

———. "Gengenstandslose Kunst?" *Universitas*, IX (1954), 1297.

———. "A Letter to Dr. Alfred Neumeyer," *Magazine of Art*, XXXIX (1946), 196.

———. "Vom Bewusstsein der Gesichte," *Genius*, I (1919), 39–45.

———. "Written after condemnation to death," *Der Sturm*, I (1910), No. 26.

———. "Zum Expressionismus," *Freie deutsche Kultur* (May–June, 1944), p. 3.

Kraus, Karl. "Kokoschka und der Andere," *Die Fackel*, XIII (1911), 22.

Kubin, Alfred. "Aus meinem Leben," *Ararat*, II (1921).

Kuhn, Alfred. "Edvard Munch und der Geist seiner Zeit," *Cicerone*, XIX (1927), 139–147.

Lancaster, Clay. "Oriental Contributions to Art Nou-

veau," *The Art Bulletin*, XXXIV (1952), 297–310.

Langer, Suzanne K. "Art: The Symbol of Sentience," *New World Writing*, IV (1953), 50–55.

Lankheit, Klaus. "Zur Geschichte des Blauen Reiters," *Cicerone* (1949), 110–114.

Laporte, P. M. "Lovis Corinth and German Expressionism," *Magazine of Art*, XLII (1949), 301–305.

Lasker-Schüler, Else. "Oskar Kokoschka," *Der Sturm*, I (1910), 166.

Lindsay, Kenneth. "The Genesis and Meaning of the Cover Design of the First *Blaue Reiter* Exhibition Catalogue," *Art Bulletin*, XXXV (1953), 47–50.

———. "Kandinsky in 1914 New York: Solving a Riddle," *Art News*, LV (1956), 32–33.

Lühdorf, Hans. "Wilhelm Morgner," *Westfalen*, XXX (1952), 53–57.

Lux, A. J. "Kunst und Ethik," *Der Sturm*, I (1910), 13–14.

———. "Kunstschau-Wien, 1908," *Deutsche Kunst und Dekoration*, XXIII (1909), 53.

McCausland, Elizabeth. "Max Beckmann," *Parnassus*, X (1938), 28–29.

Macke, August. "Die Masken," *Der Blaue Reiter* (1912), 21–27.

Mann, Thomas. "Ein Maler—ein Dichter. Ein Brief an Wolfgang Born," *Der Wiener Kunstwanderer*, I (1933), No. 10.

Marc, Franz. "Anti-Beckmann," *Pan*, II (1912), 556.

———. "Die Futuristen," *Der Sturm*, III (1912), 187.

———. "Ideen über Ausstellungen," *Der Sturm*, III (1912), 66.

———. "Die konstruktiven Ideen der neuen Malerei," *Pan*, II (1912), 530.

———. "Die neue Malerei," *Pan*, III (1912), 616–618.

———. "Die Wilden Deutschlands," *Der Blaue Reiter* (1912), 5–7.

———. "Zur Sache," *Der Sturm*, III (1912), 79–80.

Marinetti, Filippo. "Manifest des Futurismus" (first published in Paris, 1909), *Der Sturm*, III (1912), 828–829.

Marsale, L. de (pseud. for E. L. Kirchner). "Über Kirchners Graphik," *Genius*, III (1921), 250–263.

———. "Über die plastischen Arbeiten Kirchners," *Cicerone*, XVII (1925), 694–695.

———. "Zeichnungen von E. L. Kirchner," *Genius*, II (1920), 217–234.

Matisse, Henri. "Notizen eines Malers," *Kunst und Künstler*, VII (1909), 335–347.

Michaelis, Karin. "Der tolle Kokoschka," *Kunstblatt*, II (1918), 361–366.

Michalski, Ernst. "Die Entwicklungsgeschichte des

Jugendstils," *Repertorium für Kunstwissenschaft,* XLVI (1925), 133–149.

Michel, Wilhelm. "Münchner Graphik: Holzschnitt und Lithographie," *Deutsche Kunst und Dekoration,* XVI (1905), 437–457.

Molzahn, Johannes. "Das Manifest des absoluten Expressionismus," *Der Sturm,* X (1919), 90–93.

Myers, Bernard. "Ernst Ludwig Kirchner and die Brücke," *Magazine of Art,* XLV (1952), 20–26.

Neumeyer, Alfred. "Oskar Kokoschka," *Magazine of Art,* XXXVIII (1945), 261–264.

Osborn, Max. "Berliner Sezession, 1911," *Kunstchronik,* XXII (1910–1911), 385–390.

Poort, Hermann. "Ernst Ludwig Kirchner," *Kunstblatt,* X (1926), 331–349.

Purrmann, Hans. "Van Gogh und Wir," *Kunst und Künstler,* XXVI (1927–1928), 175–181.

Rannit, Aleksis. "M. K. Čirulionis," *Das Kunstwerk,* I (1946–1947), 46–48.

———. "Un pittore astratto prima di Kandinsky," *La Biennale,* VIII (1952).

Raphael, Max. "Aus dem Palau-Tagebuch," *Kunstblatt,* II (1918), 161–175.

Rilke, Rainer Maria. "Ein Brief Rainer Maria Rilkes über Paul Cézanne und Oskar Kokoschka," *Die graphischen Künste,* LIII (1930), 23–26.

———. "H. Vogeler," *Deutsche Kunst und Dekoration,* X (1902), 320.

Rosenberg, Jakob. "German Expressionist Printmakers," *Magazine of Art,* XXXVIII (1945), 300–305.

Rosenhagen, Hans. "Die 5. Ausstellung der berliner Secession," *Die Kunst,* VII (1902), 433–443.

Sauerlandt, Max. "Die deutschen Museen und die deutsche Gegenwartskunst," *Museum der Gegenwart,* I (1930), 4–16.

———. "Emil Nolde," *Zeitschrift für bildende Kunst,* XLIX (1913–1914), 181–192.

———. "Erich Heckel-Aquarelle von der Schleswigen Ostseeküste," *Genius,* III (1921).

———. "Holzbildwerke von Kirchner, Heckel und Schmidt-Rottluff," *Museum der Gegenwart,* I (1930), 101–111.

Schardt, Alois J. "Das Übersinnliche bei Paul Klee," *Museum der Gegenwart,* I (1930), 36–46.

Scheffler, Karl. "Berlin, Neue Sezession," *Kunst und Künstler,* VII (1910), 525.

———. "Berliner Sezession—die Zweiundzwanzigste Ausstellung," *Kunst und Künstler,* IX (1911), 486.

———. "Erich Heckel," *Kunst und Künstler,* XVI (1918), 249–256.

———. "Erklärung," *Kunst und Künstler,* IX (1911), 210–211.

———. "Ernst Ludwig Kirchner," *Kunst und Künstler,* XVIII (1920), 217–230.

———. "Karl Schmidt-Rottluff," *Kunst und Künstler,* XVIII (1920), 247–280.

———. "Oskar Kokoschka," *Kunst und Künstler,* XVII (1919), 123.

Scheyer, Ernst. "Expressionism in Holland," *Maandblad Voor Beeldende Kunsten,* Dec., 1950, 286–305.

———. "German Expressionism," *Baltimore Museum News,* XI (1947), No. 4.

———. "Kokoschka in Köln," *Cicerone,* XXI (1929), 243.

Schiefler, Gustav. "Das Werk Edvard Munchs," *Kunstblatt,* I (1917), 9–18.

Schmalenbach, Werner. "Ernst Ludwig Kirchner," *Werk,* XXXV (1948), 18–23.

Schmidt, Paul F. "Blütezeit der Dresdner Brücke," *Aussaat,* II (1947), 49–55.

———. "Erich Heckels Anfänge," *Zeitschrift für Bildende Kunst,* LV (1920), 257–264.

———. "Die Expressionisten," *Der Sturm,* III (1911), 734–736.

———. "Heinrich Campendonk," *Cicerone,* XVII (1925), 498–505.

———. "Die internationale Ausstellung des Sonderbundes," *Zeitschrift für Bildende Kunst,* XXIII (1912), 229–238.

———. "Max Beckmann," *Cicerone,* XI (1919), 675–684.

———. "Neue Graphik von Max Beckmann," *Cicerone,* XV (1923), 180–184.

———. "Otto Mueller," *Blätter der Galerie Ferdinand Möller,* VII (1930), 1–6.

———. "Das Recht auf Romantik," *Kunstblatt,* IV (1920), 321–325.

———. "Romantik der Gegenwart," *Feuer,* III (1922), 225.

Schreyer, Lothar. "Die neue Kunst," *Der Sturm,* X (1919), 66–70, 83–90, 103–106, 118–125.

Selz, Peter. "The Aesthetic Theories of Wassily Kandinsky and Their Relationship to the Origin of Nonobjective Painting," *The Art Bulletin,* XXXIX (1957), 127–136.

———. "E. L. Kirchner's 'Chronik der Brücke,'" *College Art Journal,* X (1950), 50–54.

———. "Kirchner's Self Portrait as Soldier in Relation to Earlier Self Portraits," *Allen Memorial Art Museum Bulletin* (Oberlin, Ohio), XIV (1957), 91–97.

Servaes, Franz. "Ein Streifzug durch die wiener Malerei," *Kunst und Künstler,* VIII (1910), 587–598.

Sievers, J. "Die XXII Ausstellung der Berliner Sezession," *Cicerone,* III (1911), 383–384.

Signac, Paul. "Neoimpressionismus," *Pan*, IV (1898), 55–62.

Sydow, Eckart von. "Erich Heckel als Graphiker," *Cicerone*, XIII (1921), 1–15.

———. "Karl Schmidt-Rottluff," *Cicerone*, X (1918), 75–80.

Tesar, L. E. "Der Fall Oskar Kokoschka und die Gessellschaft," *Die Fackel*, XII (1911), 31–39.

Thwaites, J. A. "The Blue Rider: A Milestone in Europe," *The Art Quarterly*, XIII (1950), 13–20.

———. "Max Beckmann—Notes for an Evaluation," *The Art Quarterly*, XIV (1951), 275–282.

Tietze, Hans. "Jung-Österreichische Maler," *Genius*, II (1920), 63–74.

———. "Oskar Kokoschka," *Zeitschrift für Bildende Künste*, XXIX (1918), 83.

———. "Oskar Kokoschka," *Der Ararat*, III (1921), 219–224.

———. "Oskar Kokoschkas neue Werke," *Die bildenden Künste*, II (1919), 249.

Trust (pseud. for Herwath Walden). "Der Sumpf von Berlin," *Der Sturm*, II (1911), 651–652.

Valentiner, W. R. "Expressionism and Abstract Art," *The Art Quarterly*, IV (1941), 210–234.

———. "Karl Schmidt-Rottluff," *Cicerone*, XII (1920), 455–476.

Velde, Nele van de. "Ein Tag bei Kirchner auf der Staffelalp," *Genius*, II (1920), 282–292.

Vriesen, Gustav. "Der Maler August Macke," *Westfalen*, XXX (1952), 31–52.

Walden, Herwath. "Kunst und Leben," *Der Sturm*, X (1919), 2–3.

Westheim, Paul. "Erich Heckel," *Das Kunstblatt*, I (1917), 161–179.

———. "Kunst in Frankreich," *Kunstblatt*, V (1921), 353–363.

———. "Künstlerisches Denken," *Kunstblatt*, I (1917), 353–360.

———. "Der Maler Oskar Kokoschka," *Kunstblatt*, I (1917), 233–241.

———. "Zur Psychologie des Holzschneidens," *Die Neue Rundschau*, XXXI (1920), 1055–1061.

Wiese, Erich. "Otto Mueller," *Museum der Gegenwart*, I (1930), 138–142.

Wilckens, Leonie von. "Über die Farbe bei Kokoschka," *Das Kunstwerk*, V (1951), 60.

Wingler, Hans Maria. "Oskar Kokoschkas pädagogische Konzeption," *Das Kunstwerk*, V (1951), 46–49.

Wölfflin, Heinrich. "Adolf von Hildebrand," *Kunst und Künstler*, XVI (1918), 6–20.

Wolfradt, Willi. "Holzschnitte von Gerhard Marks," *Kunstblatt*, VII (1923), 141–147.

———. "Otto Mueller," *Die Kunst für Alle*, XLIV (1929), 121–125.

Worringer, Wilhelm. "Art Questions of the Day," *The Monthly Criterion* (Aug., 1927).

———. "Kritische Gedanken zur neuen Kunst," *Genius*, II (1920), 221–236.

———. "Zur Entwicklungsgeschichte der modernen Malerei, Die Antwort auf den Protest deutscher Künstler," *Der Sturm*, II (1911), 587–598.

Zahn, Leopold. "Oskar Kokoschka," *Das Kunstwerk*, II (1948), 29–35.

Exhibition Catalogs

(arranged chronologically)

GENERAL

Sonderbund. "Internationale Austellung des Sonderbundes Westdeutscher Kunstfreunde und Künstler zu Cöln," 1912. Cologne: 1912.

Erster Deutscher Herbstsalon. Berlin: Der Sturm, 1913. (Introduction by Herwath Walden.)

International Exhibition of Modern Art. ("Armory Show") New York: 1913. (Preface by Arthur B. Davies.)

Expressionisten: Ostern 1919. Düsseldorf: Galerie Alfred Flechtheim, 1919.

Die Abstrakten. Grosse Berliner Kunstaussellung, Berlin: 1926.

Société Anonyme, New York. International Exhibition of Modern Art. Brooklyn: Brooklyn Museum, 1926. (Introduction by Katherine Dreier.)

The Arthur Jerome Eddy Collection of Modern Painting and Sculpture. Chicago: The Art Institute, 1931–1932. (Introduction by Daniel Catton Rich.)

Contemporary German Art. Boston: The Institute of Modern Art, 1939.

German Expressionism (Booth Collection). Baltimore: Baltimore Museum of Art, 1945. (Foreword by Ernst Scheyer.)

Société Anonyme. New Haven: Yale University Gallery of Fine Arts, 1950. (Compiled by Katherine Dreier and Marcel Duchamp.)

German Expressionism. Minneapolis: University of Minnesota, 1951.

Expressionisme (Haubrich Collection). Amsterdam: Stedelijk Museum, 1951. (Introduction by L. Reidemeister.)

Um 1900. Zürich: Kunstgewerbemuseum, 1952. (Introduction by Hans Curjel.)

Galerie des 20. Jahrhunderts. Berlin, 1953. (Introduction by Adolf Jannasch.)

Deutsche Kunst—Meisterwerke des 20. Jahrhunderts. Lucerne: Kunstmuseum, 1953. (Introduction by Ludwig Grote.)

20th Century German Graphic Art. Chicago: Allan Frumkin Gallery, 1954. (Introduction by Peter Selz.)

German Expressionist Prints. Los Angeles: Los Angeles County Museum, 1954. (Introduction by Ebria Feinblatt.)

A Hundred Years of German Painting 1850–1950. London: The Tate Gallery, 1956. (Introduction by Alfred Hentzen.)

German Watercolors, Drawings and Prints. (A loan exhibition sponsored by the Federal Republic of Germany and circulated by the American Federation of Arts, 1956.) (Introduction by Leonie Reygers.)

ARTISTS' GROUPS

Brücke.
Dresden: Galerie Arnold, 1910.
Hamburg: Galerie Commeter, 1912.
Berlin: Galerie Fritz Gurlitt, 1912.
"Munch und die Künstler der Brücke." Bremen: Kunsthalle, 1920. (Arranged by J. B. Neumann.) (Introduction by Emil Waldmann.)
"Paula Modersohn und die Maler der Brücke." Bern: Kunsthalle, 1948. (Introductions by Arnold Rüdlinger and W. F. Arntz.) (Contains "Chronik der Brücke.")
Hannover: Kestner Gesellschaft, 1953. (Important catalog of portfolios and "Chronik der Brücke.")

Neue Künstlervereinigung München.
Munich: Moderne Galerie Thannhauser, 1911. (First catalog.)
Munich: Moderne Galerie Thannhauser, 1912. (Second catalog.)

Der Blaue Reiter.
"Die erste Ausstellung der Redaktion Der Blaue Reiter." Munich: Moderne Galerie Thannhauser, 1911–1912.
"Die zweite Ausstellung der Redaktion Der Blaue Reiter: Schwarz-Weiss." Munich: Hans Goltz, 1912.
Berlin: Der Sturm, 1912.
Munich: Haus der Kunst, 1949. (Introduction by Ludwig Grote.)
Basel: Kunsthalle, 1950. (Introduction by Ludwig Grote.)
New York: Curt Valentin Gallery, 1954–1955.

Cambridge, Massachusetts: Busch-Reisinger Museum, 1955.

The Blue Four.
"Quatro Azules." Mexico: Biblioteca Nacional, 1931. (Introduction by Diego Rivera.)
"Feininger, Jawlensky, Kandinsky, Klee." Santa Barbara, California: Faulkner Memorial Art Gallery, 1932. (Arranged by Mme Galka Scheyer.)
"Feininger, Jawlensky, Kandinsky, Klee." New York: Buchholz Gallery, 1944. (With quotations from the artists.)
"Feininger, Jawlensky, Kandinsky, Klee," Pasadena, California: Pasadena Art Museum, [1955]. (Introduction by W. Joseph Fulton.)

Neue Sezession.
Berlin: Galerie Maximilian Macht, 1910. (First Neue Sezession catalog.)
Berlin: Der Sturm, 1912.

INDIVIDUAL ARTISTS

Amiet, Cuno. New York: Galerie St. Etienne, 1954. (Introduction by Otto Kallir.)

Beckmann, Max. Berlin: J. B. Neumann-Graphisches Kabinett, 1917. (Foreword by Max Beckmann.)
———. New York: Buchholz Gallery, 1946. (Introduction by Georg Swarzenski.)
———. New York: Buchholz Gallery, 1947. (Introduction by James Thrall Soby.)
*———. (Retrospective.) St. Louis, Missouri: City Art Museum, 1948. (Introduction by Perry T. Rathbone.)

Bloch, Albert. Lawrence, Kansas: The University of Kansas Museum of Art, 1955. (Edited by Edward A. Maser.) (Letter from Albert Bloch.)

Corinth, Lovis. Hannover: Landesmuseum, 1950.
———. (Retrospective.) (Traveling U. S. and Canada, 1950–1951.) (Introduction by Julius Held.)
———. New York: Curt Valentin Gallery, 1953. (Introduction by Charlotte Berend-Corinth.)

Le Fauconnier. "First American Le Fauconnier Exhibition." New York: J. B. Neumann–New Art Circle, 1948–1949. (Introduction by A. Ozenfant.)

Feininger, Lyonel. Hannover: Kestner Gesellschaft, 1932.
———. Detroit: Institute of Arts, 1941. (Introduction by Perry T. Rathbone.)
———. "Lyonel Feininger–Marsden Hartley." New York: Museum of Modern Art, 1944. (Introductions by Alfred H. Barr, Jr., and Alois Schardt.)
———. Cleveland: Museum of Art, 1951. (Introduction by Walter Gropius.)

Heckel, Erich. Hannover: Kestner Gesellschaft, 1919.

Heckel, Erich. Chemnitz: Kunsthütte, 1931.

————. Mannheim: Kunsthalle, 1950. (Introduction by Walter Passarge.)

————. Münster: Landesmuseum, 1953. (Introduction by W. Greischel.)

————. Hannover: Kestner Gesellschaft, 1953. (Introduction by Alfred Hentzen.)

Hoelzel, Adolf. (Retrospective.) Stuttgart, [1952]. (Introduction by Hans Hildebrand.)

Jawlensky, Alexey von. Düsseldorf: Galerie Alex Vomel, 1956. (Introduction by Clemens Weiler.)

————. (Retrospective exhibition.) London: The Redfern Gallery, 1956.

————. Basel: Galerie Beyeler, 1957.

Kandinsky, Wassily. (60th anniversary exhibition) Dresden: Galerie Arnold, 1926. (Eulogies by Klee, Will Grohmann, *et al.*)

————. Paris: Galerie de France, 1930. (Articles by Maurice Reynal, C. H. Zervos, *et al.*)

————. Berlin: Galerie Alfred Flechtheim, 1931. (Introduction by Alois Schardt.)

————. "Kandinsky Memorial." New York: The Museum of Non-Objective Painting, 1945.

————. Pittsburgh: Carnegie Institute, 1946. (Introduction by Hilla Rebay.)

————. Paris: Galerie René Drouin, 1949. (Introduction by Charles Estienne.)

————. Paris: Galerie Maeght, 1951. (Introductions by Max Bill, Jean Arp, Nina Kandinsky, *et al.*)

————. Cologne: Galerie Ferdinand Möller, 1953–1954. (Introduction by Ludwig Grote.)

Kirchner, Ernst Ludwig. Frankfurt: Ludwig Schames, [1919]. (Introduction by Professor Gräf: "Über die Arbeit von E. L. Kirchner.")

————. Frankfurt: Ludwig Schames, [1920]. (Notes by E. Griesebach: "Über das graphische Werk von E. L. Kirchner.")

————. Frankfurt: Ludwig Schames, 1921. (Text by L. de Marsale: "Über die Schweizer Arbeiten von E. L. Kirchner.")

————. Bern: Kunsthalle, 1933. (Introduction by Louis de Marsale.)

————. Stuttgart: Künstlerhaus Sonnehalde, 1948. Aquarelle, Zeichnungen, Druckgraphik. (Introduction by Erwin Petermann.)

————. Hannover: Kestner Gesellschaft, 1950. (Introduction by Alfred Hentzen.)

————. Hamburg, Hannover, Bremen, 1950. (Introduction by Alfred Hentzen.)

————. Cambridge, Massachusetts: Busch-Reisinger Museum, 1950–1951.

————. Zürich: Kunsthaus, 1952. (Introduction by H. Bolliger.)

————. New York: Curt Valentin Gallery, 1952. (Contains letter from E. L. Kirchner to Curt Valentin.)

————. "Gemälde und Graphik der Sammlung Dr. F. Bauer, Davos." Nürnberg: 1952. (Introduction by Ludwig Grote.)

————. Stuttgart: Würtembergischer Kunstverein, 1956. (Introduction by E. Rathke.)

————. Los Angeles: Paul Kantor Gallery, 1957. (Introduction by Gerald Nordland.)

Klee, Paul. Munich: Hans Goltz, 1920.

————. Düsseldorf: Galerie Flechtheim, 1920. (Introduction by Theodor Däubler.)

————. Hannover: Kestner Gesellschaft, 1920. (Introduction by Paul Erich Küppers.)

————. Paris: Galerie Vavin-Raspail, 1925. (Introduction by Louis Aragon.)

————. Berlin: Galerie Flechtheim, 1928. (Preface by René Crevel: "Merci, Paul Klee.")

————. Brussels: Galerie le Centaure, 1928. (Introduction by Georges Marlier.)

————. Dresden: Neue Kunst Fides, 1929. (Introduction by Rudolf Probst.)

————. New York: Museum of Modern Art, 1930. (Introduction by Alfred H. Barr, Jr.)

————. New York: J. B. Neumann–New Art Circle, 1935.

————. New York: Buchholz Gallery, 1940. (Essays by J. J. Sweeney, Julia and Lyonel Feininger.)

————. Basel: Kunstmuseum, 1940. (Introduction by Georg Schmidt.)

————. London: Leicester Gallery, 1941. (Introduction by Herbert Read.)

*————. New York: Museum of Modern Art, 1941. (Introduction by Alfred H. Barr, Jr. Essays by J. J. Sweeney, Julia and Lyonel Feininger.)

————. New York: Museum of Modern Art, 1945.

————. New York: Museum of Modern Art, 1947: "Paintings, Drawings and Prints by Paul Klee from the Klee Foundation, Berne." (Introduction by James Thrall Soby.)

————. Frankfurt: Galerie Buchheim-Militon, 1950. (Introduction by Will Grohmann; statement by Walter Gropius.)

————. Hannover: Kestner Gesellschaft, 1952. (Introduction by Alfred Hentzen.)

Kokoschka, Oskar. Berlin: Galerie Paul Cassirer, 1910.

————. Berlin: Galerie Paul Cassirer, 1918.

————. Hannover: Galerie von Garvens, 1921. (With Kokoschka's essay: "Lauschender? Erwecker des Echos der Ewigkeit.")

————. Zürich: Kunsthaus, 1927. (Introduction by W. Wartmann.)

————. London: The Leicester Galleries, 1928. (Preface by P. G. Konody.)

————. Mannheim: Städtische Kunsthalle, 1931. (Retrospective exhibition.) (Introduction by G. F. Hartlaub, essays by Walter Hasenclever, Adolf Loos, Max Liebermann, Arnold Schönberg, Hans Tietze, *et al.*)

————. Paris: Galerie Georges Petit, 1931.

————. New York: Buchholz Gallery, 1938.

————. New York: Galerie St. Etienne, 1940.

————. Zürich: Kunsthaus, 1947. (Introduction by W. Wartmann.)

————. Venice: XXIV Biennale di Venezia, 1948. (Special exhibition.) (Introduction by Edith Hoffmann.)

————. Munich: Haus der Kunst, 1950. (Catalog of graphic work by W. F. Arntz.) (Introduction by Ludwig Grote; preface by Oskar Kokoschka; essays by Paul F. Schmidt, Lothar Schreyer.)

————. Linz: Neue Galerie der Stadt Linz, 1951. (Introduction by Ernst Schönwiese, Oskar Kokoschka, Wolfgang Gurlitt, Franz Roh.)

————. Bremen: Kunsthalle, 1956. (Excerpts from letters, essays, and lectures by Kokoschka.)

Kubin, Alfred. New York: Galerie St. Etienne. 1957.

Macke, August. Cologne: Museen der Stadt Köln, 1947. "Gedächtnisausstellung."

————. New York: Fine Arts Associates, 1952. (Introduction by Gustav Vriesen.)

Marc, Franz. Berlin: Der Sturm, 1916. (Memorial exhibition.)

————. Munich: Galerie Günther Franke, 1946.

————. Munich: Moderne Galerie Otto Stangl. Aquarelle und Zeichnungen, 1949–50. (Introduction by Dr. Klaus Lankheit.)

————. New York: Buchholz Gallery, 1950. (Introduction by Robert J. Goldwater.)

Modersohn-Becker, Paula. Hannover: Kestner-Gesellschaft, 1951.

Mueller, Otto. Berlin: Paul Cassirer, 1919.

————. Berlin: Galerie Ferdinand Moeller, 1930. (Introduction by Paul F. Schmidt.)

————. Hannover: Kestner Gessellschaft, 1956. (Introduction by Werner Schmalenbach.)

Münter, Gabriele. Hannover: Kestner Gesellschaft, 1951.

Nolde, Emil. Berlin: J. B. Neumann-Graphisches Kabinett, 1916.

————. Basel: Kunsthalle, 1928. (Introduction by Georg Schmidt.)

————. Hannover: Kestner Gesellschaft, 1948. (Introduction by Alfred Hentzen.)

Pechstein, Max. Berlin: Staatsoper, 1946. (Introduction by Adolf Jannasch.)

————. Berlin: Hochschule für Bildende Künste, 1952. (Introduction by Adolf Jannasch.)

Rohlfs, Christian. Hagen: Karl-Ernst Osthaus Museum, 1946. (Introduction by Dr. Herta Hesse-Frielinghaus.)

————. Münster: Landesmuseum, 1949. (Preface by W. Greischel. Introduction by Ludwig Thormaehlen.)

————. Hagen: Karl-Ernst Osthaus Museum, 1949–1950.

————. London: The Arts Council of Great Britain, 1956. (Introduction by Hans Hess.)

Schiele, Egon. New York: Galerie St. Etienne, 1948. (Introduction by Joseph von Sternberg.)

*————. Bern: Gutekunst and Klipstein, 1956. (Introductions by Otto Benesch and Arthur Roessler.)

————. New York: Galerie St. Etienne, 1957. (Introduction by Otto Benesch.)

Schmidt-Rottluff. Munich: Hans Goltz, 1917. "Sonder-Ausstellung." (Introduction by Rosa Schapire.)

————. Dresden: Galerie Arnold, 1927. (Introduction by Will Grohmann.)

————. Chemnitz: Kunsthütte, 1929. (Introduction by Rosa Schapire.)

————. Hannover: Provinz-Museum, 1930. (Introduction by Alexander Dorner.)

————. Chemnitz: Schlossberg Museum, 1946. (Introduction by Adolf Behne, Will Grohmann, *et al.*)

Slevogt, Max. Hannover: Landesmuseum, 1952.

Unpublished Material

Beckmann, Max. "Letters to a Woman Painter." Lecture delivered at Stephens College, 1948. Copy at Ryerson Library, Art Institute of Chicago (mimeographed).

*Brisch, Klaus. "Wassily Kandinsky: Untersuchung zur Entstehung der gegenstandslosen Malerei." Ph.D. dissertation, University of Bonn, 1955.

Brücke. "Manifest der Künstlergruppe Brücke." Woodcut, Kestner Museum, Hannover.

————. "Chronik der Brücke." Complete copy compiled by E. L. Kirchner. Munich, Zentralinstitut für Kunstgeschichte.

Gabo, Naum. Lecture delivered at Institute of Design, Chicago, March, 1948. Copy in possession of Mr. Alex Nicoloff, Chicago (mimeographed).

Heckel, Erich. Letter to Peter Selz, July 16, 1952.

Hope, Henry R. "The Sources of Art Nouveau." Ph.D. dissertation, Harvard University, 1942.

Kandinsky, Wassily. Catalog of exhibitions. MS Mme Nina Kandinsky, Neuilly-sur-Seine (handwritten).

Kirchner, E. L. Sketchbook, 1906. Library, Kunsthaus, Zürich.

———. Diary: 1919–1928. In possession of Hans Bolliger, Zürich.

———. Explanatory Notes to "Peter Schlemihl,"

1928. In possession of Hans Bolliger, Zürich.

———. Short autobiography [*ca.* 1932]. MS in possession of Hans Bolliger, Zürich (typewritten).

———. Letter to Karl Nierendorf, n.d. In possession of Hans Bolliger, Zürich.

*Lindsay, Kenneth C. D. "An Examination of the Fundamental Theories of Kandinsky." Ph.D. dissertation, University of Wisconsin, 1951.

Pechstein, Max. Letter to Peter Selz, September 23, 1953.

Schmidt-Rottluff, Karl. Letter to Peter Selz, July 11, 1953.

*Selz, Peter. "German Expressionist Painting from Its Inception to the First World War." Ph.D. dissertation, University of Chicago, 1954.

INDEX

PLATES

1a.   MATTHIAS GRÜNEWALD   Isenheim altarpiece
1512–1516   Crucifixion detail: Virgin and St. John
Musée Unterlinden, Colmar, France

1b.   HEINRICH NAUEN   Pietà   1913
Detail: Virgin and St. John   Burg Drove, Rhineland

3. HANS VON MARÉES The Three Horsemen 1885–1887 Central panel of
triptych Bayerische Staatsgemäldesammlungen, Munich

2. ARNOLD BÖCKLIN Shepherd's Lament 1866 Bayerische
Staatsgemäldesammlungen, Munich

5. FRANZ VON STUCK The Sin 1895 Bayerische
Staatsgemäldesammlungen, Munich

4. MAX KLINGER Beethoven monument 1890–1900 Museum der
Bildenden Künste, Leipzig

6a. MAX LIEBERMANN   Dutch Sewing School   1876   Collection of
William Roth, New York

6b. MAX LIEBERMANN   Bathing Boys   1912   Collection of William Roth,
New York

7.   LOVIS CORINTH   Portrait of Graf Keyserling   1901   Bayerische
Staatsgemäldesammlungen, Munich

8. MAX SLEVOGT Uniforms 1903 Bayerische Staatsgemäldesammlungen, Munich

9. OTTO MODERSOHN   Bad Weather   ca. 1895   Collection of Mr. and Mrs.
Fred Grunwald, Los Angeles

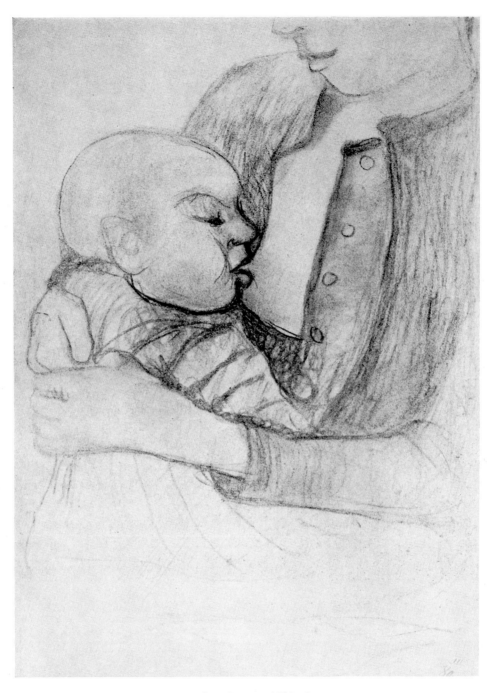

10. PAULA MODERSOHN-BECKER   Infant Nursing   1904   Drawing
Roselius Haus in der Böttcherstrasse, Bremen

11. PAULA MODERSOHN-BECKER   Old Peasant Woman   1904   Kunstmuseum, Basel

12. PAULA MODERSOHN-BECKER Portrait of Rainer Maria Rilke 1904
Roselius Haus in der Böttcherstrasse, Bremen

13. PAULA MODERSOHN-BECKER   Self-Portrait
1907   Folkwang Museum, Essen

14. PAUL GAUGUIN   The Yellow Christ   1899   Albright Art Gallery, Buffalo

15.　ODILON　REDON　Face of a Man in the Sky　1880　Drawing
The Art Institute of Chicago

16.　EDVARD MUNCH　The Cry　1893　Municipal Collections, Oslo

17.   JAN TOOROP   The Young Generation   1892   Museum Boymans, Rotterdam

18.   JAN THORN-PRIKKER   The Bride   1892   Rijksmuseum
Kröller-Müller, Otterloo, Holland

19. HENRI DE TOULOUSE-LAUTREC   Mlle Marcelle Lender au Buste   1895
Color lithograph

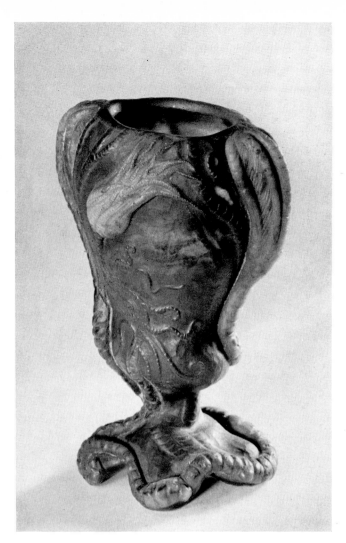

20a. EMIL GALLÉ Vase ca. 1890
Musée des Beaux-Arts, Nancy, France

20b. AUGUST ENDELL Façade of
Elvira Studio, Munich 1897

21. EDVARD MUNCH   The Kiss   1897–1902   Woodcut

22. ERNST LUDWIG KIRCHNER Self-Portrait 1904 Kunstmuseum, Basel

23.   ERNST LUDWIG KIRCHNER   Still Life   1902   Color woodcut

24. VINCENT VAN GOGH Starry Night 1889 The Museum of Modern Art, New York

25.   ERNST LUDWIG KIRCHNER   Deciduous Forest   1904   Paul Kantor Gallery, Los Angeles

26. ERNST LUDWIG KIRCHNER   Self-Portrait at Dawn   1906   Lithograph

27. KARL SCHMIDT-ROTTLUFF   Court Church, Dresden   1906   Lithograph

28.   ERNST LUDWIG KIRCHNER   Street   1907   The Museum of Modern Art, New York

29.   ERNST LUDWIG KIRCHNER   Self-Portrait with Model   1907
Kunsthalle, Hamburg

30. ERICH HECKEL Standing Nude 1908 Woodcut

31.   KARL SCHMIDT-ROTTLUFF   Windy Day   1907   Collection of Frau Dr. Rauert, Hamburg

32.   EMIL NOLDE   Flower Garden   1907   Haubrich Collection, Wallraf-Richartz-Museum, Cologne

45. ERICH HECKEL Head of a Woman
ca. 1912 Collection of W. R. Valentiner,
Raleigh, North Carolina

46.   ERICH HECKEL   To the Sick Woman   1912–1913   Triptych   Busch-Reisinger Museum,
Harvard University

47. ERNST LUDWIG KIRCHNER   Nude with Hat   1911   Haubrich Collection,
Wallraf-Richartz-Museum, Cologne

48. ERNST LUDWIG KIRCHNER Lady with Green Hat 1912 Photograph by courtesy of
Bildarchiv Rheinisches Museum, Cologne

49. ERNST LUDWIG KIRCHNER Street Scene 1912 Drawing Collection of
Mr. and Mrs. Max Zurier, Los Angeles

50. ERNST LUDWIG KIRCHNER The Street 1913 The Museum of Modern Art, New York

51.   ERNST LUDWIG KIRCHNER   The Painters of the Brücke   1925
Wallraf-Richarts Museum, Cologne

52. GUSTAV KLIMT   Portrait of Frederica Beer   1916   Collection of
F. M. Beer-Monti, New York.

53. GUSTAV KLIMT The Kiss 1908 Photograph by courtesy of
Bildarchiv der Oesterreichischen Nationalbibliothek

54a. FERDINAND HODLER Eurythmy 1895 Kunstmuseum, Bern

54b. FERDINAND HODLER The Admired Youth 1903–1904
Kunsthaus, Zurich

55. EGON SCHIELE The Self-Seer I 1910 Private collection

56.　EGON SCHIELE　The Room of the Artist at Neulengbach　1911　Private collection

57. EGON SCHIELE Sunrise 1912 Collection of Otto Kallir, New York

58. EGON SCHIELE   Girl in Green Stockings   1914   Water color
Collection of Otto Benesch, Vienna

59.   EGON SCHIELE   Portrait of Paris von Guetersloh   1918
The Minneapolis Institute of Arts

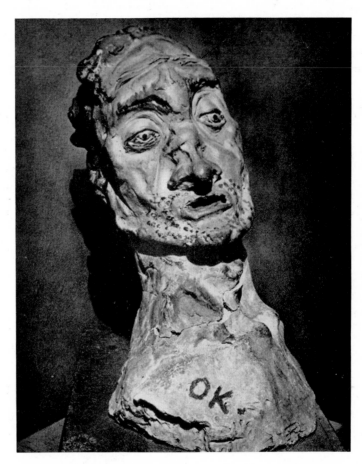

60. OSKAR KOKOSCHKA Self-Portrait 1908 Clay and
polychrome Private collection, New York

61a.   OSKAR KOKOSCHKA   The Dreaming Boys
1908   Last of a series of color lithographs

61b.   OSKAR KOKOSCHKA   Portrait of a Boy
(The Blue Boy) 1908 Collection of Mr. and Mrs.
John W. Blodgett, Jr., Grand Rapids, Michigan

62a. OSKAR KOKOSCHKA   The Trance Player
ca. 1907–1908   Musées Royaux des Beaux-Arts de
Belgique, Brussels

62b. OSKAR KOKOSCHKA   Dent du Midi   1909   Collection of M. Feilchenfeldt, Zurich
Copyright by Paul Cassirer, London

63.   OSKAR KOKOSCHKA   Portrait of Auguste Forel   1910   Städtische   Kunsthalle, Mannheim

64. OSKAR KOKOSCHKA   Portrait of Mrs. K.   ca. 1911   Collection of
Joseph H. Hirschhorn, New York

65. WASSILY KANDINSKY   Poster for the first Phalanx exhibition   1901   Color woodcut

66. WASSILY KANDINSKY   The Sluice   1902   Collection of Richard Feigen, New York

67.   WASSILY KANDINSKY   Ancient Town   1902   Collection of Mme Nina Kandinsky,
Neuilly-sur-Seine, France

68a.   WASSILY KANDINSKY   Der Blaue Reiter   1903
Formerly Collection Citroen, Amsterdam

68b.   WASSILY KANDINSKY   Improvisation No. 3   1909   Photograph by
courtesy of Bildarchiv Rheinisches Museum, Cologne

69a. ALEXEY VON JAWLENSKY
White Feathers 1909 Collection of
Adolf Erbslöh, Irschenhausen, Germany

69b. ALFRED KUBIN Crushing 1903 Drawing

70. ALEXANDER KANOLDT Cityscape ca. 1912 Private collection

71.   ADOLF ERBSLÖH   Tennis Court   1910   Photograph by courtesy of
Bildarchiv Rheinisches Museum, Cologne

72. KARL HOFER   Two Women   1907   Kunsthalle, Bremen

73.   WASSILY KANDINSKY   Poster for the first exhibition of the Neue
Künstlervereinigung, Munich, 1909   Collection of Mme Nina Kandinsky,
Neuilly-sur-Seine, France

74. HENRI LE FAUCONNIER L'Abondance
1910

75. PABLO PICASSO Head of a Woman 1909 Crayon and gouache
The Art Institute of Chicago

76a. ALEXEY VON JAWLENSKY Floating Cloud 1910 Pasadena Art Museum,
Blue-Four Collection

76b. GABRIELE MÜNTER Landscape
with White Wall 1910 Collection of
Gabriele Münter, Murnau, Germany

77. WASSILY KANDINSKY   Composition No. 2   1910   The Solomon R. Guggenheim Museum,
New York

78. WASSILY KANDINSKY   Improvisation No. 12, "The Rider"   1910
Bayerische Staatsgemäldesammlungen, Munich

79a.   FRANZ MARC   Portrait of Jean Blois Niestlé   1906
Photograph by courtesy of Curt Valentin Gallery, New York

79b.   FRANZ MARC   Deer among the Reeds
ca. 1908   Bayerische Staatsgemäldesammlungen,
Munich

80.   FRANZ MARC   Red Horses   1911   Collection of Mr. and Mrs. Paul E. Geier, Cincinnati

81.   FRANZ MARC   The Yellow Cow   1911   The Solomon R. Guggenheim Museum, New York

82. WASSILY KANDINSKY First nonobjective water color (untitled) 1910 Collection of
Mme Nina Kandinsky, Neuilly-sur-Seine, France

83.   WASSILY KANDINSKY   Trojka   1911   The Art Institute of Chicago

84. WASSILY KANDINSKY Lyrisches 1911 Museum Boymans, Rotterdam

85. WASSILY KANDINSKY   Composition No. 4   1911   Collection of Mme Nina Kandinsky,
Neuilly-sur-Seine, France

86.   AUGUST MACKE   Sunny Garden   1908   Macke estate, Bonn

87. AUGUST MACKE   Storm   1911   Saarland Museum, Saarbrücken

88.   ALBERT BLOCH   Harlequin with Three Pierrots   1911   The Art Institute of Chicago

89.   GABRIELE MÜNTER   Still Life with Queen   1912   The Art Institute of Chicago

90.   ROBERT DELAUNAY   Saint Séverin   1909   The Minneapolis Institute of Art

91. PAUL KLEE Crown Mania 1904 Etching

92a.   PAUL KLEE   Willikofun   1909   Drawing   Collection of Henry T. Kneeland
Hartford, Connecticut

92b.   PAUL KLEE   Scaffolding Is Being Loaded   1910   Drawing   Collection of
F. O. Schang, New York

93. PAUL KLEE Residential Section 1912 Drawing Formerly collection of
Curt Valentin, New York

Henri Rouſſeau.

DER BLAUE REITER

Mit etwa 140 Reproduktionen. Vier handkolor. graph. Blätter.

Bayeriſche, ruſſiſche Volkskunſt; primitive, römiſche, gotiſche Kunſt;
ägyptiſche Schattenfiguren, Kinderkunſt. — Kunſt des XX. Jahrhunderts:
Burljuck W., Cézanne, Delaunay, Gauguin, Girieud, Kandinsky,
Kokoſchka, Kubin, Le Fauconnier, Marc, Matiſſe, Münter, Picaſſo,
Henri Rouſſeau, Schönberg, van Gogh uſw.
MUSIKBEILAGEN: Lieder von Alban Berg, Arnold Schönberg,
A. von Webern. — Herausgeber: Kandinsky und Franz Marc.
Es erſcheinen drei Ausgaben: Allgemeine Ausgabe: geh. M 10.—,
geb. M 14.—. Luxus-Ausgabe: 50 Exemplare. Enthält noch zwei
von den Künſtlern ſelbſt kolorierte und handſignierte Holzſchnitte. Preis
M 30.—. Muſeums-Ausgabe: 10 Exemplare: jedem Exemplar wird
eine Originalarbeit eines der beteiligten Künſtler beigegeben. Preis
M 100.—. Nur vom Verlag direkt zu beziehen. Proſpekte koſtenlos.

R. PIPER & Co., VERLAG, MÜNCHEN.

94. Advertisement of "Der Blaue Reiter" almanac in Sonderbund catalog, 1912

95a.   MAX BECKMANN   Young Men by the Sea   1905   Private collection

95b.   MAX BECKMANN   The Sinking of the Titanic   1912   Collection of Mr. and Mrs.
Morton D. May, St. Louis

96. PIERRE GIRIEUD   Three Marys   1912   Private collection

97. EDVARD MUNCH Madonna 1895 Lithograph

98. EDVARD MUNCH   Portrait of Jappe Nilssen
1909   Photograph by courtesy of Bildarchiv
Rheinisches Museum, Cologne

99.   ERNST LUDWIG KIRCHNER   Bathers   1912   Photograph by courtesy of
Bildarchiv Rheinisches Museum, Cologne

100.   OTTO MUELLER   Bathing Women   1912   Photograph by courtesy of
Bildarchiv Rheinisches Museum, Cologne

101. FRANZ MARC The Bewitched Mill 1912 The Art Institute of Chicago

102.   FRANZ MARC   The Tower of the Blue Horses   1913   Formerly
Kronprinzenpalais, Berlin; present whereabouts unknown

103. FRANZ MARC The Unhappy Tyrol 1913–1914 Bayerische
Staatsgemäldesammlungen, Munich

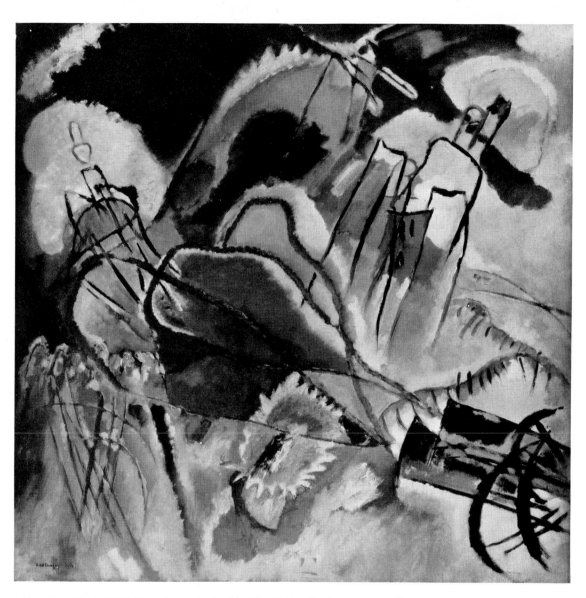

104. WASSILY KANDINSKY   Improvisation No. 30   1913   The Art Institute of Chicago

105. AUGUST MACKE Bathing Girls 1913 Bayerische Staatsgemäldesammlungen, Munich

106.   GABRIELE MÜNTER   Man in the Armchair   (Portrait of Paul Klee)   1913
Bayerische Staatsgemäldesammlungen, Munich

107a. PAUL KLEE   Rejection   1913   Drawing   Formerly Allan Frumkin Gallery,
Chicago

107b. PAUL KLEE   Suicide on the Bridge   1913
Drawing   Collection of John McAndrew,
Wellesley, Massachusetts

108.   PAUL KLEE   Flower Path   1913   Collection of Mr. and Mrs. John W. Blodgett, Jr., Grand Rapids, Michigan

109. HEINRICH CAMPENDONK   Harlequin and Columbine   1913   Collection of Mr. and Mrs.
Morton D. May, St. Louis

110.   CHRISTIAN ROHLFS   March Morning on the Ilm   1894   Photograph by courtesy of
Bildarchiv Rheinisches Museum, Cologne

111. CHRISTIAN ROHLFS   Landscape near Weimar   1902   Photograph by courtesy of
Bildarchiv Rheinisches Museum, Cologne

112. CHRISTIAN ROHLFS   Beeches in Autumn   1910   Collection of
Baron Eduard v. der Heydt, Ascona, Switzerland

113. CHRISTIAN ROHLFS Dancers 1913 Collection of Fritz Haastert, Hagen

114. CHRISTIAN ROHLFS War 1914 Formerly Folkwang Museum, Hagen

115. CHRISTIAN ROHLFS   St. Patroklus, Soest   1912   Formerly
Folkwang Museum, Hagen

116. LYONEL FEININGER Zirchow VI 1916 Formerly J. B. Neumann Gallery, New York

117.   LYONEL FEININGER   Harbor   1915   Collection of Joseph H. Hirschhorn, New York

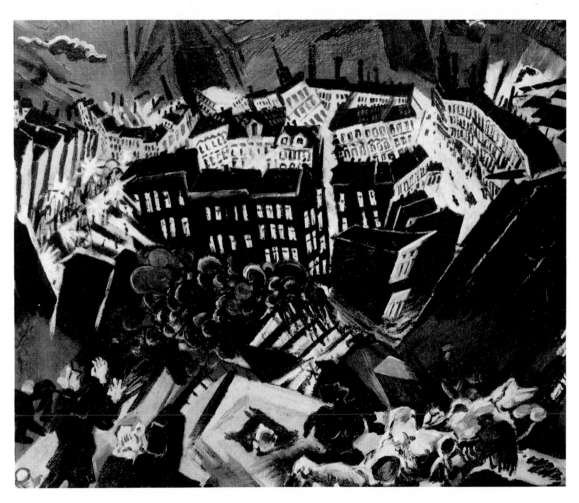

118. LUDWIG MEIDNER Burning City 1913 Collection of Mr. and Mrs. Morton D. May,
St. Louis

119.   LUDWIG MEIDNER   Self-Portrait   1916   Formerly J. B. Neumann Gallery, New York

120.   WILHELM MORGNER   Woman with Brown Wheelbarrow   1911   Private collection

121a. WILHELM MORGNER Ornamental Composition 1911 Private collection

121b. WILHELM MORGNER Adoration 1912 Private collection

122. MAX BECKMANN   Self-Portrait   1912   Allan Frumkin Gallery, Chicago

123.   MAX BECKMANN   The Division of the Cloak   1911   Lithograph

124. MAX BECKMANN The Street 1913 Collection of
Mrs. Max Beckmann, New York

125.   MAX BECKMANN   Der Krankenträger   1914   Dry point, first state

126. MAX BECKMANN   Der Krankenträger   1914   Dry point, third state

127.   MAX BECKMANN   Christ and the Woman Taken in Adultery   1917
The City Art Museum of St. Louis

128. MAX BECKMANN Self-Portrait 1919 Dry point

129. EMIL NOLDE   South Sea Dancers   1915   Collection of W. R. Valentiner,
Raleigh, North Carolina

130.   EMIL NOLDE   Three Russians   1915   Collection of Richard Feigen, New York

131a. MAX PECHSTEIN Monterosso 1913
Formerly private collection, Darmstadt

131b. MAX PECHSTEIN Palau Triptych 1917 Detail: left panel Formerly private collection,
Erfurt, Germany

132. AUGUST MACKE Girl with Fishbowl 1914 Städtisches Museum,
Wuppertal-Elberfeld, Germany

133.   PAUL KLEE   View of St. Germain   1914   Water color   Collection of F. C. Schang, New York

134. AUGUST MACKE Farewell 1914 Haubrich Collection, Wallraf-Richartz-Museum, Cologne

135. PAUL KLEE Opened Mountain 1914 Photograph by courtesy of J. B. Neumann, New York

136. PAUL KLEE House Tree 1918 Pasadena Art Museum, Blue-Four Collection

137. ERNST LUDWIG KIRCHNER   Self-Portrait   1913–1914   Formerly Curt Valentin Gallery,
New York

138.   ERNST LUDWIG KIRCHNER   Soldiers in the Shower Room   1915
The Museum of Modern Art, New York

139. ERNST LUDWIG KIRCHNER   Self-Portrait as Soldier   1915   The Dudley Peter Allen
Memorial Art Museum, Oberlin College, Oberlin, Ohio

140. KARL SCHMIDT-ROTTLUFF Self-Portrait with Hat 1919 Collection of W. R. Valentiner,
Raleigh, North Carolina

141.   HEINRICH CAMPENDONK   *Pastoral Scene*   ca. 1920   Collection of
Société Anonyme, Yale University Art Gallery

142a. OSKAR KOKOSCHKA Brother and Sister 1914 Leopold-Huesch Museum,
Düren, Germany

142b. OSKAR KOKOSCHKA The Knight Errant 1915 The Solomon R. Guggenheim Museum,
New York

143. LOVIS CORINTH   Easter at the Walchensee   1922
Private collection   Copyright by Franz Hanfstaengl, Munich

144. EDVARD MUNCH   The Dance of Life   1899—1900
National Gallery, Oslo

145. PAULA MODERSOHN-BECKER   Self-Portrait   1906
Kunstmuseum, Basel

146.   ERNST LUDWIG KIRCHNER   River Boat near Dresden   1905
Collection of Mr. and Mrs. Yoland Markson, Los Angeles

147.   ERNST LUDWIG KIRCHNER   Portrait of Dodo and Her Brother   1909
Smith College Gallery, Northampton, Massachusetts

148. ERICH HECKEL Village Ball 1908
Collection of Mr. and Mrs. S. J. Levin, St. Louis

149.   KARL SCHMIDT-ROTTLUFF   Estate in Dangast   1910
Galerie des 20. Jahrhunderts, Berlin

150. MAX PECHSTEIN   Indian and Woman   1910
Collection of Mr. and Mrs. Morton D. May, St. Louis

151. MAX PECHSTEIN   Beach at Nidden   1911
Collection of Mr. and Mrs. John C. Best, Los Angeles

152. JAMES ENSOR   The Entry of Christ into Brussels   1888
Detail   Private collection, Ostend

153. KARL SCHMIDT-ROTTLUFF Rising Moon 1912
Collection of Mr. and Mrs. Morton D. May, St. Louis

154. ERICH HECKEL   The Glass Day   1913
Collection of Marcus Kruss, Berlin

155. ERNST LUDWIG KIRCHNER   Portrait of a Woman   1911
Collection of Mr. and Mrs. Paul Kantor, Los Angeles

156.   ERNST LUDWIG KIRCHNER   Dancer   1912
Collection of Mr. and Mrs. Max Zurier, Los Angeles

157.   ERNST LUDWIG KIRCHNER   Houses in Fehmarn   1912
Collection of Mr. and Mrs. Morton D. May, St. Louis

158. EGON SCHIELE   The Bridge   1913
Galerie St. Etienne, New York

159. OSKAR KOKOSCHKA   Portrait of Dr. Tietze and His Wife   1909
The Museum of Modern Art, New York

160. WASSILY KANDINSKY   Church at Froschhausen   1906
Dalzell Hatfield Gallery, Los Angeles

161. WASSILY KANDINSKY Street in Murnau 1908
Collection of Mme Nina Kandinsky, Neuilly-sur-Seine, France

162.   FRANZ MARC   Horse in Landscape   1910
Folkwang Museum, Essen

163. ROBERT DELAUNAY Les Fenêtres 1912
Collection of Mr. and Mrs. Sidney Janis, New York

164. ALEXEY VON JAWLENSKY Infanta 1912
Collection of Mr. and Mrs. S. J. Levin, St. Louis

165. ALEXEY VON JAWLENSKY   Spanish Woman   1912
Collection of Rex de C. Nan Kivell, London

166a. FRANZ MARC - Tiger 1912
Collection of Bernhard Koehler, Berlin   Copyright by Franz Hanfstaengl, Munich

166b. FRANZ MARC Two Cats 1912
Kunstmuseum, Basel

167. UMBERTO BOCCIONI   Dynamism of a Football Player   1913
Collection of Mr. and Mrs. Sidney Janis, New York

168. FRANZ MARC   The Fate of the Beasts   1913
Kunstmuseum, Basel

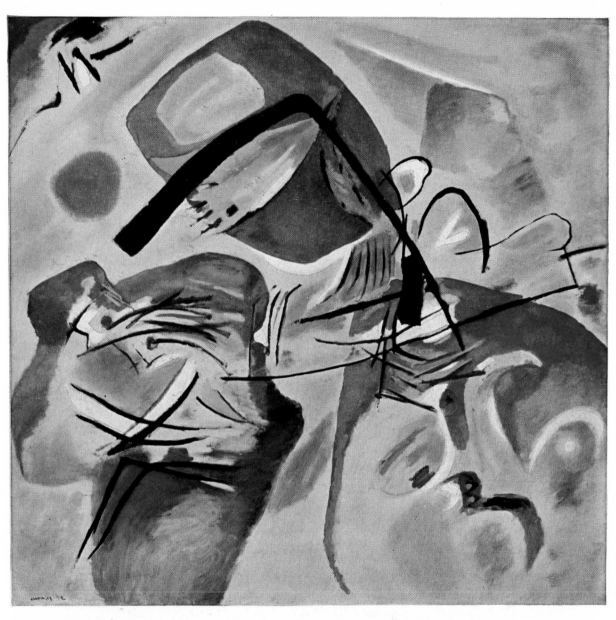

169.   WASSILY KANDINSKY   The Black Arc   1912
Collection of Mme Kandinsky, Neuilly-sur-Seine, France

170. ALEXEY VON JAWLENSKY   Sibyl   1913
Collection of Mr. and Mrs. S. J. Levin, St. Louis

171. AUGUST MACKE Sunny Path 1913
Macke estate, Bonn

172. CHRISTIAN ROHLFS Self-Portrait 1918
Rohlfs Estate, Essen

173. EMIL NOLDE Two Russians 1915
Private Collection, New York

174. EMIL NOLDE Marsh Landscape 1916
Kunstmuseum, Basel

175. AUGUST MACKE   Tunis: Bright House   1914
Water color   Macke estate, Bonn

176.   PAUL KLEE   South Wind in Marc's Garden   1915
Water color   Private collection

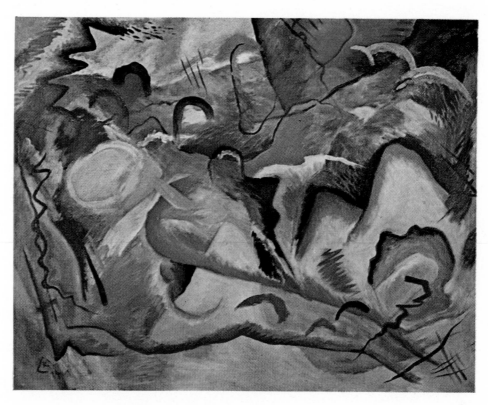

177.   WASSILY KANDINSKY   Composition   1914
Collection of Mr. and Mrs. Joseph R. Shapiro, Oak Park, Illinois

179. OSKAR KOKOSCHKA   The Tempest   1914
Kunstmuseum, Basel

180.   OSKAR KOKOSCHKA   The Slave   1920
Collection of Mr. and Mrs. Morton D. May, St. Louis